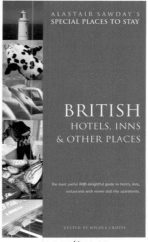

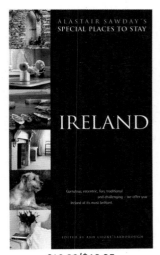

Third edition
Copyright © 2006
Alastair Sawday Publishing Co. Ltd

Published in 2006
Alastair Sawday Publishing,
The Old Farmyard,
Yanley Lane, Long Ashton
Bristol BS41 9LR
Tel: +44 (0)1275 395430
Fax: +44 (0)1275 393388
Email: info@specialplacestostay.com
Web: www.specialplacestostay.com

The Globe Pequot Press
P. O. Box 480, Guilford,
Connecticut 06437, USA
Tel: +1 203 458 4500
Fax: +1 203 458 4601
Email: info@globepequot.com
Web: www.globepequot.com

Design:
Caroline King

Maps & Mapping:
Maidenhead Cartographic Services Ltd

Printing:
Butler & Tanner, Frome, UK

UK Distribution:
Penguin UK, 80 Strand, London

US Distribution:
The Globe Pequot Press, Guilford, CT 06437

ISBN-10: 1-901970-71-x
ISBN-13: 978-1-901970-71-5

Paper and Printing: We have sought the
lowest possible ecological 'footprint' from
the production of this book, using super-
efficient machinery, vegetable inks and
high environmental standards. Our printer is
ISO 14001-registered.

The publishers have made every effort to
ensure the accuracy of the information
in this book at the time of going to
press. However, they cannot accept
any responsibility for any loss, injury
or inconvenience resulting from the
use of information contained therein.

ALASTAIR SAWDAY'S
SPECIAL PLACES

PUBS & INNS
OF ENGLAND & WALES

Contents

Alastair Sawday Publishing

We are the faceless toilers at the pit-face of publishing but, for us, the question of who we are and how we inter-react is important. For who we are shapes the books, the books shape your holidays, and thus are shaped the lives of people who own these 'special places'.
So we are trying to be a little more than 'just a publishing company'.

New eco offices
In January 2006 we moved into our new eco offices. By introducing super-insulation, underfloor heating, a wood-pellet boiler, solar panels and a rainwater tank, we will have a working environment benign to ourselves and to the environment. Lighting will be low-energy, dark corners will be lit by sun-pipes and one building is of green oak. Carpet tiles are leased: some of recycled material, most of wool and some of natural fibres. We will sail through our environmental audit.

Environmental & ethical policies
We combine many other small gestures: company cars run on gas or recycled cooking oil; kitchen waste is composted and other waste recycled; cycling and car-sharing are encouraged; the company only buys organic or local food; we don't accept web links with companies we consider unethical; we use the ethical Triodos Bank for our deposit account.

We have used recycled paper for some books but have settled on selecting paper and printer for their low energy use. Our printer is British and ISO14001-certified and together we will reduce our environmental impact.

Thanks partially to our Green Team, we recently won a Business Commitment to the Environment Award – which has boosted our resolve to stick to our own green policies. Our flagship gesture, however, is carbon offsetting; we calculate our carbon emissions and plant trees to compensate as calculated by Climate Care. In 2006 we will support projects overseas that plant trees or reduce carbon use; our money will work better by going direct to projects.

Ethics
But why, you may ask, take these things so seriously? You are just a little publishing company, for heaven's sake! Well, is there any good argument for not taking them seriously? The world, by the admission of the vast majority of scientists, is in trouble. If we do not change our ways urgently we will doom the planet and all its creatures – whether innocent or not – to a variety of possible catastrophes. To maintain the status quo is unacceptable. Business does much of the damage and should undo it, and provide new models.

Pressure on companies to produce Corporate Social Responsibility policies is mounting. We are trying to keep ahead of it all, yet still to be as informal and human as possible – the antithesis of 'corporate'. (We even have unofficial 'de-stress operatives' in the shape of several resident dogs.)

The books – and a dilemma

So, we have created fine books that do good work. They promote authenticity, individuality and high quality, local and organic food – a far cry from the now-dominant corporate culture. Rural economies, pubs, small farms, villages and hamlets all benefit. However, people use fossil fuel to get there. Should we aim to get our readers to offset their own carbon emissions, and the B&B and hotel owners too? That might have been a hopeless task a year or so ago, but less so now that the media has taken on board the enormity of the work ahead of us all.

We are slowly introducing green ideas into the books: the Fine Breakfast scheme that highlights British and Irish B&B owners who use local and organic food; celebrating those who make an extra effort; gently encouraging the use of public transport, cycling and walking. Next year we are publishing a book focusing on responsible travel and eco-projects around the globe.

Our Fragile Earth series

The 'hard' side of our environmental publishing is the Fragile Earth series: *The Little Earth Book*, *The Little Food Book* and *The Little Money Book*. They have been a great success. They consist of bite-sized essays, polemical and hard-hitting but well researched and methodical. They are a 'must have' for people from all walks of life – anyone who is confused and needs clarity about some of the key issues of our time.

Lastly – what is special?

The notion of 'special' is at the heart of what we do, and highly subjective. We discuss this in the Introduction. We take huge pleasure from finding people and places that do their own thing – brilliantly; places that are unusual and follow no trends; places of peace and beauty; people who are kind and interesting – and genuine.

We seem to have touched a raw nerve with thousands of readers; they obviously want to stay in special places rather than the dull corporate monstrosities that have disfigured so many of our cities and towns. Life is too short to be wasted in the wrong places. A night in a special place can be a transforming experience.

Alastair Sawday

Acknowledgements

I was once warned off the idea of having anything administrative to do with pub landlords. They are far too busy to answer letters or deal with outsiders. Well, I was warned. But David Hancock, the redoubtable and indefatigable editor of this third edition (not to mention the previous two), has – poor fellow – been the one to test the veracity of the warning, not I.

It has been hard, but rewarded by the delights of bringing it all together in such an unusual and successful book. And the landlords who have been quick on their keyboards have helped made it all possible. I thank them.

David has put together his own team of inspectors and, together, he and they have created this book. I salute them all – not least because their job was made even harder by our new inclusion of pub bedrooms.

Alastair Sawday

Series Editor Alastair Sawday

Editor David Hancock

Editorial Director Annie Shillito

Writing David Hancock, Jo Boissevain, Elizabeth Carter, Neil Coates, Mark Taylor

Inspections David Hancock, David Ashby, Elizabeth Carter, Colin Cheyne, Neil Coates, Rebecca Harris, Lesley Mackley, Aideen Reid, Mark Taylor, Jill Turton, Jenny White, Glyn Williams

Accounts Sheila Clifton, Bridget Bishop, Christine Buxton, Sandra Hassell, Jenny Purdy, Sally Ranahan

Editorial Jackie King, Jo Boissevain, Maria Serrano, Rebecca Stevens, Danielle Williams

Production Julia Richardson, Rachel Coe, Paul Groom, Kathy Purdy, Allys Williams

Sales & Marketing & PR Siobhan Flynn, Andreea Petre Goncalves, Sarah Bolton

Web & IT Russell Wilkinson, Chris Banks, Brian Kimberling

A word from Alastair Sawday

"Beer drinking don't do half the harm of lovemaking".
(Eden Phillpots, The Farmer's Wife).

I will adopt that notion uncritically, for I am here to celebrate beer drinking and pubs. They form a chunky part of the national heritage, not to say the national psyche.

Drinking has also occupied a chunky part of the British newspapers during the last year, with the government intending us to drink like Frenchmen. Let us hope that for every city-centre boozer spewing out drunken revellers 24 hours a day there will be another offering extra time for the quiet pleasures of its customers. Those are the ones that you will find in this splendid book.

Many of us are cynical and weary, reluctant to get involved, detached from our families and our friends and depending on our new social circle (the internet one) to satisfy us. But the pub is still there for us, a convivial place to mingle with strangers, warm our cockles and pin back our ears for the latest gossip. We can also, in many, eat well – or even magnificently. How bizarre it is that so many pubs are under threat.

If, by the way, your village pub is under threat, why not *buy* it? How many pubs have been lost because it never occurred to the locals to save

them? CAMRA has produced (with others) a fine little guide to saving your local – such as The Old Crown in Hesket, near Newmarket.

In this third edition we include a selection of inspected pub bedrooms. If we like them we mention them. Some can compete with the best hotel and B&B rooms; others are simple, but great value. None, I hope, will invite you to share the bed with a ragtag collection of fellow travellers. Things have moved on.

My attachment to the British pub has recently grown. I arrived on my bike, dripping with rain. Pressing myself towards the fireplace I raised a railway-lovers' head of steam and was dry within minutes. Nobody turned a hair. Now that is the sort of pub I like.

Alastair Sawday

Introduction

THRIVING COMMUNITY LOCALS, DIMINISHING BACKWATER GEMS AND THOSE FANTASTIC FOOD PUBS...

With Britain's fascinating pub scene evolving rapidly, research for Edition 3 has seen our inspectors trawling England and Wales in search of thriving community locals, diminishing backwater gems and those fantastic food pubs that are beginning to pepper our villages and towns.

So what's new to this edition?
We have included nearly 100 new pubs: some are quirky and little-known, others are passionate about beer and wine or champion local, seasonal and organic food. Yet others have pretty gardens, waterside settings, great walks and wonderful views. We are also won over by a genuine welcome from hands-on publicans, enthusiastic staff, history, character and charm.

The result is 620 pubs and inns that stand out from the crowd, plus a further 263 in our Worth a Visit section at the back of the guide.

● Pub Awards
These awards reflect the philosophy and ethics behind Alastair Sawday Publishing. Read on to discover the award winners for the best pubs for Local, Seasonal and Organic Foods, the best Authentic Pubs, our favourite Community Pubs and our top Pubs with Rooms.

● Inspected Rooms
Pubs wishing to include bedroom details in their entry have been fully inspected. If we found them special, we included them. Look for the room symbol, the coloured entry flag on the map, or view our special 'rooms' pages (p.30-p.44).

How we go about it
We have visited every place in this guide to check on friendliness, atmosphere and style. Reader feedback and re-inspections have seen some pubs drop out of the guide; others have been 'downgraded' to Worth a Visit (see below) as landlords change or chefs leave, and these await re-inspection.

Photo left The Howard Arms, entry 495
Photo right The Drunken Duck Inn, entry 87

Introduction

We search for the details that cannot be gleaned over the internet or phone and we write the descriptions ourselves, thus avoiding brochure-speak and tired cliché. If a pub is in, it's special, and the write-up should tell you if it's your sort of special.

Our 'Best For...' choices listed at the back are pubs that stand out as the best of their type. Among them are country locals whose owners are passionate about everything organic including the beers, a city pub with a fascinating literary past, a Yorkshire tavern whose gas lamps softly hiss, and a seaside inn with saltmarsh views, a seafood menu and stylishly simple rooms. These places are 'special'.

Photo Nag's Head Inn, entry 612

The Worth a Visit section includes those pubs that didn't make a full entry this time but are still well worth seeking out. In this section, too, you will find top-flight pubs that have recently changed hands and foodie pubs that we believe are on the up.

Feedback, please

Things are constantly evolving in the world of pubs and inns. Do let us know whether your experience at any of the pubs in this book has been a disappointment or a success, or even a bit of both – or if you hear that a pub has changed hands, or if you think a pub listed in the Worth a Visit section deserves upgrading. Your input is invaluable, as we note and act on feedback. Tell us, too, about any new pubs you have found and thought special. There is a form at the back of the book – or go to www.specialplacestostay.com and click 'contact'.

The changing pub scene

Rural pubs have had to change, improve and, in some cases, diversify in order to meet social change and the demands of today's pub-goer. Dotted across the country, in ever-decreasing numbers, are Britain's gems, truly unspoilt and refreshingly plain, many having been in the family for decades (even centuries). With the closure of village shops and halls, others have become the hub of the community, a few even owned by consortiums of villagers; a growing number operate as the local shop and post office, too.

But the key to the survival of Britain's rural pub is the provision of good food – and, more recently, the added appeal of a few cosy bedrooms. Pubs are now seen as places to go to eat, and, with the nation's spiralling interest in a healthier lifestyle, more people want food that is fresh and vital, not tired, microwaved or frozen.

Gastropubs

A term born in London and embraced by the rest of the country. In London, basic backstreet boozers continue to be transformed into thriving food/gastronomy pubs where restaurant-quality food is served in casual but contemporary surroundings. The ripple-effect out of the capital has been impressive, and the trend for young entrepreneurs and talented chefs to buy failing pubs and re-invent them as pub-bistros continues to gather pace. Now pubs are becoming a serious challenge to restaurants as a wave of casual dining envelops the nation.

Pub or restaurant – a fine line

Too many gastropubs are losing sight of their pubby roots as cash tills tot up meals rather than pints of beer. High rents dictated by owner pub companies and big breweries, combined with a steady decline in beer sales and stricter drink-driving laws, has seen food begin to dominate the rural scene, to the extent that villagers are losing their 'local' in favour of bums on seats and high food revenues.

If 90% of the tables are prepared for dining and covered in 'reserved' signs, if you are greeted with a menu and a "have you booked a table, sir", and if the pristine bar is virtually devoid of real ale handpumps, then you can be pretty sure your once-treasured boozer has metamorphosed into a restaurant.

The best food pubs in England and Wales are listed within these pages and all strike a good balance between being a restaurant/bistro and a pub. A pub is a pub when you find three or more (often local) real ales, a genuine welcome for those popping in for a pint, and an easy-going and convivial atmosphere.

Movers and shakers

In 2005, hard on the heels of Heston Blumenthal (Hind's Head Hotel, Berkshire – entry 15), Phil Vickery (King of Prussia, Berkshire – entry 32), and Nigel Haworth (Three Fishes, Lancashire – entry 257), we have seen more high-profile chefs enter the world of pub dining than ever before. TV chef and author

Introduction

Mike Robinson has worked wonders with The Pot Kiln at Frilsham, Berkshire (entry 9); Michelin-starred chef Mark Dodson left the culinary hothouse of Michel Roux's famous Waterside Inn at Bray for the charms of a thatched country pub in Devon, The Mason's Arms at Knowstone (entry 145); Steve Love sold his fine dining restaurant in Leamington Spa to work his magic at the College Arms at Lower Quinton, near Stratford-upon-Avon (entry 494); and Claude Bossi, chef-patron of the eponymous Hibiscus restaurant in Ludlow, has opened a rural outpost at the Bell Inn in Yarpole, Herefordshire (entry 216).

Local food champions

These chefs are champions of local produce and believers that gastronomy is rooted in the soil. The ingredients they use are fresh, seasonal and come from the best regional suppliers. Even some of the humble rural locals are banishing laminated menus listing deep-frozen foods in favour of fresh, homemade meals.

Pubs with rooms

More and more pubs are offering bedrooms too. Some pubs may be virtually indistinguishable from hotels, but a lively bar serving real beer as well as good food puts them in the classic inn category. Others are more humble village pubs where the enthusiasm to get things right in the bar extends to the bedrooms and bathrooms upstairs.

Room inspections – a new approach

We are known for our Special Places to Stay series and for recommending wonderful places to stay in Europe and beyond. Every entry is inspected and included only if we like it. We have no truck with 'tick' boxes or grading systems.

In previous editions of this guide we visited a limited number of pub bedrooms, yet listed details for all pubs with rooms. This led to confusion and some complaints from readers. In this edition, the only pub

Photo above The White Swan Inn, entry 569
Photo right Beaufort Arms, entry 599

the cask and, if you're lucky, soup and sandwiches! Others offer more in the way of food and facilities but remain genuinely unspoilt, classic examples of the great British pub.

Pub as hub – community pubs

A well-loved pub with a big welcome, a crackling fire and the landlord's personality etched into the very fabric of the building lifts the spirits. Add heart-warming food and fine beer and you are in heaven. To have such a pub in your village would draw any community together and certainly beats meeting in a cold, soulless village hall.

Such pubs encourage folk to settle in the area and are the life and soul of the village. They generally have thriving darts, pool and football teams and are often the first venue for raffles, carol singing, farmers' markets and polling stations. A growing number are taking on an even wider role in the community, becoming part-time post offices, shops and delicatessens as village stores become unviable and are forced to close.

It all sounds too good to be true. Yet the reality is that around 26 pubs are closing each month across Britain. Why? High rents and falling sales are forcing publicans out. Rocketing property prices make bricks and mortar more valuable that

rooms featured are those that have been inspected and found to be special. Owners pay for their bedrooms to be mentioned but it is not possible for anyone to buy their way in. Their fee goes towards the high cost of the inspection process, the production of an all-colour book and the maintenance of our web site www.specialplacestostay.com

Timeless gems

Often family-owned and unchanged down the years, in historic or unusual buildings, or buried down a city backstreet or a country lane, these belong to Britain's diminishing breed of traditional pubs. We have unearthed an interesting crop. At some, expect few frills and modern-day intrusions, just basic parlour rooms, lively banter, ale tapped from

Photo Sandy Park Inn, entry 134

the business itself, so the pub becomes ripe for conversion or sale for residential use. And many villages are becoming dormitory settlements whose villagers take little active involvement in the community. However, some pubs threatened with closure have been bought by village consortiums, with locals chipping in cash and becoming shareholders. With the right landlords at the helm these pubs thrive.

Seasonal, local and organic food

The competitive global marketplace has driven our eating habits for too long, fobbed us off with cheap food and deprived us of the ebb and flow of the seasons. But, in 2001, there was a salutary wake-up call with the foot and mouth epidemic, followed by more recent scares, such as the cancer risk associated with farmed salmon. Now, slowly, the message is filtering through: mass production comes at a cost. And, as a happy antidote to this, and a reaction to it, the number of farmers' markets continues steadily to rise, re-introducing us to 'real food' and the joys of seasonal and artisanal produce. 'Local', 'seasonal' and 'organic' are the buzz words now.

Many pubs trumpet regional and seasonal food – Cumbrian ham in Cumbria, fish from the nearest coast, asparagus in season and partridge

from the local shoot. On such menus lamb is not just lamb, it's Lancastrian and heather-reared. Cheeses are west country. Beef is Herefordshire. Smoked salmon is Irish – and, increasingly, wild. The emphasis on regionality and authenticity, so deep-rooted in Italy, France and Spain, is gaining momentum here.

Paradoxes exist. Purists raise their eyebrows at the prospect of Kenyan beans in February and Peruvian asparagus in October yet insist on freshly squeezed orange juice at breakfast. Most of us appreciate lamb all year round. And who can say whether a factory-farmed tomato is better or worse than air-freighted organic? The real battle is

Photo Red Lion Inn, entry 269

to persuade producers to move away from artificially grown, extended-shelf-life, textbook-perfect produce, and to rear poultry and animals humanely so that the meat is full of texture and taste.

What is 'Modern British' food?

Modern British cooking, first defined in 1987, puts the best British produce in the spotlight, demands a freshness of approach (let the ingredients do the talking) and shows a respect for seasonal bounty. Increasingly, 'Mod Brit' has also come to mean a nod to Mediterranean and oriental shores – hence linguine with roasted peppers and squid with lime and chilli.

'British rustic' cooking

Lately, in some of the more adventurous gastro-kitchens, an unexpected element has come into play. A number of chefs are moving away from the Mediterranean and 'fusion' fixation of the past decade and placing an emphasis on British tradition. Hence the intriguing

revival of British dishes of low or 'rustic' origin, from Lancashire hot pot to ginger parkin.

So food that was once confined to 'below stairs' turns out to be the trendiest thing on your plate. These British-rustic delicacies tend to have simple, strong flavours and go rather well with a pint. Look out for:

- Bath chap – pig's cheek, as delicious as a trotter
- faggots – meat balls that developed as a way of using up all the unwanted bits of pig, served with mushy peas
- black pudding – a large sausage made of pig's blood, suet, bread crumbs and oatmeal, sautéed and served with mash
- champ – of Irish descent: potatoes mashed, mixed with onions, lashings of butter, and served with sausages
- sausages – voguishly served with onion marmalade (also known as 'confit') and created from venison, wild boar or Cumberland pork (provenance is all)
- fish and chips, served with 'minted' mushy peas and hand-cut chips
- oxtail and kidney pudding; smoked eel on bread; potted ham with chutney; herring and potato salad
- bubble and squeak – a tasty way of using up yesterday's mashed potatoes and cooked cabbage, fried until crunchy. Originally, the dish included chopped boiled beef

Photo left The Garrison Public House, entry 297
Photo right Dartmoor Inn, entry 131

Introduction

Whatever happened to duck à l'orange?

Gastropubs Sweeping the land, the new 'bistros of Britain' are blurring the distinction between casual-chic restaurants and old-fashioned drinking dens.

Slow Food Anti fast-food movement founded in Italy, inching its way into Britain and most conspicuous in Ludlow. Based on the philosophy that food tastes better when grown organically, harvested locally and eaten in season. The movement champions artisan-producers.

- **Pan-fried** steak, sea bass etc are in; 'fried' is out. 'Deep-fried' is acceptable re calamari and cod.
- **Jus** A concentrated reduction made from meat juices and wine: gravy without the flour.
- **Coulis** A pretty puddle of fruit or vegetable purée. May disappear from menus as minimal garnish gains momentum.
- **Twice-baked soufflé** tolerates reheating at the last minute. Expect to see more in 2006.
- **Twice-baked potatoes** Baked potatoes whose flesh has been scooped out, fluffed up with butter and cheese, then baked again.
- **Trio of chops** – on every modish menu. Look out for trio of fish, trio of ice cream, trio of crème brulée.
- **Baguette** is out, ciabatta in. And sandwiches are called panini.

- **Bruschetta** – toasted Italian sourdough bread rubbed with garlic and drizzled with oil; sometimes served with melting mozzarella.
- **Polenta** – the cornmeal cooked in a similar manner to porridge is still in fashion, eaten hot with a little butter or cooled until firm, cut into squares and fried in olive oil. Often mixed with cheese.
- **Pancetta** Italian bacon, cured with salt and spices but not smoked. Good with scallops.
- **Carpaccio** Thin shavings of raw beef fillet, drizzled with olive oil and lemon juice or served with a mayonnaise or mustard sauce.
- **Duck confit** – salted duck poached slowly in fat to preserve it; rich, gamey and meltingly tender.
- **Braised lamb shank** Slow-cooked front leg – possibly the most popular dish on the gastropub menu.
- **Venison** – roast, casseroled, 'sausaged' or 'terrined'. Free-ranging game and rabbit are becoming popular alternatives to livestock reared in dubious conditions.
- **Pommes dauphinoises** – 2005's favourite potato dish: layers of thin slices cooked in a creamy, cheesy, garlicy sauce. Sometimes known as Pommes Gratin.
- **Salad** is out, 'leaves' are in and rocket rules.
- **Old-fashioned root vegetables** – very now. Beetroot is everywhere, roasted or in relish; suede, parsnip and celeriac make brilliant mash.

- **Pumpkin and squash** Another must-have – roasted or puréed.
- **Wilted spinach** – on many a fashionable menu.
- **Wild mushrooms**, garnered from the homeland's rich but neglected natural larder, these fungi fulfil every foodie's dream. Good in risotto.
- **Nursery puddings** have been restored to their rightful place, to be joined of late by lighter English desserts. Look out for walnut tart, quince tart, treacle tart, lemon posset, poached pears, fruit crumble ('Bramley' or 'plum and armagnac').
- **Panna cotta** 'Cooked cream' is an egg custard, divinely silken, served cold and accompanied by fruit.
- **Crème fraîche** – the stylish alternative to cream, adding a tangy note to sweet tarts and fruits.

What is a real ale?

Cask or keg ale – what's the difference? One's a living organism, the other isn't. After the brewing process, cask-conditioned green beer ('real ale') is put into barrels to allow a secondary fermentation, producing a unique flavour and bubbles that are natural. Mass-produced fizz, on the other hand, has been filtered and sterilised and, like lager, is dead – until the gas is pumped back to give the distinguishing bubbles. Stored in sealed containers, it tastes more like bottled beers – and is put through the same process. Their advantage? They have a longer shelf life, and are easier to dispense. However, some bottled beers still contain the life-giving yeast(s) that imbue them with character, the Belgian trappist beers being an appealing example.

In the 1960s and early 1970s the big breweries flooded the market with keg beers and lager. Then, in 1971, CAMRA (The Campaign for Real Ale) was founded. Its success in inspiring the real ale revival has been a dramatic example of a consumer group in action, forcing the brewing industry to rethink its strategy and produce real ales. The new century has seen a flowering of craft breweries across the country, with beer being brewed on farms, on industrial estates and in sheds behind pubs. The Progressive Beer Duty was introduced in 2002 to give micro-brewers a further boost; now there are over 400 independent breweries in Britain.

Photo The Cherry Tree Inn, entry 365

Introduction

Finding the right place for you

At the back of the book (p.413-p.421) we highlight pubs that stand out for a special reason. We list the best:

- Pubs for real ale
- Pubs that brew their own beer
- Pubs for local/organic food
- Pubs for cheese
- Authentic pubs
- Pubs with views
- Pubs with waterside settings
- Pubs for real fires
- Pubs for summer gardens

Quick reference indices

At the back of the book (p.422-p.427) we list those pubs with:

- wheelchair-accessible bar and wcs
- special bedrooms
- live music
- local/organic produce
- no piped music

How to use this book

Opening times

We asked owners to give the days/sessions their pub is open and closed. For those that open 'usual' pub hours, and are closed 3pm-6pm (7pm Sundays), we have left the 'Closed' field blank, listing only the variations between these hours and if they are closed particular lunchtimes and evenings. We state if the pub is 'open all day', or 'open weekends', or 'open Friday-Sunday'. We do advise that you check before setting out, especially in winter.

Meals and meal prices

We give the times meals are served and the approximate cost of main courses – in the bar and/or restaurant. Note that some pubs charge extra for side dishes, which significantly increases the 'main course' price. Where set menus are mentioned, assume these are for three courses. Note that many pubs do fixed price Sunday lunches, and that prices may change. Check when booking.

Map and directions

The map pages at the front of the book show the position, with an entry number, for each of our pubs and inns. Mauve map flags indicate pubs with rooms and orange flags the award winners. Our maps are for guidance only; use a detailed road map or you may get lost!

Photo left The Rose & Crown, entry 340
Photo right The Angel Inn, entry 521

Introduction

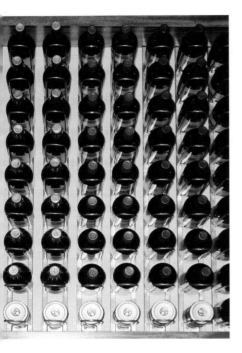

The map and entry numbers are given at the foot of the separate guide entries. The directions given are, again, for guidance.

Bedrooms, bathrooms and breakfasts

If you're thinking of staying the night in a simple pub or inn do bear in mind that an early night may not be possible if folk are carousing below. Some bedrooms do not have ensuite bathrooms; if this is important to you, check before booking. Breakfasts are generally included in the room price; again, check. Most places serve breakfast between 8am and 10am.

Photo The Rose & Crown, entry 501

Bedroom prices

Prices are per room for two people sharing. If a price range is given, then the lowest price is usually for the least expensive double room in low season and the highest for the most expensive room in high season. These may change during the year. The single room rate (or the single occupancy of a double room) generally follows. Occasionally, prices are for half board, i.e. they include dinner, bed and breakfast.

Symbols

On the inside back cover we explain our symbols. Use them as a guide, not as a statement of fact, and double-check anything that is particularly important to you.

Real Ale 🍺 identifies those pubs with a real passion for beer. It is given to pubs serving four or more real ales, including local microbrewery beers.

Wine 🍷 As food improves in pubs so does the wine quality and the selection of wines available by the glass. In many top food pubs wine sales far exceed beer sales. We give this symbol to pubs that serve eight or more wines by the glass.

Bed The 🛏 symbol is given to pubs/inns that have had their rooms inspected and that we consider special.

Children The 🏃 symbol is given to places that accept children of any age. That doesn't mean that they can go everywhere in the pub, or that highchairs and special menus (or small portions) are provided. Nor does it mean that children should be anything less than well-monitored! Call to check details such as separate family rooms, whether children are allowed in the dining room and whether there is play equipment in the garden.

Dogs The 🐕 symbol is given to places where your dog can go into some part of the pub – generally the bar and garden. It is unlikely to include restaurant areas and many pubs don't allow dogs in the bedrooms either.

Payment 💳 All our pubs and inns take cash and cheques with a cheque card. If they also take credit cards, we have given them the appropriate symbol. Check that your credit card is acceptable. Visa and MasterCard are generally fine. American Express is sometimes accepted; Diners Club hardly ever. Debit cards are widely accepted.

Smoking 🚭 Most separate dining areas will either be smoke-free or have smoking restrictions. In anticipation of the government's no-smoking legislation, an increasing number of pubs are now totally no-smoking. In such cases we state 'No smoking throughout' in italics at the end of the description.

Wheelchair ♿ We use this symbol wherever those in wheelchairs can access the bar and loos. The symbol doesn't apply to accommodation.

Walking 👟 This symbol indicates where a pub has walking information (ie. leaflets and guides) and, perhaps, maps on display for customers to peruse.

Bookings
At weekends, food pubs are often full and it is best to book a table well in advance. At other times, only tables in the dining rooms may be reserved, while tables in the bar may operate on a first come, first served basis. Always phone to check meal times. Some of the best gastropubs do not take reservations at all, desirous of holding on to their pubby origins. Arrive early and pick your table!

Photo Star & Garter, entry 467

Most pubs and inns will ask for a credit card number and a contact phone number when you telephone to book a room for the night.

Tipping
It is not obligatory but it is appreciated, particularly in pubs with restaurants.

Internet
www.specialplacestostay.com has online pages for all the pubs with bedrooms listed here and from all our other books – around 4,500 places in total. There's a searchable database, a snippet from the write-up and colour photos. New kid on the block is our dedicated UK holiday home web site, www.special-escapes.co.uk

Disclaimer
We make no claims to pure objectivity in choosing our Special Places. They are here because we like them. Our opinions and tastes are ours alone and this book is a statement of them; we hope that you will share them. We have done our utmost to get our facts right but apologise unreservedly for any mistakes that may have crept in.

We do not check such things as fire alarms, kitchen hygiene or any other regulation with which owners of properties in this guide should comply, for that is their responsibility.

And finally
Feedback from you is invaluable. With your help and our own inspections we can maintain our reputation for dependability.

Thank you to all those who have taken the time to share your opinions with us. You have helped make this edition of the book even better than the last. Please let us have your comments; there is a report form at the back of this book. Or email us at info@sawdays.co.uk

David Hancock

Photo left The Punch Bowl Inn, entry 83
Photo right Spread Eagle Inn, entry 517

Pub awards

Local, Seasonal & Organic Produce Award

Hearts soar when our inspectors come across a chalkboard menu promoting seasonal produce, perhaps farm meats, village-baked bread, locally shot game, fish and shellfish from local boats, organic wines and local brewery ale. We have seen a marked improvement in pubs actively sourcing seasonal foods from high-quality suppliers. So much so that we have introduced an award this year for our champions of local, seasonal and organic produce.

The Pot Kiln, Frilsham,
Berkshire
entry 9

The George & Dragon,
Speldhurst, Kent
entry 250

The Appletree Country Inn,
Marton, Yorkshire
entry 568

Authentic Pub Award

We have visited dozens of simple, unadulterated pubs and a host of authentic rural watering holes and those that we found to be very special have a half-page entry – many more are listed in our Worth a Visit section. The cream of the crop, all with a full-page entry, are:

The Tinners Arms, Zennor,
Cornwall
entry 61

The Queen's Head, Newton,
Cambridgeshire
entry 36

Ye Olde Gate, Brassington,
Derbyshire
entry 109

Pub with Rooms Award

For Edition 3 our inspectors visited an eclectic bunch of bedrooms, from swish country suites sporting flat-screen TVs to fresh, simple bedrooms overlooking the sea. For a list and photographs of our pubs with special rooms see pages 30-44.

This year two pubs stand out from the crowd, one hidden down lanes in a sleepy village on the Dorset/Somerset border, the other a busy roadside pub in Sussex. Under new ownership, both have been stylishly revamped in the past two years without losing their 'pubby' roots. Their food, wines and beers are excellent, their bedrooms are special.

Photo © Getty images

The Queen's Arms,
Corton Denham, Somerset, entry 430

The Halfway Bridge,
Petworth, Sussex, entry 461

Community Pub Award

Within these pages you will find some cracking rural locals run by enterprising, hard-working landlords who have succeeded in making their pub the hub of the community. Our shining examples are:

The Old Crown,
Hesket Newmarket, Cumbria
entry 96

The Halfway House,
Langport, Somerset
entry 429

The Plough & Harrow
Monknash, Glamorgan
entry 591

Buckinghamshire
The Dinton Hermit – entry 28
Charming four-posters & 'Regency' bedrooms in the old, wonky-floored part, stylish modern rooms in the converted barn.
Rooms: 13: 2 four-posters, 10 doubles, 1 twin £80–£125.
Singles from £80.
Water Lane, Ford Village, Aylesbury Tel: 01296 747473
dintonhermit@btconnect.com www.dinton-hermit.com

Cheshire
Albion Inn – entry 44
The bedrooms at the top (separate entrance) are modern, compact and comfortable, with excellent bathrooms.
Rooms: 2 doubles £65.
Park Street, Chester
Tel: 01244 340345
mike@albioninn.freeserve.co.uk www. albioninnchester.co.uk

Cornwall
The Halzephron – entry 62
Cosy bedrooms with deep-sprung beds, patchwork quilts, fresh fruit, real coffee and farmyard views.
Rooms: 2 doubles from £80.
Singles from £45.
Gunwalloe, Helston
Tel: 01326 240406 halzephroninn@gunwalloe1.fsnet.co.uk

The Plume of Feathers – entry 68
Converted stables contain stylishly simple bedrooms with generous brass beds, large-screen TVs, great bathrooms and the odd sofa.
Rooms: 5 doubles £75–£105. Singles £56.25–£78.75.
Mitchell, Truro
Tel: 01872 510387
enquiries@theplume.info www.theplume.info

The Mill House Inn – entry 73
The pub's contemporary bedrooms vary in size and have a
stylish Cape Cod feel, in sympathy with the setting.
Rooms: 9 twins/doubles £80-£100.
Singles £50.
Trebarwith, Tintagel
Tel: 01840 770200 management@themillhouseinn.co.uk
www.themillhouseinn.co.uk

Cumbria
The Mason's Arms – entry 80
Attractive, contemporary suites have beds on the mezzanine
and kitchenettes; cottages are stylish...
Rooms: 3 suites £85-£105.
2 cottages: 1 for 6, 1 for 4, £105-£155.
Strawberry Bank, Cartmel Fell Tel: 01539 568486
info@strawberrybank.com www.strawberrybank.com

Devon
Dartmoor Inn – entry 131
And so to bed... new mattresses on antique beds, soft lights and
sofas: the Dartmoor's rooms are absolutely gorgeous.
Rooms: 3 doubles £90-£115.
Lydford, Okehampton
Tel: 01822 820221
info@dartmoorinn.co.uk www.dartmoorinn.com

Sandy Park Inn – entry 134
Bedrooms above the kitchen are simple, crisp, comfortable and
quiet. Some overlook thatched roofs to fields, one opens to the
garden – another delight – beds are big and bathrooms smart.
Rooms: 5: 4 doubles, 1 twin £70. Singles £45
Sandy Park, Chagford
Tel: 01647 433267
sandyparkinn@aol.com www.sandyparkinn.co.uk

Devon

Culm Valley Inn — entry 144

Bedrooms are simple and cheerful, with white bed linen and vibrant walls.
Rooms: 3: 1 double, 1 twin, 1 family from £55.
Singles £30.
Culmstock, Cullompton
Tel: 01884 840354

Durham

The Victoria Inn — entry 151

Upstairs bedrooms are traditionally furnished and good value, breakfasts are generous and there's off-street parking and garaging. Original, timeless, welcoming.
Rooms: 5: 3 doubles, 1 twin, 1 family £60.
86 Hallgarth Street Tel: 0191 386 5269
www.victoriainn-durhamcity.co.uk

Gloucestershire

The King's Arms Inn — entry 165

Super bedrooms, one with a dressing room, all with mod cons, reflect the demands of the county set.
Rooms: 3 doubles £80.
The Street, Didmarton, Badminton
Tel: 01454 238245 kingsarms@didmarton.freeserve.co.net
www.kingsarmsdidmarton.co.uk

Bathurst Arms — entry 171

Smartened-up bedrooms provide a homely base for exploring the Cotswolds: they are clean, comfortable, freshly painted and well-equipped.
Rooms: 5 doubles £70. Singles £50.
North Cerney, Cirencester
Tel: 01285 831281
chefpilgrim@aol.com www.bathurstarms.co.uk

The King's Arms – entry 187
A diminutive stair leads to bedrooms above. Be cheered by bright wool throws, tasselled cushions, crisp white linen and Neals Yard goodies.
Rooms: 10 doubles £70-£130.
Market Square, Stow-on-the-Wold
Tel: 01451 830364 info@kingsarms-stowonthewold.co.uk
www.kingsarms-stowonthewold.co.uk

The White Hart Inn – entry 191
Beautiful bedrooms are mostly furnished with Scandinavian antiques, one is Moroccan in style, another 'New England',
Rooms: 8: 6 twins/doubles, 2 four-posters £65-£135.
Singles £55-£115.
High Street, Winchcombe Tel: 01242 602359
enquiries@the-white-hart-inn.com
www.the-white-hart-inn.com

Hampshire

The Greyhound – entry 199
Smart new bedrooms sport spotlights, auction antiques, flat-screen TVs, classy bathrooms and cosseting extras.
Rooms: 8: 3 doubles, 4 twins, 1 single £70-£100.
31 High Street, Stockbridge
Tel: 01264 810833

Herefordshire

The Bulls Head – entry 221
With understatedly stylish bedrooms, stabling for your horse *and* rough camping available, there's no excuse not to stay the night.
Rooms: 3: 2 doubles, 1 family room, £60-£65.
Craswall Tel: 01981 510616
info@thebullsheadpub.com
www.thebullsheadpub.com

Herefordshire
Three Crowns Inn – entry 225
A bedroom upstairs – peaceful, characterful, understatedly
stylish – is the icing on this very special cake.
Rooms: 1 family room from £90.
Bleak Acre, Ullingswick
Tel: 01432 820279
info@threecrownsinn.com www.threecrownsinn.com

The Cottage of Content – entry 227
Small, beamy bedrooms are carpeted and cottagey, and
bathrooms fresh and new. Good value.
Rooms: 4: 3 double, 1 twin £56-£64.
Carey, Hereford
Tel: 01432 840242
admin@cottageofcontent.co.uk www.cottageofcontent.co.uk

Leicestershire
The Queen's Head – entry 264
Then add bedrooms that have a similarly stylish feel and you
have a well-nigh-perfect, 21st-century coaching inn.
Rooms: 6: 4 doubles, 2 twins £70-£100. Singles £55.
2 Long Street, Belton, Loughborough
Tel: 01530 222359
enquiries@thequeenshead.org www.thequeenshead.org

London
Portobello Gold – entry 277
Refurbished bedrooms have small shower rooms and good beds
– ideal if the hippy in you is still active...
Rooms: 8: 6 twin/doubles, 1 suite, 1 roof terrace apartment,
£60-£180.
95-97 Portobello Road, Notting Hill Gate Tel: 020 7460 4910
reservations@portobellogold.com www.portobellogold.com

Norfolk

Saracen's Head – entry 326

Bedrooms have bold colours, sisal floors and linen curtains...
The whole mood is of quirky, committed individuality.

Rooms: 6: 5 doubles, 1 twin £85. Singles £45.
Wolterton, Erpingham Tel: 01263 768909
saracenshead@wolterton.freeserve.co.uk
www.saracenshead-norfolk.co.uk

Globe Inn – entry 332

The bedrooms are as fresh and as un-traditional as can be,
gleaming with oak floors, powerful showers and digital TVs.

Rooms: 7: 5 doubles, 2 twins £55-£115.
The Buttlands, Wells-next-the-Sea
Tel: 01328 710206
globe@holkham.co.uk www.globeatwells.co.uk

The Victoria – entry 334

There are serene bedrooms upstairs, some with views to marsh
and sea, and three luscious lodges in the grounds.

Rooms: 10 + 3: 9 doubles, 1 attic suite £110-£200.
Singles £90-£110. 3 self-catering lodges £160-£200 (max. 4).
Park Road, Holkham
Tel: 01328 711008 victoria@holkham.co.uk
www.victoriaatholkham.co.uk

King's Head – entry 336

If you're staying, the bedrooms are swish – enormous beds,
flat-screen TVs, a decanter of port as well as a mini-bar, and a
welcome-you-in plate of home-baked biscuits.

Rooms: 9 doubles £125-£175. Singles £69.50.
Great Bircham, King's Lynn
Tel: 01485 578265 welcome@the-kings-head-bircham.co.uk
www.the-kings-head-bircham.co.uk

Pubs with rooms

Norfolk

The White Horse – entry 337

Bedrooms in a wavy extension facing the tidal marshes and North Norfolk Coastal Path have generous proportions and a patio each.

Rooms: 15: 9 doubles, 6 twins £100–£115.
Main Road, Brancaster Staithe Tel: 01485 210262
reception@whitehorsebrancaster.co.uk
www.whitehorsebrancaster.co.uk

The Rose & Crown – entry 340

Inside, a warren of rooms filled with old beams and log fires, a family-friendly garden room, and five delightfully stylish bedrooms in the new wing.

Rooms: 16 twins/doubles £85–£95. Singles £50–£65.
Old Church Road, Snettisham, King's Lynn
Tel: 01485 541382 info@roseandcrownsnettisham.co.uk
www.roseandcrownsnettisham.co.uk

Northumberland

The Pheasant Inn – entry 351

Bedrooms next door in the hay barn are fresh, simple, compact and cosy – good value for money.

Rooms: 8: 4 doubles, 3 twins, 1 family, £65–£85. Singles £40–£45.
Stannersburn, Hexham
Tel: 01434 240382
stay@thepheasantinn.com www.thepheasantinn.com

Oxfordshire

The Cherry Tree Inn – entry 365

Bedrooms are contemporary and stylish, with flat-screen TVs, king-size beds and feather pillows.

Rooms: 4 doubles £65–£85.
Stoke Row, Henley-on-Thames
Tel: 01491 680430
info@thecherrytreeinn.com www.thecherrytreeinn.com

Kings Head Inn – entry 382
The bedrooms look fabulous. All are different, most have a stunning view, some family furniture mixed in with 'bits'... painted wood, great colours and lush fabrics.
Rooms: 12: 10 doubles, 2 twins, £70-£125. Singles £55.
The Green, Bledington
Tel: 01608 658365
kingshead@orr-ewing.com   www.kingsheadinn.net

Somerset

The Royal Oak Inn – entry 405
Bedrooms ramble around the first floor (one below has a private terrace) and are individual, peaceful, homely and great value.
Rooms: 10: 8 doubles, 2 twins, £65-£85. Singles £55-£65.
Luxborough, Dunster Tel: 01984 640319
info@theroyaloakinnluxborough.co.uk
www.theroyaloakinnluxborough.co.uk

Carew Arms – entry 407
Freshly decorated bedrooms are upstairs: new pine, good linen, creaking floorboards.
Rooms: 6: 3 doubles, 3 twins £79.
Crowcombe, Taunton
Tel: 01984 618631
info@thecarewarms.co.uk
www.thecarewarms.co.uk

The Greyhound Inn – entry 411
Clean, comfortable bedrooms: more hotel than individual with floral curtains and bed covers.
Rooms: 4: 2 doubles, 2 twins from £80.
Singles from £65.
Staple Fitzpaine, Taunton
Tel: 01823 480227 info@thegreyhoundinn.fsbusiness.co.uk
www.thegreyhoundinn.fsbusiness.co.uk

Somerset

Farmers Inn – entry 412

Off-beat but elegant rooms with distinctive beds (all antique) and gleaming wooden floors. Bathrooms are shiny and chic.
Rooms: 5 doubles £90-£110. Singles £70-£90.
Slough Green, West Hatch, Taunton Tel: 01823 480480
letsgostay@farmersinnwesthatch.co.uk
www.farmersinnwesthatch.co.uk

Lord Poulett Arms – entry 414

Contemporary wallpapers set the tone for super bedrooms upstairs – along with open-stone walls, brass bedsteads and seagrass floors; Roberts radios add a fun touch. Brilliant value.
Rooms: 4 twins/doubles £72. Singles £48.
High Street, Hinton St George, Crewkerne
Tel: 01460 73149 steveandmichelle@lordpoulettarms.com
www.lordpoulettarms.com

The Devonshire Arms – entry 416

Outside are a new patio and sunny walled garden; upstairs, a flurry of large, light and absolutely fabulous bedrooms.
Rooms: 9: 8 doubles, 1 family room, £70-£110.
Singles from £55.
Long Sutton, Langport
Tel: 01458 241271
mail@thedevonshirearms.com www.thedevonshirearms.com

The Manor House Inn – entry 419

After, totter out to the single-storey building where smart and generous bedrooms await; beds are hugely comfortable, shower rooms a treat.
Rooms: 3: 2 doubles, 1 twin £80. Singles £50.
Ditcheat, Shepton Mallet Tel: 01749 860276
giles@themanoratditcheat.co.uk
www.themanorhouseinn.co.uk

The Talbot Inn – entry 422
Lovely big bedrooms are staunchy traditional with deep carpets,
floral fabrics and plenty of charm.
Rooms: 8 twins/doubles £95-£145.
Singles £85.
Selwood Street, Mells, Frome
Tel: 01373 812254
roger@talbotinn.com www.talbotinn.com

Bear & Swan – entry 425
Retire to bedrooms airy and spacious; there are charming
antiques, stylish bathroom suites and an open-plan living area,
with kitchen, to share.
Rooms: 2 doubles £80. Singles £50.
13 South Parade, Chew Magna
Tel: 01275 331100
enquiries@bearandswan.co.uk www.bearandswan.co.uk

The Queen's Arms – entry 430
Bedrooms are stunning and stylish with smart bath and shower
rooms, posh smellies and breathtaking views – book the French
room!
Rooms: 5 twins/doubles £75-£120.
Corton Denham
Tel: 01963 220317
relax@thequeensarms.com www.thequeensarms.com

Sussex
Halfway Bridge Inn – entry 461
Deep beds, leather chairs, plasma screens and PlayStations "for
the boys" sit beautifully with old beams and rustic brickwork.
Rooms: 6: 2 suites from £120, 4 doubles from £90.
Singles from £55.
Halfway Bridge, Midhurst Tel: 01798 861281
hwb@thesussexpub.co.uk www.thesussexpub.co.uk

Sussex

White Horse Inn – entry 466

CD players, snowy bathrobes, hamper breakfasts... this is a Green Tourism gold award-winner, committed to sourcing local and organic wherever possible.

Rooms: 8 twins/doubles £95-£120. Singles £65-£95.
High Street, Chilgrove, Chichester Tel: 01243 535219
info@whitehorsechilgrove.co.uk www.whitehorsechilgrove.co.uk

Royal Oak – entry 470

Bedrooms are divided between a cottage, a nearby barn and upstairs at the back; all have DVD and CD players and plasma screens, brown leather chairs and big comfy beds.

Rooms: 5 doubles, 1 cottage for 4, £80-£110.
Singles £60-£70.
Pook Lane, East Lavant, Chichester Tel: 01243 527434
ro@thesussexpub.co.uk www.thesussexpub.co.uk

The Bull – entry 474

Return to white bed linen in gorgeous rooms where new and old blend as beautifully as below. Expect bold silks, walk-in rain showers and fresh lilies.

Rooms: 4 doubles £80-£100.
2 High Street, Ditchling, Burgess Hill
Tel: 01273 843147
dcworrall@hotmail.com

The Griffin Inn – entry 477

Bedrooms have an uncluttered country-inn elegance: uneven floors, country furniture, soft coloured walls.

Rooms: 13: 1 twin, 5 doubles, 7 four-posters £80-£130.
Singles £60-£80 (not weekends).
Fletching, Uckfield
Tel: 01825 722890 thegriffininn@hotmail.com
www.thegriffininn.co.uk

Warwickshire

The Howard Arms – entry 495

Gorgeous bedrooms are set discreetly apart, mixing period style and modern luxury; the double oozes old world charm, the twin is more folksy, the half-tester is almost a suite.

Rooms: 3: 2 doubles, 1 twin £97-£112. Singles £75.
Ilmington, Stratford-upon-Avon Tel: 01608 682226
info@howardarms.com www.howardarms.com

Fox & Goose Inn – entry 496

The fun spills over into bedrooms upstairs which come eccentrically dressed à la Cluedo – Plum, Scarlet, Peacock, Mustard – while bathrooms have luxurious claw-foot tubs.

Rooms: 4 twins/doubles £85-£120.
Armscote, Stratford-upon-Avon
Tel: 01608 682293
contact@foxandgoose.co.uk www.foxandgoose.co.uk

Wiltshire

Spread Eagle Inn – entry 517

Peaceful bedrooms have muted colours, white linen, original fireplaces and delightful views. Bathrooms are not state-of-the-art but perfectly plain – and spotless.

Rooms: 5 twins/doubles £70-£90. Singles £50-£60.
Stourhead, Stourton, Warminster Tel: 01747 840587
enquiries@spreadeagleinn.com www.spreadeagleinn.com

The Compasses Inn – entry 519

Bedrooms are at the top of stone stairs outside the front door and have the same effortless charm: walls are thick, windows are wonky, bathrooms are new

Rooms: 4: 2 doubles, 2 twins/doubles £75.
Lower Chicksgrove, Tisbury
Tel: 01722 714318
thecompasses@aol.com www.thecompassesinn.com

Wiltshire

The Forester Inn – entry 520
Bedrooms are fresh and lovely, with cast-iron beds, feather duvets and white linen.
Rooms: 2 doubles, £65.
Singles £50.
Lower Street, Donhead St Andrew
Tel: 01747 828038

Yorkshire

The Tempest Arms – entry 541
In the bedroom wing are recently done-up rooms, six on the ground floor, with hand-crafted furniture and bathrooms sporting Molton Brown toiletries.
Rooms: 12 twins/doubles £74.95. Singles £59.95.
Elslack, Skipton Tel: 01282 842450
info@tempestarms.co.uk www.tempestarms.co.uk

Forester's Arms – entry 547
The bedrooms are either sweet and old-fashioned or contemporary and cheerful, and there's homemade marmalade for breakfast.
Rooms: 3: 2 doubles, 1 twin £79.
Carlton in Coverdale, Leyburn
Tel: 01969 640272
chambermic@hotmail.co.uk www.the-foresters-arms.co.uk

The Boar's Head – entry 556
Up the pretty staircase to comfy bedrooms, with sherry and fresh flowers in the best.
Rooms: 25: 4 doubles, 21 twins/doubles £125-£150.
Singles £105-£125.
Ripley, Harrogate Tel: 01423 771888
reservations@boarsheadripley.co.uk
www.boarsheadripley.co.uk

The Abbey Inn – entry 560
Bedrooms are special with bathrobes, aromatherapy oils, fruit, homemade biscuits and a 'treasure chest' of wine.
Rooms: 3 doubles £95-£155.
Byland Abbey, Thirsk
Tel: 01347 868204
jane@nordli.freeserve.co.uk
www.bylandabbeyinn.co.uk

The White Swan Inn – entry 569
The handsome pub has luxurious bedrooms (plump beds, smart magazines, Penhaligon smellies)
Rooms: 21 doubles/twins/suites from £129.
Singles from £79.
Market Place, Pickering
Tel: 01751 472288
welcome@white-swan.co.uk   www.white-swan.co.uk

Wales
Conwy
Kinmel Arms – entry 584
Four dreamy suites, each with French windows to a decked seating area and a fabulous bathroom with vast towels.
Rooms: 4 suites £135-£175.
St George, Abergele   Tel: 01745 832207
info@thekinmelarms.co.uk   www.thekinmelarms.co.uk

Monmouthshire
Bell at Skenfrith – entry 595
Bedrooms are country smart with Farrow & Ball colours and beds dressed in cotton piqué and Welsh wool; plus homemade biscuits andCath Collins toiletries...
Rooms: 8: 5 doubles, 3 suites £95-£170. Singles £70-£110.
Skenfrith   Tel: 01600 750235
enquiries@skenfrith.co.uk   www.skenfrith.co.uk

Monmouthshire

Beaufort Arms – entry 599

Bedrooms – the best in the main house – are pleasing, fresh, spotless and new. Ask for one with a church view.
Rooms: 15: 7 double, 7 twin, 1 single £85-£95. Singles £60.
High Street, Raglan, Usk
Tel: 01291 690412 thebeauforthotel@hotmail.com
www.beaufortraglan.co.uk

Neath

Dulais Rock – entry 605

Up in the eaves, bedrooms are smartly cream, white and cocoa brown; two share a balcony overlooking trees, rockface and glimpses of the stunning falls.
Rooms: 3 doubles £62.50.
Main Road, Aberdulais Tel: 01639 644611
dulaisrock@tiscali.co.uk www.dulaisrock.co.uk

Pembrokeshire

The Old Point House Inn – entry 606

Three simple, fresh, white and blue bedrooms await upstairs; ask for the quiet twin with the stunning bay view.
Rooms: 3 twins/doubles £50.
Singles £25.
Angle, Pembroke
Tel: 01646 641205

Powys

The Felin Fach Griffin – entry 617

Bedrooms are in a modern style, clean and simple, with a few designer touches: tulips in a vase, check curtains, snowy white towels and linen.
Rooms: 7: 4 twins/doubles, 3 four-posters £92.50-£115.
Singles from £67.50.
Felin Fach, Brecon Tel: 01874 620111
enquiries@eatdrinksleep.ltd.uk www.eatdrinksleep.ltd.uk

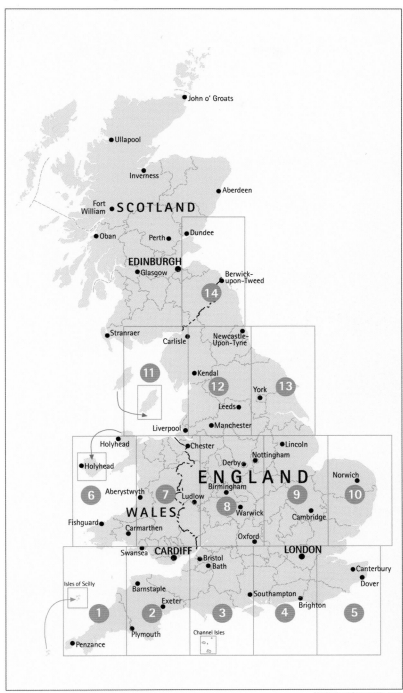

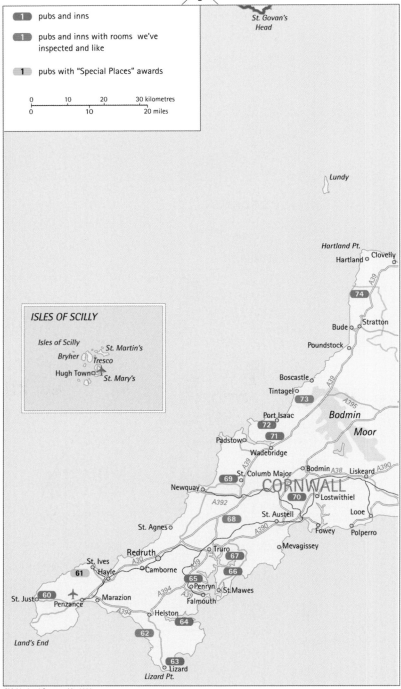

6

Map 2

47

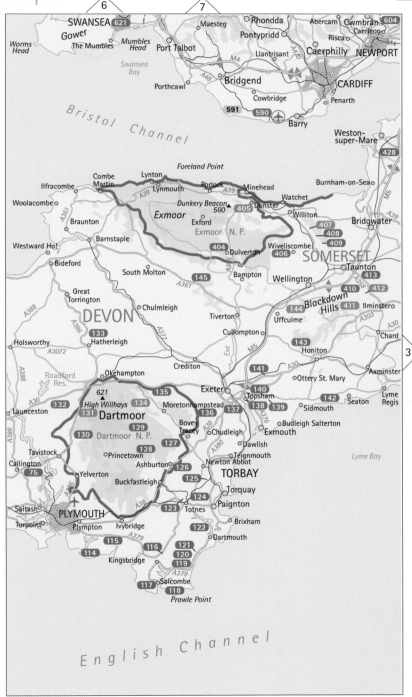

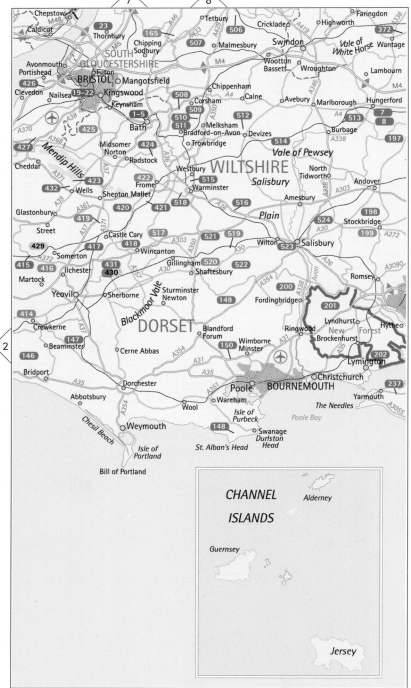

Map 4

49

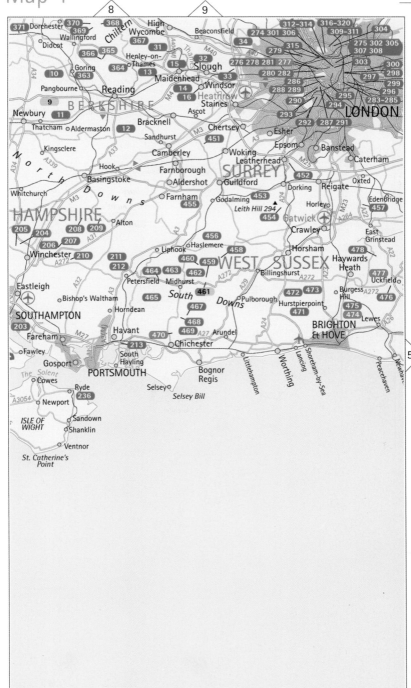

Map 5

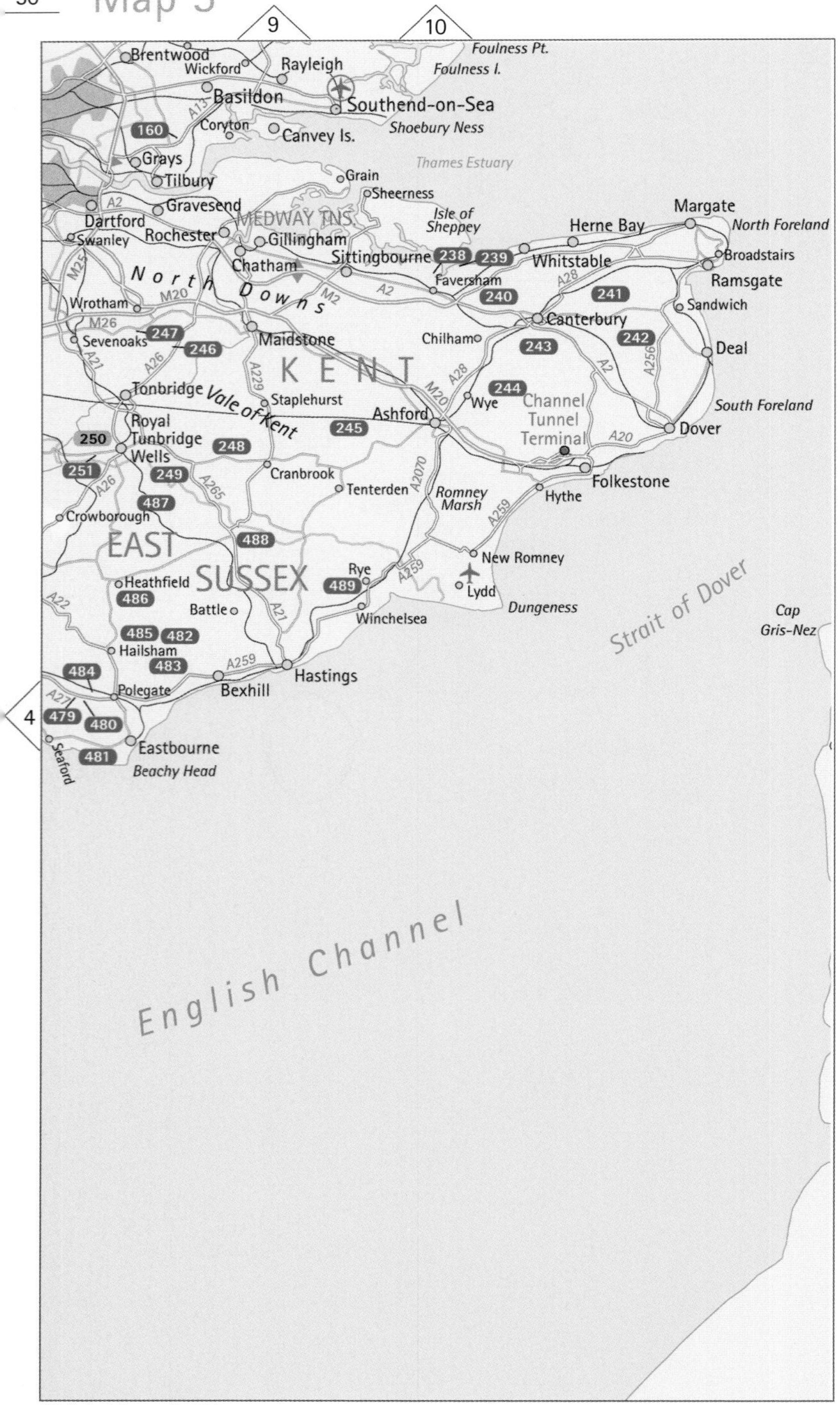
9
10
Foulness Pt.
Foulness I.
Brentwood
Wickford
Rayleigh
Basildon
Southend-on-Sea
Shoebury Ness
Coryton
Canvey Is.
160
Grays
Tilbury
Thames Estuary
Grain
Sheerness
Isle of Sheppey
A2
Gravesend
Dartford
MEDWAY TNS.
Swanley
Rochester
Gillingham
Chatham
Sittingbourne
238
239
Faversham
Whitstable
Herne Bay
Margate
North Foreland
Broadstairs
Ramsgate
North Downs
M20
M2
A2
240
A28
241
Wrotham
M26
M25
Sandwich
Sevenoaks
247
246
Maidstone
Canterbury
Chilham
243
242
Deal
A21
A26
A229
KENT
M20
A28
A2
A256
244
Wye
Tonbridge
Vale of Kent
Staplehurst
Channel Tunnel Terminal
South Foreland
Royal Tunbridge Wells
Ashford
245
A20
Dover
250
248
251
249
Cranbrook
A265
A2070
Folkestone
A26
Tenterden
Romney Marsh
Hythe
487
A259
Crowborough
EAST SUSSEX
488
New Romney
Rye
Heathfield
489
A259
Lydd
486
Battle
A21
Winchelsea
Dungeness
Strait of Dover
A22
Cap Gris-Nez
485
482
Hailsham
483
A259
484
Hastings
Polegate
Bexhill
4
A27
479
480
Eastbourne
Seaford
481
Beachy Head
English Channel

Map 6

51

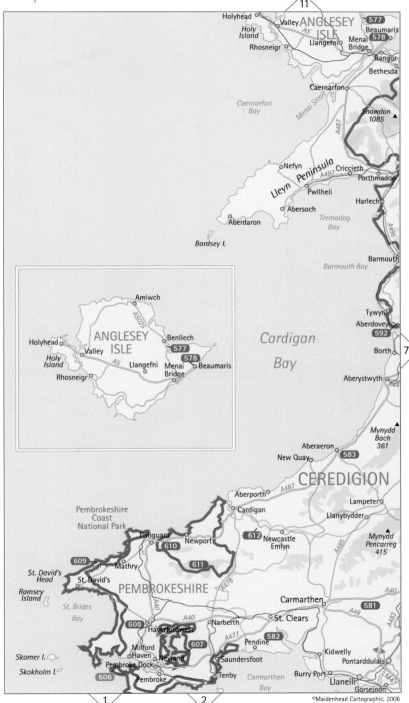

11 12

Llandudno
Colwyn Bay
Prestatyn
Rhyl
Heswall
Neston
Runcorn
Conwy
Bay
Abergele
Rhuddlan
A548
Ellesmere
Port
Frodsham
53
Conwy
Llanfairfechan
St. Asaph
584
A55
Holywell
Flint
Connah's
Quay
Chester
Helsby
51
CONWY
Denbigh
A525
FLINTSHIRE
589
Mold
Buckley
Hawarden
44
52
Tarporley
Glyder Fawr
▲ 999
Capel
Curig
Llanrwst
Bylchau
585
Llyn
Brenig
Llay
45
CHESHIRE
A51
593
Betws-y-Coed
Ruthin
Holt
47
49
Nantwich
Pentrefoelas
A5
DENBIGHSHIRE
Wrexham
588
46
Malpas
48
Blaenau
Ffestiniog
Corwen
Llangollen
586
A5
587
Ruabon
Overton
Whitchurch
A525
Ffestiniog
Snowdonia
Chirk
A5
Market
Drayton
Rhinog
Fawr
720 ▲
Trawsfynydd
National Park
Bala
Dee
Moel Sych
▲ 827
A495
Ellesmere
Wern
399
Hodnet
A41
Bala
Lake
Whittington
Oswestry
GWYNEDD
Lake
Vyrnwy
Llanfyllin
A483
Shawbury
A442
Dolgellau
A470
A458
Crudgington
Wellington
Shrewsbury
The Wrekin
407 ▲
Cader
Idris
892 ▲
Mallwyd
A458
Welshpool
Long
Mountain
408
Minsterley
SHROPSHIRE
398
Machynlleth
A487
A470
Llanfair
Caereinion
Montgomery
A489
The
Long Mynd
517
393
Church
Stretton
Much
Wenlock
397
620
6
A493
Moelfre
468
619
Caersws
Severn
Bishop's
Castle
396
Wenlock Edge
Talybont
Plynlimon
▲ 752
Newtown
A488
Craven
Arms
Brown
Clee Hill
539
395
Nant-y-
Moch Res.
Llanidloes
Clun
Forest
392
Clun
394
Ponterwyd
Llangurig
Beacon
Hill
547 ▲
Ludlow
Cleobury
Mortimer
A456
Devil's
Bridge
Llanbister
Knighton
Tenbury
Wells
A485
Rhayader
A483
214
Penybont
A44
New Radnor
216
A470
Tregaron
Bryn
Brawd
484 ▲
Drygarn
Fawr
645
Llandrindod
Wells
618
215
Kington
217
Pembridge
Leominster
A44
Bromyard
POWYS
Llyn
Brianne
A481
Weobley
218
Builth
Wells
223
225
Llanwrtyd
Wells
A483
Hay-on-Wye
219
Eardisley
A4112
A438
HEREFORDSHIRE
A40
579
Llandovery
Llyswen
617
Bronllys
A470
220
Wye
Hereford
A438
222
226
Llanwrda
580
Brecon
594
221
227
Sennybridge
Brecon Beacons
616
886 ▲
Bwlch
615
224
Pontrilas
595
228
Ross-on-Wye
Llandeilo
A4067
Usk
Black
Mountains
Crickhowell
614
613
596
229
National Park
Brecon
Beacons
Brynmawr
Abergavenny
Monmouth
Cinderford
Forest
of Dean
Coleford
Lydney
Ammanford
A465
597
A40
598
174
Pontardawe
Merthyr
Tydfil
Ebbw
Vale
Raglano
601
599
600
602
605
Neath
Aberdare
Mountain Ash
Bargoed
Abertillery
Pontypool
603
MONMOUTH-
SHIRE

Cambrian Mountains

Map 8

53

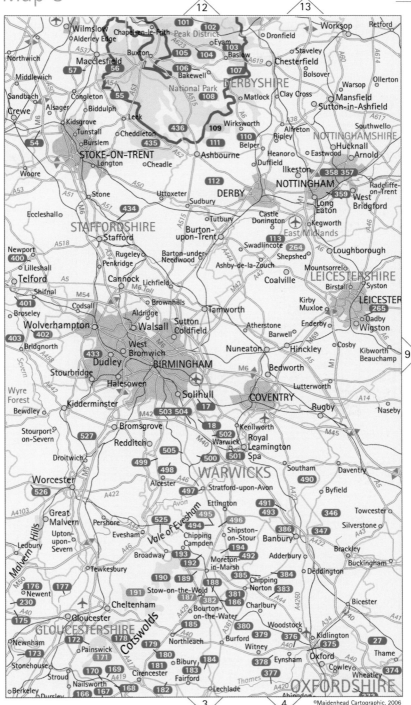

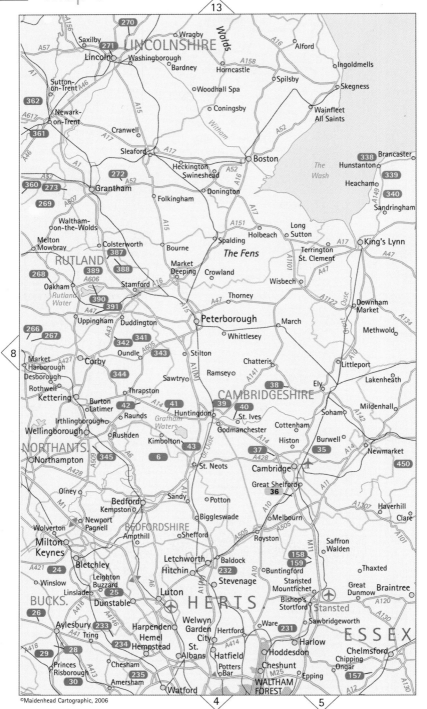

Map 10

55

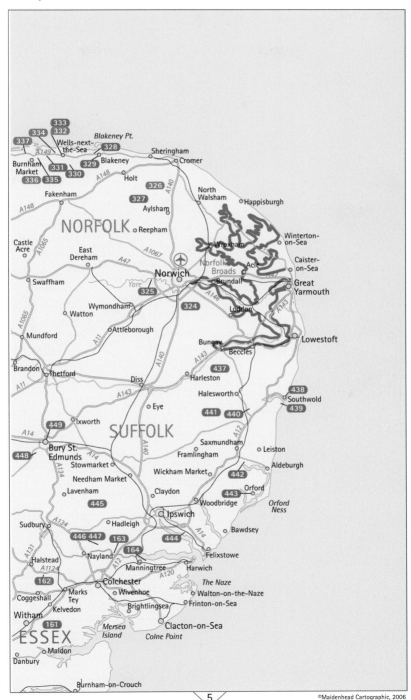

Gatehouse of Fleet
Castle Douglas
Dalbeattie
Kirkcudbright

Gretha
Longtown
Brampton
Carlisle

Wigton
Aspatria

Maryport
CUMBRIA

92 Cockermouth
Skiddaw ▲931
94
96
98 Penrith
97

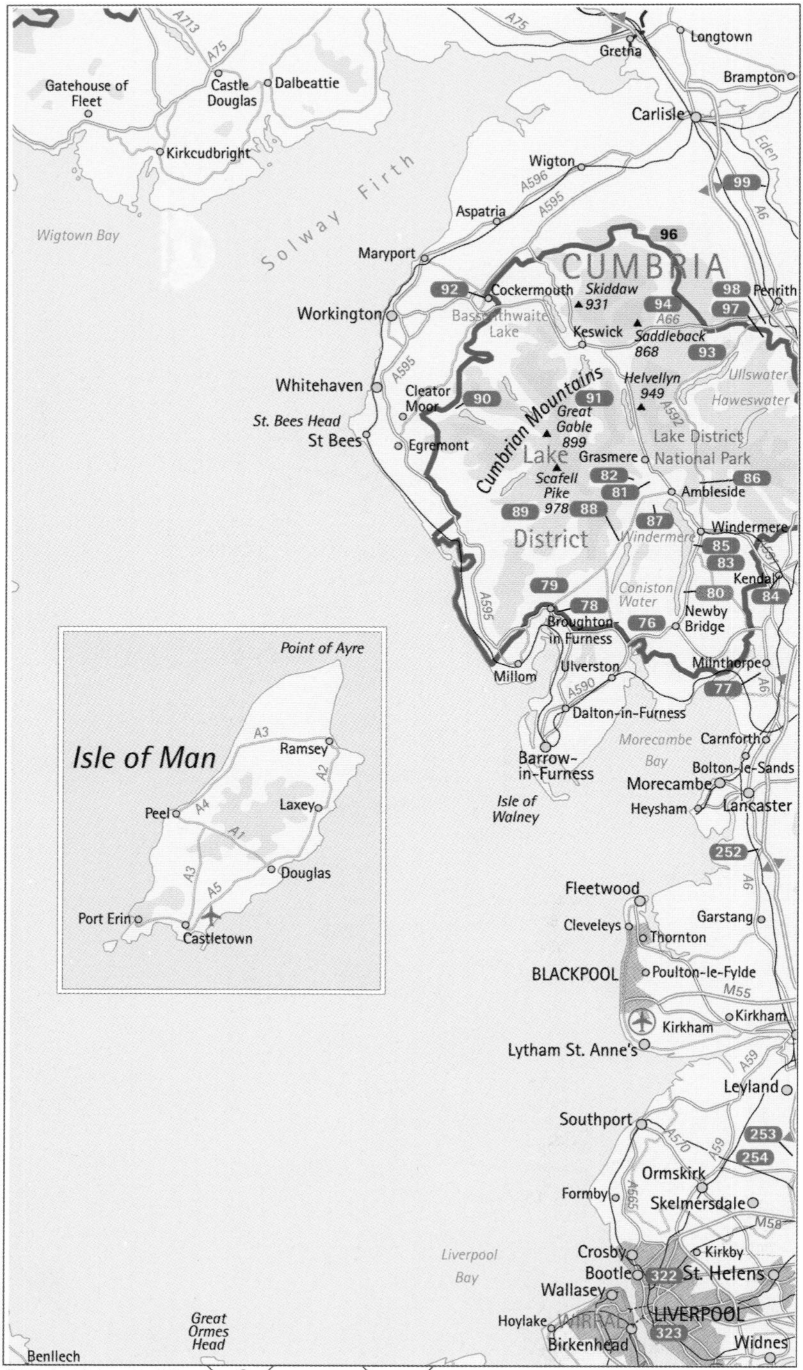

Workington
Bassenthwaite Lake
Keswick
A66
Saddleback 868
93

Whitehaven
Cleator Moor
90
91
Helvellyn 949
Ullswater
Haweswater

St. Bees Head
St Bees
Egremont
Great Gable 899 ▲
Grasmere
Lake District National Park

Scafell Pike 978 ▲
82
81
Ambleside
86

89
88
87
Windermere

Lake District
79
85
83
Kendal
84

80
Coniston Water
Newby Bridge
78
76

Broughton-in-Furness
Ulverston
Milnthorpe
77

Millom
Dalton-in-Furness
A590

Barrow-in-Furness
Morecambe Bay
Carnforth

Isle of Walney
Morecambe
Heysham
Bolton-le-Sands
Lancaster

252

Isle of Man
Point of Ayre

Ramsey
A2

Peel
A4
Laxey
A1

A3
A5
Douglas

Port Erin
Castletown

Fleetwood
Cleveleys
Thornton
Garstang

BLACKPOOL
Poulton-le-Fylde
M55

Kirkham
Kirkham

Lytham St. Anne's

Leyland

Southport
253
254

Ormskirk
Formby
Skelmersdale
M58

Crosby
Kirkby
Bootle
322
St. Helens
Wallasey
Hoylake
323
Birkenhead
LIVERPOOL
Widnes

Great Ormes Head

Benllech

Map 12

57

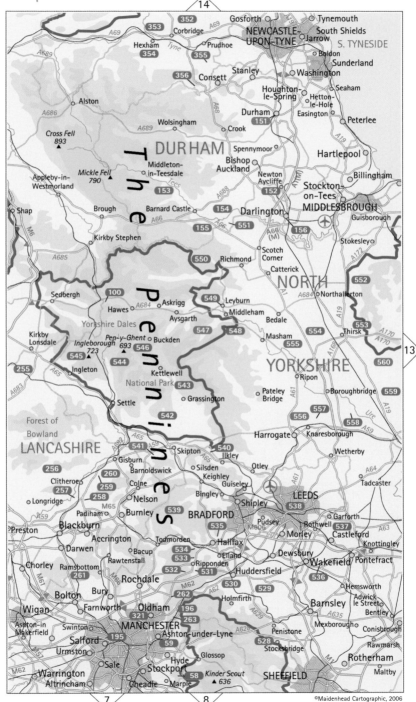

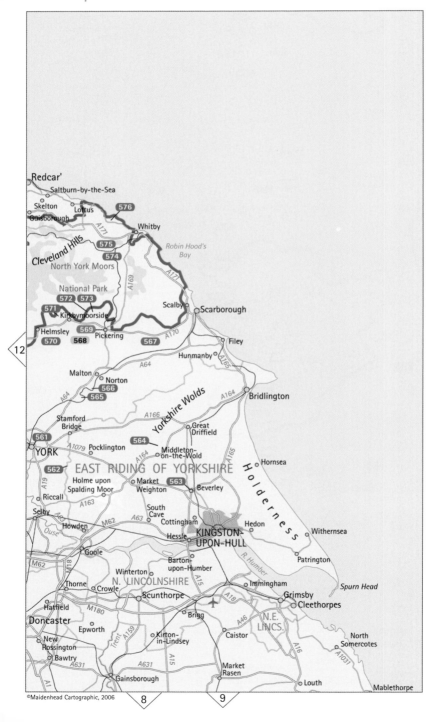

Map 14

59

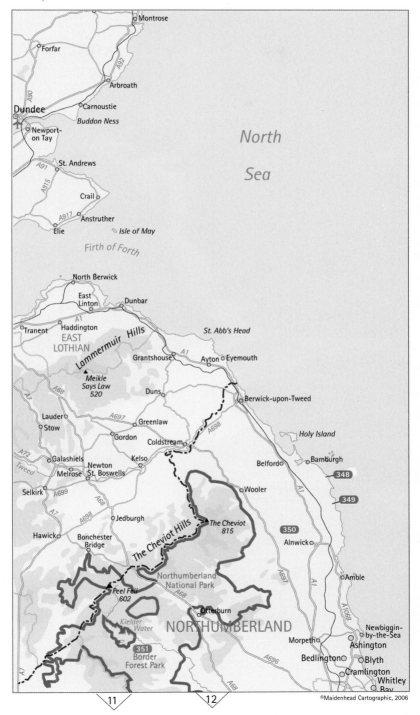

england

The Old Green Tree
Bath

Right in Bath city centre, the tiny dark pub, whose staff are fanatical about ale (at least six guest beers chalked up on the board outside), is humming with life even before midday. Deep in conversation, old regulars clutch pint jars to their chests as you squeeze through the narrow wooden-floored bar into the cabin-like non-smoking room. Undecorated since the panelling was installed in 1928, the pub is part of our heritage and has no intention of changing – Tim and Nick refuse any form of modernisation. In three little, low-ceilinged rooms, old dog-eared banknotes from across the world and a mosaic of foreign coins are stuck up with yellowing sellotape behind the bar – along with artists' work in spring and summer. The menu is far from traditional, however, with adventurous twists on old English dishes. They have a devoted following, young and old, and drink is not limited to beer: there are malts, wines, Pimms, hot toddies and good coffee. Easily a place to fall into idle chat with a stranger.

directions	Green Street, off Milson Street. Bath city centre.
meals	12pm-3pm. Main courses £5.50-£8.50.
closed	Open all day.

Mr T Bethune & M F N Luke
The Old Green Tree,
12 Green Street,
Bath,
Bath & N.E. Somerset BA1 2JZ
tel   01225 448259

map: 3 entry: 1

The Salamander
Bath

The main bar, like a Victorian apothecary, is stacked with bottles on a Welsh dresser, hand pumps gleam under the glass fluted lights and looking up is hoppy heaven. The narrow room stretches its wooden self from the Parisian café-style front window to the moody orange recesses of the back. Bath Ales dominate, though the bottled beer list is eclectic (Leffe and Erdinger, for example), and there are the usual oddities such as an old beer tap collection; the Salamander has become one of the most popular – and friendly – boozers in Bath. Up a set of creaky stairs hides the 'dining room', a light, chic restaurant space with trompe-l'oeil panels, bentwood chairs and an open kitchen where chef Kingsley Pillinger delivers delicious dishes with a global slant. There's tasty lunchtime bar food and a sophisticated dinner menu. A fine pub without the spittle.

directions	Behind Jollys in Bath city centre, off Milsom Street.
meals	12pm-2.30pm (3pm Sundays); 6.30pm-9.30pm. No food Sunday evenings. Main courses £4.95-£7.95 (lunch) £8.95-£16.95 (dinner).
closed	2.30pm-6pm.

Robert Kinsella
The Salamander,
3 John Street, Bath,
Bath & N.E. Somerset BA1 2JL
tel   01225 428889
web   www.bathales.com

map: 3 entry: 2

King William
Bath

The scruffy little corner pub has been transformed. Named after the king who was on the throne when the Duke of Wellington passed his Beer Act (in a bid to wean people off foreign spirits and support British beer, anyone with two guineas could open a beerhouse), the King William near Walcot Street has a chilled café/bar feel and a terrific range of wines and beers. They get into gastropub gear at lunch; the food's so popular Charlie and Amanda have created extra space in the intimate dining room upstairs (booking advised). Ingredients are locally sourced and largely organic, dishes are simple and modern – terrine of pigeon and rabbit, wild bass with roast fennel, local unpasteurised cheeses. Bare boards, village hall furniture, gold flock velvet curtains and background reggae and soul pull in an art-funky crowd. And the staff could not be nicer.

directions	Short walk from Walcot Street, off London Road.
meals	12pm-2.30pm; 6.30pm-10pm. No food Sun evening; Monday; Tuesday; Wed lunchtime. Main courses £4.50-£12.50 (lunch), £6.50-£14.50 (dinner). Set menu £19.50 & £24.50.
closed	3pm-5pm. Open all day weekends.

Charlie & Amanda Digney
King William,
36 Thomas Street, Bath,
Bath & N.E. Somerset BA1 5NN
tel   01225 428096
web   www.kingwilliampub.com

map: 3 entry: 3

The Star Inn
Bath

A sepia-tinted drinkers' pub oozing history. Listed on the National Inventory of Historic Pubs, it's serious boozer and museum piece wrapped into one. A pub since 1760, refitted in the 19th century, the Star is partitioned off into three numbered rooms, each with rough planks, panelled walls, ancient settles and opaque toplights. A real coal fire pumps out the heat in one room and you can still get a free pinch of snuff from the tins on the ledge above the wall... you can almost imagine the wrinkled Victorian regulars pressing their lips to their pewter tankards. To this day Bass is served in four-pint jugs which you can take away for a small deposit. There are no meals, just the odd bap from a basket on the bar – no fuss. What counts is the beer, so much so that Alan has started brewing his own Abbey Ales and has since scaled the heady heights of the real ale world to win several awards for his Bellringer tipple. A jewel.

directions	On A4 (London Road) in Bath.
meals	Fresh rolls served all day £1.60.
closed	2.30pm-5.30pm. Open all day weekends.

Alan Morgan
The Star Inn,
23 Vineyards, The Paragon, Bath,
Bath & N.E. Somerset BA1 5NA
tel   01225 425072
web   www.star-inn-bath.co.uk

map: 3 entry: 4

Bath & N.E. Somerset

The Hop Pole
Upper Bristol Road

Bath Ales have waved their magic wand over the Hop Pole, creating a space that banishes much of the usual stuffy pub masculinity while not forgetting where the roots of the real pub lie – in its ales. If you're pedalling your thirsty selves along the Bristol-to-Bath cycle path, you'd do well to meander very slightly off course and drop in here. Just out of the main throb of town, this gently sophisticated boozer has a verdant summer courtyard – all pergolas and vines – and a polished feel. Moody oranges, dark wood and a smattering of 'antique' pub furniture are made more contemporary by the extra space. It's a surprise to find this beamed dining room with its classy wooden boathouse finish – popular with foodies and families. Expect a modern British menu – crispy belly of free-range pork with sage, onion and potato rosti, chocolate marquis with crème anglais.

directions	10-minute walk from centre.
meals	7pm-9pm (12pm-2.30pm Sun); bar meals 12pm-2pm (2.30pm Sun) & 7pm-9pm (Mon-Sat). Main courses £9.95-£15.95; bar meals £3.75-£10.95.
closed	Open all day.

D. Goodyear & A. Sowden
The Hop Pole,
7 Albion Buildings,
Upper Bristol Road, Bath, BA1 3AR

tel	01225 446327
web	www.bathales.com

map: 3 entry: 5

Bedfordshire

The Plough at Bolnhurst
Bolnhurst

The pub equivalent of a phoenix from the ashes. A tavern has stood here since the 1400s, but 15 years ago the last one burnt down; tradition lives on in this happy reincarnation. The Plough subtly holds on to its heritage, employing reclaimed blackened beams and cast-iron chimney, yet overlaying this is a modern touch – stripped boards, hewn-wood bar and crisp white walls. Food is equally sophisticated. Chef-patron Martin Lee and his wife Jane have had a string of successes, and his grounding was with Raymond Blanc. Braised pork belly with black pudding mash, roast pumpkin tart… "gutsy flavours but restrained formulation" are the order of the day, and, going by the heaving crowd of happy foodies, they've got it right. Come to dine rather than pop in for a swift pint – the wine list is impressive, though the well-kept Village Bike bitter also slips down a treat. Great staff, great feel, great food. *No smoking throughout.*

directions	On B660 north of Bedford; pub in village centre.
meals	12pm-2pm (2.30pm Sunday); 7pm-9.30pm. Main courses £9.95-£17.95; set lunch £11 & £15.
closed	Sunday evenings; Monday.

Martin & Jayne Lee
The Plough at Bolnhurst,
Kimbolton Road, Bolnhurst,
St Neots, Bedfordshire MK44 2EX

tel	01234 376274
web	www.bolnhurst.com

map: 9 entry: 6

Pheasant Inn
Shefford Woodlands

It may look like it's seen better days but don't be put off: this is a cracking place with a reputation among the horse-racing set. This may explain the certain shabby gentility (rustic tiling, blood red walls, big mirrors, pine tables, heavy drapes) and certainly explains the TV tuned into the racing – often drowned out by the hubbub of jockeys and trainers. Butt's Jester, Loddon Hoppit and Wadworth 6X help charge the atmosphere, backed up by half a dozen wines by the glass. As for food, good ingredients are used in comfortingly familiar ways. Nothing is forced or pretentious and prices are reasonable. A short menu delivers simple but careful home cooking: carrot and coriander soup, lamb stew with herbed potatoes, excellent meaty burgers; for dinner, grilled fillet of turbot with rosemary roast potatoes, asparagus, ginger and shellfish sauce. It's the best M4 pit-stop for miles.

Dundas Arms
Kintbury

The Dalzell-Pipers have run this delightfully old-fashioned inn since the 1960s. At the junction of river and canal, dabbling ducks entertain diners while narrowboats glide by – no wonder the summer crowds gather on the waterside patio. All year round people come for the food; the carpeted small bar and the rear restaurant room are both a stage for David's fine country cooking. Using fresh ingredients, notably estate game and prime meats from local dealers, the short, daily-changing menus highlight potted shrimps and toast, roast duck with cider and apple sauce, tuna with tomato and chilli sauce, and favourites like ham, egg and chips and bread and butter pudding. There's a great wine list, and ale drinkers will not be disappointed with Adnam's Bitter and West Berkshire's beers – try a pint of the hoppy Good Old Boy.

directions	M4 exit 14. A338 towards Wantage, first left B4000 for Lambourn; pub on right.
meals	12.30pm-2.30pm; 7pm-9.30pm. Main courses £8.50-£16.95.
closed	Open all day.

	John Ferrand
	Pheasant Inn,
	Ermin Street, Shefford Woodlands,
	Hungerford, Berkshire RG17 7AA
tel	01488 648284
web	www.thepheasantinnlambourn.co.uk

map: 3 entry: 7

directions	1 mile off A4 between Newbury & Hungerford.
meals	12pm-2pm (bar meals); 7pm-9pm. No food Monday evenings. Main courses £12-£14; bar meals £4.95-£14.
closed	2.30pm-6pm; Sunday evenings.

	David Dalzell-Piper
	Dundas Arms,
	53 Station Road, Kintbury,
	Hungerford, Berkshire RG17 9UT
tel	01488 658263
web	www.dundasarms.co.uk

map: 3 entry: 8

The Pot Kiln
Frilsham

TV chef Mike Robinson drank his very first pint in this remote and determinedly old-fashioned ale house – and jumped at the chance to buy it. A sprucing up of the dining room has not altered the faded character of the place one jot, and you still find thirsty agricultural workers crowding the tiny, basic bar (bare tables, dartboard, doorstep sandwiches) with foaming pints of Brick Kiln Bitter from the brewery across the field. (And they nip outside for a smoke!). Perfectly lovely in summer – the garden looks onto fields and woodland – it's also wonderful in winter, when log fires and a menu strong on game come into their own. In the restaurant expect "European country cooking". That means rich pumpkin soup with fontina cheese fondue, wild rabbit slow-cooked with apples, cider and mustard, gnocchi with wild mushrooms and truffle, daube of slow-cooked oxtail, hot treacle tart. The wine list is serious and affordable, the smell of baking bread drifts through the bar and the service is everything it should be. *No smoking throughout.*

directions	In Yattendon, turn opposite church for Frilsham. Cross motorway; on for Bucklebury; on right after 0.5 miles.
meals	12pm-2.30pm; 7pm-9.30pm. No food Sunday evenings. Main courses £13-£15. Set lunch £12.50 & £14.95 (weekdays only).
closed	3pm-6pm weekdays.

SPECIAL AWARD see pages 28-29

	Mike & Katie Robinson The Pot Kiln, Frilsham, Yattendon, Berkshire RG18 0XX
tel	01635 201366
web	www.potkiln.co.uk

map: 4 entry: 9

The Bell Inn
Aldworth

Once a medieval hall house, The Bell has the style of village pubs long gone and has been in the Macaulay family for 200 years. Plain benches, varnished tables, venerable dark-wood panelling, settles and an outside gents: it's a joyfully unspoilt place to which people flock. There's an old wood-burning stove in one small room, a more impressive hearth in the public bar, and early evening drinkers cluster around a glass hatch. Fifty years ago the regulars were all agricultural workers – which may explain why piped music and mobile phones are so fervently opposed. The food fits the image and they keep it simple: crusty rolls are filled with thick slices of home-baked ham, stilton or cheddar, there are good puds and, in winter, homemade soup. Drink prices are another draw: the real ales from the local West Berkshire Brewery and the house wines are well priced, and there's a great big garden next to the cricket ground for summer.

The Angel
Woolhampton

A tropical paradise off the A4. The large Victorian-era pub may look unprepossessing, save for a few exotic plants on the terrace, but inside it's eclectic and flamboyant. The ceiling by the bar is coated with wine bottles, there are dark parquet floors, huge palms and cacti, vibrant walls (deep green, burnt yellow, terracotta) and a glamorous silver coffee machine by the bar. In the dining room, walls are lined with posters, pictures and a mural, and everywhere there are unexpected touches: a bowl of exotic fruits, white lilies, a glowing candle on every table. Furniture is dark, wooden and comfortable, from the dining room chairs to the cushioned settles. Chef-patron Andrew Taylor's menus catch the mood and come dotted with luxurious touches – cream of artichoke with shaved black truffle, penne with chorizo, roast partridge, apple tarte tatin with iced praline parfait. The wine list is superb. 'Expect the unexpected' is the motto here! *No smoking throughout.*

directions	Off B4009, 3 miles W of Streatley.
meals	11am-2.30pm (12pm-2.45pm Sun); 6pm-10pm (7pm Sun). Bar meals £2-£5.50.
closed	Mondays (except bank holidays).

H E Macaulay
The Bell Inn,
Aldworth,
Reading,
Berkshire RG8 9SE

tel   01635 578272

map: 4 entry: 10

directions	On A4 between Reading & Newbury.
meals	12pm-2.30pm; 6pm-9.45pm. Main courses £6.95-£15.95.
closed	Open all day.

Andrew Taylor
The Angel,
Bath Road, Woolhampton, Reading,
Berkshire RG7 5RT

tel   0118 971 3307
web   www.a4angel.com

map: 4 entry: 11

George & Dragon
Swallowfield

You'd slay a dragon to reach the George & Dragon's unassuming door. Though very much food-orientated, the place hasn't compromised its pubby roots and gives an open-hearted welcome to all: enjoy Fuller's London Pride, Flowers IPA and good wines. There's oodles of character in flagstones, stripped beams and timbers, exposed bricks and a winter fire in the big inglenook. Walls are warm terracotta strung with country prints; over the bar is a collection of old woodworkers' planes and blue and white crockery. It's cosy and inviting, with newspapers to browse, country furniture in the bar, and a series of connecting rooms set up for the serious business of dining. An enterprising menu raids the globe for inspiration while respecting British classics, and is supplemented by daily blackboard specials; try pan-fried red snapper, five-cheese tortellini, treacle sponge. In summer, a pretty garden for you and your (well-behaved) children.

The Horns
Wargrave

Inside the Tudor hunting lodge: beams and timbers, winter fires, solid scrubbed-wood tables and Mediterranean-hued walls festooned with rugby and cricketing pictures and cartoons. There's a sweet little snug behind the bar to discover, a new bar that overlooks the landscaped garden (with play area) and a dining room that soars like a medieval hall. Once a barn, its exposed brickwork, beams and timbers are draped in hops, hunting pictures and horns, atmospherically lit by wrought-iron chandeliers. The whole place is welcoming, friendly, convivial, with an 'easy-like-Sunday-morning' feel and not a fruit machine in sight. The regular menu is supplemented by an appealing list of daily specials, the repertoire following a traditional route with the odd nod to far-reaching shores. Puddings are deeply comforting.

directions	M4 junc. 11; A33; turn for Swallowfield.
meals	12pm-2.30pm (3pm Sundays); 7pm-10pm (9pm Sundays). Main courses £9.95-£16.95; bar meals £5.95-£7.95.
closed	Open all day.

	Paul Dailey
	George & Dragon, Church Road, Swallowfield, Reading, Berkshire RG7 1TJ
tel	0118 988 4432
web	www.georgeanddragonswallowfield.co.uk

map: 4 entry: 12

directions	Turn off A4 at Knowle Hill to Crazies Hill; 1 mile past bistro, left to Crazies Hill; left at bus shelter.
meals	12pm-2.30pm (4pm Sundays); 7pm-9.45pm. Main courses £8-£16.
closed	Sunday evenings.

	Sarah Folley
	The Horns, Crazies Hill, Wargrave, Berkshire RG10 8LY
tel	0118 940 1416

map: 4 entry: 13

The Royal Oak
Maidenhead

Modest at first glance, it has star quality inside. Nick Parkinson (son of showbiz dad Michael) may have given this small inn a contemporary and stylish lift, but he has cleverly managed to keep lots of the traditional character. There are scrubbed wooden floors and stripped beams, timbers and panelling, and a collection of cricketing mementos... along with photographs of star personalities and Dad's interviewees: Mohamed Ali, Victoria Beckham, Sting. The bar is cosy and inviting, with solid wooden furniture, an open fire and a couple of armchairs. Beyond, dining tables are laid with white linen on gingham undercloths. Filled baguettes are available at lunchtime, while the dining room's food is modern and classy, with a very good choice of wines by the glass. The Royal Oak is friendly and well-run, opening its door to drinkers and diners with equal enthusiasm.

Hind's Head Hotel
Bray

When the Tudor tavern across the road from Heston Blumenthal's Fat Duck came on the market, the triple-Michelin-starred chef snapped it up. Two years on, the old Hind's Head is once again the most genuine of village pubs (polished panelling, open fires) with one striking difference: terrific food. Expect a short slate of British classics... pea and ham soup, potted shrimps with watercress salad, oxtail and kidney pudding, roast cod with champ and parsley sauce, Heston's trademark triple-cooked chips, treacle tart. Dominic Chapman, virtuoso Fat Duck-trained chef, heads the kitchen and never loses the focus: to maximise the taste of the finest and freshest materials. (Note that side dishes are extra.) Heston's interest in food history, together with the involvement of food historians at Hampton Court Palace, may put historical English recipes on the menu. You are advised to book if you wish to sit in the restaurant end.

directions	On B3024 west of Paley Street, between A330 south of Maidenhead & Twyford.
meals	12pm-2.30pm; 6pm-10pm. Main courses £9.50-£19.50.
closed	Sunday evenings.

directions	On B3028 in Bray.
meals	12pm-2.30pm (4pm Sundays); 6.30pm-9.30pm. No food Sunday evenings. Main courses £9.50-£18.50.
closed	Open all day.

Nick Parkinson
The Royal Oak,
Paley Street, Maidenhead,
Berkshire SL6 3JN

tel   01628 620541
web   www.theroyaloakpaleystreet.com

Heston Blumenthal
Hind's Head Hotel,
High Street, Bray, Maidenhead,
Berkshire SL6 2AB

tel   01628 626151
web   www.hindsheadhotel.co.uk

map: 4 entry: 14

map: 4 entry: 15

Berkshire

Birmingham

Two Brewers
Windsor

A locals' secret revealed. In the royal
town, next to the Home Park gates and
the famous Long Walk, a dark,
atmospheric gem. Small rooms meander
around a tiny panelled bar and come
quaintly decked with dark beams,
wooden floors and scrubbed-wood
tables. One room with big shared tables
flourishes dark red walls and matching
ceilings; the other two have more
intimate seating areas. There are winter
fires, magazines to dip into and walls
crammed with interesting paraphernalia
– posters, press-cuttings, pictures,
mirrors. On a blackboard above the fire,
anecdotes commemorating each day are
chalked up in preference to the usual
menu specials. If you reserve a table you
won't go hungry: the compact menu
follows a steady pub line, with four daily
specials, roasts on Sundays and homely
puddings. Beer, champagne, cigars... and
a sprinkling of pavement tables to tempt
you after the rigours of The Big Tour.

The Malt Shovel
Barston

There's a touch of the Mediterranean
here. Never mind that the nearest
expanse of water is the Stratford upon
Avon canal: the pub is painted in
sunshiny yellows with green windows
and shutters and it serves fish – lots of it.
Eat in the bar, stylish and modern with
mirrors and light wood, the airy barn-
restaurant or the flowery garden in
summer; wherever you sit, you're in for
a treat. Try scallops on pea and mint
purée with hollandaise; Devon crab with
linguine; sea bass on crushed potato,
salami and chorizo salad with fresh
clams; Thai poached salmon on basil
sweet potatoes and garlic spinach.
Sunday lunches are particularly popular,
when, again, you will be served with
something different – venison with black
pudding, maybe. The ales are good and
so are the wines. Christopher Benbrook's
inn continues to pull the crowds.

directions	Off High Street, next to Mews.
meals	12pm-2.30pm (4pm weekends); 6.30pm-10pm (Monday-Thursday). Main courses £8-£13.50.
closed	Open all day.

directions	Off A452; 1 mile beyond village.
meals	12pm-2.30pm (4.30pm Sunday); 6.30pm-9.30pm (10pm Saturday). Main courses £11-£16.95.
closed	2.30pm-5.30pm; closed from 7pm Sundays. Open all day Saturday.

	Robert Gillespie Two Brewers, 34 Park Street, Windsor, Berkshire SL4 1LB
tel	01753 855426

	Christopher Benbrook The Malt Shovel, Barston Lane, Barston, Birmingham B92 0JP
tel	01675 443223
web	www.themaltshovelatbarston.com

map: 4 entry: 16

map: 8 entry: 17

Birmingham

The Orange Tree
Chadwick End

The flagship dining pub of the Classic Country Pubs group has a striking interior. Be seduced by earthy colours, lime-washed low beams, open log fires, big lamps, deep sofas around low tables and chunky lightwood furnishings in airy eating rooms. A gorgeous Italian-style deli counter shows off breads, cheeses and vintage oils. This tastefully rustic-Mediterranean décor with oriental touches is matched by an ambitious, Italian-inspired menu, and diners with deep pockets descend in their droves for authentic wood-fired pizzas and robust, full-flavoured meat dishes cooked on an in-view rotisserie spit, perhaps Morrocan lamb or rib-eye steak. There are also homemade pasta meals such as linguine with prawns, coriander, chilli and coconut, delicious warm salads and fishy specials. Great wines by the bottle or glass, Greene Kings ales, a heated patio dotted with stylish teak tables and all-day opening hours.

directions	On A4141 between Warwick & Solihull. On edge of village, 5 miles south of M42 junc. 5.
meals	12pm-2.30pm (4.30pm Sundays), 6pm-9.30pm. No food Sunday evenings. Main courses £7.95-£16.95.
closed	Open all day.

Paul Hales
The Orange Tree,
Warwick Road, Chadwick End,
Birmingham B93 0BN

tel	01564 785364
web	www.orangetreepub.co.uk

map: 8 entry: 18

Bristol

The Albion
Clifton

Clifton village is Georgian to the core: Bath without tourists. Boutiques, restaurants and delis abound but no-one had, until summer 2005, quite mastered the gastropub idea. Step forward Messrs Johnson, Rayner and George who have given the back alley student boozer the classiest of makeovers with a summer patio, a long bar serving Doom Bar and Butcombe, a winter log fire and a discreet wooden staircase leading to a restaurant that feels like a private room. They may have installed a pair of chefs with noteworthy pedigrees and packed the open bar with Clifton's loudest and proudest but the Albion is still a pub, its menu available at every table. There are light bites at lunch and weekend brunch (artisan and home-cured charcuterie; skirt steak, chips and béarnaise) and posh nosh at dinner (parsnip and pear soup; Cornish brill, boulangère potatoes, cockles and butter sauce). Service comes with a young smile.

directions	In centre of Clifton village. Tricky parking.
meals	12pm-3pm; 7pm-10pm. No food Sunday evenings. Main courses £5-£11 (lunch), £11-£18 (dinner).
closed	Open all day.

Miles Johnson
The Albion,
Boyces Avenue, Clifton, Bristol,
Bristol BS8 4AA

tel	0117 973 3522
web	www.thealbionclifton.co.uk

map: 3 entry: 19

Bristol

Bag o'Nails
Bristol

A five-minute walk from the harbourside and centre, this is a one-room drinkers' pub with a big reputation. Gas lamps, a tiled Victorian bar, a bare-boarded floor with three 'portholes' surveying the cellar, the odd game of draughts... it's that rare thing, a traditional boozer. And the sight of nine shiny handpumps offering real ales from across the UK makes it a honeypot for CAMRA types (take a pint home). A blackboard of 'coming soon' beers whets the appetite for future visits, there's a fabulous selection of bottled beers and ciders from independent breweries at good prices and a formidable range of ports. Dispensers for draught lager are camouflaged on the wall, the food menu stops at filled rolls for £1, and there's no jukebox, simply the landlord's radio in the background. A serious temple for all things malt and hops, but with just five tables, get there early or expect to stand at the bar.

directions	Right on Hotwells roundabout, opp. SS Great Britain.
meals	Rolls available all day.
closed	2.30pm-5.30pm; Monday lunchtimes. Open all day Friday-Sunday.

James Dean
Bag o'Nails,
141 St Georges Road,
Hotwells,
Bristol BS1 5UW
tel   0117 940 6776

map: 3 entry: 20

Bristol

Cornubia
Bristol

Hidden behind the head offices of the Soil Association is one of central Bristol's best-kept secrets. Dating from the mid 18th century, the pub used to be two Georgian houses. Now this characterful inn, in the hands of the newly formed Smiles Pub Company – owners of the excellent city Smiles Brewery Tap – is popular with office workers, *Evening Post* journalists and real ale aficionados. The carpet may be threadbare and sticky, the paintwork brown and the food basic (eg. chicken and mushroom pie with minted new potatoes), but with six real ales chalked up on the board behind the dark-wood bar and a large selection of single malts, bottled beers and local Thatchers Dry cider on draught, this is a must-stop for drinkers in search of a traditional, conversation-driven boozer with soul.

directions	5-min walk from Temple Meads station. From Victoria Street, right into The Countershop, right again into Temple Street.
meals	12pm-3pm; bar snacks 2.30pm-11pm (Mon-Fri). Main courses £2.75-£4.95; bar meals £1-£2.
closed	Saturday mornings; Sundays. Open all day Mon-Fri.

Julia Richardson
Cornubia,
142 Temple Street,
Bristol BS1 6EN
tel   0117 925 4415

map: 3 entry: 21

The Hare on the Hill
Bristol

Not much to encourage you from the outside, but step through the swing doors and you feel that you're in a pub that knows its business. Bath Ales took on this down-at-heel street corner boozer in 1998 for complete renovation – yet it feels as if it's been like this for a hundred years. Wooden floors, simple furniture and fuss-free décor lend a certain masculinity and the cosmopolitan/student crowd clearly appreciates the changes and enjoy what the landlord prides himself on: good beer and conversation. No games machines, and the TV in the corner, provided for occasional sport, barely makes an impact. The place is full of nooks and crannies so you can easily find a quiet spot to enjoy a chat and a cracking pint of Bath Gem. Homemade soups, Spanish chicken and roasts on Sundays are prepared and cooked on the spot, and it was CAMRA Pub of the Year the moment Bath Ales moved in.

White Hart Inn
Littleton upon Severn

Park at the back but go in at the front: it's worth it for the door alone. Step into a panelled vestibule with a wonderful turned staircase; marvel at huge fireplaces in big, rambling, ex-farmhouse rooms. Hops hang from main bar beams, tables, chairs and cushioned settles are scattered across flagged floors, and it's packed on Sundays. At this 16th-century pub the beers are good and the kitchen ingredients carefully sourced. Outside, a sheltered terrace and a splendid front garden for summer revels and peaceful views. No music, just vintage billiards in the back bar, shelves of books and a good family room. Greg is cook, and our butter-fried, corn-fed chicken with creamed wild mushrooms and rocket salad was generous and full of flavour. The ploughman's, the baguettes and the nursery puds looks equally good. Very nice staff, too.

directions	At top of Nine Tree Hill overlooking Stokes Croft.
meals	12pm-2pm (4pm Sundays); 6pm-9pm. Main courses £5.45-£5.95.
closed	2.30pm-5pm. Open all day Friday-Sunday.

Paul & Dee Tanner
The Hare on the Hill,
Dove Street, Kingsdown,
Bristol BS2 8LX
tel 0117 908 1982
web www.bathales.com

map: 3 entry: 22

directions	From old Severn Bridge for Avonmouth, then Thornbury. 1st left at Elberton.
meals	12pm-2pm (2.30pm Saturday); 6.30pm-9.30pm (12pm-9.30pm Sunday). Main courses £7.95-£14.95.
closed	2.30pm-6pm. Open all day Sunday.

Greg Bailey & Claire Wells
White Hart Inn,
Littleton upon Severn,
Thornbury,
Bristol BS35 1NR
tel 01454 412275

map: 3 entry: 23

Buckinghamshire

The Crooked Billet
Newton Longville

The twin talents of a former Sommelier of the Year, John Gilchrist, and head chef Emma have put the 16th-century pub on the county's culinary map. With innovative menus and a 400-bin wine list (all, astonishingly, available by the glass), you may imagine it's more restaurant than pub but it's an exemplary local with a great bar, weekly-changing ales, a log-fired inglenook and a great pubby atmosphere. Munch sandwiches, salads or steak and chips in the beamed bar at lunch, or roasted venison with spiced red cabbage and root vegetables in the restaurant – inviting with its deep red walls, candles and country prints. Delicious cheeses come with fig and walnut cake and Emma's seasonal menus make full use of produce from first-class suppliers, villagers included.

directions	From Milton Keynes A421 for Buckingham, left for N. Longville.
meals	7pm-9.30pm (12.30pm-3pm Sundays); bar meals 12pm-2pm Tues-Sat. No food Sunday eves. Main courses £11-£20; bar meals £7.50-£16.
closed	2.30pm-5.30pm; Monday lunchtimes.

	John & Emma Gilchrist The Crooked Billet, 2 Westbrook End, Newton Longville, Milton Keynes, MK17 0DF
tel	01908 373936
web	www.thebillet.co.uk

map: 9 entry: 24

Buckinghamshire

The Stag
Mentmore

Michael, once master chef at the Household Cavalry, is passionate about food and the best local produce; Jenny serves and surveys and deals with customers magnificently. The mellow stone building looks like a hunting lodge, its terrace facing Mentmore Towers, once home of the Rothschilds. Treat yourself to a champagne cocktail in the smart sloping garden in summer. In winter, when logs smoulder, the lounge bar is the place to be – small, bright and cosy with patterned sofas and carpeting, low tables and fresh flowers. Here are those excellent Charles Wells ales – Eagle and Bombardier – and good nosh, notably braised venison sausages. The low-lit, more formal restaurant is approached from the front of the building and has its own bar. On the à la carte menu are such treats as poached egg and Parma ham bruschetta with hollandaise. A host of roasts on Sundays and a stunning array of wines to choose from.

directions	Off A418, 5 miles NE of Aylesbury.
meals	12pm-2pm; 7pm-9.30pm. Bar meals £5.50-£8.50; set lunch £15; set dinner £28.
closed	Open all day.

	Jenny & Mike Tuckwood The Stag, The Green, Mentmore, Buckinghamshire LU7 0QF
tel	01296 668423
web	www.thestagmentmore.com

map: 9 entry: 25

The Five Arrows
Waddesdon

Live like a lord at this inn-hotel yards from the A41. Inside: rug-strewn wooden floors, antique furnishings and unusual paintings from Lord Rothschild's collection. It is part of the model village built in 1887 by Baron Rothschild to go with his château, Waddesdon Manor, and its Versailles-like gardens. Julian Alexander-Worster runs it for the estate and creates an indulgent mood in perfect keeping with its lofty ceilings, wood panelling, parquet floors and open fires. From a cushioned settle in the bar, enjoy a pint of Fuller's London Pride or a glass of champagne and catch up on the news. In the dining room, savour carefully sourced produce subtly transformed into escalope of pork with cream and wild mushroom sauce, roasted sea bass with fennel and Parmesan crisps, honeycomb ice cream. The magnificent wine list focuses on Rothschild interests around the world. A peaceful, sheltered garden too, and, of course, impeccable service.

The Mole & Chicken
Easington

Stunning views from the immaculate garden and a far from the beaten track location are just two of the seductive charms that await those who beat a path to the door. Once the village store and beer-and-cider pub, the pretty building at the end of the terrace has come up in the world. Rag-washed walls are decorated with hunting prints and lit candle sconces; honey-coloured beams and a hand-painted Tuscan-style floor are illuminated by two glowing log fires. This is a really cosy winter pub, so come on a damp Sunday and settle in for the day. Quirky blackboard menus list 'phishy food', 'belly warmers' and 'chicken feed' alongside old pub favourites and specials like English lamb with honey, rosemary and garlic sauce. Quench your thirst with a pint of local Vale Best Bitter, or delve into the 30-strong list of malts.

directions	From Thame B4011 to Long Crendon. There, up Carters Lane opp. Chandos Arms; follow signs.
meals	12pm-2pm; 6pm-9pm (9.30pm Friday & Saturday); 12pm-8.30pm Sundays. Main courses £9.90-£15.95.
closed	3pm-6.30pm. Open all day Sunday.

directions	6 miles west of Aylesbury on A41.
meals	12pm-2.30pm; 7pm-9pm (7.30pm-8.30pm Sundays). Main courses £13.50-£25.

	Julian Alexander-Worster The Five Arrows, Waddesdon, Aylesbury, Buckinghamshire HP18 0JE		Shane Ellis The Mole & Chicken, Easington, Long Crendon, Buckinghamshire HP18 9EY
tel	01296 651727	tel	01844 208387
web	www.waddesdon.org.uk	web	www.moleandchicken.co.uk

map: 9 entry: 26

map: 8 entry: 27

The Dinton Hermit
Ford

With a bright fire, friendly proprietors, freshly-prepared food and rural views, this 15th-century pub-hotel – named after the man who signed Charles II's death warrant – has been transformed in three short years. The old part is listed, the rest is the best of new, and small pretty windows overlook wide fields. Enjoy roast beef sandwiches and local Wychert ale in the cosy bar with its inglenook and vast cushioned settle – or book a table for in the stone-walled restaurant. On seasonal menus are black pudding with crispy bacon, sea bass served with sweet chilli, roast butternut squash risotto and fabulous wines, brandies and hand-rolled cigars. You have a garden for summer and rooms for the night: charming four-posters and 'Regency' bedrooms in the old, wonky-floored part, stylish modern rooms in the converted barn.

The Green Dragon
Haddenham

In what was once a manorial courthouse by Haddenham's pretty green, Paul Berry creates fabulous modern food. In the attractive, open-plan bar, kitted out with a laid-back medley of furniture and an open fire, relax over a pint of village-brewed Notley Ale from Vale Brewery, or one of several good wines by the glass. Menus here are imaginative and change daily. Graze on a decent lunchtime sandwich or a platter of organic cheeses – or settle down to something more substantial: perhaps pan-fried sea bass served on fennel with a fish bisque and tiger prawn sauce (they have 18 different ways with fish). Sweet tooths will be happy with a pretty plateful of peach tart tatin or a cappuccino crème brûlée. Families come for Sunday lunch served by cheerful, helpful staff – and there's a sheltered courtyard for alfresco meals. *No smoking throughout.*

directions	Off A418 between Thame & Aylesbury.
meals	12pm-2pm (3pm Sun); 7pm-9pm. Main courses £6.95-£12.95 (lunch), £10.50-£16.95 (dinner).
rooms	13: 2 four-posters, 10 doubles, 1 twin £80-£125. Singles from £80.
closed	Open all day.

See page 30 for bedroom details.

directions	2 miles from Thame; follow signs for Haddenham & Thame Parkway station.
meals	12pm-2pm, 7pm-9.30pm. Main courses £8.95-£18.00. Set dinner, 2 courses, £12.95 (Tues & Thurs).
closed	3pm-6.30pm; Sunday from 4pm.

	John & Debbie Collinswood
	The Dinton Hermit,
	Water Lane, Ford , Aylesbury,
	Buckinghamshire HP17 8XH
tel	01296 747473
web	www.dinton-hermit.com

map: 9 entry: 28

	Paul Berry & Peter Moffat
	The Green Dragon,
	8 Churchway, Haddenham,
	Buckinghamshire HP17 8AA
tel	01844 291403
web	www.eatatthedragon.co.uk

map: 9 entry: 29

Buckinghamshire

Buckinghamshire

The Polecat Inn
Prestwood

A quirky place, fun and packed with character. Chintzy curtains, low lighting and beams, button-backed chairs, cosy corners, stuffed animals, antique clocks, rugs and a fireplace stacked with logs make the yellow-painted 17th-century Polecat Inn feel more home than pub. The unusual flint bar serves several real ales, including Morland Old Speckled Hen and Marstons Pedigree, and there is an impressive selection of malts, and 16 wines by the glass. Among ticking clocks and happy banter, walkers and families tuck into tempting specials such as lamb with tomatoes, rosemary and olives, or baked haddock with smoked bacon and celeriac dauphinoise. A meringue nest filled with cream, honey, whisky, toasted nuts and raspberries might just finish you off, so take one of the walking maps thoughtfully provided by John and work off any over-indulgence in the Chiltern Hills. It's a beautifully run place, and has a gorgeous garden.

Royal Oak
Marlow

A mile yet a world away from Marlow's bustle, the old whitewashed cottage stands in a hamlet on the edge of the common. It's one of a thriving trio of dining pubs owned by David and Becky Salisbury (see the Alford Arms in Hertfordshire and the Swan in Buckinghamshire) and the relaxed yet attentive staff make it special. Beyond the rosemary-edged terrace is a stylish, open-plan bar, cheerful with terracotta walls, rug-strewn boards, scrubbed tables, cushioned pews and crackling log fires. Order a pint of local Rebellion ale or one of the 15 wines available by the glass and check out the daily chalkboard or printed menu. Innovative pub grub comes in the form of 'small plates' (chicken liver and bacon parfait) and main meals (pork belly on braised red cabbage with port wine gravy): all fresh and delicious. Sprawling summer gardens are filled with fragrant herbs and there's a sunny terrace with teak tables and smart brollies.

directions	On A4128 between Great Missenden & High Wycombe.
meals	12pm-2.30pm; 6.30pm-9pm. Main courses £8.90-£13.20; bar meals from £3.50.
closed	2.30pm-6pm & Sunday evenings.

John Gamble
The Polecat Inn,
170 Wycombe Road,
Prestwood,
Buckinghamshire HP16 0HJ
tel   01494 862253

directions	From Marlow A4155; right signed Bovingdon Green.
meals	12pm-2.30pm (3pm Sundays); 7pm-10pm. Main courses £10.75-£14.75.
closed	Open all day.

Ms Trasna Rice-Giff
Royal Oak,
Frieth Road, Bovingdon Green,
Marlow, Buckinghamshire SL7 2JF
tel   01628 488611
web   www.royaloakmarlow.co.uk

map: 9 entry: 30

map: 4 entry: 31

King of Prussia
Farnham Royal

One year on, a hugely popular pub – hardly surprising given the involvement of TV chef Phil Vickery. It's the sort of place where you wish you'd ordered absolutely everything that goes by. Spicy cauliflower stew with king prawns and Thai curried mussels may be considered pub classics these days, but pan-seared calf's liver with creamed potato, and braised duck wtih roasted beetroot purée have a timeless appeal. Puddings get the respect they deserve and include such enticements as chocolate puddle pudding and lemon meringue brulée. The décor – much of it wood – is simple and understated and there's a delightful informality about the whole operation, helped along by friendly, well-drilled service. And it's a great little place for drinkers: a small bar area dispenses real ales alongside the daily papers and magazines. *No smoking throughout.*

directions	A355 towards Slough; 3.5 miles; right into Cherry Tree Lane; right into Blackpond Lane.
meals	12pm-2.15pm (4pm Sundays); 6pm-9.15pm. Main courses £9.95-£19.50.
closed	Sunday evenings.

Phil Vickery, Chris Boot
& David Gibbs
King of Prussia,
Blackpond Lane, Farnham Royal,
Slough, Buckinghamshire SL2 3EG

tel   01753 643006

map: 4 entry: 32

The Swan at Iver
Iver

The sturdy former coaching inn on the main road had been reduced to an ugly swan – until the arrival of Dominic Green. The young chef has ripped out manky old carpets to reveal a 100-year-old parquet floor, stripped off paintwork and created a rural gastropub with a cosmopolitan feel. It is well loved. Locals enjoy Fuller's London Pride (or locally brewed Grand Union ales) in the bare boards bar, young mums drop in for coffee, city folk come for Sunday lunch. Unstuffy is the mood and the food is fresh and fabulous. Dominic may have worked in some top London places but he's not above serving burgers in the bar (from the finest ingredients, naturally) or beer-battered haddock and chips in the dining room. He can show off, too, with whole grilled lobster or duck cannette. The sheltered area outside is great for summer.

directions	M4 junc 5; B470 towards Langley & Iver; pub on High Street opposite church.
meals	11am-10.30pm (to 5pm Sundays). Restaurant closed Mondays. Breakfast 9am-11am Tuesday-Saturday. Set menu, 3 courses, £25; bar meals £7.95-9.95.
closed	Open all day.

Dominic Green
The Swan at Iver,
2 High Street, Iver,
Buckinghamshire SL0 9NG

tel   01753 655776
web   www.theswaniver.co.uk

map: 4 entry: 33

Buckinghamshire

The Swan Inn
Denham

Swap the bland and everyday for the picture-book perfection of Denham village and the stylish Swan. Georgian, double-fronted, swathed in wisteria, the building has had a makeover by David and Becky Salisbury (of the Alford Arms and the Royal Oak). Like its more established siblings, the Swan has been transformed by rug-strewn boards, modishly chunky tables, cushioned settles, big mirrors, a log fire and a fabulous terrace and garden for outdoor meals. Food is modern British. If pressed for time, choose from the 'small plates' list – seared king scallops or warm brie, black fig and baby pear salad. If you've nothing to rush for, linger over a chargrilled rib-eye steak with straw chips, herb butter and tempura shallots, accompanied by a pint of Courage Best or one of 15 wines by the glass. The owners have thought of everything, including a play area in the garden.

directions	From A412 (M25 junc. 17 or M40 junc. 1) follow signs for Denham.
meals	12pm-2.30pm (3pm Sundays); 7pm-10pm. Main courses £10.25-£14.
closed	Open all day.

David & Becky Salisbury
The Swan Inn,
Village Road, Denham,
Buckinghamshire UB9 5BH
tel   01895 832085
web   www.swaninndenham.co.uk

map: 4 entry: 34

Cambridgeshire

The Crown & Punchbowl
Horningsea

The second of Oliver Thain and Richard Bradley's pubs (the other's The Cock at Hemingford Grey) combines the traditional with contemporary zing. This large, homely set-up (two buildings, one 17th century, the other Victorian, backing onto the church and graveyard) is actually run as a restaurant; there is no bar as such – only one real ale is served – but the menu has many old-fashioned delights. Try homemade sausages with a choice of flavoured mash and sauces; beef carpaccio with rocket and parmesan; venison with garlic potatoes and blackcurrant jus; poached smoked haddock with poached egg and goat's cheese cream (there's lots of fish). For pudding try the hot chocolate fondant with ginger ice cream. With manager Richard 'Ray' Day so charming and 'on the ball', it is hard not to like such a place.

directions	Off A14, 2 miles north west of Cambridge.
meals	12pm-2.30pm; 6.30pm-9pm (9.30pm Fridays & Saturdays, 8.30pm Sundays). Main courses £9.95-£14.95; set lunch £12.95 & £15.95.
closed	2.30pm-6.30pm.

Oliver Thain
The Crown & Punchbowl,
High Street, Horningsea,
Cambridge, CB5 9JG
tel   01223 860643
web   www.cambscuisine.com

map: 9 entry: 35

The Queen's Head
Newton

It is charming and unspoilt outside and in. David and Juliet Short have run the Queen's Head for a quarter of a century and are now joined by son Robert who shares their commitment. There's a timeless appeal in the bare, almost spartan main bar where clattering floorboards, plain wooden tables, benches, aged paintings and a splendid winter fire are watched over by a fine old clock that keeps the beat. A tiny carpeted lounge with deep red walls, dark beams and well-worn, almost rickety furniture is a cosier alternative when the fire is blazing. The whole interior is unusual and utterly unspoilt, a proper background for shove-ha'penny, cribbage and beef dripping on toast. Yes, the food is simple, but deliciously so: rare roast beef sliced wafer-thin, ham on the bone, a mug of rich brown soup, locally baked bread — dispensed with slow deliberation and perfect accompaniments to Adnams ales tapped from the cask. Real-pub-lovers come from far and wide.

directions	M11 junc. 11; A10 for Royston; left on B1368.
meals	11.30am-2.30pm; 7pm-9.30pm. Main courses £2.40-£4.80.
closed	2.30pm-6pm (7pm Sunday).

SPECIAL AWARD
see pages 28-29

David & Juliet Short
The Queen's Head,
Newton, Cambridge,
Cambridgeshire CB2 5PG
tel   01223 870436

map: 9 entry: 36

Cambridgeshire

Three Horseshoes
Madingley

From the outside, the thatched pub looks old-worldy; push the door and you embrace the new century. Here is a simple, stylish, open feel in pale wooden floors and furniture, soft sage and cream paintwork, modern prints; there is space and light yet the familiar features of the old pub remain. The bar has local ales such as Cambridge Boathouse Bitter, a modern open log fire and a blackboard menu packed with Italian country dishes and imaginative combinations. Chef-patron Richard Stokes is part of John Hoskin's classy Huntsbridge Group (see entries for the Falcon Fotheringhay and the Pheasant at Keyston), and he serves fabulous food – some of the best in the region. Excellent unpretentious service matches the laid-back atmosphere of the busy bar while formality and white linen come together in the conservatory dining room, popular with business lunchers. In either room the choice of wines is superb – pity the designated driver.

directions	Off A1303, 2 miles west of Cambridge.
meals	12pm-2pm (2.30pm Sundays); 6.30pm-9.30pm. Main courses £9.50-£20.
closed	Sunday evenings.

	Richard Stokes
	Three Horseshoes, High Street, Madingley, Cambridge, Cambridgeshire CB3 8AB
tel	01954 210221
web	www.huntsbridge.com

map: 9 entry: 37

Cambridgeshire

The Anchor Inn
Sutton Gault

Wedged between the bridge and the raised dyke, the little inn was built in 1650 to bed and board the men conscripted to tame the vast watery tracts of swamp and scrub. Whether you sit under the huge Fenland sky on the terrace and take in the miles of peace and quiet, or blow in with the winter winds and hunker down in front of one of three open fires, you'll relish this excellent, independent country inn run with such panache by the Moores. Rooms are understated and stylish, filled with scrubbed pine tables and antique settles, lit by gas and candles, and the cooking is a major draw – light, imaginative and surprising. The combination of flavours is artful – roast guinea fowl with wild mushroom and tarragon cream sauce, smoked haddock brandade, seared fennel and mustard cream sauce – and the results are consistent and successful. Great wines and local beers, too.

directions	6 miles west of Ely, off B1381 in Sutton Gault.
meals	12pm-2pm (2.30pm Sundays); 7pm-9pm (6.30pm-9.30pm Saturdays). Main courses £12.50-£16.95; Sunday lunch £17 & £21.
closed	3pm-7pm (6.30pm Saturday).

	Robin Moore
	The Anchor Inn, Sutton Gault, Ely, Cambridgeshire CB6 2BD
tel	01353 778537
web	www.anchor-inn-restaurant.co.uk

map: 9 entry: 38

The Crown
Broughton

The pub sits in the shadow of the church where jackdaws spiral in the breeze to be top bird on the steeple. There's been a pub cum saddler's shop in this peaceful hamlet since medieval times; villagers saved the Crown from residential conversion in 2001 and now you find one of Cambridgeshire's best gastropubs. Inside: huge terracotta floor slabs; a long lightwood bar aimed at drinkers; white wines under ice in a vast brass trough bucket. Round the side of the chimney breast is a dining room with fresh blooms, tall woodburner and orange check curtains – impressively 21st-century. If the rich and chunky confit duck terrine and red onion ragout is anything to go by, Simon Cadge's food, refined and unshowy, is worth travelling the distance for. Happy helpful young staff are clad in black and welcome all; children have capacious lawns to play on in summer, and conkers from majestic chestnuts to plunder.

directions	Broughton is signed off A141 north east of Huntingdon.
meals	12pm-2pm; 6.30pm-9pm (9.30pm Friday & Saturday); 12pm-3pm, 7pm-9pm Sunday. Main courses £9-£14.50.
closed	Monday & Tuesday.

Simon Cadge
The Crown,
Bridge Road, Broughton,
Huntingdon, PE28 3AY

| tel | 01487 824428 |
| web | www.thecrownbroughton.co.uk |

map: 9 entry: 39

The Cock
Hemingford Grey

The young, enterprising licensees have stripped the lovely 17th-century village pub back to its original simplicity. Step directly into an attractive bare-boarded bar, cosy with low beams, log burner and traditional benches and settles at which you may sup award-winning East Anglian ales: Golden Jackal and a monthly guest beer from Nethergate Ales. For food, move into the airy, non-smoking restaurant where buttermilk walls and modern prints sit beautifully with wooden floors and tables. The menu is strong on pub classics and the chef makes his own sausages, served with a choice of mash and stilton or spring onions, and wonderful sauces (green peppercorn, mustard). Game terrine with chutney is a favourite starter and chocolate torte with berry compote is popular; fish and game dishes reveal a refreshing, modern view. The British and Irish farmhouse cheeses should not be missed.

directions	From A14 south for Hemingford Grey; 2 miles S of Huntingdon.
meals	12pm-2.30pm; 6.45pm-9.30pm (8.30pm Sundays). Main courses £9.95-£17.95; set lunch £9.95 & £12.95.

Oliver Thain & Richard Bradley
The Cock,
47 High Street, Hemingford Grey,
Huntingdon, PE28 9BJ

| tel | 01480 463609 |
| web | www.cambscuisine.com |

map: 9 entry: 40

The George Inn
Spaldwick

The rambling, buttermilk building dates from the 1500s and overlooks the village green – a quintessentially English scene. The interior is equally pleasing. Walls are aubergine and hung with contemporary art, leather sofas and chunky wood tables speak 'modern brasserie', old timbers are exposed, log fires crackle, and floors are bare boards. The cool, uncluttered styling blends beautifully with the history of the place. Modern variations on traditional dishes fit the bill – sweet potato and goat's cheese terrine with port reduction, Cornish lamb with rosemary potato fritter and lamb jus, and rhubarb and crumble parfait. This is simple, robust, hugely appealing food based on first-rate ingredients. The relaxed feel extends to the several eating areas in the rambling bar and the magnificent high raftered restaurant, and to drink there's Fullers London Pride or Theakston's Old Peculiar. Or one of a slate of 24 wines by the glass.

The Pheasant
Keyston

The Huntsbridge group is known for injecting urban chic into rural hideaways. The formula is simple enough: one remarkably self-assured chef (Jay Scrimshaw), a menu that looks to the Mediterranean and points beyond, and a classic thatched exterior. Add an enterprising list of wines and expertly kept ales and you have the Pheasant to a T. The text-book country pub does beams, open fires and comfy sofas better than anyone, and the cooking is as restorative as the surroundings, with the likes of devilled kidneys with wild mushrooms and sour dough toast, roast suckling pig served with cavolo nero and soft parmesan polenta, and fig tart with vanilla ice cream. Folk come from miles around. The January Monday to Saturday lunch menu is tremendous value, and if you don't want a full-blown meal, there's bar food and beautiful unpasteurised British cheeses. The Pheasant never forgets it's a pub and Adnams ales, together with two or three guest ales, are always on handpump.

directions	Beside A141, off A14, 7 miles west of Huntingdon.
meals	12pm–2.30pm; 6pm-9.30pm. Main courses £5.95–£15.95.
closed	Open all day.

Nick Thoday
The George Inn,
High Street,
Spaldwick, Huntingdon,
Cambridgeshire PE28 0TD
tel   01480 890293

map: 9 entry: 41

directions	Keyston off A14, halfway between Huntingdon & Kettering.
meals	12pm–2pm; 6.30pm-9.30pm. Main courses £8.50–£15.

John Hoskins & Jay Scrimshaw
The Pheasant,
Village Loop Road, Keyston,
Huntingdon, PE28 0RE
tel   01832 710241
web   www.huntsbridge.com

map: 9 entry: 42

Cambridgeshire

Tavern on the Green
Great Staughton

Clive Dixon of the Snooty Fox in Northamptonshire is edging closer to his former employer's Huntsbridge Group territory with his outpost near Grafham Water. Both the aim (to serve British dishes from fine produce) and the style (lime-washed beams, wood-burning stove) are close to the Lowick original, although this is an unassuming village pub with an intimate feel. Menus are short and to the point: steak and kidney pie and sausage and mash chalked up on a board in the bar; Cornish lamb fillets with cavalo nero, or pan-fried pollack with garlic butter on the dinner menu. As at the Snooty Fox, steaks from rib-eye to fillet are on display, cut to order, priced accordingly and served with garlic butter or peppercorn sauce. And chips. Clive's business partner David Hannigan is in charge, service is smartly dressed and friendly, Greene King IPA and Old Speckled Hen are on tap, and there are decent wines by the glass.

directions	On B645 west of A1 & St Neots.
meals	12pm-2pm; 6pm-9.30pm (7pm-9.30pm Sundays). Main courses £9.95-£14.95.
closed	Open all day.

Clive Dixon & David Hennigan
Tavern on the Green,
12 The Green, Great Staughton,
Cambridgeshire PE19 5DG

tel	01480 860336
web	theaapubcompany.com

map: 9 entry: 43

Cheshire

Albion Inn
Chester

It's an unprepossessing pub near the Chester almshouses, but wait until you get inside! There's bucket-loads of WW1 memorabilia – sepia photographs, 'Your Country Needs You' posters – flocked wallpaper, soft glowing lamps, leather sofas and a piano. Mike Mercer insists on old-fashioned good behaviour (leave the little ones at home). There are four cask ales, a flurry of malt whiskies and a decent selection of New World wines. 'Trench Rations' come in un-trench-like portions: beef and Guinness stew, Staffordshire Oatcake Special (scrummy), brandy-apricot ice cream. There's even hot chocolate on the menu – Green & Black's organic. The bedrooms at the top (separate entrance) are modern, compact and comfortable, with excellent bathrooms. A nostalgic city pub with an eccentric streak.

directions	Opposite city walls between The Newgate & River Dee.
meals	12pm-2pm; 5pm-8pm (6pm-8.30pm Sat). No food Sunday evenings. Main courses from £6.95.
rooms	2 doubles £65.
closed	3pm-5pm (6pm Sat; 7pm Sun). Open all day Friday.

See page 30 for bedroom details.

Michael Mercer
Albion Inn,
Park Street, Chester,
Cheshire CH1 1RN

tel	01244 340345
web	www.albioninnchester.co.uk

map: 7 entry: 44

The Grosvenor Arms
Aldford

Pretty Aldford, part of the vast Grosvenor Estate, is all prim cottages and farms with barleysugar-twist chimneys and chequerboard brickwork. Not far from the old church and castle is the imposing brick and Victorian half-timber village local rejuvenated by Brunning & Price as their flagship pub. Something for everyone here in this most relaxing and classy pastiche: a traditional taproom and snug with log fire, tiled floor and a wonderful old photo of drunks in the stocks, an imposing part-panelled Library Room and a verdant conservatory. There are prints and pictures, bottles and plates, sales bills and Victorian cartoons, acres of refectory and rustic kitchen tables on boards, tiles and rugs, a panoply of seating choices and a dark-wood bar groaning beneath handpumps dispensing local beers. The ever-reliable B&P menu carries something for everyone and you can eat in summer on huge tree-shaded lawns next to the village cricket pitch.

Blue Bell Inn
Tushingham

Mossy-tiled and wonkily beamed, it was rebuilt in 1667. There are ghosts (a phantom duck walled up in a bottle), a medieval spiral staircase, a Cavalier's hat found behind the inglenook, and Derek, the pub's pet sheep, who grazes the meadow where kids are free to roam. There's a beautifully lived-in, old-fashioned feel nurtured by the friendly owners. The snug behind the bar makes a superb family room; the taproom has wall benches, armchairs and huge inglenook; there are maps, old prints, horse brasses, timeworn carpets and faded patterned wallpapers. Settle down to a pint of Shropshire Gold from a Salopian brewery, served from the hatch. Food is nothing fancy but portions are generous and the meat and game come from local suppliers – lamb shank, pork with apple and calvados sauce. The garden is peaceful, the views verdant; anyone yearning for a charismatic village pub will love the Bell.

directions	6 miles south of Chester on B5130 to Farndon & Holt.
meals	12pm-10pm (9pm Sundays). Man courses £8.45-£17.95.
closed	Open all day.

Gary Kidd
The Grosvenor Arms,
Chester Road, Aldford, Chester,
Cheshire CH3 6HJ
tel   01244 620228
web   www.grosvenorarms-aldford.co.uk

map: 7 entry: 45

directions	Off A41, 3 miles north of Whitchurch. Signed.
meals	12pm-2pm; 6pm-9pm (from 7pm Sundays). Bar meals £7.25-£10.50.
closed	Mondays (except bank holidays).

Jerry & Ginette Ward
Blue Bell Inn,
Bell o' th' Hill,
Tushingham, Whitchurch,
Cheshire SY13 4QS
tel   01948 662172

map: 7 entry: 46

The Cholmondeley Arms
Cholmondeley

The gabled Victorian schoolhouse, with its unusual, octagonal bell tower, stands virtually opposite Cholmondeley Castle and Gardens. It conveniently metamorphosed into a pub when the school closed in 1982 but is still part of the Viscount's estate and keeps that airy 'schoolroom' feel with its raftered, vaulted ceilings, large windows and huge radiators. Today the rooms are nicely furnished with an auction lot of tables, pews and chairs, good colours, subtle lights, characterful old prints and a blazing log fire. Educational relics in the form of old school desks, blackboards and easels fill a gallery above the bar and antique blackboards have been put to good use – of course; one is chalked up with the daily-changing choice of first-class bar food, the other lists seven wines by the glass. Popular with suits, Barbours and a smattering of farmers.

Bhurtpore Inn
Aston

The problem with this extended old Cheshire-brick village farmhouse is just where to start. Should it be the 11 real ales? The countless bottled continental lagers and the 100 malts? The farmhouse ciders and perry? Or is it best to salivate at the marvellous, ever-changing blackboard menu? There again, time could be spent simply lapping up the fascinating décor. The pub was named after an Indian city besieged by a local army commander, and multitudinous maps, paintings and ephemera spread through the warren of rooms vividly recall this deed. Low beams sag beneath myriad water jugs, and open fires crackle in the cosy lounge, where a mongrel-mix of furniture and seating, settles, a longcase clock and absorbing local bric-a-brac add tremendous character. The home-cooked food is top quality, with local fodder to the fore, the portions generous, the choice vast, and there are curries – galore!

directions	On A49, 6 miles north of Whitchurch.
meals	12pm-2.30pm; 6.30pm-10pm (9.30pm Sunday). Main courses £8.75-£15.
closed	3.30pm-6pm.

directions	Off A530, 5 miles SW of Nantwich. Follow signs for Wrenbury from turn in Aston near pottery.
meals	12pm-2pm (2.30pm Sat); 6.45pm-9.30pm (9pm Sun). Main courses £7.95-£13.
closed	2.30pm-6.30pm. Open all day Sunday.

Carolyn Ross-Lowe
The Cholmondeley Arms,
Cholmondeley, Malpas,
Cheshire SY14 8BT
tel   01829 720300
web   www.cholmondeleyarms.co.uk

Simon George
Bhurtpore Inn,
Wrenbury Road,
Aston, Nantwich,
Cheshire CW5 8DQ
tel   01270 780917

map: 7 entry: 47

map: 7 entry: 48

The Dysart Arms
Bunbury

It is one of those rare places – all things to all people. With separate areas clustered round a central bar, it feels open and cosy at the same time. There's an inglenook packed with logs, a dining area in a library, the staff are lovely, the food is special, the beers and wines superb. Once a farm on the Dysart estate, this 18th-century brick building by the church protects a listed interior. The refreshingly airy rooms have scrubbed floorboards, yellow walls, good solid tables and chairs, pictures, prints and plants, and French windows opening to the terrace and garden. Two walls are lined with books. They're proud of their food here and rightly so: game casserole with herb dumplings, salmon and smoked haddock fishcakes with tartare sauce, roast plum and almond tart... the cheeses are taken as seriously as the cask ales (try the local Weetwood Bitter), and the wines are thoughtfully chosen. Warm, intimate, friendly... the place appears to run on well-oiled wheels.

The Pheasant Inn
Higher Burwardsley

After a hike along the Sandstone Trail, come and stand before the largest fireplace in Cheshire with a pint of Weetwood Old Dog. Or sit out on the terrace and gaze across the Cheshire Plain to North Wales. Gloriously positioned up in the Peckforton Hills, the Pheasant has been stylishly re-vamped. The old laid-back feel has survived the smartening up of the beamed and wooden-floored bars and the food, which is served in both the bar and the restaurant, lives up to the surroundings. Sizzling monkfish and tiger prawns in a sweet chilli jam with dipping bread, braised shoulder of lamb with a roasted garlic and mint gravy, and syrup pudding with creamy custard satisfy the hungriest walker, and lunchtime snacks, from simple egg and cress sandwiches to fancy crispy duck with hoi sin sauce in tomato wrap, are equally good.

directions	Off A49, 3.5 miles from Tarporley.
meals	12pm-2.15pm; 6pm-9.30pm (9pm Sundays). Main courses £6.95-£15.95.
closed	Open all day.

	Darren & Elizabeth Snell The Dysart Arms, Bowes Gate Road, Bunbury, Tarporley, Cheshire CW6 9PH
tel	01829 260183
web	www.dysartarms-bunbury.co.uk

map: 7 entry: 49

directions	A534 for Wrexham; right opp. Copper Mine pub; right for Burwardsley after 1 mile. At post office, right & follow signs.
meals	12pm-2.30pm; 5.30pm-9.30pm Mon; 12pm-9pm Tues-Thurs (10pm Fri & Sat; 8pm Sun). Main courses £6-£15.95.
closed	Open all day.

	Andrew Nelson The Pheasant Inn, Higher Burwardsley, Cheshire CH3 9PF
tel	01829 770434
web	www.thepheasantinn.co.uk

map: 7 entry: 50

The Boot Inn
Willington

Strewn with ivy and pyracantha, a country cottage turned pub. Set against wooded hills in the middle of fruit farming country ('Little Switzerland'), the village local looks west towards the Welsh Hills and south over the Cheshire plain. It's a gorgeous, sheltered spot with walks nearby. Inside, the pub has been opened up with the bar at the hub, though you still get the flavour of individual rooms. Old quarry tiles, some panelling, characterful beams and a log-burning stove pull the walkers and talkers in. And there are donkeys, dog and cats to keep children entertained. The stone-flagged dining room opens onto a garden you can spill into on warm days and there's a log fire in winter. Popular food ranges from sandwiches, baguettes and panini at the bar to local lamb with roast vegetables and sea bass deep-fried in sesame batter. Local Weetwood Ales are on draught, and there are a number of wines.

directions	Chester-Manchester A54; right for Willington; 2 miles, left at T-junc. for Boothsdale.
meals	11am-2.30pm; 6pm-9.30pm. All day weekends. Main courses £7.95-£16.95.
closed	Open all day weekends.

Mike Gollings
The Boot Inn,
Boothsdale,
Willington, Tarporley,
Cheshire CW6 0NH

tel   01829 751375

map: 7 entry: 51

The Fox & Barrel
Cotebrook

The gardens are an attraction, even in winter, and the staff are attentive, whether you're here for a swift half or a slap-up meal. Inside, a comfortable mix of tables and chairs, snug corners, interesting ornaments, pictures and prints on bay-windowed walls, a large open brick fire stacked with logs, and quarry tiles covered with traditional patterned rugs. All is spotless and welcoming. There's also a large and pleasant dining room in cream and deep green; tables are candlelit and easy on the eye, the background music – Glen Miller, perhaps – is gentle on the ear. There are several cask ales and two guest beers, good wines and enjoyable food generously served: smoked haddock and chorizo risotto, pork loin with red onion and apple chutney, steak and kidney pie, salmon with hollandaise – all homemade, of course. Service is exemplary.

directions	On A49 near Oulton Park.
meals	12pm-2.30pm (3pm Sundays); 6.30pm-9.30pm (6pm Saturdays; 9pm Sundays). Main courses £8.50-£15.50.
closed	Open all day weekends.

Chris Crossley
The Fox & Barrel,
Forest Road, Cotebrook, Tarporley,
Cheshire CW6 9DZ

tel   01829 760529
web   www.thefoxandbarrel.com

map: 7 entry: 52

Chetwode Arms
Lower Whitley

The 400-year-old, Cheshire-brick roadside inn hides a warren of small rooms and passageways. There's the bar room itself, tiny, with an open coal fire, and four more; the snuggest may be used as a small private dining room. Expect low ceilings, exposed brick and beams, fresh flowers and mirrors, oodles of atmosphere and good food too. In the dining room — opening onto a terrace that overlooks the pub's own bowling green — you'll find contented diners enjoying roast rump of lamb with rich redcurrant gravy, hearty venison casserole, and roast and smoked salmon fishcakes with homemade chips. Or, simply, lunchtime sandwiches, salads and ploughman's. There are four changing guest ales on tap, over 18 wines by the glass and a huge landscaped garden. The Chetwode is great for keen drinkers of wine and beer, and a super dining pub.

The White Lion
Barthomley

An inn since 1614 and a siege site in the Civil War, the character-oozing White Lion — all wonky black and white timbers and thick thatched roof — stands beside a cobbled cart track close to the fine sandstone church. Step in to three gloriously unspoilt rooms, all woodsmoke and charm, wizened oak beams, ancient benches and twisted walls, tiny latticed windows and quarry-tiled floors. No music or electronic games, just the crackling of log fires and the hum of conversation from hikers and locals. Lunchtime food is listed on a printed menu, with occasional specials. At scrubbed wooden tables on ancient settles, wash down your sausages and mash, hot ham and pineapple, hearty ploughman's or daily roast with a well-kept pint of Cheshire-brewed Burtonwood Top Hat — or opt for the regularly changing guest ale. Summer seating is at picnic benches on the cobbles, with pretty views onto the village. Unmissable!

directions	On A49 2 miles from M56 junc. 10.
meals	12pm-3pm; 6pm-9.30pm. Main courses £8.95-£19.95.
closed	3.30pm-6pm.

	Richard Starnok
	Chetwode Arms,
	Street Lane,
	Lower Whitley,
	Warrington, Cheshire WA4 4EN
tel	01925 730203

map: 7 entry: 53

directions	M6 junc. 16; 3rd exit for Alsager; left for Barthomley.
meals	12pm-2pm (2.30pm Sunday). Main courses from £5.25.
closed	Open all day.

	Terence Cartwright
	The White Lion,
	Barthomley,
	Crewe,
	Cheshire CW2 5PG
tel	01270 882242

map: 8 entry: 54

The Ship Inn
Wincle

The red sandstone building – one of Cheshire's oldest – houses a small and well-loved local. Its two little taprooms are utterly simple, one with half barrels as ends for its counter, the other with a stone-flagged floor and a cast-iron range. Food is taken seriously in the traditional red-carpeted dining room, ingredients are local and booking is essential at weekends. Dishes include steak and ale pie, goat's cheese and leek parcel, and apple crumble for pudding. The Ship is also known for its beers – usually four on handpump plus a traditional cider or perry – and its fruit wines. The young owners are full of enthusiasm and know what makes a pub tick. The little country garden by the car park has tables and chairs shaded by mature trees – you're on the edge of the Peaks and fine walks stretch in every direction.

directions	From Congleton A54 for Buxton for 7 miles; right at Clulow Cross for Wincle, 1.5 miles.
meals	12pm-2.30pm (3pm Sat & Sun); 7pm-9pm (6.30pm-9.30pm Fri & Sat; 5.30pm-8pm Sun). Main courses £8.95-£15.50.
closed	3pm-6.30pm Tues-Thurs, 3pm-5.30pm Fri; Mondays (except bank holidays).

Giles & Vickie Meadows
The Ship Inn,
Wincle,
Macclesfield,
Cheshire SK11 0QE
tel   01260 227217

map: 8 entry: 55

Hanging Gate
Sutton

High above Macclesfield, the high heather moors of the Dark Peak fracture into steep, finger-like ridges; this very old pub hangs from the western slope. A staircase of tiny rooms drops sharply from a sublime little tap room via brass, copper and watercolour-dressed snugs to the 'View Room', where picture windows unveil an inspiring panorama that stretches to the West Pennine Moors. Several open fires add to the timeless atmosphere created by the wizened beams, flagged and carpeted floors and cosy corners where beers from Hydes' of Manchester complement the splendid home-cooked food. Game from local estates, meat and fowl from nearby farms and fish from Manchester's Smithfield Market are crafted into unfussy, fulfilling meals with a strong local following. It's popular, too, with ramblers from the nearby Gritstone Trail and Macclesfield Forest, pausing on the compact terrace or lawns.

directions	From A54 follow signs to Langley at Fairway Motel.
meals	12pm-2pm; 7pm-9pm. No food Sunday evenings. Main courses £7.45-£12.95.
closed	3pm-7pm Mon-Fri.

Peter & Paul McGrath
Hanging Gate,
Meg Lane, Sutton, Macclesfield,
Cheshire SK11 0NG
tel   01260 252238
web   www.thegate

map: 8 entry: 56

Harrington Arms
Gawsworth

You'd barely know it was a pub. The creeper-covered, red-brick building started life as a farmhouse in 1663 and still looks as if it might be part of a working farm (it is). The outside may have grown but the inside has barely changed; it wasn't long ago that they were serving beer here only from the cask. Off the passageway are a bar and a quarry-tiled snug, just big enough to take a settle chair, a table and an open fire. Then two more public rooms: the traditionally furnished Top Parlour, and the Tap Room, a red and black quarry-tiled room with simple, scrub-top tables – where they hold Friday's folk club sessions. The Wrights have a certified organic dairy herd and their high standards are reflected in the quality of the ale they serve; it's said that you won't get a finer pint of Robinsons than at the Harrington. Lunchtime snacks are of the pork pie and slab-sandwich variety – simple and good.

Oddfellows Arms
Mellor

Amid a strand of pretty cottages on a steep, narrow lane up to the moors, this mellow, three-storey gritstone pub revels in a reputation for food and ales. Folk travel from miles around and ramblers tumble down footpaths from the tops to indulge in the eclectic offerings on the modern, well-priced menu that features a strong seafood hand, inventive vegetarian options, a huge starters-and-snacks choice and great spicy dishes. Warm up beside log-burner and open fires, watching woodsmoke curl across the low-beamed ceilings past light-streamed, lead-latticed windows. Charming Victorian photos of bucolic country folk, mirrors aplenty and unusual frames of keys adorn the walls amid pews, lived-in seating and smart oak tables. Upstairs is a modern, airy restaurant, its French ambience reflecting the origins of the enthusiastic young patron, Olivier Berton. Well-kept beers are from local craft breweries.

directions	M60 junc. 1 to Marple A626. After 6 miles, to Marple Bridge & Mellor; for 2 miles.
meals	12pm-2pm; 6.30pm-9.30pm. No food Mondays & 24 December-1st January. Main courses £7.95-£15.95.
closed	3pm-5.30pm & Mondays.

directions	On A536, 2.5 miles from Macclesfield.
meals	12pm-2pm. Sandwiches & soup £2.50-£3.
closed	2.30pm-6pm.

Ian Bailey Wright
Harrington Arms,
Church Lane,
Gawsworth, Macclesfield,
Cheshire SK11 9RR

tel 01260 223325

Olivier Berton
Oddfellows Arms,
73 Moor End Road,
Mellor, Stockport,
Cheshire SK6 5PT

tel 0161 449 7826

map: 8 entry: 57

map: 12 entry: 58

Cheshire

The Buffet Bar
Stalybridge

Only a handful of these charming Victorian establishments survive. Basic, clean and timeless, this extraordinary, narrow little bar opened in 1885 as an integral part of the busy Stalybridge Station; access is still from Platform One, served by trans-Pennine trains. Its original features include coloured glass windows, a grand, black-leaded fireplace and a moulded-wood, marble-topped old bar groaning with handpumps. Parts of the former station-master's house and ladies' waiting room add much-needed space, as does a venerable old wooden conservatory tagged on to one end. Stringing the place together is a huge collection of railway bric-a-brac: shed plates and numberplates, nameplates and lamps, totems, plans and paintings. Quirky this may be, but it's double anorak heaven here, as the Bar is renowned for its real ales: over 5,000 different beers over the past seven years and usually eight on tap. Don't miss, either, their black peas, pies and puddings.

directions	8 miles east of Manchester. On the trans-Pennine line to Leeds/York.
meals	Food available most hours. Main courses £3-£5.
closed	Open all day.

John Hesketh & Sylvia Wood
The Buffet Bar,
Stalybridge Station, Stalybridge,
Cheshire SK15 1RF
tel   0161 303 0007
web   www.buffetbar.co.uk

map: 12 entry: 59

Cornwall

The Star Inn
St Just

Entrenched in the wild landscape close to Land's End is the 'last proper pub in Cornwall'. This authentic 18th-century gem, owned by the ex-mayor of St Just and its oldest inn, proudly shirks the trappings of tourism and remains a drinkers' den. Bands of locals sink pints of Tinners Ale in the low-beamed, spick-and-span bar, old pub games thrive and the place is the hub of the local folk scene, with live music at least ten nights a month, sing-a-longs and joke-telling all part of the Monday evening entertainment. The dimly-lit bar is jam-packed with interest and walls are littered with seafaring and mining artefacts; coals glow in the grate on wild winter days. Come for St Austell ale and the 'craic', and simple, home produced food using locally sourced produce – no chips or microwaves. A free juke box, mulled wine in winter and that pub rarity: a great family room.

directions	A3071 from Penzance. On right-hand side of square in centre.
meals	12pm-3pm; 6pm-8pm. Bar meals from £2.50.
closed	Open all day.

Colin McClary
The Star Inn,
Fore Street,
St Just, Penzance,
Cornwall TR19 7LL
tel   01736 788767

map: 1 entry: 60

Tinners Arms
Zennor

Under new landlords Grahame and Richard, one of Cornwall's most historic pubs has been given a welcome shot in the arm. Close to the church in the bleak, windswept, coastal hamlet of Zennor, the 13th-century inn is pretty unspoilt with its flagstone floors, whitewashed walls, old tables and fabulously long, well-stocked bar. Cornishman Grahame spent many years in London running the ultra-fashionable Kensington Place, so the food and drink have moved sharply up a gear – Newlyn crab, local cheeses, ales from St Austell, Sharp's and Skinners, Burrow Hill ciders from Somerset. Still, the Tinners Arms remains a proper inn bursting with character and open log fires and will always be a popular stop for walkers heading for the nearby coastal paths.

Windswept Zennor is worth the visit alone; D H Lawrence was inspired to write *Women In Love* here. It's packed in summer, but you could be alone in the bar in off-season – just you and the dog.

directions	Off B3306 St Ives-St Just road, 4 miles west of St Ives.
meals	12pm-2.30pm; 6pm-9pm. Main courses £6.50-£14.50.
closed	Open all day.

SPECIAL AWARD see pages 28-29

Grahame Edwards & Richard Motley
Tinners Arms,
Zennor, St Ives,
Cornwall TR26 3BY
tel   01736 796927
web   www.tinnersarms.com

map: 1 entry: 61

The Halzephron
Gunwalloe

An opera singer running a remote smuggler's inn – irresistible! Looking out across the bay, the white-washed inn has been taking in guests (and smugglers: there's an underground passage) for 500 years. It reopened in 1958 as the Halzephron, old Cornish for 'cliffs of hell' and testament to the numerous ships dashed onto this stunning but treacherous coastline. Angela, exuberant and charming, has created numerous cosy eating areas around the bar, and a patio with a huge sea view. Food is freshly cooked and carefully presented: broccoli, bacon and blue cheese soup, seafood in a Provençal sauce served on pasta, chilli con carne, chocolate tart. Blow away the cobwebs on the cliff-top walk to Gunwalloe's 13th-century church beside the sand. Return to cosy bedrooms with deep-sprung beds, patchwork quilts, fresh fruit, real coffee and farmyard views.

directions	A3093 from Helston for The Lizard; right for Gunwalloe; 2 miles to pub.
meals	12pm-2pm; 7pm-9pm. Main courses £8.50-£15.95.
rooms	2 doubles from £80. Singles from £45.
closed	2.30pm-6pm.

See page 30 for bedroom details.

Angela Thomas
The Halzephron,
Gunwalloe,
Helston,
Cornwall TR12 7QB
tel   01326 240406

map: 1 entry: 62

The Cadgwith Cove Inn
Ruan Minor

Smack on the Cornish coastal path, in a thatched fishing hamlet on the Lizard Peninsula sits this 300-year-old smugglers' inn. The two dimly-lit little bars with two open fires, furnished simply and decked with mementos of seafaring days, have five ales on draught and pub grub from printed menus. For fresh and fishy daily specials, perhaps pan-fried sea bass with bacon and garlic or poached hake Florentine, look to the chalkboard. Mullet, sea bass, lobster and crab for delicious soup and sandwiches is landed on the beach below. Or try the plump mussels served with chunks of crusty bread – perfect after a cliff-path stroll to beautiful Church Cove and accompanied by a malty pint of Sharps Doom Bar. On Friday nights there is traditional Cornish singing: the rafters resonate to the refrain of a male voice choir. In summer, lap up the views across Cadgwith's tiny working cove from the sunny front terrace.

directions	Off A3083 between Helston & The Lizard.
meals	12pm-2pm; 7pm-9pm. Main courses £5.95-£11.95.
closed	3pm-7pm in winter.

David & Lynda Trivett
The Cadgwith Cove Inn,
Cadgwith, Ruan Minor, Helston,
Cornwall TR12 7JX
tel   01326 290513
web   www.cadgwithcoveinn.com

map: 1 entry: 63

Cornwall

The Shipwright's Arms
Helford

Helford straggles beside a tidal creek on the wood-fringed waters of the river. Reachable only by foot (park in the car park and walk down), the pretty thatched pub has a gorgeous terraced garden of flowers and palms, with picnic benches on the water's edge. It was built in 1795 as a farmhouse – the shipwright connections came later – and as a summer pub is exceptionally popular... certainly on summer evenings, once the barbecue has got going. The interior is special, staunchly traditional, with simple country furnishings and open fires, full of nautical bits and pieces. Yachtmen tie up outside and there's always a buzz. The black panelled bar dispenses Sharps Doom Bar Bitter and buffet lunches. Walk off your ploughman's on the long distance coastal path that passes the front door – or the shorter circular walk via Frenchman's Creek, a smuggler's hideaway made famous by Daphne du Maurier, thrilling at high tide.

directions	On south side of Helford river & via Helston on The Lizard peninsula.
meals	12pm–2pm; 7pm–9pm. Main courses £8–£13.75.
closed	Sunday & Monday evenings in winter.

Charles Herbert
The Shipwright's Arms,
Helford,
Helston,
Cornwall TR12 6JX

| tel | 01326 231235 |

map: 1 entry: 64

Cornwall

The Pandora Inn
Mylor Bridge

Yachtsmen moor at the end of the pontoon that reaches into the creek. The building, too, is special: thatched and 13th-century. Originally The Passage House, it was renamed in memory of the *Pandora*, a naval ship sent to Tahiti to capture the mutineers of Captain Bligh's *Bounty*. The pub keeps the traditional layout on several levels, along with some panelled walls, polished flagged floors, snug alcoves, three log fires, loads of maritime mementos – and amazingly low wooden ceilings. But it's not only the position, patio and pontoon that makes this one of Cornwall's best-loved inns; the bar food has something to please everyone, with fresh seafood dominating the 'specials' board. Arrive early in summer – by car or by boat; the place gets packed and parking is tricky. On winter weekdays it's blissfully peaceful, and the postprandial walking along wooded creekside paths easy.

directions	A39 from Truro; B3292 for Penryn & Mylor Bridge; descend steeply to Restronguet.
meals	12pm–3pm; 6pm–9.30pm. Main courses £4.25–£12.95; bar meals £4.50–£8.95.
closed	Open all day.

John Milan
The Pandora Inn,
Restronguet Creek,
Mylor Bridge, Falmouth,
Cornwall TR11 5ST

| tel | 01326 372678 |

map: 1 entry: 65

The Roseland Inn
Philleigh

Beside a peaceful parish church, two miles from the King Harry Ferry, a cob-built Cornish treasure. The front courtyard is bright with blossom in spring, climbing roses in summer. Indoors: old settles with scatter cushions, worn slate floors, low black beams and winter log fires. Local photographs, gig-racing memorabilia and a corner dedicated to rugby trophies scatter the walls. The place is spotlessly kept and run with panache by father and son team, William and Douglas Richards, and attracts locals and visitors in search of real ale and good food such as local farm meats and fish landed at St Mawes. Menu and blackboard dishes range from decent sandwiches to game terrine, scallops wrapped in bacon, shoulder of lamb, fillet steak and whole sea bass. Staff are full of smiles – even when the pub doubles as the Roseland Rugby Club clubhouse and the lads down pints of Sharps Doom Bar on winter Saturday nights.

Kings Head
Ruan Lanihorne

A pub with a heart. Niki and Andrew are warm, friendly and love what they do. Children are welcome in each of the dining rooms, dogs snooze in the bar. Find pine-backed stools, a comfy old sofa, a real fire. An impressive collection of tea cups hangs from the ceiling, a window sparkles with a display of multi-hued bottles – it's quirky and fun. Off the main bar are a second room with maps and woodburner and a homely, carpeted dining room with gleaming tables and Windsor chairs. Ales are from Skinners in Truro, fish from St Mawes, milk and cream from an organic Jersey herd. We tried a gamey venison casserole with celeriac mash and a lemon posset with zing – both delicious. The quiet little village on the old coach road from Penzance to London has a church with a Norman font and a creek that is a haven for waders and waterfowl… behind are the hills and leafy lanes of the Roseland countryside.

directions	Off A3078 St Mawes road or via King Harry Ferry from Truro (Feock) to Philleigh.
meals	12pm-2.30pm; 6pm-9.30pm. Main courses £4.25-£15.
closed	Open all day in summer.

directions	Village signed off A3078 Tregony-St Mawes road.
meals	12.30pm-2pm; 6.30pm-9pm. Main courses £7.85-£14.50.
closed	2.30pm-6pm & Mondays November-Easter.

William & Douglas Richards
The Roseland Inn,
Philleigh,
Truro,
Cornwall TR2 5NB
tel 01872 580254

Andrew & Niki Law
Kings Head,
Ruan Lanihorne,
Truro,
Cornwall TR2 5NX
tel 01872 501263

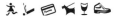

map: 1 entry: 66

map: 1 entry: 67

Cornwall

The Plume of Feathers
Mitchell

A sanctuary off a lonely stretch of carriageway. It was an inspired move of chef-patron Martyn Warner to transform the old 16th-century coaching inn where John Wesley once preached into a warm and stylish pub-restaurant with rooms. The imaginative cooking draws an appreciative crowd and, in summer, food is available all day. Low stripped beams, half-panelled walls hung with modern art, fresh flowers, candle-studded pine tables and soothing lighting make this place a pleasure to walk into to; it is novel and fun. Delightful staff serve Scottish beef and local vegetables and fish at sensible prices – take roast fillet of salmon with ratatouille risotto. The central bar is lively with TV, piped music and Sharps Doom Bar on tap. Converted stables contain stylishly simple bedrooms with generous brass beds, large-screen TVs, great bathrooms and the odd sofa. Something different from the Little Chefs and the Travel Inns you passed by.

directions	Off junction of A30 & A3076.
meals	12pm-3pm; 6pm-10pm (12pm-10pm summer). Main courses £8.25-£15.
rooms	5 doubles £75-£105. Singles £56.25-£78.75.
closed	Open all day.

See page 30 for bedroom details.

Martyn Warner
The Plume of Feathers,
Mitchell,
Truro, Cornwall TR8 5AX
tel   01872 510387
web   www.theplume.info

map: 1 entry: 68

Cornwall

The Falcon Inn
St Mawgan

Traditional pubs are an endangered breed in Holiday Land; the Falcon is one of them, and a pub-lover's delight. In an attractive village, deep in the Vale of Lanherne and a stone's throw from its tiny stream, this 16th-century wisteria-draped inn is utterly unspoilt and a summer haven for those escaping the bucket-and-spade brigade on the beach. The game-free main bar is neatly arranged and decorated with pine farmhouse tables and chairs. Andy and Jan Marshall source fish and seafood from Newlyn (fresh cod in beer batter and Fowey mussels in cider and cream) and local meats, seasonal fruits and vegetables for decent pub dishes – speciality sausages, seafood and broccoli mornay. The dining room has a rug-strewn flagged floor, a pine dresser and French windows leading out into the cobbled courtyard. Beyond the rose-covered arch is a splendid terraced garden, ideal for summer quaffing.

directions	A30 for Newquay airport; right for St Mawgan. At bottom of hill by church.
meals	12pm-2pm; 6pm-9pm (from 7pm Sunday). Main courses £7.95-£13.95.

Jan & Andy Marshall
The Falcon Inn,
St Mawgan, Newquay,
Cornwall TR8 4EP
tel   01637 860225
web   www.falconinn.net

map: 1 entry: 69

The Crown Inn
Lanlivery

You are on the bucolic Saint's Way, along which Irish drovers used to 'fat walk' their cattle from Padstow to Fowey before setting sail for France. Walkers still stop by for sustenance and a bed. Most of the 12th-century longhouse's flagged floors have been carpeted in red and blue, but the deep granite-lined clome oven remains and a country mood prevails – the Crown is the hub of the village. Five areas ramble: the largest for dining, the conservatory for the sun, and three small bars. Tasty food comes courtesy of fine Cornish produce, and is cooked to order: crab cakes with sweet chilli dip, fresh scallops, creamy fish pie, pork with mustard and cider, Cornish rib-eye steak with peppercorn sauce. There's a decent wine list, and hand-pumped ales include one brewed specially for the pub, Crown Inn Glory. Outside is a pretty garden with a view of the church tower.

St Kew Inn
St Kew Churchtown

Lost down a maze of lanes in a secluded wooded valley, the St Kew is a grand old inn that stands next to the parish church. Though its stone walls go back 600 years – it was built for the masons working on the church – it has been welcoming visitors for a mere 200. Reputedly haunted by a Victorian village girl discovered buried beneath the main bar, it is an irresistibly friendly, chatty place with a huge range and a warming fire, a dark slate floor, winged settles and a terrific unspoilt atmosphere – no pub paraphernalia here. Meat hooks hang from a high ceiling, earthenware flagons embellish the mantelpiece, fresh flowers brighten the bar. Local St Austell ales are served in the traditional way, straight from the barrel, and the famous St Kew Inn steaks are delicious. In summer, the big streamside garden is the place to be.

directions	Signed off A390 between Lostwithiel and St Blazey. Pub opposite church.
meals	12pm-2.15pm; 7pm-9.15pm; 12pm-9.30pm in summer. Main courses £5.95-£14.95.
closed	Open all day in summer.

Andy Brotheridge
The Crown Inn,
Lanlivery, Bodmin,
Cornwall PL30 5BT

tel	01208 872707
web	www.wagtailinns.com

map: 1 entry: 70

directions	From Wadebridge for Bude on A39 for 4 miles; left after golf club. 1 mile to St Kew Churchtown.
meals	12pm-2pm; 7pm-9.30pm (9pm in winter). Main courses £6.75-£11.95.
closed	2.30pm-6pm (3pm-6pm Sundays). Open all day July-August.

Justin & Sarah Mason
St Kew Inn,
St Kew Churchtown,
Bodmin,
Cornwall PL30 3HB

tel	01208 841259

map: 1 entry: 71

Cornwall

The Port Gaverne
Port Gaverne

Once an ordinary seaside hotel, now a stylish little inn. The food, cooked fresh in a modern English style – sweet pepper soup, mussels, baked wing of skate – has come on in leaps and bounds since the Sylvesters took over. The 17th-century inn is set back from rocky, funnel-shaped Port Gaverne near the pretty fishing village of Port Isaac where people come for the sea and quiet relaxation, and there's a sheltered swimming cove within seconds of the door. In the warren-like bar, snug cubby-holes warmed by a woodburner are ideal for recuperating with a pint after a hike along the coast. A wonderful stained-glass picture of a rigger leads to the formal restaurant, where an emphasis is placed on locally sourced beef, lamb and fish and fresh garden produce. And there's a choice of roasts on Sundays.

directions	From Wadebridge B3314; B3267 to Port Isaac. There to Port Gaverne. Inn up lane from cove on left.
meals	12pm-2pm; 6.30pm-9pm. Main courses £5-£10.95; set menu £25.
closed	Open all day.

Graham Sylvester
The Port Gaverne,
Port Gaverne, Port Isaac,
Cornwall PL29 3SQ

tel	01208 880244
web	www.portgavernehotel.co.uk

map: 1 entry: 72

Cornwall

The Mill House Inn
Trebarwith

You coast down a steep winding lane to the 1760s mill house in its pretty woodland setting. The bar is the best of old and new Cornish: big flagged floor, whitewashed beams, wooden tables, chapel chairs, two leather sofas by a wood-burning stove. The dining room over the mill stream has light, elegance and a bistro feel: sea blues, white linen. Settle down to soup of the day with warm crusty bread, Cornish haddock with crayfish risotto, Michaelstow beef on a bed of roast vegetables, lemon and coconut tart; the locally-sourced dishes are updated daily. Trebarwith beach, all surf and sand, is five minutes away, while coastal trails lead to Tintagel, official home of the Arthurian legends… stay a while. The pub's contemporary bedrooms vary in size and have a stylish Cape Cod feel, in sympathy with the setting.

directions	From Tintagel, B3263 south, to Trebarwith Strand.
meals	12pm-2.30pm (3pm Sundays); 7pm-9.30pm. Main courses £11.50-£15.50; bar meals £5-£11.
rooms	9 twins/doubles £80-£100. Singles £50.
closed	Open all day in summer.

See page 31 for bedroom details.

Mark & Kep Forbes
The Mill House Inn,
Trebarwith, Tintagel,
Cornwall PL34 0HD

tel	01840 770200
web	www.themillhouseinn.co.uk

map: 1 entry: 73

The Bush Inn
Morwenstow

After a blowy walk along the cliffs – where the eccentric 19th-century local vicar and poet, Robert Hawker, contemplated the sea and the greater questions – the Bush Inn, a genuinely ancient pub, makes the perfect resting place. Local farmer Rob Tape took over in July 2005 and is carefully updating the place, one of England's oldest pub buildings. Once a monastic rest-house, it dates back in part to AD950, and a Celtic piscina carved from serpentine is set in one wall. Slate-flagged floors, a huge stone fireplace and lovely old wooden furnishings in the bar preserve the timeless character of this immutable tavern. Visitors will find a new dining area and all day food that takes in local mussels, beef and lamb from neighbouring farms, fish from Widemouth Bay (sea bass with beurre blanc), and pheasant with red cabbage and game chips. Weary walkers will find excellent beer and hearty snacks. There's seating on the front lawn, and a view out to sea.

directions	Off A39, 9 miles north of Bude.
meals	11am-9.30pm. Main courses £8.50-£15.
closed	Open all day.

Rob & Edwina Tape
The Bush Inn,
Crosstown,
Morwenstow, Bude,
Cornwall EX23 9SR
tel 01288 331242

map: 1 entry: 74

Boot Inn
Calstock

Imagine being head chef at Sir Terence Conran's Blueprint Café, then leaving to help Delia Smith revamp the catering at Norwich City FC. Such stuff are dreams made of. But all Lucy Crabb wanted was a place of her own, and after a year-long search she fell for Calstock's Boot Inn. From a pub that locals eschewed, Lucy and her brother Harry have turned the Boot into one warm, welcoming tavern. People pop in for a pint, then stay for a meal. Inspired by the great produce on her doorstep, Lucy has gone for simple but mouthwatering renditions of tried and trusted favourites: cauliflower and Beenleigh blue cheese soup; South Devon sirloin steak with red wine, shallots and tarragon butter. Add in Helsett Farm organic ice creams, apple and Cornish cider brandy parfait with blackberries, and local farmhouse cheeses and you see why it's impossible to stick to just a pint.

directions	Calstock is signed off A390 west of Tavistock at Gunnislake.
meals	12pm-2.30pm; 6pm-10pm (9.30pm Sundays). Main courses £8-£14.
closed	2.30pm-6.30pm & Mondays.

Lucy Crabb
Boot Inn,
Fore Street,
Calstock,
Cornwall PL18 7RN
tel 01822 834866

map: 2 entry: 75

White Hart Inn
Bouth

The main bar has a central counter dripping with brass, jugs and hops; walls and shelves are strewn with agrarian implements, clay pipes, old photos, washboards, taxidermy, tankards and mugs. It's a friendly, sleepy-village local, where regulars mingle happily with visitors over foaming pints of Black Sheep, Jennings Cumberland and Hawkshead Bitter. There are loads of malts, too, and a no-nonsense menu that includes rare-breed meat from nearby Abbots Reading farm and local lamb cooked in fresh thyme and red wine. They source locally, and there are small portions for children. An age-polished, slopey flagged floor reflects the light from the window; grand fires at both ends are log-fuelled in cold weather. The walking's marvellous and both pub and village fit snugly into the ancient landscape of wooded valleys and tight little roads. *No smoking throughout.*

The Wheatsheaf
Beetham

A timeless air pervades the village of Beetham. The Wheatsheaf traces its origins back to the 16th century: witness the leaded windows, dark wood panelling, fine mouldings and wide open stairs. Comfortable furnishings, pictures and flowers lend a restful air. Beyond the cocooning bar is a classic tap room with a big open fire and old prints while the first-floor dining rooms have a country-house feel. Lunchtime bar food ranges from generous sandwiches to dishes like Thai-spiced crab and salmon fishcakes or Cumberland sausages with creamy mash. Pan-seared duck marinated in honey, coriander and cumin appear in the evening and fine wines from Frank Stainton of Kendal join cask ales from Jennings and a local brewer to keep drinkers happy.

directions	Off A590 Barrow road after Lakeside & Haverthwaite Steam Railway.
meals	12pm-2pm; 6pm-8.45pm. Main courses £7.25-£11.95.
closed	Monday & Tuesday lunchtimes. Open all day weekends.

Nigel Barton
White Hart Inn,
Bouth,
Ulverston,
Cumbria LA12 8JB

tel 01229 861229

map: 11 entry: 76

directions	Off A6, 1 mile south of Milnthorpe.
meals	12pm-2pm; 6pm-9pm; 6.30pm-8.30pm Sundays. Main courses £7.95-£16.95; Sunday lunch £10.95 & £12.95.
closed	2.30pm-5.30pm (6pm Sundays). Sunday evenings in winter.

Mark & Kath Chambers
The Wheatsheaf,
Beetham, Milnthorpe,
Cumbria LA7 7AL

tel 01539 562123
web www.wheatsheafbeetham.com

map: 11 entry: 77

Manor Arms
Broughton-in-Furness

Unspoilt, grey-stoned Broughton-in-Furness — complete with village stocks — is a market town that feels like a village. In a corner of its Georgian square stands the 18th-century Manor Arms, a modest inn that has been in the Varty family for 17 years. This is not a foodie's pub, though snacks are on tap all day — hot and cold rolls, homemade soup and the like. Its main fascination lies in its traditional bar and its eight handpumped ales; try Yates, Timothy Taylor's, Roosters, and more in the cellar. In their unpretentious quest for perfection, David Varty and son Scott go to some lengths to ensure the beers are in top-class condition. Cosy up on the bay window seat with children's books and games — little ones are welcome here. Logs burn in a rare 'basket' fireplace into whose oak mantel drinkers have scored their names down the centuries.

Blacksmiths Arms
Broughton Mills

An utterly unspoilt little local — there are few this good in the north of England. In the land of rugged hills and wooded valleys, you approach down a winding lane between high hedges; once you are round the final bend, the low-slung farmhouse-inn comes into view. Inside are four small, slate-floored rooms with beams and low ceilings, long settles, big old tables and several log fires. It couldn't be more 'homely' with its ornaments, dominoes and darts. The bar is strictly for drinking — indeed, there's not much room for anything else; there are three cask ales (two local, one guest) and traditional cider in summer. Across the passage, a room serving proper fresh food, snacks or full meals, and two further dining rooms that sparkle with glass and cutlery. The blackboard advertises dishes with a contemporary slant plus beef and Herdwick lamb reared in the valley. The food is seriously good, so it gets busy; in summer you can spill onto the flowery terrace.

directions	On A593, 10 miles south west of Coniston.
meals	12pm–10pm. Bar snacks £1.60–£2.40.
closed	Open all day.

David & Scott Varty
Manor Arms,
The Square,
Broughton-in-Furness,
Cumbria LA20 6HY
tel   012297 16286

map: 11 entry: 78

directions	Off A593, Broughton to Coniston.
meals	12pm–2pm; 6pm–9pm. Main courses £6.95–£11.95.
closed	Monday lunchtimes; 2.30pm–5pm Tuesday-Friday (winter only). Open all day weekends.

Michael & Sophie Lane
Blacksmiths Arms,
Broughton Mills,
Broughton-in-Furness, LA20 6AX
tel   01229 716824
web   www.theblacksmithsarms.com

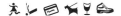

map: 11 entry: 79

Cumbria

The Mason's Arms
Strawberry Bank

Slake your thirst with damson beer. Or gin: the Lyth valley is known for its fruit. The countryside is gentle and the pub sits high on a steep wooded hillside; from the terrace you can see for glorious miles. Getting here may test your map reading skills but persevere – this is no ordinary local. Three score bottled beers are on sale – continental beer engines gleam next to ebony handpumps – with a range from nearby Hawkshead Brewery plus others. There's charm too, in open fires, old flag floors, black beams, Jacobean panelling and a family parlour. Dishes range from baked sea bass to vegetarian lasagne to succulent kleftico. Attractive, contemporary suites have beds on the mezzanine and kitchenettes; cottages are stylish; hamper breakfasts (full English if required) are provided. And the views are stunning.

directions	A5074 for Bowness; 6 miles; signs to Bowland Bridge; just beyond village.
meals	12pm-2pm (3pm Sun); 6pm-9pm (8pm Sun). All day in summer. Main courses £8-£14.
rooms	3 suites £85-£105. 2 cottages: 1 for 6, 1 for 4, £105-£155.
closed	Open all day weekends & summer.

See page 30 for bedroom details.

John & Diane Taylor
The Mason's Arms,
Strawberry Bank, Cartmel Fell,
Cumbria LA11 6NW
tel   01539 568486
web   www.strawberrybank.com

map: 11 entry: 80

Cumbria

The Britannia Inn
Elterwater

Being everyone's secret, this pub is always busy, with happy customers spilling out onto the terrace, garden and maple-shaded village green. At the centre of lovely Elterwater, with Great Langdale Beck tumbling past into the tarn close by, it's a brilliant starting point for walkers. Drinking and eating happen together in the low-ceilinged rooms, corridors and the little velvety snug – ever welcoming with old settles, oak seats, open fires and homely touches. A fine range of ales is always on tap (they have their own champion beers festival in November) and menus carry satisfying lunchtime sandwiches or tasty main dishes. In the evening, food has more of a restaurant style – Lakeland lamb marinated in mint and spices, duck with black pudding and mushroom sauce. The Britannia's atmosphere is compulsive.

directions	A593 for 3 miles; right at Skelwith Bridge onto B5343, after a mile cross cattle grid. Next left is Elterwater; in middle of village.
meals	12pm-9.30pm. Main courses £8.30-£17 (lunch from £6.75).
closed	Open all day.

C. Woodhead & C. Jones
The Britannia Inn,
Elterwater, Ambleside,
Cumbria LA22 9HP
tel   015394 37210
web   www.britinn.co.uk

map: 11 entry: 81

Old Dungeon Ghyll
Great Langdale

In frontier land, at the foot of the fells, a barn of a place… the Walkers' Bar has cattle-stall seating and a good old fireplace that could smelt steel when it gets going. To hikers ruddy from the day's exertions, full of stories of courage in the face of adversity – mist, driving rain, mobile phone failure and the like – it serves decent grub, mugs of tea, and God's own beer, Yates. An institution in the Lakes, the ODG is unavoidably fall-into-able and the atmosphere infectious, but avoid bank holidays at all costs – it would be quicker to walk back over to Borrowdale than to queue at the bar. In wild weather you feel cocooned within the substantial stone walls beneath the rafters, when it's fine there are tables outside with Tolkeinian views in every direction. The beautiful mansion next door was donated to the National Trust in 1928 and has been leased as a hotel/pub ever since.

The Punch Bowl Inn
Crosthwaite

A reassuring old inn in a gentle setting, overlooking the valley. The Punchbowl has been taken on by the owners of the famous Drunken Duck, but the old rafters are still intact and the dining room keeps its intimate corners. The long bar is stylishly slate-topped, a fitting accompaniment to flagged floors, polished dressers and immaculately chalked boards; relax here over a pint of Barngates beer and a posh ploughman's. In the restaurant are gleaming dark oak boards, swish leather chairs, white napery and a fine 18th-century stone fireplace. Popular bar dishes include brisket braised in their own Tag Lag beer served with an array of vegetables and horseradish cream; in the restaurant, chef Matt Waddington turns his talented hand to twice-cooked rabbit with a honey glaze, rosemary mousse and hazelnut and balsamic jus. Outside is a sheltered area that overlooks the church.

directions	From Ambleside, A593 for Coniston, then right on B5343. On right after 5 miles, signed, past Great Langdale campsite.
meals	12pm-2pm; 6pm-9pm. Main courses from £8.
closed	4 days at Christmas. Open all day.

Neil Walmsley
Old Dungeon Ghyll,
Great Langdale, Ambleside,
Cumbria LA22 9JY

tel	015394 37272
web	www.odg.co.uk

map: 11 entry: 82

directions	Head for Kendal on A591; 1st exit signed Barrow; follow signs for Bowness; after 2 miles, at sharp bend, right for Crosthwaite. Inn next to church.
meals	12pm-3pm; 6pm-9pm. Main courses £14.25-£24.95; bar meals £9.25-£12.75.
closed	Open all day.

Paul Spencer
The Punch Bowl Inn,
Crosthwaite, Lyth Valley,
Cumbria LA8 8HR

tel	015395 68237
web	www.the-punchbowl.co.uk

map: 11 entry: 83

Cumbria

The Watermill Inn
Ings

Fifteen years and several extensions on, the converted saw mill is Tardis-like outside. Inside: beams, open stonework, open fires and lots of traditional pubby stuff to give the impression they've been serving beer for centuries. Everyone loves the Watermill: locals, tourists, walkers, dogs. They come for the 50 malt whiskies, the heady farm ciders and the mind-boggling range of real ales served in award-winning condition. There's a sunny front bar good for families, a dimly-lit drinkers' bar and several eating areas that overlook the rushing stream. Enjoy tasty pub food locally supplied: fish and chips, chicken with mustard and rosemary, ale pie, cheddar platter. The Watermill is on the edge of good walking country and handy for Windermere, Taffy the Storyteller drops by on the first Tuesday of the month, and a late night bus back to Kendal is the icing on the cake. An on-site brewery is planned for an Easter 2006 opening.

directions	Just off A591 in Ings, midway between Kendal & Windermere.
meals	12pm-4.30pm; 5pm-9pm. Main courses £7-£14.
closed	Open all day.

Alan & Brian Coulthwaite
The Watermill Inn,
Ings, Kendal,
Cumbria LA8 9PY
| tel | 01539 821309 |
| web | www.watermillinn.co.uk |

map: 11 entry: 84

Cumbria

Hole in t'Wall
Lowside

Known in 1612 as the New Inn, the name was later changed – thanks to the landlord's habit of passing beer though the wall to the blacksmith's next door. It's a good, old-fashioned tavern, not plain but not plush, packed with tourists in season, popular with walkers all year round. The slate flagstones and fireplace have been uncovered and restored to their former glory, the black beams are hung with hops, chamber pots and pretty plates, and the flagged front terrace is a cheerful suntrap in summer. You get two bars downstairs, one long and narrow with that characterful log fire, the other small and snug with an old range, and a third room up. Food is straightforward, from prawn platter to curry of the day; there are jacket potatoes (oven-baked, not microwaved), sandwiches, chicken nuggets, real ale and mulled wine. Lake Windermere, with jetty and boat trips, is a three-minute walk.

directions	From Windermere A592; fork off right onto Fallbarrow Rd for Lowside before A592 joins A5074.
meals	12pm-2.30pm; 6pm-8pm; 12pm-7pm Fridays & Saturdays. Main courses £6.95-£7.95.
closed	Open all day.

Susan Burnet
Hole in t'Wall,
Lowside,
Bowness-on-Windermere,
Cumbria LA23 3DH
| tel | 015394 43488 |

map: 11 entry: 85

The Queen's Head Hotel
Troutbeck

The Queen's Head crouches at the foot of the Kirkstone pass, with sweeping views over moor and valley. Inside it's a warren of fascinating rooms. The flagged bar is built around a magnificently carved Elizabethan four-poster. Old instruments hang above beams, stuffed birds and beasts gaze down from mantelpiece and alcove. In the bar there's a carved giant's chair, while blazing logs in the large open fireplace are a big pull on chilly days. Food is taken seriously, and there's masses of choice. Try the homemade bread and soup or a plate of local cheeses for a quick lunch, or go for the Lowther estate venison with roast shallot and orange marmalade sauce, followed by sticky toffee pudding with toffee sauce. There's even proper food for children. The bar appeals just as much to those in search merely of a drink, with its fine cask beers (some local), and a wide choice of wines by the glass.

The Drunken Duck Inn
Barngates

At an isolated crossroads where narrow winding lanes meet stands this old inn, enfolded by high peaks and craggy tree-covered fells, small tarns and green fields enclosed by stone walls or high hedges. It is a stunning, quintessential Lakeland scene. The Duck has long been a popular watering hole among walkers and still is, in spite of its fresh contemporary face. Traditionally furnished small rooms with beams, picture-lined walls and open fires radiate from the solid bar – sheer joy for real ale enthusiasts, with home-brewed Barngates beers on handpump. And the food is utterly delicious: venison with chestnut polenta, caramelised figs and pistachio nuts; halibut with wild mushroom risotto. The chips are the best and all suppliers of fresh produce are listed. Rustic benches across the lane take in those fabulous views; residents have a secluded garden and 60 glorious acres of woodland and tarn to explore. The staff are brilliant, too.

directions	A590/A591 through Windermere. Right at mini r'bout for Troutbeck; 0.75 miles past church.
meals	12pm-2.30pm; 6.30pm-9pm. Main courses £11.95-£16.95; set menu £15.50.
closed	Open all day.

directions	From Ambleside B5286 for Hawkshead for 2.5 miles. Signed on right, up Duck Hill to crossroads for pub.
meals	12pm-2.30pm; 6pm-9pm. Main courses £13.95-£22.95. Bar meals £4.25-£7.95.
closed	Open all day.

	M. Stewardson & J. Sherratt The Queen's Head Hotel, Townhead, Troutbeck, Windermere, Cumbria LA23 1PW
tel	01539 432174
web	www.queensheadhotel.com

	Stephanie Barton The Drunken Duck Inn, Barngates, Ambleside, Cumbria LA22 0NG
tel	015394 36347
web	www.drunkenduckinn.co.uk

map: 11 entry: 86

map: 11 entry: 87

The Sun Hotel & Inn
Coniston

Coniston skirts the edge of Coniston Water – famous for Donald Campbell's world water-speed trials in *Bluebird*. Off its busy hub sits the Sun. At the front is the hotel with its Edwardian façade, at the back, the old inn. Inside, stone flags, open-stone walls, settles and a 19th-century range. It's a no-nonsense little pub, the ideal place in which to quaff a fine selection of local ales from the cask. Wines too are well-chosen with at least six by the glass. Wooden agricultural implements add to the old-fashioned Cumbrian feel, as do the stools at the bar, the dartboard and the blackboard of tasty dishes, nothing too fancy – steak and kidney cobbler, that sort of thing. For summer there's seating outside on a flagged area, and a tree-sheltered garden in front of the hotel's conservatory restaurant, with views.

The Boot Inn
Boot

Eskdale is one of England's most inaccessible valleys. Get here via the Cumbrian coastal road, or over the steep and challenging Hardknott Pass: either will be a treat. Harry and Paddington Berger took the old inn on in 1998 and have modernised comfortably. There's garden seating for sunny days and a log-fuelled bar for winter, a conservatory, a games room and hearty home cooking. Meals are served throughout the day; don't be surprised if you're asked if your appetite is "normal or starving". Expect plenty of local and organic food, game in season, and a slim but thoughtfully chosen wine list supported by four or more Cumbrian ales. In fine weather it's a joy to sit outside – as a reward, perhaps, for tackling the path to England's highest point, Scafell Pike. Dogs like it here too.

directions	100 yds up hill from bridge in centre, off A593 Ambleside road.
meals	12pm-2.30pm; 6pm-9pm. Main courses £8.50-£18.50; bar meals £3-£7.50.
closed	Open all day.

	Alan Piper
	The Sun Hotel & Inn,
	Coniston,
	Cumbria LA21 8HQ
tel	01539 441248
web	www.thesunconiston.com

map: 11 entry: 88

directions	M6 junc. 36 for Broughton-in-Furness, then for Ulpha to Eskdale & Boot.
meals	12pm-5pm (bar meals only); 6pm-8.30pm (bar meals to 9pm). Main courses £4.50-£15.
closed	Open all day.

	Harry & Paddington Berger
	The Boot Inn,
	Boot,
	Cumbria CA19 1TG
tel	01946 723224
web	www.bootinn.co.uk

map: 11 entry: 89

Shepherds Arms
Ennerdale Bridge

Beside a rushing stream in pretty Ennerdale Bridge, the immaculate Shepherds Arms strikes the balance between community pub and small hotel. It's also 'Overnight Stop 1' on Wainwright's Coast to Coast Walk, so they're used to muddy boots. Pass the peaceful lounge with fine old furnishings, settles and armchairs; then go down the Victorian tiled passage to the cosy bar – a bookcase, daily papers, an open fire; then a conservatory at the back where doors open in summer to gardens bordering the stream. The enthusiasm for real ale draws aficionados from miles and their eagerness to support local food suppliers and producers results in some fine home cooking: goat's cheese tartlet, half shoulder of fellside lamb with mint and garlic jus, rum and raisin pudding – beautifully served in a Georgian panelled dining room.

directions	East from A5086, by Ennerdale Water. In centre of Ennerdale Bridge.
meals	12.30pm-2pm; 6.30pm-9pm. Main courses £6.95-£12.95.
closed	2pm-4pm. Open all day Friday-Sunday.

	Malcolm Thomas-Chapman Shepherds Arms, Ennerdale Bridge, Cumbria CA23 3AR
tel	01946 861249
web	www.shepherdsarmshotel.co.uk

map: 11 entry: 90

The Langstrath Country Inn
Borrowdale

A magnet for walkers: from here it is just a track up the Lang Strath to the Lake District's highest peaks (but note, parking can be tricky). Donna and Gary Macrae have run this little inn for at least 15 years. Vertical timbers create cosy, stable-like corners, carpeting and a crackling fire add warmth, and there are some fascinating old photos of local characters and scenes to peer at over your pint. The slate-topped bar with its polished brass rail sports four hand-pulls for Jennings or Black Sheep ales; Torres wines are available by the glass and a couple of dozen malts enliven the varnished rack. The changing blackboard menu indicates an enthusiasm for local produce: Borrowdale trout, Morecambe Bay shrimps, Cumberland sausage, Lakeland lamb. The inn is a popular refuelling stop on both the Coast to Coast path and the Cumbrian Way.

directions	From Keswick B5289 to Borrowdale. Stonethwaite on left between Rosthwaite & Seatoller.
meals	12pm-2pm; 6pm-8pm. Main courses £7.95-£14.95.
closed	Open all day.

	Donna & Gary Macrae The Langstrath Country Inn, Stonethwaite, Borrowdale, Keswick, Cumbria CA12 5XG
tel	01768 777239
web	www.thelangstrath.com

map: 11 entry: 91

Kirkstile Inn
Loweswater

Hard to imagine a more glorious setting than that of the Kirkstile Inn, tucked in among the fells, next to an old church and a stream, a half mile from the lakes of Loweswater and Crummock. Roger Humphreys is well up to the job of hosting this legendary bar. There's a peaceful old farmhouse feel to the several low-beamed rooms, and no shortage of space. The whole place is authentic, traditional, well looked after: whitewashed walls, cosy carpeting, solid polished tables, cushioned settles, a well-stoked fire, plants, flowers and the odd horse harness to remind you of the past. Settle down with an unforgettable pint of Coniston Bluebird Bitter or their own excellent Melbreak Bitter. Five chefs deliver unfussy traditional dishes such as seafood gratin, braised shoulder of lamb and Cumberland Rum Nicky.
No smoking throughout.

Brackenrigg Inn
Ullswater

The terrace and bay windows of this 18th-century inn have breathtaking views across the water to the fells. Attention to detail is the thing here, and the service is swift and friendly. The part-panelled bar with polished old boards, darts and open fire has a homely feel, as does the carpeted lounge-dining room where families are welcome. Black Sheep and local beers are on tap, and there's a good long wine list. Menus have a modern British slant. In the bar, tuck into flat-capped mushroom topped with goat's cheese with balsamic dressing, or superb Cumberland sausage; in the restaurant, loin of pork with Bury black pudding and apple rosti, or marinated chump of Lakeland lamb served on goat's cheese mash with a roasted red pepper sauce. Sunday lunch is brilliant value, and the treacle toffee pudding is sensational.

directions	Lorton road from Cockermouth; follow signs to Loweswater.
meals	12pm-2pm; 6pm-9pm. Main courses £7-£11.
closed	Open all day.

Roger Humphreys
Kirkstile Inn,
Loweswater, Cockermouth,
Cumbria CA13 0RV

tel	01900 85219
web	www.kirkstile.com

map: 11 entry: 92

directions	M6 junc. 40 A66 for Keswick; A592 for Ullswater; Watermillock 5 miles.
meals	12pm-2.30pm; 6.30pm-9pm. Set menu £24.95; bar meals £3.95-£14.95.
closed	Open all day.

Michael Evans
Brackenrigg Inn,
Ullswater, Penrith,
Cumbria CA11 0LP

tel	01768 486206
web	www.brackenrigginn.co.uk

map: 11 entry: 93

The Mill Inn
Mungrisdale

By a tumbling burn at the foothills of Blencathra… the setting could not be more idyllic. The village inn has a solid northern feel and is there to provide a down-to-earth yet comfortable welcome. The neat, simple bar has a warming fire and a wooden counter that dispenses Jennings ales to locals and walkers. A light and airy room at the back doubles for games and families and there's a riverside garden for summer. Since their arrival a few years ago, Jim and Margaret Hodge have built up a reputation for home-cooked country dishes; they even organise an annual pie festival. Evening specials may include a pie of wild venison and fresh cranberries marinated in port, local Cumberland sausage, duck with honey, port and coriander sauce, or lamb casserole – and there are homemade scones for tea.

The Horseless Coach
The Escarpment

Can one learn to run a pub by taking a correspondence course? If so, one might begin with the Horseless Coach. The first rule, well evidenced here, is 'never run into debt if you can find something else to run into' – and this once-fine edifice-on-wheels has come to rest so far from any creditors that you are unlikely to be disturbed by bailiffs (indeed, by anyone at all). So it is for the lone drinker, and the brave one – noting Joe Lewis's dictum that a man is never drunk if he can lay on the floor without holding on. It is hard to hold on in the Horseless Coach; it is the sort of place where you may feel as though someone has stepped on your tongue with muddy boots. People do – it is muddy. There is no problem so big or so complicated that it cannot be run away from – as the owner of the Horseless Coach well knew. Mae West said that she used to be Snow White – but drifted. So did this wayward pub. But if you want to get away from life's angst, come here. *All visitors encouraged.*

directions	From M6 junc. 40, A66 for Keswick for 10 miles; right for Mungrisdale; 1.5 miles to inn.
meals	12pm-2.30pm; 6pm-8.30pm; 5.30pm-9pm weekends in summer. Main courses £7.80-£13.60.
closed	Open all day.

	Jim & Margaret Hodge
	The Mill Inn,
	Mungrisdale, Penrith,
	Cumbria CA11 0XR
tel	01768 779632
web	www.the-millinn.co.uk

map: 11 entry: 94

directions	No fixed address; often found in moonlit meadows & quiet campsites.
meals	You might find some pork scratchings. Negotiable.

	Ichabod Crane
	The Horseless Coach,
	The Escarpment,
	Cumbria
web	www.horselesscoach.com

map: entry: 95

Old Crown
Hesket Newmarket

In 2003 the old pub was bought by a cooperative of one hundred souls and is run by Lou and Linda Hogg. Its tiny front room with bar, settles, glowing coals, thumbed books, pictures, and folk music on the first Sunday of the month, squeezes in a dozen; a second room houses darts and pool; a third is a simple dining room. Not only is this the only pub where you can sample all of Hesket Newmarket's beers brewed in the barn at the back – Blencathra Bitter, Doris's 90th Birthday Ale, Helvellyn Gold – but it is the focal point of the community, even supporting the village post office whose postmistress repays in scrumptious puddings and pies. The Old Crown is also known for its bangers and mash, ham and eggs, fine curries and Sunday roasts. Its authenticity draws people from miles around – even

Prince Charles, who dropped by to launch the *Saving Your Village Pub* guide. Walkers come to explore the Caldbeck Fells; from the higher ground views reach over the Solway Firth to Scotland. Ask about brewery tours.

directions	M6 junc. 41 for Wigton on B5305. 6.5 miles turn for H. Newmarket.
meals	12-2pm; 6.30-8.30pm. No food Sun eves or Mon & Tues eves in winter. Main courses £5-£9.50.
closed	Mon & Tues lunchtimes in winter; 3-5.30pm Wed-Sat (7pm Sun).

SPECIAL AWARD
see pages 28-29

	Lewis Hogg
	Old Crown,
	Hesket Newmarket, Carlisle,
	Cumbria CA7 8JG
tel	01697 478288
web	www.theoldcrownpub.co.uk

map: 11 entry: 96

Cumbria

Cumbria

The Queen's Head Inn
Tirril

William Wordsworth and his brother sold the inn in the early 1800s to a Mr Bewsher after whom one of Tirril Brewery's ales is named. Chris Tomlinson brewed here before expanding operations at nearby Brougham Hall, but the whitewashed village inn is still the 'brewery tap' and hosts the Cumbrian Beer & Sausage Festival each August. Inside, oodles of charm: low beams, wooden settles and several open fires including a vast inglenook – logs smoulder, even, occasionally, in June. At the back is a lively bar and games room. Sit down to some well-priced food in the bar or the cosy, carpeted restaurant, where Scottish-beef stroganoff and chicken fajitas with a spicy salsa will set you up for a day on England's highest peaks. Other chalkboard specials may include whole grilled sea bream and fresh pasta. Only three miles from the M6 at Penrith – or Ullswater and its grand scenery.

The Gate
Yanwith

It was built as a toll gate in 1683 – hence the name. Known to locals as the Yat, the old pub is gaining a reputation for its food – locally sourced and served in hearty portions. The place is immaculate, the young staff are attentive and the landlord remains loyal to the pub's roots, so you may eat anywhere, as well as on the sunny shetered patio at the back. Walk in to a characterful, carpeted, dimly-lit bar, all cosy corners and roaring fire, background music and happy chatter. Beyond is a light, airy and raftered dining room, with crisply laid tables and Windsor chairs. The menu depends on fresh deliveries every day including Cumbrian meat and plenty of fish, and there's real food for children, with pizzas, beefburgers and fishcakes homemade. Wines come from an excellent wine merchant's in Kendal, beers include the fruity and full-flavoured Doris's 90th Birthday Ale. *No smoking throughout.*

directions	On B5320, 3 miles south of Penrith.
meals	12pm-2pm; 6pm-9.30pm (8.30pm Sundays). Main courses £7.95-£15.50.
closed	Open all day in summer; closed 3pm-6pm Mon-Thurs in winter.

Chris Tomlinson
The Queen's Head Inn,
Tirril, Penrith,
Cumbria CA10 2JF

tel	01768 863219
web	www.queensheadinn.co.uk

map: 11 entry: 97

directions	On B5320 south-west of A6 & Penrith; 2.5 miles from M6 junc. 40.
meals	12pm-2.30pm; 6pm-9pm. Main courses £7-£18.
closed	Open all day.

Matt Edwards
The Gate,
Yanwath, Penrith,
Cumbria CA10 2LF

tel	01768 862386
web	www.yanwathgate.com

map: 11 entry: 98

Highland Drove
Great Salkeld

Yards from the Norman church with its keep-like tower (protection against marauding Scots), an old timber porch leads into a flagged bar — cosy, warm, civilised. With open fire, polished tables, tartan, brick and timber, this is a spruce, 21st-century inn that pleases drinkers, diners and walkers. The popular Newton family have turned this into a great local and a successful restaurant. Named after the waters ('kyloes') that the cattle drovers' crossed on their way to Scottish market, the dining room has a Highland lodge feel, its great windows gazing to the lush Pennines. Tuck into salmon, red bream, duck breast or grouse, sticky toffee pudding and cranberry crème brûlée. Beers are from the cask, wines are well-chosen. Or keep things simple with Spanish potato and saffron soup and a fresh baguette at lunch.

The Moorcock Inn
Garsdale Head

Wild and remote it may be, but the locals beat a path to this pub's door. The Moorcock crouches in an isolated moorland spot at the meeting of roads from Kirkby Stephen, Sedbergh and Hawes at the top end of Wensleydale. Young new owners fell in love with the location, bought the pub in November 2005 and plan few changes. The outside looks straightforward enough but the inside is a surprise: it has been decorated with charm, originality and flair. The traditional bar area, with bar stools and solid fuel stove, is cheerfully fronted by a sofa, cushioned seating and a mix of tables, objects and plants. There's a quirky stylishness that is striking in such an unworldly setting. The bar stocks up to four cask ales, mostly local, and there's an impressive array of malts. Food is the best of traditional homemade pub grub — country terrine, Lancashire hotpot, Kilnsey trout — with a posher menu for the evening.

directions	Just off B6412 in Great Salkeld.
meals	12pm-2pm; 6.30pm-8.45pm (8.30pm Sundays). Main courses £6.50-£11.95 (lunch); £8.95-£18.50 (dinner).
closed	Monday lunchtimes; Tuesday lunchtimes if bank holiday Monday. Open all day weekends.

directions	On A684, just after Garsdale station.
meals	12pm-3pm; 6.30pm-9pm (bar snacks 10.30am-9pm). Main courses £4.50-£10.95.
closed	Open all day.

	Donald & Paul Newton
	Highland Drove,
	Great Salkeld, Penrith,
	Cumbria CA11 9NA
tel	01768 898349
web	www.highland-drove.co.uk

	Simon Tijou & Caroline Field
	The Moorcock Inn,
	Garsdale Head, Sedbergh,
	Cumbria LA10 5PU
tel	01969 667488
web	www.moorcockinn.com

map: 11 entry: 99

map: 12 entry: 100

Derbyshire

The Cheshire Cheese
Hope, Castleton

At the heart of the Hope Valley and dating back to the 16th century, the creeper-clad stone inn is traditional, totally unpretentious and rests beside the twisting road to Edale. It owes its unusual name to being a stopping point on the old salt carrying route from Cheshire to Yorkshire. The river Noe gurgles by, sweeping below Lose and Win Hills, two distinct peaks in the famously peak-less Peak District National Park; a terraced garden has views. Three small, beamed, colourwashed rooms step down through the compact and cosy interior, all discreetly bedecked with maps, mirrors, paintings, a few plates and brasses, little old settles and benches and a mix of mature furnishings. A mellow old stone fireplace warms the taproom and bar, where up to five real ales, often from microbreweries, add to the menu, and inventive home-cooked meals complement traditional pub grub.

Derbyshire

The Plough
Leadmill Bridge

Expect a big welcome from Bob and Cynthia and their team at their 16th-century free house, once a corn mill, on the banks of the river. Acres of grounds and a riverside garden high in the National Park are the perfect backdrop to a perfect inn. The atmosphere is convivial in the cosy, carpeted, split-level bar; settle down to log fires, exposed beams and stone walls, good solid furniture and, beyond, a plush country restaurant. With over 40 dishes to choose from, this is very much a diners' pub; tasty dishes, from lamb sweetbreads with pancetta to lemon sole with papardelle, are the order of the day, there's a good range of hand-pulled ales and wines for connoisseurs. You're on a main road but the large sloping gardens are lovely, and have pretty valley views.

directions	On A6187 between Chapel-en-le-Frith & Hathersage.
meals	12pm-2pm (2.30pm Saturdays); 6.30pm-9.30pm; 12pm-9pm Sundays. Main courses £6.25-£9.95; bar meals from £4.25.
closed	2.30pm-6pm. Open all day weekends.

David Helliwell
The Cheshire Cheese ,
Edale Road, Hope,
Derbyshire S33 6ZF

tel   01433 620381
web www.cheshire-cheese.net

map: 8 entry: 101

directions	On B6001, 1 mile south from Hathersage towards Bakewell.
meals	11.30am-2.30pm; 6.30pm-9.30pm (all day at weekends). Main courses £7.25-£17.95.
closed	Open all day.

Bob & Cynthia Emery
The Plough,
Leadmill Bridge, Hathersage,
Derbyshire S32 1BA

tel   01433 650319
web www.theploughinn-hathersage.com

map: 8 entry: 102

The Chequers Inn
Hope Valley, Calver

The setting is almost alpine in its loveliness – impossible to pass this pub by. Once four stone-built cottages going back to the 16th century, Jonathan and Joanne Tindall's ancient whitewashed inn has been sympathetically modernised, recently refurbished, and is full of homely touches. Pastel yellow walls, wooden floorboards, pine and country prints, cottage furniture and interesting 'objets d'art' give character to rooms that radiate off a stone-walled, timber-ceilinged bar. While blackboards promise modern bistro-style dishes – lamb shank with redcurrant suace, salmon and crab fishcakes with chilli salsa – the standard Innkeeper's Fare lists doorstep sandwiches and traditional casseroles and pies. From the raised garden behind, a path leads straight up through woods to stunning Froggatt Edge; the walking is marvellous. *No smoking throughout.*

directions	On A625 8 miles northwest of Chesterfield, 9 miles southwest of Sheffield.
meals	12pm-2pm; 6pm-9.30pm. 12pm-9.30pm Saturday (9pm Sunday). Main courses £7.75-£15.95.
closed	2.30pm-6pm. Open all day weekends.

Jonathan & Joanne Tindall
The Chequers Inn,
Froggatt Edge, Hope Valley,
Derbyshire S32 3ZJ

tel	01433 630231
web	www.chequers-froggatt.com

map: 8 entry: 103

Three Stags Heads
Wardlow Mires

Do not judge a pub by its cover. This unpretentious moorland inn with three stags' skulls fastened to the front by way of a sign may look a plain, squat, stark place on the outside (especially in driving rain), and rough within, but it's a gem. It's a walkers' pub; dressed in anything other than waterproofs and gaiters, you could feel out of place. The small, plain front bar has a coal-burning kitchen range and there's another fire in the slightly larger room next door, perfect for drying out muddy boots – and dogs, of which there are many. Pat and Geoff Fuller have a splendidly relaxed attitude and run things their way, which means restricted opening hours (so check opening days and times) and a great sense of fun. Food is wholesome, hearty and local, with just a few dishes chalked up on the board: usually pasta, often rabbit or pigeon, or steak and kidney pie, no puddings. The beers, from Abbeydale Brewery, are excellent; there may be live music at weekends.

directions	At junction of A623 & B6465 south east of Tideswell.
meals	12.30pm-4pm; 7.30pm-9.30pm. Main courses £6.50-£10.50.
closed	Monday-Thursday; Friday until 7pm. Open all day weekends & bank holidays.

Geoff & Pat Fuller
Three Stags Heads,
Wardlow Mires,
Tideswell,
Derbyshire SK17 8RW

tel	01298 872268

map: 8 entry: 104

The Red Lion
Litton

Tiny rooms hemmed in by timeworn bare-stone walls; shuttered, small-paned windows; huge stone fireplaces warming slab-floored spaces dappled with old kitchen and dining tables; worn old settles dressed with scatter cushions; fading photographs and old prints beneath comfortably undulating low ceilings. A couple of steps lead to the rear room where a collection of pottery pigs catches the eye. Step out from the dimple-tiled entrance passageway and you're on an idyllic village green, complete with mouldering stocks and a cluster of Peak District cottages and houses. Wash down hearty pub fare such as steak and kidney pie or Babbotie (minced lamb and apricots in a red wine and curry sauce) with beers from local microbreweries, an ideal preparation for – or recovery from – walks into nearby Cressbrook Dale, one of the National Park's hidden treasures.

directions	One mile east of Tideswell, off A623.
meals	12pm-2pm; 6pm-8pm (8.30pm Thursday-Saturday). No food Sunday evenings. Main courses from £5.50.
closed	Open all day Friday-Sunday. Check erratic opening hours.

Terence & Michele Vernon
The Red Lion,
Litton,
Tideswell,
Derbyshire SK17 8QU

tel 01298 871458

map: 8 entry: 105

The Bull's Head
Ashford-in-the-Water

Lovely carved settles, cushions, clocks and country prints – this is pub heaven. There are newspapers and magazines to read, light jazz hums in the background, coals glow in the grate. The busy Bull's Head has been in Debbie Shaw's family for half a century and she and Carl have been at the helm for the past five. Carl cooks, proudly serving "bistro food, not a laminated menu"; even the bread and the cheese biscuits are homemade. With a strong emphasis on local and seasonal produce, there could be lettuce and mit soup, steak and Old Stockport pie with dripping-roasted potatoes, rabbit and pear sausages on spring onion mash and red wine gravy, blueberry pie with berry sauce. Service is swift and friendly and, this being a Robinson's pub, Unicorn Best Bitter, Old Stockport and Double Hop are on handpump. Roses round the door, tables round the back, and a pretty village with a bridge from which to throw bread at the ducks. A brilliant place.

directions	Off A6, 2 miles north of Bakewell. 5 miles from Chatsworth.
meals	12pm-2pm; 6.30pm-9pm (7pm Sundays). No food Thursdays in winter. Main courses £8.50-£15.
closed	3pm-7pm Sunday

Debbie Shaw
The Bull's Head,
Church Street,
Ashford-in-the-Water, Bakewell,
Derbyshire DE45 1QB

tel 01629 812931

map: 8 entry: 106

Devonshire Arms
Beeley

Classic Peak District scenery surrounds stone-built Beeley and this splendid Georgian public house. It started life as three cottages, then became a coaching inn on the busy road from Bakewell to Matlock – and is popular today because of its proximity to Chatsworth House. Wisely open all day, it's a civilised, upmarket stopover for Chatsworth visitors and well-heeled locals – and an obvious harbour for walkers exploring the estate footpaths. All is as neat as apple pie, the three beamed rooms enticing with log fires, cushioned antique settles and tasteful prints. A separate stone-flagged tap room welcomes the booted walkers, refreshing them with expertly-kept Black Sheep and Theakston ales. Decent bar food ranges from soups and ploughman's to braised lamb knuckle with rosemary sauce, reassuringly followed by bakewell pudding. Friday is fresh fish night and on Sunday there's a sumptuous Victorian brunch (must book) complete with bucks fizz and newspapers. *No smoking throughout.*

directions	Follow signs for Chatsworth off A6 at Rowsley Bridge.
meals	12pm-9.30pm. Sunday brunch £11.75. Main courses £7.75-£16.50.
closed	Open all day.

John Grosvenor
Devonshire Arms,
Beeley,
Matlock,
Derbyshire DE4 2NR
tel   01629 733259

map: 8 entry: 107

Druid Inn
Birchover

A strange, enticing countryside of tors, crags, wooded knolls and stone circle-strewn moors erupts high above Matlock. In the midst of this morphological mayhem stands the Druid Inn. There's more than meets the eye, for a mellow stone exterior disguises an ultra-chic gastropub and a menu drawing on traditional British and the best of European – the patrons have recreated their Sheffield city Thyme Restaurant & Café concepts here. Shadows of the old village local it once was remain: a peaceful quarry-tiled snug, open fire and antique seats and beers brewed by the Leatherbritches brewery – but the general atmosphere is that of bistro-in-the-country, with blond wood to the fore, designer seating in the split-level restaurant rooms and minimalist décor. Suntrap patios among a colourful flood of planters and shrubs promise village views, and ramblers rub shoulders with epicures. *No smoking throughout.*

directions	From A6; B5056; signs for Birchover.
meals	12pm-2.30pm (3pm Sundays); 6pm-9.30pm. Sandwiches & afternoon tea 11am-5pm. Main courses £7-£15.95.
closed	Mondays in winter; Sunday from 4pm. Open all day.

Richard Smith
Druid Inn,
Main Street, Birchover,
Derbyshire DE4 2BL
tel   01629 650302
web   www.thymeforfood.co.uk

map: 8 entry: 108

Ye Olde Gate Inne
Brassington

One of the most exquisite pubs in Derbyshire, built from timber salvaged from the wrecks of the Armada. Furnishings are plain: ancient settles, rush-seated chairs, polished tables, gleaming copper pans, a clamorous antique clock, a collection of pewter. In winter a fire blazes in the blackened range that dominates the quarry-tiled main bar. In the gloomy, wonderfully atmospheric snug are a glowing range and flickering candlelight. There's a short, regularly changing blackboard menu and traditional tucker: ploughman's, filled baguettes (delicious roast beef with onions and mushrooms), game hotpot, curries, Derbyshire specialities like fidget pie (layers of ham, potatoes and cheese), lemon sponge. Come too for superbly kept Marstons Pedigree on handpump and a number of malts. Mullioned windows look onto a sheltered back garden – perfect for the popular evening barbecues that are held from Easter until October.

directions	Midway between Ashbourne & Wirksworth off B5035.
meals	12pm-1.45pm; 7pm-8.45pm. Bar meals £3.25-£15.95.
closed	2.30pm-6pm & Mondays (except bank holidays).

SPECIAL AWARD
see pages 28-29

Paul Burlinson
Ye Olde Gate Inne,
Well Street, Brassington,
Matlock,
Derbyshire DE4 4HJ
tel   01629 540448

map: 8 entry: 109

The Bear Inn
Alderwasley

The best of olde England – the sort of place that Americans travel far to find. (And it is in the back of beyond!). Enter a dressed-stone, bare-boarded, atmospheric warren. Expect a long passageway, a comfy lobby for families chatty with budgies and cockatoos, and a solid old door to a delightful snug – all high-backed settles, old pews and stools, low beams and clutches of farmers and chinwagging locals. Yet more rooms, more alcoves and carved chairs, old brass scales, gilt-framed prints, a dresser packed with porcelain, horsey ephemera, blackened cooking pots, ancient clocks and bottles, candles, stone fireplaces and aromatic log fires. The blackboard menu is long, with up to 30 main courses available all day and great Sunday roasts, there are six handpumps with a changing array of beers, and lots of wines. Great staff make this a well-nigh perfect place – but be sure to book your table for evenings and weekends.

The Red Lion Inn
Hognaston, Ashbourne

New owners took over the reins in 2005 of this endearing and enduring village local. The open-plan, L-shaped bar room quakes with quarry tiles and mature floorboards, on which stand a Pandora's box of classic tables, pews, settles and grand and simple chairs overseen by umpteen artefacts, from an HMV-style gramophone to an intriguing ship's gimbal hanging from a low-slung beam. The original and imposing wood-panelled bar sweeps between levels warmed by capacious open log fires and sports wickets dispensing ales from Marston's and some of the raft of craft breweries that have exploded in Derbyshire recently. Filling fodder, from light bites to hearty creations, includes lamb dishes that are the signature of the place. This is a fine old pub for the traditionalist – in great walking and shooting country.

directions	From B5025 east of Wirksworth, turn off at Wirksworth Moor at the Malt Shovel pub. Continue for 1 mile.
meals	12pm-9.30pm. Main courses £8.95-£16.95.
closed	Open all day.

Nicola Fletcher-Musgrave
The Bear Inn,
Alderwasley,
Belper,
Derbyshire DE56 2RD
tel   01629 822585

directions	Off the B5035 between Ashbourne & Wirksworth.
meals	12pm-2pm; 6.30pm-9.30pm. Main courses £8.95-£16.
closed	Open all day Sunday.

Jenny Waterall
The Red Lion Inn,
Main Street,
Hognaston, Ashbourne,
Derbyshire DE6 1PR
tel   01335 370396

map: 8 entry: 110

map: 8 entry: 111

The Red Lion Inn
Hollington

When Robin Hunter took over six years ago the inn was in a sorry state. His dedication has paid off: the Red Lion pulls such a crowd at the weekends that you'll need to book in advance. Modernisation has been sensitive to character and bar food keeps the traditional mood going with steak and kidney pie and sticky toffee pudding. But it is on the main daily menu that Robin gets to show off, using fresh, seasonal ingredients; try sesame tiger prawns in teriyaki marinade on gingered Swiss chard, followed by venison on swede mash with shallot and cep marmalade. While the menu revels in being wide-ranging and up-to-date, Robin's style is commendably direct and simple and his staff really make you feel at home. If you are here just for a drink, try Marstons Pedigree on handpump or a guest beer. There's a pretty garden, too.

Three Horseshoes
Breedon-on-the-Hill

Ian Davison and Jennie Ison – the team behind the Nags Head, Castle Donington – have done it again. Now the revitalised village pub has a relaxed modern atmosphere and a menu to match. Expect painted brickwork, seagrass matting, antique tables and chairs, an eclectic mix of photos and prints and masses of space. Smaller rooms include a simple quarry-tiled bar and an intimate red dining room with three tables, while pride of place goes to a handsome Victorian bar counter picked up years ago and stored in anticipation of the right setting. Kitchen and serving staff are fresh from the Nags Head so the winning formula continues: tasty seared scallops with balsamic vinegar, pork escalope with black pudding. Marston's Pedigree and Theakstons on hand pump should satisfy those in for a swift pint, and ongoing renovation will eventually restore the faded façade and create a sheltered patio.

directions	Off A52 between Derby & Ashbourne.
meals	12pm-2pm (2.30pm Sunday); 6.30pm-9pm. No food Monday lunchtimes. Main courses £10.75-£16.95; bar meals £6-£10.
closed	Monday evenings. Open all day Sunday.

	Robin Hunter
	The Red Lion Inn, Main Street, Hollington, Derbyshire DE6 3AG
tel	01335 360241
web	www.redlionhollington.co.uk

map: 8 entry: 112

directions	Follow signs off A42 between Ashby de la Zouch & Castle Donington.
meals	11.45am-2pm; 5.30pm-9.15pm. No food Sundays. Main courses £11.95-£17.95.
closed	2.30pm-5.30pm (7pm Sunday).

	Ian Davison & Jennie Ison
	Three Horseshoes, Breedon-on-the-Hill, Derby, Derbyshire DE73 8AN
tel	01332 695129
web	www.thehorseshoes.com

map: 8 entry: 113

Devon

The Ship Inn
Noss Mayo

At the head of a tidal inlet, a 16th-century pub remodelled with a nautical twist. While visiting boats can tie up alongside (with permission, of course), high-tide parking is trickier. When the tide is in, you enter via the back door on the first-floor level; when out, it's a quick stroll over the 'beach' and in by the front entrance. Downstairs are plain boards, a wooden bar, solid wood furniture and walls richly caparisoned with maritime prints. Open fires, books and newspapers add to the easy feel. Upstairs the Galley, Bridge and Library areas have views and a happy, dining buzz. The menu strikes a modern chord, and is fish-friendly, with fish stew and fresh crab sandwiches alongside Devon lamb and rhubarb and ginger crumble. They have well-kept beers from Devon breweries, many malts and eight wines by the glass: take your drink to the sunny patio at octagonal tables and make the most of the watery views. This is a civilised stop-off for walkers on the South Devon coast path.
No smoking throughout.

directions	South of Yealmpton, on Yealm estuary.
meals	12pm-9.30pm. Main courses £7-£14.
closed	Open all day.

Bruce & Lesley Brunning
The Ship Inn,
Noss Mayo, Plymouth,
Devon PL8 1EW
tel   01752 872387
web   www.nossmayo.com

map: 2 entry: 114

Devon

Dartmoor Union
Holbeton

Don't be deceived by the unassuming plaque next to the front door of this former cider press and village union room. Inside is stylish, welcoming and full of surprises. The leather sofas, chopped logs and glossy piles of *Country Living* in the flagstoned bar create a comfortable farmhouse feel, while the burgundy walls of the dining area add a bistro touch. Broad and keenly-priced daily menus appeal to all tastes, with some judicious sourcing of ingredients from head chef Ollie Luscombe. Tuck into partridge with spicy lentils and parsnip purée, roast cannon of lamb with confit garlic and red wine jus or crab crostini. Another surprise: they have just created a microbrewery in the enclosed, decked and sunny garden, producing two ales from a Kentish blend of Goldings, Brambling Cross and Fuggles hops. Beaches and walks beckon…

directions	Village signed off A379, 10 miles east of Plymouth.
meals	12pm-2pm (3pm Sunday); 6.30pm-9.30pm (9pm Sunday). Main courses £4.25-£17.95.
closed	3pm-5.30pm. Open all day Sunday.

John Stevens
Dartmoor Union,
Fore Street, Holbeton, Plymouth,
Devon PL8 1NE
tel   01752 830288
web   www.dartmoorunion.co.uk

map: 2 entry: 115

Devon

Fortescue Arms
East Allington

Tom and Werner are the 'highlights' here. Canadian Tom is maitre d' and has looked after heads of state; Austrian Werner has cheffed in starred restaurants and used to own the Old Vienna in Torquay. The Fortescue's double doors fling open in summer and you can hear the wine corks popping in the bar. Your hosts have been here mere months but are reinventing pub food – and how! Portions are generous, quick to arrive, great value and, if the rabbit and pumpkin stew is anything to go by, delicious. There's pork tenderloin filled with ham and cheese and topped with mustard sauce; prime fillet of beef with smoked oysters; red mullet baked with fennel; apfelstrudel with crème patissière; Wiener coffee ice cream. The dark panelled bar is where Tom and the bar girls hold court, the restaurant is big and inviting, and the outdoor decked area is smartly spotlit at night.

directions	Village signed off A361 between Totnes and Kingsbridge.
meals	12pm-2pm; 7pm-9.30pm. Main courses (dinner) £7.85-£17.65; bar meals £3-£6.50.
closed	2.30pm-6pm & Monday lunchtimes.

Werner Rott & Tom Kendrick
Fortescue Arms,
East Allington, Totnes,
Devon TQ9 7RA

| tel | 01548 521215 |
| web | www.fortescue-arms.co.uk |

map: 2 entry: 116

Devon

Victoria Inn
Salcombe

Separated from the rock pools and the sea by a modest car park, this fully revamped and rather civilised inn has won several awards under chef-proprietor Andrew Cannon. Local pictures and nautical *objets* acknowledge the coastal location and history – as does the menu, whose range is broad. Pop in for a swift half and a sandwich and chips or stay for a daily fish special – codling, sea bass, trout – served in generous portions. Young and cheery staff make all ages welcome and the large three-tiered garden, with super wooden play area, makes this an excellent family venue in summer. Salcombe's yachties and second-home owners mean that star-spotters may get lucky – though you might be better off having a nautical natter with the sea dogs at the bar. Flowers and white linen in the restaurant, log fires and malt whiskies in the bar, coastal walks to make the heart soar.

directions	Town centre.
meals	12pm-2.30pm; 6pm-9pm. Main courses £9.95-£17.
closed	Open all day.

Andrew Cannon
Victoria Inn,
Fore Street, Salcombe,
Devon TQ8 8BU

| tel | 01548 842604 |
| web | www.victoriainnsalcombe.co.uk |

map: 2 entry: 117

Pig's Nose Inn
East Prawle

Winding lanes with skyscraper hedges weave from the main road to the edge of the world. There are an awful lot of porcine references round these parts (South Hams, Gammon Head, Piglet Stores) and the Pig's Nose is Devon's most southerly pub. Filled with character, cosy corners and quirky ephemera, it has an atmosphere all of its own. A pie, pint and a paper at lunchtime can give way at night to the entire pub joining in a singalong; Peter's connections entice legendary acts – The Yardbirds, Wishbone Ash – to play in the adjacent fabulous hall. If your teenagers fail to join in, a ready supply of 50p coins will keep them entertained in the pool room. Lifelong friendships may be struck up by the woodburning stove as you tuck into good old pub favourites cooked up by Carlo the chef. Your hosts have a terrific sense of fun and it's infectious. The best pub in the world – or a close contender.

directions	A379 Kingsbridge-Dartmouth; at Frogmore, right over bridge opp. bakery; signs to East Prawle. Pub by green.
meals	12pm-3pm; 7pm-9.30pm. Main courses £6-£10.
closed	2.30pm-6pm; Sunday evenings & Mondays in winter.

Peter & Lesley Webber
Pig's Nose Inn,
East Prawle, Kingsbridge,
Devon TQ7 2BY
tel 01548 511209
web www.pigsnoseinn.co.uk

map: 2 entry: 118

Tradesmans Arms
Stokenham

Nick Abbot swapped a thriving Chiltern's dining pub for the good life in the South Hams. His 14th-century, part-thatched pub, formerly a brewhouse with three cottages, stands in a sleepy village inland from Slapton Sands and takes its name from the tradesmen who used to call in for a jug of ale while trekking the coastal bridlepath. You may still find a tradesman or two here today, downing a pint in the main bar. Beamed, not smart but attractively rustic, it has an open fire and antique dining tables and views that reach across the valley. Both the menu and daily chalkboard specials list some innovative pub food, all created by a local chef. As well as the usual lunchtime sandwiches, the daily-changing and seasonal selection includes fresh Brixham fish, scallops from the bay and game – perhaps venison steak with red wine sauce. You'll find five real ales on handpump, including Brakspear Bitter – Nick's favourite tipple – fondly recalling his Chiltern Hills days.

directions	1 mile from Slapton Sands & Torcross, off A379.
meals	12pm-2.30pm; 6.30pm-9.30pm. Main courses £6.95-£14.95.
closed	Open all day Sunday.

Nicholas Abbott
Tradesmans Arms,
Stokenham,
Kingsbridge,
Devon TQ7 2SZ
tel 01548 580313

map: 2 entry: 119

Devon

The Tower Inn
Slapton

Despite the drawbacks of hidden access and tricky parking, this 14th-century inn attracts not just locals but visitors from Slapton Sands. Standing beside the sinister ivy-clad ruins of a chantry tower, and built to house the artisans working on it, the pub is a flower-bedecked classic, and hugely atmospheric inside. Dark and gloomy by day, the low-beamed and stone-walled interior – all rustic dark-wood tables, old pews and fine stone fireplaces – comes into its own by night, when flickering light from candles and fires creates the cosiest possible atmosphere. Choose golden, bitter-sweet St Austell Brewery Tribute from the array of handpumps on the bar, then soak it up with a plateful of crispy fried red mullet with roasted pepper salsa. A lovely, sleepy village setting – and a super landscaped garden at the back with views of the parish church and the eerie tower.

directions	Off A379 between Torcross & Dartmouth. Signed.
meals	12pm-2pm; 7pm-9pm. Main courses £8-£15.
closed	2.30pm-6pm. Sunday evenings & Mondays in winter.

Andrew & Annette Hammett
The Tower Inn,
Slapton, Kingsbridge,
Devon TQ7 2PN

| tel | 01548 580216 |
| web | www.thetowerinn.com |

map: 2 entry: 120

Devon

Kings Arms
Strete

Tempting to visit on a dark and rainy night – but it would be a shame to miss the glorious views of Start Bay. In three years Rob Dawson has revitalized the Edwardian hotel-turned-pub, bringing a natural warmth to the place *and* a fine menu – much of it fishy. A modest bar and a few tables greet you, then up the pine stair to a mezzanine dining room. Delicious smells waft from the kitchen – of cream of celeriac soup, rib-eye steak with straw chips, poached pears with port jelly ice cream. Oysters are gathered from the river Yealm, lobsters and crabs come straight from the bay, the cheeses are local and the wines are wide-ranging, with an excellent number by the glass – surprising for such a small place. The Kings Arms and its garden fill up at summer weekends as holiday-cottagers get wind of the place, and return – for the food, the friendliness and the views.

directions	Between Dartmouth & Torcross on the A379.
meals	12pm-2pm; 6.30pm-9pm. Main courses £8.95-£16.95.
closed	Sunday evenings & Monday in winter.

Rob Dawson
Kings Arms,
Dartmouth Road, Strete,
Dartmouth, Devon TQ6 0RW

| tel | 01803 770377 |
| web | www.kingsarms-dartmouth.co.uk |

map: 2 entry: 121

Devon

The Ferry Boat Inn
Dittisham

Little has changed at this waterside pub since it was built three centuries ago. The only inn right on the River Dart, it used to serve the passenger steamers plying between Dartmouth and Totnes – you can still arrive by boat. Inside, big windows show off the view over to the wooded banks of the Greenway Estate (once Agatha Christie's home, now owned by the National Trust: shake the bell and catch the ferry). Arrive early and bag the best seats in the rustically charming, unspoilt little bar with its bare boards, crackling log fire, nautical bric-a-brac and unmissable, all-important 'high tides' board. If you happen to have overlooked the village car park, negotiated the steep lane and parked on the 'beach', then check the board before ordering your pint. Similarly, the tide dictates whether or not you can dine outside in summer… Expect a rousing welcome from landlord Ray Benson and decent home-cooked pub food. Gents can 'spray and pray' next door in the converted chapel.

directions	Off A3122, 2 miles west of Dartmouth.
meals	12pm-2pm; 7pm-9pm. Main courses £6.95-£12.
closed	Open all day.

	Ray Benson
	The Ferry Boat Inn, Manor Street, Dittisham, Dartmouth, Devon TQ6 0EX
tel	01803 722368

map: 2 entry: 122

Devon

The White Hart Bar
Dartington

Down a long, long drive past farmland and deer, Dartington Hall finally peeps into view: the college, conference centre, arts centre, dairy farm and 14th-century hall built for a half-brother of Richard II. Sneaked away in the corner of the courtyard – dotted with picnic tables in summer – is the White Hart. The bar and restaurant is informally 21st century, with chunky beams, York stone floor, smouldering log fires, round light-oak tables and Windsor chairs. Organic and local produce are the mainstay of the menus, from warm salads to sausage and mash. In the trestled dining hall: fish chowder, rack of lamb with redcurrant and rosemary sauce, bitter chocolate tart with clotted cream. Beers are from Otter Brewery, there are good wines and as many organic juices and ciders as you could wish for. Walk off a very fine lunch with a stroll through sweeping parkland that borders the Dart.

directions	Off A385, 2 miles north west of Totnes.
meals	12pm-2pm; 6pm-9pm. Main courses £5.95-£12.95.
closed	Open all day.

	John Hazzard
	The White Hart Bar, Dartington Hall, Dartington, Totnes, Devon TQ9 6EL
tel	01803 847111
web	www.dartingtonhall.com

map: 2 entry: 123

Devon

The Church House Inn
Marldon

The old village pub is a civilised place, popular with retired locals and ladies that lunch – indeed, anyone who appreciates a glass of rioja and a naturally reared Exmoor steak. With its welcoming bar, several dining areas and lovely sloping garden, this is a great all-rounder. The feel is one of a well-crafted, rustic elegance – stonework and beams, original bell-shaped windows, paintings in gilt frames, crisp table settings and smiling service. The long central bar has been partitioned into three areas, plus one four-tabled candlelit snug, perfect for a party. The chef has been here 13 years and the diners keep coming; the food is modern British and locally sourced. Some come just for a pint of well-kept Dartmoor Best and a chat by the fire. The pub originally housed the artisans who worked on Marldon Church, and its ancient tower overlooks the hedged garden.

directions	Marldon off Torquay-Brixham ring road. Pub at bottom of village, signed.
meals	12pm-2pm (2.30pm Sundays); 6.30pm-9.30pm (7pm-9pm Sundays). Main courses £5-£16.50.
closed	2.30pm-5pm (3pm-5.30pm Sundays).

Julian Cook
The Church House Inn,
Marldon,
Paignton,
Devon TQ3 1SL

tel	01803 558279

map: 2 entry: 124

Devon

Bickley Mill
Kingskerswell

The microclimate of the English Riviera is never more apparent than in the garden of this 13th-century flour mill, tucked into a hidden valley between Newton Abbot and Torquay. A large decked area is surrounded by tropical plants and trees and it all feels special and secluded – a far cry from the nearby resorts. It's been a pub since 1971, but the arrival of the Smiths has seen the place transformed. New wooden floors, chunky beams, pristine hardwood furniture and glowing log fires draw folk from afar. Families and children are especially welcome. Chef Bill Gott's strong links with Devon fish merchants and butchers make specials like Mediterranean fish stew and braised beef casserole are deservedly popular.
No smoking throughout.

directions	Follow Totnes signs through Newton Abbot onto A381; left at Park Hill Cross after garage; 1 mile to thatched cottage on right; next left, signed.
meals	12pm-2pm (2.15pm Sat); 6.30pm-9pm (9.30pm Fri & Sat); 12pm-8pm Sun. Main courses £8-£16.
closed	3pm-6.30pm (6pm Fri & Sat). Open all Sunday.

David & Tricia Smith
Bickley Mill,
Stoneycombe, Kingskerswell,
Devon TQ12 5LN

tel	01803 873201
web	www.bickleymill.co.uk

map: 2 entry: 125

Devon

Rising Sun
Woodland

The farmhouse on the edge of Dartmoor was once a tearoom. Now the plushly-furnished open-plan bar, cosy with beams and log fire, delivers Princetown Jail Ale, Luscombe cider and fine wines. Fresh market produce is what landlady Heather Humphreys likes to serve, her daily menus listing fish from Brixham, game from local estates and smoked meats and fish from Dartmouth's smokehouse. Hearty ploughman's come with a selection of four Devon cheeses, or try roasted dab with lemon and herb butter, braised lamb with red wine, garlic and redcurrant jelly, perfect flaky pastry pies generously filled with, say, lamb and apricot, and Devon apple cake with clotted cream for pudding. Children have toys and dressing-up clothes in the family room; in the big garden are swings and an old tractor. There are a sunny terrace and rolling South Hams views, too.

directions	Off A38 before Ashburton junction heading west for Plymouth.
meals	12pm-2.15pm (3pm Sundays); 6pm-9.15pm (7pm Sundays). Main courses £6.95-£14.95.
closed	Mondays (except bank holidays). Sundays 3pm-7pm.

Heather Humphreys
Rising Sun,
Woodland, Ashburton,
Devon TQ13 7JT
tel   01364 652544
web www.risingsunwoodland.co.uk

map: 2 entry: 126

Devon

The Rock Inn
Haytor Vale

Originally an ale house for quarrymen and miners, the 300-year-old Rock Inn stands in a tiny village high on Dartmoor's windswept southern slopes. Run by the same family for 20 years, this civilised haven oozes character; there are polished antique tables and sturdy settles on several levels, a grandfather clock, pretty plates and fresh flowers, cosy corners and at least two fires. Settle down with a pint of Dartmoor Best in the beamed and carpeted bar and peruse the supper menu that highlights local, often organic, produce. All that fresh Dartmoor air will have made you hungry, so tuck into beef cobbler cooked in red wine, garlic and thyme, lusciously followed by sticky toffee pudding. Lunchtime meals range from soup, sandwiches and ploughman's to local sausages in onion gravy. There's a pretty beer garden, too.

directions	At Drumbridges roundabout A382 for Bovey Tracey; B3387 to Haytor. Left at phone box.
meals	12pm-2pm; 7pm-9pm. Main courses £6.50-£16.95.
closed	Christmas Day, Boxing Day.

Christopher & Susan Graves
The Rock Inn,
Haytor Vale, Bovey Tracey,
Devon TQ13 9XP
tel   01364 661305
web www.rock-inn.co.uk

map: 2 entry: 127

Rugglestone Inn
Widecombe-in-the-Moor

Beside open moorland within walking
distance of the village – and named after
the massive Ruggle Stone nearby – is a
rustic, 200-year-old stone building
whose two tiny rooms lead off a stone-
floored passageway. Few of the hordes
who descend on this honey-pot village in
the middle of Dartmoor make it to this
rare gem. Head-ducking beams fill the
old-fashioned parlour with its simple
furnishings, open woodburner and deep-
country feel. Both rooms are free of
modern intrusions, the locals preferring
time-honoured games such as cribbage,
euchre and dominoes. The tiny bar serves
local farm cider; Butcombe Bitter and St
Austell Dartmoor Best are tapped
straight from the cask. From the kitchen
come simple bar meals, from
ploughman's lunches and homemade
soups to hearty casseroles. Across the
babbling brook at the front is a lawn with
benches and peaceful moorland views.
Heaven.

The Warren House Inn
Postbridge

High and alone, in a remote and
beautiful part of Dartmoor – a hugely
welcome sight for drivers and walkers
braving the moor. Such a treat to walk
into the warm panelled bar with its
settles and log fire – fuelled by peat until
recent years and allegedly kept alight
since 1845. In spite of the lino stone-
effect tiles, this is an attractive, no-
nonsense pub, plain, simple and honest,
and with stories to tell. Local maps,
pictures and brassware hang on the walls,
ceiling beams are dark, lighting dim and
there's a pool table in the family room.
Outside, a grassy terrace on the other
side of the road, no flowers or frills – but
the view! From this old tin miners' pub,
the third highest in England, you can see
for 20 miles on a clear day. Helen the
barmaid, cheerful and kind, settles you
in with a pint of foaming Otter Bitter
and a bowl of homemade soup, rabbit
pie, Dartmoor lamb or a hot apple pie.

directions	On B3212 2 miles north of Postbridge.
meals	12pm-4.30pm, 6pm-9pm in winter. 12pm-9pm (8.30pm Sundays) in summer. Main courses £6-£15.
closed	Open all day.

directions	600 yards from centre of Widecombe; signed.
meals	12pm-2pm; 7pm-9pm. Main courses from £6.95.
closed	3.30pm-6.30pm.

	Rod & Diane Williams Rugglestone Inn, Widecombe-in-the-Moor, Devon TQ13 7TF
tel	01364 621327

	Peter Parsons The Warren House Inn, Postbridge, Moretonhampstead, Devon PL20 6TA
tel	01822 880208

map: 2 entry: 128

map: 2 entry: 129

Devon

The Peter Tavy Inn
Peter Tavy

An atmospheric 15th-century inn on the flanks of desolate Dartmoor. Originally a tiny cottage built to house the masons working on the church, it graduated from being the parish poorhouse to an ale house, frequented for 200 years by grateful moorland walkers and local drinkers. Some years ago it was sensitively extended and is now one of Dartmoor's noted food pubs. There's masses of charm here, in black beams, gleaming, polished slate floors, long pine tables, high-backed settles and woodburners in huge hearths. Follow an invigorating walk with a pint of Princetown Jail ale and a lunchtime snack – perhaps steak and stilton pie. Food in the evening steps up a gear, with chicken stuffed with goat's cheese and tomatoes and monkfish with creamy garlic sauce on the imaginative chalkboard menu. Devon farm cider, country wines and fine malt whiskies are there for those averse to West Country ale. *No smoking throughout.*

directions	2 miles off A386, 4 miles north of Tavistock.
meals	12pm-2pm; 6.30pm-9pm. Main courses £5.75-£10.95 (lunch), £8.95-£13.95 (dinner).
closed	2.30pm-6pm (3pm Saturday & Sunday).

Chris & Jo Wordingham
The Peter Tavy Inn,
Peter Tavy,
Tavistock,
Devon PL19 9NN
tel   01822 810348

map: 2 entry: 130

Devon

Dartmoor Inn
Lydford

Karen and Philip Burgess are self-confessed foodies and their rambling dining pub turns out some serious surprises. In flight-of-fancy rooms are up-dates on gourmet evenings and seasonal celebrations, a Parisian bistro supper or a Brazilian jazz night. Evening menus match the occasion and are seasonal; locals take advantage of monthly set lunches. (And mobile phones are wisely discouraged!). In November you might start with squash soup and chive cream, move on to slow-cooked duck leg with lentils and juniper. Walkers and dogs stride in from the moors and squeeze into the bar for Dartmoor Best Bitter and organic bottled cider. And so to bed... new mattresses on antique beds, soft lights and sofas: absolutely gorgeous. *No smoking throughout.*

directions	On A386 between Okehampton & Tavistock.
meals	12pm-2.15pm; 6.30pm-9.15pm. Main courses £11.75-£19; bar menu £5.75-£13.50; set menus £13.75 & £16.50.
rooms	3 doubles £90-£115.
closed	Sunday evenings; Mondays.

See page 31 for bedroom details.

Philip & Karen Burgess
Dartmoor Inn,
Lydford, Okehampton,
Devon EX20 4AY
tel   01822 820221
web www.dartmoorinn.com

map: 2 entry: 131

The Harris Arms
Lewdown

An unusually delightful place where you are welcomed on the way in and thanked on the way out. The passion Andy and Rowena have for food and wine is infectious and the awards they are gathering is proof of their commitment. Expect a long bar, a fire at one end, a patterned carpet, maroon walls and a big strawberry blond cat named Reg. A large new decked area at the back has rich rolling views. The Whitemans are members of the Slow Food movement so real food is their thing: cheeses are the west country's finest, fish and meat come from exemplary suppliers, Dunn's Dairy supplies the organic milk and cream, fruit and veg are from Dartmoor Provisions and wines from small growers. Flavoursome food is what the Cornish chef delivers. Whether it be fish cakes on creamed leeks or steak and frites from the griddle, it is consistently good and little portions can be ordered for little people. Great value.

Duke of York
Iddesleigh

Built to house the 14th-century stonemasons working on the church next door, the thatched Duke of York is a cracking local: heart-warming food, real ale and a big welcome from farmer-pub landlord Jamie Stuart and his wife. Pass a parked tractor on your way in to find farmers, shooters and the odd slaughterman parleying in the single bar over pints of Cotleigh Tawny tapped from the cask. Scrubbed oak tables have fresh flowers and candles, there are village photographs on the walls, banknotes on the beams, rocking chairs by the blazing log fire – it's a rustic, enchanting place. With fish fresh from Clovelly and Brixham and locally sourced beef, lamb and pork, diners enjoy the heartiest home cooking: tureens of homemade soup, steak and kidney pudding, lamb chops with rosemary and garlic gravy, whole baked sea bass with lemon butter, glorious puddings. The all-day breakfasts are not for the faint-hearted either.

directions	On old A30 between Lewdown & Lifton; leave A30 at exit for Broadwoodwidger and head south.
meals	12pm-3pm; 6pm-9pm. Main courses £7.50-£8.95 (lunch), £8.95-£13.75 (dinner).
closed	Mondays (except bank holidays).

Andy & Rowena Whiteman
The Harris Arms,
Portgate, Lewdown,
Devon EX20 4PZ

tel	01566 783331
web	www.theharrisarms.co.uk

map: 2 entry: 132

directions	On B3217 between Exbourne & Dolton, 3 miles NE of Hatherleigh.
meals	8am-10pm. Main courses £8-£12; set menu £22.
closed	Open all day.

Jamie Stuart & Pippa Hutchinson
Duke of York,
Iddesleigh,
Winkleigh,
Devon EX19 8BG

tel	01837 810253

map: 2 entry: 133

Devon

Sandy Park Inn
Chagford

You'll like it the moment you step in. Benched snugs and oriental rugs, worn flagstones and crackling logs, delicious smells and a happy hum. And it gets lively on Friday and Saturday nights. The restaurant is in two parts, cosy like the rest, daily specials are chalked up on a board above the fire and chef Huge Leech's food is "creative-brasserie". We chose well: a rich and flavoursome pasta carbonara, a fresh seared tuna steak and a warm treacle tart. Simon has been here just over a year and is extending his list of wines, while ales are Otter, St Austell and two guests. It's so lovely you'd be mad to leave – so stay! Bedrooms above the kitchen are simple, crisp, comfortable and quiet. Some overlook thatched roofs to fields, one opens to the garden – another delight – beds are big and bathrooms smart. Teign Valley makes a lovely walk, Castle Drogo is up the road and the magical moors beckon.

directions	On A382, 5 miles south of A30 & Whiddon Down.
meals	12pm-2.30pm; 6pm-9.30pm. No food Sunday evening. Main courses £7-£11.
rooms	5: 4 doubles, 1 twin £70. Single £45.
closed	Monday lunchtimes. Open all day.

See page 31 for bedroom details.

Simon Saunders
Sandy Park Inn,
Sandy Park, Chagford,
Devon TQ13 8JW
tel 01647 433267
web www.sandyparkinn.co.uk

map: 2 entry: 134

Devon

The Drewe Arms
Drewsteignton

Long, low and thatched, in a pretty village square above the wooded slopes of the Teign valley, the Drewe Arms is better known as Auntie Mabel's. Why? In honour of Mabel Mudge, once Britain's longest-serving landlady, who retired in 1996 aged 99. No longer quite in the time-warp it once was, it does remain an unpretentious and well-loved local. Beer straight from the cask is served from two hatchways, one opening to a front room with rustic benches and tables; a second room across the flagged passageway has sturdy old pine tables and a roaring log fire. Mabel's Kitchen, now the dining room, keeps the original dresser and old black cooking range. Home-cooked food using fresh local produce is listed on a daily-changing blackboard menu. Stride off through National Trust woodland to Castle Drogo – the walks are wonderful.

directions	Off A382, 2 miles south of A30, 8 miles west of Exeter.
meals	12pm-2pm; 6.30pm-9pm. Main courses £7.95-£14.

David & Lisa Jermey
The Drewe Arms,
The Square,
Drewsteignton, Exeter,
Devon EX6 6NQ
tel 01647 281224

map: 2 entry: 135

The Nobody Inn
Doddiscombsleigh

We remember an excellent cheese and wine lunch ten years ago and little has changed… the Butcombe bitter is still racked on an up-turned crate behind the bar. Nick Borst-Smith also has his own wine company (800 bins), the wines of the moment standing on an uneven counter; pick up a bottle and the others glide into place. Settles and tables are crammed into every corner, horse-brasses brighten low beams, there's an inglenook glowing with logs and a part of the bar dates from Tudor times. Choose a tranche of pork and apple pie followed perhaps by chocolate truffle cake… Sweet and spicy Nobody soup is made from chicken stock, vegetables and local fruit; smoked eel comes from Dartmouth; local quail is stuffed with rice and apricots; there are Devon cheeses and 240 whiskies, and their own Nobody's beer comes in old pint glasses. The village is buried down a maze of lanes but it's not hard to find and worth the detour.

The Puffing Billy
Exton

Martin Humphries has turned this old railway inn into a shrine for local produce. Polished wooden floors, leather sofas and crackling log fires set the tone, while the bright whitewashed walls are colourfully peppered with photos of the pub's producers and suppliers. And a large serving hatch allows certain tables to watch the theatre of the open kitchen, where a band of enthusiastic chefs toil to perfect dishes such as crispy Crediton duckling embellished with fondant potato, baby turnips, apples and fig jus. Or wild orange risotto; crispy brill with leeks, butternut squash and aubergine caviar cream; chocolate and orange mousse. Traditionalists will be happy to hear that pub classics, sandwiches and baguettes are not ignored. A small grassed area is perfect for summer barbecues and the place is rammed to the rafters on jazz nights. Friendly to families, too.

directions	Off A38 at Haldon Racecourse exit, then 3 miles.
meals	7.30pm-9.30pm (Tuesday-Saturday); bar meals 12pm-2pm; 7pm-10pm. Main courses £6.90-£12.50.
closed	2.30pm-6pm (3pm-7pm Sunday).

	Nick Borst-Smith
	The Nobody Inn,
	Doddiscombsleigh, Exeter,
	Devon EX6 7PS
tel	01647 252394
web	www.nobodyinn.co.uk

map: 2 entry: 136

directions	Off A376 between M5 junc 30. & Exmouth; pub close to Exton railway station.
meals	11am-3pm; 6pm-9.30pm. Main courses £6-£18.
closed	Sunday evenings; Mondays.

	Martin Humphries
	The Puffing Billy,
	Station Road, Exton, Exeter,
	Devon EX3 0PR
tel	01392 877888
web	www.thepuffingbilly.com

map: 2 entry: 137

Devon

The Bridge Inn
Topsham

Cut across the bridge too fast and you miss one of Devon's last traditional ale houses. Unchanged for most of the century – and in the family for as long – the 16th-century Bridge Inn is a 'must' for ale connoisseurs. And for all who appreciate a genuine pub furnished in the old-style, all high-back settles and ancient floors. (The Queen chose the Bridge for her first official 'visit to a pub'.) Years ago it was a brewery and malthouse; Caroline's great-grandfather was the last publican to brew his own here. This is beer-drinker heaven – lager lovers should note their favourite tipple is banned – with up to ten real ales drawn from the barrel. There's cider and gooseberry wine, too. Cradle your pint to the background din of local chatter in the Inner Sanctum, under a grandfather clock by a blazing log fire. With bread baked at the local farm, home-cooked hams, homemade chutneys and cracking cheeses, the sandwiches and ploughman's are the best. *No smoking throughout*

directions	In Topsham A376 for Exmouth; Elmgrove Road into Bridge Hill.
meals	12pm-2pm. Bar meals £2-£5.90.
closed	2pm-6pm (7pm Sundays).

Caroline Cheffers-Heard
The Bridge Inn,
Topsham,
Exeter, Devon EX3 0QQ
tel   01392 873862
web   www.cheffers.co.uk

map: 2 entry: 138

Devon

Digger's Rest
Woodbury Salterton

Months of searching led the Rushtons to this 500-year-old, fat-walled former cider house built of stone and cob. It is the quintessential thatched Devon inn. A good looking makeover swiftly followed, the timbered interior was revived: fresh yellow décor, new carpets, an eclectic mix of old dining tables, subtle wall lighting, tasteful prints. Arrive early to bag the sofa by the log fire. In addition to the local Otter and guest ales, the impressive list of wines (ten by the glass) and the relaxing atmosphere, there are organic soft drinks, Italian Gaggia coffee, soothing piped jazz, baby-changing facilities, daily newspapers and a brilliant pub menu that employs the best local produce. Treat yourself to Brixham fish (pan-fried scallops with bacon, on dressed leaves), Devon Ruby Red beef (21-day hung rib-eye with herb butter), and local Kenniford Farm pork, roasted for Sunday lunches. And there's a landscaped patio garden.

directions	Off A3052, 3 miles east of Exeter & 3 miles from M5 junc. 30.
meals	12pm-2pm (all day weekends); 7pm-9.30pm. Main courses £7.75-£12.50.
closed	Open all day weekends.

Steve & Sarah Rushton
Digger's Rest,
Woodbury Salterton, Exeter,
Devon EX5 1PQ
tel   01395 232375
web   www.diggersrest.co.uk

map: 2 entry: 139

The Blue Ball
Sandygate

The Blue Ball is a popular place – though it is more informal eatery than traditional pub. Handy for the motorway, the colourwashed, thatched, roadside inn offers a welcoming respite to any savvy traveller. Brasserie-style food is generous and well presented, while a separate restaurant menu struts its stuff in the evening. There's an earthy pubbiness to the dimly-lit front bar, with its flagstones, low beams, reassuring settles and log fire. Pink walls may add a cosmopolitan touch, but the old handsaws hung around the fire reinforce its essential rusticity. A further bar has a lighter feel with polished floorboards; a contemporary dining room extension brings things bang up to date: an airy atmosphere, blond-wood furniture, cord carpeting and modern art. A great open-hearted village local, and, with a play area in the garden, family-easy too.
No smoking throughout.

directions	M5 exit to Sidmouth. At r'bout on Sidmouth road, double-back towards m'way. Left 200 yards down lane.
meals	12pm-2.30pm; 6.30pm-9.30pm. Main courses £4.95-£16.95.
closed	4pm-7pm Sundays.

Colin & Janice Sparks
The Blue Ball,
Sandygate,
Exeter,
Devon EX2 7JL

tel   01392 873401

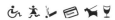

map: 2 entry: 140

The Jack in the Green
Rockbeare

Bustle and buzz in the dark wood bar, and good local brews on tap – Otter Ale, Cotleigh Tawny, Branscombe Vale Bitter. But this is more restaurant than pub: "For those who live to eat," reads the sign. In a series of smart, brightly lit, blue-motif carpeted rooms, chef Matthew Mason's bar menu goes in for modern and mouthwatering variations of tried and trusted favourites: braised faggot with creamed potato, steamed venison pudding with port and juniper jus… even the ploughman's is impressive. More ambition on display in the restaurant, where seared fillet of salmon with sorrel and hollandaise sauce and crisp fried confit of Creedy Carver duck legs with plum squash make for succulent seasonal choices. For summer there's courtyard seating. Paul Parnell has been at the helm for years and he and his staff do a grand job. Good for company dinners too.

directions	5 miles east of M5 (exit 29) on old A30 just past Exeter Airport.
meals	12pm-2pm (2.30pm Fri & Sat); 6pm-9pm (10pm Fri & Sat); 12pm-9.30pm Sun. Main courses £9.50-£19.50.
closed	3pm-5.30pm Mon-Fri (3pm-6pm Sat); 25 December-6 January.

Paul Parnell
The Jack in the Green,
Rockbeare,
Exeter, Devon EX5 2EE

tel   01404 822240
web   www.jackinthegreen.uk.com

map: 2 entry: 141

Devon

Masons Arms
Branscombe

Approach straggling Branscombe down narrow lanes (good for honing reversing skills) to this creeper-clad inn. The 14th-century bar has a traditional feel with dark ship's timbers, stone walls, slate floor and central fireplace that cooks spit-roasts to perfection. Quaff pints of Otter Bitter or Jack Rat scrumpy by the fire; on warm days, make for the sun-trapped terrace. Nothing is too much trouble for the staff, whose prime aim is for you to unwind. Local produce, including fresh crab and lobster landed on Branscombe's beach, is the focus of the modern British menu. There's creamy seafood chowder and Lyme Bay mackerel, salt-baked brill and organically reared beef fillet with pepper sauce. The pebbly beach is a 12-minute stroll across National Trust land and wonderful coastal path walks await the adventurous.

directions	Off A3052 between Sidmouth & Seaton.
meals	12pm-2pm; 7pm-9pm. Main courses £6.95-£14.95; set menu £25.
closed	Open all day everyday in summer & all day weekends in winter.

	Colin & Carol Slaney
	Masons Arms,
	Branscombe, Seaton,
	Devon EX12 3DJ
tel	01297 680300
web	www.masonsarms.co.uk

map: 2 entry: 142

Devon

The Drewe Arms
Broadhembury

Nigel Burge runs a relaxed ship – the secret of his long success. The 15th-century thatched Drewe is the cornerstone of a thatched Devon village. By the fire are the day's papers and magazines; on the bar, local Otter ales tapped straight from the cask and wines beyond reproach. It's a captivating little place. Beams are oak-carved, walls plank-panelled, there are country tables, wood carvings, walking sticks, flowers and a log-fired inglenook that crackles in winter. Food is way above average for a country pub, with fish from Brixham and Newlyn. Go for Scandinavian-style gravadlax with dill and mustard, or skate wings served in the traditional manner with a caper sauce. Plenty of classy modern touches, too: stilton and smoked haddock rarebit comes in both small and large portions, there's brill with horseradish hollandaise, and hand-dived scallops that are seared to perfection. All this, and a garden that's as dreamy as a country garden can be.

directions	M5 junc. 28; A373 Honiton to Cullompton.
meals	12pm-2pm; 7pm-9.15pm. Main courses £10-£20.
closed	Sunday evenings.

	Kerstin & Nigel Burge
	The Drewe Arms,
	Broadhembury,
	Honiton,
	Devon EX14 3NF
tel	01404 841267

map: 2 entry: 143

Culm Valley Inn
Culmstock

Don't be put off by the unkempt exterior of Richard Hartley's pub by the river Culm. It may not be posh but there's a warm and easy feel: deep pink-washed walls, glowing coals, flickering candles. From ragged bar stools the locals sample flavoursome microbrewery beers while the gentry drop by for unusually good food. Easy-going chef-patron Richard and his efficient band make this place zing. Look to the chalkboard for south coast seafood, weekend fish specials such as monkfish with crispy ginger and garlic noodles, Ruby Red Devon beef and wild boar from nearby farms or tapas. From the English elm bar you can order from a fantastic array of rare and curious spirits, French wines from specialist growers or local beers tapped from the cask. Bedrooms are simple and cheerful, with white bed linen and vibrant walls.

directions	On B3391, 2 miles off A38 west of Wellington.
meals	12pm-2pm; 7pm-9.30pm. No food Sunday evenings. Main courses £8-£18.
rooms	3: 1 double, 1 twin, 1 family from £55. Singles £30.
closed	3pm-7pm. Open all day weekends and in summer.

See page 32 for bedroom details.

Richard Hartley
Culm Valley Inn,
Culmstock,
Cullompton,
Devon EX15 3JJ
tel   01884 840354

The Mason's Arms
Knowstone

Leaving windswept Exmoor behind, arrive through fern or twisting lane. Wood is stacked against the 13th-century walls, you are drawn to enter. The dim, low, flagged bar, with inglenook and elaborate burner, fills with dogs and drinkers in Wellington boots, here for a natter and a pint of Cotleigh Tawny ale. But who would imagine, down worn stone steps, a cosy lounge with deep sofas and a restaurant extension with a ceiling mural? Served at a jumble of candlelit tables is food fit for kings. Mark Dodson spent 18 years working at the celebrated Waterside Inn, 13 of those as head chef. So short menus accompanied by French wines major in classic French and British dishes and are concocted from the finest regional produce; try pan-fried foie gras with sultanas and pears, Devon ruby red beef with parsnip purée, monkfish with balsamic and orange sauce. And the rear terrace has wonderful views to Exmoor. One to watch.

directions	M5 junc. 27; A361 for Barnstaple; Knowstone signed after 20 miles. Into village, right at bottom of hill & pub on left.
meals	12pm-2pm; 7pm-9.30pm. Main courses £10.50-£16.50.
closed	Sunday evenings; Mondays.

Mark Dodson
The Mason's Arms,
Knowstone, South Molton,
Devon EX36 4RY
tel   01398 341231
web   www.masonsarmsdevon.co.uk

The Shave Cross Inn
Marshwood Vale

Fancy a pint of Branoc and a spicy salad of jerk chicken? Once a busy stop-off point for pilgrims and monastic visitors (who had their tonsures trimmed while staying), the cob-and-flint pub now sits dreamily off the beaten track at the end of several tortuously narrow lanes. It was rescued from closure by the Warburtons, back from the Caribbean. Life has stepped up a gear and the old tavern thrives – thanks largely to the exotic and delicious cuisine. Where else in deepest Dorset can you tuck into a zarzuela of fresh fish with a mild coconut curry sauce? There's simple pub grub for less adventurous palates, while surroundings remain strictly traditional: flagged floors, low beams, country furniture, a vast inglenook and the oldest thatched skittle alley in the country. The meandering garden, with goldfish pool, wishing well and play area, is gorgeous.

The Fox Inn
Corscombe

Clive, once an accountant, feels privileged to be running one of the most sought-after places to eat in the south-west. Everything about this 17th-century inn makes you feel good: the food, the people, the setting – Hardy's Wessex at its most peaceful and beautiful. The beer's not bad either, and there are farm cider and excellent wines. In the old days, drovers on the road to market would dip their sheep into the stream opposite and stop off for a pint of cider... the pub only received its full licence 40 years ago. In spite of modern changes the old feel has been kept; clever additions include a slate-topped bar, a flower-filled and benched conservatory, a long table made from a single oak felled by the storms of 1987. Be charmed by stuffed owls in glass cases, gingham tablecloths, paintings, flowers, flagstones, fires and six fish dishes a day. So close to the sea, you can almost smell it.

directions	B3162 for Broadwindsor; left in 2 miles for Broadoak. Follow unclassified road for 3 miles.
meals	11am-3pm; 5pm-9.30pm (6pm-8pm Sundays in summer). Main courses £3.50-£10.50; set menus £22.50 & £26.
closed	Mondays (except bank holidays).

Roy & Mel Warburton
The Shave Cross Inn,
Shave Cross,
Marshwood Vale, Bridport,
Dorset DT6 6HW

tel	01308 868358

map: 3 entry: 146

directions	From Yeovil, A37 for Dorchester for 1 mile; right for Corscombe for 5.5 miles. On left on outskirts.
meals	12pm-2pm; 7pm-9pm (9.30pm Friday-Sunday). Main courses £8.25-£18.25.
closed	3pm-7pm.

Clive Webb
The Fox Inn,
Corscombe, Dorchester,
Dorset DT2 0NS

tel	01935 891330
web	www.fox-inn.co.uk

map: 3 entry: 147

Dorset

The Square & Compass
Worth Matravers

The name honours all those who cut stone from the nearby quarries. Built as a farm in the 17th century, this splendid old pub has been in the family for 90 years and remains gloriously unchanged. A narrow (and rare) drinking corridor leads to two hatches from where young Charlie Newman draws Ringwood and Badger ales straight from the cask. With a pint of farmhouse cider and a homemade pastie – that's all they sell – you can chat in the flagged corridor or settle in the sunny parlour with its painted wooden panels, old tables, wall seats, local prints and cartoons. The woodburner will warm you on a wild night. The rustic, stone-walled main room has live music; there's cribbage and shove-ha'penny; the family's fossil museum is next door. High on the edge of the village, gazing out across fields to the sea, the pub and its sunny front terrace – dotted, from time to time, with free-ranging chickens – is a popular stop for coastal path hikers. A treasure.

directions	B3069 east of Corfe Castle; through Kingston; right for Worth Matravers.
meals	Pasties and pies only.
closed	Open all day Saturday & July-September.

	Charlie Newman
	The Square & Compass,
	Worth Matravers,
	Swanage,
	Dorset BH19 3LF
tel	01929 439229

map: 3 entry: 148

Dorset

The Museum Inn
Farnham

In a village with roses round every door is the Museum Inn, one of the finest in the south of England. Vicky, Mark and their (mostly) Aussie staff have created a blissfully warm and happy place to be: she does bubbly, he does laid-back. The refit of the big 17th-century bar has kept the period feel – all flagstones, inglenook, fresh flowers and fashionably mismatched tables and chairs. It is usually jam-packed with smart country folk and their dogs and is best out of season. Expect cosy alcoves to hide in, a gorgeous, book-filled drawing room to browse and a smart, white-raftered dining room. New chef Danny Turner is Michelin-trained and his dishes range from mini fishcakes with hollandaise sauce to slow-roasted Dorset lamb shoulder with buttered spinach and aioli. Dark chocolate brownies come with bitter chocolate sauce, hot lime sponge with custard.

directions	From Blandford, A354 for Salisbury for 6.5 miles; left for Farnham.
meals	12pm-2pm; 7pm-9.30pm. Main courses £13-£16.50.

	Vicky Elliot & Mark Stephenson
	The Museum Inn,
	Farnham, Blandford Forum,
	Dorset DT11 8DE
tel	01725 516261
web	www.museuminn.co.uk

map: 3 entry: 149

Dorset

Coventry Arms
Corfe Mullen

A converted 15th-century watermill with its own island, and a fisherman for a landlord. John Hugo's freshly caught trout are sometimes reeled in by customers and may end up on your plate. Fish is a bit of a speciality – turbot with tomato and herb linguine, roast monkfish with baby leeks and herb butter sauce – with the menu focusing on fresh ingredients cooked simply and well. The local butcher makes sausages and faggots to the pub's own recipe and game comes from the local estates. Ploughman's and salads are equally good. Comfortably rustic rooms ramble around the main bar, a display of antique fishing reels hangs above the beer barrels and local ales are pulled straight from the cask. There are low beams, logs in the grate, weekly musicians and tables by the stream: John's waterside pub is loved by all – don't miss the annual beer and seafood festivals.

directions	A31 between Dorchester & Wimborne; 2 miles from Wimborne.
meals	12pm-2.30pm; 6pm-9.30pm. All day on Sundays. Main courses £8.50-£16.
closed	3pm-5.30pm. Open all day weekends.

John Hugo, David Armstrong Reed
Coventry Arms,
Mill Street,
Corfe Mullen, Wimborne,
Dorset BH21 3RH
tel   01258 857284

map: 3 entry: 150

Durham

The Victoria Inn
Durham

Imagine an old Victorian public house with small rooms, high ceilings, marble fireplaces, etched and cut glass and a vast collection of Victoriana. Once upon a time, shawled women popped in for a porter or in search of an errant husband, now it's frequented by builders, students, academics. Virtually unaltered since it was built in 1899, the Vic has been in the Webster family for 30 years and has a strong local following. The three traditional rooms are spick and span; above the bar servery is an unusual gallery with shining figurines and ornaments of Queen Victoria and the Prince Consort. Simple snacks are available but it is the Darwins Ghost Ale and other local and Scottish beers, the whiskies and the camaraderie that makes this place enticing. Upstairs bedrooms are traditionally furnished and good value, breakfasts are generous and there's off-street parking and garaging. Original, timeless, welcoming.

directions	5-minute walk over Kingsgate Bridge from cathedral, castle & market place.
meals	12pm-3pm (toasted sandwiches only).
rooms	5: 3 doubles, 1 twin, 1 family £60.

See page 32 for bedroom details.

Michael Webster
The Victoria Inn,
86 Hallgarth Street,
Durham DH1 3AS
tel   0191 386 5269
web   www.victoriainn-durhamcity.co.uk

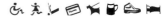

map: 12 entry: 151

Durham

Durham

The County
Aycliffe

Having won a Raymond Blanc scholarship in 1995, and worked with Gary Rhodes in London, Andrew Brown brought his skills north and restored the fortunes of a once rundown pub overlooking Aycliffe's pretty green. The patterned carpeting and faded walls have gone; in their place are bare boards, fresh walls and a pleasing minimalist feel. The award-winning food draws an eager crowd, while the open-plan bar is still the focal point of the community. Eat here, or in the stylish bistro. There are open sandwiches at lunchtime, and sausages with black pudding mash; in the bistro, crab and prawn risotto with lobster sauce, confit shoulder of lamb with Mediterranean vegetables and mint couscous, grilled tuna with fennel and a tomato ragout. The touch is light, bringing out textures and flavours superbly. Several real ales are on handpump, wines are mostly New World, and service is swift, young and friendly.

The Rose & Crown
Romaldkirk

Few country inns match one's expectations as well as the Rose & Crown. Built in the 1750s when Captain Bligh, Romaldkirk's famous son, was a young sprite, this dreamy inn is gently informal and utterly unpretentious. In the small bar, warmed by an open fire while a few trophies peer down, locals sit at settles and browse the *Stockton Times*. A shiny brass door latch reveals more: an elegant lounge where a grandfather clock sets a restful pace, and a panelled dining room for more formal fare. Food is scrummy — from scallop, bacon and wild mushroom risotto to steak and kidney pie with Theakston gravy. Outside, a village green, with church and unblemished stone cottages, opens onto countryside as good as any in Britain. Alison and Christopher are easy-going perfectionists and the all-pervading sense of tradition is the perfect antidote to England's fickle clime.

directions	North of junc. 59 A1 (M), by A167.
meals	12pm-2pm; 6pm-9.15pm (bar meals 6pm-7pm only). Main courses £13.50-£17.95; bar meals from £7.50
closed	Sunday evenings.

Andrew Brown
The County,
13 The Green, Aycliffe,
Darlington, Durham DL5 6LX

tel	01325 312273
web	www.the-county.co.uk

map: 12 entry: 152

directions	From Barnard Castle, B6277 north; right in village towards green; on left.
meals	12pm-1.30pm; 6.30pm-9.30pm (7pm Sundays). Main courses £7.50-£11.25 (lunch). £8.95-£14.50 (dinner).
closed	3pm-5.30pm.

Christopher & Alison Davy
The Rose & Crown,
Romaldkirk, Barnard Castle,
Durham DL12 9EB

tel	01833 650213
web	www.rose-and-crown.co.uk

map: 12 entry: 153

Durham

Durham

Bridgewater Arms
Winston

A Victorian schoolhouse with views rising across fields to distant woods is the slightly quirky setting for this fun and welcoming modern bar and restaurant. The memory of the old school is carefully retained in the bar, with its high ceiling, decorative leaded windows, shelves of books and photos of past pupils. The names of the children that took part in the 1957 production of *Jack and the Beanstalk* are inscribed in big letters above the bar and add charm and a sense of recent history to the room. Adjoining half-panelled dining rooms are warmly decorated and furnished in contemporary style. Blackboards and daily printed menus place firm emphasis on the local, seasonal, fresh and organic, the choice of dishes ranging from traditional Yorkshire with a modern twist to Asian-inspired. Try simply the egg and Parma ham sandwich and a pint of Timmy Taylor's for lunch – exceptional!

The Morritt Arms Hotel
Greta Bridge

Old-fashioned peace and quiet are the keynotes of the Dickens Bar of this well-loved coaching inn; the novelist stayed here while researching *Nicholas Nickleby*. The imposing building, right by the old stone bridge, invitingly floodlit after dark, has been welcoming travellers on the long road from Scotch Corner over Bowes Moor to Carlisle and Scotland since the 17th century. It's a warm and stylish stopover: the interior is effortlessly homely, polished block floors are graced with colourful rugs and deep chintz armchairs front open log fires in panelled lounges – a cosy spot for afternoon tea and homemade cakes. The Dickens Bar has three local cask ales, views across the lawn to the river, and a wonderful mural painted in 1946 by John Gilroy, who selected well-known local figures and created a Dickensian theme around them. Bar snacks in the bar, elaborate modern dishes in the restaurant and bistro.

directions	A67 between Darlington and Barnard Castle. In the village of Winston.
meals	12pm-2pm; 5.30pm-9pm. No food Sunday evenings. Main courses £9.50-£17.

Claire & Barry Dowson
Bridgewater Arms,
Winston, Darlington,
Durham DL2 3FY
tel   01325 730302
web   www.bridgewaterarms.com

map: 12 entry: 154

directions	Off A66, 10 miles west of Scotch Corner.
meals	12pm-3pm; 6pm-9.30pm. Main courses £8.70-£21.50; set menus £14.50 & £30.
closed	Open all day.

Barbara-Anne Johnson
The Morritt Arms Hotel,
Greta Bridge, Barnard Castle,
Durham DL12 9SE
tel   01833 627232
web   www.themorritt.co.uk

map: 12 entry: 155

Durham

Number Twenty 2
Dartington

It is young, yet it is Darlington's most classic Victorian pub. Just off the town centre, the Traditional Alehouse & Canteen looks no different from the neighbouring shopfronts. Inside, a high ceiling and raised areas in the front bays give a vault-like impression; indeed, Number Twenty 2 is licensed for the sale of ales and wines only (no spirits). The odd cask provides a useful place to rest your glass. Of the five regular beers three are their own, there are five changing guests and a good choice of wines chosen for easy quaffing; it's a civilised place frequented by local business folk. At the back of the long bar is a seating area known as the "canteen" at lunchtimes. Food is good and uncomplicated – wholemeal sandwiches, a pasta dish, roast salmon, locally reared Angus sirloin with fries and salad. Number Twenty 2 is closed on Sundays, but for the rest of the week Darlington has a very fine local.

Essex

The Viper
Mill Green

Isolated, but not lonely, this little pub is deep in magnificent woodland on an empty road. The snug, neat, open-plan front bar is warm and jolly – the place has been in the family since 1938 and they are determined to keep things simple. Locals will tell you, with a well-placed pride in their traditions, that these two plain simple rooms have stayed unchanged, bar the odd lick of paint, for 60-odd years. One blackboard lists a regularly changing selection of East Anglian real ales, such as Adnams Broadside, Mighty Oak Oscar Wilde or Ridleys IPA; another lists a decent choice of wine. The classic, good-value bar snacks are served at lunchtime only – sandwiches, soup, chilli, ploughman's – with the popular real-ale sausages at weekends. The setting is so quiet you can ignore the nearby road; tables on the lawn overlook a cottage garden, resplendent in summer with flowers and shrubs. Super woodland and common-land walks start from the door.

directions	Just west of Darlington town centre. Coniscliffe Road leads into A67 to Barnard Castle.
meals	12pm-2pm. Main courses £4.95-£9.95.
closed	Sundays. Open all day.

Ralph Wilkinson
Number Twenty 2 ,
22 Coniscliffe Road,
Darlington,
Durham DL3 7RG

tel   01325 354590

map: 12 entry: 156

directions	From A12 for Margaretting; left up Ivy Barn Lane; pub at top.
meals	12pm-2pm (4pm weekends). Main courses £2.75-£5.95.
closed	Open all day weekends.

Denise & Harry Torris
The Viper,
The Common,
Mill Green, Ingatestone,
Essex CM4 0PT

tel   01277 352010

map: 9 entry: 157

Axe & Compasses
Arkesden

At the heart of an absurdly pretty village of thatched, timbered cottages with a stream running down its middle, the 400-year-old building resembles the perfect English pub. The rambling interior is a classic too: beamed ceilings, timbered walls, panelling, regiments of horse brasses gleaming in the light from little lamps, open fires, comfy sofas — and that's just the lounge bar. From the well-loved, lived-in feel to the attentive service, the place is nigh-perfect. It's all down to the Christou family, with father Themis at the head, whose pride in his pub over the past 13 years and respect for the traditions of English inn-keeping puts many English landlords to shame. Local Greene King ales are excellent; food is either the best of English — steak and kidney pie, lamb's liver and bacon, chicken supreme, wing of skate — or recognises the family's Greek Cypriot roots, with moussakas and Greek salads. It is all fresh, apparently effortlessly cooked and generous.

The Cricketers
Clavering

It achieved fame as the family home and training ground of Jamie Oliver and, as such, draws a few passers-by... but this big 16th-century inn on the edge of Clavering handles its glory with good humour. Trevor and Sally Oliver's pub has low beams, original timbers and a contented, well-cared for air; light floods in, reflected in the highly polished tables and gleaming brass and glass. A serious commitment to seasonal food is obvious the moment you see the printed menu: orecchiette with roasted pumpkin, confit duck with sweet plum sauce, loin of local pork with rosemary and apple sauce, venison with blackberry, clove and orange sauce. The daily changing blackboards give tempting options including fish, seasonal game and superb steaks. Another blackboard lists good value wines of the month, many served by the glass.

directions	On B1038 between Newport & Clavering.
meals	12pm-2.15pm; 7pm-9.30pm. No food Sunday evenings in winter. Main courses £8.95-£16.95; Sunday lunch £17.

Themis & Diane Christou
Axe & Compasses,
Arkesden, Saffron Walden,
Essex CB11 4EX

tel	01799 550272

map: 9 entry: 158

directions	On B1038 between Newport & Buntingford.
meals	12pm-2pm; 7pm-10pm. Main courses £8-£16.
closed	Open all day.

Trevor Oliver
The Cricketers,
Clavering, Saffron Walden,
Essex CB11 4QT

tel	01799 550442
web	www.thecricketers.co.uk

map: 9 entry: 159

The Bell Inn
Horndon-on-the-Hill

Christine is an original fixture of this Great Inn of England: her parents ran the Bell for years. John is a key figure, much admired in the trade, as is Joanne, their loyal manager of many years. The flagstoned bar, with oak panelled walls and French wood carvings, bustles at lunchtime. Bare flags or boards covered in rugs, an open fire, a grandfather clock, fine prints, ancient hot-cross buns hanging from beams – all bring warmth and gregariousness. In contrast the breakfast room is light and airy, with elegant white table and chair coverings. In the evenings, black-clad waiters serve an interesting array of dishes under the watchful eye of Master Sommelier Joanne. You could have beef fillet with bernaise sauce and tempura king prawns, or sea bass with truffle potato and chorizo. Fat chips come with balsamic mayonnaise and the food picks up awards, as do Christine's flower arrangements. Stylish.

directions	From M25, A13 for Southend for 3 miles; B1007 to Horndon-on-the-Hill.
meals	12pm-1.45pm; 6.45pm-9.45pm. No food bank holiday Mondays. Main courses £8.50-£14.50.
closed	2.30pm-5.30pm (3pm Saturday; 4pm-7pm Sunday).

John & Christine Vereker
The Bell Inn,
High Road, Horndon-on-the-Hill,
Essex SS17 8LD

tel	01375 642463
web	www.bell-inn.co.uk

map: 5 entry: 160

The Swan
Little Totham

In a village of 300 souls who have no shop, post office or bus service, the highpoint has to be the village pub. Little Totham is lucky: Valerie and John Pascoe take their role as publicans seriously and their pretty, listed, 400-year-old cottage inn is as convivial as can be. There are quiz nights, special live music events of country and Irish music, a choice of old pub games, an impressive award-winning array of real ales and old-fashioned pickled eggs on the bar. Lunchtime food ranges from toad-in-the-hole to scampi and chips to roast on Sundays with all the trimmings. No glamour, no frills, just a lovely, lively local with low beams, open fires, soft lighting and bar room chat. Once you're here it's a job to tear yourself away. There's a splendid dining room too, ideal for family gatherings, and the front beer garden is a lively spot in summer.

directions	Leave A12 at Rivenhall for Great Braxted, right onto B1022, then immed. left into Loamy Hill Road; 2 miles, on right, in village centre.
meals	12pm-2.30pm. No food evenings & Mondays. Main courses £4.95-£8.95.
closed	Open all day.

John & Valerie Pascoe
The Swan,
School Road, Little Totham,
Essex CM9 8LB

tel	01621 892689
web	www.theswanpublichouse.co.uk

map: 10 entry: 161

The Carved Angel
Earls Colne

The pub is 15th-century, though modern beams now mix with the originals. Contemporary lighting, colours and prints create an informal eatery where good food is served with good cheer. Not that drinkers are discouraged: locals happily nurse pints of Adnams, Greene King and Carved Angel Bitter (brewed for the pub) in the bar. Dishes range from traditional staples of, say, sausage and herb mash, to the more modern confit duck with caramelised apple and burgundy and sage reduction, and there is a good value, express-lunch menu of two or three courses. You can sit either at a table in the light, bright, modern conservatory, or in the snug, low-beamed rooms. Covered decking with outside heaters is an attractive, summer evening option. The civilised, clubby pool room is brilliant – standard-setting stuff. *No smoking throughout.*

The Sun Inn
Dedham

With a sunny yellow theme running throughout, the timbered Tudor ceilings, panelled walls, planked floors, log fires in grand grates and board games on old tables take you back centuries. Piers Baker's food, on the other hand, is entirely modern, and he changes his dishes according to season and suppliers. Ideas come from far and wide, as seen in stunningly fresh renditions of Tuscan sausages with baked polenta and black cabbage, roast partridge with red onion jam, and Bramley apple and caramel fool. Fish (almost) always comes from British waters, beef and pork is reared naturally. Come for fair prices, beers from small breweries, midweek autumn and winter wine tastings with dinner and children's portions of whatever takes their fancy. Busy in the tourist season, the Sun is a quiet, warm refuge on a winter's day, and refreshingly smoke-free with one designated smoking room.

directions	On A1124 between Colchester & Halstead.
meals	12pm-2pm (2.30pm weekends); 7pm-9pm (10pm Fridays & Saturdays). Main courses £7.95-£15.95; set menu from £9.95.
closed	3pm-6.30pm (from 3.30pm weekends).

Michael & Melissa Deckers
The Carved Angel,
Upper Holt Street, Earls Colne,
Essex CO6 2PG

tel	01787 222330
web	www.carvedangel.com

map: 10 entry: 162

directions	From A12 towards Dedham & Stratford St Mary; pub 2 miles.
meals	12pm-2.30pm (3pm weekends); 6.30pm-9.30pm (10pm Friday & Saturday). Main courses £8.50-£14.
closed	Sunday from 6pm. Open all day.

Piers Baker
The Sun Inn,
High Street, Dedham,
Colchester, Essex CO7 6DF

tel	01206 323351
web	www.thesuninndedham.com

map: 10 entry: 163

Essex

The Mistley Thorn
Mistley

In Constable country: an unexpectedly chi-chi village, its Georgian cottages gathered around the river estuary with bobbing boats and green hills beyond. David and Sherri (who has a cookery school next door) run a happy ship: staff are young and on the ball, there are plenty of locals tossed into the mix, and some impeccably well-behaved children. The mood is more laid-back city wine bar than country pub, colours are soft and easy, the tables are of various shapes, candles flicker, modern art rubs along well with the odd antique and food is taken seriously. There's lots of good local fish and seafood – a melt-in-the-mouth gravadlax, mussels with fennel and red pepper, chunky fishcakes, brilliant chips – and a pudding list that includes the gooiest-ever pecan pie and a cheesecake from Sherri's mum. A confidently-run family operation with a great weekend buzz. *No smoking throughout.*

directions	Mistley on B1352, off A137 between Colchester & Ipswich.
meals	12pm-2.30pm (3pm Sundays); 6.30pm-9.30pm. Main courses £8-£15.
closed	3.30pm-6.30pm Sunday.

Sherri Singleton & David McKay
The Mistley Thorn,
High Street, Mistley,
Colchester, Essex CO11 1HE

| tel | 01206 392821 |
| web | www.mistleythorn.co.uk |

map: 10 entry: 164

Gloucestershire

The King's Arms Inn
Didmarton, Badminton

This fine roadside village inn sports slate floors, Cotswold stone lintels, terracotta walls, hops on beams and oak settles in the bar, and a separate, cheekily-bright dining room adorned with lithographs of the area. There's a big old fireplace for winter, darts and dominoes, too, a walled garden and a boules pitch that people travel some distance for. For a light lunch, served in rustic rolls or as a salad, order Wiltshire ham and coleslaw or crispy bacon, tomato and melted brie. 'Something for everyone' on the daily menu might include local game or lamb with mint, garlic and parmesan risotto and thyme jus. Super bedrooms, one with a dressing room, all with mod cons, reflect the demands of the county set. You'll find Uley Bitter alongside oft-changing guest ales: 'If they don't serve beer in heaven, then I'm not going', reads the sign behind the bar.

directions	On A433 between Tetbury and M4, junc. 18.
meals	12pm-2pm (2.30pm weekends); 7pm-9.30pm (9pm Sundays). Main courses £11.95-£15.95.
rooms	3 doubles £80.
closed	3pm-6pm Monday-Thursday. Open all day Friday-Sunday.

See page 32 for bedroom details.

Jo Hampton-Stone
The King's Arms Inn,
The Street, Didmarton, Badminton,
Gloucestershire GL9 1DT

| tel | 01454 238245 |
| web | www.kingsarmsdidmarton.co.uk |

map: 3 entry: 165

Gloucestershire

Tipputs Inn
Horsley

A handsome Bath stone freehouse in a little town once noted for the wool trade; now it attracts riders, walkers and the young at heart. Its reincarnation is brightly modern with sanded boards throughout, bar tables bunched around a smart woodburner at one end and well-spaced, mosaic-ed tables in the galleried restaurant. Choose from large printed menus – light bites are served throughout the day (sandwiches till 6pm) and more stylish dishes for lunch and dinner. How about cured gravlax with flavoured vodka and lemon juice, hoisin-glazed duck leg with stir-fry bean sprouts, noodles and sweet chilli sauce, and orange and almond cake with clotted cream for pudding? Bite-sized additions include spiced Greek olives and several variations on garlic bread – popular at Happy Hour. There are a dozen decent house wines, and well-kept ales from the likes of Abbott, Ruddles and IPA.

directions	On A46 2 miles south of Nailsworth.
meals	11am–10pm. Main courses £6.95–£16.25.
closed	Open all day.

Chris Wright
Tipputs Inn,
Bath Road, Horsley, Nailsworth,
Gloucestershire GL6 0QE
tel 01453 832466
web www.foodclub-uk.com

map: 8 entry: 166

Gloucestershire

The Trouble House
Tetbury

Busy road, another pub: but you would miss a Michelin star if you drove past this one. Rhodes-trained chef-patron Michael Bedford is another cook who has swapped the glamour of the city for doing his own thing in a country pub. The food is unfussy, exemplary modern British. For a snack go for smoked haddock and whisky soup – or fragrant homemade bread and scrumptious cheese. For something more substantial, Hereford rib-eye steak with sensational chips and a melt-in-the-mouth béarnaise… then, perhaps, orange and rosemary syrup cake. The wine list is accessible and serious and the brilliant thing is, you don't have to book. Just get there early and choose a scrubbed pine table in a cosy corner. Everything is done with simplicity and integrity and that includes the interior of bare boards, cream walls and open fires. And the Trouble? The framed news clippings will explain all that.

directions	On A433, 3 miles north east of Tetbury.
meals	12pm–2pm; 7pm–9.30pm. Main courses £14–£17.
closed	3pm–6.30pm (7pm in winter); Sunday evenings & Mondays.

Michael & Sarah Bedford
The Trouble House,
Cirencester Road, Tetbury,
Gloucestershire GL8 8SG
tel 01666 502206
web www.troublehouse.co.uk

map: 8 entry: 167

Gloucestershire

The Tunnel House Inn & Barn
Coates

Follow the bumpy track down from the church, "and don't give up," said the passer-by upon our enquiry. We didn't; the setting is idyllic – one of John Betjeman's favourite places. Emerge via the portico tunnel of the Stroudwater canal to find a sweet Bath stone house in the clearing; it was built in the 1780s to house the canal workers. Its latest conversion has been beautifully considered. Not only are there wheelchair-accessible toilets but a delightfully quirky, bareboarded décor: scrubbed tables and huge sofas in front of a fire, a cacophony of bric-a-brac in the bar (most on the ceiling!), an Ogygian juke box with decent tunes. In the lovely light dining room choose from a seasonal menu: beef and horseradish sandwiches, spiced potted pheasant, Old Spot sausages, haddock and chips, sticky toffee pudding. Uley Bitter and Archers' Best will keep ale fans happy, and there are several wines. Outside, a big garden with open-field views – great for kids – and a very smart terrace.

directions	Between Coates & Tarlton.
meals	12pm-2.30pm; 6.30pm-9.30pm. Main courses £8-£13.
closed	Open all day Friday-Sunday.

Andrew Freeland
The Tunnel House Inn & Barn,
Tarlton Road, Coates, Cirencester,
Gloucestershire GL7 6PW

tel	01285 770280
web	www.tunnelhouse.com

map: 8 entry: 168

Gloucestershire

The Bell at Sapperton
Sapperton

This elegant pub attracts drinkers, foodies, ramblers and riders: note the tethering rail. There's a delightful rustic-modern mood inside – rug-strewn flagstones, stripped beams and woodburners, modern art on stone walls, country prints, fresh flowers, newspapers to browse. Sup on local Uley and Butcombe ales, dine on fresh local produce and rare breed and organic meats. The monthly menus or daily specials are chalked up above the fireplace and we find the food consistently good: fresh breads and olives, spiced corn chowder with cumin scones and rouille, braised Old Spot belly of pork, shank of Forest of Dean lamb, and daily fresh fish. Puddings and cheese boards really are first class, Sunday roast lunches hugely popular and you have 16 wines by the glass. Summer eating can be outside on the glorious front terrace and spills over into the sun-trapping courtyard.

directions	Off A419, 6 miles west of Cirencester.
meals	12pm-2pm; 7pm-9.30pm (9pm Sundays). Main courses £11.50-£16.95.
closed	2.30pm-6.30pm (3pm-7pm Sunday).

Paul Davidson & Pat Le Jeune
The Bell at Sapperton,
Sapperton, Cirencester,
Gloucestershire GL7 6LE

tel	01285 760298
web	www.foodatthebell.co.uk

map: 8 entry: 169

Gloucestershire

White Horse Inn
Frampton Mansell

Wonderful: a quirky-chic bar and restaurant, with good ales and first-class food. Emma and Shaun Davis have filled it with candlelit tables on seagrass floors, modern art on vibrant walls, Indian and Nepalese curios inspired by their travels. Expect an informal atmosphere and a big smile from Emma, who pulls pints of Uley Bitter and oversees happy eaters in the restaurant. Fresh food is the mainstay of Shaun's imaginative and seasonal modern menus: traceable meats come from Butts Farm down the road, fish from Looe is delivered twice a week. Bread is baked daily, and you can tuck into duck leg confit with puy lentils and thyme jus, followed by sea bass with spicy couscous and caper and lemon sauce. All this and lobsters, oysters, crabs and clams fresh from the tank, puddings to entice you (apricot bread and butter pudding) and eight wines by the glass. It may not be very lovely and it may be next to a petrol station in the middle of nowhere – but what a pity to pass it by.

directions	On A419, 6 miles W of Cirencester.
meals	12pm-2.30pm (3pm Sundays); 7pm-9.45pm. Main courses £10.95-£25.95; bar meals £4.95-£8.95.
closed	Sunday from 4pm.

Shaun & Emma Davis
White Horse Inn,
Cirencester Road,
Frampton Mansell, Stroud, GL6 8HZ
tel 01285 760960
web www.cotswoldwhitehorse.com

map: 8 entry: 170

Gloucestershire

Bathurst Arms
North Cerney

Young James Walker has worked hard in breathing new life into this handsome inn on the Bathurst Estate. Once unloved, the 17th-century building now has warmth and energy as locals, walkers and passing travellers drop in for pints of Wickwar Cotswold Way and decent pub food. The stone-flagged bar is the hub of the place, warmed by a crackling log fire and cosy with old beams and rustic furnishings. Eat here or head next door to James's pride and joy, the revamped restaurant, replete with open kitchen and a sitting area that displays a very "organic" wine list – choose a bottle from the shelf. Allotment vegetables, Cerney goat's cheese, game from Withington and local farm beef are championed on seasonal menus – try the beef and ale pie with suet crust. Smartened-up bedrooms provide a homely base for exploring the Cotswolds: they are clean, comfortable, freshly painted and well-equipped.

directions	Beside A435 Cirencester-Cheltenham road, 4 miles north of Cirencester.
meals	12-2pm (2.30pm Fri-Sun); 6-9pm (9.30pm Sat; from 7pm Sun). Main courses £7.95-£14.95.
rooms	5 doubles £70. Singles £50.

See page 32 for bedroom details.

James Walker
Bathurst Arms,
Cirencester,
Gloucestershire GL7 7BZ
tel 01285 831281
web www.bathurstarms.co.uk

map: 8 entry: 171

The Butcher's Arms
Sheepscombe

Hidden away in the folded hills and
valleys of the glorious Cotswolds, the
17th-century Butcher's Arms is not easy
to find. But persevere down these
twisting, Gloucestershire lanes – it's
worth it. A favourite with Laurie Lee,
this has everything you would hope for
from a village pub: friendly welcome,
well-kept beer – Wye Valley, Otter &
Moles – and a good choice of traditional
and modern pub food. The rustic bar is
hung with old banknotes, postcards and
brass, and leads into two tiny, no-
smoking dining rooms. Try the handmade
sausages on a leek and mustard mash
with onion gravy, or ham, egg and chips,
or a daily special of mixed game braised
in cranberries and port. Picnic tables are
scattered across the front courtyard and
the precipitous garden has superb views
over the village. Look out for the unusual
pub sign with a carving of a butcher and
pig over the Guild of Butchers' coat of
arms – and don't set your watch by the
clock over the bar.

The Red Hart Inn at Awre
Gloucestershire

Martin and Marcia's 15th-century
freehouse with Georgian additions is in a
tucked-away farming village between the
Severn and the Forest of Dean. The Red
Hart is rambler-, dog- and child-friendly,
has open fires, hearty meals, real wines,
real ales and a lovely welcome. Expect
flagstones and carpeted floors, pine
tables and chairs, old beams, stone
fireplaces, some wattle and daub. The
food is good, very good, and almost all
the ingredients come from within five
miles of the inn; 'from plough to plate' is
the philosophy. Gloucester Old Spot
pork, rabbit and turkey from the village,
game from Lydney Park – they all wash
down beautifully with a pint of Wye
Valley Butty Bach or a local guest ale.
Cider is made in the village, there are
ten wines by the glass and a good beer
garden for summer. Follow the riverside
walks from the maps outside, then foot it
back to the whitewashed inn for genuine
old-fashioned cheer.

directions	Off A46 north of Painswick.
meals	12pm-2.30pm; 7pm-9.30pm (12pm-9.30pm Sunday). Main courses £4.25-£9.25 (lunch), £7.50-£15 (dinner).
closed	3pm-6.30pm. Open all day Sunday.

directions	Off A48, 3 miles south of Newnham.
meals	12pm-2pm; 6.30pm-9pm (from 7pm Sundays). Main courses £12.95-£25.95; bar meals from £7.95.
closed	Sunday evenings; Mondays October-March.

	Johnny & Hilary Johnston
	The Butcher's Arms,
	Sheepscombe, Painswick,
	Gloucestershire GL6 7RH
tel	01452 812113
web	www.cotswoldinns.co.uk

	Martin Coupe & Marcia Griffiths
	The Red Hart Inn at Awre,
	Awre,
	Newnham on Severn,
	Gloucestershire GL14 1EW
tel	01594 510220

map: 8 entry: 172   map: 8 entry: 173

The Ostrich Inn
Newland

In the pretty village of Newland, the Ostrich is where the beer drinkers go. Across from All Saints Church, the famous 'Cathedral of the Forest', you'll rub shoulders with all sorts before a log fire; huntsmen and trail bikers pile in for the massive portions of delicious food, from the Newland bread and cheese platter to rib-eye steak with lashings of fresh béarnaise. The nicotine-brown ceiling that looks in danger of imminent collapse is supported by a massive oak pillar in front of the bar where the locals chatter and where 1940s jazz CDs keep the place swinging. The weekly menu, served throughout the pub, takes a step up in class, and is excellent value. Energetic landlady Kathryn and her cook Sue keep the place buzzing. To the back is a walled garden — and the loos, 'just by there', beyond the coal sacks and guarded by the pub pooch Alfie.

The Glasshouse Inn
Longhope

If you are an aficionado of Bass and Butcombe, Weston's ciders and all good, nature-blessed produce, you have to come here. Ramshackle tables and open log fires are considered modern at this converted 16th-century brick cottage where glass was once blown in wood-fired ovens and cider pressed in the shed. Guinness adverts, cartoons and horseracing prints decorate the place as do autographed England rugby shirts — and the chiming clock never serves as an invitation to leave. Say landlords Steve and Jill: "We buy the best available produce locally, so our lady cooks can provide our customers with generous portions of tasty, interesting homemade food." There's a lovely calm atmosphere at the Glasshouse Inn, and youngsters under 14 are welcome in the garden during the summer months.

directions	Signed on lane linking A466 at Redbrook & at Clearwell between B4228 Coleford & Chepstow road.
meals	12pm-2.30pm; 6.30pm-9.30pm (from 6pm Saturdays). Main courses £12-£18; bar meals £5.50-£9.
closed	3pm-6.30pm.

Kathryn Horton
The Ostrich Inn,
Newland, Coleford,
Gloucestershire GL16 8NP
tel 01594 833260
web www.theostrichinn.com

map: 7 entry: 174

directions	Signed from A40 at Longhope, between Gloucester & Ross-on-Wye.
meals	11.30am-2pm (from 12pm Sunday); 6.30pm-9pm. Main courses £6.50-£13.50.
closed	3pm-6.30pm & Sunday evenings.

Steve & Jill Pugh
The Glasshouse Inn,
May Hill, Longhope,
Gloucestershire GL17 0NN
tel 01452 830529

map: 8 entry: 175

Gloucestershire

The Kilcot Inn
Kilcot

The smart blue and sand painted exterior bodes well, then step in to a happy tumble of exposed stone walls, flagged floors, a Tudor beam and three quirky 'tree-stump' chairs before a central fire. There's an open feel to this cosy inn, with the large bar dominating the drinking side. Beers include Cats Whiskers, Hobgoblin and Bass on handpump; there are a couple of ciders, including Weston's Old Rose, and decent wines. The restaurant area has deep blue walls, varnished pine furniture and Windsor chairs, a new tapestry on the wall; it's ideal for both romantic suppers and big family do's. Meat and vegetables are locally sourced and dishes range from lamb shank in rosemary and sun-dried tomato gravy to meringue nests filled with maple and walnut ice cream. Lunchtime bar food is simpler: jacket potatoes, baguettes, sausage and chips. Work it all off with a good walk — and bring the dogs and children.

directions	Kilcot signed off B4421 between Newent & Gorsley.
meals	12pm-2.30pm; 6.30pm-9pm (7pm Sundays). All day in summer. Main courses £7.95-£14.95; bar meals £4.95-£7.95.
closed	Open all day.

Sue Harper
The Kilcot Inn,
Ross Road,
Kilcot, Newent,
Gloucestershire GL18 1NG
tel   01989 720663

map: 8 entry: 176

Gloucestershire

The Boat Inn
Ashleworth

This extraordinary, tiny pub has been in the family since Charles II granted them a licence for liquor and ferry — about 400 years! It's a gem — a peaceful, unspoilt red-brick cottage on the banks of the Severn and an ale-lover's paradise. Settle back with a pint of Beowulf, Church End or Archer's in the gleaming front parlour — colourful with fresh garden flowers, huge built-in settle and big scrubbed deal table fronting an old kitchen range — or in the spotless bar. On sunny summer days you can laze by the languid river (with a covered 'shed' for smokers). Adjectives are inadequate: this place is cherished. Real ale straight from the cask, Weston's farm cider, a bar of chocolate, a packet of crisps... but don't feed Sam, he's on a diet. There's no 'jus' here; lunchtime meals are fresh filled rolls with homemade chutney. Perfect. *No smoking throughout.*

directions	On A417 1.5 miles from Hartpury, between Gloucester & Ledbury.
meals	Filled rolls £1.50-£2, lunchtimes only.
closed	Mondays; Wednesday lunchtimes; 2.30pm-7pm (3pm weekends).

Ron Nicholls
The Boat Inn,
Ashleworth Quay, Ashleworth,
Gloucester, GL19 4HZ
tel   01452 700272
web   www.boat-inn.co.uk

map: 8 entry: 177

Gloucestershire

The Five Mile House
Cirencester

In 300 years the interior has changed not a jot: bare wooden floors, open fires, two curving settles, newspapers, cribbage. There's a flagstoned 'poop deck' of a snug for locals and a galley a few steps below; a more genteel wardroom – the owners' private parlour for a century or more – stands across the hall. Review here the pick of the day's produce, as it appears in baked codling fillets, lamb with rosemary jelly, stilton, spinach and mushroom lasagne. The rest of the menu keeps things simple: homemade soups and pâtés, local trout and plain grills accompanied by a sauce of your choice. All is cooked to order by Joe and his team. Deserving more consideration than the proverbial swift half, the beer, which includes guests and Taylor's Landlord, is seriously good. You can hardly go wrong here, with serene views from the garden to the valley below. Above, the busy main road – now mercifully concealed by a bank and burgeoning hedgerows.

directions	On A417, turn at D. Abbots Services; pub down the road past the petrol station.
meals	12pm-2.30pm, 6pm-9.30pm; 7pm-9pm Sundays. Main courses £8.50-£15.50.

Jo & Jon Carrier
The Five Mile House,
Lane's End, Old Gloucester Road,
Duntisbourne Abbots, Cirencester,
Gloucestershire GL7 7JR

tel   01285 821432

map: 8 entry: 178

Gloucestershire

Seven Tuns Inn
Chedworth

As you nudge the brow of the hill and look down on the Seven Tuns, you know you've found a goodie. In 1610, and for a few centuries after that, it was a simple snug; then they diverted the river and built the rest. Part-creepered on the outside, it rambles attractively inside, past open fires, aged furniture, antique prints and a skittle alley with darts. After a gentle walk to Chedworth's Roman Villa, buried in the wooded valley nearby, there's no finer place to return to for a pint of Young's Bitter. Mingle with cyclists, walkers and locals in the little lounge or rustic bar. If you're here to eat you can do so overlooking the garden through two gorgeous mullioned windows; a little further, across the road, is a raised terrace by a waterwheel and babbling brook. Good food is listed on daily menus, from pub ploughman's to corn-fed chicken with rosti potatoes. This is still the village hub, just as it should be.

directions	Off A429, north of Cirencester.
meals	12pm-2.30pm (3pm Sunday); 6.30pm-9.30pm. Main courses £7-£12.
closed	Open all day weekends.

Alex Davenport-Jones
Seven Tuns Inn,
Queen Street,
Chedworth, Cirencester,
Gloucestershire GL54 4AE

tel   01285 720242

map: 8 entry: 179

Inn at Fossebridge
Fossebridge

A vast two-acre lake, hog roasts in summer and Harvey the friendly black labrador – such details set the Inn at Fossebridge apart. Throw in roaring fires, real ales and a family-friendly feel and you have somewhere worth going out of your way for on a Sunday. (You may expect three roasts and all the best trimmings from a French chef.) The Jenkins family run this thriving coaching inn and its merry team. In the wooden-floored, stone-walled bars – one with darts board and stag's head – loads of rustic character, and a gentler Georgian feel to the dining room, where dressers guard antique china. And there's a cosy, check-sofa'd sitting room – the mood here is laid-back country house. Outside is just as fine: a great decked and fenced terrace to the side and a five-acre garden bordering the river Coln, replete with perch- and carp-filled lake. *No smoking throughout.*

The Village Pub
Barnsley

It's the 'jeans and twinset' twin of the Barnsley House hotel opposite: a smart village pub. An old favourite of locals and faithfuls from far and wide, this civilised boozer has it all: seasonal food based on the best local produce, good-quality beers and wines. There's even a service hatch to the heated patio at the back, so you can savour your sauvignon until the sun goes down. Cotswold stone and ancient flags sing the country theme; past bar and open fires, quiet alcoves provide a snug setting that will entice you to stay. On a typical dinner menu there may be potted rabbit with celeriac and mustard, roast cod with salad nicoise, and lamb's sweetbreads with wild mushroom risotto cake. Pudding-lovers will appreciate the rum baba or the chocolate and espresso tart – delicious. With award-winning cooking and such authenticity, who could wish for more? *No smoking throughout.*

directions	Beside A429 between Cirencester and Northleach.
meals	12pm-3pm; 6.30pm-10pm; 12pm-10pm Sunday. Main courses £8.95-£16.95.
closed	Open all day.

Robert & Liz Jenkins
Inn at Fossebridge,
Fossebridge, Cheltenham,
Gloucestershire GL54 3JS

| tel | 01285 720721 |
| web | www.fossebridgeinn.co.uk |

map: 8 entry: 180

directions	A419 for Gloucester; right onto B4425 for Bibury; village 2 miles.
meals	12pm-2.30pm (3pm weekends); 7pm-9.30pm (10pm Friday & Saturday). Main courses £11-£16.
closed	3.30pm-6pm Monday-Thursday. Open all day Friday-Sunday.

Tim Haigh & Rupert Pendered
The Village Pub,
Barnsley, Cirencester,
Gloucestershire GL7 5EF

| tel | 01285 740421 |
| web | www.thevillagepub.co.uk |

map: 8 entry: 181

Falcon Inn
Poulton

Look out for this old cream stone pub as you swing round the bends through the village. Young owner Jeremy Lockley has given wing to this bird's potential – a superb gastropub for Gloucestershire. One eating area faces an open theatre kitchen, creating plenty of room for private dining without spoiling the feel of the traditional village bar and fireside tables at the front. Chef William Abraham does not go in for towering lunches: simplicity is the key to his near-perfect seared scallops with pea purée with crispy prosciutto and mint vinaigrette. Main courses graduate to rare-breed rib-eye steak with a chive and peppercorn butter. Whatever you choose, try the hand-cut real chips dusted with sea salt (children cannot resist them), along with memorable guest beers such as West Berkshire's Good Old Boy, or one of several equally well-chosen wines by the glass.

directions	Beside A417, midway between Ampney Crucis & Fairford, 5 miles east of Cirencester.
meals	12pm-2pm; 7pm-9pm. Main courses £8.95-£16.95; bar meals from £3.50.
closed	Sunday evenings.

Jeremy Lockley
Falcon Inn,
London Road, Poulton, Cirencester,
Gloucestershire GL7 5HN

| tel | 01285 850844 |
| web | www.thefalconpoulton.co.uk |

map: 8 entry: 182

The Victoria Inn
Eastleach Turville

The golden-stoned Victoria pulls in the locals – whatever their age, whatever the weather. Propping up the bar, welly-clad with dogs or indulging in great home-cooked grub by the log fire, the locals and their laughter suggest a whale of a time is had by all. If frolic you must, this is the place to do it: summer brings river tug-o-war and the village's Frolic Day. (The highlight of which involves a large oak tree, children in sacks and a loaf of treacle-coated bread.) Refreshments are available for all from proprietors Stephen and Susan Richardson who, in spite of opening up the rooms, have kept much of the character and cosiness of the low-ceilinged pub. And who could fail to enjoy warm smoked chicken, steak and mushroom pie and lamb shank on minty mash, accompanied by Arkells on handpump? There are picnic tables out front, from where you can look down onto the pretty stone cottages and the churches of the village below. A lovely spot following a country stroll.

directions	Off A361 between Burford & Lechlade.
meals	12pm-2pm; 7pm-9.30pm (9pm Sundays). Main courses £7.25-£14.50.
closed	3pm-7pm.

Stephen & Susan Richardson
The Victoria Inn,
Eastleach Turville,
Fairford,
Gloucestershire GL7 3NQ

| tel | 01367 850277 |

map: 8 entry: 183

The Swan at Southrop
Southrop

Its fans include Sir Terence Conran and Simon Hopkinson – the handsome Georgian Swan is the jewel in the Cotswolds' crown. Chef James Parkinson trained under Simon Hopkinson at Bibendum and his seasonal, unshowy, British-European menu reads like the index of one of his mentor's classic cookbooks – potted shrimps, grilled entrecôte with béarnaise sauce, pommes frites and green salad, panna cotta with raisins in armagnac, sticky date pudding with clotted cream. An excellent wine list matches a tasty selection of local real ales, accompanied by scrumptious bar 'snacks' such as steak baguette with red onion, rocket and aïoli, and a cheese ploughman's. A roaring log fire, a sober décor, a relaxed mood and a skittle alley for locals – this is the village inn on the village green that everyone dreams of.

directions	2 miles west off A361 between Burford & Lechlade.
meals	12pm-2.30pm (3pm weekends); 7pm-9.30pm (10pm weekends). Main courses £9.50-£15.
closed	Sunday evenings in winter.

Graham Williams, James Parkinson & Ian MacKenzie
The Swan at Southrop,
Southrop, Lechlade,
Gloucestershire GL7 3NU

tel	01367 850205

map: 8 entry: 184

The Wheatsheaf
Northleach

The fine old coaching inn on the Fosse Way was in an unloved state when the Harvard-Walls brothers took it on in 2002; now it's a great little pub with a passionate chef and a genuine, down-to-earth feel. Pass the piles of logs by the back door to enter a long, light space divided into three. Off a plain flagstoned bar are a charming dining area hung with botanical prints and a stripy-carpeted, sofa'd snug with an open fire. Beers are well-kept, nine wines come by the glass and the food is simple and special. Come for impeccable ingredients and, if the local farm sausages with red onion mash are anything to go by, fulsome flavours. Such care and attention to detail – even the flowers decorating the puddings are edible. A much-loved local with an exceptionally warm and open feel, and a sweet, small garden at the back with a pretty village view.

directions	Off A429, between Stow & Burford.
meals	12pm-3pm; 7pm-9.30pm (12pm-4pm; 7pm-9pm Sunday). Main courses £7-£17; bar meals from £5; set menus £12 & £15.
closed	Open all day.

Gavin & Caspar Harvard-Walls
The Wheatsheaf,
West End, Northleach,
Gloucestershire GL54 3EZ

tel	01451 860244
web	www.wsan.co.uk

map: 8 entry: 185

Gloucestershire

The Horse & Groom
Upper Oddington

Cotswold stone, hanging baskets, hefty beams and flagstone floors, chunky logs around the double fireplace... is this the pub from central casting? Given that it's 500 years old, the publican ought to be a spry old character. Instead, this is a first-pub venture for incomers Simon and Sally Jackson, who have rejuvenated without losing traditional charm. There's a good selection of guest ales, some from nearby microbreweries, including Wye Valley Best, Butty Bach and Hereford Pale Ale, Barley Mole and Banks's Best. The menu takes a Cook's tour of Europe, with a good serving of trad-English: salmon, chablis and shallot fishcake with salsa verde, lamb tagine, rabbit casserole, braised pork belly, game from the Adlestrop Estate. Produce is organic and local whenever possible, breads and puddings are all homemade. No fewer than 25 wines are available by the glass.

directions	Village signed off A436 east of Stow-on-the-Wold.
meals	12pm-2pm; 6.30pm-9pm (7pm-9pm Sundays). Main courses £9.50-£17.50.
closed	3pm-5.30pm. Open all day Friday-Sunday.

Simon & Sally Jackson
The Horse & Groom,
Upper Oddington,
Stow-on-the-Wold, GL56 0XH
tel   01451 830584
web   www.horseandgroom.uk.com

map: 8 entry: 186

Gloucestershire

The King's Arms
Stow-on-the-Wold

The honey-stone building in the charming town centre is old; Charles II stayed here during the Civil War. Downstairs is the bar, unfussy with open-stone walls and wooden furniture, leather sofa, magazines, ten wines by the glass, seven malts and Old Speckled Hen. Upstairs, the wonky-floored, candlelit dining room, its lovely mullioned windows overlooking a floodlit church. At high-back Arts & Crafts chairs, diners are served by smiling Swedes. There's a Scandinavian influence here, a Norwegian chef in charge and dill-flavoured fishcakes and smorgasbord platters on the menu. (Should you prefer pastas, risottos and tiramisu, the sous-chef is Italian.) A diminutive stair leads to bedrooms above, cheered by bright wool throws, tasselled cushions, crisp white linen and Neals Yard goodies. Outdoor seating is planned for 2006.

directions	Off A429, in centre of Stow-on-the-Wold.
meals	12pm-5pm; 7pm-10pm. Main courses £11.50-£16.50. Bar meals £4-£9.75.
rooms	10 doubles £70-£130.
closed	1 week in October (Horse Fair). Open all day.

See page 33 for bedbedroom details.

David Burr
The King's Arms,
Market Square, Stow-on-the-Wold,
Gloucestershire GL54 1AF
tel   01451 830364
web   www.kingsarms-stowonthewold.co.uk

map: 8 entry: 187

Gloucestershire

The Fox Inn
Lower Oddington

Amid the grandeur of old Cotswold country houses, the Fox evokes a wonderful sense of times past, gently at odds with the fast pace of modern life. Low ceilings, worn flagstones, a log fire in winter, good food and an exemplary host... people love it here. The comfortably stylish bar has scrubbed pine tables topped with fresh flowers and candles; newspapers, magazines and ales are on tap; rag-washed ochre walls date back years; no wonder the locals are happy. Eat here or in the elegant, rose-red dining room, or on the delightful garden terrace, heated on cool nights. Imaginative, sometimes elaborate dishes include wild rocket, olive and parmesan tart, carrot, coriander and ginger soup, lamb tagine, rib-eye steak with mustard butter, dark chocolate torte. Before you leave, explore the honey-stone village and 11th-century church, known for its magnificent frescos.

directions	From Stow A436 for 3 miles.
meals	12pm-2pm; 6.30pm-10pm; 7pm-9.30pm Sundays. Main courses £7.95-£13.75.
closed	3pm-6.30pm (7pm Sunday).

Ian MacKenzie
The Fox Inn,
Lower Oddington,
Stow-on-the-Wold, GL56 0UR
tel   01451 870555
web www.foxinn.net

map: 8 entry: 188

Gloucestershire

Horse & Groom
Bourton-on-the-Hill

Having recently saved this Cinderella boozer from being turned into a private home, landlords Tom and Will Greenstock — whose parents run the exemplary Howard Arms at Ilmington — have created a dining pub of note. The charming, listed, Georgian building may be on an A road, but once inside, tranquillity reigns. Log fires burn at either end of the bar, while original period features, wooden furniture, vintage posters and enthusiastic, fresh-faced staff add to the inviting feel. Food, too, surpasses the pub norm, the blackboard-only menu being continually updated. Local produce dominates in dishes such as griddled Old Spot pork medallions with apple, pear and black pudding, while cask ales include such stalwarts as Wye Valley Dorothy Goodbody's and Everard's Tiger. *No smoking throughout.*

directions	Beside A44, 2 miles west of Moreton-on-Marsh.
meals	12pm-2pm (2.30pm Sunday); 7pm-9pm (9.30pm Friday & Saturday). Main courses £9.50-£15.
closed	Sunday evenings; Monday lunchtimes.

Tom & Will Greenstock
Horse & Groom,
Bourton-on-the-Hill,
Moreton-in-Marsh, GL56 9AQ
tel   01386 700413
web www.horseandgroom.info

map: 8 entry: 189

Gloucestershire

The Plough Inn
Cheltenham

Horses from the local stables gallop past, local shoots lunch here, race-goers dine. The rustic walls of The Plough are lined with photographs of meetings at nearby Cheltenham: this place is dedicated to country pursuits. Cheltenham week is bedlam, and a marquee is erected in the garden, but – because of the food – every week is busy. The cooking has a loyal following, and the dining room is famous for its asparagus suppers. Aberdeen Angus fillet in a brandy and black peppercorn sauce tastes every bit as good as it looks. There are good local beers, real ciders and well-chosen wines. The building has been an inn since the 16th century, probably dates from the 13th and was once a courthouse, so bars are darkly cosy with low beams, flagstones and smouldering fires. In spite of its success, The Plough still pulls in the locals. Children will make a bee-line for the play fort in the garden.

directions	B4077 between Stow & Tewkesbury.
meals	12pm-9pm. Main courses £6.95-£14.95.
closed	Open all day.

Craig & Becky Brown
The Plough Inn,
Ford, Temple Guiting, Cheltenham,
Gloucestershire GL54 5RU

tel	01386 584215
web	www.theploughinnatford.co.uk

map: 8 entry: 190

Gloucestershire

The White Hart Inn
Winchcombe

Swedish ownership has brought vibrant chic and warm hospitality to this 400-year-old English inn. The style is rural Scandinavian: scrubbed wooden floors, sisal matting, big windows and Gustavian blue-grey furniture. Nicole employs solely Swedish staff; all take it in turns to serve, clean, or cook authentic food, be it Sunday roasts or marinated herring. The pubby front bar is lively with locals supping Old Speckled Hen, accompanied by a crusty baguette or a steak from the grill. They've even introduced Santa Lucia, a winter festival of song and candles… there's an all-day bar menu and a pizzeria downstairs for those of a more southern persuasion. Beautiful bedrooms are mostly furnished with Scandinavian antiques, one is Moroccan in style, another 'New England', and Winchcombe is a Costwold dream.

directions	From Cheltenham, B4632 to Winchcombe. Inn on right.
meals	Bar snacks 8am-11pm; à la carte from 6pm; smörgåsbord Friday & Sunday lunch. Main courses £12.95-£18.95; bar meals £5.95-14.95.
rooms	8: 6 twins/doubles, 2 four-posters £65-£135. Singles £55-£115.
closed	Open all day.

See page 33 for bedroom details.

Nicole Burr
The White Hart Inn,
High Street, Winchcombe,
Gloucestershire GL54 5LJ

tel	01242 602359
web	www.the-white-hart-inn.com

map: 8 entry: 191

The Churchill Arms
Paxford

The Churchill is fun. Walk into the bar to a hub of happy chatter. Leo and Sonya are right to be proud of their creation — one guest described it as "Fulham in the country", and the locals downing their well-kept Hook Norton like it that way. There is a popular quiz night on Sundays and Aunt Sally teams make good use of the garden in summer, but the food is the draw; no bookings, so arrive early. Whether it's tagliatelle with mussels, tomato and chorizo, pot-roast partridge with red wine and thyme, monkfish with pea purée and pinenut gremolata or pear and frangipane tart, you're in for a serious treat. The L-shaped dining room/bar is full of rustic charm — books, prints, cushioned pews, a roaring woodburner in the inglenook. Beams, old radiators and uneven floors: a relaxed and engaging mix.

directions	A44 through Bourton-on-Hill; right to Paxford, via Blockley.
meals	12pm-2pm; 7pm-9pm. Check Sunday evening food times in winter. Main courses £10.50-£13.50.

Leo & Sonya Brooke-Little
The Churchill Arms,
Paxford, Chipping Campden,
Gloucestershire GL55 6XH

tel	01386 594000
web	www.thechurchillarms.com

map: 8 entry: 192

Eight Bells
Chipping Campden

It was built to house masons building the nearby church — and to store the bells. Royalty has passed through the door; even, rumour has it, William Shakespeare. The tiny Cotswold stone building holds its history close — 14th-century beams and standing timbers, flagstones, a priest's hole — but the focus today is the food. Walkers in socks by the fire wolf down lunchtime sandwiches, Hook Norton Best and Old Hooky, while the hot menu combines modern and traditional ideas. Local ingredients are used to vibrant effect in thick-cut roasted prime English ham studded with cloves and glazed with honey, or brace of pheasant with wild mushroom, cream and brandy sauce. For veggies there's baked aubergine stuffed with goat's cheese and spinach on tagliatelle. The large, flower-filled terraced garden is a sun-trap in summer.

directions	Just off High Street near church.
meals	12pm-2pm (2.30pm-3pm Fridays-Sundays); 6.30pm-9pm (9.30pm Fridays-Saturdays). Main courses £9.75-£14.95.
closed	Open all day.

Neil & Julie Hargreaves
Eight Bells,
Church Street, Chipping Campden,
Gloucestershire GL55 6JG

tel	01386 840371
web	www.eightbellsinn.co.uk

map: 8 entry: 193

Gloucestershire

The Farriers Arms
Todenham

A treasure: a couple of tables in front, a private dining room in the 'library', a restaurant for 25, a few tables on the pretty back terrace, and enthusiastic new owners as we went to press. It's cosy, cheerful and reassuringly old-fashioned. Polished flagstones, hop-hung beams, deep orange walls and an inglenook with a woodburner; add great beers, real cider and perry, 11 wines by the glass, an enjoyable blackboard menu and colouring books for kids and you have one special little pub. The Farriers is jam-packed on Sundays (lunch must be booked), and the draw is the high quality pub food: fresh ingredients with tasty sauces. There are homemade burgers, local sirloin steaks, fresh soups, poached pears and ice cream. The mellow-stone village is as pretty as the pub.

Greater Manchester

The White Hart
Lydgate

Decay was settling in at this 18th-century ale house overlooking Saddleworth Moor when Charles Brierley took it over 13 years ago. It has since been transformed into a charming restaurant-pub. Relax in the bar with a glass of Timothy Taylors Landlord, toast your toes by the wood-burning stove and admire its colourful lack of clutter, or have your drink in a room lined with Tibetan photographs. Try British cheeses, a platter of oysters, homemade 'Saddleworth' sausages (five, with five different kinds of mash). Or move upstairs to the restaurant, where delicacy combines with robustness in some unusually fine cooking: chilli squid with saffron and garlic mayonnaise, braised lamb with pickled red cabbage, pan-fried cod with tomato compôte. This is a beautiful village where, on a fine day, you can stretch your eyes all the way to the distant Cheshire Plain.

directions	Signed from Moreton-in-Marsh & from A3400.
meals	12pm-2pm; 7pm-9pm (9.30pm Fridays & Saturdays). Main courses £7.95-£16.95. Bar snacks from £3.
closed	3pm-6.30pm.

Nigel & Louise Kirkwood
The Farriers Arms,
Todenham, Moreton in Marsh,
Gloucestershire GL56 9PF

tel	01608 650901
web	www.farriersarms.com

map: 8 entry: 194

directions	From Oldham E on A669 for 2.5 miles. Before hill right onto A6050; 50 yds on left.
meals	12pm-2.30pm; 6pm-9.30pm; 1pm-7.30pm Sundays. Main courses £12.50-£17.
closed	Open all day.

Charles Brierley
The White Hart,
51 Stockport Road, Lydgate,
Oldham, OL4 4JJ

tel	01457 872566
web	www.thewhitehart.co.uk

map: 12 entry: 195

Greater Manchester

The Swan
Dobcross

Immerse yourself in the epitome of a traditional Yorkshire village pub – in a lush, comely landscape that formed part of the West Riding until 1974. Slabbed stone floors and colourwashed ceilings pitch like a dinghy in a storm, and rooms warmed by huge log fires hive off in all directions from the lobby bar – sparingly dressed with toby jugs, local paintings and some fascinating old documents concerning the building, once the village court and goal. Outside, the tiny patio overlooks an absurdly picturesque village square from which lanes plummet down into the Tame Gorge, backed by forebidding moors. On the door lintel are the initials of the Wrigley chewing-gum family who once lived here. Today's visitor can chew on good homemade curries and more adventurous fare, helped down by the full range of Jennings' beers and guests.

Hampshire

Marco Pierre White's Yew Tree Inn
Highclere, Newbury

The staff, smartly turned out in long white aprons, may look dauntingly posh, but rest assured, they're courteous and friendly. A contemporary and sympathetic makeover stitches the elegant dining room into the old fabric and character of this building, with its inglenooks, timbers and light, uncluttered walls. A spent magnum of Bollinger may stand alongside bowls of crisps and nuts on the bar, but there's ale on tap, scrubbed tables softened by lamplight and an informal feel. Still, the Yew Tree is more restaurant than pub, the dining room's crisp white napery contrasts stylishly with its backdrop of exposed brick and timber, and chef Neil Thornley's menu, the best of modern British – risotto of local crayfish and chives, sage-crusyed calf's liver, cauliflower purée, sauce diable – is overseen by Marco Pierre White.

directions	Off A670, 4 miles north-east of Oldham near Uppermill; signs for Saddleworth, then Dobcross.
meals	12pm-2pm (2.30pm Sunday); 5.30pm-8pm. No food Sunday evenings. Main courses £5.75-£9.75.
closed	3pm-5:30pm (3.30pm Thursday-Sunday).

Richard Holborn
The Swan,
The Square,
Dobcross, Oldham,
Greater Manchester OL3 5AA

tel   01457 873451

map: 12 entry: 196

directions	Exit M4 junc. 13 onto A34 for Newbury, A343 Andover road for Highclere. Just after village.
meals	12pm-2.30pm (3pm Sundays); 6pm-10pm. Main courses £8.50-£19.50.
closed	2.30pm-7pm (7.45pm Fri & Sat); Sunday evenings.

Marco Pierre White
Marco Pierre White's Yew Tree Inn,
Hollington Cross, Andover Road,
Highclere, Newbury, RG20 9SE

tel   01635 253360
web   www.theyewtree.net

map: 3 entry: 197

Hampshire

The Peat Spade
Longstock

It's a short drive through the glorious Test Valley to Longstock, a straggling village of heavily thatched cottages with this striking gabled Victorian pub at its heart. Behind the little, lozenge-paned windows the feel is more private home than country pub, with a series of neatly furnished eating areas around an uncluttered bar. New owners continue to deliver a near-perfect version of country-pub food, working to a short menu and buying local, seasonal and organic from first-class suppliers to offer tea-smoked trout salad, confit duck leg with caramelised quince, or calf's liver with organic bacon. Handpumped beers include the locally-brewed Ringwood Fortyniner. With the Test Way footpath almost passing the door and the famous trout stream only 100 yards away, it is popular with walkers and fishermen. The latter will find a rural outpost of the Rod Box tackle shop in the car park. Secluded rear terrace for summer sipping.

directions	Off A3057, 1 mile north of Stockbridge.
meals	12pm-2pm; 6.30pm-9.30pm (7pm-9pm Sun). Main courses £7.50-£13.90.
closed	Sunday evenings; Mondays.

Lucy Townsend
The Peat Spade,
Longstock, Stockbridge,
Hampshire SO20 6DR
tel   01264 810612
web www.peatspadeinn.co.uk

map: 3 entry: 198

Hampshire

The Greyhound
Stockbridge

Civilised, one-street Stockbridge is England's fly-fishing capital, and the colour-washed Greyhound draws both fishing folk and foodies. This 15th-century coaching inn is a dapper, food-and-wine-centred affair – and of some pedigree; chef Helene Schoeman produces modern dishes based on impeccable produce. Charming staff serve roast sea bass with shellfish linguine and sauce nero, and beef fillet with smoked bacon dumpling and cep consommé; lighter bar meals take in eggs Benedict and smoked chicken Caesar salad. There's a lounge with low beams, armchairs and a log fire, and an open-plan dining area with stripped floors and big trestle-style tables. Smart new bedrooms sport spotlights, auction antiques, flat-screen TVs, classy bathrooms and cosseting extras. A small garden overlooks the Test: rest here with a glass of chilled chablis or cast a line.

directions	On A30, 10 miles west of Winchester.
meals	12pm-2.30pm; 7pm-9.30pm. Main courses £11.50-£22; bar meals £7.50-£15.
rooms	8: 3 doubles, 4 twins, 1 single £70-£100.
closed	Open all day.

See page 33 for bedroom details.

Tim Fiducia
The Greyhound,
31 High Street, Stockbridge,
Hampshire SO20 6EY
tel   01264 810833

map: 3 entry: 199

The Rose & Thistle
Rockbourne

A thatched Hampshire dream with a dovecote and a rose-tumbled garden. Like many rural pubs, it started life as two cottages so the two huge fireplaces come as no surprise. It is a perfect mix of heavy oak beams and timbers, carved benches and flagstoned or tiled floors. Add country-style fabrics, dried flowers, tables strewn with magazines and you have a thoroughly enchanting place to return to after a visit to Rockbourne's Roman villa. Tim Norfolk has built up a good reputation for his steaks and sauces and his ever-changing blackboard specials make use of fresh local produce: estate game in season, south-coast fish. At lunchtime you might find it hard choosing between smoked salmon and scrambled eggs, prawns by the pint and a classic steak and kidney pudding. The more elaborate evening menu favours fish, such as monkfish wrapped in pancetta. The village of Rockbourne is also delightful.

The Royal Oak
Fritham

A small, ancient, thatched, secluded New Forest inn and an ale-lover's delight. There's no truck with fruit machines or muzak here: the atmosphere is one of quiet, old-fashioned bonhomie. Locals sup pints and exchange stories around the bar; ramblers and dogs are equally welcome. Huge fires glow through the winter and the smell of logs seduces one to linger. Neil and Pauline McCulloch believe in local produce and deliver honest, unpretentious pub lunches: ploughman's with homemade pâté, home-baked pies, soups, quiches, no chips. Though rustically simple, the three small rooms are well turned out, with light floorboards, solid cottagey tables and spindleback chairs, homely touches, darts, dominoes and cribbage. Beers are drawn straight from the cask – Cheriton Pots, Hop Back Summer Lightning, Ringwood Best. Also: a large garden for summer barbecues and a September beer festival.

directions	3 miles NW of Fordingbridge, off B3078.
meals	12pm-2.30pm; 7pm-9.30pm. Main courses £8.25-£19.75.
closed	Sunday evenings from 8pm November-March.

	Tim Norfolk The Rose & Thistle, Rockbourne, Fordingbridge, Hampshire SP6 3NL
tel	01725 518236
web	www.roseandthistle.co.uk

map: 3 entry: 200

directions	M27 junc. 1; B3078 to Fordingbridge; turn for Fritham after 2.5 miles. Follow signs.
meals	12pm-2.30pm (3pm weekends). Main courses £4.50-£6.00.
closed	Open all day weekends.

	Neil & Pauline McCulloch The Royal Oak, Fritham, Lyndhurst, Hampshire SO43 7HJ
tel	023 8081 2606

map: 3 entry: 201

Hampshire

The East End Arms
East End

The name may conjure up images of a Londoner's local, but this is about as far from the average city boozer as you can get. Hidden down narrow New Forest lanes, it's winningly unpretentious; owned by John Illsley of the band Dire Straits, its walls are lined with photographs of the famous. Walkers, wax jackets and the odd gamekeeper congregate in the earthy Foresters Bar — or in the lounge/dining room, carpeted-comfortable with sturdy tables, sofa and log fire. Good, no fuss, value-for-money dishes flow from the kitchen; homemade beef pie or rare beef platter may be chalked up for lunch; in the evening, a printed menu trumpets whole lemon sole with caper and basil sauce, and braised rabbit with grain mustard sauce. In the small garden are picnic benches and a big green brolly. At first glance this plain little pub might not warrant a second; in fact, it's all a pub should be.

directions	Off B3054, 3 miles east of Lymington; follow signs for Isle of Wight ferry & keep going.
meals	12pm-2.30pm; 7pm-9.30pm (10pm Friday & Saturday). No food Sunday evenings. Main courses £8-£12.
closed	Open all day weekends.

	C. Savart & J. Willcock
	The East End Arms,
	East End, Lymington,
	Hampshire SO41 5SY
tel	01590 626223
web	www.eastendarms.co.uk

map: 3 entry: 202

Hampshire

White Star Tavern & Dining Rooms
Southampton

Placing the city on the gastropub map, the former seafarers' hotel has been stylishly revived. Large etched windows carry the White Star logo, while a cluster of lounges round a lofty, dark wood bar are kitted-out with suede banquettes, leather armchairs and retro mirrors. Open fires add warmth. The raised dining room has impressive wooden panelling, an open-to-view kitchen and the original chandeliers; reclaimed wooden dining furniture, black leather banquettes and shipping photographs add to the metropolitan mood. Up-to-the-minute dishes should hit all the right notes — game terrine with beetroot salad, lobster linguine, warm chocolate fondant with pistachio ice cream — while the bar flaunts cocktails, champagnes, wines by the glass and real ales. Pavement tables are just the thing for fine-weather drinking, accompanied by the papers.

directions	A33 to Southampton city centre & head for Ocean Village & Marina.
meals	12pm-2.30pm (3pm Friday & Saturday); 6pm-9.30pm (10pm Friday & Saturday); 12pm-9pm Sundays. Main courses £7.50-£15; set menus £9.95, £12.95 & £14.95.
closed	Open all day.

	Mark Dodd & Matt Boyle
	White Star Tavern & Dining Rooms,
	28 Oxford Street, Southampton,
	Hampshire SO14 3DJ
tel	023 8082 1990
web	www.whitestartavern.co.uk

map: 4 entry: 203

The Wykeham Arms
Winchester

The old Wykeham is English to the core, full of its own traditions and neatly hidden away between the cathedral and the city's famous school. Ceilings drip with memorabilia, the walls are packed with pictures and fiercely loyal, bow-tied Winchester types chat, pint in hand. It's grand too, a throwback to the past and brimming with warm colours and atmosphere. There are small red-shaded lamps on graffiti-etched desks (ex-Winchester College), three roaring fires and two dining rooms. At heart it remains a pub, but it's easy to mistake it for something smarter – viz. the Latin prose in the gents. Food is not cheap, but superb, from upmarket sandwiches to daily-changing dishes, perhaps sea bass and scallops with saffron cream. When they tried to take the roasted rack of Hampshire Down lamb off the menu once, a small scale rebellion erupted. The local Gales ales are good, the wine list is long and the staff young and laid-back.

The Plough Inn
Sparsholt

Children frolic in the flowery garden's wooden chalet and play-fort while grown-ups can relax and enjoy the views. The beer's good, too, with Wadworths ales on draught. Walkers come here for a lunchtime snack of beef-and-horseradish sandwiches with relish. Inside, the pub is smart and open-plan, with pine tables, hop-garlanded beams and an open log fire. The 200-year-old cottagey front rooms are particularly cosy places to have dinner and the enthusiastic tenants, Richard and Kathryn Crawford, with a loyal and hard-working team, run this busy pub with good humour. Blackboards proclaim the dishes of the day; favourites, like lamb's liver and bacon, are given a modern twist, and restaurant-style main courses show imagination and flair. Try cod with olives, crushed potato and herb oil, followed by fruits of the forest crumble. Wines are taken seriously and 12 are available by the glass.

directions	Near Winchester College; call for directions; parking tricky.
meals	12pm-2.30pm; 6.30pm-8.45pm. No food Sunday evenings. Main courses £10.75-£18.50. Set lunch £6-£9.
closed	Open all day.

Peter & Kate Miller
The Wykeham Arms,
75 Kingsgate Street,
Winchester,
Hampshire SO23 9PE
tel   01962 853834

map: 4 entry: 204

directions	Off B3149 Winchester to Stockbridge road.
meals	12pm-2pm; 6pm-9pm (9.30pm Fridays & Saturdays; 8.30pm Sundays). Main courses £7.95-£16.95.

Richard & Kathryn Crawford
The Plough Inn,
Sparsholt,
Winchester,
Hampshire SO21 2NW
tel   01962 776353

map: 4 entry: 205

Chestnut Horse
Easton

In the beautiful Itchen valley, this rather smart 16th-century pub was done up by experienced chef-landlord John Holland some time ago. A decked terrace leads to a warren of snug rooms around a central bar, warmed by log fires and cheered by a vast collection of jugs, teapots and country pictures. At night it is cosy and candlelit; you can eat either in the low beamed Red Room, with its wood-burning stove, cushioned settles and mix of dining tables, or in the panelled and plate-filled Green Room. On weekdays before 7.30pm try the two or three course menu (Caesar salad, confit of duck with green beans, treacle and lemon tart – all good value). Or tuck into fresh crab, homemade steak and kidney pudding or beer-battered fish and chips. Great local ale from Itchen Valley Brewery and decent wine and champagne by the glass. Decked rear terrace for summer sipping.

Bush Inn
Ovington

Down a meandering lane alongside the clear running waters of the river Itchen, the 17th-century inn is brimful of character – a jewel in the county crown. In winter it's dark and atmospheric, with a roaring log fire (Real-fire Pub of the Year 2001, no less), walls and ceilings are painted dark green and lit by gas lamps and candles on tables. In summer the cottagey garden comes into play, and there's the added bonus of a stroll along an idyllic stretch of the river. Cottage furniture and high-backed pews fill the series of small rooms around the bar, while walls are hung with fishing and country paraphernalia; among these, a stuffed four-pound salmon's head. The atmosphere is calm, cosy and friendly, the clientele well-heeled. The kitchen deals in fresh local produce and presents its appealing modern menu with flair – venison steak, perhaps, with spiced red cabbage and a whisky and sherry vinegar sauce – but there are simpler dishes too.

directions	1 mile off B3047 (Winchester to Alresford), 4 miles E of Winchester.
meals	12pm-2pm; 6.30pm-9.30pm; 12pm-8pm Sundays (4pm winter). Main courses £10.95-£16.95; set menu £10-£14.95 before 7.30pm
closed	Sunday from 4pm in winter. Open all day.

directions	Off A31 between Winchester & Alresford.
meals	12pm-2.15pm; 7pm-9pm (9.30pm Friday & Saturday). No food Sunday evenings. Main courses £9-£16.50.

John Holland
Chestnut Horse,
Easton,
Winchester,
Hampshire SO21 1EG
tel 01962 779257

Nick & Cathy Young
Bush Inn,
Ovington,
Alresford,
Hampshire SO24 0RE
tel 01962 732764

map: 4 entry: 206

map: 4 entry: 207

The Yew Tree
Lower Wield

Tim Manktelow-Gray and head chef
Penny arrived from the Masons Arms,
Branscombe in 2004 and their
experience is revitalising this hard-to-
find restaurant-inn. Once again folk are
beating a path to its rather smart door.
The re-worked, stone-flagged bar and
the fresh dishes daily chalked up on the
board are proving a hit with walkers,
retired locals and ladies who lunch.
Their own Yew Tree Bitter goes down
a treat with gargantuan ham and mustard
sandwiches, salad and crisps, not to
mention deep tureens of celery, potato
and stilton soup. Splash out on a good
wine to accompany scallops with
pernod, whole sea bass with citrus
dressing, or Hungarian spicy meatballs
with tagliatelle. On summer weekends
it's especially buzzy and the beer flows as
the local cricket team play on the pitch
opposite. If cricket's not your thing,
retreat to the peaceful garden with its
gentle, rolling Hampshire views.

The Sun Inn
Bentworth

Stonehenge Pigswill, Badger Tanglefoot,
Brakspears Bitter, Cheriton Pots...
a parade of hand pumps (eight in all)
pulls the beer buffs in. There's charm,
too: this friendly, flower-decked local
was once a pair of 17th-century cottages.
Surprisingly little has changed. On
ancient bricks and bare boards find a
rustic mix of scrubbed pine tables and
oak benches and settles; beams are hung
with horse brasses, walls adorned with
prints and plates; there are fresh and
dried flowers, candelight and smart
magazines. Three cosy log-fired
inglenooks warm the interlinking bars.
Food is mostly perfect English: onion
and cider soup, liver and bacon casserole,
lamb chops, Sunday roasts, wicked
puddings. Hidden down a tiny lane on the
edge of a village in deepest Hampshire
the Sun Inn could scarcely be more rural.
There's a garden at the back and
footpaths radiate from the door.

directions	4.5 miles north of Alresford, off B3046.
meals	12pm-2pm; 6.30pm-9pm (8.30pm Sunday). Main courses £7.95-£16.95.
closed	Mondays.

Tim Manktelow-Gray
& Penny Appel-Billsberry
The Yew Tree,
Lower Wield, Alresford,
Hampshire SO24 9RX
tel   01256 389224

map: 4 entry: 208

directions	Off A339, 2 miles from Alton.
meals	12pm-2pm; 7pm-9.30pm. Main courses £6-£12.95.
closed	Open all day Sunday.

Mary Holmes
The Sun Inn,
Sun Hill,
Bentworth, Alton,
Hampshire GU34 5JT
tel   01420 562338

map: 4 entry: 209

The Flower Pots Inn
Cheriton

Ramblers and beer buffs beat a path to Pat and Jo Bartlett's door, where award-winning pints of Pots Ale and Diggers Gold are brewed in the Cheriton Brewhouse to the side. Open fires burn in two traditional bars: one a wall-papered parlour, the other a quarry-tiled public bar with scrubbed pine and an illuminated, glass-topped well. Ales are tapped from casks behind the counter hung with hops, and drunk to the accompaniment of happy chat; music and electronic games would be out of place here. In keeping with the simplicity of the place, the menu is short and straightforward: baps with home-cooked ham, sandwiches toasted or plain, home-cooked hotpots, spicy chilli with garlic bread, hearty winter soups. Curry-lovers come on Wednesday evenings for authentic Punjabi dishes; Morris dancers drop by in summer.

The White Horse Inn
Priors Dean

Locally known as 'The Pub with No Name' – there being no sign in the cradle on the nearby road – this isolated pub is fiendish to find. But worth the effort for it is a wonderful 17th-century farmhouse pub of utterly simple charm. Untouched by modernity, the two splendid bars have open log fires, a motley collection of old tables, a wealth of memorabilia from old clocks to farming implements and a rich, warm patina on the walls, achievable only by age. The ticking of a grandfather clock and the gentle motion of the rocking chairs in front of the fire transport the visitor to an earlier age. First World War poet Edward Thomas used to drink here and the pub inspired his first published work, *Up in the Wind*. The White Horse stands 750 feet up on the top of the Downs, with peaceful views rolling out on every side. Expect up to eight real ales on handpump, a traditional pub menu and a decent range of wines.

directions	Off A272 east of Winchester on B3046.
meals	12pm-2pm; 7pm-9pm. No food Sunday evenings & bank holiday evenings. Main courses £4.50-£8.
closed	2.30pm-6pm (7pm Sundays).

Joanna & Patricia Bartlett
The Flower Pots Inn,
Cheriton,
Alresford,
Hampshire SO24 0QQ
tel 01962 771318

map: 4 entry: 210

directions	Between Petersfield & Alton. 6 miles from Petersfield, beyond Steep.
meals	12pm-2.30pm; 6.30pm-9.30pm; 7pm-9pm Sundays. Main courses £8.95-£15.50.

Paul & Georgie Stuart
The White Horse Inn,
Priors Dean, Petersfield,
Hampshire GU32 1DA
tel 01420 588387
web www.stuartinns.com

map: 4 entry: 211

Harrow Inn
Steep

The 16th-century Harrow is a gem. Unspoilt, brick-and-tiled, it hides down a sleepy country lane that dwindles into a footpath by a little stream. Formerly a drovers' stop, it has been in the McCutcheon family since 1929 and they keep it today very much as it must always have been. Two small bar rooms have boarded walls, a brick inglenook fireplace cosy in winter, scrubbed wooden tables and a hatch-like serving counter behind which barrels of local ale rest on racks, with bundles of drying flowers hanging above. There's a small orchard garden, and some weather-worn rustic benches and tables to the front — only the distant hum of the hidden A3 disturbs the bucolic calm. Food is limited to generously-filled sandwiches, a split-pea and ham soup full of fresh vegetables served with great chunks of bread, a ploughman's platter of home-cooked ham, homemade treacle tart. Loos are a quick dash across the lane.

The Royal Oak
Langstone

Twitchers regularly beat a path to the door of this wonderful waterside pub. The views across Chichester Harbour are stunning and it's magical on a fine summer's evening to listen to the plaintive call of the curlew across the water. From your bench at the water's edge you can watch the tide ebb and flow and study the waders in the mudflats; at very high tide the water laps the front door. The pub, licenced since 1725, was once a row of 16th-century cottages lived in by workers at Langstone Mill next door; they used to have a 'tidal licence' allowing travellers a drink while waiting for the tide to ebb. These were the days before the bridge to Hayling Island was built. When inclement weather forces you inside and away from the view you'll find rambling rooms with flagstone and pine floors, beams, and open fires. There are four real ales, traditional pub food (go for Sunday lunch) and sandwiches all day.

directions	A272 at Steep west of Petersfield, left opp. garage; left at church; cross A3 to reach pub.
meals	12pm-2pm; 7pm-9pm. Main courses £3.60-£10.50.
closed	2.30pm-6pm & Sunday evenings in winter.

Claire & Wisa McCutcheon
Harrow Inn,
Steep,
Petersfield,
Hampshire GU32 2DA
tel   01730 262685

map: 4 entry: 212

directions	Beside Chichester harbour, off A3023 before bridge to Hayling Island.
meals	12pm-2.30pm; 6pm-9pm. Snacks all day. Main courses £5.95-£12.95.
closed	Open all day.

Chris Ford
The Royal Oak,
19 Langstone High Street,
Langstone, Havant,
Hampshire PO9 1RY
tel   023 9248 3125

map: 4 entry: 213

The Riverside Inn
Aymestrey

Edward IV had a celebratory noggin here after a decisive incident nearby in the Wars of the Roses. He was declared King soon afterwards. It is much altered: there's an easy mix of antiques, fresh flowers, hops and pine. Menus change with the seasons and the seductive dishes include locally-smoked salmon with cream cheese parcels, confit of duck legs with pak choi, and roast Ludlow venison with red cabbage and sloe gin sauce. Wander from the bar into linked rooms with log fires; order a pint of Wye Valley Ale from nearby Stoke Lacy or a house wine from Italy, Chile, Australia. And look for the map of the kitchen gardens from which so much of the fruit and vegetables come: an interesting idea which we wish others would copy. The setting is bucolic, tucked back from a stone bridge over the river Lugg, alive with river trout, with waterside seats and a lovely terraced garden.

The Stagg Inn
Titley

It took some courage for Steve Reynolds to take on a tiny village pub in the back of beyond and, defying all odds, become a Herefordshire food hero. What strikes you is the attention to detail on the daily boards: the only thing you're not told is the name of the bird from which your pigeon breast (perfectly served with fig and port sauce) came. And most of the produce is organic. They fully deserve their Michelin star, the very first for a British pub. There are seared scallops on parsnip purée with black pepper oil, traditional roast grouse with game chips and bread sauce, trio of crème brûlée (vanilla, coffee, cardamom) and an ancient Caerphilly that arrives in the mail because the lane leading to the farm where it's made is impassable. The intimate bar is perfect and dog-friendly, there's beer from Hobsons, cider from Dunkerton's and some very classy wines.

directions	On A4110 18 miles north of Hereford.
meals	12pm–2.15pm; 7pm–9.15pm. Main courses £12.95–£15.95; bar meals £7.25–£11.95.
closed	Sunday evenings; Mondays in winter.

Richard & Liz Gresko
The Riverside Inn,
Aymestrey, Leominster,
Herefordshire HR6 9ST

tel	01568 708440
web	www.theriversideinn.org

map: 7 entry: 214

directions	On B4355 between Kington & Presteigne.
meals	12pm–2pm; 6.30pm–10pm. Main courses £12.50–£16.50; bar meals from £7.50 (not Sat eve).
closed	Sunday evenings; Mondays.

Steve & Nicola Reynolds
The Stagg Inn,
Titley, Kington,
Herefordshire HR5 3RL

tel	01544 230221
web	www.thestagg.co.uk

map: 7 entry: 215

Bell Inn
Yarpole

The pub car park fills up fast these days. And a peep through the window reveals chefs in pristine whites yelling out "service" as great-looking dishes are ferried off to tables. The kitchen is in the hands of Rob Walker, former chef of one of Ludlow's starred restaurants. Now the daily chalked-up menu flourishes 'real' scampi with mushy peas and ploughman's with robust fillings. Crispy crab cakes rub shoulders with coq au vin, and there's butternut squash and chestnut lasagne for vegetarians. But it's still a village pub where locals meet over a pint of Wye Valley, dogs doze and children play in the large leafy garden. Large and reassuringly traditional, there are plush red benches, patterned carpets, beams, horse brasses and a roaring log fire – and you can eat where you like, in the bar or the lofty-beamed dining room. Children have mini-portions of real food, heavenly homemade marshmallows come with your coffee and the staff are charming.

The New Inn
Pembridge

Perfect for English heritage lovers with big appetites. The food is generously portioned, the building is as old as can be (1311), and Pembridge is a remarkable survivor; its market hall could be in deepest France. It is a simple but great pleasure to amble in to this ancient inn, order a drink and squeeze into the curved back settle in the flagstoned bar. You could film a period drama in here it's so history-laden, and when the fireplace logs are lit, it's heaven. Yet this is a real local, with photos of village shenanigans up on the wall and a darts board put to good use. Upstairs has floral carpets, books and sofa – a reassuring spot in which to tuck into reassuringly familiar prawn and avocado salad, creamed kidneys with sherry on toast and home-baked ham with mustard mash. Jane is evidently happy doing what she does best.

directions	Yarpole signed off B4361 between Ludlow & Leominster.
meals	12pm-2.30pm (3pm Sundays); 6.30pm-9.30pm. Main courses £10.25-£13.95; bar meals from £5.25. Set lunch £10.95 & £14.
closed	Mondays.

Claude & Claire Bossi
Bell Inn,
Yarpole,
Leominster,
Herefordshire HR6 0BD
tel 01568 780359

map: 7 entry: 216

directions	Just off A44 in Pembridge. In centre next to Market Square.
meals	12pm-2pm; 6.30pm-9pm (7pm Sundays). Main courses £6.75-£12.50; bar meals £2.75-£4.95.
closed	2.30pm-6pm (from 3pm summer).

Jane Melvin
The New Inn,
Market Square,
Pembridge,
Herefordshire HR6 9DZ
tel 01544 388427

map: 7 entry: 217

Salutation Inn
Weobley

Lording it at the top end of a village green that goes back to the Middle Ages, the old cider house creaks with age. Drop by for a pint of Butty Bach from the Wye Valley Brewery, a local Stowford cider or a glass of Aussie wine. Stay on, for ham, omlette and chips, homemade soup or the award-winning steak and ale pie. The lounge bar is divided by standing timbers and is nicely pubby, particularly in winter with logs burning in the grate. For dinner there's the Oak Room, its old booths separated by glass partitions; book a table and feast on Herefordshire fillet steak and sweet Welsh rump of lamb. Desserts are decidedly top drawer: brioche and butter pudding with orange, vanilla and star anise custard, whole roast baby pineapple with coconut parfait, a trio of crème brulée. Warm days encourage drinkers into the courtyard and a decked terrace.

The Old Black Lion
Hay-on-Wye

Heaven for historians, antique-book-lovers and foodies in equal measure. Oliver Cromwell lodged here while laying siege to Hay Castle and the main building is packed with oak beams, ancient artefacts and conspiratorial nooks and crannies. New owner Dolan plans to change little at this busy dining pub. The Wye Valley Brewery provides their own Black Lion bitter. Seasonal bar favourites keep the kitchen working flat out through every session with fairly priced herb-crusted rack of spring lamb with Mediterranean tart; local produce such as Brecon game and Wye salmon play their part. The 20-seat restaurant steps upmarket for those with more time and money to spare at night: Caesar salad with anchovies, fallow venison loin with parsnip purée and a bottle of decent wine. Expect to pay accordingly.

directions	Off A480 north west of Hereford.
meals	12pm-2.30pm; 6.30pm-9.30pm. Best to call to check in low season. Main courses £8.25-£15.95.
closed	Open all day (except 3pm-7pm January).

Mike Tai
Salutation Inn,
Market Pitch, Weobley,
Hereford, Herefordshire HR4 8SJ

tel	01544 318443
web	www.thesalutationinn.co.uk

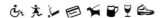

map: 7 entry: 218

directions	2-minute walk from centre of Hay.
meals	12pm-2.30pm; 6.30pm-9.30pm. Main courses £8.95-£17.50.

Dolan Leighton
The Old Black Lion,
26 Lion Street, Hay-on-Wye,
Herefordshire HR3 5AD

tel	01497 820841
web	www.oldblacklion.co.uk

map: 7 entry: 219

The Pandy Inn
Dorstone

Going way back to 1165, a half-timbered, Herefordshire gem – another contender for 'oldest pub in the land'? Inside are heavy beams, a well-worn flagstoned floor, much smoke-stained stone, a vast oak lintel over the old log grate and an intimate dining room beyond the red velvet curtain. This is the county of Dorothy Goodbody and Butty Bach ales, Old Rosie and 'cloudy' scrumpy. On the menu are mussels, big Hereford beef steaks and seasonal British specials, while for hungry walkers there are filled baguettes, hearty vegetable soup and homemade chicken-liver pâté with first-class bread. Families feel welcome here and children may spill into the garden with its picnic tables and play area in summer. You are in the so-called Golden Valley, so set off for Abbey Dore, Arthur's Stone or bookish Hay-on-Wye, just a short drive away.

The Bulls Head
Craswall

Craswall is not so much a village as a tangle of country lanes below the Black Hill of Bruce Chatwin fame. Down a small flight of steps discover stone floors, a hatch in the wall and a real fire; the drovers' inn, 400 years old, has barely changed since the arrival of electricity. And the dimly-lit, time-warp lower bar becomes a rustic-chic 'lemon room' of equal charm. For summer there's a big, lush, enclosed garden – safe for children – with wonderful green views. Using locally sourced produce, heart warming food takes in the famous Craswall pie, home-baked chunky bread 'huffers', game dishes, well-hung steaks and vegetarian dishes. Helped along with a fine wine, farmhouse cider or pint of Butty Bach straight from the cask, passing hikers should stride off fully fuelled. With understatedly stylish bedrooms, stabling for your horse *and* rough camping available, there's no excuse not to stay the night. Special.

directions	Signed from B4348 Hereford to Hay-on-Wye, 5 miles from Hay.
meals	12pm-2.30pm; 7pm-9.30pm. Main courses £7.50-£14.95.
closed	Mondays in winter. Open all day Saturday.

directions	On country lanes between B4350 at Hay-on-Wye & A465 at Pandy.
meals	12pm-9.30pm (8.30pm Sundays) Main courses £5.75-£15.95.
rooms	3: 2 doubles, 1 family, £60-£65.
closed	Mondays in winter. Open all day.

See page 33 for bedroom details.

	Bill Gannon The Pandy Inn, Dorstone, Hay-on-Wye, Herefordshire HR3 6AN
tel	01981 550273
web	www.pandyinn.co.uk

	Sandra Durose The Bulls Head, Craswall, Herefordshire HR2 0PN
tel	01981 510616
web	www.thebullsheadpub.com

map: 7 entry: 220

map: 7 entry: 221

The Ancient Camp Inn
Eaton Bishop

With stunning views of the Wye, snaking below this whitewashed, 19th-century cider house, the Ancient Camp Inn takes its name from an Iron Age fort that once stood here. The delightful Mackintoshes, who lived in France for 18 years, have brought with them a Gallic-trained chef and a love of simple, delicious food that wouldn't look out of place in a classic French bistro – local beef, fresh fish and just-picked vegetables grown by a former postman living down the road. No surprise either to find that the décor is more than just a little French-influenced. Traditional flagstones, beams and stone walls are complemented by French posters and antique furniture, and the low-ceilinged dining room, sitting room and snug bar flow into each other warmly – cream sofas, white walls, lilies in an enamel jug. *No smoking throughout.*

The Crown & Anchor
Lugwardine

Locals, families, couples, walkers – all sorts gather here, drawn by the happy buzz. Three miles from the centre of Hereford, the old pub is friendly, countrified and atmospheric. Intimate rooms are cosy with red quarry tiles scattered with rugs, solid pine tables, corner settles and comfy sofas in corners. Pastoral prints dot the walls, bookshelves spill with books, bottles and jars. There's a big log fire and a hop-decorated bar from which Butcombe, Worthy Pedigree and Timothy Taylor beers flow; Nick offers malts from Oban and Talisker and a good few wines, and Julie oversees an excellent kitchen. Whether you choose a cheddar sandwich or a fillet of pollock with parsley sauce and mash, it will be fresh and good. There's plenty for vegetarians, too, and bread and butter pudding with custard. The garden, overlooking the car park, is pretty in summer.

directions	From Hereford A465 to Abergavenny. After 0.5 miles right to Ruckhall & Belmont Golf Course. Cross small bridge, right for Ruckhall; inn signed.
meals	12pm-2pm; 7pm-9pm. Main courses £10.95-£14.50.
closed	Sunday evenings; Monday; Tuesday.

directions	From Hereford A438 to Ledbury. In Lugwardine first left into Cotts Lane.
meals	12pm-2pm; 7pm-10pm. Main courses £7-£12.
closed	Open all day.

Charles & Kathryn Mackintosh
The Ancient Camp Inn,
Ruckhall, Eaton Bishop, Hereford,
Herefordshire HR2 9QX

tel	01981 250449
web	www.theancientcampinn.co.uk

Nick & Julie Squire
The Crown & Anchor,
Cotts Lane, Lugwardine,
Hereford,
Herefordshire HR1 4AB

tel	01432 851303

map: 7 entry: 222

map: 7 entry: 223

Carpenter's Arms
Walterstone

A marvellous little chapel-side pub in the middle of nowhere, with great views up to Hay Bluff. Vera has been dispensing Wadworth 6X from behind the corner hatch for 20 years and spoils you rotten; all get a generous welcome, from locals to walkers to babies. Through an ancient oak doorway is a tiny bar with a log-fired range, and a dining area to the side. Floors are Welsh slate, settles polished oak, tables cast iron, curtains pink, walls open stone; it's as cosy and cared for as can be. On the menu are fishcakes and salad, chicken breast stuffed with stilton and wrapped in bacon, syrup and stem ginger pudding – proper homemade food, some organic. Beer is served from the drum, cider and perry from the flagon. In summer you may spill into the grassy garden at the end of the car park and gaze up at the Sugarloaf mountain; then pull on the hiking boots and climb it. Gentler walks take you along beautiful Offa's Dyke.

directions	Village signed from Pandy; Pandy signed from A465 from Abergavenny.
meals	12pm-2pm; 7pm-9pm. Main courses £8-£12.
closed	Open all day.

	Vera Watkins
	Carpenter's Arms,
	Walterstone,
	Hereford,
	Herefordshire HR2 0DX
tel	01873 890353

map: 7 entry: 224

Three Crowns Inn
Ullingswick

The Three Crowns is worth any number of missed turns. Hop-strewn beams and settles in the bar, open fires, candles on tables, cribbage – all that you'd expect of an old-fashioned inn. Walk into a flagstoned bar to find the day's lunch or early evening specials chalked up to tempt you; since chef-landlord Brent Castle arrived we've not had a poor meal. And there are some unusual dishes, such as steamed mussels Portugaise and rump of lamb with chive mash and a shallot madeira sauce. Ingredients are likely to be organic and local, extras, like home-baked bread and cafetière coffee, are delicious. With a new restaurant extension this may sound more restaurant than pub, but there's always a table set aside for drinkers. The Wye Valley ale is delicious, and there's Hereford cider and the odd bargain wine too. A bedroom upstairs – peaceful, characterful, understatedly stylish – is the icing on this very special cake.

directions	1 mile from A465, north-east of Hereford.
meals	12pm-2.30pm; 7pm-9.30pm. Main courses £8.75-£14.50.
rooms	1 family room from £90.
closed	2.30pm-7pm & Mondays.

See page 34 for bedroom details.

	Brent Castle
	Three Crowns Inn,
	Bleak Acre, Ullingswick,
	Herefordshire HR1 3JQ
tel	01432 820279
web	www.threecrownsinn.com

map: 7 entry: 225

The Butchers Arms
Woolhope

Martin produces thoroughly reliable food from his fully-modernised kitchen, and there are log fires and smiling Cheryl to settle you in. Surrounded by walking country, opposite Marcle Ridge and close to the Forestry Commission's Haugh Woods, this is a half-timbered 'magpie' house that goes back to the 14th century – and the ceiling beams just about reach the level of your nose. Taken over by returning locals it has undergone a restoration that it deserved long ago. From the central bar, cosy with Windsor armchairs and hung with Weston's cider lithos and sepia prints, French windows slide open to a charming terrace with roses and a garden that stretches down to the village brook – eat out here. In the evening, dine by candlelight in the tiny non-smoking restaurant from a menu that tempts with big salads in summer and, in winter, local game.

directions	Off B4224 between Hereford & Ross-on-Wye.
meals	12pm-2pm; 6.30pm-9pm. Main courses £7.25-£16.95.
closed	3pm-6.30pm.

Martin & Cheryl Baker
The Butchers Arms,
Woolhope,
Hereford,
Herefordshire HR1 4RF
tel   01432 860281

map: 7 entry: 226

The Cottage of Content
Carey

Svenia does friendly 'front of house' and Paul cooks – with imagination. They've been here a year and are working their socks off to put this historic thatched pub in the depths of Herefordshire on the map. Décor is pared-down traditional: flagstones in the bar, polished wood beyond, Windsor chairs, pine tables and pews. Beams are hung with horse-and-hop impedimenta, paintings are for sale, light jazz plays in the background and one area merges merrily into another. Walkers, families, retired holiday makers, locals with dogs – there's room for all. Vegetables are organic, produce local and the menu is tempting in its simplicity: home-baked ham and eggs, entrecôte of beef, panna cotta with a berry compote, warm walnut tart and clotted cream. Small, beamy bedrooms are carpeted and cottagey, and bathrooms fresh and new. Good value.

directions	A40 west of Ross-on-Wye, then A49 towards Hereford; signs for Hoarwithy, then Carey.
meals	12pm-2pm; 7pm-9.15pm. Main courses £8.95-£15.50.
rooms	4: 3 double, 1 twin £56-£64.
closed	2.30pm-6.30pm (3pm-7pm Sunday); Monday; Tuesday lunchtime in winter.

See page 34 for bedroom details.

Svenia Wolf & Paul Franklin
The Cottage of Content,
Carey, Hereford,
Herefordshire HR2 6NG
tel   01432 840242
web   www.cottageofcontent.co.uk

map: 7 entry: 227

The Lough Pool Inn
Sellack

The words 'Lough' and 'Pool' are almost synonymous and, perversely, the pool and stream by which the pub once stood, deep in the bosky folds of Herefordshire, have long run dry. The Lough Pool has survived a recent change of ownership and is going from strength to strength. A cosy fire, a glowing bar, head-ducking beams and a refreshingly unshowy dining room – solid tables, comfortable chairs – in which to enjoy daily-changing dishes. The menu is a successful balance of comfort food and modern treatments of superb ingredients, whether it be simple Ross rarebit with apple and hazelnut salad or roast tranche of brill with dauphinoise potatoes and new season kale. Stock-in-trade are good real ales from Wye Valley Brewery, strong draught ciders, wines by the glass of surprising quality; try the French fizz. A relaxed and civilised place to be.

The Mill Race
Walford

A real surprise to push open the 'ecclesiastical' door and find yourself in a boldly stylish space. The central log fire is the focus of the room, a blackboard proudly lists the local suppliers and a stainless steel kitchen glistens beyond the granite-topped bar. Relax in a black bucket chair as you browse the papers, perch at the bar on a chrome and wood stool or gaze on the Herefordshire hills from the terrace. An eclectic choice of music may play in acknowledgement of a mostly-young clientele, but foodies of all ages come here for the chef, Aaron Simms, who trained at Le Manoir aux Quatres Saisons. Printed menus change seasonally and nothing is showy – it's the best of modern British pub food. For lunch there are steak burgers with onion marmalade and quiche of the day, for dinner, 'real' prawn cocktail, wild mushroom risotto and Herefordshire steak and kidney pie. It looks great on the plate and it's jolly good value.
No smoking throughout.

directions	Off A49, 3 miles north-west of Ross-on-Wye on the Ross-Hoarwithy road.
meals	12pm-2.15pm; 7pm-9.30pm. Main courses £10.75-£15.25; bar meals from £3.75.
closed	Sunday evenings; Mondays October-February.

David & Janice Birch
The Lough Pool Inn,
Sellack,
Ross-on-Wye,
Herefordshire HR9 6LX

tel   01989 730236

map: 7 entry: 228

directions	Walford is on B4234 3 miles south of Ross-on-Wye.
meals	12pm-2.30pm; 6.30pm-9.30pm. Main courses £5.95-£16.95.
closed	3pm-5pm. Open all day Friday-Sunday.

Rebecca Bennett
The Mill Race,
Walford, Ross-on-Wye,
Herefordshire HR9 5QS

tel   01989 562891
web   www.millrace.info

map: 7 entry: 229

Herefordshire

Penny Farthing Inn
Aston Crews

Worth a detour – a 17th-century inn and former blacksmith's shop standing high on an escarpment above the Wye, with the Malvern Hills as a backdrop. The food is cockle-warming, and there has been plenty of praise for the fresh fish (flag snapper and Cajun-spiced swordfish, Thai fishcakes and chargrilled tuna), country-style bowls of lamb knuckles in rich-scented gravy, game in season and Hereford beef steaks from local farms. There are a few ales of high quality (Wadworth 6X and Greene King Abbot and one guest), wines from Tanners and cups of fresh coffee re-filled at the table before you've had a chance to ask. Eat informally in the bar or at plainly-set tables in the cottagey restaurant. This is a great all-rounder that would appeal to young, old and everything in-between – and your dog, who has a cheery coal-effect fire to curl up by. There are views from the garden and footpaths from the door: stride out to discover this green and under-sung county.

directions	Off A40 at traffic lights in Lea. Signed Aston Crews.
meals	12.30pm-2pm, 6.30pm-9pm. Main courses £4.95-£7.95 (lunch), £7.95-£14.95 (dinner).
closed	Sunday evenings & Monday lunchtimes.

Derek & Debbie Royston
Penny Farthing Inn,
Aston Crews,
Herefordshire
HR9 7LW
tel   01989 750366

map: 8 entry: 230

Hertfordshire

The Fox & Hounds
Hunsdon

London chefs quitting fabulous establishments to set up in rural pubs may be an increasing trend, but few have managed it with the aplomb of James Rix. Witness a comfy laid-back bar with log fire, leather sofas and local ales from Tring Brewery. Then tuck into something simple like a ploughman's, a plate of Spanish charcuterie or a classic calf's liver and mash with bacon and onion gravy. But note also the funky country-house-on-a-shoestring dining room that tosses together polished old tables with a crystal chandelier and deals in pigeon breast with foie gras, and linguine with clams, chilli, garlic and parsley – a starter or a main. Whether eating in the bar or dining room, do not miss out on the homemade foccacia – it merely emphasisis the attention paid to the smallest detail. A treat to see an old pub in the right hands, and the garden at the back comes into its own its own in summer. Booking is recommended.

directions	Off A414 between Harlow & Hertford on B1004.
meals	12pm-3pm (4pm Sunday); 6pm-10.30pm. Main courses £7-£16.
closed	Sunday evenings; Mondays.

James Rix
The Fox & Hounds,
2 High Street, Hunsdon,
Hertfordshire SG12 8NH
tel   01279 843999
web   www.foxandhounds-hunsdon.co.uk

map: 9 entry: 231

Fox Inn
Willian

Willian locals have been making the most of The Fox since it opened last year. It has good lighting, a solid, comfortable feel and a modern menu that showcases British ingredients including fish from the north Norfolk coast. The Fox could beat many neighbourhood restaurants into a cocked hat but part of its charm is that it is still a place where beer drinkers feel welcome (and shares this ethos with Cliff Nye's other pub, the White Horse at Brancaster). A cool, formal dining room sits astride a relaxed bar, where Cromer crabs and smoked salmon sandwiches add glamour to a menu that includes cod, chips and pease pudding. The restaurant is a mix of French bistro and British pub: pork fillet stir-fry on sesame soy noodles, chargrilled rib-eye with smoked potato rosti. This Fox is one you'd do well to hunt down.

The Valiant Trooper
Aldbury

A pretty village in a pretty setting. A Roman road – the Ridgeway Path – runs past, and the Saxon name means 'old fort'. Named in honour of the Duke of Wellington, said to have held a meeting here during the Napoleonic wars, the dear little brick and tiled cottage has been a pub since 1752. Now it caters for booted ramblers, diners escaping town and families (there's a little play house in the garden). You'll find dark beams on rough-plaster walls, bare brick, blazing log fires, tiled floors, an old-fashioned feel and a big welcome from landlord Tim O'Gorman, who's been pleasing customers for over 20 years. Walkers can slake a thirst with a decent pint of ale from a chalked-up choice of five and refuel on ciabatta sandwiches. The light and airy stable restaurant groans with lunchers on Sundays. Come for roasts and sound English dishes: peppered mackerel with horseradish relish, and bread and butter pudding.

directions	A1 junc 9 for Letchworth; 1st left into Baldock Lane; pub 1.5 miles.
meals	12pm-2pm (3pm Sun); 6.45pm-9.15pm. No bar food evenings & Sunday lunchtimes. No restaurant food Sunday evenings & Mondays. Main courses £8.95-£18.50; bar meals £6.95-£10.95.
closed	Open all day.

directions	North of Berkhamsted off B4506 towards Aldbury Common.
meals	12pm-2.15pm; 6.30pm-9.15pm. No food Sunday & Monday evenings. Main courses £8-£12; bar meals £5.
closed	Open all day.

Cliff Nye
Fox Inn,
Baldock Lane, Willian, Letchworth,
Hertfordshire SG6 2AE
tel   01462 480233
web   www.foxatwillian.co.uk

Tim O'Gorman
The Valiant Trooper,
Trooper Road,
Aldbury, Tring,
Hertfordshire HP23 5RW
tel   01442 851203

map: 9 entry: 232

map: 9 entry: 233

The Alford Arms
Frithsden

It isn't easy to find, so be armed with a detailed map or precise directions before you set out – David and Becky Salisbury's gastropub is worth any number of missed turns. It's in a hamlet enfolded by acres of National Trust common land – bring your boots! Inside, two interlinked rooms, bright, airy, with soft colours, fresh flowers, scrubbed pine tables on wooden or tiled floors, and prints on the walls. Food is taken seriously and ingredients are as organic, free-range and delicious as can be. On a menu that divides dishes into small plates and main meals, there are Thai mussels with coconut broth, chargrilled calf's liver on chorizo and haricot bean ragout, treacle tart with lemongrass crème fraîche. Wine drinkers have the choice of 15 by the glass, while service is informed, friendly and alert. Arrive early on a warm day to take your pick of the teak tables on the sun-trapping front terrace, shaded by posh brollies.

The Bricklayers Arms
Hogpits Bottom

When The Bricklayers came onto the market Alvin Michaels pounced, eager to restore the fortunes of his run-down local. Within two weeks the regulars had given him the thumbs up; now he and his staff are run off their feet. He's been in catering all his life and has no problem whatever turning out home-smoked fish with lemon coriander butter, mushroom stuffed quail with balsamic jus, sea bass and scallop soufflé with Provencal sauce – or good old steak and kidney pie, all delicious. As well as installing skilled kitchen staff, Alvin has also remodelled the interiors and removed some less than sympathetic earlier renovations. The pretty, 18th-century building has low beams, a log fire and, now, white-painted, timbered walls. There's an excellent selection of beers, over 50 wines, ports and cognacs. As for the exotically named Hogpits Bottom, 'hog' is a dialect word for shale.

directions	A4146 Hemel Hempstead to Water End; 2nd left after Red Lion to Frithsden; left after 1 mile at T-junc., then right; on right.
meals	12pm-2.30pm (3pm Sundays); 7pm-10pm. Main courses £11.25-£14.25.
closed	Open all day.

directions	M25 junc. 20; A41; 1st left to Chipperfield; 1st right to Flaunden.
meals	12pm-3pm (4pm Sundays); 6.30pm-9.30pm. Main courses £5.95-£15.95.
closed	Open all day.

	David & Becky Salisbury The Alford Arms, Frithsden, Hemel Hempstead, Hertfordshire HP1 3DD
tel	01442 864480
web	www.alfordarmsfrithsden.co.uk

	Alvin Michaels The Bricklayers Arms, Hogpits Bottom, Flaunden, Hertfordshire HP3 0PH
tel	01442 833322
web	www.bricklayersarms.com

map: 9 entry: 234

map: 9 entry: 235

The Seaview Hotel
Seaview

Seaview is an island institution – smart, buzzing, by the sea and full of thirsty sailors. The gaily-parasoled terrace, with its railings, mast and flag, is like the prow of a boat; in the back bar, learn your knots; in the front, brush up your semaphore. When the weather is warm, have a pre-dinner drink in the front garden and watch the sun go down over the Solent – perfect. Then wander past portholes, ships' wheels, lanterns and sails for a plateful of roast monkfish with crab mash and chilli sauce in the restaurant; the food is pricey but praiseworthy. In the bar, order island-brewed Goddard's Special and the famous hot crab ramekin; if you're here on a Sunday, don't miss the roast. Afterwards, retire to a sitting room for binoculars and views of the sea. Ask for details about wine-tasting, cycling and adventure breaks.

The New Inn
Shalfleet

Built in 1746 on the site of a church house, this old fishermen's haunt is worth more than a passing nod – especially if you are on the 65-mile, coastal path trail. Or have arrived by boat and moored at Shalfleet Quay. The place now draws a cheery mix of tourists, walkers and sailors to a spick-and-span bar with 900-year-old flagstones, beams and old fireplaces, and a series of pine-tabled dining rooms decked with nautical bits and bobs. Refreshment includes pints of island-brewed ales and fabulously fresh seafood marked up on the daily-changing chalkboard. The huge platter is a treat; other (considerably cheaper) fish choices might include sea bass cooked with lemon or simply grilled plaice. Mouthwatering fresh crab and lobster are landed at Newtown Quay; the crab sandwiches are memorable, as is the lobster salad. And carnivores are not forgotten, with prime steak, game in season and traditional pub grub.

| directions | B3330 from Ryde; left into Puckpool Hill for Seaview. |
| meals | 12pm-2.30pm; 7pm-9.30pm. Main courses £6.95-£14.95. |

Andrew Morgan
The Seaview Hotel,
High Street, Seaview,
Isle of Wight PO34 5EX
| tel | 01983 612711 |
| web | www.seaviewhotel.co.uk |

map: 4 entry: 236

| directions | On A3054 between Yarmouth & Newport. |
| meals | 12pm-2.30pm; 6pm-9.30pm. Main courses £7-£16. |

Martin Bullock
The New Inn,
Main Road, Shalfleet, Yarmouth,
Isle of Wight PO30 4NS
| tel | 01983 531314 |
| web | www.thenew-inn.co.uk |

map: 3 entry: 237

Shipwright's Arms
Faversham

It's been called the loneliest pub in the world. Surrounded by salt marshes, the below-sea-level-building and boatyard are protected by a dyke from inundation by the tidal creek above. Its isolation calls for self-sufficiency: water is still drawn from a well and propane gas used for cooking. Plain and simple just about sums up the three tiny bar rooms separated by standing timbers and wooden partitions, all warmed by open fires or stoves and with booths formed by black-panelled settles. Furniture is ancient and there's no shortage of boating paraphernalia. Beers are from Kent brewers Goachers and Hopdaemon and are expertly kept, food sustains sailing folk and walkers on the Saxon Shore Way, and Derek and Ruth are lovely people. Join the summer crowd in the garden and sup a pint on the sea wall.

The Sportsman
Seasalter

Slip off to Seasalter for a meal you won't forget. Brothers Phil and Steven Harris's pub is a gastronomic haven amid wastes of marshland, faded beach huts and caravan sites with the North Sea somewhere behind. In defiance of the pub's bleak surroundings, happy eaters fill the three large, light-filled rooms, spreading across the stripped pine floors, pine wheelback chairs, chunky tables built from reclaimed wood and winter log fire. It's simple, fresh, unprecious: red stools at a cream-boarded bar, neat lighting, modern prints on white walls and a glassed-in front porch, a good place for soaking up the winter sun. The blackboard menu is short and sweet with everything seasonal and with an understandable emphasis on fish. So, fantastic food at reasonable prices, such as Thornback ray with balsamic vinaigrette, new-season lamb with pommes Anna, roast baby pineapple and coconut sorbet… There are good wines by the glass and, on handpump, Shepherd Neame beers.

directions	From A2 for Sittingbourne. Through Ospringe, right at r'bout on to western link road; right at end (T-junc.). Right again opp. school in 0.25 miles. Cross marsh to pub.
meals	12pm-2.30pm; 7pm-9pm. No food Sunday evenings. Main courses £5.95-£12.95.
closed	Mondays in winter.

Derek & Ruth Cole
Shipwright's Arms,
Hollowshore,
Faversham,
Kent ME13 7TU

tel	01795 590088

map: 5 entry: 238

directions	On coast road between Faversham & Whitstable.
meals	12pm-2pm; 7pm-9pm. No food Sunday evenings & Mondays. Main courses £11-£17.
closed	Open all day Sunday.

Phil Harris
The Sportsman,
Faversham Road,
Seasalter, Whitstable,
Kent CT5 4BP

tel	01227 273370

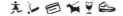

map: 5 entry: 239

The Dove
Dargate

In winter, woodsmoke hangs in the air, in summer, it's the heady scent of roses. This is an idyllic rural pub in the gloriously named Plum Pudding Lane. Enter through a series of small rooms with bare-boarded floors, scrubbed wooden tables and plain solid chairs to a hop-garlanded bar and winter fire. Nigel Morris cooks with skill and imagination using the freshest ingredients he can get his hands on. It's not your usual pub grub and raw materials are mostly regional: pheasant and partridge from local shoots, lemon sole, plaice and hake from Hythe. There could be roast shank of lamb, or a smashing confit of duck. Lunchtime snacks include soups, baguettes and a never-off-the-menu marinated chicken with mint. The sheltered, formal garden has tables under fruit trees, a swing for children, a dovecote with doves. Remember to book to eat, especially in the evening. There are Shepherd Neame ales on handpump and a short, good-value wine list.

The Red Lion
Stodmarsh

A genuine country pub reached down rutted lanes that wind through bluebell woods. The tiny, 15th-century rooms have bare boards, log fires, garlands of hops, fresh flowers and candles on every table… and prints, framed menus from France, old wine bottles, milk churns, trugs and baskets, tennis rackets, straw hats and two lazy cats. Then there's Robert Whigham, one of life's characters; the perfect landlord. A basket of freshly-laid eggs (chickens in the garden), locally-made chutney and a sign for the sale of locally-smoked ham add to the rural feel. Greene King IPA and Old Speckled Hen are tapped direct from barrels behind the bar and everyone here is a regular – or looks like one. The blackboard menu changes every couple of weeks depending on what's available from local farms and shoots, food arrives on huge, individually painted plates and the quality is high.

directions	Off A299, 4 miles south west of Whitstable.
meals	12pm-2pm; 7pm-9pm. Main courses £5-£18.
closed	Mondays (except bank holidays when closed Tuesdays).

Nigel & Bridget Morris
The Dove,
Plum Pudding Lane,
Dargate, Canterbury,
Kent ME13 9HB
tel   01227 751360

map: 5 entry: 240

directions	Off A257 Canterbury to Sandwich road.
meals	12pm-2.30pm; 7pm-9.30pm. Main courses £12.95-£17.95.
closed	Open all day.

Robert Whigham
The Red Lion,
High Street, Stodmarsh,
Canterbury, Kent CT3 4BA
tel   01227 721339
web   www.red-lion.net

map: 5 entry: 241

The Griffin's Head
Chillenden

Jerry and Karen's hugely attractive Shepherd Neame pub – a Wealden hall house from the 14th century – will charm you. Dominated by a log fire in the tiny, flagstoned, central bar and back-to-back with its doppelganger hearth in the snug, attractive restaurant, this is a superb winter pub. Pale beams and standing timbers are everywhere, ceilings are low and the beams above the bar are a mass of glass beer mugs. Lovers of fizz know they've come to the right place the moment they step in and spot the blackboard listing champagne. Wine is taken seriously too, with a fair choice by the glass – three reds, three whites; you can always try a taster before you commit. Good country cooking is of the creamy garlic mushrooms, steak and kidney pie, roast partridge in cranberry sauce variety, and very delicious it is too. In spring the gorgeous garden is surrounded by wild roses. Popular with the Kent cricketing fraternity.

The Granville
Lower Hardres

From the same stable as the Sportsman in Seasalter, the Granville mirrors its older sibling, comfortably straddling the divide between restaurant and pub. Rugs are strewn, cream walls bear tasteful lithographs, leather sofas fill one corner – this is an attractively laid-back place to drop in on for a pint or a well-chosen wine. Overseeing it all is Gabrielle Harris, aided by chef Jim Shave heading an open-to-view kitchen that deals in classically modern, uncontrived dishes. These are chalked up on a blackboard in the bar, tried-and-trusted favourites like rock oysters with hot chorizo; slow-roast partridge with chocolate sauce; baked cod with parsley sauce; a mouthwatering hot chocolate pudding. Those looking for a light lunch will find excellent antipasti and cheese ploughman's. The ingredients are impeccably sourced, the cooking a match, and there's a big beer garden. Great for walkers, foodies and families.

directions	A2 from Canterbury; left on B2068 for Wingham; Chillenden signed.
meals	12pm-2pm; 7pm-9pm. Main courses £7.95-£15.95; bar meals £5.95-£7.95.
closed	Sunday evenings. Open all day.

Jeremy Copestake
The Griffin's Head,
Chillenden,
Canterbury,
Kent CT3 1PS

tel   01304 840325

map: 5 entry: 242

directions	On B2068 just outside Canterbury.
meals	12pm-2pm (2.30pm Sundays); 7pm-9pm. No food Sunday evenings. Main courses £9.95-£16.95.
closed	Open all day.

Phil & Gabrielle Harris
The Granville,
Street End,
Lower Hardres, Canterbury,
Kent CT4 7AL

tel   01227 700402

map: 5 entry: 243

Froggies at the Timber Batts
Bodsham

Winding lanes lead to Bodsham, with glorious views of the North Downs. Wander into the splendidly rural Timber Batts – built in 1485 – and you are in for a surprise. Along with the bar menu is a slateboard of regional and seasonal British mixed with French specialities: | at traditional tables under hop-hung tables treat yourself to local game, Rye Bay fish, stuffed mussels, duck leg confit and tarte tatin. The house wine comes from Loire vineyard of owner-chef Joel Gross's cousin. In winter, nurse a whisky by one of three fires, in summer enjoy the garden with its lush Kentish views. And make the most of delicious local and French produce at the last-Sunday-of-the-month market in the car park.

Dering Arms
Pluckley

Pluckley is possibly the most haunted village in England (16 ghosts at the last count) and the gothicky Dering Arms contributes its share. The former hunting lodge is hidden down country lanes almost two miles from the village. Owner/chef James Buss has given this civilised place a fantastic reputation for food and drink. Stone floors, blazing logs, old wooden tables and chairs and two bars garlanded with hops, farming implements, guns and prints – feast amid it all on fine produce and fish that will have you hooked: fillets of plaice with crisp Serrano ham and beurre noisette or a whole crab salad. Or dine more formally in the pretty restaurant, candlelit at night. The blackboard also lists seasonal game, pie of the day, confit of duck. Dering Ale on handpump is brewed for the pub by Goachers of Maidstone; wines and whiskies galore.

directions	B2068 for Canterbury; left for Wye & Bodsham; 1st left fork; 1.5 miles; right for Wye; right for Bodsham; 300 yds up on top of hill.
meals	12pm-2.30pm (12.30pm Sunday); 7pm-9.30pm. Main courses £14-19; Sunday lunch £16 & £20. No food Sunday evenings.
closed	3pm-6.30pm; Mondays (except bank holidays when closed Tuesdays). Open all day weekends.

directions	8 miles west of Ashford (M20 south junc. 8). Signed from Pluckley, by railway station.
meals	12pm-2pm; 7pm-9.30pm. Main courses £8.45-£15.95.
closed	3.30pm-6pm (7pm Sundays).

	Joel Gross Froggies at the Timber Batts, School Lane, Bodsham, Wye, Kent TN25 5JQ
tel	01233 750237
web	www.thetimberbatts.co.uk

	James Buss Dering Arms, Station Road, Pluckley, Ashford, Kent TN27 0RR
tel	01233 840371
web	www.deringarms.com

map: 5 entry: 244

map: 5 entry: 245

The Swan on the Green
West Peckham

West Peckham may be the back of beyond – albeit a well-heeled beyond – but there's nothing backward about Gordon Milligan's 16th-century pub. People are drawn by its growing reputation for good food and beer that comes from the microbrewery parked outside. The décor is fresh, contemporary and open-plan: blond wood, rush-seated chairs, big flowers, modern black and white photographs. Under the Swan Ales label, half a dozen brews are funnelled from the central bar: Ginger Swan, Swan Mild, Trumpeters Best, Whoopers Pale Ale. The printed menus are a compendium of updated pub classics and the likes of haddock, tomato and root vegetable chowder, red mullet with mussel broth, and crispy duck confit with red wine jus. In spite of clear gastropubby leanings, Gordon and his team have created a balanced mix of drinking bar – replete with locals – and dining areas. You may even borrow a rug and eat on the village green.

The Harrow
Ightham Common

The continuing, hands-on approach of John Elton and Claire Butler is reaping rewards. Their Kent ragstone country pub looks the part, with cottage garden flowers outside and old benches, candlelight and a roaring winter fire within. The cooking is based on sound supplies, from local game to wild mushrooms, and the food adds enough spice to provoke interest without being overpowering: mustard and chive sauce with home-baked ham, fillet of chicken with Cajun spices. Some of the starters might make a meal in themselves: spicy vegetable and lentil soup comes with a whole loaf, and tomato and anchovy salad is a heaped pile. A separate restaurant, that spreads into a small conservatory, has a more formal feel to match the starched white cloths on the bookable tables. It's first-come, first-served for tables in the bar – and this is a popular place!

directions	From A26 north, 2nd left off B2016.
meals	12pm-2.15pm; 7pm-9.15pm. No food Sunday and Monday evenings. Main courses £6.50-£10.95.
closed	Sunday evenings in winter.

directions	Ightham Common signed off A25.
meals	12pm-2pm; 6pm-9pm. Main courses £8.50-£16.
closed	Sunday evenings & Mondays.

	Gordon Milligan
	The Swan on the Green,
	The Village Green, West Peckham,
	Maidstone, Kent ME18 5JW
tel	01622 812271
web	www.swan-on-the-green.co.uk

	John Elton & Claire Butler
	The Harrow,
	Ightham Common,
	Sevenoaks,
	Kent TN15 9EB
tel	01732 885912

map: 5 entry: 246

map: 5 entry: 247

The Three Chimneys
Biddenden

Ramble through tiny, unspoilt rooms – all rough panelling, stripped brick, faded paintwork, old flags, ancient timber and several smouldering fires. During the Napoleonic wars French officers imprisoned nearby were allowed to wander as far as the point where the three paths – 'trois chemins' – met (hence the name)... so, nothing to do with chimneys at all (of which there are only two). The cooking is modern, in contrast to the rest, and tasty; try parmesan and herb-crusted loin of lamb followed by chocolate and praline torte with pistachio ice cream. You may eat in the bars, apart from the spartan public one, and in the charming restaurant, built 20 years ago to look like a barn from reclaimed wood. In summer, tables spill out onto a stylish and sheltered patio. They get the balance just right here between pub and restaurant – prop up the bar for as long as you like. There's farm cider and Adnams Best Bitter drawn straight from the cask.

The Swan at the Vineyard
Lamberhurst

Real ale, real flowers, real food and real English wines – from Lamberhurst, naturally. A complete remodelling in late 2005 has made the most of the building's 15th-century origins (low ceilings, beams, worn brick walls, boards and flagstones), added an extra dining room and moved and improved the previously cramped bar area. Vanessa and Sean Arnett have put in a lot of hard work to achieve this mellow look, incorporating slate walls, leather sofas and dining chairs, modern wrought-iron light fittings and lots of church candles. Folk are drawn by the friendly and relaxed atmosphere, the blazing winter fires, the local ales and wines, as well as the adventurous dishes: duo of meatballs with classic beef glaze and sautéed mushrooms; pork medallions with caramelised apple and brandy sauce on dauphinoise. The outside terrace overlooking the children's adventure playground is a summer treat.

directions	On A262 2 miles west of Biddenden.
meals	12pm-2pm; 6.30pm-9.45pm (9pm Sundays). Main courses £11.95-£18.95.

Craig Smith
The Three Chimneys,
Hareplain Road,
Biddenden,
Kent TN27 8LW
tel   01580 291472

directions	From A21 in Lamberhurst, B2100 for Wadhurst; right at x-roads.
meals	12pm-2.15pm; 6pm-9.30pm. Main courses £8.50-£17.50; bar meals £6.50-£9.95.
closed	Open all day Friday-Sunday.

Sean & Vanessa Arnett
The Swan at the Vineyard,
The Down, Lamberhurst,
Kent TN3 8EU
tel   01892 890170
web   www.theswanatthevineyard.com

map: 5 entry: 248

map: 5 entry: 249

George & Dragon
Speldhurst

"We try to buy from people not companies,'" says Julian Leefe-Griffiths — before launching into an exuberant description of the produce he finds in the local woods, and the beers that come from microbrewers Westerham. Meat, game and vegetables are local and often organic; cheeses come mostly from Sussex. Julian realises that rescuing one of the oldest inns in southern England from years of mediocrity is no easy task, but he's made a very fine start; already there are plush new loos, a smart front terrace and a lovely rear garden. It's a characterful old pub, too, worth popping into for its massive flagstones, doors, inglenook and beams. But chef Max Leonard's gutsy food is the biggest treat: crisp, salty sea purslane cooked with creamy soft scallops, wood sorrel with

seared local wood pigeon breast, smoked eel on toast with poached duck egg and confit garlic, Valrhona chocolate tart with chocolate mousse. The atmosphere is easy, the staff friendly, and Chiddinstone Castle and Penshurst Place are delightfully close by.

directions	In centre of village opposite church.
meals	12pm-2.30pm (3pm Saturday, 4pm Sunday); 7pm-10.30pm (11pm Saturday). No food Sunday evenings. Main courses £9.50-£16.

SPECIAL AWARD
see pages 28-29

Julian Leefe-Griffiths
George & Dragon,
Speldhurst Hill,
Speldhurst, Tonbridge,
Kent TN3 0NN
tel   01892 863125

map: 5 entry: 250

Kent

The Hare
Langton Green

As you negotiate the green and the surrounding roads in the quest for somewhere to park, you'd be forgiven for thinking The Hare is hardly Kent's best-kept secret. Don't be put off. The feel inside is stylish and relaxed and the food among the best in the area. Large, light rooms create marvellous eating areas, with gleaming, well-spaced tables on polished floorboards, and character from old prints, paintings, books – and a collection of chamber pots dangling over broad doorways! The blackboard menu has pub classics such as steak and ale pie with braised cabbage and good sandwiches (crab, avocado and lemon mayonnaise), plus more ambitious dishes like shoulder of lamb with red wine sauce, and slow-roast belly-pork with dauphinoise potato. Cheerful staff dispense Greene King Abbot Ale and guest beers such as Ruddles County and Archers. Wine is taken seriously too; the well-balanced wine list has 16 by the glass.

directions	On A264 3 miles west of Tunbridge Wells.
meals	12pm-9.30pm (9pm Sundays). Main courses £7.50-£17.95.
closed	Open all day.

Chris Little
The Hare,
Langton Green,
Tunbridge Wells, Kent TN3 0JA

| tel | 01892 862419 |
| web | www.brunningandprice.co.uk |

map: 5 entry: 251

Lancashire

Bay Horse Inn
Forton

The Wilkinsons have been in the saddle for a number of years during which their son Craig has become an accomplished chef. Lancashire produces some marvellous ingredients and Craig takes full advantage of them in his modern British cooking; specialities include fish pie with cheese mash, Lancashire hotpot of Bowland lamb with pickled red cabbage, and roast Lune Valley venison with honey sauce. Although the Bay Horse considers itself to be a gastropub, there's a traditional pubby atmosphere and a range of cask beers. Interconnecting areas are comfortably furnished with a mix of old chairs and cushioned seating in bay windows, the dining room sparkles and the bar is warm and inviting with its low beams, soft lighting and open fire in winter. Gentle background jazz adds to the relaxed mood and the service is friendly and professional. Beware: the inn is easy to miss on the corner of a country lane.

directions	From M6 junc. 33; A6 for Preston, 2nd left; pub on right.
meals	12pm-1.45pm; 7pm-9.15pm. No food Sunday evenings. Main courses £10.95-£17.95.
closed	3pm-7pm (4.30pm-9pm Sundays); Mondays.

Craig Wilkinson
Bay Horse Inn,
Forton, Lancaster,
Lancashire LA2 0HR

| tel | 01524 791204 |
| web | www.bayhorseinn.com |

map: 11 entry: 252

Lancashire

Mulberry Tree
Wrightington

The old wheelwright's workshop has become a freehouse and restaurant with a Wrightington-born chef who headed the kitchen at Le Gavroche. A big jewel in Lancashire's crown, it's a vast, rambling place with a fresh, modern look to match the cooking. There's a smart lounge with a long bar, a private dining room and an open-plan eating area – subtly lit, softly hued, warmly carpeted. Whether you order something simple like rump steak with pepper sauce from the bar, or book for a serious meal, you'll be impressed by the presentation and the finesse. Start with Tuscan white bean soup with pesto, move onto breast of wood pigeon with wild mushrooms and rich merlot sauce. Lush puddings include bread and butter pudding with apricot coulis, and rhum baba with chantilly cream. Chef-patron Mark Prescott's verve in the kitchen makes the Mulberry Tree one of the best gastropubs in the north-west. *No smoking throughout.*

directions	M6 junc. 27; B5250 for Eccleston; 2 miles, on right.
meals	12pm–2pm; 6pm–9.30pm (10pm Fri & Sat); 12pm–9.30pm Sundays. Main courses £10.95–£18.50; Sunday lunch £22.50.
closed	Open all day Sunday.

Mark Prescott
Mulberry Tree,
9 Wrightington Bar,
Wrightington, Wigan,
Lancashire WN6 9SE
tel 01257 451400

map: 11 entry: 253

Lancashire

The Eagle & Child
Bispham Green

There's an old-fashioned pubbiness here *and* a sense of style – an informality touched with zing. The candlelit main bar welcomes you in with its rug-strewn flagged floors, well-used tables and chairs, hop-flower-decked beams and open fire, and the other two rooms are equally engaging – one hessian-carpeted with burgundy walls, the other cosy, with a cast-iron fireplace. Hand pumps line the bar (with beers from lesser-known brewers like Anglo-Dutch), the shelves parade an army of malts, and the wine cellar has some fine and unusual offerings, including English fruit wines. The staff seem to enjoy themselves as much as the customers and the food has won awards: olive and tomato bread pizza, loin of lamb with chorizo mash, seafood tagliatelle. The pub's reputation lies, too, with its cask ales, and a weekend beer festival in May packs the place out with beers and beer buffs.

directions	From M6 junc. 27, A5209 for Parbold; right along B5246; left for Bispham Green. Pub in 0.5 miles.
meals	12pm–2pm; 5.30pm–8.30pm (9pm Fridays & Saturdays); 12pm–8.30pm Sundays. Main courses £8.50–£16.
closed	2pm–5.30pm. Open all day Sunday.

Martin Ainscough
The Eagle & Child,
Malt Kiln Lane,
Bispham Green, Ormskirk,
Lancashire L40 3SG
tel 01257 462297

map: 11 entry: 254

The Lunesdale Arms
Tunstall

A soft, wide, undulating valley, the Pennines its backdrop – this is the setting of The Lunesdale Arms. A traditional pub with a fresh, modern feel: Pimms in the summer, mulled wine in the winter, good ales and good cheer. Comfort is deep: big sofas and wood-burning stoves, cushioned settles in yellow and blue, newspapers to browse and oil paintings to consider – even to buy. A big central bar separates drinkers (three local cask ales, whiskies and wines) from diners. Sit down to locally-reared produce, home-baked bread and seasonal, often organic, vegetables at tables away from the bar. Emma Gillibrand delivers wholesome food full of flavour – organic leek soup, corn-fed chicken breast stuffed with leeks and roquefort cheese, soaked lemon sponge and custard – and encourages children to have small portions. The Lunesdale is a great local for all ages, with a popular games room.

directions	M6 junc. 34; A683 for Kirkby Lonsdale.
meals	12pm-2pm (2.30pm weekends); 6pm-9pm. Main courses £7.50-£13.50.
closed	Mondays (except bank holidays). Open all day Saturday.

Emma Gillibrand
The Lunesdale Arms,
Tunstall, Kirkby Lonsdale,
Lancashire LA6 2QN

tel	01524 274203
web	www.thelunesdale.co.uk

map: 12 entry: 255

The Inn at Whitewell
Whitewell

The owner was advised not to touch this inn with a bargepole, which must qualify as among the worst advice ever given because you'll be hard-pressed to find anywhere better than this.. The old deerkeeper's lodge sits just above the River Hodder with views across parkland to rising fells in the distance. Merchants used to stop by and fill up with wine, food and song before heading north through notorious bandit country; the hospitality remains every bit as good today and the most that will hold you up is a stubborn sheep. The long restaurant and an outside terrace drink in the view – which will only increase your enjoyment of cornfed Goosnargh chicken, peppered beef salad, homemade ice creams and great wines, including their own well-priced Vintner's. In the bar, antiques, bric-a-brac, log fires, old copies of *The Beano*, creamy fish pie and local bangers. Marvellous.

directions	M6 junc. 31a; B6243 east through Longridge; follow signs to Whitewell for 9 miles.
meals	12pm-2pm; 7.30pm-9.30pm. Main courses £12-£22; bar meals from £3.50.

Charles Bowman
The Inn at Whitewell,
Whitewell,
Forest of Bowland,
Clitheroe, Lancashire BB7 3AT

tel	01200 448222

map: 12 entry: 256

The Three Fishes
Mitton

The producers, suppliers and growers are the heroes of this venture, named and proclaimed on the back of every menu. Quite rightly – the region is a hotbed of food artisans. This 17th-century village pub in the lovely Ribble Valley reopened in 2004; under the auspices of Nigel Haworth of Michelin-starred Northcote Manor it is taking gastropubbery to a mouthwatering new level. The long whitewashed public house has been restyled in rustic-smart 21st-century fashion and is vast: up to 130 people inside, a further 60 out. Walls are pale brick, floors stone, furniture sober, lighting subtle and winter logs glow. Wines are gorgeous, local pints and real ciders are served and the food is generous and delicious. Lunchtime prawn sandwiches, buttered crumpet with crumbly Lancashire curd, slow-baked succulent pigs' trotters, hotpot from heather-reared lamb, orange and bitter chocolate pudding. *No smoking throughout.*

The Freemasons Arms
Wiswell

Nothing fazes Ian Martin. He cooks brilliantly, serves great ales and must have one of the finest wine lists in the country. All this in a tiny pub in a village in Lancashire. Formerly three small cottages, one of which was a free masons' lodge, its small beamed bars are simply and freshly decorated in green, pink and white with not a flounce in sight – just fresh flowers and modern art. The cooking is equally contemporary, allowing the flavours and textures to speak for themselves. Smoked bacon and lentil soup followed by salmon fishcakes with homemade tartare sauce make for a fantastic value two-course lunch. Bowland pork comes with black pudding and cider sauce, braised lamb with flagelot beans and rosemary. There are fine cheeses and the vintage clarets – some 120 of them – go back 30 years. Extraordinary.

directions	From M6 junc. 31 onto A677. Turn onto A59 for Whalley. Mitton off A59.
meals	12pm-2pm (8.30pm Sun); 6pm-9pm (9.30pm Fri & Sat). Main courses £8.50-£15.
closed	Open all day.

directions	From A59 2 miles south of Clitheroe take A671 to Blackburn. After 0.5 miles first left to Wiswell.
meals	12pm-2pm; 6pm-9pm; 12pm-8pm Sundays. Main courses from £6.95; set lunch, 2 courses, £9.95.
closed	Mondays & Tuesdays. Open all day Sunday.

Nigel Haworth & Craig Bancroft
The Three Fishes,
Mitton Road, Mitton,
Lancashire BB7 8PQ
tel 01254 826888
web www.thethreefishes.com

Ian Martin
The Freemasons Arms,
8 Vicarage Fold,
Wiswell, Whalley,
Lancashire BB7 9DF
tel 01254 822218

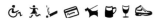

map: 12 entry: 257

map: 12 entry: 258

Assheton Arms
Downham

Assheton is the family name of the Lords of Clitheroe and Downham is their village. It has remained splendidly preserved since the 16th century, its stone cottages strung out along a stream; not long ago it remodelled itself as Ormston in the BBC TV series *Born and Bred*. In the best traditions of country life, the pub stands opposite the church – it's the community's hub. The rambling, low-beamed bar bustles more often than not with both village regulars and hikers fresh from a walk up Pendle Hill. Diners drop by for the delicious scallops in garlic butter, the grilled sea bass with ginger and spring onion and the rib-sticking puddings. The atmosphere of an old inn has been preserved, right down to the huge stone fireplace and the horse brasses on the walls. Sit at solid oak tables on wing-back settles and bask in the absence of electronic games. In summer the front terrace entices you out to its serene pastoral views.
No smoking throughout.

directions	Off A59, 3 miles NE of Clitheroe.
meals	12pm-2pm; 7pm-10pm; 12pm-10pm Sundays in summer. Main courses £7.75-£22; bar meals from £5.
closed	3pm-7pm. Open all day Sunday.

	David Busby
	Assheton Arms,
	Downham, Clitheroe,
	Lancashire BB7 4BJ
tel	01200 441227
web	www.assheton-arms.co.uk

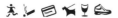

map: 12 entry: 259

The Black Bull
Rimington

It looks normal but step inside: traditional rooms are filled with railway models and transport memorabilia. Unusual, yes, but carpeted, wallpapered, polished and comfortable. No jukebox – that would be too modern! – just mellow background music. Pop in for a sandwich and a pint of Theakston's Draught Bitter, or stay for a mustard glazed sirloin of beef; everyone's welcome, and nothing is too much trouble for Barbara Blades and her team. There are a number of malt whiskies and some very good wines, while blackboards in the cosy, log-fired bar reveal that the food is taken most seriously. Chef Gary Newsome has an inventive approach to the fish that is delivered daily (smoked salmon parcel with scrambled egg and truffle, seared sea bass), his spotted spiced syrup sponge is legendary and there's an Express Lunch if you're in a hurry. No beer garden, but beautiful views at the front to Pendle Hill.

directions	In middle of Rimington village; signed from Chatburn or Gisburn on A59.
meals	12pm-2.30pm; 7pm-9.30pm. No food Sunday evenings. Main courses £5.95-£14.95.
closed	3pm-7pm & Mondays.

	Barbara Blades
	The Black Bull,
	Rimington, Clitheroe,
	Lancashire BB7 4DS
tel	01200 445220
web	www.theoffice.demon.co.uk/blackbull

map: 12 entry: 260

Lancashire

Strawbury Duck
Turton

In a secluded hamlet amid reservoirs and wooded cloughs, this magical former station hotel is something of a legend among ramblers. Outside it is an odd mix of pseudo black and white and mellow gritstone, inside it is a revelation of flagged floors, log fire and eccentric furniture (one table is an organ bellows), threaded around a dimly lit, L-shaped bar. The whole place is atmospherically gloomy, with winter woodsmoke drifting along wavy old beams and dressed-stone walls. Those doughty escapees from the wild moors (and visitors drawn from far and wide) have the blissful choice of at least five real ales, many from local microbreweries, and the chance to sample the ever-reliable meals, from filling stalwarts to the inn's own specials. Tables on the patio and in the garden make an enviable summer evening's retreat.

directions	Blackburn Road from Edgworth (just N. of Bolton). After 0.5 miles signed left down Hob Lane (left); drive across the reservoir dam.
meals	12pm-9.30pm (8pm Sundays). Main courses £7.50-£15.
closed	Open all day.

Daniel Byrne
Strawbury Duck,
Overshores Road,
Turton, Edgworth,
Lancashire BL7 0LU
tel   01204 852013

map: 12 entry: 261

Lancashire

The Rams Head Inn
Denshaw

High on the moors between Oldham and Ripponden – you're on the border here – with glorious views, the inn is two miles from the motorway but you'd never know. Unspoilt inside and out, there's a authentic, old-farmhouse feel. The small rooms, cosy with winter log fires, are carpeted, half-panelled and beamed and filled with interesting memorabilia. Until recently beer was served straight from the cask; there's still an old sideboard behind the bar to remind you of former days. Blackboards announce a heart-warming selection of tasty and well-priced food cooked to order: game and venison in season, seafood specialities and great steaks. Even the bread and ice creams are homemade. A wonderfully isolated Lancashire outpost, staffed by people who care, and with a farm shop and tea rooms in the offing. Well-behaved children are very welcome – but watch the open fires!

directions	M62 junc. 22 for Oldham & Saddleworth; 2 miles on right.
meals	12pm-2.30pm; 6pm-10pm; 12pm-8.30pm Sundays. Main courses around £9.95.
closed	Mondays (except bank holidays); 2.30pm-6pm. Open all day Sunday.

Mr G R Haigh
The Rams Head Inn,
Denshaw,
Saddleworth,
Lancashire OL3 5UN
tel   01457 874802

map: 12 entry: 262

Lancashire

The Church Inn
Uppermill

Next to the church on the way to the moors – it's not easy to find. Julian Taylor brews their own Saddleworth beers and is involved in everything. At the top end of the long curved bar are a grand fire and some window tables; at the other end, a big log burner in an old fireplace, with a heavily framed mirror above. Seating is a mix of padded benches, settles, chairs and a pew named Hobson's Choice. There's a fine atmosphere: lofty beams, leaded windows, lamps on sills, nightlights on tables, brass plates, Staffordshire jugs, fresh flowers. The soft background music is entirely bearable. Eat in the no-smoking dining room with valley views: the food is honest, unpretentious and good value, as are the beers. The inn is home to the world-famous Saddleworth Morris Men and several events take place here including the Rush Cart Festival on the August bank holiday weekend. A friendly place loved by all ages.

directions	Saddleworth signed from Oldham. From Uppermill go up New Street for 1 mile. On left, next to church.
meals	12pm-2.30pm; 5:30pm-9pm (12pm-9pm Saturdays, Sundays & bank holidays). Main courses £3.50-£11.95.
closed	Open all day.

Julian & Christine Taylor
The Church Inn,
Church Lane,
Uppermill, Saddleworth,
Lancashire OL3 6LW
tel   01457 820902

map: 12 entry: 263

Leicestershire

The Queen's Head
Belton

Take a village pub by the scruff of its neck and renovate it from top to toe. The result: a cool, relaxed drinkers' bar, all leather sofas and low-slung tables, a bistro with an open fire and dining room of wood, suede and leather. Then add bedrooms that have a similarly stylish feel and you have a well-nigh-perfect, 21st-century coaching inn. The Weldons deserve applause for not losing sight of tradition: the Queen's Head serves its own beer, from the local Wicked Hathern brewery, plus ales from the Castle Rock Brewery and outstanding wines. Printed menus and blackboard dishes point to diverse, even inspirational ideas, from burgers and relish in the bar to black-leg chicken with thyme sauce in the restaurant. Watch out for the summer Real Ale and Gourmet Barbecue weekend, and the Champagne and Lobster night. Great staff, too.

directions	In Belton, just off B5234.
meals	12pm-2.30pm (4pm Sun); 7pm-9.30pm (10pm Fri & Sat). No food Sun evenings. Main courses £13.50-£17; set lunch £10-£15.
rooms	6: 4 doubles, 2 twins £70-£100. Singles £55.
closed	3pm-7pm; Sun eves from 5pm.

See page 34 for bedroom details.

Henry & Ali Weldon
The Queen's Head,
2 Long Street, Belton,
Loughborough, LE12 9TP
tel   01530 222359
web   www.thequeenshead.org

map: 8 entry: 264

The Cow & Plough
Oadby

A pub-restaurant housed in the former milking sheds of a working farm just outside Leicester. Barry and Elizabeth Lount founded it in 1989 and filled it with good beer and a hoard of brewery memorabilia: the two back bars are stuffed with period signs, mirrors and bottles. It later became an outlet for their range of Steamin' Billy ales (named after Elizabeth's Jack Russell who 'steamed' after energetic country pursuits). When the foot and mouth epidemic closed the farm's visitor centre, the Lounts established a restaurant there instead. Most of their dishes are made with local produce such as pheasant or rack of Market Harborough pork. The pub has built up a great reputation, winning awards and becoming a place for shooting lunches; it's also popular with the Leicester rugby team. And there's a conservatory with piano and plants and beams decked with dried hops.

directions	On B667 north of town centre & A6.
meals	12pm-2pm (5pm Sunday); 7pm-9pm. No food Sundays & Monday evenings. Main courses £8.95-£14.95; Sunday lunch £11.95 & £14.95; bar meals from £4.95.
closed	3pm-5pm. Open all day weekends.

Barry Lount
The Cow & Plough,
Stoughton Farm Park, Oadby,
Leicester, Leicestershire LE2 2FB
tel   0116 272 0852
web   www.steamin-billy.co.uk

map: 8 entry: 265

The Bell
East Langton

Peter Faye took over the pretty 16th-century village pub and its on-site brewery in 2003; the Caudle Bitter and Bowler Strong are a treat. In upmarket Langton village, approached via a delightful cottage garden — with barbecues in summer — The Bell draws a loyal crowd. Subtle changes have brought a fresh look to the long stone-walled bar with its low beams, uneven floors and winter log fire; expect seagrass floors, checked blinds, stripped pine tables, delicious aromas and a happy buzz. Peter, "a keen amateur", is serious about his food, and his daily menus, agreeably short, are devoted to the freshest produce. Caught-that-day cod is lightly battered and served with homemade chips and minted mushy peas, mussels are simmered in garlic, white wine and cream, confit of duck leg comes with gingered greens. Seasonal vegetables are generally separately charged.
No smoking throughout.

directions	From A6, turn for East Langton on B6047.
meals	12pm-2pm; 7pm-9.30pm. No food Sunday evenings and Mondays in winter. Main courses £9.50-£16.95.
closed	2.30pm-7pm (6pm Fridays; 6.30pm Saturdays).

Peter Faye
The Bell,
Main Street, East Langton,
Market Harborough,
Leicestershire LE16 7TW
tel   01858 545278

map: 9 entry: 266

The Baker's Arms
Thorpe Langton

A sleepy-village treasure with oodles of atmosphere beneath 16th-century thatch. A series of intimate little areas have been kitted out with cottagey scrubbed pine tables, antique pews and settles, paintings and prints on warm terracotta walls. The Baker's is more foodie than boozey though the pubbiness remains and if you're looking for a pint of Baker's Dozen you won't be disappointed. But most come for Kate Hubbard's first-rate cooking (do book) and use of impeccable produce. Chalked up daily on the boards are pan-fried scallops with a honey, mustard and lemon dressing, confit of duck leg and breast with parsnip and apple compote, baked sea bass with spinach, mushrooms and prawn jus, white chocolate and raspberry trifle. Wines, too, are good, and may come mulled in winter. Great staff make the Baker's Arms close to perfect.

Fox & Hounds
Knossington

Open all day for Adnams and Marston's Pedigree (rare hours for such a rural spot) and with quiz nights and cards for the regulars, this is one lively local. Brian Barker and his sister Claire Ellis are instrumental in having created a mood of warmth at a stylishly remodelled 17th-century boozer in upmarket Knossington. Two fires are lit in winter, ceiling spots sparkle, there are soft contemporary colours and simple scrubbed pine tables (just four in the bar, five in the non-smoking dining room). Chef Brian's background includes a stint as personal chef to Sir Elton John, and his philosophy demands good quality ingredients and precision: enjoy lamb rump with roasted aubergines and artichokes, skate wing with lemon, capers and shallot dressing, white peach tart with vanilla ice cream and traditional roasts on Sundays. And make room for the Colston Bassett stilton.

directions	On A6, 10 miles south of Leicester.
meals	12pm-2pm (weekends only); 6.30pm-9.30pm. Main courses £10.95-£16.95.
closed	Weekday lunchtimes; Sunday & Monday evenings.

Kate Hubbard
The Baker's Arms,
Thorpe Langton,
Market Harborough, LE16 7TS
tel 01858 545201
web www.thebakersarms.co.uk

map: 9 entry: 267

directions	Through Oakham on A606, take Braunston Road after r'way crossing; on for 4 miles.
meals	12pm-3pm; 7pm-9.30pm. No food Monday or Tuesday lunchtimes. Main courses £8.95-£13.75; set lunch, 2 courses, £9.95 (Wed-Sat).
closed	Open all day.

Claire Ellis & Brian Baker
Fox & Hounds,
6 Somerby Road, Knossington,
Melton Mowbray, LE15 8LY
tel 01664 454676
web www.foxandhounds.biz

map: 9 entry: 268

Leicestershire

Red Lion Inn
Stathern

Quirky stylishness and cheerful service. The rambling Red Lion feels like a home, with its books and papers, deep sofas and open fires; gamekeepers frequent the flagstoned bar. A trusted network of growers and suppliers fills the kitchen with game from the Belvoir estate, cheeses from the local dairy, fruits and vegetables from nearby farms. Menus are on blackboards dotted around, with a choice that leaps between fashion and tradition: confit duck salad; fish and chips and mushy peas; sea bream, pesto mash, chorizo sausage and cherry tomatoes; Hill Farm roast leg of lamb with swede purée; glazed curd tart with armagnac ice cream. The set Sunday lunch is fantastic value. The wine list is imaginative; beers include village-brewed Brewsters Bonnie and Grainstore Olive Oil from Oakham, and children have homemade lemonade. The outdoor play area will delight them, too.

directions	Off A607 north east of Melton Mowbray; through Stathern; past Plough; pub signed on left.
meals	12pm-2pm (4pm Sundays); 6pm-9.30pm. Main courses £10-£15; Sunday lunch £16.50.
closed	Sundays from 5.30pm. Open all day Friday & Saturday.

B Jones, M Welford & S Hope
Red Lion Inn,
Red Lion Street, Stathern,
Leicestershire LE14 4HS
tel 01949 860868
web www.theredlioninn.co.uk

map: 9 entry: 269

Lincolnshire

Farmers Arms
Lincoln

Trumpeting 30 by the glass, this pub loves its wines. Andrew Bennett runs wine courses, visits Europe and Africa to buy and ensures that whether you like your vintage crisp and dry or rich and opulent, oaked or unoaked, fizzy or floral, there's something here for you. This plush pub's second passion is food and the seasonal menus look enticing. Twice-baked soufflé is whipped up from creamy, nutty Lincolnshire Poacher and accompanied by tomato and chive salad, Lincolnshire sirloin steak is served with sautéed field mushrooms, espresso crème brûlée comes with brandy snap curls, impressive cheeses include Yellow Belly – made by a local farmer. Once past the plum plastic canopies and the mock stone balustrade you enter a cosy but capacious cavern, all swirly carpets, traditional pub furniture, sofas and lamps. Staff are cheerful and helpful, customers range from gentleman farmers to ladies that lunch, and the whole place feels animated and convivial. *No smoking throughout.*

directions	On A46 between Lincoln & Market Rasen.
meals	12pm-2.30pm; 6.30pm-9.15pm. Main courses £7.95-£17.95.
closed	2.30pm-6.30pm; Sunday evenings & Mondays.

Andrew Bennett & Vicky Herring
Farmers Arms,
Welton Hill, Lincoln,
Lincolnshire LN2 3RD
tel 01673 885671
web www.farmers-arms.co.uk

map: 9 entry: 270

Wig & Mitre
Lincoln

When Captain Hope left the army in the year of the Silver Jubilee, he and Valerie decided to open a pub in Lincoln. Here they still are, some three decades on, sandwiched between the cathedral and the courts. (They could have called it the Mitre & Wig: though lawyers dine here, the first pint was drawn by the Bishop of Lincoln.) Downstairs has a French café feel: old oak boards, exposed stone, sofas to the side; a civilised place for late breakfast and the papers. Upstairs, a cosy series of dining rooms and an open fire. In the Seventies it was hard to find decent food in a pub, let alone one in Lincoln. Valerie's kitchen became one of the most exciting in the area, serving a mix of dishes – baked cheese and spinach soufflé, rack of lamb with garlic flageolet ragout – strongly influenced by French and Mediterranean cooking. Was this the first gastropub? The regular visits of visiting High Court judges have, of course, nothing to do with the late supper licence.

directions	On Steep Hill leading down from Castle.
meals	8am-10.30pm. Main courses £10.95-£19.50; set lunch £11 & £13.95.
closed	Open all day.

Valerie Hope
Wig & Mitre,
30-32 Steep Hill, Lincoln,
Lincolnshire LN2 1TL
tel   01522 535190
web   www.wigandmitre.com

map: 9 entry: 271

Houblon Inn
Oasby

The word 'civilised' springs to mind, as befits the pedigree of the place; the pub is named after John Houblon, first governor of the Bank of England and honoured on the back of the £50 note. Hollyhocks round the door, rubble stone and pretty sash windows greet you; low beams, stone walls and cosy bar await. By chance, 'houblon' also means 'hop' in Flemish – and lovers of real ale will not be disappointed. Belly Dance, Oldershaw Old Boy and Surrender may take your fancy as you perch at the bar and scan the simple yet stylish menu – pigeon breast or risotto to start, maybe lamb rump with roast shallots to follow. Owners Eddie and Hazel make this pub – passionate, gentle people who left 'the smoke' years ago and thrive on the business. Locals, foodies and lovers of real ale track them down wherever they go. Sitting at the heart of a conservation village, it's honest, unaffected and intelligently run.

directions	From A1, B6703 to Ancaster; right to Welby, follow road to Oasby.
meals	12pm-2pm; 6.30pm-9.30pm. No food Sunday evenings. Main courses £6.50-£14.95.
closed	3pm-6.30pm (7pm Sunday) & Mondays (except bank holiday lunchtimes).

Eddie Simmonds & Hazel Purvis
Houblon Inn,
Oasby,
Grantham,
Lincolnshire NG32 3NB
tel   01529 455215

map: 9 entry: 272

Lincolnshire

The Chequers Inn
Woolsthorpe-by-Belvoir

A coaching inn for 200 years, the Chequers has built a reputation over the last five as a top dining pub; Uma Thurman dropped by when filming at Belvoir Castle. There's contemporary luxury with deep comfort, a flurry of open fireplaces, three dining areas and two bars, leather sofas, linen drapes and Farrow & Ball colours. You have three ales on handpump, 24 wines by the glass, 50 whiskies, several fruit pressés and a humidor on the bar. Robust dishes – roast rabbit leg stuffed with garlic and apricot, rib-eye steak on black olive rosti with mustard hollandaise – taste as good as they look, the Monday evening set menu is very reasonable and small helpings are available. In summer the pub hosts the village cricket team on what must be one of the slopiest pitches in England. The Vale of Belvoir is as beautiful as it sounds.

directions	Off A52, west of Grantham.
meals	12pm-2.30pm (4pm Sundays); 7pm-9.30pm (6pm-8.30pm Sundays in summer). £8-£15; Sunday lunch, 2 courses, £10.95; set menus £10.95 & £12.50 (Mondays).
closed	3pm-5.30pm. Sunday evenings in winter. Open all day Sundays in summer.

Justin & Joanne Chad
The Chequers Inn,
Main St, Woolsthorpe-by-Belvoir,
Grantham, Lincolnshire NG32 1LU
tel   01476 870701
web   www.chequers-inn.net

map: 9 entry: 273

London

French House
Soho

As the French House does not serve pumped ale, it would not, by some lights, qualify as a pub – but no guide to British inns and public houses would be complete without it. The legendary Soho haunt, once patronised by members of the Free French, has been – and still is – befriended by famous Londoners (Freud, Melly), international figureheads and a welter of journalists, writers and bohemians who spend their days and nights in Soho. Dylan Thomas lost the only manuscript of *Under Milk Wood* here while on a bender. Despite the gentrification of Soho and the pub's renown, 'The French' has a delightfully scuffed-around-the-edges feel and attracts a friendly, bacchanalian crowd from many walks of life. There's bar food in the small, packed, smoky bar, and a short French menu in the charmingly panelled restaurant upstairs. But this is first and foremost a drinking den (half pints of John Smith's, Guinness) and a vastly atmospheric one at that.

directions	Nearest tube: Leicester Square.
meals	12pm-3pm; 5.30pm-11pm; bar meals 12pm-3pm. No food Sundays. Main courses £14.95-£17. Bar meals £2.50-£5.
closed	Open all day.

Lesley Lewis
French House,
49 Dean Street,
Soho,
London W1D 5BG
tel   020 7437 2477

map: 4 entry: 274

The Seven Stars
Holborn

Nudging the backdoor of the Royal Courts of Justice, the Seven Stars is something of a barristers' den. Here since 1602, it was originally the haunt of Dutch sailors, and named after the seven provinces of the Netherlands; having survived the Great Fire by a whisker it's been here longer than the courts themselves. Recently it was transformed by the exotically named Roxy Beaujolais, landlady, head chef and *Full On Food* television presenter. The glorious single bar has hung on to its boarded floors, low beams, old mirrors and narrow wood settles; framed vintage legal film posters line the red walls. The menu is short and bistro-like: poached chicken and aïoli, chargrilled rib-eye steak sandwich, dill-cured herring and potato salad. Adnams and Harveys bitters are the house beers and there is a very decent selection of wines. The utterly old-fashioned, diminutive, "near perfect" Seven Stars is now being extended – but get here early if you want a seat!

directions	Nearest tubes: Chancery Lane; Temple.
meals	12pm-9pm. Main courses £8-£12.50.
closed	Bank holidays. Open all day.

Roxy Beaujolais
The Seven Stars,
53 Carey Street,
Holborn,
London WC2A 2JB
tel   020 7242 8521

map: 4 entry: 275

The Westbourne
Notting Hill

Come to see and be seen! Sebastian Boyle and Olly Daniaud took the place some years ago and gave it a thorough going over. Westbourne Park Villas promptly became the trendiest place in England and it's worth arriving early... 11am perhaps. London's beau monde amasses throughout the day at this shabby-chic gastropub, keen to dish out for Belgian beers and scrummy food. In the main bars is a collection of old tables and chairs, with some lush sofas at the back; walls spill over with posters, photos and original art. The terrace at the front with its gas heaters is an all-year drinking spot – and just about handles the overflow. Cooking is robust modern British and the ingredients used are the freshest: oysters, game terrine with onion marmalade, pot-roasted pheasant, Old Spot pork chop with butter beans, chorizo, black cabbage and red wine sauce. All sorts love it here – including those who've been coming for 30 years.

directions	Nearest tube: Westbourne Park.
meals	12.30pm-3pm (3.30pm weekends); 7pm-10pm (9.30pm Friday-Sunday). Main courses £9-£12.50.
closed	Monday lunchtimes. Open all day.

Wood Davis
The Westbourne,
101 Westbourne Park Villas,
Notting Hill, London W2 5ED
tel   020 7221 1332
web   www.thewestbourne.com

map: 4 entry: 276

London

Portobello Gold
Notting Hill

A fun little place off Ladbroke Grove – a bar, a restaurant, an internet café and a place to stay. Sit out on the pavement in wicker chairs and watch the fashionistas stroll by. Or hole up at the bar with a pint of Guinness and half a dozen oysters, as Bill Clinton did on a presidential visit to Britain. Tiled floors, an open fire, monthly exhibitions of photography on the walls and a putting green on the roof terrace. At the back, the restaurant with its retractable glass roof feels like a comfortable jungle. Dine – to the sweet song of canaries – on roast sea bass with rosemary and garlic (seafood's a speciality), venison casserole or spaghetti with mushroom ragout. Linda writes about wine, so you'll drink well too. Refurbished bedrooms have small shower rooms and good beds – ideal if the hippy in you is still active, or you're after a quirky place to eat, drink and stay.

directions	Nearest tube: Notting Hill Gate. Follow signs for Portobello Market.
meals	10am-10pm (from 12pm Sundays). Main courses £5-£12.95; set menu £20.50.
rooms	8: 6 twin/doubles, 1 suite, 1 roof terrace apartment, £60-£180.
closed	Open all day.

See page 34 for bedroom details.

Michael Bell & Linda Johnson-Bell
Portobello Gold,
95-97 Portobello Road,
Notting Hill Gate, London W11 2QB

tel	020 7460 4910
web	www.portobellogold.com

map: 4 entry: 277

London

Ladbroke Arms
Holland Park

The warm glow emanating from the sage sash windows is enough to tempt anyone into the Ladbroke Arms. Cream-painted and ginger hessian walls, benches plump with autumnal-hued cushions, long shiny tables, paintings, books, good wines and beers to please enthusiasts: Fuller's London Pride, Greene King IPA and Abbot Ale, Adnams Bitter. The intimate Ladbroke takes its food seriously, too, the chef buying cheese twice weekly from a touring supplier and placing orders with a fishing fleet every day. The bar sparkles with olive oils, vinegars and bottled fruit; in the raised restaurant area, stylish diners savour richly flavoured dishes such as chorizo and chickpea broth, warm salad of pork confit with salsa verde and pan-fried veal kidneys with girolles and watercress salad. Sunday roasts are a favourite among those who live close by; the hot chocolate fondant pudding is legendary. Sup under the parasols in summer as Notting Hillbillies smooch by.

directions	Nearest tubes: Notting Hill Gate; Holland Park.
meals	12pm-2.30pm (3pm weekends). 7pm-9.45pm. Main courses £9.50-£14.50.
closed	Open all day.

J Shubrati
Ladbroke Arms,
54 Ladbroke Road, Holland Park,
London W11 3NW

tel	020 7727 6648
web	www.capitalpubcompany.com/ladbroke.htm

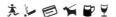

map: 4 entry: 278

Paradise by Way of Kensal Green
Kensal Rise

The name was poached from G K
Chesterton. Locals may have been taken
aback when the arty bar first opened;
now the area is full of trendies who little
realise that The Paradise – all fairy lights
and candles, background jazz and blues –
stands on the site of the oldest pub in
Brent. A statue of a fallen angel on the
wall stares down in surprise on the
battered reproduction Regency sofas,
wrought-iron garden tables and chairs,
and vast palm fronds growing in even
vaster planters. The bar itself is small and
not the most comfortable but there's still
a pubby feel. The place doesn't take itself
too seriously in spite of attracting the
odd C-list celebrity; pop in for a pint of
real ale and to look at the papers, or stay
for a meal (must book). The menu is
modern European with an oriental twist
and the food extremely good: Thai green
curry, penne with grilled aubergine,
artichoke hearts, tomatoes and black
olives, beef fillet with peppercorn sauce.
A great place to spend a Sunday.

The Scarsdale
Kensington

We can be grateful to the French
builder who believed Napoleon would
invade and built The Scarsdale as living
quarters for the French army. The
immaculate Edwardes Square could
only have been built by the French. This
is a delightful little pub with a summer
terrace of hanging baskets and bags of
Victorian character. The old stained
glass, dark panelling and burgundy walls
provide a distinguished foil for old
paintings in heavily gilded frames and
various empty magnums of champagne,
while the happy hum of drinkers flows
from cosy corners as easily as the ales.
Fabulous smells emanate from the
kitchen hatch heralding the arrival of
Aberdeen Angus rib-eye steak with
sauce béarnaise, expertly followed by
hot chocolate pudding. Eat in the busy
bar or in the swagged dining room; sit
in the garden and feel you're in the
country. You could happily go on a first
date here, or bring the parents.

directions	Nearest tube: Kensal Green.
meals	12.30pm-4pm; 7pm-11pm; 12.30pm-9pm Sundays. Main courses £8-£9; set menu £10.
closed	Open all day.

Paul & Sarah Halpin
Paradise by Way of Kensal Green,
19 Kilburn Lane,
Kensal Rise,
London W10 4AE
tel   020 8969 0098

map: 4 entry: 279

directions	Nearest tube: High Street Kensington.
meals	12pm-10pm (9.30pm Sundays). Main courses £8-£14.
closed	Open all day.

Ray & Sarah Dodgson
The Scarsdale,
23a Edwardes Square,
Kensington,
London W8 6HE
tel   020 7937 1811

map: 4 entry: 280

London

Churchill Arms
Kensington

It's hard to say which comes first in the popularity stakes, the publican or the pub: Gerry O'Brien is an influential figure and this is a terrific pub. The Churchill is not only a shrine to the great prime minster but to Gerry's collection of memorabilia and his irrepressible Irish humour. To the left of the counter in the bar – smoky, cosy with open fire – is Chamber Lane (115 chamber pots suspended from the ceiling) while the walls of the leafy, glass-roofed Thai restaurant – once, unbelievably, a garage – display his prized butterflies. Never mind the tourists; come for great Guinness and beers, oriental feasts that don't break the bank, bags of atmosphere and a big dollop of tradition. On the annual celebration of Sir Winston's birthday unsuspecting drinkers are amazed to see everyone dressed in 40s style; sausage and mash can be bought for a shilling and the evening's takings go to the Cabinet War Office Museum. You have been warned!

directions	Nearest tube: High Street Kensington.
meals	12pm-9.30pm. Main courses £5.85.
closed	Open all day.

Gerry O'Brien
Churchill Arms,
119 Kensington Church Street,
Kensington,
London W8 7LN

tel   020 7727 4242

map: 4 entry: 281

London

The Anglesea Arms
South Kensington

The raised heated terrace, historic lamp posts, wooden benches and hanging baskets are a temptation for any passer-by. And one can't help wondering whether Dickens, who lived at No 11, and Lawrence, at No 9, were similarly drawn. Original panelling, etched glass, dark floral wallpaper, heavy velvet curtains and scrubbed wooden tables – it's wonderfully, traditionally cosy. Settle down to a pint of Adnams or browse the Sunday papers over creamy hot chocolate. The little restaurant downstairs, away from the lively main bar, is a quiet snug in which to savour traditional English cooking. The menu, built around fresh and local supplies, lists carrot, lime and coriander soup, duck pie with red wine, battered haddock with homemade chips and pea purée, and hearty roasts on Sundays. Puddings are equally down-to-earth – apple and plum crumble, bread and butter pudding. Deeply, comfortingly English.

directions	Nearest tube: South Kensington.
meals	12pm-3pm (5pm weekends); 6.30pm-10pm (6pm weekends; 9.30pm Sundays). Main courses £8.95-£13.95.
closed	Open all day.

Jenny Podmore
The Anglesea Arms,
15 Selwood Terrace,
South Kensington, SW7 3QG

tel   020 7373 7960
web   www.angleseaarms.com

map: 4 entry: 282

Swag & Tails
Knightsbridge

Hidden down a pretty mews in one of the smartest parts of town, the little whitewashed pub with black shutters and well-clipped topiary is an easy walk – even in your Manolos – from the Harvey Nichols-Harrods drag. Escape the crowds and rest weary feet in the warm, yellow-and-blue interior where wooden floors and swagged curtains make a fresh and glamorous alternative to the heavy trimmings of your usual Knightsbridge pub. The attractive tiled conservatory at the back – less noisy and smoky than the main bar – is a delightful spot in which to tuck into seared king scallops with lemon dill sauce or roast venison with crushed sweet potatoes. The food is stylish, modern and very good. Staff are full of smiles and, if it takes an explorer to find this little place, the wonderful photograph of Nare's Arctic expedition of 1875 – a present from landlady Annemaria to her husband – is a fitting first reward for your perseverance.

Nags Head
Knightsbridge

Once known as the smallest pub in London, the Nags Head expanded in Victorian times, but modestly. This wooden-floored, panelled and rambling boozer may be tiny but it has vast personality. The bar is low enough to serve passing gnomes, hence the sunken floor behind, allowing bar staff to meet seated drinkers eye to eye. Walls and ceilings are packed with interesting memorabilia, including a squadron of nicotine-stained matchstick bi-planes and a 'What the Butler Saw' machine – operational in exchange for a donation to the pub's charity pot. No fruit machines, no mobile phones, but music hall songs from the 20s and 30s, open fires and Tudor beams; it's a great little place to quaff Adnams ales or a glass of Aspall's Suffolk cider. Downstairs, on checked cloths, a great spread of home-cooked meats, pies, cheeses and salads can be scoffed at lunchtime, along with other hot 'Kitchen Favourites', like steak and mushroom pie. A prince among paupers.

directions	Nearest tube: Knightsbridge.
meals	12pm-3pm; 6pm-10pm. Main courses £7.50-£14.95.
closed	Weekends; bank holidays. Open all day.

Annemaria Boomer–Davies
Swag & Tails,
10-11 Fairholt Street,
Knightsbridge, London SW7 1EG
tel 020 7584 6926
web www.swagandtails.com

map: 4 entry: 283

directions	Nearest tubes: Knightsbridge; Hyde Park Corner.
meals	11am-9.30pm. Main courses £6.50-£10.50.
closed	Open all day.

Kevin Moran
Nags Head,
53 Kinnerton Street,
Knightsbridge,
London SW1X 8ED
tel 020 7235 1135

map: 4 entry: 284

The Grenadier
Belgravia

Down a cobbled alley on the Grosvenor estate, the tiny Grenadier is unmissable with its fanfare of patriotic paintwork, tumbling flowers and sentry box – a magnet for tourists and their cameras. Uneven steps lead to a charismatic interior with a military theme, a reflection of this little watering hole's past. Originally the Duke of Wellington's officers' mess, it later became a popular place for King George IV to enjoy a pint; later it was frequented by Madonna. The dimly-lit Mess Bar, with smouldering coal fire, is stuffed with memorabilia: gleaming breast plates, swords, bearskins and bugles. Behind, in the restaurant, squeeze in and settle down to beef Wellington or fish and chips at battle-themed bench seats and tables dressed in starched white linen. In September, the ghost of an officer – accidentally flogged to death after cheating at cards – returns to haunt the place, while the infamous Bloody Marys are best sampled on Sundays, from a specially erected bar. A small place with a big heart.

directions	Nearest tube: Hyde Park Corner.
meals	12pm-2.30pm (3pm Sundays); 6pm-9pm. Main courses £5-£10.75.
closed	Open all day.

Christopher Buckley
The Grenadier,
18 Wilton Row,
Belgravia,
London SW1X 7NR
tel   020 7235 3074

map: 4 entry: 285

The Builders Arms
Chelsea

You wouldn't expect such an exquisite little pub in the back streets off the King's Road. Enter and be seduced: the country-living-room feel is so enticing you could move in. Enjoy a sauvignon or a pint of London Pride against a background of large puffy armchairs, low table lamps, walls in soft greens and creams and a ruby-red snug behind the bar. 'Never trust a builder without a tattoo' reads the sign on the wall, but the people here (and their pooches) are as immaculate as the interior. The Builders is a stylish pub, even if labelling the loos 'Builders' and 'Ballerinas' is a touch twee, and the food is delicious modern British well presented: smoked haddock, grilled calf's liver with bacon and sweet potato confit, grilled rib-eye steak with garlic and parsley butter. The area is a shoppers' dream – but avoid the Builders on Friday lunchtimes: it's packed!

directions	Nearest tubes: Sloane Street; South Kensington. Behind King's Road, between Sydney Street & Chelsea Green.
meals	12pm-2.30pm (3pm Saturday, 4pm Sunday); 7pm-10pm (9.30pm Sunday). Main courses £7.50-£13.95.
closed	Open all day.

Rupert Clevely
The Builders Arms,
13 Britten Street, Chelsea,
London SW3 3TY
tel   020 7349 9040
web   www.geronimo-inns.co.uk

map: 4 entry: 286

Chelsea Ram
Chelsea

A quiet residential street off the Lots Road seems an unlikely place to find a corner pub bursting with bonhomie. It used to be a junk shop; now the fine arched shop windows with etched glass are complemented by soft and subtle mustards and terracottas, tongue-and-groove cladding, a dark green wooden bar and colourful local art. A carpeted area to the back has small alcoves, soft lighting and shelves of thumbed books – an intimate spot in which to be treated to some truly enticing, Roux-inspired food. Smoked haddock and spinach perhaps ("posh fish pie"), or grilled lamb cutlets with salsa verde, followed by chocolate pudding with Baileys sauce. The scrubbed wooden tables are a great place for lively card games (please bring your own) over coffee. Close to the large storage depot of Bonhams the auctioneers, this popular pub is well worth the few minutes' walk from the end of the King's Road.

directions	Nearest tubes: Fulham Broadway; Sloane Square.
meals	12.30pm-3pm (12pm-4pm Sundays); 7pm-10pm (9.30pm Sundays). Main courses £3.95-£11.95.
closed	Open all day.

James Symington
Chelsea Ram,
32 Burnaby Street,
Chelsea,
London SW10 0PL
tel   020 7351 4008

map: 4 entry: 287

The Atlas
Fulham

Up high, golden letters on wooden panelling proclaim London Stout, Burton Bitter and mild ales. The Atlas is a great little place in which to delve into more modern brews: Fuller's London Pride, Caledonian Deuchars IPA, Adnams Broadside. A glazed wooden partition – a prop for the 'Wine of the Moment' blackboard – divides the bar in two. Other Thirties' features remain: floorboards, attractive black and white tiling around the foot of the bar and three brick fireplaces, two of which add a glow in winter. The third, its mantelpiece piled high with lemons and limes, has been converted into a serving hatch for dishes that change twice daily – grilled sardines and Tuscan sausages, pot-roast poussin; the wine list trumpets 24 wines by the glass. Doors lead to a walled suntrap garden (open May to October) where puffa-jacketed folk flock under the rain and wind cover. In spite of its modest frontage on a residential street, the pub is next to a big Pay & Display, so not hard to find.

directions	Nearest tube: West Brompton.
meals	12.30pm-3pm; 7pm-10.30pm (10pm Sundays). Main courses £7.50-£13.
closed	Open all day.

George & Richard Manners
The Atlas,
16 Seagrave Road, Fulham,
London SW6 1RX
tel   020 7385 9129
web   www.theatlaspub.co.uk

map: 4 entry: 288

London

The White Horse
Fulham

The pub on the green is reputed to have the best-kept beers in Europe: Mark Dorber's knowledge of real ale is the fruit of years working with the best tasters. The ever-changing list of guest ales above the log fire is within reading distance of some deeply comfortable sofas, while bar food is of the best sort, from ploughman's with unusual cheeses to fried bass with garlic mash. Even better, the menu suggests the best accompanying liquor; how about a crisp Bavarian wheat beer with your smoked salmon and scrambled eggs... a delicious alternative to a macon chardonnay. Inside, terracotta walls, slatted wooden blinds, lovingly polished pumps and beer memorabilia; outside, a big terrace overlooking the green and a Sunday barbecue. Dubbed 'The Sloany Pony' the pub may be a hotbed of Fulhamites but it's also a shrine to beer; come for the glorious two-day festival in November when real ale enthusiasts descend from all over the globe.

directions	Nearest tube: Parsons Green.
meals	12pm-10.30pm.
	Main courses £7.75-£13.95.
closed	Open all day.

Mark Dorber
The White Horse,
1-3 Parson's Green, Fulham,
London SW6 4UL
tel   020 7736 2115
web   www.whitehorsesw6.com

map: 4 entry: 289

London

The Idle Hour
Barnes

'The trouble with the Rat Race is, even if you win you're still a rat'. Thus reads the sign outside. The Idle Hour is a small haven – tucked away down a dark, secret alley – where rats don't race and time stands still. The hour can all too easily be idled away over a cocktail or Grolsch as you sit stylishly amid fat dripping candles and a bizarre mix of clocks set at different times. Stephen Thorp (relaxed owner/designer/barman/chef) has put as much thought and effort into the fresh, contemporary décor as the predominantly organic menu. Sundays at the Idle Hour are legendary; a delightful place to laze by the fire with a Bloody Mary before tucking into whole roast organic lamb served in the roasting pan and accompanied by utensils for a 'carve-it-yourself' meal. Just like home but without the washing up... with sticky toffee pudding to follow who knows what time you'll leave? A gentle, unpretentious and civilised place.

directions	Nearest rail: Barnes; Barnes Bridge.
meals	1pm-3.30pm (Sundays only);
	7pm-9.45pm.
	Main courses £7.95-£12.95.
closed	Weekday lunchtimes.
	Open all day Sunday.

Stephen Thorp
The Idle Hour,
62 Railway Side, Barnes,
London SW13 0PQ
tel   020 8878 5555
web   www.theidlehour.co.uk

map: 4 entry: 290

Cat's Back
Putney

Down a hidden backstreet, surrounded by new waterside development, an unexpected gem. You'll sense an appealing eccentricity here, as you sit among cosy-red walls, mismatched tables, African masks, a disco glitter ball, a portrait of Audrey Hepburn and all manner of flotsam and jetsam – presents from regulars and treasures picked up on the family's travels. (That's Roger, Venetia, Ella and dog Sonny.) It's mellow and fun and everyone and his hound pops by – locals, builders, business people. At night, moody candlelight and chilled music – Bob Marley perhaps – with live acts on the first Sunday of every month. In this part of town you may expect good food; there are organic meats and vegetables, light homemade batters, hand-cut chips and potted shrimps with toast. Red, yellow and green lights in the stairwell lead to a lovely sash-windowed restaurant and a small but lavish private dining room beyond. Extraordinary.

The Earl Spencer
Southfields

Its spit 'n' sawdust days are over, its Edwardian interior restored. Now, to a clean backdrop of deep cream and dark blue, gilded ceiling mouldings and a winter fire, you can discover some of the best pub food in south London. Mark Robinson and his team bake bread twice a day, have a smokery on the premises and a bunch of cookery books on the bar. Above the central fireplace the blackboard is chalked up with a seasonal menu and inventive dishes pop up every day: chargrilled squid with chorizo, tomato and garlic; duck rillette with gherkins and chutney; daube of beef with green beans and horseradish; shoulder of lamb to be shared among four; poached pear, honey and brandy parfait. Proprietor Jonathan Cox has not forgotton the drinkers, so there are good wines by the glass and Hook Norton, Shepherd Neame and Hoegaarden on tap. Fresh flowers and papers, laid-back staff, happy drinkers, contented dogs – a place to unwind.

directions	Nearest tube: Putney.
meals	12pm-3pm; 6.30pm-10.30pm. Main courses £8.50-£11.50; bar meals from £3.75.
closed	Open all day.

Roger Martin
Cat's Back,
86 Point Pleasant,
Putney, London SW18 1NN

| tel | 020 8877 0818 |
| web | www.thecatsback.com |

map: 4 entry: 291

directions	Nearest tube: Southfields.
meals	12.30pm-2.30pm (3pm Sundays); 7pm-10pm (9.30pm Sundays). Main courses £7.50-£13.50
closed	Open all day.

Jonathan Cox
The Earl Spencer,
260-262 Merton Road,
Southfields, London SW18 5JL

| tel | 020 8870 9244 |
| web | www.theearlspencer.co.uk |

map: 4 entry: 292

London

The Ship
Wandsworth

Drinking a pint of Young's Special next to a concrete works doesn't sound all that enticing, but the riverside terrace by Wandsworth Bridge is a dreamy spot. Chilly evenings still draw the crowds to this super old pub, cosy with its warm-red and sage-green walls, and its conservatory with central chopping-board table and wood-burning stove. No music, just happy chat, newspapers, tall blackboards and fresh flowers. Charles and Linda Gotto hand over to Young's in July 2006; until then, they will continue to supply ingredients for a swish, fresh menu from their organic farm – Shorthorn beef, rare breed pork and lamb, eggs. Summer barbecues find grilled swordfish and lobsters alongside organic sausages and Angus rib-eye steaks. At peak times expect 'who can be the loudest' Fulhamites to pack out the front bar – but don't be put off. The Ship opens its arms to all, and families merrily congregate in summer.

directions	Nearest rail: Wandsworth.
meals	12pm-10.30pm (10pm Sundays). Main courses £8-£14.35.
closed	Open all day.

Charles Gotto
The Ship,
Jews Row, Wandsworth,
London SW18 1TB

tel	020 8870 9667
web	www.theship.co.uk

map: 4 entry: 293

London

The County Arms
Wandsworth

A fireplace with a crackling fire and tartan wing chairs… it's not the Highlands, just the lowlands of Wandsworth Common. And a great weekend place for families. This pub has been very well restored – the brass shines, the stained glass glows and the pints of Young's Winter Warmer flow. Beyond, in the roomy restaurant, fireside customers tuck into a menu where quality and simplicity reign. Chunks of fresh bread accompany thick wholesome soups, while from the open kitchen hatch come dishes such as roast cod on saffron mash with herb butter, wild mushroom risotto, and dark chocolate and tia maria mousse. Summer brings popular barbecues as the pub's restaurant overflows to the shaded rattan chairs outside. A long party table with an awning makes a great corner for alfresco celebrations and a double deckchair is the perfect resting place for couples to share a chilled pint.

directions	Nearest rail: Wandsworth; Earlsfield.
meals	12pm-10pm. Main courses £6.95-£16.95.
closed	Open all day.

Justin Whitehead
The County Arms,
345 Trinity Road, Wandsworth,
London SW18 3SH

tel	020 8874 8532
web	www.countyarms.co.uk

map: 4 entry: 294

The Fox & Hounds
Battersea

As you pass beneath yet another dripping railway bridge you might wonder if the trek from Chelsea was worth it. But the moment the bright little corner pub comes into view you'll feel spirits rise. With its excellent beers and its photos of pints on cream walls, the place appears to be a shrine to the golden brew. No longer the old boozer it once was, it's still a popular hangout for the locals – and, along with its sister pub, The Atlas, a foodie destination. As Mediterranean-style dishes flow from the open-to-view kitchen, food-loving train-spotters will think they've gone to heaven and back as they watch the Connex South Central trains whizz by. Try hake and fennel tagine, smoked haddock and saffron risotto, and rib-eye steak with sweet potato mash and salsa verde. There's a great atmosphere here, and a good little garden for summer.

directions	Nearest rail: Clapham Junction. Left towards lights; up Lavender Hill. At Police Station left onto Latchmere Rd.
meals	12.30pm-3pm; 7pm-10.30pm (10pm Sunday). No food Tues-Thurs lunchtimes. Main courses £7.50-£13.
closed	3pm-5pm & Monday lunchtimes. Open all day Friday-Sunday.

George & Richard Manners
The Fox & Hounds,
66 Latchmere Road,
Battersea, London SW11 2JU
tel 020 7924 5483
web www.thefoxandhoundspub.co.uk

map: 4 entry: 295

The Fentiman Arms
Kennington

Toffee-coloured walls, a relaxed mood, well-thumbed books and games – a perfect place in which to "nurse your hangover on Saturday morning with the Fentiman brunch menu". This happy pub, designed by proprietor Rupert Clevely's wife Jo, echoes the cosmopolitan themes and earthy colours of their beloved South Africa. Come rain or shine, smart London regulars gather over pints of Bombardier and a menu that stretches way beyond the confines of brunch. Scallops, prawns and squid with a lime and lemon caramel, roast chicken with Jerusalem artichoke purée and borlotti beans, and date and walnut slice with rum ice cream can be enjoyed in cosy corners against fat velvet cushions and suede bolsters. The upstairs function room, the Fentiroom, with high ceilings and large windows, is a popular place for big gatherings; so too is the trendy outdoor terrace, brilliant for summer drinking and dining. Plan to arrive early on Sundays!

directions	Nearest tubes: Oval; Vauxhall.
meals	11am-2.45pm (4pm Sat); 12pm-4pm Sun; 7pm-10pm (9.30pm Sunday). Main courses £8.95-£14.95.
closed	Open all day.

Rupert Clevely
The Fentiman Arms,
64 Fentiman Road,
Kennington, London SW8 1LA
tel 020 7793 9796
web www.geronimo-inns.co.uk

map: 4 entry: 296

London

The Garrison Public House
London Bridge

Do dinner and a movie – there's a rough-and-ready cinema downstairs with films on Sunday nights, and a great little restaurant up. Gastropub veterans Clive Watson and Adam White have taken on an old boozer, kept the engraved glass windows and remodelled the rest into a light, airy, bare-boarded space. The furniture is silver-sprayed, lamps and objects fill every cranny. Fresh food, from apricots to Orkney mussels, arrives daily from the market down the road, and is incorporated into dishes that are elaborate but not overly so. A glass of rioja or a bottle of St Peter's goes down very well with rib-eye steak with watercress and roquefort butter, or roast cod with shrimp and chive sauce. And the pub is open daily for breakfast. The kitchen is open, staff are attractively laid-back, decibels are high, tables are crammed; the Fashion Museum is up the road and fashionistas stop for lunch. Forget hushed conversation: the place bounces with bonhomie.

directions	Nearest tube: London Bridge.
meals	8am-12pm; 12.30pm-3.30pm; 6.30pm-10pm (9am-11.30am; 12.30-4pm; 6.30pm-9.30pm weekends). Main courses £9-£14.
closed	Open all day.

Clive Watson & Adam White
The Garrison Public House,
99 Bermondsey Street,
London Bridge, London SE1 0PA
tel   020 7089 9355
web www.thegarrison.co.uk

♿ 🚶 🍽 🐶 🍷 👞

map: 4 entry: 297

London

Anchor & Hope
Southwark

One of the first bistropubs to champion below-stairs food. Come for some of the plainest yet gutsiest cooking in London; chefs Jonathan Jones and Harry Lester are names to watch. They describe the food as 'English bistro', and give or take the odd foreign exception (a chorizo broth, a melting pommes dauphinoise), it is just that. The menu is striking in its simplicity: pigeon terrine, smoked sprats with horseradish and lemon, slip soles with anchovy butter, rabbit with pearl barley and sherry, almond and nectarine tart. The beer comes from the Charles Wells brewery, the wine list has 18 by the glass. Staff are youthful – and may be rushed. Décor is 1930s sober and the restaurant area glows by candlelight. At the far corner of the rambling bar is the tiny theatre kitchen where you can watch the stars at work. No bookings, massively popular, but arrive at 6pm and you should get a table.

directions	Nearest tubes: Southwark; Waterloo.
meals	12pm-2.30pm; 6pm-10.30pm. Bar meals all day. Main courses from £10.
closed	Sundays & Monday lunchtimes. Open all day.

Robert Shaw
Anchor & Hope,
36 The Cut,
Southwark,
London SE1 8LP
tel   020 7928 9898

♿ 🚶 🍽 🐶 🍻 🍷

map: 4 entry: 298

Greenwich Union
Greenwich

Master brewer Alastair Hook has turned this Greenwich boozer into a shrine to his lagers and beers. The golds and browns of the interior reflect the hues of the glorious ales he painstakingly creates at the nearby Meantime Brewery; his Red, White, Golden, Amber and Chocolate beers slip down so easily that Sainsbury's has made them part of their range. (If you're not sure which pairs with which food, helpful staff behind the bar will give you a taster.) And this quirky little pub is a great place to eat, the Italian chef willing to concoct tapas at short notice. He is also a dab hand at sauté of mussels with saffron, chives and orange zest, roasted chicken breast with sweet shallots, and chestnut gnocchi with porcini mushrooms. Sandwiches include homemade 'piadina' (flat bread from Romagna) served with brie and rocket salad. All are welcome including families and dogs, and the weekend brunches are deservedly popular.

directions	Exit Greenwich station, left & 2nd right (Royal Hill), pub on right.
meals	12.30pm-10pm (10am-9pm weekends). Main courses £5.90-£8.90.
closed	Open all day.

Alastair Hook
Greenwich Union,
56 Royal Hill, Greenwich,
London SE10 8RT
tel 020 8692 6258
web www.meantimebrewing.com

map: 4 entry: 299

London

The Gun
Docklands

It's fiendishly difficult to find, but persevere. The front room, dominated by a dark panelled bar, is hugely atmospheric – a planked floor, settles and battered leather sofas, the smell of truffles in the air – while the restaurant area is pristine with white napery. A loose nautical theme runs through the prints and paintings (Lady Hamilton stayed in an upstairs room). Bag a table by the fire; settle in till the sun sets over the river; the candlelit terrace is spectacular. In the bar, a reassuring selection of pub favourites – rare-breed pork sausages with Old Spot bacon and apple and onion gravy, fish pie with sauce Mornay – while the restaurant menu is fiercely modern: rib-eye steak with snails, confit of salmon with butter bean cassoulet. Weekend brunch from 10.30am to 1pm is hugely popular – do book; summer barbecues in the new beer garden trumpet Billingsgate fish.

directions	Just off A1206 (Prestons Road); turn into Managers Street, then right turn at the end.
meals	12pm-3pm; 6.30pm-10.30pm. Sat/Sun brunch 10.30am-1pm. Bar meals all day. Main courses £11-£18; bar meals £4-£12.
closed	Open all day.

Tom & Ed Martin
The Gun,
27 Coldharbour, Docklands,
London E14 9NS
tel 020 7515 5222
web www.thegundocklands.com

map: 4 entry: 300

London

The Princess
Clerkenwell

Bare boards, bare tables, modern art and modern walls – another Clerkenwell boozer turned gastropub. This one is cool and charismatic, romantically candlelit at night, and its simple, honest cooking is hard to beat. In downstairs' one-room-serves-all bar, British classics nudge Mediterranean dishes on the menu: choose fish 'n' chips or risotto. Or book a big table for a long, lazy, entirely British Sunday lunch. If you're after slightly more formal surroundings and more adventurous cooking, trip up that spiral staircase in the corner to the restaurant above. Some daring and accomplished dishes – pan-fried queen scallops with piri piri butter and rocket; duck breast with roast pumpkin pilau, harissa and mint yogurt – are served by attentive and likeable staff. Timothy Taylor and Fuller's London Pride are on handpump if you're popping in for a drink, and they make the best Bloody Marys in town.

directions	Nearest tube: Farringdon.
meals	12.30pm-3pm (1pm-4pm Sunday); 6.30pm-10.30pm. No food Sunday evenings. Main courses £11.95-£14.95; bar meals £5-£10.50.
closed	Open all day.

Zim Sutton
The Princess,
76 Paul Street,
Clerkenwell,
London EC2A 4NE
tel   020 7729 9270

map: 4 entry: 301

London

The White Swan
Holborn

It had spent the previous ten years as the Mucky Duck. In 2003, brothers Tom and Ed Martin transformed the bird and restored the original name. The bar, with a vast mirror on one wall, evokes a classic, city pub feel. At plain tables on fashionably unpolished boards, City traders savour real ales (there are three) and fine wines (over 20 by the glass). Upstairs is a smart restaurant with some unusually good modern European cooking ranging from the robust (rump of lamb with crushed olive-oil potatoes and salad niçoise) to the subtle (fricassée of monkfish with fennel, chervil and truffle oil). Cheese and wine lists are encyclopaedic, and guess what: regulars have lockers to store their unfinished spirits. The bar menu veers from a pint o'prawns to seasonal dishes… with a bit of luck you'll find seared rabbit with roast tomatoes, chorizo, basil and crème fraîche on yours. The accompanying homemade focaccia is wonderful.

directions	Nearest tube: Chancery Lane.
meals	12pm-3pm; 6pm-10pm. Set lunch £25, dinner £28; bar meals from £6.
closed	Saturday & Sunday. Open Monday-Friday all day.

Tom & Ed Martin
The White Swan,
108 Fetter Lane, Holborn,
London EC4A 1ES
tel   020 7242 9696
web   www.thewhiteswanlondon.com

map: 4 entry: 302

Black Friar
Blackfriars

Across the Thames from the Tate Modern, the only Art Nouveau pub in London – perhaps the world. It was built in 1905 and the fact that it exists today is almost entirely due to Sir John Betjeman and his Sixties' campaign to save it from demolition. The building's amazing wedge shape is an echo of those narrow medieval streets, long since replaced. It stands, soaked in history, on the site not only of a Dominican Friary but also of the courthouse in which Henry VIII achieved the annulment of his marriage to Catherine of Aragon. Art Nouveau mosaics romp over walls inside and out; in the arched room off the saloon, green and red marble alabaster is embellished with cavorting friars. It gets packed at lunchtimes and evenings so go off-peak if you possibly can. No piped music, no plush – just bare boards, unpretentious pub grub and good solid ales from Adnams and Fullers. But it's the architecture that's the star here – there is no other like it. *No smoking throughout.*

The Eagle
Clerkenwell

Still mighty, after all these years – though recent reports tell of uppity service and some resting on laurels. No tablecloths, no reservations – just delicious food ordered from the bar. With its real ales and decent choice of wines, the appeal is as much for drinkers as for diners and at peak times it heaves. The atmosphere is media-bohemian and the offices of the *Guardian* lie next door. In spite of the laid-back appeal of scuffed floors, worn leather chairs, mix-and-match crockery, background Latin music and art gallery upstairs, the Eagle's reputation rests on its edible, seasonal bounty. The long bar counter is dominated by a stainless steel area at which ravishingly beautiful Mediterranean vegetables, cuttlefish and pancetta are prepared. Pasta, risotto, peasant soups, spicy steak sandwiches... still worth the trek to get here.

directions	Nearest tube/rail: Blackfriars.
meals	12pm-9pm. Main courses £5.50-£7.50.
closed	Open all day.

David Tate
Black Friar,
174 Queen Victoria Street,
Blackfriars,
London EC4V 4EG
tel 020 7236 5474

map: 4 entry: 303

directions	Nearest tube: Farringdon.
meals	12.30pm-3pm (3.30pm weekends); 6.30pm-10.30pm. Main courses £8-£12.
closed	Sunday evenings. Open all day.

Michael Belben
The Eagle,
159 Farringdon Road,
Farringdon,
London EC1R 3AL
tel 020 7837 1353

map: 4 entry: 304

Coach & Horses
Clerkenwell

Gone are the days when the Coach & Horses was a corner boozer; now the Edwardian pub fills with a mod-media crowd. Savour a pint of London Pride in the small panelled bar – or alfresco in summer – as you check out the blackboard listing some of the scrummiest gastropub food in London. The chef, Scott Walsh, devises British dishes with youthful enthusiasm and fresh ingredients burst with flavour: stilton and thyme potato cakes with apple chutney; pint pots of prawns and oysters by the dozen. Rare-breed meats are traditionally reared at Long Ghyll farms in Lancashire, fish is delivered daily. The bar specialises in malt whiskies and attentive staff lay on nibbles of toasted pumpkin seeds in keeping with the pub's logo, a pumpkin pulled by four mice. Note: most tables have a reserved sign on them on busy nights, so drinkers are confined to the bar.

The Well
Clerkenwell

Tom and Ed Martin's pub empire has grown. But this bright, breezy little local has not let its younger siblings – the White Swan, Holborn and the Gun, Isle of Dogs – overshadow it. Step under the deep blue awnings on this dull stretch of St John Street and enter a light-filled room of bare brick and chunky wooden furniture. The brunch menu draws the weekend locals for excellent renditions of eggs Benedict and smoked salmon with scrambled eggs, alongside such modern pub staples as venison pie with root vegetables. During the week there's more of a Mediterranean feel: rabbit leg with borlotti beans and salsa verde, risotto with gorgonzola. And it's good value, from the homemade bread to the raspberry and almond tart. The private basement bar is all contemporary fittings and dark, moody lighting – more classy Clerkenwell than plain gastropub. Service is friendly and knowledgeable.

directions	Nearest tube: Farringdon.
meals	12pm-3pm; 6pm-10.30pm; 10.30am-10.30pm Saturday; 10.30am-9.30pm Sunday. Main courses £9.95-£14.95. Weekend brunch menu £5.50-£13.50.
closed	Open all day.

directions	Nearest tube: Farringdon.
meals	12pm-3pm; 6pm-10pm. Main courses £10.75-£14; bar meals £6-£10.
closed	Saturday lunchtimes; Sunday evenings. Open all day.

Giles Webster
Coach & Horses,
26-28 Ray Street,
Clerkenwell, London EC1R 3DJ
tel   020 7278 8990
web   www.thecoachandhorses.com

map: 4 entry: 305

Tom & Ed Martin
The Well,
180 St John Street,
Clerkenwell, London EC1V 4JY
tel   020 7251 9363
web   www.downthewell.com

map: 4 entry: 306

Jerusalem Tavern
Clerkenwell

There's so much atmosphere here you could bottle it up and take it home – along with one of the beers. Old Clerkenwell has reinvented itself; the quaint little 1720 tavern, a former coffee house, epitomizes all that is best about the place. Its name is new, acquired nine years ago when the St Peter's Brewery of Suffolk took it over and stocked it with their ales and fruit beers. Step in to a reincarnation of a nooked and crannied interior, all bare boards and plain tables, candlelit at night with a winter fire; arrive early to bag the table on the 'gallery'. Lunchtime food is simple and English – bangers and mash, a roast, a fine platter of cheese – with ingredients coming daily from Smithfield Market down the road. There's a good selection of wines by the glass but this is a drinker's pub: staff are friendly and know their beer, and the full, irresistible range of St Peter's ales is all there, from the cask or the specially designed bottle.

directions	Nearest tube/rail: Farringdon Road.
meals	12pm–3pm. Main courses £5–£8.
closed	Saturday & Sunday. Open all day.

Colin Coroy
Jerusalem Tavern,
55 Britton Street, Clerkenwell,
London EC1M 5UQ

| tel | 020 7490 4281 |
| web | www.stpetersbrewery.co.uk |

map: 4 entry: 307

The Peasant
Islington

An impressive, Victorian gin palace with the original horseshoe bar, a blazing fire in the corner and acres of ceiling. Over five years the Wright brothers built up a reputation for splendid food, wines, beers and cocktails; now they have improved what was already a slick and sophisticated operation, and brought in new blood to spice up the menus. Expect the freshest ingredients and a few surprises: grilled kangaroo with globe artichoke stuffed with shiitake mushrooms and peanuts; roast cod on fennel; a fabulous South American brunch (must book). Tapas and mezze are served downstairs alongside the daily papers – chickpea salad, marinated olives, good cold meats, decent bread. The restaurant, too, has had a shake-up: a light, very pretty first-floor room with a painted corner bar and a conservatory with a balcony attached. Brilliantly positioned for antique shops, markets and visiting the Design Centre or Sadler's Wells.

directions	Nearest tubes: Angel; Farringdon.
meals	12pm–11pm (9.30pm Sundays). Main courses £9.50–£15.80; bar food & brunch £4.50–£10.70; tapas from £2.50.

Gregory & Patrick Wright
The Peasant,
240 St John Street, Islington,
London EC1V 4PH

| tel | 020 7336 7726 |
| web | www.thepeasant.co.uk |

map: 4 entry: 308

London

Drapers Arms
Islington

The Islington Labour Party was founded in the meeting room upstairs. Islington, the Labour Party and The Drapers have come a long way in the 100-odd years since but today's Labour group would be just as happy here as their forebears. In the old days, there was probably only beer, sandwiches and Clause 4 on the menu; today's deliberations are more likely to be accompanied by gnocchi with tiger prawns or perfect foie gras (it's not great for veggies), washed down with an Amarone della Valpolicella at £69 a bottle. There are, of course, less pricey vintages on offer... and delicious roasts on Sundays. In a quiet side street off Upper Street, the once ramshackle Drapers has rejoiced in its renaissance ever since Paul McElhinney took over. It has won a hatful of awards for its food and is friendly, airy and scrupulously clean. A nice place in which to settle down on a comfy leather sofa with a jug of Bloody Mary. Outside is a lovely little garden.

directions	Nearest tube: Highbury & Islington.
meals	12pm-3pm; 7pm-10.30pm (6.30pm-9.30pm Sundays). Main courses £9-£16.
closed	Open all day.

Paul McElhinney
Drapers Arms,
44 Barnsbury Street, Islington,
London N1 1ER
tel 020 7619 0348
web www.thedrapersarms.co.uk

map: 4 entry: 309

London

The House
Islington

The old Belinda Castle has become The House. Robert Arnott is a Marco Pierre White protegé; people come for the character and the cooking. Mirrors gleam on pale lemon walls, one slice of the wedge-shaped building is given over to white-clothed tables, candles and twinkly lights, the other is a chic and charming bar, with a real fire. Food is simple, gutsy, characterful, and the set lunches superb value. Try omelette Arnold Bennett, roast salmon with cannelloni of scallop, risotto of herbs with deep-fried onion rings, whole baby plaice wth brown shrimp butter, corn-fed chicken with chestnuts, wild mushrooms and pancetta – or simple shepherds pie. And save space for Valrhona hot chocolate pudding with espresso ice cream. It's Islington-cool, far from hushed, and smoky in the bar, but you could relax with anyone here – and pop in for a pint of handpumped ale. Great staff, too.

directions	Nearest tubes: Highbury & Islington; Essex Road.
meals	12pm-2.30pm (3.30pm weekends); 6pm-10.30pm (6.30pm-9.30pm Sundays). Main courses £9.50-£22.50; set lunch £14.95 & £17.95.
closed	Monday lunchtimes. Open all day.

Barnaby Meredith
The House,
63-69 Canonbury Road, Islington,
London N1 2DG
tel 020 7704 7410
web www.inthehouse.biz

map: 4 entry: 310

The Duke of Cambridge
Islington

Geetie Singh is on a mission to raise people's awareness of food and where it comes from. At the Duke, the first all-organic London pub, 'organic' and 'sustainable' are the watchwords and British rustic the style. Wines, beers, spirits are certified organic and they buy as locally as they can to cut down on food miles. Most of the beers are brewed in nearby Shoreditch, meat comes from two farms, fish is purchased from sustainable sources. Impeccable produce, not a whiff of self-righteousness and menus that change twice a day. And you can smoke in the bar. It's a sprawling, airy space with a comfortable, easy, shoestring minimalism; take your fill of herring fillets with braised puy lentils and grain mustard sauce, venison steak with redcurrant jus, crusty bread, fruity olive oil, chocolate tart – in here, or in the big non-smoking restaurant. Recent reports suggest staff are less obliging than they could be.

directions	Nearest tube: Angel.
meals	12.30pm-3pm (3.30pm Saturday & Sunday); 6.30pm-10.30pm (10pm Sunday). Main courses £9.50-£16.
closed	Open all day.

Geetie Singh
The Duke of Cambridge,
30 St Peter's Street, Islington,
London N1 8JT

tel	020 7359 3066
web	www.dukeorganic.co.uk

map: 4 entry: 311

London

The Crown & Goose
Camden

You might wonder where the border lies between bohemian and unkempt and some would argue that this popular little pub lies on the wrong side. However, the laid-back inhabitants of Camden Town (where Dickens had Bob Cratchit live) don't mind one bit... people are as happy here browsing the papers as gossiping with friends. There's one big room with an elaborate wooden bar and a vaguely Victorian mishmash of tables, sofas and chairs, an open fire and music in the background. Walls are largely bare but carry the odd piece of art; look out for an unusual bronze. Service is exuberant and warm, the beer plentiful and well-priced, the food modern British. Tuck in, upstairs (must book) or down, to delicious renditions of wild-boar sausages with roasted vegetables and beetroot and apple relish; and Cuban burgers with jalapeno salad. Some say the chips are the best in town.

directions	Nearest tube: Camden Town.
meals	12pm-3pm; 6pm-10pm; 12pm-10pm Fridays & Saturdays (9pm Sundays). Main courses £8-£10.
closed	Open all day.

Joe Lowry
The Crown & Goose,
100 Arlington Road,
Camden,
London NW1 7HP

tel	020 7485 8008

map: 4 entry: 312

London

The Lansdowne
Primrose Hill

The buzzy Lansdowne is worth crossing postcodes for. Amanda Pritchett was one of the founders of the trail-blazing Eagle; later she set up the Lansdowne and followed a similar gastropub route. It's laid-back, open-plan and atmospherically lit, with big wooden tables and dark green décor – and manages, at least downstairs, to keep its pubby feel, in spite of the emphasis on dining. Upstairs is an elegant and charming 60-seat restaurant where a trendy crowd is treated to adventurous food – Jerusalem artichoke and red onion risotto, sea bass en papillotte, belly of pork with mash and shallots, paprika squid. Though the serious dining goes on up here, you can also eat down where the decibels are high, the atmosphere shambolic and everyone loves the pizzas (kids included). There are two draught ales and one real cider, but really this is a wine, lager and olives place. Outside in summer is a little oasis to which you can retreat and leave the city behind.

London

The Engineer
Primrose Hill

Victorian superstar Isambard Kingdom Brunel, whose silhouette decks the sign, once had an office here. Today the place is run by a painter and an actress. Behind the half-stuccoed 1850 edifice lies a cheerful, friendly gastropub with a smart bohemian feel and an outstanding reputation for food. It is particularly strong on fish cooked with a touch of the Mediterranean – sea bass with minted couscous and aubergine relish, say – but there are organic rib-eye with bearnaise, fat homemade chips and creamy and chocolately desserts to swoon over too. Wines look to the New World and beer is excellent. Eat up or down: the front bar is relaxed, bright and buzzing, the restaurant upstairs has white plates on white cloths, mirrors in gilt frames and art for sale. In summer, the large lush garden catches the sun. There's a good mixed crowd here though the majority are hip and young. The service is often praised, and the parking is easy.

directions	Nearest tube: Chalk Farm.
meals	12pm-3pm; 7pm-10pm. Main courses £8-£15.
closed	Monday lunchtimes. Open all day.

Amanda Pritchett
The Lansdowne,
90 Gloucester Avenue,
Primrose Hill,
London NW1 8HX
tel 020 7483 0409

map: 4 entry: 313

directions	Nearest tube: Camden Town.
meals	All day menu 9am-11pm. Main courses £10.95-£16.25.
closed	Open all day.

Karen Northcote
The Engineer,
65 Gloucester Avenue,
Primrose Hill, London NW1 8JH
tel 020 7722 0950
web www.the-engineer.com

map: 4 entry: 314

London

The Salt House
St John's Wood

A mere scuttle from the Beatles' zebra crossing, the Salt House brings a bit of sleepy Suffolk to the metropolis. The meats are rare breed, the day-boat fish is caught by Andy in Looe and practically everything is homemade. Head chef Enrico Sartor is Sardinian and his team Italian, so the occasional swearing from the kitchen will seem lyrical and exotic. The homemade pastas, bread and seafood dishes are genuinely superb. The ale is by Greene King, the wine list is excellent value and wide-ranging. The building is 18th century, quaintly listing and utterly beautiful. Lofty, intricate, 200-year-old windows, scrubbed wooden tables and leather sofas make the bar a cosy, stylish space. The function room has a roaring open fire; so has the restaurant at the back, secluded and elegant. Add the outside tables with awnings, heaters and space and you have one special pub.

London

Dartmouth Arms
Dartmouth Park

The pub has style *and* a sense of humour. Sitting unobtrusively in a Highgate side street the Dartmouth Arms may look smart but unexceptional but inside is another story. There's huge personality – and the predominant theme is copper: in water pipes, bar top and mirror frames. In the back room there's bold kitsch in a copper statue, fish in a TV-set tank and champagne bottles hanging from a chandelier. Furnishings are chic: a pine bar, black padded chairs, half-panelled walls painted vibrant red. Landlord Nick is passionate about food and beer. There are three perfectly kept cask ales, a mind-boggling choice of ciders, ten wines by the glass and a modern British menu displayed on copper boards. There's food for everyone here: roast vegetable and goat's cheese tart, leek and Caerphilly sausages with tomato sauce and mash, pan-fried organic salmon and Spanish, English and Greek platters. The background music is noisy at times and the pub attracts a lively crowd.

directions	Nearest tube: Maida Vale.
meals	10am–10pm. Main courses £8.95–£18.95.
closed	Open all day.

Ryder Butler & Charles Leatham
The Salt House,
63 Abbey Road,
St John's Wood,
London NW8 0AE
tel 020 7328 6626

map: 4 entry: 315

directions	Nearest tube: Tufnell Park.
meals	11am–10pm (from 10am Saturdays & Sundays). Main courses from £7.
closed	Open all day.

Nick May
Dartmouth Arms,
35 York Rise, Dartmouth Park,
London NW5 1SP
tel 020 7485 3267
web www.dartmoutharms.co.uk

map: 4 entry: 316

The Junction Tavern
Kentish Town

From the stainless-steel, open-to-view kitchen flows food that is modern European and wide-ranging – from roast belly pork with bacon, black pudding and prune and brandy jus to Spanish-style seafood stew with aïoli. The daily menu is market-based and well-priced, particularly at weekday lunchtimes when main courses are pleasingly affordable. Word has spread: at weekends you book; the place heaves. Young staff are friendly and attitude-free. The interior is high-ceilinged, corniced, wood-panelled, with big leather sofas and an open fire. While half the pub is restaurant, the rest is old-fashioned bar, serving beers (note the August beer festival) and good wines. Enjoy a fresh glass of manzanilla in the garden in summer (or in winter, thanks to the heaters), or in the conservatory in spring. Jacky Kitching and partner Chris Leech have a background in restaurants and their experience shows.

Holly Bush
Hampstead

Down a Hampstead cul-de-sac the faithful flock. The stables once owned by painter George Romney have become a hugely loved pub. A labyrinth of corridors leads to cosy corners, painted settles and big tables set with board games and pints of Harvey's Sussex. Ale rules at the Holly Bush, where chef Marco cooks not with wine but with beer. The open-hatched kitchen is centre-stage, the aromas of beef and Harvey's pie proving a sore temptation for drinkers to become diners. Adnam's rarebit – followed, possibly, by hot chocolate, marmalade and malt whisky fondant – is set to educate the beer lover's palate. Dishes are seasonal and fresh, with game and organic meat from Winchelsea and a superb selection of English cheeses. Upstairs in the dining room, elegant with pistachio walls, wooden floors and fresh lilies, the celebration of all things British continues – in style.

directions	Nearest tubes: Kentish Town; Tufnell Park.
meals	12pm-3pm (4pm weekends); 6.30pm-10.30pm (9.30pm Sundays). Main courses £9.50-£14.50.
closed	Open all day.

	Jacky Kitching & Chris Leech The Junction Tavern, 101 Fortess Road, Kentish Town, London NW5 1AG
tel	020 7485 9400
web	www.junctiontavern.co.uk

map: 4 entry: 317

directions	Nearest tube: Hampstead.
meals	12.30pm-4pm; 6.30pm-10pm (Saturday 12.30pm-10pm, 9pm Sunday). Main courses £5-£15.
closed	Open all day.

	Nicolai Outzen Holly Bush, 22 Holly Mount, Hampstead, London NW3 6SG
tel	020 7435 2892

map: 4 entry: 318

The Flask
Highgate

The Flask's lights gleam so invitingly you can see why Dick Turpin stopped off with his horse. (He's also supposed to have hidden in the cellars.) Thirsty travellers now enjoy Fuller's Jack Frost from an array of real ales, where beer pulls are marked with handwritten labels and you choose between tankard and glass. The warren of little rooms may be 350 years old but its candlelit nooks and crannies have a modern feel. A vaulted sitting area with high chopping board tables and handmade paper lamps makes for a friendly place in which to indulge in stylish takes on old pub favourites: a pint jug of Atlantic shell-on prawns, homemade sausages with parsnip mash, handmade pies and sticky toffee pudding with toffee sauce. In summer, locals and walkers from Hampstead Heath come for outdoor barbecues, while 'doggie treats' invigorate weary pets from behind the bar. Much loved, mobbed in summer, it can be hard to find a free table.

The Bull
Highgate

A meeting place for friends, colleagues, families; something for everyone here. The plain listed Georgian façade gives way to an inspired interior – coffee-coloured leather banquettes, cream walls, painted bullfights – and the menu, too, unveils hidden surprises. The knowledgeable staff will be happy to advise on wine and food; head chef Jeremy Hollingsworth – ex Quo Vadis – transforms fresh, seasonal and high quality ingredients into rustic-simple dishes that have huge depth of flavour. Leave the aromas behind and ascend the twisting stair, its walls strikingly embellished with animal silhouettes, to the first-floor cherry wood bar – sleek yet pub-cosy. Fall into a fat luxurious sofa and melt into the fire, catch Sky Sport on the large flat-screen TV, try your hand at a vintage American pool table. Barnaby Meredith's latest venture (his first was The House in Islington) is a vibrant and chic retreat.

directions	Nearest tube/rail: Archway; Highgate.
meals	12pm–3pm; 5pm–10pm; 12pm–10pm Saturday (9.30pm Sunday). Main courses £7–£14.50.
closed	Open all day.

Ena O'Neil
The Flask,
77 Highgate West Hill,
Highgate, London N6 6BU

| tel | 020 8348 7346 |
| web | www.theflaskhighgate.com |

map: 4 entry: 319

directions	Nearest tube: Highgate.
meals	12pm–2.30pm (3.30pm weekends); 6pm–10.30pm. Main courses £11.95–£16.95; set lunch £14.95 & £17.95.
closed	Monday lunchtimes. Open all day.

Barnaby Meredith
The Bull,
13 North Hill, Highgate,
London N6 4AB

| tel | 0845 456 5033 |
| web | www.inthebull.biz |

map: 4 entry: 320

Manchester

The Bridge
Manchester

Beneath Manchester's rapidly developing skyline stands this haven. The Bridge has morphed from ugly-duckling city tavern into wood-and-brass gastropub, and chef-patron Robert Owen Brown's ceaseless quest for organic and local raw materials has resulted in some accomplished cooking. Gorge on black pudding, spring onion and dry-cure bacon duck egg omelette — topped with Mrs Kirkham's tasty Lancashire cheese — in the laid-back, half-panelled bar, sprinkled with sofas and loafers and a generous display of potted plants. Or decant to the secluded, candlelit restaurant area for a sampling of Robert's renowned game dish of the day. Expect decorative fire-blacked and tile fireplaces, contemporary paintings and hangings, cream and crimson brick walls, easy-on-the-ear music — and busy staff ferrying dishes and braces of real ale to movers, shakers and shoppers in the city's vibrant heart.

directions	Near the Crown Courts, People's History Museum & Salford Central Station.
meals	12pm-3pm; 5.30pm-9pm; 12pm-5pm Sundays. Main courses £8.95-£13.95.
closed	Sunday evenings; bank holidays. Open all day.

	Robert Owen Brown The Bridge, 58 Bridge Street, Manchester M3 3BW
tel	0161 834 0242
web	www.thebridgemanchester.co.uk

map: 12 entry: 321

Merseyside

The Baltic Fleet
Liverpool

Alone on a dockland corner, this landlocked Fleet's Victorian fabric remains unchanged with no concessions to poshness — and people like it that way. The small marble-topped bar counter is crammed with handpumps (most ferrying beers brewed in the engine room below) and furnishings are engagingly timeworn: settles, plain chairs, marble-topped tables. Two rooms beyond offer more comfort. The first has a lunchtime servery for baguettes, toasties and Scouse soup, its walls lined with pictures of Liverpool's past and Simon Holt's forebears — traders and shipowners when the Baltic was built. The second is a snug in the 'bows' with that Liver Building view; hole up here in front of the fire and imagine sailors swapping tales. An honest outpost with cheerful, hard-working staff; the more engaging the longer you stay.

directions	Liverpool city centre, opposite Albert Dock.
meals	12pm-2.30pm Monday-Friday. Bar meals £2.50-£3.95.
closed	Open all day.

	Simon Holt & Mark Yates The Baltic Fleet, 33a Wapping, Liverpool, Merseyside L1 8DQ
tel	0151 7093116
web	www.wappingbeers.co.uk

map: 11 entry: 322

Merseyside

The Philharmonic
Liverpool

The Phil was built by Liverpool brewers Robert Cain & Co in the style of a gentlemen's club: a place for bodily refreshment after the aesthetic excitements of the Philharmonic Hall opposite. There's ornate Victorian extravagance at every turn, impossibly high ceilings, elaborate embellishment, etched glass; the gents is decked in marble and mosaic, its porcelain fittings of historical importance. Sweep through the columned entrance into the imposing, mosaic-tiled central bar, gawp at the scale. Beyond, a succession of small rooms and snugs separated by mahogany partitions, then a Grand Lounge with a stately frieze and table service for lunch: settle down to baked potatoes or fish and chips. In spite of the remarkable surroundings the Philharmonic is very popular with students. It is a great pub serving excellent beers, wines and whiskies and a huge dose of cheer.

directions	City centre; between the cathedrals at corner of Hardman Street.
meals	12pm-6pm (3pm in summer); 12pm-3pm weekends (5.30pm in summer). Main courses £4.95-£7.95.
closed	Open all day.

Marie-Louise Wong
The Philharmonic,
36 Hope Street,
Liverpool,
Merseyside L1 9BX
tel   0151 7072837

map: 11 entry: 323

Norfolk

The Wildebeest Arms
Stoke Holy Cross

In the 1990s Henry Watt decided to introduce good food to this country inn – a rarity then. Now the Wildebeest Arms is one of the most popular dining pubs in Norfolk. The 19th-century building may look no great shakes, but the atmosphere is special. Sympathetically modernised to create one long room split by a central bar, there are rich yellow walls, dark oak beams, fresh flowers on polished tables, a roaring fire and an African theme to match the pub's name. Ales include Adnams, there's a choice of wines by the glass alongside an interesting list, and the menu is up-to-the-minute with everything freshly made. Tuck into the rich delights of pot-roast duck breast with cocotte potatoes, crispy Alsace lardon and sautéed cabbage with redcurrant jus. Chef Daniel Smith may enjoy a bit of leonine bravura, but he is equally at home with old English favourites like sausage and mash and sticky toffee pudding.

directions	Off A140, 3 miles south of Norwich.
meals	12pm-2pm; 7pm-10pm. Main courses £9.95-£18.50; set menus £14.95 & £18.50.

Henry Watt
The Wildebeest Arms,
82-86 Norwich Road,
Stoke Holy Cross, Norwich,
Norfolk NR14 8QJ
tel   01508 492497

map: 10 entry: 324

King's Head
Bawburgh

Norwich is just over the hill, but you'd never know it: pretty Bawburgh stands in rural seclusion, straddling the idly flowing river Yare, an old mill and the 17th-century King's Head at its heart. Unprepossessing, yet with a distinctive terracotta façade, Anton Wimmer's old pub is full of charm. Head-cracking low beams, thick upright timbers, bulging walls and big blazing fires blend well with wooden floors, sunny yellow walls and contemporary squashy sofas and chairs in the refurbished bar areas. John's a bit of a whizz in the kitchen, baking bread from local organic flour and using local game, meats and seafood in imaginative menus. There's braised oxtail with horseradish and dumplings at lunch, and Suffolk ham, hand-cut chips and free range eggs. In the evening, splash out on marinated scallops and confit of duck. Further delights are East Anglian beers, a mind-boggling choice of wines by the glass, piped jazz and a heated terrace.

Saracen's Head
Wolterton

Real ale, fine food, good wines, a delightful courtyard and walled garden, Norfolk's bleakly lovely coast – this is why people come. But the food is the deepest seduction. Typical starters are Morston mussels with cider and cream, or fricassée of wild mushrooms. Expect Cromer crab, venison and local game; vegetarians will be pampered with baked avocado with sweet pear and mozzarella. Then Robert works his magic on old favourites such as treacle tart. In this 1806 coaching inn modelled on a Tuscan farmhouse, the bar is as convivial as a bar could be. There's a parlour room for residents, with a big open-brick fireplace, deep red walls, colourful plastic tablecloths and candles in old wine bottles. Bedrooms have bold colours, sisal floors and linen curtains – in keeping with the quality of the food. The whole mood is of quirky, committed individuality, in the middle of nowhere.

directions	Off B1108 (Watton Road) west of Norwich, 1 mile from A47.
meals	12pm-2.30pm (12.30pm-4pm Sun); 6.30pm-9.30pm. No food Sun & Mon eves. Main courses £10.50-£17.50; bar meals £7-£12.50.
closed	Open all day.

directions	From A140, signs for Erpingham. Pass church; follow road to Carthorpe & Wolterton.
meals	12.30pm-2.15pm; 7.15pm-9pm. Main courses £10-£15.
rooms	6: 5 doubles, 1 twin £85. Singles £45.
closed	3.30pm-6pm (7pm Sunday).

See page 35 for bedroom details.

Anton Wimmer
King's Head,
Harts Lane, Bawburgh,
Norwich, Norfolk NR9 3LS
tel   01603 744977
web   www.kingshead-bawburgh.co.uk

Robert Dawson-Smith
Saracen's Head,
Wolterton, Erpingham,
Norfolk NR11 7LZ
tel   01263 768909
web   www.saracenshead-norfolk.co.uk

map: 10 entry: 325

map: 10 entry: 326

The Walpole Arms
Itteringham

Enjoying fine food and wine is an adventure, a voyage of discovery – so says Richard Bryan, ex-producer of 'Masterchef', co-owner of this famous Norfolk pub. Exploration, one assumes, carries less guilt than indulgence. Sweating over a hot stove is Andy Parle, once head chef to Alastair Little. His daily menus are utterly seasonal and delight in fresh local produce – Cromer crab, Morston mussels, venison from the Gunton estate, farm-fresh fruits and vegetables – and typically take in fish soup with rouille, lamb shank with baked ratatouille and dauphinoise, confit duck leg with borlotti beans, chorizo, fennel and tomato, and pear and frangipane tart. You can eat in the bar, with rough brick walls, beamed ceilings, standing timbers and big open fire, or in the stylish dining room. There are fine East Anglian ales from Adnams and Woodfordes, a first-class list of wines, and masses of outside space for kids.

The Anchor
Morston

Taste the salty sea – Morston mussels, Thornham oysters, Blakeney crab – and wash it down with Norwich's Winter Brewery Golden ale... or just a nice cup of Royal tea. All a village pub should be, this flintwork and whitewashed building on the popular coast road does the north Norfolk shores proud. It's a warren of intimate, loved and lived-in rooms, each with its own story to tell: cheery jade green walls, a random collection of tables and chairs, bedpans, old fishing pics and faded newspaper clippings. There's even a cosy old 'front room' resplendent with stuffed birds and armchairs. Around every corner are enthusiastic birders, chattering locals and relaxed tourists lapping it up. Honest pub cooking with fine local ingredients matches the decent beers and inexpensive wines. On a sunny day stretch out in the secluded beer garden, drawing deeply on the bracing air. Book a seal trip while you sup.

directions	From Aylsham towards Blickling, then 1st right to Itteringham.
meals	12pm-2pm (2.30pm Sundays); 7pm-9pm. Main courses £8.50-£16.
closed	4pm-7pm Sunday.

Richard Bryan
The Walpole Arms,
The Common, Itteringham,
Norwich, Norfolk NR11 7AR

tel	01263 587258
web	www.thewalpolearms.co.uk

map: 10 entry: 327

directions	In the centre of Morston on the A149, 2 miles west of Blakeney.
meals	12pm-2.30pm; 6pm-9pm; 12pm-8pm Sundays. Main courses £8.95-£18.95.
closed	Open all day.

Nick Handley
The Anchor,
The Street, Morston, Holt,
Norfolk NR25 7AA

tel	01263 741392
web	www.glavenvalley.co.uk

map: 10 entry: 328

White Horse Hotel
Blakeney

The smart hub of this small coastal village attracts its share of switched-on custom; Blakeney is the jewel in north Norfolk's crown. The lamp-lit windows of the bar beckon; Adnams Bitter and Woodforde's Wherry are served to those in search of a pint. But stay for more: dressed local crab, filled ciabattas, sea bass with crayfish butter and rocket salad are all served in the polished bar, while local Cley Smokehouse smoked salmon, Morston mussels and seasonal ingredients are given a decidedly contemporary treatment in the sunny-coloured restaurant. With its airy conservatory and sheltered courtyard, Dan Goff's friendly inn is a pleasant place to rest weary limbs following a bracing coast path walk. At the bottom of the steep, narrow high street are marshes of sea lavender, mudflats with samphire and natural mussel beds; there are skylarks and redshanks, and seals a ferry ride away.

Carpenter's Arms
Wighton

Locals and visitors love this pub for all the right reasons: good beer, good food and a popular landlord. It looks modest enough from the outside – three knocked-together cottages in traditional knicker-pink render. But a courageous hand with the paint pot has transformed the interior: a jolly blue in the hallway, tables and chairs painted terracotta, navy and duck-egg blue, and luscious walls in a dining room that would make Barbie blink. Kelims, leather-style sofas and a pyrex bowl of grapefruit create a happy mish-mash of textures; a huge, double-sided woodburner heats the bar and dining room (in summer there's a grassy sun-trap round the back, with picnic tables). A pint of well-kept Nelson's Revenge slips down a treat with chicken liver parfait and red onion marmalade, and the cream of tomato soup is properly homemade. 'Frankie' the landlord, well-known from the Hoste Arms in Burnham Market, is a delight to meet.

directions	Just up from quay, in village; off A149 10 miles west of Sheringham.
meals	12pm-2.15pm (bar meals only); 6pm-9pm. Main courses £10.95-£18.95; bar meals £7.95-£12.95.
closed	1 week in January.

directions	Village signed off A149 at Wells-next-the-Sea.
meals	12pm-2.30pm (6pm Sunday); 7pm-9pm. No food Sunday evenings. Main courses £7.95-£12.95.
closed	Open all day.

Dan Goff
White Horse Hotel,
4 High Street, Blakeney,
Norfolk NR25 7AL
tel 01263 740574
web www.blakeneywhitehorse.co.uk

Stephen Franklin
Carpenter's Arms,
High Street, Wighton,
Wells-next-the-Sea,
Norfolk NR23 1PF
tel 01328 820752

map: 10 entry: 329

map: 10 entry: 330

The Lord Nelson
Burnham Thorpe

Once The Plough, the pub changed its name two years after the Battle of Trafalgar to commemorate Burnham Thorpe's most famous son (Nelson threw a dinner for the village here to celebrate his return to sea). It hasn't changed a great deal in 400 years: ancient benches and settles, worn brick, tile floors, a serving hatch instead of a bar, distinguish this marvellous place. If a tot of Nelson's Blood (a devilish concoction of 100 percent proof rum and spices) doesn't tempt, order a pint of Woodforde's or Greene King tapped from the cask. Nelson memorabilia reaches into every corner of the small, characterful rooms – and into the Victory Barn restaurant where the annual Trafalgar Night Dinner is held on October 21st before an open fire. All in all, a unique local asset, with a family-friendly garden, imaginative food (red mullet with roast peppers and cointreau cream) and a past that is well respected by licensees David and Penny Thorley.

directions	Off A149, B1155 & B1355; 2 miles south of Burnham Market.
meals	12pm-2pm; 7pm-9pm. No food Sunday evenings. Main courses £8.95-£18.95.
closed	Mondays in winter.

David & Penny Thorley
The Lord Nelson,
Walsingham Rd, Burnham Thorpe,
Kings Lynn, Norfolk PE31 8HN

tel	01328 738241
web	www.nelsonslocal.co.uk

map: 10 entry: 331

Globe Inn
Wells-next-the-Sea

The renovation of the Globe on pretty, leafy Buttlands Green has been masterminded by the owners of the Victoria at Holkham. Now the old coaching inn has two bars and a restaurant that serves unstuffy modern food: spring lamb with fresh asparagus, grilled lemon sole, venison and (rare treat) wild partridge from the Holkham estate. On sunny days you can take your plates and your pints (Adnams and Woodfordes) out into the large and sunny courtyard; in winter, settle in to the atmospheric 'new' bar – a warm mish-mash of old furniture, big woodburner and antique lighting. Children and dogs like it here too, what with child-size pies and walkies on the hugest beach ever. Sunday brunch is fun and the bedrooms are as fresh and as un-traditional as can be, gleaming with oak floors, powerful showers and digital TVs.

directions	In the centre of Wells-next-the-Sea.
meals	12pm-2.30pm; 6.30pm-9.30pm; 12pm-8pm Sunday. Main courses £7.95-£10.95; bar meals from £4.
rooms	7: 5 doubles, 2 twins £55-£115.
closed	Open all day.

See page 35 for bedroom details.

Tom Coke
Globe Inn,
The Buttlands, Wells-next-the-Sea,
Norfolk NR23 1EU

tel	01328 710206
web	www.globeatwells.co.uk

map: 10 entry: 332

Norfolk

Crown Hotel
Wells-next-the-Sea

The interior of this handsome 16th-century coaching inn has been neatly rationalised yet is still atmospheric with its open fires, bare boards and easy chairs. And it's run by an enterprising landlord who knows how to cook. Order pub food at the bar and eat it in the lounges, the lovely modern conservatory or the Sun Deck: a hearty serving of Brancaster mussels, perhaps, with locally brewed Adnams Bitter. Bold colours, modern art and attractively laid tables give life to the restaurant too, where local ingredients are translated into global ideas: flash fried squid with bacon and black pudding; cod with ginger, lemongrass and lime; Thai marinated duck with seared scallops and chilli jam. A happy, relaxed place, with a welcome for dogs and families too. Beaches and bracing salt marsh walks are only minutes away.

directions	On B1105, 10 miles north of Fakenham.
meals	12pm-2.30pm; 6.30pm-9.30pm. Main courses £8.50-£14; set menu £29.95.
closed	Open all day.

Chris Coubrough
Crown Hotel,
The Buttlands, Wells-next-the-Sea,
Norfolk NR23 1EX

tel 01328 710209
web www.thecrownhotelwells.co.uk

Norfolk

The Victoria
Holkham

Tom and Polly (Viscount and Viscountess) Coke took on the pub on the family's estate a few years ago. The building is early 19th century and the interior is exotic. Stone flags and polished floors, velvet sofas and leather armchairs, huge bowls of fruit, a buzzing bar, a feel of anticipation... It functions best in summer: walkers come straight off Holkham beach and into the courtyard or garden for barbecues and a pint of Woodforde's Wherry. In a dining room redolent with lilies, unobtrusive young staff ferry in crabs from Cromer, game from the estate and great steaming nursery puddings; children get their own two-course menu. There are serene bedrooms upstairs, some with views to marsh and sea, and three luscious lodges in the grounds. Sands and skylarks are a stroll away – at their finest out of season.

directions	On A149, 2 miles west of Wells-next-the-Sea.
meals	12pm-2.30pm; 7pm-9.30pm. Main courses £7-£16.
rooms	10 + 3: 9 doubles, 1 attic suite £110-£200. Singles £90-£110. 3 self-catering lodges £160-£200 (max. 4).
closed	Open all day.

See page 35 for bedroom details.

Paul Brown
The Victoria,
Park Road, Holkham,
Norfolk NR23 1RG

tel 01328 711008
web www.victoriaatholkham.co.uk

The Hoste Arms
Burnham Market

As the brochure says, pub and owner are made for each other (that's Paul they are talking about): "both have struggled to avoid being popular country attractions". Brilliantly too – The Hoste has won almost every prize going. It's a luxurious place that has a genius of its own – successful mixtures of bold colour, sofas to sink into, panelled walls, an art gallery, log fires, a real buzz. And food to delight, anywhere and anytime. The 'modern British with Pacific Rim influences' menu changes every five weeks – partridge with butternut squash and liquorice sauce, roasted ham hock, Burnham Creek oysters, spiced bream. The Burnhams comprise seven villages on the north Norfolk coast of which Burnham Market is the loveliest. And it is perfectly placed for some of the most unspoilt coastline in north Norfolk.

King's Head
Great Bircham

If you fancy urban sleek in the wilds of Norfolk, come to this grand, white-fronted Victorian pub with a snazzy makeover. The reception area is über-modern Soho: spotlighting, suede sofas, iconic flower art. The bar has a sleek satin metal counter, dark wood, green tweed, designer logs. But it's a friendly place for a simple pint of Woodforde's Wherry, or a glass of rosé accompanied by smoked haddock kedgeree. The restaurant is all striped banquettes and dark wood tables – and summer dining in the smart courtyard – with chef Ben Handley serving modern British food with a cosmopolitan flourish: Thornham oysters or marinated venison, seared Szechuan tuna with a sushi roll and pickled Vietnamese coleslaw. If you're staying, the bedrooms are swish – enormous beds, flat-screen TVs, a decanter of port as well as a mini-bar, and a welcome-you-in plate of home-baked biscuits.

directions	Village centre, on B1153 between A148 at Hillington & Brancaster.
meals	12pm-2pm; 7pm-9pm. Main courses £9.75-£15.10.
rooms	9 doubles £125-£175. Singles £69.50.
closed	Open 7am-11pm.

See page 35 for bedroom details.

directions	By green & church in village centre.
meals	12pm-2pm; 7pm-9pm. Main courses £8.95-£16.50.
closed	Open all day.

P. & J. Whittome & E. Tagg
The Hoste Arms,
The Green, Burnham Market,
Norfolk PE31 8HD

tel	01328 738777
web	www.hostearms.co.uk

Carrie Harvey
King's Head,
Great Bircham, King's Lynn,
Norfolk PE31 6RJ

tel	01485 578265
web	www.the-kings-head-bircham.co.uk

map: 10 entry: 335

map: 10 entry: 336

The White Horse
Brancaster Staithe

Enter the dapper white pub, pass the front bar – lively with locals enjoying East Anglian ales – and head for the conservatory restaurant with its astonishing views. The White Horse is chic with muted tones, driftwood finds, contemporary paintings and fresh flowers. Local oysters, crabs, mussels and fish – maybe baked bream with a cassoulet of puy lentils – are matched by exemplary steaks, lamb and pork. Bedrooms in a wavy extension facing the tidal marshes and North Norfolk Coastal Path have generous proportions and a patio each; the roof is grassed over so that the fine-weather sun deck, dining room and some of the main house bedrooms (ask for the split-level room at the top, with telescope) have a clean view all the way to Scolt Head Island. Huge sunsets, fine food, big breakfasts, and a proper welcome for children and dogs.

directions	On A149 between Hunstanton & Wells-next-the-Sea.
meals	12pm-2pm; 7pm-9.15pm. Bar food 2.30pm-4pm weekends; 6.30pm-9pm Sun-Thurs. Main courses £9.75-£15.95.
rooms	15: 9 doubles, 6 twin £100-£115.
closed	Open all day.

See page 36 for bedroom details.

Cliff Nye
The White Horse,
Main Road, Brancaster Staithe,
Norfolk PE31 8BY

| tel | 01485 210262 |
| web | www.whitehorsebrancaster.co.uk |

map: 10 entry: 337

The Orange Tree
Thornham

Up a notch or three from your average watering hole, this place knows what a contemporary foodie pub should be. From funky wicker fencing fronting the garden to sage-splashed walls, the approach from the village green says it all. Step inside – to chunky seagrass floors, light wood, bright walls and log-stuffed fireplaces. Snuggle up at a cheeky *table à deux* at the bar, or retire to one of two relaxed dining rooms. There's a faint waft of Norfolk 'money' on the air, but something for everyone on the Ivy-esque menu – from crisp confit pork belly to a perfect cheeseburger. This is a fabulous area for food, and the pub sources locally and well. Spitfire, Tiger and IPA Greene King are on handpump, and the wine list does a decent job, mostly mid-market and New World. Children have an up-market play area... come for urban chic, a particularly happy feel and great food.

directions	On A149 in village centre; from Hunstanton, pub on left-hand side.
meals	12pm-2.30pm; 6.30pm-9pm (9.30pm Fridays & Saturdays); 12pm-6pm Sundays. Main courses £8.25-£12.95; bar meals from £4.50.
closed	Open all day.

Chris Hinde
The Orange Tree,
High Street, Thornham,
Hunstanton, Norfolk PE36 6LY

| tel | 01485 512213 |
| web | www.theorangetreethornham.co.uk |

map: 9 entry: 338

Gin Trap Inn
Ringstead

Locate the champion conker tree and spot the plough shares above the door. Deep in lazy lavender country, the 17th-century coaching house is a trendy, touristy place popular with all: visitors, families and ladies that lunch. You may sit out at the front on a fine day and watch the world go by, or relax in the sunny walled garden. Inside is a bold décor: gin-trap light fittings, dark green carpets, low black beams and a crackling log fire in winter; in the restaurant, softer coffee and cream hues, church candles and linen napkins. Grilled puffballs grab your eye on the menu, along with local pumpkin and pesto soup, beer-battered haddock, and irresistible bread and butter pudding. Chef Simon Reynolds has an impressive pedigree, and the wines are pleasing, as are the real ales – Adnams, Woodforde's Wherry, guest ales. Once replete, head for the car park and browse the art gallery there.

directions	Ringstead signed off A149 at Heacham, north of King's Lynn; pub on right along High Street.
meals	12pm-2pm (2.30pm Saturdays & Sundays); 6pm-9pm (9.30pm Fridays & Saturdays). Main courses £9-£18; bar meals from £5.
closed	Open all day in summer.

Don & Margaret Greer
Gin Trap Inn,
High Street, Ringstead,
Hunstanton, Norfolk PE36 5JU

tel	01485 525264
web	www.gintrapinn.co.uk

map: 9 entry: 339

The Rose & Crown
Snettisham

Roses round the door and twisting passages within, it is gloriously English. Homemade burgers with red onion relish and fish and chips with minted mushy peas (delicious) should please the traditionalists, but the menu soon spirals into the dizzy realms of pressed wild salmon with caviar cream, or seared calf's liver with fried polenta, baby gem lettuce and fig vinaigrette. It's great value. In spite of 30 wines on the list, half available by the glass, the Rose & Crown is still proud to be a pub; fine beers on handpump and a hands-on feel. The walled garden was once the village bowling green and children will like the wooden play fort and the weeping willows. Inside, a warren of rooms filled with old beams and log fires, a family-friendly garden room, and a flurry of delightfully stylish bedrooms.

directions	Village signed off A149 north of King's Lynn; pub on side street off main village road.
meals	12pm-2pm (2.30pm weekends); 6pm-9pm (9.30pm Fri & Sat). Main courses £8.95-£14.75; bar meals from £4.75.
rooms	16 twins/doubles £85-£95. Singles £50-£65.
closed	Open all day.

See page 36 for bedroom details.

Anthony & Jeannette Goodrich
The Rose & Crown,
Old Church Road, Snettisham,
King's Lynn, Norfolk PE31 7LX

tel	01485 541382
web	www.roseandcrownsnettisham.co.uk

map: 9 entry: 340

The Falcon
Oundle

The Falcon is a smashing place serving wonderful food. Discreetly, stylishly modernised, it keeps its pubby feel – darts in the tap bar, an open fire in the main bar and well-kept Adnams on handpump. The extras are undoubtedly spoiling: high-back tapestry-covered chairs, candlelight and fresh flowers. Richard III was born in Fotheringhay Castle and Mary Queen of Scots was executed here; now the castle is a mound, but the medieval church is worth a visit and the Falcon picks up on the history in the prints in the bar. For a change of mood, head for the elegant, double conservatory with its impressive church views; it has the same monthly-changing menu and a more contemporary feel: light and open, with Lloyd Loom chairs. Ray Smikle's cooking is stylishly simple, whether it's Portland crab salad, roast monkfish with salsa verde, chargrilled Dexter beef with horseradish butter or caramelised lemon tart. Wines are as good, with a tempting 18 by the glass. *No smoking throughout.*

directions	Off A605 4 miles NE of Oundle.
meals	12pm-2pm; 6.30pm-9.30pm.
	Main courses £9.95-£14.95.

	Ray Smikle & John Hoskins
	The Falcon,
	Fotheringhay, Oundle,
	Peterborough, PE8 5HZ
tel	01832 226254
web	www.huntsbridge.com

map: 9 entry: 341

The Queen's Head
Bulwick

A mellow old stone pub in a lovely village – you'll wish this was your local. The simple beamed and flagstoned bar rambles into several country-styled dining rooms, all nooks and crannies, bright walls and fresh flowers. This may be the owners' first pub venture, but their natural friendliness and instinct to keep things simple has worked in their favour. Bar food features the very good Grassmere Farm ham with local free range eggs, or try a steak and stilton toasted sandwich with hand-cut chips washed down with Rockingham Ales from the village microbrewery. The short à la carte menu is full of more extravagant enticements: chicken and goat's cheese wantons; trio of salmon, cod and sea bass; confit of belly pork with pea purée, black pudding and grainy mustard jus.

directions	Just off A43, between Stamford & Corby.
meals	12pm-2.30pm; 6pm-9.30pm.
	No food Sunday evenings.
	Main courses £9.95-£13.95.
closed	Mondays.

	Geoff Smith & Angela Partridge
	The Queen's Head,
	Main Street,
	Bulwick, Corby,
	Northamptonshire NN17 3DY
tel	01780 450272

map: 9 entry: 342

The Chequered Skipper
Oundle

Ashton is a glorious, rural, stone-and-thatch village, its houses casually arranged around an ample village green. The mellow pub blends in perfectly, yet is just 100 years old (and has burnt down twice to boot). This explains the generous open-plan interior – a modern fireplace in the bistro area, striking wooden pillars and honey-coloured beams in the bar. Whether choosing from the blackboard or the printed à la carte, food is utterly contemporary and adopts a best-bits-from-everywhere approach, ranging from Thai spiced fishcake with sweet chilli sauce and whole lemon sole with lemon butter, to whole partridge pot-roasted in port with root vegetables and herbs, and good old spotted dick and hot custard for afters. Wash it down with any one of a regularly changing slate of local and regional ales, say Old Tosspot, or Oliver's Army, or an excellent wine, and you might find yourself checking out the house prices.

Snooty Fox
Lowick

If it weren't for the sign, the pub could be mistaken for a manor house. Which it was, four centuries ago. Nowadays it's patronised by locals as both pub (Greene King IPA, Fuller's London Pride) and restaurant. The bar, with polished dining tables, caramel leather sofas and open fire, is separate from the dining room proper; both are a good size, beamed, flagged and open-stone-walled. And it's notably family friendly, with a toy box for children. But what really sets the Snooty Fox apart is chef-patron Clive Dixon. A slate of pub favourites such as cottage pie, homemade pork pie with chutney and bangers and mash are served in the bar, while in the restaurant there's a more upmarket rotisserie-grill menu – superb dry-aged steaks are cut to order – as well as other good things like braised belly pork with parmesan polenta, and fresh crab tagliatelle. Foodie heaven.

directions	Off A605, 1 mile from Oundle.
meals	12pm-2pm; 7pm-9.30pm. Main courses £10.95-£15.50; bar meals from £7.20.

Ian Campbell
The Chequered Skipper,
Ashton, Oundle, Peterborough,
Northamptonshire PE8 5LD

tel   01832 273494
web   www.chequeredskipper.co.uk

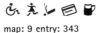

map: 9 entry: 343

directions	A14 junc.12; follow A6116 for 2 miles.
meals	12pm-2pm; 6pm-9.30pm (7pm-9.30pm Sundays). Main courses £10.50-£13.95.
closed	Open all day.

Clive Dixon & David Hennigan
Snooty Fox,
Main Street, Lowick,
Northamptonshire NN14 3BH

tel   01832 733434
web   theaapubcompany.com

map: 9 entry: 344

Northamptonshire

Northamptonshire

The Wollaston Inn
Wollaston

Hard to believe that back in the 60s and 70s this was the legendary Nag's Head music venue: U2 played here, and John Peel DJ'd. But then the local Doc Martens factory closed, and when the boots walked, so did the pub's rockin' clientele. When Chris Spencer and Andrew Parton took it on two years ago it was a real dive. Their aim was to clean up its act, and the result is as far from spit-and-sawdust as you can get – the walls are too creamy, the ceilings too high, the leather sofas too comfy. The beer garden is now a courtyard patio with bay trees in terracotta pots. Chef Chris is serious about his food, and especially seafood which changes daily. That doesn't mean pretentious: he won't have any truck with "drizzling", or "beds" of this or that. Instead, he does a "Mediterranean saffron fish stew" and hake steak – as well partridge, venison, ploughman's and steamed syrup pudding. The wine list is one to wade around in.

Royal Oak
Eydon

Everyone's welcome at the small and unpretentious Royal Oak. Walkers drop by to refuel, children are welcome in the games room (skittles, darts), dogs trot around freely. No music, just the hum of happy eaters. The menu – fresh, short, regularly changing – is the big attraction and you'll find not only the best of British – rich tomato soup, Gloucester Old Spot belly pork stuffed with black pudding, Cornish hake supreme – but also a touch of the exotic (eg. spicy vegetable tagine). The pretty, 17th-century honey-stone pub has old flagstones, exposed stone walls, a woodburner in the inglenook and a Sunday-papers-and-a pint feel. The long bar is propped up by ale-quaffing regulars, the rest is made over to the games room and three small eating areas. There are picnic seats out in front and Eydon, though only seven miles from the motorway, feels as remote as can be.

directions	Village signed off A509 south of Wellingborough.
meals	11am-6pm; 5pm-11pm. Main courses £6.50-£10 (lunch), £13-£20 (dinner).
closed	Open all day.

Andrew Parton & Chris Spencer
The Wollaston Inn,
87 London Road, Wollaston,
Northampton, NN29 7QS
tel 01933 663161
web www.wollaston-inn.co.uk

map: 9 entry: 345

directions	Off A361 midway between Banbury & Daventry.
meals	12pm-2pm; 7pm-9pm. No food on Mondays. Main courses £10.95-£16.

Justin Lefevre
Royal Oak,
6 Lime Avenue,
Eydon,
Northamptonshire NN11 3PG
tel 01327 263167

map: 8 entry: 346

Northamptonshire

George & Dragon
Chacombe

It's an old pub – the building dates from 1640 and has been added to over the centuries – but a relative newcomer given that Chacombe appears in the Domesday Book. One wonders what they did for a drink until 1640. There's a great atmosphere at the George & Dragon, with its flagstones, low beams, simple furnishings, crackling log fire and mellow front festooned with flowers in summer. Like so many successful country pubs, it's reputation has been built on its food. Roast beef sandwiches, game terrine with plum compote, Norfolk crab calad, lamb Wellington, bread and butter pudding – this is good, comforting, English food. Almost all the ingredients are local, and there are real ales from Everards and seven wines by the glass. Chacombe is a delightful conservation village and a world away from the M40 just over the hill.

Northumberland

Olde Ship Hotel
Seahouses

The Glen dynasty has been at the helm of this nautical gem for close on a century. The inn sparkles with maritime memorabilia to remind you of Seahouses' fine heritage and the days when Grace Darling rowed through huge seas to rescue stricken souls. Settle into the cosy and atmospheric main bar by the glowing fire with a decent pint – there are eight ales to choose from – and gaze across the harbour to the Farne Islands and the Longstone Light (later, take the ferry). In the smaller 'cabin' bar you can get stuck into some enjoyable, home-cooked food – fresh crab soup and sandwiches, wild boar terrine with cumberland sauce, liver and onion casserole, hearty fish stew, apple crumble. The place positively creaks with history – retreat here after a bracing coastal walk to Bamburgh Castle.

directions	M40 junc. 11; A361 for Daventry; Chacombe signed in 1 mile.
meals	12pm-2.30pm; 6pm-9.30pm. Bar meals £6.50-£14.50.
closed	Sunday evening. Open all day.

Richard Philips
George & Dragon,
Silver Street, Chacombe, Banbury,
Northamptonshire OX17 2JR
tel 01295 711500
web www.flockinns.co.uk

map: 8 entry: 347

directions	B1340 off A1 8 miles north of Alnwick; inn above harbour.
meals	12pm-2pm; 7pm-8.30pm Main courses £6.50-£10.30.
closed	Open all day.

A & J Glen, D Swan & J Glen
Olde Ship Hotel,
9 Main Street, Seahouses,
Northumberland NE68 7RD
tel 01665 720200
web www.seahouses.co.uk

map: 14 entry: 348

The Ship Inn
Low Newton-by-the-Sea

A deeply authentic coastal inn with tongue and groove boarding and flooring, old settles, scrubbed tables and a solid-fuel stove. Step in and you step back 100 years: landlady Christine Forsyth fell in love with the simplicity of the place and gives you provender to match. Good local beers (Wylam Gold Tankard and Landlord's Choice) and fair trade coffee and chocolate go well with a menu built around the best local produce – simple, fresh, satisfying. Local hand-picked-crab rolls (stotties), lobster from yards away, Craster kippers from two miles down the coast, ploughman's with local unpasteurised cheddar or New Barns free-range ham. In the evenings there's often a choice (venison, grilled red mullet) but book first. Park on a compulsory plot back from the beach and take the short walk to the sand, green and pub – worth every step.

The Tankerville Arms
Eglingham

Exploring the rolling acres between Northumberland's dramatic coastline and the wild Cheviot Hills? Charming Eglingham has the best pub for miles. The long, stone-built tavern, a boon for ramblers and cyclists, cheerfully mixes traditional and new. In the lounge and bar are carpeted and stone-flagged floors, blackened beams, coal fires, plush seating and old-fashioned dominoes; in the kitchen, a modern approach. John Blackmore, owner and cook, chalks up blackboard menus featuring fresh, local, seasonal ingredients – ham and duck confit terrine with toasted brioche; black pudding tart with goat's cheese, roasted vegetables and garlic sauce. Food goes traditional in good sandwiches and Sunday lunchtime roasts, served in one of the cosy bars or in the converted barn restaurant. Children are welcome and drinkers kept happy with a range of thoroughly respectable ales, including the local Hadrian and Border brews, and a well-balanced list of wines.

directions	From Alnwick B1340 for Seahouses for 8 miles to crossroads; straight over, follow signs.
meals	12pm-2:30pm; phone for evening opening & food times in winter. Main courses £6.50-£22.
closed	4pm-6pm Monday-Thursday. Open all day weekends & school holidays.

directions	On B6346 towards Charlton & Wooler, 7 miles from Alnwick.
meals	12pm-2pm; 6.30pm-9pm. Main courses £7.50-£14.
closed	Mondays; Tuesdays; Wednesday lunchtimes January-early March.

Christine Forsyth
The Ship Inn, The Square,
Low Newton-by-the-Sea,
Alnwick, NE66 3EL
tel   01665 576262
web   www.theshipinnnewtonbythesea.co.uk

John Blackmore
The Tankerville Arms,
15 The Village, Eglingham,
Alnwick,
Northumberland NE66 2TX
tel   01665 578444

map: 14 entry: 349

map: 14 entry: 350

The Pheasant Inn
Stannersburn

Everything shines at this little stone inn. Walls carry old photos of the local community: from colliery to smithy, a vital record of their past heritage. The bars are wonderful – brass beer taps glow, anything wooden has been polished to perfection, the clock above the fire keeps perfect time and the Timothy Taylor's and Theakston's Black Sheep Bitter are expertly kept. Robin and Irene offer homemade soups and steak and kidney pies for lunch while in the evening things step up a gear: steaks cooked to your liking, fish simply grilled and served with herb butter, roast Northumbrian lamb. Bedrooms next door in the hay barn are fresh, simple, compact and cosy – good value for money. You are in the glorious Northumberland National Park, so no traffic jams, no rush; hire bikes and cycle round the lake, sail or ride.

directions	From Bellingham to Kielder Water 8 miles. On left, before K. Water.
meals	12pm-2.30pm (2pm Sun); 7pm-8.30pm. Main courses £7.50-£13.95.
rooms	8: 4 doubles, 3 twins, 1 family, £65-£85. Singles £40-£45.
closed	Mondays & Tuesdays November-March.

See page 36 for bedroom details.

Walter & Robin Kershaw
The Pheasant Inn,
Stannersburn, Hexham,
Northumberland NE48 1DD
tel   01434 240382
web   www.thepheasantinn.com

map: 14 entry: 351

Queens Head Inn
Great Whittington

A warm refuge in a wild country of moors, sheep and vast skies. The mellow bar is charming, its hunting mural satisfactorily yellowed by coal fires and smokers since it was painted by a 17-year-old in 1934. Gleaming beer engines disburse Nick Stafford ales, one specially brewed for the pub; hunting prints hint at local interests; a background tape plays. Toast your toes from the carved oak settle before the fire, then up steps to a traditional lounge and another log-filled grate for those bitter Northumbrian days. Beyond is a big, pine-furnished dining area. Staff are gently charming and people come for the food; chef Norman Dodds uses fresh, local produce, including local beef and lamb. As well as exceptional filled rolls, daily menus may include seared scallops with bacon and green bean salad, and halibut on baby spinach with fennel and tomato-scented fumé.

directions	Off B6318, 4 miles north of Corbridge.
meals	12pm-2pm (2.30pm Sunday); 6.30pm-9pm. Main courses £9.95-£18.95.
closed	2.30pm-6pm; Sunday evenings & Mondays.

Ian Scott
Queens Head Inn,
Great Whittington,
Corbridge,
Northumberland NE19 2HP
tel   01434 672267

map: 12 entry: 352

Rat Inn
Anick

Locals from 50 miles away target the old Rat, celebs and overseas visitors come and go. The hard-to-find old drovers' inn may not be venerable but it has an irresistible appeal. It's half-pub, half-cafeteria, the sort of place where everyone, kids included, is made welcome. Inside are three areas: a shabby sun room curiously dotted with animal figurines, a charming snug beside a gleaming dark-oak bar, and a central dining area with student-like servery. Logs and coal hogs encourage warmth and good cheer, staff are smiley, and unflappable Joan D'Adamo must be the youngest granny in the world. Sustaining food consists of monster steaks, traditional pies, rabbit, mince and ale dumplings and fish in summer; real ales are ever changing with a core of five hand-pulled. Ragged shrubs tumble over the walls outside, dahlias line the roadside in jaunty abandon, tables and chairs abound and views are far-ranging.

Dipton Mill
Hexham

Less than a ten-minute drive out of town along a rollercoaster road, Geoff Brooker's old inn squats in a deep hollow next to a stone bridge and a babbling brook. Formerly a mill house built around 1750, it's been updated but has hung on to much of its old character. Within the tiny interior is a single warm and intimate bar with panelled walls, low ceilings, small leaded windows and blazing winter log fires — comfortingly traditional. Food is home-cooked: warming soups and steak and kidney pie, or ploughman's with a rare choice of British and local cheeses. Real-ale fans will know that the Dipton Mill is the brewery tap for Hexhamshire Brewery ales, Geoff being both landlord and head brewer. Outside: a big walled garden with a wooden bridge over the mill stream. A wintery word of warning: if there's ice or snow, although you may get down the hill you may not get up again!

directions	Off A69 between Corbridge & Hexham, 2 miles east of Hexham
meals	11am-3pm; 6pm-9pm. Main courses £7.25-£19.50. Bar meals from £4.95.
closed	Sunday evenings.

David & Joan D'Adamo
Rat Inn,
Anick,
Hexham,
Northumberland NE46 4LN
tel 01434 602814

map: 12 entry: 353

directions	From Hexham B6306 for Blanchland; 2nd right onto Dipton Mill Road to Whitley Chapel & Racecourse; pub 2 miles on.
meals	12pm-2.15pm; 6.30pm-8.30pm. Main courses £4.75-£7.30.
closed	2.30pm-6pm; Sunday evenings.

Geoff Brooker
Dipton Mill,
Dipton Mill Road,
Hexham,
Northumberland NE46 1YA
tel 01434 606577

map: 12 entry: 354

The Feathers Inn
Hedley on the Hill

Marina Atkinson has seen a few changes to the British pub scene in her 25 years – yet has not lost sight of The Feathers' old-fashioned pubby feel. It is a rare treat west of Newcastle to find such an authentic little place. In the two bars are old beams, exposed stonework, Turkey rugs, open fires and a cottagey feel. Furnishings are simple but comfortable: red benches and settles, ornaments and soft lights. So restful – you'd feel as much at home browsing the papers here as enjoying a fireside chat. Beer is excellent, with four cask beers from local or microbreweries; wines are taken as seriously. The food – Greek beef casserole, tortillas and croustades, ginger pudding – is home-cooked and vegetarian- and vegan-friendly. Menus change twice a week, and dishes are deliberately unfussy: Marina puts the focus on freshness and flavour. Hedley on the Hill is as charming as its name.

The Manor House Inn
Carterway Heads

No wonder it's a popular place. Cheerful young staff, tasty food, a good bar with four cask ales and a cask cider, eight wines by the glass, a raft of malts. The large, light lounge bar, with wood-burning stove and blackboard menu, is a great spot for meals, though there's a dining room if you prefer. Chicken liver pâté comes with onion marmalade, scallops with chilli jam, pigeon breast with mushroom and juniper sauce. In the smallish public bar, modestly furnished with oak settles and old pine tables, is a big open fire; owners Chris and Moira Brown add a further warm touch. Take your pint of Theakstons Best into the garden in summer where the eye sweeps over the Derwent valley to the Durham moors. There's a shop/delicatessen selling a wide range of goodies – puddings, chutneys, ice cream – much of it home-produced.

directions	From Consett, B6309 north to New Ridley; follow signs to Hedley on the Hill.
meals	12pm-2.30pm (weekends & bank holidays only); 7pm-9pm. No food Monday evenings. Main courses £7.95-£10.50.
closed	Weekday lunchtimes (except bank holidays).

directions	Beside A68 at junction with B6278; 3 miles west of Consett.
meals	12pm-9.30pm (9pm Sundays). Main courses £6-£17.
closed	Open all day.

Marina Atkinson
The Feathers Inn,
Hedley on the Hill,
Stocksfield,
Northumberland NE43 7SW
tel 01661 843607

Moira & Chris Brown
The Manor House Inn,
Carterway Heads,
Shotley Bridge,
Northumberland DH8 9LX
tel 01207 255268

map: 12 entry: 355

map: 12 entry: 356

Nottinghamshire

Ye Olde Trip to Jerusalem
Nottingham

Another pub that is the oldest in England! The building dates from the 1600s and the name is older still. Certainly there has been brewing on the site since the 1170s (to supply the needs of the castle above) and the crusaders probably met here en route to Jerusalem. An amazing place carved into solid rock on which the castle sits; drinking here is like drinking in a cave, only warmer. There are rickety staircases, ancient chimneys that were cut up through the rock to assist medieval brewing, a cursed galleon, hairy with dust because the last three people who cleaned it died, and Ring the Bull, a pub game which involves swinging a ring on a string over a bull's horn. The Rock Lounge, with its sandstone ceiling and chimney, is aptly named, while the cellars stretch more than 100 feet beneath the castle. The Trip (meaning 'resting place') serves Hardys & Hansons to a mixed crowd — locals, tourists, students — and the food is standard pub stuff.

directions	From inner ring road follow A6005 'The North' to Castle Boulevard; right into Castle Road.
meals	11am-6pm (12pm-6pm Sunday). Main courses £5-£8.
closed	Open all day.

Mark Kent
Ye Olde Trip to Jerusalem,
1 Brewhouse Yard, Nottingham,
Nottinghamshire NG1 6AD

tel	0115 947 3171
web	www.triptojerusalem.com

map: 8 entry: 357

Nottinghamshire

Cock & Hoop
Nottingham

The 'Lace Market' is undergoing a revival — and it's a treat to find such a fine free house in the city centre. Opposite the law courts — transformed, now, into an award-winning museum — the old ale house once gave sanctuary to judges preparing for the hangings that took place outside. The pub is a happier place today, shoppers, beer-lovers and city workers making a bee-line for what is one of the cosiest places in town. Women feel happy to pop in on their own, families descend at weekends. There are two rooms, one at ground level, one below. Below is larger and softly lit; ground-level has an open fire and a tiny bar. Both have wooden panelling and bare-brick walls, plush new furnishings, armchairs, benches and club chairs. Friendly staff know all about the whiskies and wines and there's an unexpectedly good selection of both. Beers include Black Sheep and London Pride, food comes from the stylishly informal hotel next door. *No smoking throughout.*

directions	From city centre, follow brown signs for Lace Market; next to Lace Market Hotel.
meals	12pm-3pm; 5.30pm-7.30pm (12pm-9pm Sunday). Main courses £5.50-£8.95.
closed	Open all day.

Mark Cox
Cock & Hoop,
25 High Pavement, Nottingham,
Nottinghamshire NG1 1HE

tel	0115 852 3231
web	www.cockandhoop.co.uk

map: 8 entry: 358

The Victoria
Beeston

A large picture of Queen Victoria rules the main bar of this unpretentious and bustling city-suburb pub. It's an ex-Victorian railway hotel with bags of character, and its awesome raft of ales, wines by the glass and malt whiskies pulls in a crowd. The food's good, too, with a menu strong on vegetarian options. The civilised main bar, with fire, newspapers on racks and etched windows, sets the tone for the other rooms, all plainly painted in magnolia with woodblock flooring and scrubbed dark-wood or brass-topped tables. Blackboards give the food and booze headlines. You get roast pork Catalan, braised beef in ale and veggie dishes to delight even non-vegetarians (winter vegetable bourguignon, pasta with goat's cheese and rocket pesto). At the back, there's a heated marquee area for cooler summer nights; dine as the trains go by. Service is efficient and friendly. Try to catch the summer festival of ale, food and music.

Martin's Arms
Colston Bassett

An Elizabethan farmhouse morphed into an ale house around 1700, and an inn 100 years later. Today it is a deeply civilised pub. The front room exudes so much country-house charm – scatter cushions on sofas and settles, crackling logs in Jacobean fireplaces, 18th-century prints – that the bar seems almost an intrusion. Fresh, seasonal menus change daily. Bar snacks include special sandwiches, warm salads and splendid ploughman's lunches with Colston Bassett stilton from the dairy up the road (do visit). In the restaurant, the highlight of the winter menu is Park Farm Estate game shot by Salvatore the chef. Polish it all off with raspberry and mascapone shortbread with stem ginger. Behind the bar is an impressive range of well-kept real ales, cognacs, wines and malts from Adnams. The staff are hugely welcoming, the garden backs onto the Colston Bassett Estate and you can play croquet on the lawn in summer. Superb.

directions	Off A6005 at the bottom of Dovecote Lane. Follow signs to station.
meals	12pm-8.45pm (7.45pm Sundays). Main courses £6.50-£10.95.
closed	Open all day.

directions	Off A46, east of Nottingham. Take Owthorpe turning.
meals	12pm-2pm; 6pm-10pm. Main courses £7.50-£18.95; bar meals £10-£13.
closed	Sunday evenings.

Neil Kelso
The Victoria,
Dovecote Lane, Beeston,
Nottinghamshire NG9 1JG
tel   0115 925 4049
web   www.victoriabeeston.co.uk

Lynne Bryan Strafford
& Salvatore Inguanta
Martin's Arms,
School Lane, Colston Bassett,
Nottinghamshire NG12 3FD
tel   01949 81361

map: 8 entry: 359

map: 9 entry: 360

Nottinghamshire

Waggon & Horses
Halam

The Whites have built up a fantastic reputation for their food. You can tell how keen they are just by looking at the menu with its exhortations to try each dish. The specials board announces whole roast partridge with a mushroom, port and thyme sauce and Cornish bream with smoked salmon and scallops; even the lunchtime rolls are worth travelling for. Members of the Campaign for Real Food, William and Rebecca get almost everything locally; fish comes daily from Cornwall. The pub is small, beamed and softly lit with low ceilings and bold walls. In the cosy but open-plan bar, rush-seated chairs pull up to sturdy tables; there's the odd settle and masses of cricket memorabilia, and an exotic metal grill separates the bar from the smoke-free dining area. It's a Thwaites' tied house, friendly and expertly run – they even do catering for parties.

directions	Off B6386 in Southwell for Oxton.
meals	12pm-2.30pm (3pm Sunday); 6pm-9.30pm. No food Sunday evenings. Main courses £8-£14. Set lunch & early evening menu, £11.50 & £14.50.
closed	3pm-5.30pm. Open all day weekends.

William & Rebecca White
Waggon & Horses,
Mansfield Road, Halam, Newark,
Nottinghamshire NG22 8AE

tel	01636 813109
web	www.thewaggonathalam.co.uk

map: 9 entry: 361

Nottinghamshire

Caunton Beck
Caunton

Having hatched the hugely successful Wig & Mitre in Lincoln, Valerie looked for a rural equivalent and found one in pretty little Caunton. The pub was lovingly reconstructed from the skeleton of the 16th-century Hole Arms and then renamed. A decade on and it is a hugely popular pub-restaurant, opening at 8am for breakfast – start your day with freshly squeezed orange juice, espresso coffee, smoked salmon and scrambled eggs. Later, there are sandwiches, mussels with pickled ginger and coriander laksa and pot-roasted guinea fowl. The puddings (make space for lemon and thyme posset) are fabulous. It's all very relaxed and civilised, the sort of place where newspapers and magazines take precedence over piped music and electronic wizardry. Come for country chairs at scrubbed pine tables, rag-rolled walls and a fire in winter, or parasols on the terrace in summer. Well-managed ales are on handpump.

directions	6 miles NW of Newark past sugar factory on A616.
meals	8am-11pm. Main courses £8.50-£18.50; set menus £11 & £13.95.
closed	Open all day.

Valerie Hope
Caunton Beck,
Main Street, Caunton,
Newark,
Nottinghamshire NG23 6AB

tel	01636 636793

map: 9 entry: 362

The White Lion
Crays Pond

The Pierreponts may have moved on but head chef Andrew Hill remains at the stove and the new owners plan to change little at this thriving pub-restaurant. A well-heeled Henley and Goring crowd is drawn by the imaginative and daily-changing menus that mix old favourites such as fillet steak with garlic butter and chips with new ideas like tom yar seafood broth or whole red mullet with fennel and basil compote. Everthing is made freshly and in-house, from the pasta to the ice cream. Simple tables are topped with fat white candles in a dining room where deep red walls are lined with unusual prints and the floor is jauntily strewn with rugs. There's also a light and airy conservatory extension. Relax over the papers in the small bar with a pint of Greene King and a bowl of marinated olives, dip daintily into a pint of prawns or chew on a thick steak sandwich.

The Three Tuns
Henley-on-Thames

Long gone are the days when the Three Tun's last orders prompted the first fights of the night. Few would have dared step inside; now it's more wine bar than pub. Soft cream hues and old beams, arresting antiques, some for sale, and homemade goodies to take home. Funky chairs by a fireplace add a contemporary splash; fossils add whimsy. This eclectic mix extends to the food prepared by Kieron. It's seasonal, fresh, of the very best quality and served on crisply clothed tables. Linger over lunchtime's Spanish white onion and crème fraîche tart, Mrs King's port pie, and fillet steak sandwich with sauté potatoes. Evenings at the Foodhouse introduce seafood and salsa verde risotto, roast young grouse, and baked apple and vanilla caramel. Wines are global, the Brakspear is well-kept, and there are an elegant courtyard and funky bar at the back. A small place with a big personality, on Henley's fine market square.

directions	3 miles N of Pangbourne on B471.
meals	12pm-2pm; 6pm-9pm. No food Sunday evenings. Main courses £9.95-£19.95. Set menus £13.95 & £16.95.
closed	Mondays. Open all day.

Celine Steger
The White Lion,
Crays Pond, Goring Heath,
Oxfordshire RG8 7SH

tel	01491 680471
web	www.whitelioncrayspond.com

map: 4 entry: 363

directions	In central square.
meals	12pm-2.30pm; 7pm-9.30pm. Main courses £5-£17.
closed	3pm-5.30pm. Open all day Friday-Sunday.

Kieron Daniels
The Three Tuns,
5 Market Place,
Henley-on-Thames,
Oxfordshire RG9 2AA

tel	01491 573260

map: 4 entry: 364

The Cherry Tree Inn
Stoke Row

This pub exudes 17th-century charm and 21st-century luxury. From the bar's minimalist good looks – low beams and brick walls, bare boards and flags, chunky wooden tables and muted earth tones – to gorgeous bedrooms in the barn, it's no regular inn. And the blackboard listing imaginative dishes reinforces that impression. There's braised shank of Chiltern lamb with garlic and herb mash; wild mushroom linguine; grilled squid and chorizo salad with roast peppers. Puddings are classics – treacle tart, strawberry pavlova with a raspberry sorbet – with local cheeses an alternative. Beers are from Brakspear, there's a very decent selection of wines by the glass and the attractive front lawn and terrace make a lovely spot for relaxing outdoors. Bedrooms are stylish and contemporary, with flat-screen TVs, king-size beds and feather pillows.

directions	Off B481 Reading to Nettlebed road, 5 miles west of Henley.
meals	12pm-3pm (4pm weekends); 7pm-10.30pm. Main courses £5.95-£8.95 (lunch), £9.25-£14.95 (dinner).
rooms	4 doubles £65-£85.
closed	Open all day.

See page 36 for bedroom details.

Richard Coates & Paul Gilchrist
The Cherry Tree Inn,
Stoke Row, Henley-on-Thames,
Oxfordshire RG9 5QA

tel	01491 680430
web	www.thecherrytreeinn.com

map: 4 entry: 365

The Crooked Billet
Henley-on-Thames

Dick Turpin apparently courted the landlord's daughter and Kate Winslet had her wedding breakfast here. Pints are drawn direct from the cask (there is no bar!) and the rusticity of the pub charms all who manage to find it: beams, flags and inglenooks, old pine, walls lined with bottles and baskets of spent corks. In the larger room, red walls display old photographs and mirrors; shelves are stacked with books... by candlelight it's irresistible. You come here to eat and the menu is Italian/French provincial, and long: bouillabaisse, beef fillet with seared foie gras and red wine jus, venison with roast figs and port and juniper sauce, dark chocolate tart with mint ice cream. It's founded on well-sourced raw materials and bolstered by a satisfying wine list. Occasional jazz, and a big garden bordering the beech woods where children can roam. Talking of children, the pub cooks the village school meals. *No smoking throughout.*

directions	5 miles W of Henley, off B481 Reading to Nettlebed road.
meals	12pm-2.15pm; 7pm-10pm (12pm-10pm Saturday & Sunday). Main courses £12-£20; set menus £13.50 & £16.45.
closed	Open all day weekends.

Paul Clerehugh
The Crooked Billet,
Newlands Lane, Stoke Row,
Henley-on-Thames, RG9 5PU

tel	01491 681048
web	www.thecrookedbillet.co.uk

map: 4 entry: 366

The Bull & Butcher
Turville

Landlady Lydia Botha ensures this little pub quenches the thirsts of all who come to visit one of the most bucolic film locations in Britain – it sits beneath the Chitty Chitty Bang Bang windmill, the village is the setting for *The Vicar of Dibley* and suspects from *Midsomer Murders* have propped up the bar. Bags of atmosphere, and style, in cream walls, latched doors, a glass-topped 50-foot well, fresh flowers. Busy with Londoners at weekends, it's a jolly place in which to down a pint of Brakspear's finest or take a tipple of homemade sloe gin. Food is good modern British: fresh crayfish tails, 'all beef monster pie', steak & kidney suet and great Sunday roasts. No piped music, no games, no pubby paraphernalia, just fine 17th-century beams, working log fires and friendly people. There's a garden for fine days and great walks through the Chiltern beech woods.

directions	M40 junc. 5; through Ibstone; for Turville at T-junction.
meals	12pm-2.30pm (4pm Sunday); 6.30pm-9.30pm (7pm-9pm Sundays). Main courses £7.50-£14.95.
closed	Open all day.

Lydia Botha
The Bull & Butcher,
Turville, Henley-on-Thames,
Oxfordshire RG9 6QU
tel 01491 638283
web www.thebullandbutcher.com

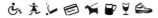

map: 4 entry: 367

Fox & Hounds
Christmas Common

In a hamlet in the hills – a few grand houses and this 15th-century brick and flint cottage: the civilised Fox and Hounds. Once it was a rustic rural ale house, but Brakspears have transformed it into a thriving food pub under the guidance of chef-landlord Kieron Daniels. Despite the changes, the 'Top Fox' (on its escarpment) has lost none of its charm and character. Enter a beamy bar full of simple benches, cosy corners, logs glowing in a vast inglenook always lit, cribbage and cards and pints of Brakspear tapped direct from the cask. The foodie action takes place in the restaurant, with its wooden floors, open-to-view kitchen, quirky rustic décor and French windows to the garden. Farm-reared meats and local fruit and vegetables result in such dishes as mussel and brown shrimp risotto, roast partridge with cranberry gravy, squid, bok choi and miso broth. Make time for walks through the beech woods, look up for soaring red kites.

directions	From M40 junc. 5 follow old A40.
meals	12pm-2.30pm (3pm Sundays); 7pm-9.30pm. Main courses £7-£13; £5 weekday lunch.
closed	Open all day in summer.

Kieron Daniels
Fox & Hounds,
Christmas Common,
Watlington,
Oxfordshire OX49 5HL
tel 01491 612599

map: 4 entry: 368

Oxfordshire

The Goose
Britwell Salome

At first glance, the 16th-century pub on the main through road of the village might not warrant a visit. Yet those in the know will tell of light, remodelled interiors and fabulous food and wine. Calming colours, pale floorboards and matting, comfy armchairs and a fireside sofa create a civilised backdrop for this high-rolling, gastropub adventure. Owner-chef Michael North's innovative daily menus reflect the seasons; dive-caught scallops with home-dried tomatoes; roast local partridge with bubble-and-squeak; Scottish halibut with green herb risotto. Bar meals include soup, sandwiches and beefburgers, the flavours shine, and the service is from a young, professional team. The lightwood bar and white-linen-dressed tables further add to the chilled-out yet friendly feel. The back room (no smoking) continues the theme, and an enclosed garden with proper wooden furniture is tidily hidden at the back.

directions	On B4009 south of Watlington, 5 miles from M40 junc. 6.
meals	12pm-2.30pm; 7pm-9pm. Main courses £16-£18; bar meals £8-£12; set menus £15 & £18.
closed	3pm-6.30pm; Sunday evenings.

Michael North
The Goose,
Britwell Salome,
Watlington,
Oxfordshire OX49 5LG
tel   01491 612304

map: 4 entry: 369

Oxfordshire

The Lord Nelson
Brightwell Baldwin

The sleepy back-lane setting of Brightwell Baldwin lives up to expectations; cottages tumbling down the hill, a church perched on a bank, a rambling old inn festooned with flowers – and flags on Trafalgar Day. The creamy yellow façade and front veranda catch the eye, enticing you into a civilised 16th-century interior, all wooden floors, wonky beams, logs fires, cosy corners and charm. Antiques, fine old prints and Nelson memorabilia keep the eye entertained. Most come to eat and eat well you can; there's chicken liver parfait with homemade chutney, monkfish with mustard beurre blanc, lemon tart with raspberry coulis. Retire to the womb-like snug (deep sofas, table lamps, a country-house feel) for coffee and a little doze. And there's more – Brakspear on tap, 20 wines by the glass, friendly, smiley service and a wonderful rear terrace for summer sipping.

directions	Village signed off B4009 between Benson & Watlington.
meals	12pm-2.30pm; 6.30pm-10pm (7pm-9.30pm Sunday). Main courses £12.95-£18.95; set lunch £10.95.

Roger & Carole Shippey
The Lord Nelson,
Brightwell Baldwin, Watlington,
Oxfordshire OX49 5NP
tel   01491 612497
web   www.lordnelson-inn.co.uk

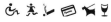

map: 4 entry: 370

Oxfordshire

North Star
Steventon

Despite the owner's hammering of the ancient walls with a JCB in a fit of New Year pique, the 15th-century interior has remained miraculously intact. Enter a narrow corridor to four small rooms whose creaky latched doors have numbers — a throwback to the days when inns were taxed by the room. Freehouse ales are served straight from the barrel through a hatch, there's no central heating, three open fires, and an L-shaped settle filling the low-ceilinged main bar. This used to be a popular venue for the old boys of the village; it's still a fine stop for a horse and rider. You get bar food at lunchtimes and microbrewery beer, tables outside, and a front gateway through an ancient yew. Recent photographs of the pub's restoration show workmen reconstructing the ancient walls (wattle and daub with horsehair plaster) overseen by the resident ghost.

directions	Exit A34 at Didcot/Milton junc. for Steventon; right at lights; through village. Left at causeway; follow road.
meals	12pm-2.30pm. Bookings only for evening meals & Sunday lunch. Main courses £2.50-£6.95.
closed	3pm-7pm; Mondays (except bank holidays). Open all day Friday-Sunday.

Kerry Tyrrell & Michael Toplis
North Star,
2 Stocks Lane, The Causeway,
Steventon, Abingdon, OX13 6SG
tel 01235 831677
web www.northstarpub.co.uk

map: 4 entry: 371

Oxfordshire

The Boar's Head
Ardington

If it's not the sweet smell of lilies, it's the irresistible aroma of fresh bread. With daily baking to tempt them, villagers arrive for a pint of the best then put in their orders — sun-dried tomato, granary, with or without olives. Here are good ales, fine wines and a welcome for kids. In a bar cosy with low beams, scrubbed wooden tables, checked curtains and log fires, sit down to a first-class seasonal menu created by a chef-patron who knows what's what. Bruce Buchan is inventive with fish from Newlyn and market-fresh produce from Newbury and Wantage — assiette of Cornish scallops, duck breast with chorizo, rosti and port sauce, hot pistachio soufflé. Even the local black pudding has won prizes. His wife Kay keeps this lovely little pub running with friendly efficiency. A 400-year-old special place in a timeless estate village. Come to unwind.

directions	On A417, 2 miles east of Wantage.
meals	12pm-2pm; 7pm-9.30pm (10pm Fridays & Saturdays). Main courses £14-£19; bar meals £8-£13.
closed	3pm-6.30pm.

Bruce & Kay Buchan
The Boar's Head,
Church Street, Ardington,
Wantage, Oxfordshire OX12 8QA
tel 01235 833254
web www.boarsheadardington.co.uk

map: 3 entry: 372

Oxfordshire

The Mole Inn
Toot Baldon

The Mole has proved a hit with Oxford foodies who have flocked to experience the pub's renaissance... it is packed most days. Now there are an impeccable stone exterior, landscaped garden and ravishing bar. Be embraced by stripped beams and chunky walls, black leather sofas, logs in the grate and a dresser that groans with breads and olive jars. Chic rusticity continues into three dining areas: fat candles on blond wooden tables, thick terracotta floors and the sun angling in on a fresh plateful of roast Oxfordshire lamb with garlic mash and rosemary jus. Daily specials point to a menu that trawls the globe for inspiration, and whether you go for light salad and pasta bowl lunches or rib-eye steak, sauté potatoes and dressed salad, you'll eat well. Scrumptious ice creams, British cheeses, good wines, local Hook Norton ale and polite staff complete the picture.

directions	From A4074, 5 miles south of Oxford; turn at Nuneham Courtenay for Marsh Baldon & Toot Baldon.
meals	12pm-2.30pm; 7pm-9.30pm; 12pm-4pm, 6pm-9pm Sundays. Main courses £7.95-£17.50.
closed	Open all day.

Gary Witchalls
The Mole Inn,
Toot Baldon, Oxford,
Oxfordshire OX44 9NG
tel 01865 340001
web www.themoleinn.com

map: 8 entry: 373

Oxfordshire

Old Red Lion
Tetsworth

Hungry and on the M40? Then head here. You can't miss the pub – bright pink with a big lion painted above the door and bang opposite the village green. It's a fun place, quirky and individual, reflecting the enthusiastic owners' background in film and TV. Salmon-pink walls are dotted with big mirrors, eye-catching paintings and shelves filled with books. A lion's head looms behind the bar, the wooden floor clatters, there's the odd armchair or sofa in a corner, board games on rustic pine tables and eclectic piped jazz wafting through to the dining area at the back – and the 'library', a private dining room filled with books. The pub has an upmarket yet relaxed feel and the food is good – lunchtime pies and grills, roast belly pork, beef Wellington, lazy Sunday lunch. The Monday suppers are a steal at £5, and the Tuesday jazz nights are fantastic and free.

directions	On A40 south of Thame, 3 miles from M40 junc. 6.
meals	12pm-2.30pm; 6pm-9pm (12pm-9pm Sunday). Main courses £4.95-£9.95 (lunch), £9.75-£16.95 (dinner).
closed	Open all day Saturday, Sunday & in summer.

Bluey & Stewart Richards
Old Red Lion,
40 High Street,
Tetsworth, Thame,
Oxfordshire OX9 7AS
tel 01844 281274

map: 8 entry: 374

White Hart
Wytham

Who says the traditional and the contemporary don't mix? At the White Hart – once a rural, Thames-side drinkers' den, now practically in Oxford – bold colours and modern art mingle with flagged floors and stone fireplaces. And the different areas have distinctive characters: the 'Parlour' room has a French feel with painted floors and furniture and a central bread block laid with fresh loaves; the cosy bar has exotic coloured walls and velvet cushions. The upstairs bar is quite different, all open brickwork, plain floorboards, log fire and walls bearing framed tomatoes. The rustic terrace has Greek terracotta woodburners and a 15th-century dovecote. There are real ales and a raft of wines by the glass in the bar and modern cooking from the kitchen. Monthly specials, described as "divine", might include braised lamb shank with spearmint jus, and roast halibut on saffron and herb risotto with tomato confit and green chilli salsa.

directions	A34 to Oxford, off at Botley interchange.
meals	12pm-3pm (3.30pm Saturday; 4pm Sunday), 6.30pm-10pm (9pm Sunday). Main courses £10.95-£15.95.
closed	4pm-6pm. Open all day weekends.

David Peevers
White Hart,
Wytham,
Oxford,
Oxfordshire OX2 8QA
tel 01865 244372

map: 8 entry: 375

The Boot Inn
Barnard Gate

It's not often you can down a pint of Hook Norton in a cosy Cotswold pub while pondering David Beckham's shoe size, Jasmin Le Bon's ankle and the flexibility of Roger Bannister's soles. The Boot's walls are covered with a rare collection of celebrity footwear, and the list is long: Stirling Moss, Henry Cooper, Prue Leith, Rick Stein. Expect standing timbers, bare board floors, good country tables, candlelight at night and a huge log fire… a deliciously traditional atmosphere in which to settle back and enjoy some fresh, flavourful cooking: monkfish with lime and ginger butter and polenta chips, bouillabaisse with aioli, fillet steak with garlic butter. After a slice of dark chocolate cheesecake there is an overwhelming temptation to don a pair of Ranulph Fiennes's record-breaking Polar bootliners and turn into an armchair explorer by the fire.

directions	Off A40; 4 miles from Oxford.
meals	12pm-2pm (2.30pm Saturdays; 3pm Sundays); 7pm-9.30pm (10pm Fridays & Saturdays). Main courses £7.95-£15.95.
closed	Open all day weekends.

Craig Foster
The Boot Inn,
Barnard Gate, Eynsham,
Oxfordshire OX29 6XE
tel 01865 881231
web www.theboot-inn.com

map: 8 entry: 376

Oxfordshire

The Trout at Tadpole Bridge
Buckland Marsh

Down here by the river, one could almost expect to bump into Ratty and Toad toasting their toes in front of the wood-burning stove. The Trout is a drinking fisherman's paradise. Walls are adorned with bendy rods, children are welcomed, and your dogs may join the pub's. Landlord and chef Chris Green knows breeds, cuts and quality of meat better than most; with lamb from the Blenheim estate, game from his family's farm and veg grown at the back, you can expect a treat, perhaps pork loin with prune, apple and leek stuffing, or Angus sirloin with garlic and parsley butter. With his father in charge of the wine, Chris concentrates on the food – wholesome dishes with a dash of fun. In summer the riverside garden comes alive as drinkers in search of real ale arrive by boat. Pitch your tent at the pub's waterside camping site and catch a glimpse of *Wind in the Willows* magic.

directions	Off A420 between Oxford & Swindon.
meals	12pm-2pm; 7pm-9pm. Main courses £8.95-£16.95.
closed	Sunday evenings; 1st week of February.

Christopher Green
The Trout at Tadpole Bridge,
Buckland Marsh, Faringdon,
Oxfordshire SN7 8RF

tel	01367 870382
web	www.troutinn.co.uk

map: 8 entry: 377

Oxfordshire

Masons Arms
South Leigh

A quintessentially English inn – with attitude – in somnolent South Leigh. Who would guess there's a gentlemen's club here? This is 'Gerry Stonhill's Individual Masons Arms'; dogs, children and mobile phones are unwelcome, vegetarians visit 'by appointment only', and some folk arrive by helicopter (ask about the nearest helipad!). Fifteenth-century flagstone floors, crackling log fires, dark hessian walls clad with paintings, old oak tables, spent wine bottles and scattered cigar boxes on shelves. There are three Dickensian rooms to explore and be charmed by, and a cosily clubby whisky-and-cognac-stocked bar. Burton Ale comes from the barrel and the wines are French. This is a smoking establishment, naturally, with Cuban cigars proffered at the end of the meal. Food is proper English, and superb: potted shrimps, wild smoked salmon, casseroles, roast duck, Angus steaks and the juiciest fish from the market, brought to the table to be admired before it's cooked.

directions	3 miles south east of Witney off A40 towards Oxford.
meals	12.30pm-2.30pm; 7.30pm-10.30pm. Main courses £10-£25.
closed	Monday & Sunday evenings.

Gerry Stonhill
Masons Arms,
South Leigh,
Witney,
Oxfordshire OX29 6XN

tel	01993 702485

map: 8 entry: 378

Royal Oak
Ramsden

From opening time on, the jolly banter of the Royal Oak's regulars can be heard from the doorstep outside. Blazing winter fires, piles of magazines and well-thumbed books by the inglenook make this a fine place for a pint of real ale; tuck into a corner filled with plump scatter cushions. Some brilliant food can be had in the pubby bar – open-stone walls, cream and soft-green windows – as well as in the restaurant extension beyond, where glass doors open onto a pretty terrace with wrought-iron chairs in summer and outdoor heaters to keep you snug. With dishes such as crab and salmon fishcakes, pan-fried calf's liver with bacon, garlic potatoes and wild mushroom sauce, chocolate and brandy ice cream and lovely Sunday roasts you cannot go wrong. Well-behaved children are welcome, as are dogs. The village is a stunner.

Shaven Crown Hotel
Shipton-under-Wychwood

Stone-mullioned windows, ancient faded tapestries, grand fireplaces and suits of armour... not your average local. This marvellous Tudor stone building, built to a medieval design, is still loved by villagers today, and its history is fascinating – a monastic hospice turned royal inn. When Henry VIII disbanded the monasteries, Elizabeth I gave the 'Crown Inn' back to the village; the locals still come first. Boules championships pull in the crowds in summer, while the Christmas sloe gin competition with courtyard pig roast brings pink cheeks to the faithful. To the passing traveller, the Shaven Crown is a marvellous place in which to savour both medieval architecture, cracking Hook Norton beers, and mixed game terrine with pear chutney or pot roasted pheasant with rich gravy in the cosy Monk's Bar.

directions	On B4022, 3 miles from Witney.
meals	12pm-2pm; 7pm-10pm. Main courses from £8.
closed	2.30pm-6.30pm (from 3pm Saturday, to 7pm Sunday).

directions	On A361, 4 miles NE of Burford.
meals	12pm-2pm (2.30pm weekends); 6pm-9.30pm (9pm Sun). Main courses £9.95-£13.50; bar meals £7.95-£8.95.
closed	2.30pm-5pm. Open all day weekends.

Jon Oldham
Royal Oak,
Ramsden,
Chipping Norton,
Oxfordshire OX7 3AU
tel   01993 868213

Philip Mehrtens
Shaven Crown Hotel, High Street,
Shipton-under-Wychwood,
Oxfordshire OX7 6BA
tel   01993 830330
web   www.theshavencrown.co.uk

map: 8 entry: 379

map: 8 entry: 380

The Chequers
Chipping Norton

Eye-catching with an immaculate stone frontage, smart green paintwork and stylish stone urns, the 18th-century Chequers stands smartly on the village lane. The Goldings took it on in 2003 – it had been closed for five years – and months of refurbishment followed before the reincarnation was unveiled. Prepare for a dramatic, airy and open-plan interior: bare boards and pine tables, cleverly partitioned dining areas, stone walls, roaring woodburner and stacked logs, chunky tables topped with candles and flowers. Soaring rafters, modern oak tables and a vast dresser racked with wine bottles are the wow factors in the dining extension. No music, just a buzz when busy, and excellent food – smoked haddock kedgeree, fisherman's pie, rib-eye steak with red wine sauce, stewed plums in armagnac. Book for the crispy duck night (Thursday) and roast Sunday lunches. Upstairs are a lounge and private dining area.

Kings Head Inn
Bledington

Achingly pretty Cotswold stone cottages around a green with quacking ducks, a pond and a perfect pub with a cobbled courtyard. Archie is young, affable and charming with locals and guests, but Nic is his greatest asset – a milliner, she has done up the bedrooms on a shoestring and they look fabulous. All are different, most have a stunning view, some family furniture mixed in with 'bits' she's picked up, painted wood, great colours and lush fabrics. The bar is lively – not with music but with talk – so choose rooms over the courtyard if you prefer a quiet evening. The flagstoned dining room with pale wood tables is elegant and inviting, and there are lovely unpompous touches like jugs of cow parsley or dahlias from the garden. Expect steaks, stews, fish pies, vegetarian options and roasts on Sundays. Or just tuck into a toasted panini, a ploughman's and a homemade pud.

directions	Churchill on B4450 between Chipping Norton & Stow-on-the-Wold.
meals	12pm-2pm (3pm Sundays); 7pm-9.30pm. Main courses £9.50-£16.
closed	Open all day.

directions	Burford-Stow A424; right to Idbury; Bledington, signed.
meals	12pm-2pm; 7pm-9.30pm. Main courses £8.95-£16.95; bar meals from £4.
rooms	12: 10 doubles, 2 twins, £70-£125. Singles £55.
closed	3pm-6pm (6.30pm Sundays).

See page 37 for bedroom details.

Peter & Asumpta Golding
The Chequers,
Church Road, Churchill,
Chipping Norton,
Oxfordshire OX7 6NJ
tel   01608 659393

Archie & Nicola Orr-Ewing
Kings Head Inn,
The Green, Bledington,
Oxfordshire OX7 6XQ
tel   01608 658365
web   www.kingsheadinn.net

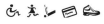

map: 8 entry: 381

map: 8 entry: 382

Oxfordshire

The Crown Inn
Church Enstone

With six years as head chef at the Three Choirs Vineyard behind him, Tony decided to seek out his own place. With his wife Caroline, he headed for the Cotswolds and this striking 17th-century inn. It's a mellow local-stone dream, festooned in creepers and off the beaten track in a sleepy village close to the river Glyme. Walk in to a cosy, cottagey bar, smartly comfortable with old pine tables on a seagrass floor, rough stone walls, and a log fire crackling in the inglenook. At lunchtime, walkers and weekenders come for pints of Hook Norton and generous plates of home-cooked pub grub; warming soups, Dexter beef and Hooky pie, fish and chips and the like are listed on the blackboard. Cooking moves up a gear in the evening. Fish is Tony's speciality, so look out for sea bass with scallops, chilli and garlic dressing. Food is fresh and locally sourced and Sunday lunch is deservedly popular.

directions	3.5 miles south east of Chipping Norton.
meals	12pm–2pm; 7pm–9pm. Main courses £7–£15.
closed	Sunday evenings; Monday lunchtimes.

Tony & Caroline Warburton
The Crown Inn,
Mill Lane, Church Enstone,
Chipping Norton, OX7 4NN

tel	01608 677262
web	www.crowninnenstone.co.uk

map: 8 entry: 383

Oxfordshire

The Falkland Arms
Great Tew

In a perfect Cotswold village, the perfect English inn. Five hundred years on and the fire still roars in the stone-flagged bar under a low timbered ceiling slung with jugs, mugs and tankards. Here, the hop is treated with reverence: ales are changed weekly and old pump clips hang from the bar. And tradition runs deep; they stock endless tins of snuff with splendid names like Irish High Toast and Crumbs of Comfort. In summer, Morris Men jingle in the lane outside and life spills out onto the terrace at the front, and into the big garden behind. This lively pub is utterly down-to-earth and in very good hands. The dining room is tiny and intimate with beams and stone walls; every traditional dish is home-cooked. It's all blissfully free of modern trappings – nowhere more so than in the bar, where mobile phones meet with swift and decisive action.

directions	Off A361 between Banbury & Chipping Norton.
meals	12pm–2pm (bar meals only); 7pm–8pm. No food Sunday evenings. Booking essential for evenings. Main courses £7.50–£14.95.
closed	2.30pm–6pm (from 3pm Saturdays; 3pm–7pm Sundays). Open all day weekends in summer.

Paul Barlow-Heal
The Falkland Arms,
Great Tew, Chipping Norton,
Oxfordshire OX7 4DB

tel	01608 683653
web	www.falklandarms.org.uk

map: 8 entry: 384

Mason's Arms
Swerford

At one time the village of Swerford was owned by a hilariously-named henchman of William the Conqueror, one Robert D'Oily, but there's not a glimpse of a crocheted doily or a Toby jug in today's pub. It may be low on roadside appeal, but inside's chic-cottage décor would knock the clips off a makeover show designer's cue-board: duck-egg blue beams, clotted-cream walls and olive checked curtains, with rugs and seagrass matting across the floor. A wardrobe is stacked with wine bottles, background music plays, the central bar stacks up locals nursing their Brakspear's Special. And the food? It's locally-sourced best-of-British, including the old-fashioned bits. Chef-patron Bill Leadbeater, who has worked for Gordon Ramsay, delivers braised shin of beef, user-friendly steaks and roast shoulder of Oxford Down lamb. Children are not pandered to with nuggets'n'chips but offered mini-portions – and a garden to romp in.

directions	On A361 north east of Chipping Norton.
meals	12pm-2.15pm; 7pm-9pm. Main courses £10.95-£13.95; bar meals £6.50-9.95; set menus £9.95 & £10.95.

Bill & Charmaine Leadbeater
Mason's Arms,
Banbury Road, Swerford,
Chipping Norton, OX7 4AP
tel   01608 683212
web   www.masonsarms.co.nr

map: 8 entry: 385

Olde Reindeer Inn
Banbury

Oliver Cromwell held court in the heavily wood-panelled Globe Room during the Civil War. The panelling was dismantled in 1909, almost sold to America, then returned in 1964... it is a magnificent feature in Banbury's oldest pub. Owned by Hook Norton and run by Tony and Dot Puddifoot, the backstreet local has a reputation for very decently priced, home-cooked lunches, simply but perfectly done. Specialities include steak and ale pie, bubble-and-squeak in a Yorkshire pudding and delicious pies. The bar is cosy polished oak boards, solid furniture and a magnificent, carved, 17th-century fireplace, log-fuelled in winter. Hook Norton ales are served as well as country wines, including apricot and damson, that rival the beer in popularity. Parsons Street is tiny and runs off the Market Square yet the Reindeer is unmissably signed.

directions	In town centre, just off Market Square.
meals	11am-2.30pm. No food Sunday lunchtimes. Main courses £4-£6.75.
closed	Sunday evenings. Open all day.

Tony Puddifoot
Olde Reindeer Inn,
47 Parsons Street,
Banbury,
Oxfordshire OX16 5NA
tel   01295 264031

map: 8 entry: 386

The Jackson Stops Inn
Stretton

James and Sharon Trevor strike just the right balance between the familiar and the novel in this exemplary village pub, and have built up a core of regulars in the few years they have been here. Sharon's warm style ensures that everything runs smoothly in the bare-bones bar and the quirky-rustic dining rooms; James's cooking matches the mood. The menu spans scallops with black pudding, mash and garlic sauce and well-timed pan-fried halibut with boulangère potatoes, while first-rate puddings include glazed lemon and pine nut tart and vanilla pana cotta. Open fires, evening candles, fresh flowers and a rambling corridor linking rooms add to the charm, while in the tiny bar (two scrubbed tables and several benches) Oakham ales are on tap. The old thatched building was formerly known as the White Horse, but the estate agent's sign remained outside the pub for so long that the name stuck.

The Olive Branch
Clipsham

There are so many blackboards here you might think that Sean Hope, Ben Jones and Marcus Welford were school teachers unable to let go. But it's the simplest way to list the speciality wines, the cigars and the daily lunches. The Olive Branch is not your usual chi-chi ex-boozer: its Michelin star is pinned to a relaxed pub personality, the casual mood contrived by closely arranged tables, a medley of books, furniture and a roaring log fire. The adjoining barn is a small party room, and there's a sheltered patio. The menu roams through tempura-battered tiger prawns with chilli mayonnaise to chocolate brownies, but British cooking is a strong point. Fish and chips and roast rib of beef are given a delectable modern edge, real ales are taken seriously with weekly guests – Shepherd Neame Spitfire, Greene King Abbot – and the wines are exceptional. What's more, you can take away from the "pub shop" list. Superb.

directions	From A1 take B668 for Oakham & Stretton. Pub 0.5 miles on.
meals	12pm-2:30pm; 7pm-10pm. Main courses £7.25-£13.50.
closed	2.30pm-6.30pm; Sunday evenings; Mondays.

James & Sharon Trevor
The Jackson Stops Inn,
Rookery Lane,
Stretton, Oakham,
Rutland LE15 7RA

tel	01780 410237

map: 9 entry: 387

directions	2 miles off A1 at Stretton (B668 junction).
meals	12pm-2pm (3pm Sunday); 7pm-9.30pm. Main courses £10.50-£16.95; set lunch £13.50 & £16.50.
closed	Open all day Sunday.

B. Jones, S. Hope & M. Welford
The Olive Branch,
Main Street, Clipsham,
Rutland LE15 7SH

tel	01780 410355
web	www.theolivebranchpub.com

map: 9 entry: 388

Rutland

Fox & Hounds Inn
Exton

Exton is an unspoilt village of thatched houses and honey-coloured stone. On the sycamored village green sits the creeper-covered Fox & Hounds, looking more like an exquisite manor than the coaching house it used to be. Valter and Sandra Floris arrived three years ago, she a local girl, he the Italian chef. No modish gastropubbery here, but they do have a reputation for food in both English and Italian styles: authentic pizzas and pastas as well as more formal dishes such as roast lamb shank with sweet potato mash. Or Valter combines the two, as in his roast leg of Rutland venison with polenta and a chianti jus. The lounge bar is country-smart with armchairs and sofa gathered round a roaring log fire; there's a deep-red walled dining room and a long public bar with darts. The large walled garden is brilliant for alfresco dining, and kids.

directions	Off A606 between Stamford & Oakham.
meals	12pm-2pm; 6.30pm-9pm. No food Sunday evenings. Main courses £7.25-£14.25.

Valter & Sandra Floris
Fox & Hounds Inn,
19 The Green, Exton,
Oakham, Rutland LE15 8AP
tel 01572 812403
web www.foxandhoundsrutland.co.uk

map: 9 entry: 389

Rutland

Finch's Arms
Upper Hambleton

Alone on its peninsula surrounded by Rutland Water, the Finch's has the greatest of rural views. Colin Crawford, who took over nine years ago, could have sat back and twiddled his thumbs and people would still have poured in. But he has not been idle, and has created a terrific team in the kitchen led by David Bailey. Décor in the Garden Room is ultra-elegant, with food to match; choose from steamed wild mushroom and spinach pudding with confit potato, or fillet of beef with rosti potato, baby artichokes and claret sauce. Or sausages with mash and onion... the bar and restaurant menus change frequently. There's a small, bustling bar with log fires, a fine selection of ales, a great wine list, and a garden and a hillside terrace for summer with wonderful watery views. Staff are friendly and efficient.

directions	Off A606, east of Oakham.
meals	12pm-2.30pm; 6.30pm-9.30pm; 12pm-8pm Sundays. Main courses £9.95-£15.95; set lunch (weekdays) £9.95 & £11.95.
closed	Open all day.

Colin & Celia Crawford
Finch's Arms, Oakham Road,
Upper Hambleton, Oakham,
Rutland LE15 8TL
tel 01572 756575
web www.finchsarms.co.uk

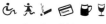

map: 9 entry: 390

Rutland

The Old Pheasant
Uppingham

Earlier renovation knocked down a few walls and has left an odd, rambling shape, but Richard and Nikki have introduced a clean, simple décor and a neutral colour scheme to complement bare brick, heavy beams, open fire and polished tables. It's still a pubby pub, with local Grainstore Brewery ales served alongside Timothy Taylor and Jennings, and friendly too, but the emphasis is on food. The menu is short, refreshingly to-the-point and changes continually, with a welcome number of old-English dishes such as steak and kidney suet pudding. There's a swish streak too: fillet of turbot comes roasted with crispy bacon and herb butter (fish is a strong point), Medbourne honey duck breast is served with blackcurrant sauce and dauphinoise. Choose to eat in the restaurant, in the bar or in the pretty courtyard in summer.

directions	On A47 between Leicester & Peterborough, east of Uppingham.
meals	12pm-2pm; 6.30pm-9pm (12pm-2.30pm, 7pm-8.30pm Sunday). Main courses £9-£16.
closed	3pm-5pm (3.30pm-6pm Sunday). In winter, 3pm-6pm (3pm-5pm Saturday, 3.30pm-6pm Sunday).

Richard Graham
The Old Pheasant,
Main Road, Glaston,
Uppingham, Rutland LE15 9BP

tel	01572 822326
web	www.theoldpheasant.co.uk

map: 9 entry: 391

Shropshire

The Waterdine
Llanfair Waterdine

"We've come for a ploughman's and been asked to wait while they bake some fresh rolls," said a customer. Ken's food would be worth the wait and booking is a must for both lunch and dinner. Take a look at the tiny kitchen garden packed with herbs: a hint of what is to come. Crab cannelloni with chive sauce, rack of Shropshire lamb with Provençal vegetables, roast turbot on leek confit with girolle mushroom, Valhrona chocolate mousse – take your fill in the conservatory or dining room. Bar food, too, shows skill and finesse: baked black pudding with cider sauce, root vegetable soup, rump of Longhorn beef with red wine, shallot and mushroom sauce. The garden, bordered by the river, is tailor-made for summer pleasure, to be enjoyed with a tasty drop of Woods' seasonal ales, a fine cider or perry. Takeaway homemade pickles and preserves will have you dashing back for more.

directions	Off B4355, 4 miles west of Knighton.
meals	12pm-1.45pm; 7pm-9pm. Main courses £7.50-£15; set menus £17.50-£27.50.
closed	Sunday evenings; Mondays (except bank holidays).

Ken Adams
The Waterdine,
Llanfair Waterdine, Knighton,
Shropshire LD7 1TU

tel	01547 528214
web	www.waterdine.com

map: 7 entry: 392

Bottle & Glass
Picklescott

Come via All Stretton – it's worth it for the views. In the wilds of Shropshire, in a village of under a hundred souls, is this archetypal English country inn. Cross the front terrace and enter a beamed, oak-corsetted lounge bar, warm and inviting with log fires, fresh flowers, chunky candles and merry landlord. There's an eating area with dark pink walls, a second bar with cushioned bar stools and wooden settles and, for the literary-minded, a bookcase full of novels. Classical music plays gently in the background as walkers and locals take their fill of Hobson's Bitter and Shropshire Lad. The menu is extensive and helpings are hearty, so tuck into lunchtime rolls and ploughman's and good, simple, homemade soups, dumpling stews and steak and Guinness pies. Bow-tied, jolly-jumpered Paul Stretton-Downes U.A.A. (Unencumbered by Academic Achievement) makes this place special.

The Unicorn Inn
Ludlow

With its trio of Michelin-starred restaurants, Ludlow deserves at least one pub serving proper pub tucker. The Unicorn hides at the bottom end of town on the east bank of the river Corve as you approach the Shrewsbury road and, unlike its more distinguished neighbours, does not have to be booked weeks in advance. Along with well-priced bar snacks there's proper food and plenty of it (local rabbit in mustard sauce, seafood medley for two, boozy fruit cake ice cream). You eat before a log fire in the panelled, ancient-beamed bar, at red-clothed tables in the dining rooms or in the beer garden by the stream in summer. Ceremony here is about as out-of-place as Formula One tyres on a family Ford: no wonder it remains popular. And the beer is expertly kept.

directions	Village signed off A49 north of Church Stretton.
meals	12pm-2pm; 6pm-9pm. No food Sunday evenings; Mondays in winter. Main courses £8.50-£14.
closed	2.30pm-6pm (7pm Sunday); Sunday evenings in winter.

directions	From A49, B4361 to Ludlow. After lights & bridge, bear right; bear left up hill. Next right after lights at bottom of hill. 50 yds on left.
meals	12pm-2.15pm; 6pm-9.15pm; 12pm-2pm, 6.30pm-9pm Sunday. Main courses £6.95-£13.50.

Paul & Jo Stretton-Downes
Bottle & Glass,
Picklescott,
Church Stretton,
Shropshire SY6 6NR
tel 01694 751345

Mike & Rita Knox
The Unicorn Inn,
Lower Corve Street,
Ludlow, Shropshire SY8 1DU
tel 01584 873555
web www.theunicorninnludlow.com

map: 7 entry: 393

map: 7 entry: 394

Fighting Cocks
Stottesdon

As you negotiate tractors and horses on the lane to get here, you pass the farm that supplies the kitchen with its excellent meat. Sandra Jeffries wears multiple hats: jolly landlady, enthusiastic chef, manager of the great little shop next door. Step into the bar and choose a velour-topped perch – or a settle or a sofa by the fire. The décor is haphazard, the carpet red-patterned, the piano strewn with newspapers and guides (the ancient rolling hills of Shropshire beckon) and the copper-topped bar hung with pewter tankards. Up steps is a room for smokers, darts, dominoes and TV. The dining room is as unpretentious as can be and a proper match for the cooking; make the most of gamey (or spicy) casseroles, organic salmon, scrummy pies and beautiful nursery puddings. Plans are afoot to extend the ramshackle 'garden' at the back. A true community pub.

Crown Country Inn
Munslow

The thistles that grew around The Crown's front door have long gone. Richard and Jane Arnold bought this listed Tudor inn (variously a courtroom, doctor's surgery and jail in previous lives) in a parlous state. Now it's a happier place, where locals gather for a chat and a pint of Cleric's Cure at dark polished tables in a winter-cosy, log-stoved bar. The upstairs function room and outside terrace are also well-used. The secret of the inn's success is revealed on the rustic walls of the bar, adorned with food awards and a map of suppliers: proprietor and chef Richard is passionate about local produce and the menu is stuffed with it. Try crostini ('little toasts') of local black pudding with Wenlock Edge Farm bacon, or griddled local sirloin steak with organic smoked butter. And the cheeseboard is a treat of lesser-known British cheeses – including Hereford Hop, rolled in hops.
No smoking throughout.

directions	Village signed off A4117 & B4363 east of Ludlow at Cleobury Mortimer.
meals	12pm-2pm; 7pm-9pm. No food Mondays, weekday lunchtimes & Sunday evenings. Main courses £7.95-£13.95.

Sandra Jeffries
Fighting Cocks,
1 High Street, Stottesdon,
Bridgnorth,
Shropshire DY14 8TZ
tel   01746 718270

map: 7 entry: 395

directions	On B4368 to Bridgnorth, at extreme western end of Munslow.
meals	12pm-2pm; 6.45pm-8.45pm (6.30pm-8.30pm Sunday). Main courses £7.50-£16.
closed	2pm-6.45pm (6pm Sunday); Mondays.

Richard & Jane Arnold
Crown Country Inn,
Munslow, Craven Arms,
Shropshire SY7 9ET
tel   01584 841205
web   www.crowncountryinn.co.uk

map: 7 entry: 396

Shropshire

The Wenlock Edge Inn
Wenlock Edge

A E Housman's 'blue remembered hills' set the scene, high on a limestone ridge. Daniel and Julia's inn has a terrace with that view – and a beer garden – and a conservatory. This is walking and riding country, so set off down one of the many bridleways and come back hungry: you can look forward to some great food at the Wenlock. The menu is largely based on locally available produce, and the chef, being a Shropshire Lad, knows what's what. In the bar are old-fashioned ginger beer and lemonade, Hobson's real ale and guests such as Archers Golden – each a fine accompaniment to the day's homemade soup, oak-roasted Bradon salmon, steak and ale pie, beef stroganoff and rack of Shropshire lamb cooked in garlic and red wine – plus fresh vegetables in generous portions. Vegetarians are looked after, too. Settle into a cosy corner by the log stove.

Shropshire

The Riverside Inn
Cressage

There's a great buzz in this cosy, comfortable huntin', shootin' and fishin' inn – standing on a magnificent bend of the Severn and looking out over open country towards the Wrekin and beyond. The Riverside Inn is worth seeking out for its open fires in winter and its dining conservatory with the amazing view all year round. Seasonal monthly menus might include starters of roasted parsnip soup or salmon and prawn salad; main dishes could be haddock veronique, cod with tarragon and pernod or game casserole and dumplings – and there's port to accompany your cheese. Make the most of the Salopian beers, the country fruit wines and the homemade sorbets and ice creams – it's all good value. For summer: a pretty garden smartly furnished with patio and that view – and you can fish from the bank for salmon and trout.

directions	On B4371 between Much Wenlock & Church Stretton.
meals	12pm-2pm; 7pm-9pm. Main courses £7.50-£13.25.
closed	Monday; Tuesday lunchtime; 2.30pm-7pm Wednesday-Sunday.

Daniel & Julia Christ
The Wenlock Edge Inn,
Hilltop, Wenlock Edge,
Much Wenlock TF13 6DJ
tel 01746 785678
web www.wenlockedgeinn.co.uk

map: 7 entry: 397

directions	On A458 Shrewsbury road.
meals	12pm-2.30pm; 6.30pm-9.30pm. Main courses £7.15-£10.95.

Peter Stanford Davis
The Riverside Inn,
Cound, Cressage,
Much Wenlock,
Shropshire SY5 6AF
tel 01952 510900

map: 7 entry: 398

Shropshire

Shropshire

The Burlton Inn
Burlton

Gerry Bean's philosophy here is tried and successful: keep it simple. Well-stocked with real ales from Wye Valley and Salopian and wines of the month, the central bar has assorted pine tables in front of an open log fire. Recent additions 'in response to popular demand', include kitchen and dining room improvements, and a sun-trap terrace with posh tables and chairs. Yet the Burlton remains both intimate and personal. The staff are super and there's nothing wrong with the food either, from home-cooked gammon or rare roast beef sarnies to roast rack of lamb with apricot and mustard glaze – or plaice fillets with smoked salmon, chablis and prawn cream. All are chalked up daily. Neither the building itself nor the road it stands on are the prettiest, but the minute you enter you know the warmth of the place is genuine – just like its owner.

The Fox
Chetwynd Aston

As you wander from room to room – each sunny space radiating off the central bar – you realise just how vast this 1920s pub is. Yet there are plenty of nooks to be private in. Fires crackle in magnificent fireplaces, heavy cast-iron radiators add warmth, Turkey rugs are scattered on stained-wood floors and summer promises a great big garden with rolling views. Pews, solid oak tables and chairs – there's a happy mix of furniture and a bistro feel here. It's a grown-ups' pub and attracts urban rather than country folk, appreciative of a good selection of wines by the glass and three regularly changing guest ales. Staff are charming, customers happy and the food looks great. Choose a table, then browse the daily-changing menu: there are ploughman's with local cheeses, venison pie with apple chutney, Shropshire lamb with roast potatoes, warm chocolate brownies and very good coffee.

directions	On A528 Wrexham road, 8 miles north of Shrewsbury.
meals	12pm-2pm; 6.30pm-9.45pm (7pm-9.30pm Sundays). Main courses £8.95-£16.95.
closed	Bank holiday Monday lunchtimes.

Gerald Bean
The Burlton Inn,
Burlton,
Shrewsbury,
Shropshire SY4 5TB
tel   01939 270284

map: 7 entry: 399

directions	Just off A41 south of Newport,
meals	12pm-10pm (9.30pm Sunday). Main courses £7.95-£14.45.
closed	Open all day.

Sam Cornwall
The Fox,
Pave Lane, Chetwynd Aston,
Newport, Shropshire TF10 9LQ
tel   01952 815940
web   www.brunningandprice.co.uk

map: 8 entry: 400

All Nations
Madeley

The old Victorian pub could be an extension of the Industrial Open Air Museum on the other side of the bridge. Once smothered with ivy, now spruce and white, it looks more family house than pub. But step across the threshold and you're into timeworn-tavern territory — cast-iron tables, leatherette benches, coal fire at one end, log fire at the other. Old photographs of Ironbridge strew the walls, secondhand paperbacks ask to be taken home (donations to charity accepted), dogs doze and spotless loos await — outside. It's a chatty, friendly ex-miners' ale house and some of the locals could have been here forever: an old boy by the fire clutching a pewter tankard, another in yellow waders. Drink is own-brew, well-kept, low-cost Dabley from the hatch, plus three others and a cider, while the menu encompasses two sorts of roll — black pudding or cheese and onion, with tomato on request. The sort of place you need to catch before it's gone.

Hundred House Hotel
Norton

Henry is an innkeeper of the old school, with a great sense of humour — he once kept chickens, but they didn't keep him. Having begun its life in the 14th century, the place rambles charmingly inside as well as out. Enter a world of blazing log fires, soft brick walls, oak panelling and quarry-tiled floors. Dried flowers hang from beams, herbs sit in vases, blackboard menus trumpet prime Shropshire sirloin, chicken blanquette with lemon and sage, grilled tuna in Moroccan spices. In the restaurant, Sylvia's wild and wonderful collage art hangs on wild and wonderful walls, and there's live music in the barn. Wander out with a pint of Heritage Mild and share a quiet moment with a few stone lions in the beautiful garden, full of unusual roses, herbaceous plants and a working herb garden with over 50 varieties — a real summer treat.

directions	Off Legges Way, near entrance to Blists Hill Museum.
meals	Filled rolls £1.50.
closed	4pm-5pm. Open all day Thursday-Sunday.

Jim Birtwistle
All Nations,
20 Coalport Road,
Madeley, Telford,
Shropshire TF7 5DP
tel   01952 585747

map: 8 entry: 401

directions	Midway between Bridgnorth & Telford on A422.
meals	12pm-2.30pm; 6pm-9.30pm (7pm-9pm Sundays). Main courses £7.95-£18.95.
closed	3pm-5.30pm.

The Phillips Family
Hundred House Hotel,
Bridgnorth Road, Norton, Telford,
Shropshire TF11 9EE
tel   01952 730353
web   www.hundredhouse.co.uk

map: 8 entry: 402

Shropshire

Pheasant Inn
Linley Brook

The only traffic you're likely to encounter on the way here are a couple of horses clip-clopping along – or, if things hot up a bit, a tractor. The Pheasant has been here for centuries and is wondrously unspoilt. Expect a wood-burning stove and an open fire, wooden benches, pub tables and a carpeted floor... and fox masks, fox brushes and polished horse brasses on low beams. In a second room, past the hatch, are bar billiards. Simon and Liz Reed are landlord and landlady and run the Pheasant single-handedly; they cook, clean, serve, stoke the fire *and* find time to chat to customers. There's no piped music and everything shines. Walkers and locals pop in for a quiet pint and simple, very good pub food: toasted sandwiches, local gammon and steaks, treacle suet pudding. Even the beers have names that belong to another age: Wye Valley Butty Bach, Salopian Heaven Sent, Cannon Muzzle Loader and Shropshire Gold.

directions	Just off B4373 Bridgnorth-Broseley road, 4 miles north of Bridgnorth.
meals	12pm-2pm; 7pm-9pm. Main courses £5.95-£7.95.
closed	2.30pm-6.30pm (from 3pm Saturday).

Simon & Liz Reed
Pheasant Inn,
Linley Brook, Bridgnorth,
Shropshire WV16 4TA
tel   01746 762260
web   www.the-pheasant-inn.co.uk

map: 8 entry: 403

Somerset

Woods Bar & Dining Room
Dulverton

It hasn't been a pub for ever – indeed, it used to specialise in tea and cakes – but it is in the centre of a lively little village, and wine buffs and foodies have much to be grateful for. Landlords Sally and Paddy are helpful, friendly and welcome families and dogs. A stable-like partition divides the space up into two intimate seating areas, beyond which is a smart, soft-lit, deeply cosy bar: two woodburners, lots of pine, a few barrel tables and stags' heads on exposed stone walls. Outside, a small paved area and a couple of cast-iron tables. Ales include Exmoor Gold, Otter (Devon's largest brewer) and St Austell – but the wines are the thing here, with many by the glass. A Dutch chef delivers some fine modern British dishes, with the emphasis on food in season. Hard to resist breast of pheasant with chestnut purée and port sauce – or a slab of Montgomery's cheddar with homemade chutney.

directions	From Tiverton, A396 N; left on B3222 for Dulverton; near church & bank.
meals	12pm-2pm; 7pm-9.30pm (9pm Sundays). Main courses £6.95-£14.95.

Sally & Paddy Groves
Woods Bar & Dining Room,
4 Bank Square,
Dulverton,
Somerset TA22 9BU
tel   01398 324007

map: 2 entry: 404

The Royal Oak Inn
Luxborough

Five miles south of Minehead, as the pheasant flies, is Luxborough, tucked under the lip of the Exmoor's Brendon hills. This is hunting country and from September to February beaters and loaders traditionally lunch at The Oak. Two low-beamed, log-fired, dog-dozed bars (with locals' table) lead to a warren of dining rooms kitted out with polished dining tables and hunting prints on deep green walls. (In spate, the river Washford has been known to take a detour!). A shelf heaves with walking books and maps; the owners lend them freely, all are returned. A chef who trained in Alsace delivers first-class food: generous starters, fish from St Mawes, vegetables from local growers, game aplenty. For those lucky enough to stay, bedrooms ramble around the first floor (one below has a private terrace) and are individual, peaceful, homely and great value.

Three Horseshoes
Langley Marsh

A proper, traditional local and proud of it. Come for good beer and good food, kept and cooked by John and Marella. He's an MG man (owns four) and the pub is full of memorabilia, steering wheels, display cases, Dinky toys, and a unique collection of black and white photos of the racing greens. Otter Bitter and others are tapped from the cask. Lunches and dinners have been described as "home-cooked food from heaven". Pies, soup and sandwiches, daily specials – lamb steak in mint and yogurt – all freshly made, no chips, nothing frozen, and veg from the garden. Just so you see how seriously they take it, they list their suppliers on the back of the menu. In the bustling front room, polished tables, dark wallpaper dotted with banknotes, table skittles, dominoes, darts and a piano; in the dining room, old settles; in the garden, tables and sloping lawns.

directions	Luxborough signed off A396 from Dunster.
meals	12pm-2pm; 7pm-9pm. Main courses £11.95-£14.95.
rooms	10: 8 doubles, 2 twins, £65-£85. Singles £55-£65.
closed	2.30pm-6pm (7pm Sundays).

See page 37 for bedroom details.

directions	Off B3227 Wiveliscombe; turn in front of White Hart towards Huish Champflower; 1 mile on right.
meals	12pm-1.45pm; 7pm-9.30pm. Main courses £5.50-£11.95.
closed	2.30pm-7pm. Mondays in winter.

James & Siân Waller, Sue Hinds
The Royal Oak Inn,
Luxborough, Dunster,
Somerset TA23 0SH
tel 01984 640319
web www.theroyaloakinnluxborough.co.uk

map: 2 entry: 405

John & Marella Hopkins
Three Horseshoes,
Langley Marsh,
Wiveliscombe,
Somerset TA4 2UL
tel 01984 623763

map: 2 entry: 406

Carew Arms
Crowcombe

Supposedly retired, Reg Ambrose is assisting son Simon in reviving this pub in the shadow of the Quantock Hills. It was, and still is, a mammoth task. But the outside loos have been spruced up and the old skittle alley transformed; now it's a bar-dining room whose French windows lead to a sunny back terrace and a garden with tables and gentle woodland views. The front room, with its hatch bar, flagstones, plain settles, pine tables with benches and vast inglenook remains delightfully unspoilt. Down pints of Exmoor Ale, engage in lively conversation and enjoy Cornish seafood casserole, grilled lamb cutlets with braised onions, locally farmed beef steaks and orange trifle. Freshly decorated bedrooms are upstairs: new pine, good linen, creaking floorboards. There's Sunday jazz once a month and children and dogs get a proper welcome.

Blue Ball Inn
Triscombe

Not so long ago the Blue Ball was 'rolled' down the hill a few yards; now the old thatched buildings join the ancient stables below. Thanks to craftsmen's skills and plenty of vision, it has metamorphosed into a rather smart pub and new owners Gerald and Sue Rogers plan to keep it that way. Climb the fabulous beech stairs to a swishly-carpeted central bar that leads to two inviting dining areas, each with open fires, country furnishings and fabrics and high-raftered ceilings. Menus are imaginative, produce local. Treat yourself to wild sea bass fillet with Lyonnaise potatoes and roasted tomato sauce or pan-fried Quantock rabbit spiced with lemongrass. At the bar, lunchtime crusty rolls and excellent cheese ploughman's make this a popular walkers' pit-stop. There are four ales, wines by the glass and local farm ciders – in summer taken out in the decked garden with views across Taunton's vale.

directions	Off A358 between Taunton & Minehead.
meals	12pm-2pm; 7pm-9.30pm. No food Sun eves October-March. Main courses £9-£16.
rooms	6: 3 doubles, 3 twins £79.
closed	3.30pm-5pm (4pm-7pm Sunday). Open all day Saturday; open all day Sunday April-September.

See page 37 for bedroom details.

directions	From Taunton A358 for Minehead; past B. Lydeard right to Triscombe.
meals	12pm-2pm; 7pm-9.30pm (9pm Sun). No food Sunday & Monday evenings in Jan, Feb & Nov. Main courses £7.95-£16.95.
closed	3pm-7pm.

	Reg Ambrose
	Carew Arms,
	Crowcombe, Taunton,
	Somerset TA4 4AD
tel	01984 618631
web	www.thecarewarms.co.uk

map: 2 entry: 407

	Gerald & Sue Rogers
	Blue Ball Inn,
	Triscombe, Bishops Lydeard,
	Taunton, Somerset TA4 3HE
tel	01984 618242
web	www.blueballinn.co.uk

map: 2 entry: 408

The Rising Sun Inn
West Bagborough

In 2002 the Sun rose from the ashes of a fire, and once again shines brightly. Constructed around the original 16th-century cob walls and magnificent door, its reincarnation is bold and craftsman-led, with 80 tons of solid oak timbers and windows and a slate-floored bar. Add Art Nouveau features, spotlighting, swagged drapery and a Victorian replica of Judge Jeffrey's chair (he supposedly stayed following the Rebellion), and you have a very smart pub indeed. There's Exmoor Gold and Cotleigh Tawny to savour, modern art to buy, and, high in the rafters, a dining room with views that unfurl to Exmoor and the Blackdown Hills. It's an impressive setting for very impressive food: lamb tagine, bouillabaisse, seared venison with sherry vinegar sauce, sirloin steak with horseradish hollandaise, iced passionfruit parfait with strawberry jus.

The Blagdon Inn
Blagdon Hill

The Rushtons have a knack of finding the right pub in the right location. Now the old cider house on the edge of the Blackdown Hills – handy access for the M5 – is a stylish gastropub flourishing a modern menu and fresh, local produce. Step inside to thick stone walls, flagged and polished wooden floors, a blazing log fire fronted by leather tub chairs, and old dining tables in cosy eating areas. Fresh flowers and daily papers are further welcome touches. West Country produce, organic if available, is the mainstay of the productive kitchen: fish comes from Brixham and Looe, eggs and meat are free-range, the Ruby Red rib-eye, hung for 21 days, is served with hand-cut chips and the steak and kidney pie has a delicious shortcrust topping. Add great local beers and organic soft drinks and you have one perfect pub.

directions	Off A358 Taunton-Minehead road, 8 miles north-west of Taunton.
meals	12pm-2pm; 7pm-9pm. Main courses £5.95-£9 (lunch), £9.50-£15.50 (dinner).
closed	Mondays (except bank holidays).

Rob & Chris Rainey
The Rising Sun Inn,
West Bagborough,
Taunton, Somerset TA4 3EF

tel	01823 432575
web	www.theriser.co.uk

map: 2 entry: 409

directions	M5 junc. 25 into Taunton; Trull road out of town, then Honiton Road for 3 miles; pub on right.
meals	12pm-2pm; 6.30pm-9.30pm (9pm Sunday). Main courses £7.95-£14.95.
closed	Open all day weekends.

Steve Rushton
The Blagdon Inn,
Blagdon Hill, Taunton,
Somerset TA3 7SG

tel	01823 421296
web	www.blagdoninn.co.uk

map: 2 entry: 410

Somerset

The Greyhound Inn
Staple Fitzpaine

A classic English country pub, its walls bedecked with collages of pictures and fishing memorabilia to create an atmosphere of warmth and hospitality. Let the eye wander while sitting at wooden tables nicely worn from frequent use and decorated simply with vases of wild flowers. Interconnecting bars with open fires and flag-stoned floors are perfect for enjoying cask marque real ales, Somerset ciders and fresh local produce on a seasonal menu; children get smaller portions of the same good stuff. Then "retreat in good order", as one boxing print wisely suggests, to clean, comfortable bedrooms: more hotel than individual with floral curtains and bed covers. All this in deepest Somerset with walks through forestry to Castle Neroche and stunning views from the Blackdown Hills.

directions	A358 for Ilminster; 4 miles; right for Staple Fitzpaine. Left at T-junc; 1.5 miles; on right at x-roads.
meals	12pm-2pm; 7pm-9.30pm (9pm Sunday). Main courses £8-£18.
rooms	4: 2 doubles, 2 twins from £80. Singles from £65.
closed	2.30pm-6pm. Open all day Sunday & race days in Taunton.

See page 37 for bedroom details.

Ivor & Lucy Evans
The Greyhound Inn,
Staple Fitzpaine, Taunton,
Somerset TA3 5SP
tel 01823 480227
web www.thegreyhoundinn.fsbusiness.co.uk

map: 2 entry: 411

Somerset

Farmers Inn
West Hatch

Country-cosy with class. Debbie, Giles and two French chefs have revived this old inn; the wine list is lovingly compiled, cask ales are on tap and guest beers are increasing as demand grows. There's an open rambling feel and a generous bar, small and large tables with wheelback chairs, comfy leather sofas around the woodburner, a mass of stacked logs, the odd bench or pew. Food is imaginative and beautifully presented, whether it be Welsh rarebit with crispy bacon or shark steak with black rice and wilted spinach. Homemade bread and olives come as a complimentary nibble. Stay the night in off-beat but elegant rooms with distinctive beds (all antique) and expansive, gleaming wooden floors. Bathrooms are shiny and chic. And the garden has great views.

directions	Turn off A358 south of Taunton at Nag's Head pub, follow brown 'inn' sign for 2 miles.
meals	12pm-2pm (2.30pm weekends); 7pm-9pm (9.30pm Fri & Sat). Main courses £10-£15.50; bar meals £4.50-£9.50.
rooms	5 doubles £90-£110. Singles £70-£90.
closed	3pm-7pm Saturday & Sunday.

See page 38 for bedroom details.

Debbie Lush
Farmers Inn,
Slough Green, West Hatch,
Taunton, Somerset TA3 5RS
tel 01823 480480
web www.farmersinnwesthatch.co.uk

map: 2 entry: 412

Canal Inn
Wrantage

Blink and you could miss the rustic whitewashed pub by the A378 – closed for years until Pedro and Clare picked up on its potential in 2003. It's much more than the no-frills ale house it appears to be. Enjoy the best local ales for miles – foaming pints of Blackdown Ditch Water – in the bare-boarded bar, or sample Somerset scrumpy-style ciders and a host of Belgian beers. Yet the key to its success in winning favour with the community is its passion for local produce. Menus proudly list the small suppliers, all within a five-mile radius – eggs and veg from Mr & Mrs Titman, vintage local cheeses, allotment veg. A farmers' market in the bar on the last Saturday of the month brings customers and suppliers together. So food miles are kept to a minimum and trade receives a boost – ingenious. Regular fish nights, Monday fish and chips (eat-in or take-away), music nights and an annual beer festival complete the picture.

directions	Beside A378 towards Langport, 2 miles east of A378 Taunton-Ilminster road
meals	12pm-2pm; 6.30pm-9pm. Main courses £6-£10 (lunch), £10-£15 (dinner).
closed	2.30pm-5pm (7pm weekends); Monday lunchtimes.

Pedro Aparacion & Clare Paul
Canal Inn,
Wrantage, Taunton,
Somerset TA3 6DF
tel   01823 480210
web   www.thecanalinn.com

map: 2 entry: 413

Lord Poulett Arms
Hinton St George

There's an upbeat yet elegant feel to this wonderful 400-year-old inn. And it sits in a ravishing village. Traditional trappings – hops, pewter tankards, country antiques – rub shoulders with quirky bits: *Carry On* posters on the wall, a hammock in the divine summer garden, a chess set laid out to play. Floors are bare flags or age-worn boards, the bar is simple and uncluttered, there's space and intimacy at the same time, a huge old fireplace crackling with logs, cider from the jug. The chef trained in Japan so the Dorsetshire fish and the Exmoor game might come with an oriental touch. Try spinach and pea soup, wild sea bass with exotic mushrooms in a sake and teriyaki sauce, Lovington's ice creams and west country cheeses. Contemporary wallpapers set the tone for super bedrooms upstairs – along with open-stone walls, brass bedsteads and seagrass floors; Roberts radios add a fun touch. Brilliant value, friendly to dogs.

directions	Village signed off A30, west of Crewkerne.
meals	12pm-2pm; 7pm-9pm. Main courses £9-£15.
rooms	4 twins/doubles £72. Singles £48.
closed	3pm-6.30pm & Monday lunchtimes.

See page 38 for bedroom details.

Steve Hill
Lord Poulett Arms,
High Street, Hinton St George,
Crewkerne, Somerset TA17 8SE
tel   01460 73149
web   www.lordpoulettarms.com

map: 3 entry: 414

Rose & Crown Inn (Eli's)
Huish Episcopi

Quirky, unspoilt and in the family for 140 years. The layout has evolved, gradually taking over the family home. There's no bar as such – you choose from the casks – but who cares when the locals are so lovely, the cider so rough and the beer so tasty. Walk in and you step straight back to the Fifties. There are worn flagstones and aged panelling, cottagey doors and coal fires in five low parlours radiating off a central tap room. The 'gentleman's kitchen' is the oldest and cosiest, the pool, darts and juke box room the largest and newest. They do crib nights and occasional quiz nights and Morris dancers drop by in summer. The food is brilliant value: creamy winter vegetable soup, a tasty pork, apple and cider cobbler, chicken breast with tarragon, chocolate and rum torte. Everyone's happy and children like the little play area outside.

directions	300 yards from St Mary's Church. On left-hand side towards Wincanton on leaving Huish.
meals	12pm-2pm, 5.30pm-7.30pm. No food Sunday evenings. Main courses £5.95-£6.75.
closed	2.30pm-5.30pm Monday-Thursday. Open all day Friday-Sunday.

Eileen Pittard
Rose & Crown Inn (Eli's),
Huish Episcopi,
Langport,
Somerset TA10 9QT
tel   01458 250494

map: 3 entry: 415

The Devonshire Arms
Long Sutton

Behind the country hotel façade, a striking modernity. Step off the village green and into an open-plan space of chunky blond-wood tables, brown leather sofas, west country photographs and stylish twiggery. The Devonshire Arms is three-quarters restaurant, one-quarter pub, there are Belgian beers on draught, four guest ales and a good wine list. The food's fabulous, the hosts are engaging and the prices are fair. Choose from ploughman's with homemade chutney, luxury venison burgers or fish with home-cut chips, linger over a slow-roast shoulder of lamb with mustard mash or baked feta cheese and parsnips with beetroot confit and spiced lentils. Puddings include panna cotta, sorbets include cassis... not a glimmer left of the old pub's previous existence. Outside are a new patio and sunny walled garden; upstairs, a flurry of large, light and absolutely fabulous bedrooms.

directions	By village green.
meals	12pm-2.30pm; 7pm-9.30pm. No food Sunday eves in winter. Main courses £11-£16.50; bar meals £3.95-£9.95.
rooms	9: 8 doubles, 1 family room, £70-£110. Singles from £55.
closed	Open all day in summer.

See page 38 for bedroom details.

Philip & Sheila Mepham
The Devonshire Arms,
Long Sutton, Langport,
Somerset TA10 9LP
tel   01458 241271
web   www.thedevonshirearms.com

map: 3 entry: 416

Red Lion
Babcary

A lattice of hot white bread with unsalted butter arrives unannounced and with a cheery smile – and the girls will keep a benign eye out for you right through from starters to coffee. Best to book at weekends. This is a Somerset revival that combines the best of pub tradition with excellent food. There is a single central bar with a locals' snug behind dispensing real ale, local cider and house wines from France and Oz. To one side, hair-cord carpets, sofas and the cast-iron stove lend a welcome to the bright bar/lounge, while to the far right a dozen well-spaced country dining tables plainly set out on original flagstone flooring are part of an immaculate reconstruction. Daily menus offer as little or as much as you'd like, from small or large Caesar salads to homemade burger with tomato relish, salmon fillet with shellfish cream, and lamb rosettes with glazed garlic and rosemary.

directions	Off A37 & A303 7 miles north of Yeovil.
meals	12pm-2.30pm; 7pm-9pm (9.30pm Fridays & Saturdays). Main courses £6.95-£16.
closed	2.30pm-6pm & Sunday evenings.

Clare & Charles Garrard
Red Lion,
Babcary,
Somerton,
Somerset TA11 7ED
tel   01458 223230

map: 3 entry: 417

The Montague Inn
Shepton Montague

With scarcely another dwelling in view, the 17th-century public house still looks like the grocer's it once was. It also happens to neighbour one of the south-west's largest organic farms; your eggs and vegetables couldn't be fresher. Small remains beautiful, with real ales straight from the cask, log fires in the bar, candles on stripped pine tables and grey-green carpeting and matching paintwork. There are two bars and both the restaurant and rear terrace have garden and country views. The food is simple yet imaginative: granary sandwiches, maybe, with Old Spot sausages and red onion confit and a ploughman's lunch with Exmoor blue cheese. And there's true quality in dishes such as Quantock duck with aubergine and olive relish and Somerset rib-eye steak with pepper and cognac sauce on the daily à la carte. Good for a special meal, then, and a relaxing country lunch away from it all.

directions	Off A359 2 miles east of Castle Cary, towards Bruton.
meals	12pm-2.30pm; 7pm-9pm. Main courses £6.50-£12.50 (lunch), £12.50-£17.50 (dinner).
closed	Sunday evenings; Mondays.

Sean & Suzy O'Callaghan
The Montague Inn,
Shepton Montague,
Wincanton,
Somerset BA9 8JW
tel   01749 813213

map: 3 entry: 418

The Manor House Inn
Ditcheat

The focus of Ditcheat life has a just-renovated feel – the landlord swept in with a youthful broom in 2004 – but authenticity will follow. In the bar – big, unscuffed and open plan – there's a good fire blazing. Settle back with something tasty from Bath Ales and tune in to chatter of weather, sump oil and stock. Skittles clatter in the background – the skittle alley has had a makeover too – as enticing aromas demand you check out the chalked boards. There are baked avocados filled with Mediterranean vegetables and topped with a parmesan crust, and chargrilled steaks with stilton sauce or peppercorn and brandy. After, totter out to the single-storey building where smart and generous bedrooms await; beds are hugely comfortable, shower rooms a treat. In the morning, discover a picture-perfect village amid gently rolling hills.

The Three Horseshoes
Batcombe

Down a web of country lanes, the Woods' honey-stoned coaching inn sits by the church. Step into a long, low bar, its beams painted cream, its pine scrubbed, its pink-sponged walls hung with local landscapes. There are cushioned window seats and an inglenook with a wood-burning stove. It's a truly relaxing place that appeals as much to locals in for a pint of Butcombe as to diners and families; there's a summer terrace and a great play area for children. The modern British menu uses local organic produce and is full of promise: start with duck liver terrine with onion marmalade, move on to shoulder of local lamb with red wine jus, or sea bass fillet with tomato and herb salsa, finish with white chocolate and rum mousse. If you're here for the ale, don't miss the chance of a quenching pint of Bats in the Belfry from Blindmans Brewery in nearby Leighton.

directions	Between A37 & A371, in Ditcheat next to church.
meals	12pm-2pm; 7pm-9.30pm. No food Sunday evenings. Main courses £8.95-£16.95; bar meals £5.25-£11.95.
rooms	3: 2 doubles, 1 twin £80. Singles £50.
closed	3pm-5.30pm. Open all day Fri-Sun.

See page 38 for bedroom details.

directions	Off A359 between Frome & Bruton, 7 miles south west of Frome.
meals	12pm-2pm; 7pm-9.30pm. No food on Mondays. Main courses £7.95-£16.95.
closed	Mondays in winter; 3pm-6.30pm.

Giles Pushman
The Manor House Inn,
Ditcheat, Shepton Mallet,
Somerset BA4 6RB
tel 01749 860276
web www.themanorhouseinn.co.uk

Bob & Shirley Wood
The Three Horseshoes,
Batcombe, Shepton Mallet,
Somerset BA4 6HE
tel 01749 850359
web www.three-horseshoes.co.uk

map: 3 entry: 419

map: 3 entry: 420

Seymour Arms
Witham Friary

Plain but special, scruffy but unspoilt. Purpose-built in 1866, along with farm buildings on the Duke of Somerset's estate, the Seymour Arms has barely changed. Through the imposing porticoed entrance, into a corridor and along to the old hatch bar; to the right, a snug with snooker and bags of smoky atmosphere, to the left, a proper-sized main room. Original flagstones, simple patterned walls, benches and panelling painted an old-fashioned green, a couple of tables, an open fire. That's it. No food – you're here for a pint and a civilised chat. Well-kept beer is Ushers Best plus an occasional guest, and they sell more cider than beer. Outside is a good big grassy space with the usual picnic tables, unvarnished and mossy, and a children's play area. The pub is on the edge of the village but the views, of copse, cottages and fields, are lovely. The landlord is friendly, and opens on Christmas morn. Marvellous.

The Talbot Inn
Mells, Frome

Even in thick fog the village is lovely. Huge oak doors open to a cobbled courtyard and rough-boarded tithe barn bar on one side, and dining rooms and bedrooms on the other. Inside, a warren of passageways, low doorways, nooks, crannies and beams – all you'd hope for from a 15th-century inn. Butcombe Bitter flows from the cask and there are wines galore including five by the glass; it's a great drinking pub and, with a garden with views, a magnet for tourists in summer. Soak up any excess with a platter-full of tagliatelli with smoked salmon and asparagus in tarragon cream sauce. Dinner under the hop-strewn rafters highlights fresh Brixham fish such as brill fillets in nut-brown butter. Roger Elliott's effortless hospitality and easy charm is a further plus; lovely big bedrooms are staunchly traditional with deep carpets, floral fabrics and plenty of charm.

directions	From Frome A362 for Radstock; left signed Mells.
meals	12pm-2.30pm; 6.45pm-11pm. Main courses £6.50-£14.50.
rooms	8 twins/doubles £95-£145. Singles £85.
closed	2.30pm-6.30pm (3pm-7pm Sundays).

See page 39 for bedroom details.

directions	From A361, near junc. of A359 to Bruton, turn for Trudoxhill, on to Witham Friary.
meals	No food served.
closed	2.30pm-6pm.

John & Jean Dovel
Seymour Arms,
Witham Friary,
Frome,
Somerset BA11 5HF

tel   01749 850742

Roger Elliott
The Talbot Inn,
Selwood Street, Mells,
Frome, Somerset BA11 3PN

tel   01373 812254
web   www.talbotinn.com

map: 3 entry: 421

map: 3 entry: 422

The Hunters' Lodge
Priddy

Pulling up at the windswept Priddy crossroads high on the Mendip Hills, you'd be mad to ignore this starkly rendered old building. A little pearl lies within. It's been in the same family since 1840 and Mr Dors is its proudest fixture, administering ale to cavers, pot-holers, hikers and the odd local for over 30 years. Lively chatter drowns the ticking clock and the crackling fire. The pristine main bar is delightfully devoid of a modern make-up – just simple wooden benches and tables, a shove-ha'penny board, old photographs on the walls, Butcombe bitter, Blindman's Mine Beer and a varying Third Choice fresh from the barrel. There's a lounge bar and a rear room for families, equally plain. Food is straightforward, homemade, tasty, great value. Folk in muddy boots come for just-made bowls of chilli, cauliflower cheese, faggots and peas and chunks of bread and cheese. An unpretentious treat.

Tucker's Grave Inn
Faulkland

If only the essence of Tucker's could be bottled and preserved; 'to be used as emergency tonic for the despairing' the label would read. In an unassuming, almost-unsigned 17th-century stone building, Tucker's is defiantly informal. An unprecedentedly narrow, extremely wiggly corridor leads in from the garden door; it's like walking into someone's living room as you stoop to enter the warmth. No bar, no fridge, just four beer casks and containers of local cider sitting in their jackets in the bay (no draught) and a stack of crisp boxes against the wall. You could pour your own beer... but that privilege is reserved for real regulars. A small open fire lends cosiness to the no-frills room next to the tiny wooden serving room. The interiors are as basic as they come but the atmosphere is roaring at weekends. In the words of one regular: "you can't come here without chatting to someone". And now there's a new skittles room in the big back garden.

directions	1.5 miles up Priddy-Wells road; look out for the TV mast.
meals	11.30-2.30; 6.30-11pm. Dishes from £2.80.
closed	2.30pm-6.30pm (7pm Sunday)

Mr Dors
The Hunters' Lodge,
Priddy,
Wells,
Somerset BA5 3AR

| tel | 01749 672275 |

map: 3 entry: 423

directions	A366 Radstock-Frome; left onto A362; through Faulkland, pub near next junction.
meals	Sandwiches from £1.50.

Glenda & Ivan Swift
Tucker's Grave Inn,
Faulkland,
Radstock,
Somerset BA3 5XF

| tel | 01373 834230 |

map: 3 entry: 424

Bear & Swan
Chew Magna

It is a four-square Victorian pub in the middle of Chew Magna – a desirable village in fine walking country. Some years ago the Pushman family rescued it from dereliction and have created a roomy and airy bar and a damned good restaurant. Reclaimed floorboards, nestling tables, wooden pews, big log fires -a simple but sophisticated feel. In the restaurant are oriental rugs and ladderback chairs, candlelight and flowers, bottles racked on the wall. Beers (Butcombe and Bath Ales), 40 wines and an irresistible menu draw people from near and far. Terrine of pork and pigeon, rack of lamb, pearl barley pie, peppered pavé of salmon and perfect summer pudding. The menu changes daily, ingredients are locally sourced, much is organic and the staff are delightful. Retire to airy and spacious bedrooms; there are charming antiques, stylish bathroom suites and an open-plan living area, with kitchen, to share.

The Black Horse
Clapton-in-Gordano

A cracking pub. The Snug Bar once doubled as the village lock-up and, if it weren't for the electric lights and motors in the car park, you'd be hard pushed to remember you were in the 21st century. All flagstone and dark moody wood, the main room bears the scuffs of centuries of drinking. Settles and old tables sit around the walls, and cottage windows with dark, wobbly shutters let a little of the outside in. The fire – a focus – roars in its vast hearth beneath a fine set of antique guns, just the sort of place to pull off muddy boots. Sepia prints of parish cricket teams and steam tractors clutter the walls and cask ales pour from the stone ledge behind the wide hatch bar. The food is unfancy bar fodder, with the odd traditional special. Ale is what's important and that's what takes pride of place; beneath a chalkboard six jacketed casks squat above drip pans; there are fine wines too. There's plenty of garden; well worth leaving the motorway for.

directions	On B3130 between A37 & A38.
meals	12pm-2pm; 7pm-10pm. No food Sunday evenings. Main courses £4-£17.
rooms	2 doubles £80. Singles £50.
closed	Open all day.

See page 39 for bedroom details.

Nigel & Caroline Pushman
Bear & Swan,
13 South Parade, Chew Magna,
Somerset BS40 8SL
tel 01275 331100
web www.bearandswan.co.uk

map: 3 entry: 425

directions	M5 junc. 19 for Portbury & Clapton. Left into Clevedon Lane.
meals	12pm-2pm. No food Sundays. Main courses £3.50-£5.
closed	2.30pm-5pm. Open all day Friday-Sunday.

Nicholas Evans
The Black Horse,
Clevedon Lane,
Clapton-in-Gordano,
Somerset BS20 7RH
tel 01275 842105

map: 3 entry: 426

The Crown
Churchill

Once a coaching stop between Bristol and Exeter, then the village grocer's, now an unspoilt pub. Modern makeovers have passed this gem by and beer reigns supreme, with up to ten ales tapped from the barrel. For years landlord Tim Rogers has resisted piped music and electronic games; who needs them in these little beamed and flagstoned bars? A wooden window seat here, a settle there... the rustic surroundings and the jolly atmosphere draw both locals and walkers treading the Mendips hills. Bag a seat by the log fire, cradle a pint of Bath SPA or RCH PG Steam Bitter, be lulled by the hum of regulars at the bar. If you're here at lunchtime you'll find a short, traditional, blackboard menu: warming bowls of soup, thick-cut rare roast beef sandwiches, baked potatoes, winter casseroles, treacle pud. Evenings are reserved for the serious art of ale drinking, and it's packed at weekends, especially in summer.

Queen's Arms
Bleadon

A curious spot, for the ineffable Weston-super-Mare is just round the corner. But just behind the village begin the Mendip Hills, whose bleak winter walks challenge the most hardy, and whose wild and beautiful woodland and fields sing in summer. The Queen's Arms, like many, is not especially seductive from the outside, but cheerfully sweeps you in to four terracotta rooms, much chat and laughter and some jolly good food. There are hunting prints on the walls, wood in the burners, candles in bottles and a menu that covers pub grub to delicious calf's liver and bacon with leek mash and port gravy, and a scrumptious Bailey's bread and butter pudding. Ales come from the barrel (Butcombe Bitter, Blonde & Gold and Bath Gem), cider is Thatchers, staff are swift and Daniel and Jess run the place with good humour — not least on Sunday quiz nights.

directions	From Bristol A38 to Churchill, right for Weston S.M. Immed left in front of Nelson Pub, up Skinners Lane, pub on bend.
meals	12pm-2.30pm (3pm weekends); limited bar snacks in evenings. Main courses £3.40-£7.50.
closed	Open all day.

directions	A370 from Weston-s-Mare; left for Bleadon; 50 yds from church.
meals	12pm-2pm (2.30pm Sundays); 6.30pm-9.30pm. Main courses £8.95-£14.95; bar meals from £3.50.
closed	2.30pm-5.30pm. Open all day Friday-Sunday.

Tim Rogers
The Crown,
The Batch, Churchill,
Congresbury,
Somerset BS25 5PP

tel   01934 852995

Daniel Pardoe & Jess Perry
Queen's Arms,
Celtic Way, Bleadon,
Weston-super-Mare BS24 0NF

tel   01934 812080
web   www.queensarms.co.uk

map: 3 entry: 427

map: 2 entry: 428

Halfway House
Pitney Hill

Somerset's mecca for beer and cider aficionados. No music or electronic wizardry to distract you from the serious business of sampling up to eight ales tapped straight from the drum, heady Hecks' ciders, and bottled beers from around the globe. Local clubs gather for chess, music, hockey; real-pub-lovers return again and again. In the two simple and homely rooms is a friendly, happy buzz: there are old benches and pews, scrubbed tables, stone-slabbed floors, three crackling log fires and the daily papers to nod off over. A quick lunchtime pint can swiftly turn into two hours of beer-fuelled bliss — so blot up the alcohol with spicy bean and tomato soup, a ploughman's lunch served with huge slabs of crusty bread and ham, a beef and beer casserole or a salmon steak straight from the pub's smokery. In the evenings the Halfway's revered homemade curries are gorgeous and go down extremely well with pints of Butcombe, Branscombe and Hop Back ales.

directions	Beside B3153, midway between Langport & Somerton.
meals	12pm-2.30pm; 7pm-9.30pm. No food Sundays. Main courses £4.95-£9.50.
closed	3pm-5.30pm (7pm Sundays).

SPECIAL AWARD see pages 28-29

Julian Litchfield
Halfway House,
Pitney Hill, Langport,
Somerset TA10 9AB
tel　01458 252513
web　www.thehalfwayhouse.co.uk

map: 3 entry: 429

The Queen's Arms
Corton Denham

Stride across rolling fields with Dorsetshire views, feast on Corton Denham lamb, retire to a perfect room. Buried down several twisting border lanes, this elegant 18th-century pub is also great for a pint and a homemade pie. Londoners Rupert and Victoria Reeves saw its potential, snapped it up and revamped without losing the countrified feel. The bar is delightful with rug-strewn flagstones and bare boards, pew benches, deep sofas and crackling fire. In the warm and cosy dining room – big mirrors on terracotta walls, new china on old tables – guests dine on imaginative dishes distinguished by fresh ingredients from local suppliers. Try roasted figs with warmed goat's cheese on toasted ciabatta with a glass or two of Jim Barry's Auzzie shiraz, or honeyed pork loin on bubble-and-squeak followed by a comforting crumble. Bedrooms are stunning and stylish with fresh checks or sumptuous silks, perfect bath and shower rooms, posh smellies and breathtaking views – book the French room! A friendly labrador, Butcombe on tap, comfort and authenticity.

directions	Signed off B3145, 3 miles north of Sherborne, off A303.
meals	12pm-3pm (4pm Sat & Sun), 6pm-10pm (9.30pm Sun). Main courses £4.90-£11.50.
rooms	5 twins/doubles £75-£120.
closed	3.30-6pm. Open all day weekends.

Rupert & Victoria Reeves
The Queen's Arms,
Corton Denham,
Somerset DT9 4LR

tel	01963 220317
web	www.thequeensarms.com

See page 39 for bedroom details.

map: 3 entry: 430

The Camelot
South Cadbury

Formerly known as The Red Lion, this secluded village pub was taken over by cheese legend Jamie Montgomery in the summer of 2004. It has become a must-visit for walkers all year round and for shooting parties during the game season. Enter on a frosty November lunchtime and you'll be met by a row of Barbours, muddy boots, dogs and guns. It all makes for a great atmosphere, matched by real ales served from the keg, serious wines, solid cooking – including a wide range of *zakuski* (Russian tapas) – and, of course, a cheeseboard like no other. The pub's close proximity to the South Cadbury Environs Project also means that fossils and findings jostle for attention among the trophies won by the Montgomerys for their cheeses, while empty magnums of champagne line the window ledges. A cracking good pub, packed with both character and locals.

Wookey Hole Inn
Wookey Hole

On the edge of the Mendip hills: a traditional façade, a funky décor, excellent food and no end of choice behind the kitsch-with-style bar. The whole place throngs, particularly on summer weekends when the big garden comes into its own. It's also relaxed and properly child-friendly with toys and wax crayons for doodling on (paper) tablecloths. Terracotta tiles, open fires, stripped wood and wooden panelling, splashes of strong colour, arty lamps, photos and interesting *objets*. The atmosphere is laid-back, the cool levels boosted by live jazz at Sunday lunch times (and occasional Friday nights), and the food, which has good local and organic credentials, is seriously tasty and imaginative: asparagus tips wrapped in parma ham with saffron hollandaise and a herb salad, pan-fried, crispy-skinned sea bass with scallops and wild rice, smoked local lamb burgers. The puddings are seductive, too.

directions	Just off A303, 6 miles west of Wincanton.
meals	12pm-2.30pm; 6.30pm-9.30pm. Main courses £10.50-£15; bar meals £4.50-£12.
closed	3pm-6.30pm. Open all day weekends.

Jamie & Zizi Montgomery
The Camelot,
Chapel Road, South Cadbury,
Somerset BA22 7EX
tel   01963 440448
web www.thecamelot.co.uk

directions	Follow brown tourist signs for Wookey Hole off A371 or A39 in Wells.
meals	12pm-2.30pm (3pm Sunday); 7pm-9.30pm. Main courses £6.50-£10 (lunch), £11-£18 (dinner).
closed	Sunday after 3pm.

Mark Hey
Wookey Hole Inn,
Wookey Hole, Wells,
Somerset BA5 1BP
tel   01749 676677
web www.wookeyholeinn.com

Crooked House
Coppice Mill

Local big-wigs found coal here in about 1800 and started mining; shortly thereafter the pretty, 18th-century red-brick farmhouse fell into a hole. It has been buttressed ever since, but it is the most crooked building you are ever likely to experience and makes falling over a distinct possibility the moment you walk through the door. Inside are two wonky little bars: take your pick, both are a challenge. The grandfather clock, although upright, looks as if it is about to fall over, the red-tiled floors swim as you cross them, the bottled beers roll uphill. The whole place is faintly surreal and brings *Alice in Wonderland* to mind. The pub serves real ales such as Banks Bitter, farm cider and standard pub grub in a large (uncrooked) dining room, and sits in its own big garden near Himley Court.

directions	Off B4176 between Gornalwood & Himley.
meals	12pm-2.30pm; 5.30pm-9pm (9.30pm Fridays & Saturdays; 8pm Sundays). All day in summer. Main courses £6-£9.
closed	3pm-5pm. Open all day in summer.

	Brett Harrison
	Crooked House,
	Coppice Mill,
	Himley,
	Staffordshire DY3 4DA
tel	01384 238583

map: 8 entry: 433

The Holly Bush Inn
Salt

Geoffrey Holland came to the Holly Bush some years ago and has turned it into a thriving local. Indeed, all the emphasis is local, especially where food is concerned. Cheeses, vegetables, meat and game (hear the shoot from the pub garden) are local and almost exclusively organic; herbs are fresh from the garden. Even a few of the recipes, such as the 'oatcakes' (pancakes not biscuits), are strictly Staffs. Only the fish and some of the beers (the Boddingtons comes from Manchester) are from further afield. But people travel miles for the salmon with hollandaise sauce and the very popular steak and ale pie. The 'second oldest licensed pub in the country' is a characterful little place, quirky even – its menu is designed in the form of a Victorian newspaper – with separate cosy areas, open fires and the odd carved beam and settle. There are picnic tables on the big back lawn and the village, listed in the Domesday Book, should charm you.

directions	Off A51 south of Stone & A518 north east of Stafford.
meals	12pm-9.30pm (9pm Sunday). Main courses £7.95-£11.95.
closed	Open all day.

	Geoffrey Holland
	The Holly Bush Inn,
	Salt, Stafford,
	Staffordshire ST18 0BX
tel	01889 508234
web	www.hollybushinn.co.uk

map: 8 entry: 434

Staffordshire

Yew Tree
Cauldon

The Old Curiosity Shop meets *The Antiques Road Show*. For over 40 years, landlord Alan East has squirreled away enough artefacts to make Michael Aspel weep. Behind the tiny leaded windows of this unassuming, 300-year-old pub every space is filled: longcase clocks and flintlocks, penny-farthings and valve radios, synphonions and polyphons (insert 2p and retire), old pews and marvellously carved benches. Pianolas lie half-buried in their paper-scroll programs (there's one playing most of the time)... Wedgwood would find ceramics he may have handled (and his four-poster bed), and Queen Victoria her hosiery. Look for the Serpent (a medieval church instrument); wince at the ACME dog carrier. A floor-to-ceiling treasure trove – plus local pork pies, hot baps and sandwiches, Bass, Burton Bridge Bitter and Grays Mild.

Staffordshire

The George
Alstonefield

Green sward ripples endlessly in this remote limestone village with its old church perched on a plateau between the remarkable gorges of the rivers Dove and Manifold. Set amidst this verdant Eden, the George is an ultra-reliable local, maturing gently these past 40 years under the guidance of Richard Grandjean and is now run by his daughter and son-in-law. Small, timeless rooms of beams, quarry tile and log fire carry benches and Britannia tables, fascinating old photos and polished plate. It's an unhurried place, where everyone knows everyone else (or soon will), ramblers cram the benches and tables out front and time passes slowly. Complement this vision with homemade chow to savour – nothing fancy, just fine filling pub food – and a couple of real ales from regional breweries. The non-smoking dining room, all scrubbed pine tables, piano, antiques, watercolours and stuffed fish, is ideal for families, as is the peaceful rear courtyard shaded by an immense ash.

directions	Off A523 Leek to Ashbourne road at Waterhouses.
meals	Snacks 70p-£3.50.
closed	2.30pm-6pm (from 3pm weekends; to 7pm Sundays).

Alan East
Yew Tree,
Cauldon, Waterhouses,
Stoke-on-Trent,
Staffordshire ST10 3EJ
tel 01538 308348

map: 8 entry: 435

directions	Village signed off A515, 7 miles north of Ashbourne.
meals	12pm-2pm; 7pm-9pm. Main courses £6.50-£12.95.
closed	Open all day weekends.

Ben & Emily Hammond
The George,
Alstonefield, Ashbourne,
Staffordshire DE6 2FX
tel 01335 310205
web www.thegeorgeatalstonefield.com

map: 8 entry: 436

St Peter's Hall
St Peter South Elmham

John Murphy bought the 13th-century moated manor in 1996 to brew beer using water from the site's 60-metre bore. Now St Peter's thrives, brewing and bottling its exemplary range of bitters, fruit ales and porters. Take the weekend brewery tour or venture into the medieval hall to eat and drink like kings. The lofty stone-flagged dining hall is filled with original Brussels tapestries, fine stone fireplaces and 17th- and 18th-century furnishings: sup at candlelit tables from French choir stalls or a bishop's chair. The Library bar is more homely. It's a intriguing setting in which to show off some intriguing beers, with food to match. The weekly-changing menus reveal simple enticement: St Peter's steak and ale pie, Alsace bacon and egg salad, smoked chicken salad with sun-blush tomatoes and parmesan.

The Crown
Southwold

The Crown has an eye for metropolitan sophistication. Ceilings are elegantly beamed, the walls of the big, laid-back bar are colourwashed and uncluttered – fitting for a town known as Kensington-on-Sea. The food comes as bar snacks in full modern-brasserie mode: tempura Brancaster oysters, tapas, confit duck leg, roast pumpkin and parmesan risotto. Fresh flowers sit on kitchen-style tables, there are newspapers to read, Adnams ales on handpump and fine wines to try. There's no pretentiousness and a fascinating mix of customers – suits, locals, trendies, grannies, families. A smaller, pubbier panelled back bar keeps hard-core traditionalists happy, and there's a smart, sunny, slightly more self-conscious restaurant. All in all, The Crown has succeeded in being simultaneously a simple pub, a brasserie-wine bar and a restaurant with serious aspirations.

directions	Follow brown amenity signs from Flixton or A144, between Bungay & Halesworth.
meals	12pm-2.30pm; 7pm-9pm. Mon-Fri bar meals only. Restaurant Sat night & Sun lunch only. Main courses £10-£15; bar meals £4.95-£15.
closed	Open all day in summer and weekends in winter.

directions	In centre of Southwold.
meals	12pm-2pm; 6.30pm-9.30pm. Main courses £10-£17; set menu £29.
closed	Open all day.

	Stuart Cox
	St Peter's Hall,
	St Peter South Elmham,
	Bungay, Suffolk NR35 1NQ
tel	01986 783113
web	www.stpetersbrewery.co.uk

	Francis Guildea
	The Crown,
	High Street,
	Southwold,
	Suffolk IP18 6DP
tel	01502 722275

map: 10 entry: 437

map: 10 entry: 438

The Anchor
Walberswick

Seeking sea air, beer guru Mark Dorber (landlord of the White Horse, Parsons Green) and wife Sophie have headed for the Suffolk coast and this faded Adnams boozer. Sand, stone and aqua tones have replaced the traditional pubby décor, and the staff make a brilliant team. To the sound of the sea crashing on the beach beyond, the vast lawn hosts summer barbecues and the homemade burgers draw an appreciative crowd. Sophie's lunch and dinner menus overflow with produce sourced from a rich vein of organic farms, village allotments and top local butchers; even the children's food is organic. Menus also match beer with food. Try a pint of Bitburger Pils with griddled mackerel on sweet chilli stir-fried vegetables, Adnams Broadside with a melting Irish stew, Adnams Best with beer battered haddock and jalopeno tartare sauce. The veggie dishes are an equal treat.

The Queens Head
Bramfield

Another chef-landlord with an interest in provenance – and Mark Corcoran's menus make reassuring reading. Recent dishes include pan-fried king scallops wrapped in pancetta with salsa verde; grilled sardines with tzatziki; lamb cooked Greek-style and served with spicy couscous. Rest assured that half the ingredients will be organic and locally sourced. Lighter bites may include goat's cheese soufflé and homemade soups; accompanying salads are simple and delicious. All this plenty is served in a high-raftered bar with dark timbered walls, scrubbed pine tables and a fireplace ablaze with logs in winter. A rustically cosy non-smoking room lies next door. There are small portions for children and the drinks are exemplary: Adnams ales, ciders and wines and local elderflower pressé. Make time for the lovely terraced courtyard and garden with bantams and bower – and Bramfield's thatched church with its unusual bell tower.

directions	From A12 south of Southwold; B3187 to Walberswick.
meals	12pm–3pm; 6pm–9pm (all day July & August). Main courses £7.75–£12.75.
closed	4pm–6pm. Open all day July & August.

Mark & Sophie Dorber
The Anchor,
Main Street, Walberswick,
Southwold, Suffolk IP18 6UA
tel 01502 722112
web www.anchoratwalberswick.com

map: 10 entry: 439

directions	2 miles N of A12 on A144 Halesworth road.
meals	12pm–2pm; 6.30pm–10pm; 7pm–9pm Sundays. Main courses £5.95–£14.95.
closed	2.30pm–6.30pm; 3pm–7pm Sundays.

Mark & Amanda Corcoran
The Queens Head,
The Street, Bramfield,
Halesworth, Suffolk IP19 9HT
tel 01986 784214
web www.queensheadbramfield.co.uk

map: 10 entry: 440

Suffolk

King's Head
Laxfield

Known locally as the Low House because it lies in a dip below the churchyard, the 600-year-old thatched pub is one of Suffolk's treasures. Little has changed in the last 100 years and its four rooms creak with character – all narrow passageways and low ceilings. The simple parlour is dominated by a massive three-sided, high-backed settle in front of an open fire and there's no bar – far too new-fangled a concept for this place; instead, impeccable Adnams ales are served from barrels in the tap room and locals bang their empty glasses to summon the barman. In keeping with the timeless atmosphere, food is rustic, hearty and homemade, the short, daily-changing blackboard menu listing soup, sandwiches, hot dishes and puddings. It's the sort of place where traditional folk music often starts up spontaneously, while summer brings Morris men. At the back, the secluded garden has been created from a former bowling green.

directions	From Laxfield church, left down hill for 50 yards. Left; pub on right.
meals	12pm–2pm; 7pm–9pm. No food Sunday evenings in winter. Main courses £5.50–£14.95.

George & Maureen Coleman
King's Head,
Gorams Mill Lane,
Laxfield,
Suffolk IP13 8DW
tel   01986 798395

map: 10 entry: 441

Suffolk

Crown Inn
Snape

A Suffolk gem. A well-preserved 15th-century inn with beams and brick floors only a stroll from the Maltings concert hall and a short drive from the Minsmere bird sanctuary. It claims to have the finest example anywhere of a double Suffolk settle, known as the 'old codgers'; for this it is worth the trip alone. But the real old codgers have long gone: this popular food pub now attracts the Aldeburgh set, who come for Diane Maylott's modern brasserie-style food. Key to The Crown's success is an insistence on fresh, local produce, particularly fish, game and organic vegetables. But despite the foodie emphasis, there is still a deliciously pubby atmosphere here, in among the dark beams, old brick floors and roaring log fires. And both the real ales and the wines (11 by the glass) are supplied by Suffolk's most respected brewery, Adnams, who own the place.

directions	Off A12, A1094 following Aldeburgh, right turn signed Snape. Pub at bottom of the hill.
meals	12pm–2pm; 7pm–9pm. Main courses £9.25–£15.95.

Diane Maylott
Crown Inn,
Bridge Road, Snape,
Saxmundham,
Suffolk IP17 1SL
tel   01728 688324

map: 10 entry: 442

Suffolk

Crown & Castle
Orford

Ruth's sense of style has created a most distinctive bistro inn out of this late-Victorian building. Certainly not a village local but the welcome is friendly to all, dogs included, the atmosphere relaxed, and the food sublime. The fire in the hall lures you in, deep sofas urge you to stay. Floorboards clatter, quirky paintings amuse and the bar is as convivial as any to nibble on tapas and quaff a pint of Adnams. In the kitchen, Cromer crab, Orford skate and lobster, local game and Gloucester Old Spot pork are splendidly taken care of: the cooking is robust and it's quite impossible to resist hot bitter chocolate soufflé with local Jersey cream. In summer a casual lunch on the terrace is heaven. The old Norman castle-keep stands proud across the road and you are minutes on foot from the river Alde, the comely village, the wild river marshes and Havergate Island's admirable avocets.

| directions | Leave A12 at Woodbridge; A1152 & B1084 to Orford. |
| meals | 12pm–2pm; 7pm–9pm (9.30pm Saturdays). Main courses £11.50–£17. Set lunch from £14. |

David & Ruth Watson
Crown & Castle,
Orford, Woodbridge,
Suffolk IP12 2LJ
tel 01394 450205
web www.crownandcastle.co.uk

map: 10 entry: 443

Suffolk

The Ship
Levington

The Levington Ship is a 14th-century thatched beauty overlooking the River Orwell. This alone makes it a popular watering hole, the low-ceilinged bar and flower-festooned rear terrace filling quickly with yachting types, locals and townies escaping to the country for lunch. Naturally, the bar emphasises a nautical theme, with pictures of barges, lifebuoys and a ship's wheel on the walls. Over the past few years chef-patron Mark Johnson's imaginative cooking has made its successful mark, his chalkboard menus, changed twice a day, listing fresh fish and locally reared meats – notably venison from the Suffolk Estate – as well as seasonal salads and local vegetables. Exemplary French cheeses come from the Rungis Market in Paris and superior real ales from East Anglian brewers Adnams and Greene King. Wonderful riverside walks await those who have had one glass too many – and those who haven't.

directions	A12/A14 junction to Woodbridge; follow signs for Levington.
meals	12pm–2pm; 6.30pm–9.30pm (12pm–4pm, 6.30–9pm Sunday). Main courses from £7.95–£15.
closed	3pm–5.30pm Saturday. Open all day Sunday.

Stella & Mark Johnson
The Ship,
Levington,
Ipswich,
Suffolk IP10 0LQ
tel 01473 659573

map: 10 entry: 444

The Swan
Monks Eleigh

The polished, wooden floored interior is not unlike that of a bistro, but Nigel and Carol Ramsbottom's 16th-century thatched Swan is still a pub at heart. There's a large bar, Adnams on handpump and a good line in wines by the glass. The modernised interior is invitingly open with recessed ceiling lights, soft sage tones and a winter log fire. Yet most folk come to eat. Nigel, in the kitchen, has created a menu to please both the traditionalist and the adventurer, so dishes include simply grilled fillets of plaice with creamy leeks and new potatoes, grilled sea bass with orange and beetroot salad, whole roast teal with braised red cabbage, fabulous rice pudding. Fish can be relied upon to be beautifully fresh – raw materials are as local as possible – and puddings should not be resisted. Service, by Carol, is a lesson in how these things should be done: efficient, knowledgeable, cheerful and charming.

The Angel Inn
Stoke-by-Nayland

Soft lamplight glows in the window of this 16th-century inn in 'Constable country'. The bar divides into two: a busy, traditional sitting area with carved beams, open brickwork, log fire and polished oak tables, and a pleasant sitting room with deep sofas, wing chairs and grandfather clock. Fresh flowers and candles, fine prints and paintings, a few antique pieces and a dark-green décor add to the appeal. The Angel fills early and its imaginative menus announce plenty of fresh fish (seared fillet of sea bass marinated in orange and ginger, local smoked trout salad) plus game from the Denham estate; start with cream of cauliflower and ham soup, end with iced dark chocolate bombe. The galleried restaurant was once a brewhouse. On warm evenings tables are laid on the terrace at the back.

directions	On B1115 between Lavenham & Hadleigh.
meals	12pm-2pm; 7pm-9pm. Main courses £9.50-£16.50.
closed	3pm-7pm; Mondays & Tuesdays.

Nigel & Carol Ramsbottom
The Swan,
The Street, Monks Eleigh,
Lavenham, Suffolk IP7 7AU

tel	01449 741391
web	www.monkseleigh.com

map: 10 entry: 445

directions	On B1068 8 miles north of Colchester; off A12.
meals	12pm-2pm; 6.30pm-9.30pm (5.30pm Sundays). Main courses £7.75-£16.50.
closed	Open all day.

Neil Bishop
The Angel Inn,
Polstead Street, Stoke-by-Nayland,
Suffolk CO6 4SA

tel	01206 263245
web	www.horizoninns.co.uk

map: 10 entry: 446

The Crown
Stoke-by-Nayland

Several low-ceilinged but rambling rooms, one with a view of the kitchen, are decked in muted colours; the mood is warm, appealing and refreshingly music-free. There's space to prop up the bar and down a pint from Suffolk brewers Adnams, while the seasonal menu is a sympathetic combination of traditional and contemporary. Several chefs dispatch exuberant renditions of pressed tomato cake with peppered goat's cheese, steak and kidney pudding, braised pheasant in a cider and cream sauce with roasted celeriac chips, hot seafood platter. Polish it all off with pear, apple and hazelnut crumble and homemade custard, or Colne Valley wild cherry ice cream. The food is fairly priced and there's an outstanding wine list, with wines matched to the food and bottles to take home from the shop. And a glorious terrace with stunning views.

The Beehive
Horringer

Look out for the beehive at the front! Housed within these converted 19th-century cottages is a local of the very best kind. It's well modernised yet the higgledy-piggledy feel remains, along with low beams and worn flagstone floors oozing character. Several country-smart rooms interlink — expect soft lighting, old prints, candlelight, linen napkins, a woodburning stove. Greene King ales are on handpump but people come for more than the beer. Blackboards announce the daily menu, perhaps a lunchtime snack of Suffolk ham with salad and homemade chutney, or roast belly of Suffolk pork with apple and orange gravy; desserts are equally good. Several good wines are served by the glass. The place can fill up quickly so do book, especially at weekends — the pub's popularity is proof of Gary and Diane Kingshott's hospitality. Ickworth House, in the same pretty village, owned by the National Trust, awaits discovery. *No smoking throughout.*

directions	Just off B1087 in Stoke-by-Nayland.
meals	12pm-2.30pm, 6pm-9.30pm (10pm Saturdays); Sundays 12pm- 9pm. Main courses £8.50-£14.95.
closed	Open all day.

Edward Olwer Inns Ltd.
The Crown,
Stoke-by-Nayland,
Colchester,
Suffolk CO6 4SE
tel   01206 262001

map: 10 entry: 447

directions	3 miles south west of Bury St Edmunds on A143.
meals	12pm-2pm; 7pm-9pm. No food Sunday evenings. Main courses £9.95-£15.
closed	2.30pm-7pm.

Gary & Diane Kingshott
The Beehive,
The Street,
Horringer, Bury St Edmunds,
Suffolk IP29 5SN
tel   01284 735260

map: 10 entry: 448

Old Cannon Brewery
Bury St Edmunds

Brewing is a slow process, says Richard Eyton-Jones, and he should know; for the past six years he has been the chief brewer and owner of this admirable revitalisation of a Victorian brewhouse-cum-pub. Bare boards clatter, wooden tables are plain, a huge mirror vies with two gleaming stainless steel brewing kettles for decoration. The atmosphere is young, refreshingly friendly and further enlivened by pints of own-brew Old Cannon Best, Gunner's Daughter and Black Pig Porter. A surprisingly contemporary mix of dishes such as local sausages with onion gravy, grilled wing of skate with lemon grass and caper butter, and roast duck with sloe gin is to be expected. A cobbled courtyard beyond the old coach arch has swish tables and chairs for summer sipping. You are a five-minute walk from the town and its treasures.

Star Inn
Lidgate

The garden is glorious on a summer's day. For winter there are two blazing fires — and two snugs, each the centrepiece of an ancient-beamed bar. Indeed, the pretty Star, built in 1588, is one of the oldest buildings in the village — two cottages knocked into one. It is also as English as can be, yet landlady Maria Teresa Axon comes from Catalonia in Spain. The rich aromas that greet you may just as well come from boeuf en daube or venison in port as from Spanish-style roast lamb, fabada asturiana (Asturian pork and bean stew) or parillada of fish. Bring a good appetite as portions will be generous, and do book; proximity to Newmarket brings racing types in droves. There are darts and dominoes to get stuck into, Greene King beers on handpump — ask about the unusual handles — and Spain is deliciously represented in brandies and wines.

directions	From A14, Bury exit, for centre, left at r'bout to Northgate St; right at Cadney Lane & into Cannon St.
meals	12pm-2pm; 6.30pm-9.30pm. No food Sunday & Monday evenings. Main courses £10-£15.
closed	3pm-5pm (7pm Sunday); Monday lunchtimes.

Richard Eyton-Jones
Old Cannon Brewery,
86 Cannon Street,
Bury St Edmunds, Suffolk IP33 1JR
tel   01284 768769
web   www.oldcannonbrewery.co.uk

map: 10 entry: 449

directions	On B1063, 7 miles south east of Newmarket.
meals	12pm-2pm (2.30pm Sundays); 7pm-10pm. No food Sunday evenings. Main courses £14.50-£16.50; set lunch, 2 courses, £12.50.

Maria Teresa Axon
Star Inn,
The Street, Lidgate,
Bury St Edmunds,
Suffolk CB8 9PP
tel   01638 500275

map: 9 entry: 450

The Inn at West End
West End

Wine importer Gerry Price draws them in from all over Surrey. Stylishly revamped dining areas are light and modern with classy yellow walls, wooden floors and fine fabrics. The feeling is relaxed and friendly – quiz nights, film club, boules; the homely bar has a wood-burning stove; handpumped ale comes from Fuller's and Courage and the list of wines is huge, with a recent and welcome nod to Portuguese shores. Monthly menus have modern British choices ranging from starters like homemade chicken liver pâté served with toast and a port and herb butter to maize-fed chicken breast in a herb and tomato cream jus. A pastry chef masterminds a small but select choice of desserts; cheeses are farmhouse best. Add great lunchtime sandwiches, excellent value set lunches, regular Saturday lunchtime wine-tasting sessions and popular wine dinners and you have a superbly-run pub.

The King William IV
Mickleham

Open fires, fresh flowers, slab sandwiches and amazing views are a few of the reasons people make the steep, stepped climb – unless you're lucky enough to park in the lane. The old alehouse was originally built for Lord Beaverbrook's estate staff – a hilltop eyrie from which Chris and Jenny Grist have created a popular little pub, particularly in summer, when all and sundry spill into the terraced garden. There's a serving hatch to outside, a thoughtful touch for walkers with muddy boots. In winter it's super-snug, a place that just about squeezes in two bare-boarded bars. The real badgers have gone (see the photos on the walls) but their namesake ale remains on tap as well as ales from The Hogs Back Brewery. Equal attention is paid to food: chips are banned – but who cares, when superb garlic bread, homemade pies and best-ever puddings are brought steaming to the table?

directions	On A322 towards Guildford, 2 miles from M3 junc. 3.
meals	12pm-2.30pm (3pm Sundays); 6pm-9.30pm (9pm Sundays). Main courses £7.95-£16; set menus £9.75-£19.75.
closed	3pm-5pm Monday-Friday. Open all day Saturday & Sunday.

Gerry & Ann Price
The Inn at West End,
42 Guildford Road, West End,
Surrey GU24 9PW
tel   01276 858652
web   www.the-inn.co.uk

map: 4 entry: 451

directions	From junc. 9 M25, A24 for Dorking. Just before Mickleham, pub on hill above Frascati restaurant.
meals	12pm-2pm; 7pm-9.30pm (12pm-5pm Sundays). Main courses £6-£14.
closed	Open all day Sunday.

Chris & Jenny Grist
The King William IV,
Byttom Hill, Mickleham,
Dorking, Surrey RH5 6EL
tel   01372 372590
web   www.king-williamiv.com

map: 4 entry: 452

Stephan Langton
Abinger Common

Jonathan Coomb has not looked back since swapping the London restaurant scene for a pub at the bottom of leafy Leith Hill, with a handful of cottages and a romantic old hammer pond for company. For years a favourite walkers' watering hole, this isolated country pub at the end of a very long lane is a suitably rural spot for Jonathan's robust style of cooking. In the kitchen, beyond the plain but log-warmed bar, he takes delivery of some first-class produce from local suppliers, bakes bread, rolls out pasta, whisks up ice cream. Walkers come here to devour bowls of hearty goulash soup, Catalan squid salad and a superb peach melba, while evening additions may include chargrilled tuna with spiced aubergine, tabbouleh and raita, maize-fed chicken with girolles, and rib-eye steak with chips and horseradish cream. Accompany these superb-value treats with a well-kept pint of Adnams, then head off to explore Surrey's finest walks.

The Plough
Coldharbour

The smell of woodsmoke wafting from the Plough's chimneys is impossible to resist, and the friendly greeting as you enter makes this a second good reason to stop off for a pint. Nothing is too much trouble. Three open fires are kept smouldering from breakfast until closing-time and delicious dishes are cooked with fresh and local produce – steak and ale pie, beef Wellington with rosemary potatoes, banoffee pie. Landlady and ex-nurse Anna keeps her finger firmly on the kitchen pulse, while her husband Rick runs the pub's tiny microbrewery with equal aplomb. With wonderful home-brews – Tickety-Boo, Crooked Furrow, Tallywacker and a new hoppy beer, Hoppily Ever After, brewed for a family wedding – it's no wonder one local restored an antique lamp in exchange for two pints and another skied six miles to get here for lunch.

directions	A25 from Dorking. 2 miles outside Westcott left; 2 miles to Friday Street village; left, right at pond.
meals	12.30pm-2.30pm; 7pm-10pm. No food Sunday evenings & Monday. Main courses £7.50-£13.75.
closed	3pm-5pm & Mondays. Open all day Saturday.

directions	4 miles from Dorking.
meals	12pm-2.30pm; 6.30pm-9.30pm. Main courses £6.95-£15.95.
closed	Open all day.

	Jonathan Coomb
	Stephan Langton,
	Friday Street,
	Abinger Common, Dorking,
	Surrey RH5 6JR
tel	01306 730775

	Richard & Anna Abrehart
	The Plough,
	Coldharbour, Dorking,
	Surrey RH5 6HD
tel	01306 711793
web	www.ploughinn.com

map: 4 entry: 453

map: 4 entry: 454

Surrey

The Stag
Lower Easing

Once through Easing you come across a small bridge with a warning that heavy loads might lead to its demise. We trust this won't happen, as the pretty stone structure built by 13th-century monks forms an essential link to The Stag. With a lease dating back to 1771, this is an attractive, atmospheric place to stop off for some liquid refreshment and extremely good home cooking: pork with rosemary, mushroom risotto, banoffee pie. In spring and summer the garden, with teak-furnished terrace by the water, makes a languorous spot for quaffing Shepherd Neame Spitfire – or one of 15 wines by the glass. In winter, there are several cosily traditional rooms and two open fires; the weir outside the River Room provides a gurgling accompaniment. The friendly Stag likes children and dogs; the huge dog bowls at the entrance, belonging to residents Dotty and Bea, merely hint at their size.

directions	A3 south; 5 miles after Guildford, Eashing signed left at services. Left at garage; over bridge; on right.
meals	12pm-2.30pm (3pm Sundays); 6pm-9.30pm. No food Sunday evenings. Main courses £11.25-£17.50.
closed	Monday evenings from 7pm. Open all day.

Marilyn Lackey
The Stag,
Lower Eashing,
Godalming,
Surrey GU7 2QG
tel 01483 421568

map: 4 entry: 455

Surrey

The Swan Inn
Chiddingfold

Out of the ashes the Swan has risen. The remodelling of the 14th-century coaching inn has introduced a sparkling dining room and a cool bar – wood floors, chunky tables – but its origins have not been forgotten. Hogs Back TEA and Fuller's London Pride are served for those in for a pint; the bar menu delivers ham, egg and chips and calf's liver and bacon. And there are snails, carpaccio of beef, goat's cheese soufflé and fishcakes with smoked salmon sauce too – a successful juggling of popular and modern. In the dining room a well-presented menu lists a superb choice, from seared foie gras with truffle dressing to fillet steak with shallot sauce and homemade chips. All in all this is a happy, relaxed revival of an old inn. And a prettily landscaped terraced garden tempts you outdoors on a warm day.

directions	South of village green beside the A283 between Guildford & Petworth.
meals	12pm-2.30pm; 6.30pm-10pm. Main courses £13-£17; bar meals £7-£12.
closed	Open all day.

Daniel Hall & Darren Tidd
The Swan Inn,
Petworth Road, Chiddingfold,
Guildford, Surrey GU8 4TY
tel 01428 682073
web www.swaninnandrestaurant.co.uk

map: 4 entry: 456

Surrey

The Hare & Hounds
Lingfield

This whitewashed roadside pub may not look particularly beguiling but step inside and you know you've come to a special place. With proprietor-chef Fergus's collection of quirky objects filling every corner, the Hare & Hounds has an idiosyncratic feel. While the fireside burgundy sofa makes an ideal spot for perusing the tempting menu, the bustle of the bar can be surveyed from a throne-like chair, one of a pair: the other half lives at home with Fergus, fitting for the king of the kitchen. And there's a wooden elephant seat too. His specialities include scallops with saffron and vanilla sauce, and roast suckling pig with sage and onion mash and apple and sultana chutney. Diners are as happy among the yuccas of the main bar as beneath the huge floral paintings (the work of Fergus's artist wife) in the lovely dining room. In summer nurse a pint of Flowers Original in the split-level, partly-decked garden.

directions	From A22 towards Lingfield Racecourse into Common Road.
meals	12pm-2.30pm (3.30pm Sundays); 7pm-9.30pm. Main courses £7.50-£15.95.
closed	Sunday evening from 8pm. Open all day.

Fergus Greer
The Hare & Hounds,
Common Road,
Lingfield,
Surrey RH7 6BZ
tel   01342 832351

map: 4 entry: 457

Sussex

The Stag
Balls Cross

The quintessential Sussex pub – some might say (and often do) it's the best pub in the world. Under 16th-century beams by a crackling log fire, or in the big garden in summer, riders, walkers and locals enjoy a natter over well-kept Badger and Sussex Bitter. Wholesome home-cooked food is another draw, and the lavish piles of crispy whitebait and pint-glass servings of pink prawns are particularly tempting. A sweet shop in a former life, this little inn still welcomes children: in a set-aside room youngsters play undisturbed. There is also plenty for adults: the Stag has its own darts team, jazz nights outdoors in summer, carol singing in winter and visits from the travelling Mummers all year round. There's a 17th-century stone-floored bar and a dining room that's carpeted and cosy. And a handy tethering post for those who come by horse.

directions	2 miles from Petworth on Kirdford road.
meals	12pm-2pm; 7pm-9pm. No food Sunday evenings. Main courses £7-£15.

Hamish Hiddleston
The Stag,
Balls Cross,
Petworth,
Sussex GU28 9JP
tel   01403 820241

map: 4 entry: 458

Sussex

Hollist Arms
Lodsworth

Villager and proprietor George Bristow rescued this lovely pub a few years ago, injecting fresh enthusiasm among the staff and stuffing the menu with local and seasonal ingredients, which draw diners from miles around. Prawn and crayfish knickerbockers, duck breast in soy sauce with ginger and a melt-in-the-mouth cottage pie – all are first-class. Villagers prop up the – very long – bar for a well-kept pint of King's Horsham Best, while civilised sofas by a huge inglenook settle other dedicated drinkers in for the night. The smaller, more intimate rooms of this former smithy have been kept: one, a cosy claret-coloured private dining room, another a sweet snug with soft green armchairs, blazing fire and tables piled high with magazines and games. Children are welcome and there's a garden for summer. From the hand-cut, local-farm potato chips to the colourwashed walls, pretty feather-patterned curtains and soothing classical sounds, this watering hole oozes magic.

directions	Halfway between Midhurst & Petworth; signed off A272.
meals	12pm-2pm; 7pm-9pm. Main courses £7.95-£13.95.
closed	Open all day Sunday.

George Bristow
Hollist Arms,
The Street,
Lodsworth, Petworth,
Sussex GU28 9BZ
tel 01798 861310

map: 4 entry: 459

Sussex

The Lickfold Inn
Lickfold

The glorious 15th-century bricks bulge in a riot of herringbone, there's a sofa plump with tweed cushions and the daily papers sit beside the huge central inglenook: this is a deliciously atmospheric place. The Hickeys have settled in well and provide a popular menu and daily specials built around fresh local produce that changes with the seasons – venison with braised red cabbage and madeira jus, wild sea bass with chilli herb crust, seafood linguine, roast pork open sandwich. Diners can relax downstairs in a cosy setting where fat cream candles reflected in the latticed windows give comfort and cheer; a more formal dining area upstairs with sumptuous silk curtains brings a contemporary twist to the medieval framework. There's a super heated terrace at the back and rambling terraced gardens.

directions	Off A272, thro' Lodsworth; on to bottom of road; on left.
meals	12pm-2.30pm; 7pm-9.30pm. No food Sun evenings Oct to April. Main courses £12.95-£21.
closed	3.30pm-5.30pm. Sun evenings (except last Sunday of month); Mondays (except bank holidays).

Andrea & James Hickey
The Lickfold Inn,
Lickfold,
Petworth,
Sussex GU28 9EY
tel 01798 861285

map: 4 entry: 460

Halfway Bridge Inn
Halfway Bridge

The mellow old coaching inn is in safe hands of the Sutherlands, owners of the Royal Oak at East Lavant. Keeping the classic three-room layout and the warren of cosy corners and split levels, they have introduced a stylish and contemporary feel – scrubbed tables, cushioned benches, big lilies and fat candles. The food is good, too: a satisfying mix of traditional and modern. Find a seat by the open fire and settle down to a menu that promises first-rate fish from Billingsgate alongside steak and kidney pie. Thirsts are quenched by local Sussex beers and a number of wines by the glass. Outside is a sheltered patio with posh tables and brollies. This is a lovely spot so stay a night or two – the old stables have been converted into excellent rooms where deep beds, leather chairs, plasma screens and PlayStations "for the

boys" sit beautifully with old beams and rustic brickwork. Bath and shower rooms – big mirrors, top lotions and potions – are an equal treat.

directions	On A272 halfway between Midhurst & Petworth.
meals	12pm-2.30pm; 6pm-9.30pm (12pm-3pm, 6pm-9pm Sundays). Main courses £9-£18; sandwiches £5.25.
rooms	6: 4 suites from £120, 2 doubles from £90. Singles from £55.
closed	Open all day.

SPECIAL AWARD
see pages 28-29

Nick Sutherland
Halfway Bridge Inn,
Halfway Bridge, Midhurst,
Sussex GU28 9BP

tel   01798 861281
web   www.thesussexpub.co.uk

See page 39 for bedroom details.

map: 4 entry: 461

Sussex

Duke of Cumberland Arms
Henley

In spring the Duke looks divine, its brick and stone cottage walls engulfed by flowering wisteria — and beyond is the terraced garden, with its babbling trout pools and huge Weald views. Latch doors lead to two tiny bars that creak with character — painted tongue-and-groove walls, low ceilings, ancient scrubbed tables and benches, and log fires in the grate. Gas lamps, old indentures and the odd stuffed bird add to the atmosphere. Choose a pint of Adnams, Youngs, Broadside or Brakspear, to name but a few, drawn straight from the cask, or a glass of farmhouse cider. Landlords Christina and Gaston Duval's popular daily menu relies on fresh local produce, including trout from their spring-fed pools and delectable roasts, notably from Sussex lamb and organic beef — brought as a joint to the table.

directions	From Fernhurst towards Midhurst; pass pub on right; next left to Henley; follow road, on right.
meals	12pm-2.30pm; 7pm-9.30pm. No food Sunday or Monday evenings. Main courses £8.95-£15.75.
closed	Open all day.

Gaston & Christina Duval
Duke of Cumberland Arms,
Henley,
Midhurst,
Sussex GU27 3HQ
tel   01428 652280

map: 4 entry: 462

Sussex

The King's Arms
Fernhurst

A main road setting, on a dangerous corner south of the village, for this distinctive, 17th-century stone pub. An unusual tiled porch runs the length of the building and a wisteria-clad terrace (used for barbecues and wine tastings) shields the lovely cottage garden from the road. At the helm for a decade, Michael and Annabel Hirst have got the balance right between 'gastro' and 'pub'. Food is the thing here, but folk calling in for a drink have five ales and a slate of wines by the glass. History is evident in head-cracking beams, oak tables and a fireplace ablaze with winter logs in the spick-and-span, L-shaped bar. Graze on salmon and crayfish linguine from the chalkboard, or potato, celeric and truffle soup. Linger longer over lamb shank with honey roast parsnips, red wine and rosemary sauce, followed by chocolate fudge custard and almond florentine.

directions	On A286 just south of Fernhurst towards Midhurst.
meals	12pm-2.30pm; 7pm-9.30pm. Main courses £10.75-£16.75; bar meals £5-£10.
closed	3pm-5.30pm (6.30pm Saturdays) & Sunday evenings.

Michael & Annabel Hirst
The King's Arms,
Midhurst Road, Fernhurst,
Midhurst, Sussex GU27 3HA
tel   01428 652005
web   www.kingsarmsfernhurst.com

map: 4 entry: 463

The Keepers Arms
Trotton

A slice of Hungry Man's Hock in the kasbah? In this fabulous pub nothing seems impossible. The well-travelled owner, Jennifer Oxley, has created a pub that buzzes with life. Ethnic weavings and fabrics adorning the walls, a papier mâché zebra head by the bar, an African mask over the blackboard, gorgeous candelabra on the restaurant tables – all add colour, texture and fun. Choose your candlelit corner carefully: each one is evocative of a different continent or mood… and the huge squishy fireside sofas are the obvious refuge for Sunday lunchtime lounge lizards. Despite the exuberance, food and ales are taken seriously and are extremely good. On a menu packed with good hearty stuff you might find the best game pie in the land (venison, pheasant, partridge and wild duck) and a summer seafood platter that overflows with lobster, crab, giant crevettes and oysters. Book the corner kasbah if you can. *No smoking throughout.*

The Three Horseshoes
Elsted

Low beams, latched doors, high settles, deep-cream bowed walls, fresh flowers, cottage windows, big log fires and home-cooked food: all that you'd hope for, and more. Built in 1540 as a drovers' ale house, it has no cellar, so staff pull ales from the barrel instead; the line of metal casks is visible in the lower open-timbered bar, formerly a butcher's shop and still with the ceiling hooks. Local seafood, meat and game appear on a tempting country menu – summer lobster and crab, pheasant in cider with shallots and prunes, steak and kidney in Guinness pie – and are served in snug little rooms. In the main dining room with its wood-burning stove you can't miss the flock of chickens in china, pottery and wood. Landlady Sue has a passion for poultry and in summer her feathered friends cluck cheerily outside among the drinkers with their golden pints. The South Downs views are fabulous. *No smoking throughout.*

directions	On A272 between Midhurst & Petersfield.
meals	12pm-2pm; 7pm-9pm. Main courses £6.50-£14.
closed	3pm-6.30pm; Sunday evenings; Mondays.

Jenny Oxley
The Keepers Arms,
Trotton,
Midhurst, Sussex GU31 5ER
tel 01730 813724
web www.keepersarms.co.uk

map: 4 entry: 464

directions	From Midhurst A272 for Petersfield; Elsted signed left in 2 miles.
meals	12pm-2pm; 7pm-9pm (8.30pm Sundays). Main courses £7.95-£14.95.
closed	2.30pm-6pm.

Sue Beavis & Michael Newton
The Three Horseshoes,
Elsted,
Midhurst,
Sussex GU29 0JY
tel 01730 825746

map: 4 entry: 465

White Horse Inn
Chichester

A lovely whitewashed coaching inn, lying low with views up the South Downs. Enjoy a Ballards as ducks bob on the rejuvenated pond. But the celebrated cellar is the biggest draw: more than 600 wines on the list, 14 by the glass. The bar is clad in old wine boxes. And the food stands up to comparison; in the simple bar you can tuck into fish soup or hand-picked Selsey crab, in the crisp-linened restaurant you might find homemade oxtail ravioli, Chilgrove pheasant, and an exotic star-fruit and Earl Grey cheesecake. Fresh, excellent bedrooms in a detached annexe have CD players, snowy bathrobes and continental hamper breakfasts – and you may use the walled garden. What's more, this is a Green Tourism gold award-winner, committed to sourcing local and organic wherever possible; fittingly the old helipad has been replanted with wild flowers. An excellent stopover for visitors to Goodwood. *No smoking throughout.*

directions	On B2141 towards Petersfield; 6 miles north of Chichester.
meals	12pm-2pm; 7pm-10pm. Main courses £10.50-£19.
rooms	8 twins/doubles £95-£120. Singles £65-£95.
closed	Sunday evenings; Mondays.

See page 40 for bedroom details.

Charles & Carin Burton
White Horse Inn,
High Street, Chilgrove,
Chichester, Sussex PO18 9HX
tel   01243 535219
web   www.whitehorsechilgrove.co.uk

map: 4 entry: 466

Star & Garter
Goodwood

If fresh fish and seafood appeal then take a trip down winding Sussex lanes to this 18th-century brick-and-flint pub. Hidden in the folds of the South Downs, the old ale house now draws the well-heeled from Goodwood and Midhurst. Seafood platters groan with whole Selsey lobster and crabs, scallops, wild salmon, crevettes and prawns. There are big bowls of mussels, whole baked bass, comforting steak and kidney pud and, in season, a mouthwatering game grill, with partridge from West Dean, pigeon from East Dean and local wild boar sausages. Drink fine Sussex ales straight from the cellar in the single, wooden floored room, where hops adorn stripped beams, old village photographs line bare-brick walls and daily papers fill the rack by the door. In summer, spill out onto the sun-trap patio, then check out the summer Shellfish Bar for fresh crab and lobster to take home.

directions	Village signed off A286 between Midhurst & Chichester at Singleton.
meals	12pm-2.30pm; 6pm-10pm. Main courses £10.50-£17; bar meals £5-£7.50.
closed	Sunday evenings; Mondays. Open all day weekends.

Oliver Ligertwood
Star & Garter,
East Dean, Goodwood,
Chichester, Sussex PO18 0JG
tel   01243 811318
web   www.starandgarter.co.uk

map: 4 entry: 467

The Fox Goes Free
Charlton

King William III may have stopped off at The Fox Goes Free to refresh his royal hunting parties; this little pub, hidden in the South Downs, is now home to some of the best real ales from local microbreweries. In winter, visitors settle down by the big blazing fire under beamed ceilings for a pint of Ballards Best and the pub's own beer, Fox Goes Free; in summer there's a garden with sweeping views of never-ending, sheep-grazed farmland. Traditional bar food includes home made steak and kidney pie; in the restaurant – once a stable for Goodwood race horses – fresh local produce includes smoked salmon with Westbourne bakery bread, brace of local pigeon breast with rosemary parmentier potatoes, minted crème brûlée. Goodwood racecourse and the Festival of Speed venue are just up the hill and there are miles of downland walks from the front door.

Anglesey Arms at Halnaker
Halnaker

Laid back, relaxed, refreshingly free of airs and graces, a Georgian brick pub in an affluent part of West Sussex. It's not a pie-and-a-pint pub or a chips-with-everything roadside diner – just a cracking good local run by Roger and Jools Jackson, genuinely committed to keeping it charming and old-fashioned. Expect varnished and stripped pine, flagstones, beams and panelling, crackling log fires, locals downing pints at the bar – in short, a lovely lived-in feel. Food may not be fancy but it's fresh and home-cooked using great local produce – crab and lobster from Selsey, organic South Downs lamb, organic, well-hung beef from Goodwood Estate, venison and game birds from local shoots. Even the ciders, wines and spirits are organic. A great little local, with inter-pub cricket, golf and quizzes and regular 'moules and boules' events in the two-acre garden.

directions	From Chichester follow A286 towards Midhurst. At Singleton right to Charlton.
meals	12pm-2.30pm; 6.30pm-10pm; all day weekends. Main courses from £11.95; bar meals from £7.
closed	Open all day.

David Coxon
The Fox Goes Free,
Charlton, Goodwood,
Sussex PO18 0HU

tel	01243 811461
web	www.thefoxgoesfree.com

map: 4 entry: 468

directions	On A285, 4 miles north east of Chichester.
meals	12pm-2.30pm; 6.30pm-9.30pm. Main courses £7.95-£15.95.
closed	3pm-5.30pm. Open all day Saturday (June-August) & Sunday.

Roger & Jools Jackson
Anglesey Arms at Halnaker,
Halnaker, Chichester,
Sussex PO18 0NQ

tel	01243 773474
web	www.angleseyarms.co.uk

map: 4 entry: 469

Royal Oak
Chichester

There's a comfortable, cheery, wine-bar feel to the Royal Oak, and it's as rural as can be. Inside, a modern-rustic look with traditional touches prevails: stripped floors, exposed brickwork, dark leather sofas, open fires, racing pictures on the walls. Pop in for a glass of wine at a scrubbed pine table, or a pint of Badgers or Sussex Best. The dining area is light and airy, with a conservatory, and you can overflow onto the front terrace, warmed by outdoor heaters on summer nights; you face a road but this one goes nowhere. Six chefs deliver a satisfying mix of traditional and modern: Scottish rump beefburgers, veal schnitzel, wild mushroom risotto. Bedrooms are divided between a cottage, a nearby barn and upstairs at the back; all have DVD and CD players and plasma screens, brown leather chairs and big comfy beds. You are brilliantly placed for Chichester's theatre, and the boats at pretty Bosham.

directions	From Chichester, A286 for Midhurst. After 2 miles right for East Lavant. Over bridge; on left.
meals	12pm-2.30pm; 6pm-9pm. Main courses £10.50-£18.
rooms	5 doubles, 1 cottage for 4, £80-£110. Singles £60-£70.
closed	Open all day.

See page 40 for bedroom details.

Nick Sutherland
Royal Oak,
Pook Lane, East Lavant,
Chichester, Sussex PO18 0AX
tel 01243 527434
web www.thesussexpub.co.uk

map: 4 entry: 470

The Fountain Inn
Ashurst

The 16th-century Inglenook Bar is a snug place to be on a cold and rainy night, as Paul McCartney and Wings thought when they made their Christmas video here. When the fireplace decides 'to blow' you're transported back centuries. In the flagstoned and candlelit bar, aromatic with woodsmoke from that wafting fire, be treated to wholesome food (steak and ale pie, homemade beef burgers, nursery puds), along with a great selection of wines and five real ales. No need to bother with the wine list – just wander into the corridor where, on an ancient wonky wall, the bottles themselves are on display. Although the annual classic car and motorbike meeting attracts those from afar, The Fountain firmly remains a local. The community spirit comes into its own in September when locals bring their ripe apples along to be transformed into alcoholic nectar by the pub's cider press.

directions	On B2135, 4 miles north of Steyning.
meals	11.30am-2pm; 6pm-9.30pm. No food Sunday & Monday evenings. Main courses £7-£14.95.
closed	2.30pm-6pm (3pm-7pm Sunday). Open all day Saturday.

Craig Gillet
The Fountain Inn,
Ashurst,
Henfield,
Sussex BN44 3AP
tel 01403 710219

map: 4 entry: 471

The Green Man
Partridge Green

William Thornton used to drive past this run-down boozer and dream of taking it over. It came on the market, he snapped it up, renovated with energy and redecorated with style. Now William is behind the bar, busily overseeing a place full of cosy corners, prints on walls, big wooden tables and a woodburning stove. Even the pub garden reflects William's personal touch – wonderful Spanish-tiled plant holders on the walls, Bali furniture with simple parasols on the lawn, a herb garden. Against this vibrant backdrop good food is a big draw. William enthuses about the menu and not surprisingly; his love of Spain comes through in tapas dishes and olive oil and good bread on the table, though roast pork belly with wholegrain mustard mash and updated pub staples (say, fillet steak beefburger with hand-cut chips and onion bap) are favourites too.

Royal Oak
Wineham

A rural survivor, the part-tiled, black-and-white-timbered cottage almost lost down a country road is six centuries old and has been refreshing locals for the last two. It is unspoilt in every way. In the charming bar and tiny rear room are brick and bare-boarded floors, a huge inglenook with winter log fires and sturdy, rustic furniture. Antique corkscrews, pottery jugs and aged artefacts hang from low-slung beams and walls; Jack the tabby lives on the bar counter – an immovable fixture. Tim Peacock, who has been in charge for 35 years, draws Harveys Best and guest beers straight from the cask (no pumps) and, in keeping with ale house tradition, limits the menu to good, freshly-made sandwiches, generous ploughman's, and hearty soups on chilly days. No music or electronic hubbub, just traditional pub games. Picnic tables on the grass at the front overlook the peaceful road.

directions	On B2135 south of A272 & east of A24 junction.
meals	12pm-2pm (2.30pm Sundays); 7pm-9.30pm. Main courses £8.95-£18.95. Set lunch £14.95.
closed	Sunday evenings; Mondays (except bank holidays).

William Thornton
The Green Man,
Church Road, Partridge Green,
Horsham, Sussex RH13 8JT
tel 01403 710250
web www.thegreenman.org

map: 4 entry: 472

directions	Off A272 between Cowfold & Bolney.
meals	11am-2.30pm; 5.30pm-11pm. Bar meals £2.50-£5.
closed	2.30pm-5.30pm (6pm Saturday; 7pm Sunday).

Tim Peacock
Royal Oak,
Wineham,
Sussex BN5 9AY
tel 01444 881252

map: 4 entry: 473

The Bull
Ditchling

Inside: a dark, cosy space warmed by cheery fires and candlelight. The rambling and atmospheric bar hasn't changed for years; the other areas have been stylishly transformed: pine, parquet and modern prints on mellow walls. And there's food to match: pot-roasted rabbit with cider, rosemary and crème fraîche; fresh ciabatta filled with oaked smoked salmon and horseradish cream. Game comes from the Balcombe estate, lamb from Ditchling farms and most dishes (including sensational Sussex pond pudding!) come in half portions for children. You can eat – or drink – wherever you like, including the snug at the back. Bring bikes and try out the high-level trails on the South Downs, return to white bed linen in gorgeous rooms where new and old blend as beautifully as below. Expect bold silks, walk-in rain showers and fresh lilies.

The Jolly Sportsman
East Chiltington

Deep in the Sussex countryside, a little place with a passion for its beers, food and wine. Brewery mats pinned above the bar demonstrate chef-proprietor Bruce Wass's support of the micro-breweries, while his food has been described as "robust, savoury, skilled and unpretentious." In the stylish restaurant, where oak tables are decorated with flowers and candles, visitors natter over plates piled high and irresistibly: game pâté with onion marmalade, haunch of venison with port and juniper sauce, ripe French cheeses. Pull up a chic chair in front of the bar's open fire and enjoy winter snifters from Bruce's impressive whisky collection (including rarities bought at auction). Outside, ancient trees give shade to rustic tables, and the idyllic garden has a play area for children. A team of talented enthusiasts run this pub; the Moroccan-tiled patio tables were even made by the pub's own 'washer-upper'.

directions	In centre of village, by mini-r'bout at central crossroads.
meals	12pm-2.30pm (4pm Sunday); 7pm-9.30pm. No food Sunday evening. Main courses £9.50-£15.50.
rooms	4 doubles £80-£100.
closed	Open all day.

See page 40 for bedroom details.

Dominic Worrall
The Bull,
2 High Street,
Ditchling, Burgess Hill,
Sussex BN6 8SY
tel   01273 843147

map: 4 entry: 474

directions	From Lewes A275; B2166 for East Chiltington.
meals	12pm-2pm (3pm Sundays), 6pm-9.15pm (10pm Fridays & Saturdays). Main courses £8.95-£15.85.
closed	2.30pm-6pm; Sundays from 4pm; Mondays. Open all day Saturday.

Bruce Wass
The Jolly Sportsman,
Chapel Lane, East Chiltington,
Lewes, Sussex BN7 3BA
tel   01273 890400
web   www.thejollysportsman.com

map: 4 entry: 475

The Peacock
Piltdown

This is a pub of character — full of drunken beams without a right angle in sight. Travellers have sought out its gracious rooms in search of sustenance for 450 years; now it's filled with locals and families. Piltdown Man aficionados might also wish to drop by: the greatest archaeological hoax of all time took place down the road in 1912. The menu looks promising and all is homemade, from crab and coriander cakes to banoffee pie and summer barbecues. Beams are low, furniture a mix of settles and repro, and peacocks feature among the knick-knacks, most strikingly in a piece of needlepoint dated 1889. The often-lit inglenook, its uneven lintel hung with horse brasses and horse tack, is worth the trip alone. The back garden is safe for children, with a slide; picnic tables at the front survey gentle Sussex countryside.

The Griffin Inn
Fletching

The Pullan family run the Griffin with gentle passion. There are delicious open fires, 500-year-old beams, oak panelling, settles, red carpets, photos on the walls… this inn has been allowed to age. There's a small club room for racing on Saturdays and two cricket teams play in summer. Bedrooms have an uncluttered country-inn elegance: uneven floors, country furniture, soft coloured walls, free-standing Victorian baths, huge shower heads, crisp linen. Those in the coach house and next door are quieter. The seasonal menu changes daily: breast of pheasant wrapped in parma ham with confit pheasant leg and chestnut spring roll, maybe. In summer, a jazz duo plays in the smart garden against the backdrop of a ten-mile view, and they lay on a spit-roast barbecue every Sunday.

directions	From East Grinstead, A22 south; right at Nutley for Fletching. Straight on for 3 miles into village.
meals	12pm-2.30pm (3pm weekends); 7pm-9.30pm. Main courses £10.50-£20; bar meals from £5.50.
rooms	13: 1 twin, 5 doubles, 7 four-posters £80-£130. Singles £60-£80 (not weekends).
closed	Open all day.

See page 40 for bedroom details.

directions	Just south of Piltdown, 0.75 miles south of A272.
meals	12pm-2.30pm; 6pm-9.30pm. Main courses £7.95-£17.75.
closed	Open all day June-September.

Matthew Arnold
The Peacock,
Shortbridge,
Piltdown, Uckfield,
Sussex TN22 3XA
tel   01825 762463

Nigel, Bridget & James Pullan
The Griffin Inn,
Fletching, Uckfield,
Sussex TN22 3SS
tel   01825 722890
web   www.thegriffininn.co.uk

map: 4 entry: 476

map: 4 entry: 477

The Coach & Horses
Danehill

With ale on tap from Harveys in Lewes, fresh fish from Seaford and lamb from the fields opposite, this is a very fine pub. The central bar is its throbbing hub, original wooden panelling and open fires accompanying the gentle pleasure of mulled wine in winter-cosy rooms. During the rest of the year the big raised garden (with hedged-off play area) comes into its own; spread yourselves on the new terrace under the boughs of a spreading maple. Whatever the weather, the food attracts folk from far and wide. In the stable block restaurant a changing seasonal menu from chef Chris Start places the emphasis on quality rather than quantity – in grilled local trout with baby leeks and lobster oil, fried herb gnocchi, slow-braised venison with beetroot and juniper berries, dark chocolate parfait. Harvey the golden retriever is a final reminder that this rural pub is a true local.

Rose Cottage Inn
Alciston

In walking country close to the South Downs Way, this 17th-century, wisteria-clad cottage is on a quiet lane to nowhere. Run by the Lewis family since 1960, it's a bolthole for ramblers and locals in search of a decent pint and fresh local fish. There are cosy bars brimful with prints, bric-a-brac and farming implements, neatly furnished with sturdy tables and cushioned pews. It's a lovely place to eat; the good food includes locally shot game and home-produced fruits and vegetables. Varied menus parade ploughman's lunches, homemade soups and daily specials like rabbit and bacon pie. And always a steamed pudding. To drink? A pint of Harveys Best or local cider – most enjoyable out on the front terrace on fine summer days. Jasper, the African grey parrot, puts in regular lunchtime appearances at the bar.

directions	Off A272 1 mile from Danehill towards Chelwood Gate.
meals	12pm-2pm; 7pm-9pm. No food Sunday evenings. Main courses £8.95-£13.50; set lunch £12.50 & £16.50.
closed	4.30pm-6pm Saturdays; 5pm-7pm Sundays.

Ian Philpots
The Coach & Horses,
Coach & Horses Lane,
Danehill,
Sussex RH17 7JF
tel   01825 740369

map: 4 entry: 478

directions	Off A27 midway between Lewes & Eastbourne.
meals	11.30am-3pm; 6.30pm-11pm. Main courses £6.25-£13.50.
closed	3pm-6.30pm.

Ian Lewis
Rose Cottage Inn,
Alciston,
Lewes,
Sussex BN26 6UW
tel   01323 870377

map: 5 entry: 479

The Cricketers Arms
Berwick

Walkers seek refuge from the breezy
South Downs; so do visitors to Berwick
Church and Charleston. The 500-year-
old, brick and flint, creeper-clad pub is
utterly unspoilt outside and in. An ale
house for the past 200 years, it has three
delightfully unpretentious rooms with
beams and half-panelled walls dotted
with cricket bats. Blazing log fires,
scrubbed tables and wall benches on
worn, quarry-tiled floors add to the
pleasure of being here; all feels friendly
and unhurried. Harveys ales are tapped
from the cask in a back room and the
food is perfectly straightforward pub
grub, perhaps ham and eggs, battered
cod and chips or fresh local crab. Try
your luck at playing the Sussex coin
game, Toad-In-Ye-Hole. Surrounded
by a cottage garden resplendent with
foxgloves and roses, the Cricketers is
equally charming in summer.

The Tiger Inn
East Dean

In the flickering candlelight of the old
pub, where records go back nine
centuries, landlord Nicholas Denyer
explains why he sometimes has to say
'no': no mobile phones, no bookings, no
piped music. It's the size of the main bar
– all low beams, ancient settles and open
fire – that dictates the 'no's', and makes
it such an unusual and delightful place to
be – particularly after a wild walk up by
Beachy Head. Beside a cottage-lined
green in a fold of the South Downs, the
Tiger Inn is a great supporter of the
community: Harveys ales come from
nearby Lewes, lamb and beef for
casseroles and stews from the farm up
the hill. Freshly dressed crab is local too,
delectably served with lime-dressed
leaves and buttery new potatoes. The
ever-changing blackboard offers home-
cooked dishes and 20 varieties of the
famous ploughman's lunch, including
local sheep's cheeses and smoked meats
from the Weald smokery.

directions	Just off A27 Lewes to Polegate road near Berwick church.
meals	12pm-2.15pm; 6.30pm-9pm (12pm-9pm weekends & July-August). Main courses £6.25-£11.95.
closed	Open all day weekend & July-August.

	Peter Brown
	The Cricketers Arms,
	Berwick, Polegate,
	Sussex BN26 6SP
tel	01323 870469
web	www.cricketersberwick.co.uk

map: 5 entry: 480

directions	0.5 miles from A259 at East Dean, in village centre.
meals	12pm-2pm; 6.30pm-9pm (6pm-8pm Sundays). Main courses £7.50-£9.95.
closed	Open all day weekends.

	Nicholas Denyer
	The Tiger Inn,
	The Green, East Dean,
	Eastbourne,
	Sussex BN20 0DA
tel	01323 423209

map: 5 entry: 481

The Horse & Groom
Rushlake Green

An idyllic setting for a small, traditional, personally-run pub. Sue and Mike Chappell set out to attract people looking for more than a pint and a packet of crisps. The menu is long and tempting, the blackboards listing organic salmon fishcakes, Thai tiger prawn curry, chump of English lamb on dauphinoise potatoes, steak and kidney pudding. Generosity is a strong point, and Sue insists that all dishes include a healthy selection of fresh vegetables. Harveys, Shepherd Neame Masterbrew and seasonal guests are on handpump and they have half a dozen wines and champagne by the glass. Two small bars glow with horse brasses; the Gun Room restaurant is nicely traditional with its Windsor chairs, log fire and hunting trophies; the garden — handmade furniture and Weald views — is one of the nicest places for dining out in Sussex.

The Lamb Inn
Wartling

In next to no time, landlord Rob and his chef wife Alison have transformed this little pub into a place known for great ales, excellent food and good cheer. There's a bar with a woodburner, a beamy no-smoking snug with chunky candles and fresh flowers, a dining room with enough space for comfy sofas around a log fire and no music just chatter. Specialising in fresh fish and local produce, the menu includes fillet of local Limousin beef and roasted four-rib rack of Southdown lamb. A good selection of cheeses should follow, along with desserts like crème brûlée — no wonder people are beating a path to The Lamb's door. Make a mental note of this secluded pub if you are planning a visit to nearby Herstmonceux Castle: the drive across the Pevensey Levels is definitely well worth it.

directions	From Heathfield A265 for Burwash; B2096 for Battle. Right at Chapel Cross.
meals	12pm-2.15pm; 7pm-9.30pm (9pm Sunday). Main courses £7.95-£21.
closed	3pm-5.30pm (7pm Sunday)

Mike & Sue Chappell
The Horse & Groom,
Rushlake Green,
Heathfield, Sussex TN21 9QE

tel	01435 830320
web	www.thebestpubsinsussex.co.uk

map: 5 entry: 482

directions	A259 to Polegate & Pevensey; 1st exit for Wartling; on right after 3 miles.
meals	11.45am-2.15pm (12pm-2.30pm Sundays); 7pm-9pm. Main courses £6.95-£15.95.
closed	2.30pm-6pm.

Robert & Alison Farncombe
The Lamb Inn,
Wartling,
Hailsham,
Sussex BN27 1RY

tel	01323 832116

map: 5 entry: 483

Giants Rest
Wilmington

Most East Sussex pubs are supporters of Harveys brewery in Lewes and this is no exception; local produce is on the menu, too. Adrian's wife Rebecca is chef, and her wild rabbit and bacon pie, home-cooked ham with bubble-and-squeak and fruit crumbles are popular. It's hardly old by rural standards, but the high ceilings, the black and cream Hedges & Butler wallpaper, the pine dressers, the ferns and the candlelight seem the perfect backdrop for a plate of Victorian trifle. Menus for Burns Night or New Year are offered at normal prices as a 'thank you' to the regulars and served in front of a log fire. Furnishings include pews and pine tables at the long bar, and there are puzzles or games on every table. Work up an appetite – or walk off that trifle – with an invigorating downland stroll to view the impressive Long Man figure carved into the South Downs.

directions	On A27 just past Drusilla's roundabout.
meals	12pm-2pm; 7pm-9pm. Main courses £5.50-£11.
closed	Open all day weekends in summer.

Adrian & Rebecca Hillman
Giants Rest,
Wilmington,
Sussex BN26 5SQ
tel   01323 870207

map: 5 entry: 484

Merrie Harriers
Cowbeech

Roger Cotton changed little on his arrival at this listed clapboarded building in any way, except for greatly upgrading the food. Food lovers travel that extra mile for chef Killian Callendar's delicious "new British dishes" – fillet of Sussex beef rolled in cracked black pepper, rack of lamb with lavender mash and cassis jus – and the occasional, colourful Mediterranean dish, such as parma ham with roasted figs. Sandwiches are a cut above the average, the menus change monthly, the produce is as local as can be, and the award-winning Sunday lunches have a family following. In the peaceful heart of the Weald, the Merrie Harriers is an unpretentious, unshowy pub, quietly friendly and welcoming to dogs (in the bar) and children. The simple, part-panelled bar has a huge brick inglenook with logs at the ready, the red-carpeted restaurant extension has countryside views, and there's a nice garden at the back.

directions	Cowbeech signed off A271; in village centre, 2 miles from Herstmonceux.
meals	12pm-2pm (2.30pm Sundays); 7pm-9pm. Main courses £8.95-£16.95.
closed	4pm-6pm weekends.

Roger Cotton
Merrie Harriers,
Cowbeech, Hailsham,
Sussex BN27 4JQ
tel   01323 833108
web   www.merrieharriers.co.uk

map: 5 entry: 485

The Star Inn
Old Heathfield

Head for the church and the Star is next door. Built as an inn for pilgrims in the 14th century, with a rough, honey-stone façade, it has gained a few creepers over the centuries and its atmospheric interior has mellowed nicely. Low-beamed ceilings, wall settles and panelling, huge log-fuelled inglenook, rustic tables and chairs — it's cosy, candlelit and winter inviting. The appeal in summer is the peaceful, award-winning garden, bright with flowers and characterful with hand-crafted furniture; the gorgeous view across the High Weald towards the South Downs was once painted by Turner. Popular bar food focuses on fresh fish from Hastings and Pevensey. A chalkboard lists the daily-changing choice, perhaps tiger prawns with couscous, cod and chips or roast duck breast marinated in sweet chilli, with noodles. To drink, try Harveys Sussex Bitter from Lewes. Allow time to visit the impressive church with its fine early-English tower.

Best Beech Inn
Wadhurst

A nice little country inn — warm and glowing. The small lounge bar is busy with sofas and armchairs pulled up around copper-topped tables and the walls are a deep red — not stylish, but cosy. The open bistro has rugs on red tiles, white cloths on tables, big mirrors and horsebrass-hung beams; the residents' bar and more formal dining room are less inspiring. A French brigade rules the kitchen, under the keen eye of Roger Felstead who swept into the delapidated 17th-century inn and transformed it four years ago. Settle in with a pint of Harveys Gold and a bowlful of chunky fries (worth the visit alone) — or claim a table in the bistro and enjoy platefuls of smoked salmon, Cajun chicken on skewers and juicy sirloin steaks. There are tapas and filled ciabattas for the more modest. Rooms ramble, fires glow and Roger and his team are as welcoming to strangers as locals.

directions	From A265, left onto B2096, then 2nd right.
meals	12pm-2.15pm; 7pm-9.30pm. Main courses £7.50-£16.95; bar meals from £4.75.
closed	3pm-5.30pm (from 4pm Sundays)

Fiona Airey & Mike Chappell
The Star Inn,
Church Street, Old Heathfield,
Sussex TN21 9AH

tel	01435 863570
web	www.thebestpubsinsussex.co.uk

map: 5 entry: 486

directions	One mile from Wadhurst, B2100 Mayfield Lane to Mark Cross.
meals	12-2pm; 7-9pm. No food Sunday evening. Main courses £11.95-£17.95; bar meals £4.95-£14.95.
closed	3pm-7pm Sunday.

Roger Felstead
Best Beech Inn,
Mayfield Lane, Wadhurst,
Sussex TN5 6JH

tel	01892 782046
web	www.bestbeech.net

map: 5 entry: 487

The Curlew
Bodiam

You could do a lot worse than round off a visit to Bodium Castle with lunch at the old hop-pickers' ale house. Chef Simon Lazenby took over this spruced-up, weatherboarded pub in the summer of 2004, swept the hop garlands from the beams, decluttered the interior and wisely retained the existing brigade in the kitchen. In the smart homely bar the woodburner glows, Harveys Sussex Bitter is on handpump and the wine list flies the flag for Britain (wines from Lamberhurst vineyard join the global list). Various menus highlight lunchtime baguettes (stuffed, perhaps, with locally smoked salmon), sausages with creamy mash and caramelised onion gravy, and extra-mature fillet steak with red onion rösti. There may be pear and apple crumble with honeycomb ice cream for dessert – or a mini selection of all the desserts for the undecisive (or just plain greedy). Colour spills from tubs and borders in summer.

Globe Inn
Rye

In a modest, weather-boarded pub on the outskirts of Rye, Javed Khan has taken the gastropub hallmarks of plain wooden décor and modern kitchen and turned them into something rather special. The small, intimate, open-plan bar-dining room has a feeling of space, thanks to wide glass doors flung open in fine weather and a delightful terraced patio and garden. It's a cosy, convivial, cosmopolitan place to spend an evening or a lunchtime, with comfy leather sofas, wooden tables and chairs and chalked-up blackboard specials. A varied, locally sourced and well-priced menu offers everything from flash-fried mackerel with chilli mayonnaise and Rye deli platter to heart-warmers such as Wickham Manor Farm sausages with mash and onion gravy. A buzzing atmosphere, friendly staff, Old Speckled Hen and Harvey's Sussex Best on handpump, and good-value wines with each and every one of the 32 bins available by the glass.

directions	On B2244 Hawkhurst-Sedlescombe road; on the Bodiam crossroads.
meals	12pm-2pm (Sunday 2.30pm); 6.45pm-9.30pm. Main courses £13.95-£18.95; bar meals £7.50-£12.95.
closed	Sunday & Monday evenings.

Simon Lazenby
The Curlew,
Junction Road, Bodiam,
Robertsbridge, Sussex TN32 5UY
tel 01580 861394
web www.thecurlewatbodiam.co.uk

map: 5 entry: 488

directions	From Rye, A268 over railway bridge; right into Military Road.
meals	12pm-2.30pm; 7pm-9.30pm. Main courses £8.50-£13.95. Sunday lunch £13 & £16.
closed	3pm-5pm & Mondays (except bank holidays).

Javed Khan
Globe Inn,
10 Military Road, Rye,
Sussex TN31 7NX
tel 01797 227918
web www.theglobe-inn.com

map: 5 entry: 489

Warwickshire

Warwickshire

The Holly Bush Inn
Priors Marston

Well hidden down a village lane, an English rose – the Holly Bush Inn. Inside this large and idiosyncratic pub the feel is half Soho bar, half country boozer; not many pubs have a cigar humidor and an oil painting of Ali G. Seating in the flagged bar is in a series of alcoves stuffed with sofas and armchairs, or at tables in the large open area with walls of vibrant terracotta and exposed stone, while a blazing log fire and a woodburner bring winter cheer. Well-priced food – spicy parsnip and Bramley apple soup, roast pheasant with herb mash, fish and chips, curries and steaks – accompanies the good beers, wines and real ciders. On Wednesday night you can have a pint and a simple dish for a fiver! There are darts, TV, a friendly dog and a garden for the summer. It's a rambling, gorgeous place.

The Inn at Farnborough
Farnborough

Turning a neglected inn into a pub-restaurant was an exciting prospect for chef Anthony and his wife Joanna. Their vision and dedication led to a change of name, a stylish revival and menus created daily from the best local suppliers. It's not just the food that is irresistible but the warm yellow walls, subtle lighting, open fires, rustic floors and fresh flowers. The food is gorgeous: local Dexter beef with red wine and shallots, lamb confit with pea and mint purée and rosemary jus, salmon fishcakes with hollandaise… Or there's a good value lunchtime and early evening menu. Add fine wines by the glass, posh bar nibbles, Havana cigars, smiley staff and a fabulous landscaped garden… not everyone will be enamoured of the background music but it would be hard to find a more civilised pub. There's even a private dining room, with jaunty red walls, zebra-print chairs and a juke box.

directions	Off A361 just before Byfield, 12 miles from Banbury.
meals	12pm-2pm; 6.30pm-9.30pm (from 7pm Sundays). Main courses £5-£12.95.
closed	2.30pm-5.30pm; 3pm-6pm Saturdays; 3.30pm-7pm Sundays.

Richard Saunders
The Holly Bush Inn,
Holly Bush Lane,
Priors Marston, Southam,
Warwickshire CV47 7RW
tel 01327 260934

map: 8 entry: 490

directions	From junction 11 on M40 follow signs for Banbury. At 3rd r'bout right onto A423 for Southam.
meals	12pm-3pm; 6pm-10pm (12pm-10pm Sunday). Main courses £8.95-£19.95; set menus £10.95 & £12.95.
closed	Open all day weekends.

Anthony Robinson
The Inn at Farnborough,
Farnborough, Banbury,
Warwickshire OX17 1DZ
tel 01295 690615
web www.innatfarnborough.co.uk

map: 8 entry: 491

The Fox & Hounds Inn
Great Wolford

The Tomlinsons' gorgeous, honey-coloured pub has been trading since 1540 and dozes contentedly in a tiny community on the edge of the Cotswold hills. Its blackboard is chalked up with some irresistible-sounding dishes, excellent Hook Norton ale and a long list of whiskies. Enjoy juicy figs with finely sliced Parma ham, venison medallions in port wine with poached pears, spaghetti with cockles, clams and garlic cream sauce, and fabulous puddings in the oak-panelled bar. Low beams are hung with bunches of dried hops, there are candlelit tables on flagstoned floors and old settles, a huge stone fireplace that crackles with logs in winter, an ancient bread oven and hunting prints on the walls. It couldn't be cosier, or more welcoming – a perfect country pub. There's also a good terrace for the summer.

The Castle Inn
Edgehill

A splendid site! Charles I raised his battle standard here, before the battle of Edge Hill, and the pub sits inside the octagonal tower, built to commemorate the 100th anniversary of the battle. Unique and unusual, it opened as a pub in 1822, and later was bought by the Hook Norton Brewery. From the viewing balcony or the great big garden, spectacular views sweep over the steep scarp to the plain below and away to the Malvern Hills, some 40 miles away. In the public bar are darts, pool and a fruit machine; the octagonal walls of the lounge bar are decorated with all the Civil War maps and memorabilia you could wish for. Food is traditional English – sandwiches, steaks, home made beef and ale pie – washed down with perfect pints of Old Hooky, real cider and country wines. Malts are taken seriously, too.

directions	Off A3400 between Shipston-on-Stour & Long Compton.
meals	12pm-2pm; 6.30pm-9pm. No food Sunday evenings. Main courses £9-£17.
closed	2.30pm-6pm & Mondays.

Paul & Veronica Tomlinson
The Fox & Hounds Inn,
Great Wolford, Moreton-in-Marsh,
Warwickshire CV36 5NQ
tel 01608 674220
web www.thefoxandhoundsinn.com

map: 8 entry: 492

directions	Off A422, 6 miles NW of Banbury.
meals	12pm-2pm; 6.30pm-9pm. Main courses £5.75-£7.95.
closed	2.30pm-6pm. Open all day summer weekends.

Tony, Sue & Rory Sheen
The Castle Inn,
Edgehill, Banbury,
Warwickshire OX15 6DJ
tel 01295 670255
web www.s-h-systems.co.uk/hotels/castle2

map: 8 entry: 493

College Arms
Lower Quinton

Standing proud on a green opposite a church, this fabulous building dates from the 1500s and was once owned by Henry VIII. For centuries after that, it was owned by Magdalen College, Oxford. Claire Love and her husband, Steve, a Roux scholar who made his name at Love's Restaurant in Leamington Spa, took on the pub in summer 2005. Peerless technique and fair prices have foodies flocking to the cool contemporary restaurant, bewitched by velvety butternut squash risotto, ham hock terrine with smoked pineapple purée, roast cod with baby artichokes and fish cream, and iced mango parfait. Menus trumpet pub classics too, steaks are prime-aged Aberdeen Angus and there's a mouthwatering selection of antipasti. The small flagstoned snug to the left of Henry's Bar (named after the king *and* the Loves' dog, Harry) is a cosy spot for a pint of Hook Norton and a relaxed chat. *No smoking throughout.*

The Howard Arms
Ilmington

The place buzzes with good-humoured babble as well-kept beer flows from the flagstoned bar. Logs crackle in a vast open fire; a blackboard menu scales the wall above; a dining room at the far end has great swathes of bold colour and fresh flowers. Gorgeous bedrooms are set discreetly apart, mixing period style and modern luxury; the double oozes old world charm, the twin is more folksy, the half-tester is almost a suite. The garden has a stream, and the village, tucked under a lone hill, has an unusual church and two greens. Round off an idyllic walk with twice-baked courgette and parmesan soufflé, chargrilled Old Spot pork with wild mushrooms and cider, and Mrs G's toffee meringue. Fabulous food, good people, a lovely interior. *No smoking throughout.*

directions	Village signed off B4632, south of Stratford-upon-Avon.
meals	12pm-2pm (2.30pm Sunday); 7pm-9pm (10pm Friday & Saturday). Main courses £10-£18.50; bar meals £6-£11.50.
closed	Open all day weekends.

directions	Off A3400 between Stratford & Shipston-on-Stour; 2 miles NW of Shipston.
meals	12pm-2pm (2.30pm Sun); 7pm-9pm (9.30pm Fri & Sat); 6.30pm-8.30pm Sun. Main courses £9.50-£15.
rooms	3: 2 doubles, 1 twin £97-£112. Singles £75.
closed	3.30pm-6.30pm Sundays.

See page 41 for bedroom details.

Steve & Claire Love
College Arms,
Lower Quinton,
Stratford-upon-Avon CV37 8SG
tel 01789 720342
web www.collegearms.co.uk

Robert & Gill Greenstock
The Howard Arms,
Lower Green, Ilmington,
Stratford-upon-Avon CV36 4LT
tel 01608 682226
web www.howardarms.com

map: 8 entry: 494

map: 8 entry: 495

Fox & Goose Inn
Armscote

A really lovely little pub, with bags of atmosphere and rather good food. New owners have planned few changes, wisely: with a reputation such as this, there's no need. Regulars gladly gather here, nursing pints by the bar or tucking into sausages. Imagine the nicest sort of country pub décor — wooden floors, warm colours, scrubbed pine tables and a woodburner that glows from two sides. To expectant diners in a separate room jolly staff ferry tempting (and well-priced) platefuls of sweet pepper and red onion risotto, roasted organic salmon and celery and stilton sausages... and dark Belgian chocolate pots and tartes au citron. The fun spills over into bedrooms upstairs which come eccentrically dressed à la Cluedo — Plum, Scarlet, Peacock, Mustard — while bathrooms have luxurious claw-foot tubs with candleholders and Lady Godiva lotions. And there's a big elegant garden.

The One Elm
Stratford-upon-Avon

Stratford has a reputation for great pubs and drama, and was the birthplace of the first ever Slug and Lettuce. In the narrow building that The Slug once occupied stands The One Elm. Owned by Peach Pubs (of Warwick's Rose & Crown), it, too, is a cracker. The bar is light, airy and wooden-floored, and the décor modern and stylish, with leather sofas and bar stools reminiscent of Giacometti sculptures. In the bar downstairs there are good beers and great wines; outside, an attractive, sheltered terrace; at the back, the restaurant, with a private, secluded mezzanine and a short but mouthwatering menu. There's a chargrill section, a risotto of the week, skate with mash and a deli board that's available all day. The One Elm has a chic cosmopolitan feel and, being slightly off the tourist trail, is used by a local crowd. The staff are friendly and serve you from breakfast through until closing time.

directions	Off A3400, 7 miles south of Stratford-upon-Avon.
meals	12pm-2.30pm; 7pm-9.30pm. Main courses £9.95-£16.95.
rooms	4 twins/doubles £85-£120.

See page 41 for bedroom details.

Sarah Watson
Fox & Goose Inn,
Armscote, Stratford-upon-Avon,
Warwickshire CV37 8DD

tel	01608 682293
web	www.foxandgoose.co.uk

map: 8 entry: 496

directions	In town centre on corner of Guild Street & Shakespeare Street.
meals	12pm-10pm (9.30pm Sundays). Main courses £8.50-£15.
closed	Open all day.

Victoria Moon
The One Elm,
1 Guild Street,
Stratford-upon-Avon CV37 6QZ

tel	01789 404919
web	www.peachpubs.com

map: 8 entry: 497

The King's Head
Aston Cantlow

It is said that Shakespeare's parents had their wedding reception at the King's Head. One can imagine the scene at this long, low, rambling country inn with its small leaded windows, flagged floors and inglenook crackling with logs; perhaps they even tucked into the famous Duck Supper, a house speciality. More up-to-date delicacies join the menu today, and all is tasty, from the rare roast beef sandwiches with celeriac and horseradish to the baked fillet of cod with curly fennel, radish and chervil ceviche, and the iced mango parfait. Elderly ladies chat over pots of tea and diners come from miles around, notably well-heeled Brummies. In the bar, stylish with lime-washed beams, scrubbed pine and painted brick walls hung with boozy cartoons, are real ale and good wines. There's a small garden for summer, the village creaks with history and the walks start from the door. Hugely atmospheric — and loved by American visitors.

directions	Off A46 at Aston Cantlow.
meals	12pm-2.30pm; 7pm-10pm (9pm Sundays). Main courses £9.95-£14.50.
closed	3pm-5.30pm. Open all day Saturday & Sunday.

Peter & Louise Sadler
The King's Head,
21 Bearley Road, Aston Cantlow,
Stratford-upon-Avon,
Warwickshire B95 6HY
tel   01789 488242

map: 8 entry: 498

The Bell
Tanworth-in-Arden

First it was a row of cottages, then a hotel. In the 1930s it was taken on by Jack Hood the boxer — now the pub on the green is post office, delicatessan, restaurant and B&B all rolled into one. The main bar is contemporary and sleek: furniture from Italy, textured cushions, soft lighting, modish taupes and creams. The dining room has a boudoir glow, all silvery papered walls, vast chandelier and chocolate fountain (!), the deli is at the end of the bar, the conference room doubles up as a Sunday school. It may be swish but it's flamboyant too, and fun — just like its owner, Ashley Bent. The chef is Sudanese so the menu trumpets Moroccan chicken with couscous and fatouche salad alongside goat's cheese bruschetta, honey-glazed lamb and Bramley apple pie. And they do a great Sunday roast. *No smoking throughout.*

directions	A435 for Evesham, 2 miles; B4101 for Hockley Heath; 3rd turning on right signed Tanworth; opposite village green.
meals	12pm-2pm (3pm Sunday); 6.30pm-9pm (9.30pm weekends). Main courses £9.95-£15.95; Sunday lunch, 2 courses, £13.95.
closed	Open all day.

Ashley Bent
The Bell,
The Green, Tanworth-in-Arden,
Henley-in-Arden B94 5AL
tel   01564 742212
web   www.thebellattanworthinarden.co.uk

map: 8 entry: 499

Warwickshire

The Crabmill
Preston Bagot

The lovely, rambling, A-frame building, all tiny leaded windows and wonderfully wonky beams, once contained a cider press. A pub for the following two centuries, today it's a busy gastro haven with a dining room for every mood – one, fresh and pistachio-green, scented with lilies, another deep red, its walls hung with plump nudes, another a candlelit mushroom-cream. There's a steely bar with sand-blasted glass panels, great flagstones and a winter fire and, at the back, a split-level lounge with wooden floors, deep leather sofas and a landscaped garden that heads off into open countryside. And a stylish decked area for summer drinking. The food is justifiably popular, the menu imaginative and colourful, from croque monsieur and Cornish pasty to roast halibut with parsley and shallot rosti, steamed greens and lobster sauce. Fresh herbs are imported from France.

directions	From Henley-in-Arden on A4189 towards Claverdon.
meals	12pm-2.30pm; 6.30pm-9.30pm; 12pm-3.30pm Sundays. Main courses £11.95-16.95.
closed	Sunday evenings. Open all day.

Sarah Robinson
The Crabmill,
Preston Bagot, Claverdon,
Warwickshire B95 5DR
tel   01926 843342
web   www.thecrabmill.biz

map: 8 entry: 500

Warwickshire

The Rose & Crown
Warwick

The brainchild of Peach Pubs, the flagship Rose & Crown opens with bacon sarnies for breakfast and stays open all day. Enter a cheery, airy, wooden-floored front bar with red and white walls, big leather sofas, low tables and a crackling winter fire. To the back is the big and bustling eating area, and there's a private room that can be booked for parties and meetings. Almost all of the staff trained at Raymond Blanc's Petit Blanc restaurants; the food is good. Served all day, the tapas-style portions of cheeses, hams, marinated anchovies, mixed olives and rustic breads slip down easily with a pint of Fuller's London Pride or a glass of wine, while hot dishes are modern British with a Mediterranean slant, as in roast hake and shellfish broth, coq au vin with mash and green beans, and braised shank of lamb risotto. It's young and fun and Warwick has history in spades.

directions	In Warwick centre, on market place.
meals	8am-9.30pm. Main courses £8.50-£15; bar meals from £5.
closed	Open all day.

Victoria Moon
The Rose & Crown,
30 Market Place, Warwick,
Warwickshire CV34 4SH
tel   01926 411117
web   www.peachpubs.com

map: 8 entry: 501

The Case is Altered
Five Ways

No food, no musak, no mobiles and a Sopwith Camel propeller suspended from the ceiling. This is a Warwickshire treasure. There's even a vintage bar billiards machine, operated by sixpences from behind the bar. In the main room are stone floors, leather-covered settles and walls covered in yellowing posters offering beverages at a penny a pint. Jackie does not open her arms to children or dogs; this is a place for adult conversation and liquid refreshment. Devotees travel some distance for the pork scratcings and the expertly-kept beer, and the bar is so small you can't help but join in the chat. The sign used to show lawyers arguing but the name has nothing to do with the law; it used to be called, simply, 'The Case' and was so small that it was not eligible for a licence. It was made larger, whisky was introduced, the name was changed, and everyone was happy. They've been that way ever since.

The Punchbowl
Lapworth

The Punchbowl looks pubby enough from the outside, and functions as such with a big fire and beamed bar dispensing Banks Bitter and Marston Pedigree: a perfect place to sit, relax and unwind. So it's a surprise to discover that the building is new – the original burnt down ten years ago. James Feeney and Stephen Smith have a flair for design, and from simple materials have created a contemporary opulence: candelabra on long wooden tables, modern canvasses and ornate mirrors on bare brick, windows swept by crushed velvet. Food is a strength. Menus are printed on brown paper, and the cooking embraces many ideas, be it a contemporary gratin of scallops with a hazelnut and coriander crust or a classic sirloin of beef with mushroom sauce – or comfort food in the shape of fish and chips and rack of lamb. The outside patio is great for summer drinking.

directions	Lapworth off B4439; pub near station.
meals	12pm-2.30pm; 6.30pm-10pm (12pm-3.30pm, 7pm-9pm Sunday). Main courses £9.95-£16.95.
closed	Open all day.

directions	Follow Rowington off A4177 & A4141 junction, north of Warwick.
meals	No food served.
closed	2.30pm-6pm (2pm-7pm Sundays).

	Jackie & Charlie Willacy
	The Case is Altered,
	Case Lane,
	Five Ways, Hatton,
	Warwickshire CV35 7JD
tel	01926 484206

	James Feeney & Stephen Smith
	The Punchbowl,
	Mill Lane, Lapworth,
	Warwickshire B94 6HR
tel	01564 784564
web	www.thepunchbowllapworth.co.uk

map: 8 entry: 502

map: 8 entry: 503

Warwickshire

The Boot Inn
Lapworth

The Boot was here long before the canal that runs past the back garden. With its exposed timbers, rug-strewn quarry floors, open fires and papers to peruse it marries old-fashioned charm with rustic chic. Under the guidance of Paul Salisbury and James Eliot, the down-at-heel boozer underwent a transformation and became one of the first gastropubs of the Midlands nearly a decage ago; it has been pulling them in ever since. People come from miles around for the buzz – the feel is still very much 'friendly local' – and to sample the fabulous food. Menus have a distinct touch of Mediterranean and Pacific rim: leek, spinach and mozzarella risotto, duck confit and white bean cassoulet, seared squid with sweet chill and leaves. Ingredients are as fresh as can be and seafood dishes are a speciality. Eat in the bars or in the white-beamed dining room upstairs, and in summer go alfresco: there's a lovely terrace to the side.

directions	Off M42 junc. 4 for Hockley Heath; Lapworth signed.
meals	12.15pm-2.30pm; 7pm-10pm (9pm Sundays). Main courses £8-£14; set lunch £15 & £19.50.
closed	3pm-5.30pm. Open all day weekends.

Paul Salisbury & James Eliot
The Boot Inn,
Old Warwick Road, Lapworth,
Warwickshire B94 6JU
tel   01564 782464
web   www.thebootatlapworth.co.uk

map: 8 entry: 504

West Midlands

The White Lion
Hampton-in-Arden

A farmhouse in the 17th century, this listed timber-framed building has been a pub since the 1830s, and stands by the road that meanders through the leafy village. It's a proper village inn, all stripped pine, well-polished furniture, settles and real fires. Choose between the small lounge and the even smaller, but splendidly cosy, public bar – the whole place is warm, well-maintained and welcoming, and the local Brew X1 packs the locals in. (It's also a great stop-off point on the way to the Birmingham NEC.) Lunchtime bar snacks range from bowls of chips to paninis filled with sausage and caramelised onion to straightforward ham and eggs. The dining room has been given a lighter and more contemporary look with mirrors on walls and smart Lloyd loom chairs, and provides a decent choice of modern brasserie dishes.

directions	3 miles from NEC & aiport, for Hampton-in-Arden.
meals	12pm-2.30pm; 7pm-9pm (9.30pm Fri & Sat). No food Sundays. Main courses £9.95-£13.95; bar meals £6.50-£7.50.
closed	Open all day.

Caroline Furby
The White Lion,
High Street,
Hampton-in-Arden, Solihull,
West Midlands B92 0AA
tel   01675 442833

map: 8 entry: 505

Wiltshire

The Wheatsheaf
Oaksey

Ancient on the outside, dark-beamed and inglenooked inside, down a narrow lane – the classic English country pub. Local beer drinkers and smokers are made welcome, but, with cooking like this, it would be silly to come merely to booze. Peep around the corner from the bar and tradition ends – the dining room has pale wood and sisal floors, cream walls and modern prints, and good-looking food served on big white plates. Chef-patron Tony Robson-Burrell's imaginative country dishes reflect current trends, so whether you choose gammon, egg and chips (with sticky pineapple) in the bar, or a confit duck leg with parmesan mash, choucroute and marjoram sauce in the restaurant, you eat well. Salad-lovers should relish smoked Coln trout with pecorino and fresh lime. Real ales include Old Hooky and Ruddles, children and dogs are welcome and there's a lovely, friendly feel.

directions	Oaksey signed off A429 at Crudwell, 5 miles north of Malmesbury.
meals	12pm-2pm (2.30pm Sunday); 6.30pm-9pm (9.30pm Friday & Saturday). No food Sunday evenings & Mondays. Main courses £10.95-£15.95; bar meals £6.50-£8.95.

Tony Robson-Burrell
The Wheatsheaf,
Oaksey,
Malmesbury,
Wiltshire SN16 9TB
tel   01666 577348

map: 3 entry: 506

Wiltshire

The Vine Tree
Norton

With a fine store of ales and over 30 wines by the glass the old watermill is a watering hole in every sense. It may be hidden away but the faithful – and their dogs – return. We would too, for the food and the beer. Roasted root vegetable and mango parcels, delicately spiced and served with a light curry sauce, are devoured in seconds. There's wild mushroom risotto, too, and partridge, liver and fresh bream. Surroundings are cosy: deep red walls, candlelight and beams, a wood-burning stove. Treat yourselves to an intimate dinner in the miniscule upstairs room. In summer relax and gaze at the immaculate Cotswolds from the terrace – a delicious spot with urns of flowers and a fountain. Or join the children at play in the big garden. This vine tree has a rich harvest for guests to reap – no wonder Clementine looks so content.

directions	A429 for Cirencester. After 1.5 miles left for Norton. There, right; for Foxley. Follow road; on left.
meals	12pm-2pm (2.30pm Saturday; 3.45pm Sunday); 7pm-9.30pm (9.45pm Friday & Saturday; 9pm Sunday). Main courses £8.95-£15.
closed	Open all day Sunday.

Charles Walker & Tiggi Wood
The Vine Tree,
Foxley Road, Norton,
Malmesbury, Wiltshire SN16 0JP
tel   01666 837654
web   www.thevinetree.co.uk

map: 3 entry: 507

Quarrymans Arms
Box

Though once a row of simple cottage dwellings, this has been a pub since the 18th century – a friendly, quirky little place. As the name suggests, it once served the stone miners from the local quarry. The mines may be long-gone, but history lingers in the shape of fascinating maps, photos and some lethal-looking stonecutting equipment hanging on the walls. In pride of place near the bar: a framed front page Box quarry story from a 1934 edition of the *Daily Sketch* asks: 'Is this the world's toughest job?'. Food on the changing blackboard menus is more traditional than gastropub, but is straightforward and tasty. Good Wiltshire home-cured ham, steak and ale pie, calf's liver with mustard mash and other staples are perfect fuel for walkers, cyclists and pot-holers intent on visiting the disused mines. And the landscaped garden has fantastic views.

The Flemish Weaver
Corsham

Until their arrival in 2003, Nathalie and Jeremy had not run a pub before. You'd never guess! The couple have turned the listed old building in the busy market town into a friendly local with a kitchen worth seeking out. And so proud are they of their food suppliers that a roll-call of them appears on a board. The slate-floored bar is stylish, its darkwood tables topped with fresh flowers, local artists' work on cream walls and glowing logs in the grate. Food is modern and unshowy – free-range pork steaks (from a local farm, naturally) are served simply and tastily in a cider sauce, salmon fillet comes on a bed of watercress with orange vinaigrette – while well-kept Moles, Banks's and a weekend guest ale come straight from the barrel. In a county with few good market-town pubs, the Flemish Weaver is a great new addition. *No smoking throughout.*

directions	Just off A4, on hillside to right of village; phone for directions.
meals	12pm-3pm; 6pm-9pm. Main courses £7.50-£14.50; bar meals £2.50-£7.25.
closed	Open all day Friday-Sunday.

John & Ginny Arundel
Quarrymans Arms,
Box Hill, Box, Corsham,
Wiltshire SN13 8HN

tel	01225 743569
web	www.quarrymans.plus.com

map: 3 entry: 508

directions	In town centre, close to entrance to Corsham Court.
meals	12pm-2.30pm; 7pm-9.30pm. No food Sunday evenings. Main courses £4.25-£11.95.
closed	3pm-5.30pm (2.30pm-7pm Sunday).

Jeremy Edwards &
Nathalie Bellamy
The Flemish Weaver,
63 High Street, Corsham,
Wiltshire SN13 0EZ

tel	01249 701929

map: 3 entry: 509

Wiltshire

The Pear Tree Inn
Whitley

With its mellow farmhouse feel, the Pear Tree strikes the perfect balance between fine restaurant and traditional pub. Outside, a well-tended garden and teak-furnished terrace, inside, the feel of home. There are flagstones, beams, exposed stone, latch doors, fires, a delightful mix of furniture and cushioned window seats. The Pear Tree is a civilised spot where over 20 wines are served by the glass, along with Bath Ales Gem, changing guest beers and speciality teas. Dining rooms have a lofty, barn-like quality; country furniture stands on jute matting and glasses sparkle by candlelight. Menus announce stylish modern dishes based around well-sourced ingredients — braised neck of lamb with polenta, parmesan and puy lentils, warm pear and almond tart with rosemary ice cream — all served by polite and cheerful staff.

directions	A350 for Melksham to Beanacre; right onto Westlands Lane; at T-junc, onto B3353; immed. right to Whitley; right again into Top Lane.
meals	12pm-2pm (2.30pm Sun); 6.30pm-9pm (10pm Fri & Sat, 7pm-9pm Sun). Main courses £11.50-£20; bar meals from £4.50.
closed	Open all day Sunday.

Martin & Debbie Still
The Pear Tree Inn,
Top Lane, Whitley,
Melksham,
Wiltshire SN12 8QX

tel 01225 709131

map: 3 entry: 510

Wiltshire

The Tollgate Inn
Holt

All would pay the toll — were there one — to sample the delights of the Tollgate Inn. An exceptionally warm and convivial bar and lounge, comfy sofas on rugged tiles, a log-burning stove and planked pine tables. Newspapers, magazines and homely touches encourage you to linger over a handpumped pint of Exmoor or a glass of sauvignon. The two dining areas have distinct personalities. The smaller room off the bar downstairs has a traditional appeal; upstairs, in the former chapel of the weavers who worked below, is the restaurant — high black rafters, large open fire, an eclectic décor. Chef Alexander Venables' pedigree shines through in dishes that make the most of local produce (suppliers are named with the menu) and daily fish from Brixham. Typically, pigeon breast on black pudding and lentil ragout, roast hake with red pepper confit, beef Wellington with red wine sauce, and hot chocolate pudding.

directions	On B3107 between Bradford-on-Avon & Melksham.
meals	12pm-2pm; 7pm-9pm. Main courses £12-£17; set menus £10.95 & £12.95.
closed	3pm-5.30pm. Sunday evenings; Mondays.

A Ward-Baptiste & A Venables
The Tollgate Inn,
Ham Green, Holt, Bradford on Avon,
Wiltshire BA14 6PX

tel 01225 782326
web www.tollgateholt.co.uk

map: 3 entry: 511

The George & Dragon
Rowde

Behind the unpromising exterior hides a low-ceilinged bar, its stone fireplace ablaze in winter, its half-panelled walls lined with old paintings, its antique clock ticking away the hours. Furnishings are authentically period, there are wooden boards in the dining room, carpets in the bar, plenty of dark timber and plum-painted walls. The kitchen's chutneys and preserves are for sale, international bottled beers and organic ciders line the shelves and handpumped Butcombe Bitter can be found on the bar. Experienced new owners are maintaining the pub's reputation for fish delivered fresh from Cornwall — with the odd concession to meat eaters. Blackboards list the day's specials — perhaps steamed black bream with spinach and garlic — and puddings to diet for. Relax in the pleasant garden in summer, or wander along the Kennet & Avon Canal. *No smoking throughout.*

The Three Tuns
Great Bedwyn

Life-size models of the Blues Brothers sit at either end of the bar and set the tone. This is a cracking village pub a stone's throw from the Kennet & Avon Canal. Old buildings — one the village bakery, the other the morgue — were knocked through to create an alehouse in 1756. Get here early to bag a table in the wonderful bar where original floorboards, hefty oak beams and brick inglenook (ablaze in winter) blend beautifully with more contemporary clutter; every inch of wall and ceiling space is covered. Peruse the old farming implements, tools, jugs and teapots over a pint; chuckle at the chalkboards listing funny quotes and 'Bush Telegraph' newspaper cuttings. Locals, walkers and gamekeepers enjoy homemade food in whopping portions: wonderful meat pies, Irish stew, pigeon and quail, and rare roast beef on Sundays, all made from fresh, local produce.

directions	On A342, 2 miles west of Devizes.
meals	12pm-3pm (4pm weekends), 7pm-10pm. Snacks only Mon eves. Main courses £9-£17.50. Set lunch £13.50 (Tues-Sat).
closed	3pm-7pm (from 4pm weekends); Sun eves; Mon lunchtimes.

Chris Day, Michelle & Philip Hale
The George & Dragon,
High Street, Rowde,
Devizes,
Wiltshire SN10 2PN
tel   01380 723053

map: 3 entry: 512

directions	Great Bedwyn signed off A4 between Hungerford & Marlborough.
meals	12pm-2pm (2.30pm Sundays); 7pm-9pm. Main courses £7.95-£15.95.
closed	Sunday evenings from 5pm.

Alan & Jan Carr
The Three Tuns,
High Street,
Great Bedwyn, Marlborough,
Wiltshire SN8 3NU
tel   01672 870280

map: 3 entry: 513

The Millstream
Marden

A modern bar-restaurant that opens all day and serves champagne by the glass: not what you'd expect in the Vale of Pewsey? A recent makeover of an old pub, The Millstream keeps bags of character and a range of handpumped ales. Mustard walls, pale beams, log-burners and open fires lend a fresh appeal to the open-plan space. There's a snug with a single table off to one end, and a non-smoking dining area at the other. This picks up the vibe from the bar, but is a gentler place to be, with its upholstered chairs and calming views over the lawn to the river. The daily-changing modern British menu uses local produce, much of it organic, and fish from Looe; the wine list is long. Go for red mullet with fennel, orange and mussels, duck with lentils, wild rocket and cherries, and a strawberry and raspberry Eton mess. Staff in black aprons serve with smiles; on warm days you may sup on the terrace.

The Angel Inn
Upton Scudamore

A blaze of summer colour on the smart, sheltered decked area; beams and a huge log burner in the terracotta-coloured bar; contemporary art and sofas in the split-level restaurant. It's a comfortable and sophisticated environment for Tony and Carol Coates' blackboard menu that delivers a straightforward bistro style and is up-to-date without attempting anything too outrageous. The appeal is that the food doesn't stray too far from its pubby roots – informality and decent sized portions are among the attractions – yet is able to produce the likes of pork and coriander burger with home-pickled onions. Fish dishes star, in the form of seared Brixham scallops, whole plaice on the bone, grilled sardines. An exemplary cherry bakewell makes a satisfying finish. There are Wadworth 6X and Butcombe on tap and several wines of the month chalked up on the board by the bar.

directions	Off A302 5 miles from Devizes.
meals	12pm-3pm; 7pm-9.30pm (12pm-4pm, 6.30pm-9pm Sundays). All day bank holidays. Main courses £4-£15.
closed	Mondays (except bank holidays). Open all day.

Mrs Nicola Notton
The Millstream,
Marden, Devizes,
Wiltshire SN10 3RH

| tel | 01380 848308 |
| web | www.the-millstream.co.uk |

map: 3 entry: 514

directions	Village signed off A350 Warminster-Westbury road.
meals	12pm-2pm; 7pm-9.30pm. Main courses £10.50-£14.95; bar meals £3.65-£8.95.

Tony & Carol Coates
The Angel Inn,
Upton Scudamore, Warminster,
Wiltshire BA12 0AG

| tel | 01985 213225 |
| web | www.theangelinn.co.uk |

map: 3 entry: 515

George Hotel
Codford

By George! The old roadside inn has been given a new lease of life. Boyd McIntosh and Joanne and Robert Fryer used to practise their art at the revered Howard's House in Teffont Evias. Here, Boyd delivers dishes from a compact modern menu: wild sea bass with black olive potato and red pepper fondant, steamed turbot with watercress risotto, corn-fed chicken with mushroom risotto. Joanne is a dab hand at front of house – and her influence is stamped over the understatedly contemporary interiors. Floors are parquet, tiled or pale-carpeted, walls are warmly hued and the furniture is stylishly simple. The bar has a blond-wood counter, there are lush plants, mirrors and a sitting room full of deep sofas. The vase of lilies on the bar adds a civilised touch, as do candles on tables; the winter fires are the icing on the cake.

Spread Eagle Inn
Stourhead

Mellow and 18th century it may appear but peep inside and you see slate or coir floors, Farrow & Ball colours and understated jugs of garden flowers on old pine tables. In the bar a wood-burning stove is merry and the seats are comfy; you can eat here or in the restaurant that doubles as a sitting room. Red walls, large modern paintings and old prints create a mood that is cosy and warm. The higgledy-piggledy stairs are great if you're nimble and the bedrooms peaceful – muted colours, white linen, original fireplaces, delightful views. Bathrooms are perfectly plain – and spotless. Food is English and delicious: Wiltshire ham with sweet mustard, fillet of Cornish cod with shrimp and parsley sauce, warm treacle tart. The village is charming, and you can pretend that enchanting Stourhead with its lake and follies is yours when the hoards have gone home.

directions	Off B3092 signed Stourhead Gardens. Pub below main car park on left at entrance to garden; own parking.
meals	12pm-2.30pm; 7pm-9pm. Main courses £6.95-£13.
rooms	5 twins/doubles £70-£90. Singles £50-£60.
closed	Open all day.

See page 41 for bedroom details.

directions	Off A36 between Salisbury & Warminster.
meals	12pm-2pm; 7pm-9.30pm. Main courses £8.95-£16.95.
closed	Tuesdays & Sunday evenings in winter.

Boyd McIntosh, Joanne Fryer
& Robert Fryer
George Hotel,
High Street, Codford St Peter,
Warminster, Wiltshire BA12 0NG

tel   01985 850270

map: 3 entry: 516

Karen Lock
Spread Eagle Inn,
Stourhead, Stourton,
Warminster, Wiltshire BA12 6QE

tel   01747 840587
web   www.spreadeagleinn.com

map: 3 entry: 517

The Cross Keys
Corsley

Two crackling log fires in winter, a landscaped beer garden in summer and ales from Wadworth all year round. The convivial bar is tailor-made for quiet drinking, the front dining room, with its wooden floors and fresh flowers on pine tables, is somewhat posher. This is primarily a dining pub, so there's an intimate restaurant too, inviting with log fire, green dresser, scrubbed oak tables, gleaming glasses and chunky candles. Three huge blackboards list the oft-changing menus. Find smoked bacon and woodland mushroom baguettes, baked potatoes with posh fillings and deep-fried scampi tails at lunchtime; on Sundays, fine roasts. Dinner promises asparagus in season, chargrilled ostrich steak with mustard mash, and duck breast with plum compote. There's a skittle alley being refurbished, and a function suite in the offing. *Children over 12 welcome.*

directions	Off A3098 east of Frome at Chapmanslade.
meals	12pm-2.15pm; 7pm-9.30pm. Main courses £13.50-£20; bar meals £7.75-£10.
closed	3pm-6.30pm.

Fraser Carruth & Wayne Carnegie
The Cross Keys,
Lye's Green, Corsley,
Wiltshire BA12 7PB
tel   01373 832406
web   www.crosskeyscorsley.co.uk

map: 3 entry: 518

The Compasses Inn
Lower Chicksgrove

In the middle of a village of thatched cottages, the old inn's roof is like a sombrero, shielding the upper-floor windows that peer sleepily over the lawn. Duck into the sudden darkness of the flagstoned bar and be prepared for a wave of nostalgia as your eyes adjust to a long wooden room, its cosy booths divided by farmyard salvage: a cartwheel here, some horse tack there. At one end is a piano, at the other a brick hearth. The pub crackles with Alan's enthusiasm – he's a great host. People come for the food, too: figs in red wine topped with goat's cheese and chorizo; slow-roasted lamb shank with garlic. Bedrooms are at the top of stone stairs outside the front door and have the same effortless charm: walls are thick, windows are wonky, bathrooms are new. And the serenity of Wiltshire lies just down the lane.

directions	From Salisbury, A30; 3rd right after Fovant for L. Chicksgrove; 1st left down track lane to village.
meals	12pm-3pm; 7pm-9pm. No food Sunday evenings. Main courses £5.25-£15.95.
rooms	4: 2 doubles, 2 twins/doubles £75.
closed	Sundays from 8.30pm; Mondays (except bank holidays when closed Tuesdays).

See page 41 for bedroom details.

Alan & Susie Stoneham
The Compasses Inn,
Lower Chicksgrove, Tisbury,
Wiltshire SP3 6NB
tel   01722 714318
web   www.thecompassesinn.com

map: 3 entry: 519

Wiltshire

The Forester Inn
Donhead St Andrew

Tiny lanes frothing with cowparsley twist down to this fine little pub in Donhead St Andrew. Martin is living his dream – his passion is wine – and has revitalised the 600-year-old inn. Rustic walls, black beams and a log fire in the inglenook combine with fashionable terracotta walls, local art and planked floors; colours are muted, there's not an ounce of flounce and locals still prop up the bar of a late weekday lunchtime. Foodies come from far for Tom Shaw's cooking – seared trout with crab risotto and bouillabaisse sauce, 'a trio of lamb chops' with bubble-and-squeak, goat's cheese omlette, tomato tarte tatin – and fine puddings cooked to order, slowly. Bedrooms are fresh and lovely, with cast-iron beds, feather duvets and white linen. There's a pretty garden with views, five ales on tap, cider from Stowford Press and 17 gorgeous wines by the glass.

directions	A30 between Shaftesbury & Salisbury. Through Ludwell turning for Donhead on left after 2 miles.
meals	12pm-2pm (3pm Sunday), 7pm-9pm. Main courses £7.95-£18.
rooms	2 doubles, £65. Singles £50.
closed	Open all day Saturday & Sunday June-August.

See page 42 for bedroom details.

Martin Hobbs
The Forester Inn,
Lower Street,
Donhead St Andrew,
Wiltshire SP7 9EE

tel 01747 828038

map: 3 entry: 520

Wiltshire

The Angel Inn
Hindon

New owners again for this 1750 coaching inn in beautiful Hindon and early indications suggest that the Angel is back on form, thanks to experienced chef-landlord John Harrington. Behind the Georgian exterior is a stylish bar area in earthy tones with wooden floors, chunky tables, deep sofas and a glowing log fire. The more formal restaurant is softened by candles and fresh flowers. Good British cooking draws folk from afar: watch the team at work in the glass-fronted kitchen. At lunch: crab and smoked salmon fishcakes with sweet chilli and red pepper dressing, cod in lemon and beer batter, Wiltshire ham, egg and chips. Cooking moves up a gear in the evenings, the daily menu listing, say, roast monkfish with creamy saffron, mussel and king prawn chowder, or venison with redcurrant and port sauce. A teak-tabled courtyard and a gorgeous village at the door entice you out.

directions	From A303, left 7 miles after main A36 Salisbury junction. Inn at crossroads in village.
meals	12pm-2.30pm; 7pm-9.30pm. No food Sunday evenings. Main courses £7.95-£14.75.
closed	3.30pm-5pm. Open all day Friday & Saturday.

John & Lyn Harrington
The Angel Inn,
High Street, Hindon, Salisbury,
Wiltshire SP3 6DJ

tel 01747 820696
web www.theangelinn.com

map: 3 entry: 521

Wiltshire

The Horseshoe
Ebbesbourne Wake

The Ebble valley and Ebbesbourne Wake have escaped the intrusions of modern-day life, dozing down tiny lanes close to the Dorset border. A bucolic charm pervades the village inn that has been run as a "proper country pub" by the Bath family for over 30 years. Climbing roses and honeysuckle cling to the 17th-century brick façade, while the traditional layout of two bars around a central servery still survives. Old farming implements and country bygones fill every available cranny and a mix of rustic furniture is arranged around the crackling winter fire. Beer is tapped straight from the cask and food is hearty and wholesome, prepared by Pat Bath using local meat and vegetables and game from local shoots. Tuck into fresh fish bake, liver and bacon casserole, ploughman's, nursery puddings and three roasts on Sundays. Rustic benches and flowers fill the garden.

directions	A354 south of Salisbury, right at Coombe Bissett; follow valley road for 8 miles.
meals	12pm-2pm; 7pm-9.30pm. No food Monday evenings. Main courses £9.25-£15.
closed	Sunday evening; Monday lunchtime (except bank holidays).

Anthony & Patricia Bath
The Horseshoe,
Ebbesbourne Wake,
Salisbury,
Wiltshire SP5 5JF
tel   01722 780474

map: 3 entry: 522

Wiltshire

Haunch of Venison
Salisbury

A tiny, ancient, city-centre pub of great character; it dates from 1320 when it was built as a church house for nearby St Thomas's. A trio of rooms, jammed with shoppers, businessmen and tourists in a bare-boarded, music-free atmosphere. The rooms are affectionately known as the Horsebox (tiny), the House of Commons (chequered stone floor, beams, carved benches and minuscule, pewter-topped bar) and, lording it on the first floor, the sloping-floored House of Lords – the restaurant. The fireplace is ancient (and not always lit) but the food is modern British; warm up with wild haunch of venison with creamed potatoes, parsnips and juniper jus. Note the small side window displaying a mummified hand and a pack of 18th-century playing cards, spookily discovered in 1903. There's an amazing collection of malt whiskies crammed behind the bar, and a rare set of antique taps for gravity-fed spirits.

directions	Opposite Poultry Cross, off Market Square.
meals	12pm-2.30pm; 6pm-10pm. No food Sunday evenings. Main courses £6.90-£15.90.
closed	Open all day.

Anthony & Victoria Leroy
Haunch of Venison,
1-5 Minster Street, Salisbury,
Wiltshire SP1 1TB
tel   01722 411313
web   www.haunchofvenisonsalisbury.co.uk

map: 3 entry: 523

Wiltshire

Worcestershire

The Malet Arms
Newton Tony

Formerly a bakehouse for a long-lost manor, the old flintstone pub draws walkers and cyclists from miles around. Expect cracking ales, robust country cooking and a cheerful welcome from Noel and Annie Cardew. In the low-beamed bar, cosy with rustic furnishings, blazing winter logs, old pictures and interesting bits and pieces, sit back and sup a pint of Wadworth 6X drawn from the casks (a modern rarity!) or local Stonehenge Heelstone. Hearty food, listed above the fireplaces, reflects the rural setting, with locally-shot game a winter favourite. Fill your boots with a rich stew of pheasant and pigeon in Guinness, or a local-beef burger; follow with Annie's speciality – old English puddings (Cumbrian tart, Canterbury pie). In summer, knock a few boules about with the locals in the usually dry bed of the 'bourne' rivulet outside the door, or watch the pub cricket team on the playing field opposite.

The Fleece
Bretforton

'No potato crisps to be sold in the bar.' So ordered Lola Taplin when The Fleece was bequeathed to the National Trust after 500 years in her family. It's the sort of tradition that thrives in the Pewter Room where you can enjoy fresh local food, real ales from Uley and Weston's Old Rosie Herefordshire cider. Homemade steak and ale pie, cod in beer batter, faggots and mash and locally-culled rhubarb in pies and crumbles will tempt you. But there is so much more: summer festivals twirl with Morris dancers and asparagus auctions, and the gorgeous original farmyard is a fine setting for hog roasts and musical events. The black-and-white timbered building is as stuffed as a museum with some fabulous historical artefacts, stone flagged floors, big log fires, ancient beams and a wonderful pewter collection. Leave the 21st century behind – by about half a millenium.

directions	B4035 from Evesham for Chipping Campden. In Bretforton bear right into village. Opp. church in square.
meals	12pm-2.30pm (4pm Sundays); 6.30pm-9pm. No food Sunday evenings. Main courses £5.95-£10.95.
closed	Open all day Friday-Sunday & every day June-September.

directions	Off A338; 6 miles north of Salisbury.
meals	12pm-2.30pm; 6.30pm-10pm (from 7pm Sundays). Main courses £7.95-£14.

Noel & Annie Cardew
The Malet Arms,
Newton Tony,
Salisbury,
Wiltshire SP4 0HF

tel   01980 629279

map: 3 entry: 524

Nigel Smith
The Fleece,
The Cross, Bretforton, Evesham,
Worcestershire WR11 7JE

tel   01386 831173
web   www.thefleeceinn.co.uk

map: 8 entry: 525

The Talbot
Knightwick

It's run by two sisters, Annie and Wiz, chef-owners with a dedication to all things self-sufficient. Hops for their micro-brewed beers are grown right here and organic produce comes from the farmers' market they host every second Sunday morning. Their genuine commitment to using fresh local food pulls a crowd; the fresh crab bisque, raised pies and spotted dick are legendary. Fresh fish comes from Cornwall and scallop beignets are wrapped in nori seaweed (hardly local, but delicious). The pot-roast lamb recipe comes from Alnwick Castle in Northumberland, and the wild duck – drizzled with the meat juices, a little grand marnier and served over mashed potato – suggests a touch of genius in the kitchen. Out of the way, but no matter; make a night of it and enjoy black pudding for breakfast!

The Chequers
Cutnall Green

On the site of an ancient coaching inn, the Chequers was rebuilt 70 years ago. You'd never guess: its open fires, comfy sofas and snug little booths have evolved as smoothly as its menu. While the thirsty gather round the church-panel bar with foaming pints of Timothy Taylor's, the hungry head for the dining room – cosy and candlelit with deep red walls, pale exposed beams and a huge display of wines. Make the most of a vibrant 'mod Brit' menu from award-winning chef Roger Narbett; the food bursts with flavour. There's roasted pumpkin and sweet potato soup, spiced lamb with Brinjal pickle potatoes, banana daiquiri crème brûlée, and a classy light bites menu. And if the liqueur coffees catch your fancy, slip off and savour one in the Garden Room, whose sleek, striped, coffee-coloured curtains resemble an upside-down cappuccino. New heated patio for alfresco dining.

directions	From Worcester A44 for Leominster; 8 miles on, through Cotheridge & Broadwas; right on B4197; on left.	directions	3 miles north of Droitwich Spa on A442 towards Kidderminster. M5 exit 5.
meals	12pm-2pm; 6.30-9.30pm (7pm-9pm Sundays). Main courses £12-£17.	meals	12pm-2pm (2.30pm Sunday), 6.30pm-9.15pm (7pm-9pm Sunday). Main courses £9.75-£13.50.
closed	Open all day.	closed	4pm-7pm Sunday.

Annie Clift
The Talbot,
Knightwick, Worcester,
Worcestershire WR6 5PH
tel   01886 821235
web   www.the-talbot.co.uk

Roger & Jo Narbett
The Chequers,
Kidderminster Road, Cutnall Green,
Droitwich, Worcestershire WO9 0PJ
tel   01299 851292
web   www.chequerscutnallgreen.co.uk

map: 8 entry: 526   map: 8 entry: 527

Ye Olde Mustard Pot
Midhopestones

Bilberry- and bracken-clad slopes rise above the wooded valley of the Little Don. In a peaceful hamlet amid a latticework of stone walls, the Pot is a beacon for the pub-goer in search of fine fodder in this corner of Yorkshire. Rejuvenated some four years ago, a tangle of heavily-beamed, slab-floored rooms ramble between dressed stone walls – from secluded alcoves to traditional restaurant. Look out for Roland tinkling the ivories! Settle into settles beside huge log fires or slump into comfy sofas with a pre-prandial cocktail, eyeing up the discrete fishing ephemera or the collection of mustard pots. The first-class ingredients may have been grazing local pastures or filling local allotments just a day or two previously; for the beer buff are beers from the Wentworth brewery. Outside, sun-kissed patios and lawns encourage one to linger.

directions	Off A616, 13 miles north-west of Sheffield.
meals	12pm-9pm (8pm Sunday). Main courses £8.50-£13.95.
closed	Mondays (except bank holidays). Open all day.

Andrew & Alison Hodgkiss
Ye Olde Mustard Pot,
Mortimer Road, Midhopestones,
Sheffield, Yorkshire S36 4GW
tel   01226 761155
web   www.yeoldemustardpot.co.uk

map: 12 entry: 528

The Three Acres Inn
Shelley, Huddersfield

A dining pub par excellence: everything ticks over beautifully. The bar is a work of art, brimful of bottles, pumps, flowers, with old fishing reels and tackle hanging picturesquely above. Seating is comfy pub style, the smart polished tables are craftsmen-made, and there's a large solid fuel stove to warm the central space. Separate areas around the bar have a sea of tables set for dining (white linen, shining glasses); one area specialises in seafood. The overall feel is roomy yet intimate and hugely inviting, with plants, flowers, mirrors, old prints, a baby grand. A sizeable team prepares all the food on site, from coquilles St Jacques to braised oxtail and shin of beef with root veg and Yorkshire pud – and runs the on-site delicatessen. Well-kept beers on pump, scores of fine wines, over 50 whiskies and great sandwiches.

directions	5 miles SE of Huddersfield & off A629; signs for Kirburton on B6116; signs for Emley Moor Mast; 0.5 miles south of mast, on minor road above Shelley.
meals	12pm-2pm; 6.30pm-9.30pm. Main courses £11.95-£16.95.
closed	24 December-2 January.

Neil Truelove & Brian Orme
The Three Acres Inn,
Roydhouse, Shelley, Huddersfield,
Yorkshire HD8 8LR
tel   01484 602606
web   www.3acres.com

map: 12 entry: 529

The Sair Inn
Linthwaite

Clinging to the side of the Colne Valley, the Sair Inn oozes character, timelessness and a warren of small coal-fired rooms. Floors of rippling flagstone or scuffed boards carry tables, pews and chairs from The Ark. Massive winter fires ensure that Vulcan would feel at home; Pandora would be delighted by the artefacts and oddments. It is a Yorkshire treasure, enhanced by welcoming locals and traditional pub games; the old pub Joanna allows impromptu entertainment, side rooms allow escape from the hubbub and the front paved terrace is a fine place on a summer weekend. Beers? – to die for, created in the brewhouse near the pub; any or all of a dozen and more. Fodder? Patrons flock from leagues around to savour the ambience of this iconic idyll, so concerns about catering are the last thing on anyone's mind. It's uncompromising, not one for shrinking violets, and 'grand' – in the Wallace and Grommit sense.

The Old Bridge Inn
Ripponden

A Christmas-card image of a cobbled lane, an ancient packhorse bridge and a little low inn… this is the setting of The Old Bridge Inn. Family involvement over several decades has resulted in a thoroughly civilised, unspoilt little local; a friendly one, too. Three carpeted, oak-panelled, split-level rooms – suitably dimly lit – are furnished with a mix of old oak settles and rush-seated chairs. The small, green-walled snug at the top is atmospheric; the bar has a lofty ceiling with exposed timbers and a huge fireplace with log-burning stove; the lower room is no-smoking and good for dining. The buffet lunches are as popular as ever, while the evening menu announces sound English cooking using local produce (Hubberton rib-eye steak with port and shallot sauce, duck with quince and rosemary sauce) with a modern slant. The bar is well-used by local folk who come for Timothy Taylor's Best and Black Sheep beers, and wines are good too.

directions	Off A62 in Linthwaite; up Hoyle Ing (past oil tanks painted with sheep; turn opposite); 400 yds up steep hill.
meals	No food served.
closed	Lunchtimes Monday-Friday. Open all day weekends.

Ron Crabtree
The Sair Inn,
Hoyle Ing, Linthwaite,
Huddersfield,
Yorkshire HD7 5SG

tel   01484 842370

map: 12 entry: 530

directions	4 miles from junc. 22 M62 in Ripponden.
meals	12pm-2pm; 6.30pm-9.30pm. No food Saturday or Sunday evenings. Main courses £7.25-£10.75.
closed	3pm-5.30pm. Open all day weekends.

Tim & Lindsay Eaton Walker
The Old Bridge Inn,
Priest Lane, Ripponden,
Sowerby Bridge, Yorkshire HX6 4DF

tel   01422 822595
web   www.porkpieclub.com

map: 12 entry: 531

The Old Bore
Rishworth

The Pennines might seem bleak in winter – but drop down to Rishworth and there's a treat in store. Chef-proprietor Scott Hessel has warmed a 200-year-old pub, renamed it The Old Bore and claims it is anything but. The carved oak bar is flanked by two softly-lit dining rooms brimming with antlers, stuffed birds, old prints, Victorian screens, gilt mirrors, wine boxes and champagne bottles. The à la carte piles it on, too: pigeon and chestnut pithivier pie with foie gras sauce; an Asian style crisp belly pork with salt and pepper squid; slow-cooked Ryburn lamb with flageolets, garlic and parsley. The two-course lunch had parsnip soup topped with chocolate powder, and roast pumpkin and chorizo risotto. A menu of 15 'mains' and 'specials' threatens overload for a charming old pub on the Oldham road, but Scott Hessel has cooked his way from London to West Yorkshire with originality and flamboyance.

directions	M62 junc. 22; A672 for Halifax; 4 miles, then left at lights in Rishworth.
meals	12pm-2.15pm; 6pm-9.30pm (10pm Sat); 12pm-4pm; 6pm-8pm Sun. Main courses £9.95-£18.95.
closed	Saturday lunchtimes; Mondays.

Scott Hessell
The Old Bore,
Oldham Road, Rishworth, Halifax,
Yorkshire HX6 4QU

tel	01422 822291
web	www.oldbore.co.uk

map: 12 entry: 532

The Millbank
Mill Bank

Savour a pint and a rolling moorland view. The Millbank, clinging to the side of a steep hill, has a stripped-down, architect-scripted interior that combines flagstones and log fires with modern paintings and bold colours. Its friendly, cosmopolitan style is echoed in the food, prepared by Chez Nico-trained Glenn Futter, who creates daily wonders with fresh local produce. There might be roast scallops or warm venison salad for starters, suckling pig with black pudding fritter or Holy Island lobster ravioli with asparagus. And then there are the spoiling puddings, the fine Yorkshire cheeses, the guest beers and the Yorkshire ales (Timothy Taylor's Landlord for one), the excellent wines, the malt whiskies and the first-class snacks in the bar. The steeply terraced garden has lead planters fashionably stuffed with box topiary and bamboo, and those views.

directions	Off A58 between Sowerby Bridge & Ripponden.
meals	12pm-2.30pm (12.30pm-4.30pm Sun); 6pm-9.30pm (10pm Fridays & Saturdays, 8pm Sundays). Main courses £9.95-£15.95; bar meals £4.95-£15.95.
closed	3pm-5.30pm; Monday lunchtimes; 2-9 January. Open all day Sunday.

Glenn Futter & Joe McNally
The Millbank,
Mill Bank Road, Mill Bank,
Sowerby Bridge, Yorkshire HX6 3DY

tel	01422 825588
web	www.themillbank.com

map: 12 entry: 533

Travellers Rest
Sowerby

Caroline Lumley took over this old pub on the moors and started from scratch: she has worked wonders. The inn has kept its big fireplaces and cast-iron stoves, flagged bar, exposed stone walls and ancient beams, now sanded; Caroline has added atmospheric lighting, background sound, sofas, cushions and throws. It's a happy mix of traditional and contemporary and the result is a pub that appeals both to locals and diners from further afield. The pleasant dining room is two archways from the bar, with well-dressed tables and fine valley views. The blackboard menu highlights scrumptious English dishes – puff pastry chicken and tarragon pie, warm chocolate fondue with marshmallows – while in the stylish bar you can choose between Timothy Taylor's on tap and a champagne cocktail. From the terrace, stunning views over the Calderdale and the desolate moors.

Shibden Mill Inn
Shibden Mill

There's still a pubby feel to this rambling old inn – although it's known for its restaurant. John Smiths, Theakstons and two rotating guests manage to keep drinkers happy in front of several open fires, and the wine list is long. The deep green valley setting within sound of the mill stream makes for an idyllic summer drinking spot. Unstuffy integrity lies behind this venture, from the front-of-house warmth to the modern British kitchen. Inventive menus promise roast pigeon and beetroot risotto, wild turbot with blue cheese soufflé and mussel broth, venison, vanilla mash and chocolate sauce, and toffee parfait, caramelised banana and banoffee reduction. Fruit and veg come from local Hill Top Farm. Cosy gate-leg tables and sofas in the bars, crisp napery in the dining room, and jams and chutneys for sale make this a high-class act.

directions	West of Sowerby Bridge on A672; 5 miles west of Halifax. Signed.
meals	12.30pm-2.30pm (3pm Sunday); 6pm-9.30pm (10pm Saturday); 5pm-8.30pm Sundays. Main courses £8.50-£16.
closed	Mondays (except bank holidays) & Tuesdays; Wednesday-Friday lunchtimes; 3pm-5pm weekends.

directions	Off A58 Halifax-Leeds, near A6036 junction.
meals	12pm-2pm; 6pm-9.30pm; 12pm-7.30pm Sunday. Main courses £8.95-£16.95.
closed	2.30pm-5.30pm. Open all day weekends.

	Caroline Lumley Travellers Rest, Steep Lane, Sowerby, Halifax, Yorkshire HX6 1PE
tel	01422 832124

	Glen Pearson Shibden Mill Inn, Shibden Mill, Halifax, Yorkshire HX3 7UL
tel	01422 365840
web	www.shibdenmillinn.com

map: 12 entry: 534

map: 12 entry: 535

Yorkshire

Kings Arms
Heath

Enter Heath and step back years. A string of wool merchants' houses, 100 acres of heathland, a couple of tethered ponies... who would guess that Wakefield was down the road? In the heart of Yorkshire's most unspoilt village is the equally unspoiled King's Arms. In a dark, rich network of tap rooms and snugs, softly hissing gas lamps cast an amber glow on oak-panelled walls, yellowed ceilings and low beams, while a magnificent Yorkshire range is the best of several open coal fires. It's no museum – just a superbly old-fashioned pub that serves Clarks Classic Blond, and Stella for non-believers. Pub grub includes omelettes, curries and beef ale pie; there's no music but a quiz night on Tuesdays. Attached is a serviceable restaurant, at the back is a conservatory that breaks the spell. The gardens, enclosed by high hedges and safe for children, have gentle moorland views.

directions	Heath signed off A655.
meals	12pm-2pm; 7pm-9pm (8.30pm Sundays). Main courses £9.85-£13.50; bar meals £5.25-£8.50.
closed	3pm-5.30pm in winter. Open all day in summer.

Alan Tate
Kings Arms,
Heath Common, Heath,
Wakefield,
Yorkshire WF1 5SL
tel 01924 377527

map: 12 entry: 536

Yorkshire

The Chequers Inn
Ledsham

Fires glow, horse brasses gleam... this honey-stone-village inn could be in the Dales. In fact, you're a couple of miles from the A1: a great lunchtime stopover. A warren of panelled, carpeted rooms radiating off a central bar is cosy with log fires and plush red upholstery; faded sepia photographs are a reminder of an earlier age. Rare handpumped ales from the Brown Cow Brewery at Selby do justice to good English food of Yorkshire proportions: steaming platefuls of lamb shank, steak and mushroom pie, guinea fowl... and just when you think you're replete, along comes a treacle sponge pudding. The pub is old, deeply traditional, welcoming travellers since the 18th century. And it's closed on Sundays, a tradition that goes back to 1832 when the lady of Ledsham Hall was so incensed by a drunken farmer on her way to church that she insisted the pub close on the Sabbath.

directions	From A1 south exit at junction with A63. Left & follow signs for Ledsham.
meals	12pm-2.15pm (12pm-9.15pm Saturdays). Main courses £5.85-£16.95.
closed	Sunday; 3pm-5pm Mondays-Fridays. Open all day Saturday.

Chris Wraith
The Chequers Inn,
Claypit Lane, Ledsham,
South Milford, Yorkshire LS25 5LP
tel 01977 683135
web www.thechequersinn.f9.co.uk

map: 12 entry: 537

Whitelocks
Leeds

Fixtures and fittings have changed little since Victorian times – a remarkable achievement for a pub off bustling Briggate. The narrow bar is dominated by a tile-fronted counter with its original, marble-topped Luncheon Bar. Fine old button-backed leather banquettes come with panelled, mirrored dividers, while copper-topped tables, stained glass and several grand mirrors add to the traditional mood. There is no piped music and the place is surprisingly quiet given its city centre position, though it fills up fast at peak times. Five handpulled ales, good wines and a mix of traditional and up-to-date dishes make this a real find. There's also a carpeted dining room with dark banquettes and upholstered chairs at linen-covered tables, and an open fire to add to the atmosphere. Be comforted by sandwiches, steak and ale pie and roast lunches.

directions	Next to Marks & Spencer in Central Leeds shopping area.
meals	11am–7pm; 12pm–5pm Sunday. Main courses £4.25–£7.65.
closed	Open all day.

Darren Hancock
Whitelocks,
Turks Head Yard,
Briggate, Leeds,
Yorkshire LS1 6HB
tel   0113 245 3950

map: 12 entry: 538

The Pack Horse
Widdop

This old whitewashed inn sags beneath weathered gritstone tiles at this gloriously remote spot. Once, water engineers had a whale of a time constructing reservoirs to slake the thirst of the local textile industry – the pub's stone walls sport old plans and photos of their endeavours. Today's thirsts are those of ramblers on the Pennine Way and riders on the new Pennine Bridleway, which briefly meet right behind the pub. Four or five real ales to enjoy alongside whopping portions of crispy roast duck, rack of lamb and a whole side of grilled plaice makes this a popular spot. Two thickly beamed rooms off a passageway bar, with cavernous log fires, horsey ephemera and a comfy rag-tag of furnishings encourage you to take time out and have a natter – this is a great pub with grand food, not a dining pub with good beer.

directions	From A646 in Hebden Bridge take the road at the Fox & Goose, signed for Heptonstall and Slack. In Slack fork right for Widdop.
meals	12pm–2pm (2.30pm Sundays); 7pm–9pm (9.30pm weekends). Main courses £5.95–£10.95.
closed	Mondays (except bank holidays); weekday lunchtimes October–Easter. Open all day Sunday.

Andrew Hollinrake
The Pack Horse,
Widdop,
Hebden Bridge,
Yorkshire HX7 7AT
tel   01422 842803

map: 12 entry: 539

The Fleece
Addingham

A gorgeous old place run with flair and passion. The surroundings provide atmosphere, the friendly licensees add something special, and the food's good, too. Bags of character comes from big open fires, solid tables and old settles on flagged floors, beamed and boarded ceilings, exposed stone, white walls. It's a big space that at peak times gets busy, but in summer you can spill out onto tables on the paved terrace at the front and watch the world go by. Chris Monkman has brought a refreshing enthusiasm for local, seasonal food with him: Wharfedale lamb, braised oxtail, ocean-fresh fish. Even the children's menu is brilliant: home-battered fish, omelettes, one-minute steak, moules marinieres, grilled goat's cheese salad. Plenty of choice and it's all good value, with local cheeses playing a major role. Three of Yorkshire's best beers are always available, there's a thoughtful selection of wines, and a number of whiskies, too.

directions	2 miles north of Ilkley on A65-A650.
meals	12pm-2.15pm; 6pm-9.15pm (12pm-8pm Sundays). Main courses £6.75-£13.
closed	Open all day.

Chris Monkman
The Fleece,
Main Street,
Addingham, Ilkley,
Yorkshire LS29 0LY
tel   01943 830491

map: 12 entry: 540

The Tempest Arms
Elslack

A rambling 18th-century stone inn in rolling countryside, mid-way between Skipton and Colne. In the various areas of bar and lounge are exposed stone, old timbers and a stylish feel: settles, plump cushions, Annie Tempest cartoons, three log fires and Molly the lab. Drinkers may choose from up to four Yorkshire cask ales and several good wines by big or small glass. There's a fair mix of customers here: locals, walkers and business folk. Have a light meal in the bar or fancier dishes in the dining room; they do excellent club sandwiches, red Thai fish soup, crispy pork with thyme-roasted potatoes, sumptuous puddings, fine local cheeses. Staff are friendly and professional. Revamped bedrooms, with hand-crafted furniture and bathrooms sporting Molton Brown toiletries, are in the wing; six are on the ground floor.

directions	Off A56 between Skipton & Colne.
meals	12pm-2.30pm; 6pm-9pm (9.30pm Saturdays); 12pm-7.45pm Sundays. Main courses £8.50-£13.95; bar meals from £4.75.
rooms	12 twins/doubles £74.95. Singles £59.95.
closed	Open all day.

See page 42 for bedroom details.

Veronica Clarkson
The Tempest Arms,
Elslack, Skipton,
Yorkshire BD23 3AY
tel   01282 842450
web   www.tempestarms.co.uk

map: 12 entry: 541

Yorkshire

The Angel Inn
Hetton

The old drovers' inn remains staunchly, reassuringly traditional — but with a stylish restaurant and wines that have come, over the years, to rival the handpumped Yorkshire ales. There's even a 'cave' for private-party tastings. There are nooks, crannies, beams and crackling fires, and thought has gone into every detail, from the antique furniture in the timbered rooms (one with a magnificent oak-panelled bar) to the fabrics and the colours. Enjoyable food ranges from filo 'moneybags' of seafood in lobster sauce — the fish comes fresh from Fleetwood — to Yorkshire lamb and rosemary sausage with juniper-scented red wine sauce. Or Goosnargh duck breast with braised red cabbage. The glorious up-hill-and-down-dale drive to get here is part of the charm, and it is best to book. It's a much-loved place, yet the owners have not rested on their laurels.

directions	Off B6265, 6 miles north of Skipton.
meals	12pm-2.15pm (2.30pm Sundays); 6pm-9.30pm (10pm Saturday; 9pm in winter). Main courses £8.50-£15.95. Early Bird menus £13.20 & £16.50; Sunday lunch, 3 courses, £20.90.

Bruce Elsworth
The Angel Inn,
Hetton, Skipton,
Yorkshire BD23 6LT
tel 01756 730263
web www.angelhetton.co.uk

map: 12 entry: 542

Yorkshire

The Tennant Arms
Kilnsey

The striking edifice of Kilnsey Crag has drawn climbers for decades. Equally beguiling is the strand of buildings forming the Tennant Arms, where the best of Yorkshire hospitality has been dispensed since stage coaches first plied through the Dales. At its heart is a capacious flagged bar, replete with vast stone fireplace and intricately carved wood overmantle, age-burnished furnishings, settles and benches. Radiating from here, lounges, a snug and a restaurant all characterfully decorated: rugs and seagrass, paintings and conversation-inducing ephemera. One feature you can't miss is the fine collection of Edwardian taxidermy — the delight of gamekeepers and the bane of the nascent RSPB. Beers such as Tim Taylor's and Black Sheep bitters complement a home-cooked menu based largely on local produce (there's a fish farm next door), imaginatively prepared and served in big portions.

directions	4 miles north of Grassington on B6160.
meals	12pm-2pm; 6pm-9pm. All day Sunday & bank holidays. Main courses £7.50-£15.50.
closed	Open all day.

Stephen Whyte
The Tennant Arms,
Kilnsey, Skipton,
Yorkshire BD23 5PS
tel 01756 752301
web www.thetennantarms.co.uk

map: 12 entry: 543

The Falcon Inn
Arncliffe

Tucked into the top corner of Littondale, one of the most remote and unspoilt of Yorkshire's dales. Several generations of Millers have been licensees here and they have preserved an inn and a way of life almost lost. The fine bay-windowed and ivy-clad building looks more like a private house than a village local... expect few frills and old-fashioned hospitality. The entrance passageway leads to a small hallway at the foot of the stairs – there's a tiny bar counter facing you, a small, simple lounge, a log fire and sporting prints on the walls. A sunny back room looks out across the garden to open fells. Beer is served, as ever, straight from the cask in a large jug, then dispensed into pint glasses at the bar. At lunchtime, call in for pie and peas, sandwiches and ploughman's lunches.

The Old Hill Inn
Chapel-le-Dale

A proper, wild-country tavern – with terrific beer and food. It used to be a farmhouse, then a doss-house for walkers and potholers; now it's a comfortable old inn, a warm, safe haven in a countryside of crags, waterfalls, moors and an occasional stone dwelling. Via the porch enter the bar – a large room with open-stone walls, bare boards, old pine tables and big log fire. Six pumps deliver ales in top condition – Black Sheep Bitter, Dent Bitter, Aviator – while blackboards announce food that is well above average pub grub, enjoyed in the candlelit intimacy of the diminutive dining rooms. From Sabena come parsnip and apple soup, pheasant casserole in season and homemade bread; from master confectioner Colin, warm chocolate pudding and lemon tart. His sugar sculptures alone are worth the trip!

directions	Off B6160 16 miles N of Skipton.
meals	12pm-2pm. Snacks £2.50-£4.50.
closed	3pm-7pm. Reduced winter opening times; phone to check.

	Robert Miller The Falcon Inn, Arncliffe, Skipton, Yorkshire BD23 5QE
tel	01756 770205
web	www.thefalconinn.com

directions	On the B6255 between Ingleton and Ribblehead.
meals	12pm-2.30pm; 7pm-9pm. Main courses £8.25-£13.95.
closed	Mondays; Tuesday-Friday lunchtimes.

	Sabena Martin The Old Hill Inn, Chapel-le-Dale, Ingleton, Yorkshire LA6 3AR
tel	015242 41256

map: 12 entry: 544

map: 12 entry: 545

The White Lion Inn
Cray

For centuries the White Lion has stood surrounded by moorland high in the Pennines, serving local farmers and cattle drovers. It still does, though walkers have replaced the drovers. In the main bar are deep, upholstered settles and dark, plain tables – the ideal setting for straightforward ploughman's lunches, pork casseroles and homemade steak and mushroom pies – best washed down with a well-kept pint of Taylor's Landlord, Moorhouses Bitter or Copper Dragon Golden Pippin. At quiet times the crackle of the logs on the fire and the ticking of the clock are all you hear and the owners' relaxed style permeates the whole place. There are plenty of spots for summer eating outside by the tumbling stream. Some of Wharfedale's footpaths pass by the door, and the views are all you'd hope for, and more.

Forester's Arms
Carlton in Coverdale

A few miles past Middleham with its castle and racing stables, Coverdale is not exactly the forgotten Dale but is probably the least touted. And the Forester's is the quintessential Dales inn. Not just because of its log fires, low ceilings and flagstone floors; its drinking rooms are friendly and there's a darts team in the snug. The pub has young, keen and well-travelled landlords in Mike and Claire Chambers, who serve food as flavoursome as the ales; a lively kitchen delivers treats such as cod with brown shrimp butter, roe deer steak with brandy pepper sauce and steamed nursery puddings. Everyone feels happy here: locals, walkers, families, dogs. The bedrooms are either sweet and old-fashioned or the best of contemporary; two are ensuite and there's homemade marmalade for breakfast. Characterful and worth a detour.

directions	A1 exit A684 for Leyburn. Through Leyburn on A684. Left for Carlton.
meals	12-2pm; 6.30pm-8.30pm (7pm-8.30pm in winter). Main courses £9.95-£15.50.
rooms	3: 2 doubles, 1 twin £79.
closed	Monday; Tuesday lunchtimes. 2pm-6.30pm Tuesday-Saturday.

See page 42 for bedroom details.

directions	20 miles north of Skipton on B6160.
meals	12pm-2pm; 5.45pm-8.30pm. Main courses £7.95-£11.95.
closed	Open all day.

Kevin & Debbie Roe
The White Lion Inn,
Cray, Skipton,
Yorkshire BD23 5JB
tel 01756 760262
web www.whitelioncray.com

map: 12 entry: 546

Mike & Claire Chambers
Forester's Arms,
Carlton in Coverdale, Leyburn,
Yorkshire DL8 4BB
tel 01969 640272
web www.the-foresters-arms.co.uk

map: 12 entry: 547

The Blue Lion
East Witton

The Blue Lion has a big reputation locally; so big it followed our inspector round Yorkshire – "you must go there," everyone said. Paul and Helen came here several years ago, and have mixed the traditions of a country pub with the elegance of a country house. This is a bustling, happy place that serves superlative food and no one seems in a hurry to leave. Aproned staff, polished beer taps, stone-flagged floors, open fires, newspapers on poles, big settles, huge bunches of dried flowers hanging from beams, splashes of fresh ones. The two restaurants have boarded floors and shuttered Georgian windows, two coal fires, gilt mirrors and candles everywhere. Food is robust and heart warming; local game, braised leg of lamb with garlic mash; beef and onion suet pudding. East Witton has an interesting plague tale, Jervaulx Abbey is a mile away, there's tennis next door and a lush, enclosed garden at the back.

Sandpiper Inn
Leyburn

In 1999 former Roux scholar Jonathan Harrison swapped a slick city kitchen for an old stone pub in the Yorkshire Dales. In cosy alcoves beneath low black beams, locals and walkers put the world to rights over pints of Black Sheep and Theakston ale opposite chalkboards listing Jonathan's daily menus: fishcakes with chive and parsley sauce, club sandwiches, omelette Arnold Bennett. Cooking moves up a gear in the simple stylish dining room as in-season game, Wensleydale heifer beef and home-grown herbs and veg come into play. Loosen belts before delving into roasted lobster and tomato soup, braised rabbit with wild mushrooms and thyme, raspberry and almond tart with clotted cream. Malt whisky lovers will eye the 100 bottles behind the bar appreciatively.

directions	From A1, A684 for Bedale; on for 12 miles.
meals	12pm-2.30pm; 6.30pm-9pm (9.30pm Friday & Saturday; 10pm in summer). Main courses £8.95-£13.95 (lunch), £9.75-£16.75 (dinner); bar meals £4-£6.95.
closed	3pm-6.30pm (7pm Sundays); Mondays.

directions	From Leyburn, A6108 for 3 miles to East Witton.
meals	12pm-2pm; 7pm-9pm. Main courses £10-£18.
closed	Open all day.

Paul & Helen Klein
The Blue Lion,
East Witton, Leyburn,
Yorkshire DL8 4SN

tel	01969 624273
web	www.thebluelion.co.uk

Jonathan & Michael Harrison
Sandpiper Inn,
Market Place, Leyburn,
Yorkshire DL8 5AT

tel	01969 622206
web	www.sandpiperinn.co.uk

map: 12 entry: 548

map: 12 entry: 549

Yorkshire

Yorkshire

The Red Lion Inn
Arkengarthdale

Here is Langthwaite, a cluster of stone dwellings so perfectly huddled that film companies flock. Over the humpback bridge the Red Lion looks as it has for ever – give or take the odd shutter. Outside are picnic tables, inside, a mix of traditional front room and shop (postcards, ice cream). All is carpeted and cosy with upholstered wall seats around cast-iron tables, a fire sometimes lit, and a small snug where children are welcome at lunchtime. Fascinating to look at all the maps and books on the area, and the film photos and darts and quoits trophies that line the bar shelves, almost obscuring the pumps. Black Sheep Best Bitter and Riggwelter are served in admirable condition – after 40 years, Rowena Hutchinson knows what makes a good pint. Sandwiches, pies and sausage rolls are on tap throughout pub hours - swiftly devoured after a morning out on the unspoilt moors.

The Oak Tree Inn
Hutton Magna

A tiny cottage at the end of a row, masquerading as a pub, the Oak Tree has been snapped up by Alastair and Claire Ross – happy to swap London for the Dales. Alastair trained at the Savoy and he and Claire have created a gem. The front bar has old wooden panelling and whitewashed stone, an attractive medley of tables, chairs and pews, newspapers, fresh flowers and an open fire. The dark green dining area at the back is softly lit, its tables separated by pews. All is delightful and informal. There's plenty of good food to be had in this part of Yorkshire and in three years the Oak Tree has made a niche for itself. Game appears regularly on the menu in season and the produce is as fresh as can be – in terrine of chicken, ham and foie gras; sea bream with crab and ginger cannelloni and shellfish sauce; baked vanilla cheesecake. Booking is recommended, especially at weekends.

directions	From Reeth in Swaledale towards Arkengarthdale; right over bridge to Langthwaite; on left.
meals	11am-3pm (12pm Sunday); 7pm-11pm. Bar meals only.
closed	3pm-7pm.

Rowena Hutchinson
The Red Lion Inn,
Langthwaite, Arkengarthdale,
Richmond, Yorkshire DL11 6RE
tel   01748 884218
web   www.redlionlangthwaite.co.uk

map: 12 entry: 550

directions	Off A66, 6.5 miles west of Scotch Corner.
meals	6.30pm-9pm. Main courses £13-£15.50.
closed	Monday; Tuesday-Sunday lunchtimes

Alastair & Claire Ross
The Oak Tree Inn,
Hutton Magna, Richmond,
Yorkshire DL11 7HH
tel   01833 627371
web   www.elevation-it.co.uk/oaktree

map: 12 entry: 551

Golden Lion
Osmotherley

There's never a dull moment at the old stone inn overlooking the village green and market cross. It bustles with booted walkers at lunchtime and hums with well-dressed diners at night. This thanks to the talents of Christie Connelly and Belal Radwan. Get there early to bag a seat in the wood-panelled bar with pew bench seating, raised open fire and flickering evening candlelight. Nurse a pint of Timothy Taylor's Landlord or a first-class wine by the glass, as you choose from a refreshingly simple menu. Nothing is over-ambitious; the chef simply gives you fresh ingredients well put together and well presented. Start with fish soup or pâté with apricot relish, move on to chicken Kiev or calf's liver with onions and mash, finish with a calorific pudding. From beautiful Osmotherley on the flanks of the Cleveland Hills walkers head for the famous Coast to Coast Walk: don your hiking boots.

Carpenter's Arms
Felixkirk

It's warm, cheeful, attractive and fun. Oriental fans by the fire and other oddities are dotted around the heavily beamed interior, along with pictures, books and antique carpentry tools. The long, panelled, barrel-fronted bar has three sections and bar stools, while rustic tables are cheerful with gingham. Beyond is the dining room, more formal with its white cloths, shining glassware and comfortable period dining chairs. A couple of Yorkshire beers are accompanied by some especially good wines by the glass and the menu is long: chunky fish soup with aïoli, baked Queen scallops, Thai beef and oriental vegetable tortilla with sour cream and chives, vanilla pod cheesecake – and simple baguettes at lunchtime. This mother and daughter team and their young staff add a bit of spice that makes a visit huge fun. The village on the edge of the moors has a floodlit church.

directions	Off A19 10 miles north of Thirsk & Northallerton.
meals	12pm-3.30pm; 6pm-10pm. Main courses £6.50-£13.95.
closed	2.30pm-6pm. Open all day weekends.

Christie Connelly
Golden Lion,
6 West End,
Osmotherley,
Yorkshire DL6 3AA

tel   01609 883526

map: 12 entry: 552

directions	From Thirsk A170 to Sutton Bank; 1st left for Felixkirk. Pub 2 miles.
meals	12pm-2pm; 7pm-9pm. Main courses £7.50-£8.95 (lunch); £11.95-£15.95 (dinner).
closed	3pm-6.30pm; Sunday evenings; Mondays.

Karen & Linda Bumby
Carpenter's Arms,
Felixkirk, Thirsk,
Yorkshire YO7 2DP

tel   01845 537369
web   www.carpentersarmsfelixkirk.co.uk

map: 12 entry: 553

Nags Head
Pickhill

Three racecourses within a 15-minute drive, golf and shooting nearby – sporting guests from all walks of life predominate at this popular country inn. Behind, a manicured lawn; inside, a delightful surprise. Dark beams, snug fires and polished brass distinguish the tap room, where Black Sheep is on handpump; head for the lounge bar or mellow, picture-lined dining room if you wish to eat. If the formula holds few surprises it's because that's what customers have come to expect, and the Boynton family have been here over 30 years. That's not to damn with faint praise, only to acknowledge that generous and unaffected cooking using fresh local produce can be better than high-risk experimentation under the guise of innovation. Tuck into deep-fried Whitby haddock with thick chips and mushy peas, Swaledale lamb, Eton Mess. Staff, courteous and beavering, add to the general sense of well-being.

directions	Pickhill off A1, west of Thirsk.
meals	12pm-2pm; 6pm-9.30pm. Main courses £8.95-£17.
closed	Open all day.

Edward & Janet Boynton
Nags Head,
Pickhill, Thirsk,
Yorkshire YO7 4JG
tel   01845 567391
web   www.nagsheadpickhill.co.uk

map: 12 entry: 554

Freemason's Arms
Nosterfield

The Freemason's whitewashed exterior may suggest an ordinary village pub but over the years an extraordinary assemblage of items has been added to the traditional décor: 1900s enamel advertisements, veteran agricultural implements, Union flags, miners' lamps, a piano, and beams littered with calling cards and old bank notes. It's a low-beamed place with inter-connecting rooms, some flagged floors, two open fires, pew seating, soft lighting, candlelight – traditional, unspoilt, cosy, fascinating. It's also a downright good pub, with at least four local cask ales on offer, and a blackboard to tantalise the hungry: partridge in rowan berry sauce, pink liver and onions with bacon. Kris Stephenson enjoys buying locally and dishes up fresh produce with flair. Eat in the bar, or at one of the bigger tables in the far room, perfect for dining. Just the spot after a day at the Ripon races.

directions	On B6267 for Masham, 2 miles off A1.
meals	12pm-2pm; 7pm-9pm. Main courses £8-£15.
closed	Mondays. Open all day Sunday.

Kristian Stephenson
Freemason's Arms,
Nosterfield,
Ripon,
Yorkshire DL8 2QP
tel   01677 470548

map: 12 entry: 555

The Boar's Head
Ripley

The Boar's Head sits four-square in this peaceful, pretty Model Estate village. Its sitting rooms are carpeted and draped: pink and green sofas, button-back armchairs, glass-topped tables, ancestor oils with brass lights over, an evening fire. There are games to play, newspapers, and a parasoled garden where you are served long summer drinks by delightful staff. The restaurant is candlelit at night and the food rich and generous: Yorkshire beef, guinea fowl and Nidderdale lamb. Simpler fare in the bistro: game terrine with prune and thyme chutney, wild boar sausages with pastrami mash. Up the pretty staircase to comfy bedrooms, with sherry and fresh flowers in the best. (More rooms lie across the street.) Visit the castle gardens and the National Hyacinth Collection as a guest of the hotel; umbrellas and wellies are put out on rainy days.

directions	From Harrogate, A61 north for 3 miles; left at r'bout for Ripley.
meals	12pm-2.30pm (2pm winter); 6.30pm-9.30pm. Main courses £9.95-£15.95. Set dinner, 3 courses, from £30.
rooms	25: 4 doubles, 21 twins/doubles £125-£150. Singles £105-£125.
closed	Open all day.

See page 42 for bedroom details.

Sir Thomas Ingilby
The Boar's Head,
Ripley, Harrogate,
Yorkshire HG3 3AY
tel   01423 771888
web   www.boarsheadripley.co.uk

map: 12 entry: 556

The General Tarleton
Ferrensby

Chef-patron John Topham and wife Claire run the old coaching inn (named after the only successful British general to fight in the American War of Independence) with an easy charm. The rambling, low-beamed, nooked and crannied bar-brasserie mixes rough stone walls with red ones, there are shiny oak tables and a roaring fire. You have Black Sheep Bitter on handpump, 16 well-chosen wines by the glass and uncomplicated dishes based on the finest local produce. The brasserie-style menu ranges from mouthwatering eggs benedict and warm confit duck salad to seared King scallops and black pudding with creamed leeks and palm sugar dressing. There's dark chocolate timbale for grown-ups and banana split for children. The very cosy dining room, formerly a granary, has a formal look – all white napery and high-backed chairs, with a menu to match.

directions	From A1 junc. 48; A6055 for Knaresborough; by road in Ferensby.
meals	12pm-2.15pm; 6pm-9.15pm (8.30pm Sundays). Main courses £9.25-£15.95; set menu £29.50.

John Topham
The General Tarleton,
Boroughbridge Road, Ferensby,
Knaresborough, Yorkshire HG5 0PZ
tel   01423 340284
web   www.generaltarleton.co.uk

map: 12 entry: 557

Crown Inn
Great Ouseburn

Warmth, timelessness and good cheer. An enthusiastic team oversees a merry mix of locals, drinkers, cyclists, families and anyone out for a good meal. (Five chefs take care of 300 at Sunday lunch!). Solid Yorkshire bonhomie is woven into the very fabric of this place. In the bar: a cacophony of memorabilia, polished brass, old pictures, softly-lit corners and a large open fire; to the back, a strikingly modern dining room, all dark bentwood chairs, halogen lights and fronds of palm. The food is generous and a very good notch above the norm, whether you're here for the cod loin with roast plum tomatoes and cocote potatoes or the rack of rump of lamb with creamed leeks and port wine jus. Rhubarb crumble, glazed lemon tart, Yorkshire cheeses, ten wines by the glass, 40 malts, Black Sheep on handpump, real fires – and a play area for children in the garden.

The Durham Ox
Crayke

It stands at the picturesque top of the Grand Old Duke of York's hill. In the immaculate L-shaped bar, flagstones and deep rose walls, worn leather armchairs and settles, carved panelling and big fires. There are two more bars to either side, where well-heeled locals enjoy a pint of Theakston, and a dapper, blue-walled restaurant that draws all and sundry, including Ampleforth parents out for lunch. Chalkboards above the stone fireplace list baked Queen scallops, rack of local lamb with minted mash, roasted vegetables and juniper jus, baked whole bass stuffed with lemons and rosemary, and sticky toffee pudding with toffee sauce. The Bar Bites menu and the Sunday roasts are inevitably popular. Priced bin-end bottles line the old dresser in the bar, there's a deli selling homemade goodies, a garden with a marquee for summer functions, and jazz on Thursdays.

directions	On B6265 midway between Boroughbridge & Green Hammerton.
meals	12pm-2.30pm; 5.30pm-9pm; 12pm-9pm Sundays. Main courses £12.50-£16; bar meals £8.50-£16.
closed	Monday-Wednesday lunchtimes; 3pm-5pm Thursday; 2.30pm-5pm Friday. Open all day weekends.

John Smith
Crown Inn,
Great Ouseburn,
York,
Yorkshire YO26 9RF
tel   01423 330430

directions	Exit right off A19 York-Thirsk. Through Easingwold to Crayke.
meals	12pm-2.30pm; 6pm-9.30pm (10pm Saturday, 8.30pm Sunday). Main courses £11.95-£18.95; bar meals from £5.25.
closed	Open all day weekends.

Michael Ibbotson
The Durham Ox,
Crayke, York,
Yorkshire YO61 4TE
tel   01347 821506
web   www.thedurhamox.com

map: 12 entry: 558

map: 12 entry: 559

The Abbey Inn
Byland Abbey

The monks of Ampleforth who built this farmhouse would surely approve of its current devotion to good food; whether they'd be as accepting of its devotion to luxury is another matter. The delightful inn overlooks the ruins of a 12th-century abbey; one overseas visitor asked the Nordlis when they were going to start on the renovation. Jane loves to see the look on people's faces as they enter the restaurant, a glorious flagstoned space that's lit by a skylight and full of Jacobean-style chairs and antique tables. Rambling, characterful bars have big fireplaces, oak and stripped deal tables, carved oak seats on polished boards. Food is British-based and interesting: venison with winter berry sauce or griddled, peppered rib-eye steak with jacket wedges. Traditional bedrooms are special with bathrobes, aromatherapy oils, fruit, homemade biscuits and a 'treasure chest' of wine.

directions	A1 junc. 49; A168 for Thirsk for 10 miles; A19. Left after 2 miles to Coxwold; left to Byland Abbey.
meals	12pm–2pm; 6.30pm–9pm. Main courses £6.95–£16.50.
rooms	3 doubles £95–£155.
closed	3pm–6.30pm; Sunday evenings; Monday lunchtime.

See page 43 for bedroom details.

Jane & Martin Nordli
The Abbey Inn,
Byland Abbey, Thirsk,
Yorkshire YO61 4BD
tel 01347 868204
web www.bylandabbeyinn.co.uk

map: 12 entry: 560

The Blue Bell
York

Unlike most city pubs, the Blue Bell is exactly as it's always been. Its narrow brick frontage on Fossgate, not far from The Shambles and open-air market, is quite easy to miss; once you've found the old pub, you step into a long corridor that runs through to the back. On the right, a little bar with red-tiled floor and high ceilings, wooden panelling, Edwardian stained-glass, a cast-iron, tiled fireplace, settle seating on two sides and iron-legged tables – one round, covered in copper, the other long, dressed in red formica, more Fifties than Edwardian. 'Ladies only' used to be allowed into the narrow back lounge; now its cosy red carpet can be trod on by all. Original fireplaces, polished panelling dotted with interesting old pictures... the place is a delight, and there's a terrific range of cask beers and wines to boot, as well as a surprisingly sophisticated choice of tapas. Rumour has it the bar takes more money per square foot than any other public house in the country!

directions	In York city centre.
meals	12pm–8.30pm. Tapas dishes from £2.
closed	Open all day.

Jim Hardie
The Blue Bell,
53 Fossgate,
York,
Yorkshire YO1 9TF
tel 01904 654904

map: 13 entry: 561

St Vincent Arms
Sutton-upon-Derwent

Humming with happy chat, the public bar is the heart of the place, sporting panelled walls lined with brass plates, warm red curtains and tartan carpet. There are up to eight cask beers to choose from and no background music or electronic gadgetry — just an old radiogram. To the left of the lobby is a smaller, snugger bar decorated in pale green with matching tartan carpet; this leads into several attractive small eating areas. Food ranges from sandwiches or hot brie and bacon on ciabatta to scallops in garlic butter, mussels (recommended), steak au poivre, jam roly-poly. if you're not into ale (eight brews on handpump) there are several wines by the glass. The St Vincent Arms is a great little local and the staff seem to enjoy themselves as much as the customers — you can't ask for more.

The White Horse Inn (Nellie's)
Beverley

You could pass the White Horse by, its brick front and old pub sign do not stand out on busy Hengate. Inside is more beguiling — be transported back 200 years (the building itself is even older). Known as 'Nellie's', it's a wonderfully atmospheric little place; your eyes will take a while to become accustomed, so dim are the gas-lit passages. Little has changed in these small rooms with their old quarry tiles, bare boards, smoke-stained walls and open fires. Furniture is a mix of high-backed settles, padded benches, simple chairs, marble-topped cast-iron tables, old pictures and a gas-lit pulley-controlled chandelier. Locals love the place, and its prices. Food is straightforward and good value: sandwiches, bangers and mash, steak and ale pie, spotted dick with custard. Charles Wesley preached in the back yard in the 18th century and the only concession to the modern age is the games room at the back with its juke box and darts.

directions	Off North Bar, close to St Mary's Church.
meals	11am-3pm (5pm Friday & Saturday); 12pm-4pm Sunday. Main courses £3.95-£7.50.
closed	Open all day.

directions	On B1228, 8 miles SE of York.
meals	12pm-2pm; 7pm-9.30pm. Main courses £7.50-£13.

Simon Hopwood
St Vincent Arms,
Main Street,
Sutton-upon-Derwent, York,
Yorkshire YO41 4BN
tel   01904 608349

Samuel Smith
The White Horse Inn (Nellie's),
5 Hengate, Beverley,
Yorkshire HU17 8BN
tel   01482 861973
web   www.e-hq.co.uk/nellies

map: 13 entry: 562

map: 13 entry: 563

The Star
Driffield

The village is strung along the road, its handsome houses suggesting ancient prosperity. The long low Star appears to rise out of the village pond, where mallards and moorhens paddle purposefully around a tiny willow island watched by diners. Come for an idyllic setting, a young and charming staff and a revamp that is a harmonious and understated match of contemporary and traditional. The slate-floored bar / dining areas, bright with Guinness mirrors and the best of pub memorabilia, are intimate but never crowded, with a happy Sunday-papers sort of feel. The long dining room is chic-er, all modern abstracts and painted walls. On Sundays the place is full to the gunnels with foodies and families, and the smart menus suggest modern and imaginative dishes – scallop and leek risotto with mild chilli oil and fresh herbs, calf's liver with hazelnut and bacon gratin, plum and armagnac crumble.

directions	On B1246 between Pocklington & Driffield.
meals	12pm-2pm; 6.30pm-9pm. Restaurant open eves (Tues-Sat). Main courses £12.95-£18.50; lunch, 3 courses, from £20.
closed	2.30pm-6pm & Mondays.

Peter & Anne-Marie Thomson
The Star,
North Dalton,
Driffield,
Yorkshire YO25 9UX
tel 01377217688

map: 13 entry: 564

The Blacksmiths Inn
Westow

All sorts come here: smart young farmers, ladies who lunch, merry families and folk in tweeds. It's on the restaurant side of pub, attractive, understated and buzzy. There's a long, L-shaped bar with the short leg used by local drinkers. The other bit is spacious, flagged to the side, set with big old pine tables, candles and fresh flowers, and a well-fed log burner. The linked dining rooms are modern-Yorkshire-flagged with splashes of red tartan carpet. The Marshalls bought the pub in October 2005 and are dedicated to serving fresh seasonal food: Dales lamb served with caper and rosemary juices, Ryedale venison with roasted winter vegetables and sloe gin juice, 21-day aged steaks with hand-cut chips and pepper sauce. And the British cheeses are superb.

directions	A64 for Malton; right for Kirkham Abbey, then Westow; on main street.
meals	12pm-2pm Saturday (3.30pm Sunday); 6pm-9.30pm (Wednesday-Saturday). Main courses £9.95-£18.50. Early Bird weekday menus £10.95 & £12.95.
closed	Monday; lunchtimes Tuesday-Friday; 2pm-6pm Saturday; 4pm-7pm Sunday.

Gary & Sarah Marshall
The Blacksmiths Inn,
Westow, Malton,
Yorkshire YO60 7NE
tel 01653 618365
web www.blacksmithsinn.co.uk

map: 13 entry: 565

The Stone Trough Inn
Kirkham Abbey

A great find: traditionally pubby and welcoming, with excellent food. The bar is comfortable and cosy, with low beams, stone walls, two log fires, fresh flowers, and separate areas for privacy. Much care goes into running this place, and it shows. Although the range of beers and wines is excellent – and the staff delightful – it's the food that people travel the extra mile for. Adam Richardson is a talented chef, dreaming up such treats as pressed game, foie gras and parsnip terrine, halibut on smoked salmon risotto with lemon butter sauce, roast Flaxton lamb with tomato and puy lentil sauce, and hot chocolate brownie. You choose from two menus, one from the bar, the other from the restaurant. There's also a games room with pool, fruit machine, dominoes and TV. On warm days take your pint of Malton Golden Chance onto the front terrace that overlooks the gentle Derwent valley, then stroll down to Kirkham Abbey.

The Coachman Inn
Snainton

Since Helen (actress turned wine trade exec) and Pat (designer) took over, the locals, golfers and business folk have been beating a path to The Coachman's door. It's been an inn since 1776, and the bar remains charmingly old-fashioned in an Arts and Crafts way, its solid tables glowing in the firelight. The lovely dining room, running the depth of the building, is broken up by double doors and gingham sofas, its Georgian windows overlooking the pretty side garden. Expect fine food from a bright young chef; the breads, chutneys and truffles are homemade and the local ingredients – game in season, fish from Scarborough – impeccable. Dine elegantly on slow-roast belly of pork with cider, celeriac and apples, swoon over sticky toffee pudding with Guinness ice cream. Helen's wines are as good as all the rest – and her damson gin and Seville orange liqueur delicious.

directions	Between York & Scarborough, 1.5 miles off A64 near Castle Howard.	
meals	12pm-2pm (2.15pm Sundays); 6.45pm-9.30pm (6.30pm-8.30pm). Main courses £7.25-£16.50.	
closed	Mondays (except bank holidays). Open all day Sunday.	

Adam & Sarah Richardson
The Stone Trough Inn,
Kirkham Abbey,
Whitwell on the Hill, York YO60 7JS

tel   01653 618713
web   www.stonetroughinn.co.uk

map: 13 entry: 566

directions	From A170 Pickering-Scarborough road, onto B1258 for Malton.	
meals	12pm-2pm (2.30pm Sun); 7pm-9pm (9.30pm weekends). Main courses £9-£14.50.	
closed	2.30pm-7pm. Sunday evenings; Monday & Tuesday lunchtimes.	

Helen Patrick & Patricia Clairmont
The Coachman Inn,
Snainton, Scarborough,
Yorkshire YO13 9PL

tel   01723 859231
web   www.coachmaninn.co.uk

map: 13 entry: 567

The Appletree Country Inn
Marton

She chooses the wines and he cooks. Melanie and TJ are an unstoppable team and have put the Appletree onto the Yorkshire foodie map. Locals pile in for sandwiches and a pint of locally brewed Hambleton's — as much thought goes into the beers here as the wines — while the food-conscious seek out the deli counter for its breads, chutneys, chocolates and terrines. TJ's menus reflect the seasons and change every day. Perhaps Yorkshire blue cheese and pear salad, steamed monkfish tail with golden tomato risotto, Marton beef with horseradish cream and red onion marmalade, sautéed lambs sweetbreads — and a legendary chocolate pyramid. Herbs from the garden, fruits from the orchard, farm-reared meats... here are intense flavours with modern British eclecticism thrown in. Bliss in summer to relax on the orchard patio with a jug of Pimms; in the winter, it's cosy and comforting indoors: a beamed bar with ruby walls, flickering candles and log fires, and a farmhouse-style dining room. At busy times you'd be wise to book.

directions	2 miles from A170 between Kirkbymoorside & Pickering.
meals	12pm-2pm (2.30pm Sunday); 6.30pm-9.30pm (7pm-9pm Sunday). Main courses £8.50-£16.50.
closed	Closed Monday & Tuesday.

SPECIAL AWARD
see pages 28-29

Trajan & Melanie Drew
The Appletree Country Inn,
Marton, Pickering,
Yorkshire YO62 6RD

tel	01751 431457
web	www.appletreeinn.co.uk

map: 13 entry: 568

The White Swan Inn
Pickering

This old coaching inn is rather more hotel than pub, but still full of surprises. Duck in through the front door to find a cosy panelled tap room serving real Yorkshire ales (Black Sheep, local Cropton brews), and a lounge with deep burgundy walls and roaring log fire. The restaurant and private meeting room are handsomely furnished and the bedrooms are luxurious (plump beds, smart magazines, Penhaligon smellies). But the food is the big draw. All their meat comes from only seven miles away: how about seared pigeon breast and a fresh pea risotto? Or whole Whitby crab with homemade mayonniase and green salad for a summer lunch? There's a fantastic wine list, including 50 clarets from St Emilion. Stay awhile – for beach walks, the moors and a ride on the steam railway.

directions	From York, A64 to Malton, then A169 to Pickering. Left at roundabout; at lights turn right; 1st right up Market Place. On left.
meals	12pm-2pm; 7pm-9pm. Main courses £9.95-£16.95; Sunday lunch £17.95.
rooms	21 doubles/twins/suites £129-£189. Singles from £79.
closed	Open all day.

See page 43 for bedroom details.

Marion & Victor Buchanan
The White Swan Inn,
Market Place, Pickering,
Yorkshire YO18 7AA
tel 01751 472288
web www.white-swan.co.uk

map: 13 entry: 569

The Star Inn
Harome

You know you've hit the jackpot as soon as you walk into The Star – low ceilings, flagged floors, gleaming oak, flickering fire, irresistible aromas, a fat cat patrolling the bar. Andrew and Jacquie arrived in 1996 and the Michelin star in 2002. It's been a formidable turnaround for the 14th-century inn yet the brochure simply says: "He cooks, and she looks after you"… and how! Andrew's food is rooted in Yorkshire tradition, refined with French flair and written in plain English on ever-changing menus. Potted oak-smoked salmon with fresh horseradish sauce, pan-roast loin of local hare, gutsy puddings, a 'cheeseboard of the week' – and you're as welcome to have one course as three. There's a bar with a log fire and a Sunday papers-and-pint feel (drinks range from homemade schnapps to Scrumpy Jack), a coffee loft in the eaves and a fruit-treed garden, with chickens, for summer. Exceptional.

directions	From Thirsk, A170 for Scarborough. Through Helmsley; right, for Harome.
meals	11.30pm-2pm; 6.30pm-9.30pm. No food Sunday evening & Monday. Main courses £8.95-£21.50.
closed	3pm-6.30pm; Monday lunchtimes. Open all day Sunday.

Andrew & Jacquie Pern
The Star Inn,
Harome, Helmsley,
Yorkshire YO62 5JE
tel 01439 770397
web www.thestaratharome.co.uk

map: 13 entry: 570

Yorkshire

The Plough Inn
Fadmoor

It's been a welcoming refuge from the wintry moors for years. Catch sight of it from up high, smoke curling from the stack, and you feel irresistibly drawn. Inside the Plough all is as warm and reassuring as could be; the onetime row of cottage dwellings feels rambling but contained, the several small rooms immaculate with gleaming wood, rosy upholstery and rugs on seagrass floors. The food is a major draw and there are six dining areas in all, the nicest being half-panelled. All have open fires. Dishes range from cod and pancetta fishcakes with sweet chilli and ginger dressing to a mouthwatering steak, kidney and Guinness suet pudding; the soups are very good, and we liked the look of the chocolate and hazelnut terrine. Spill outside to bikes, boots, dogs and a pretty view of the village green in summer.

Yorkshire

Moors Inn
Appleton le Moors

An ancient sign hangs from a long bracket. That's all there is to identify this unassuming inn but it is unexpectedly fresh and modern inside: white walls are unadorned, a few pictures and brasses on beams add colour, there's a charcoal-grey carpet, a stripped settle, little clutter. Warmth and cosiness emanate from the big old Yorkshire range with open fire and built-in ovens at one end of the main room; there's a wood-fronted bar at the other, a number of well-designed seating areas and a small dining room. Expect well-kept beer and good food – pheasant casserole, fish pie – largely made from their own or locally sourced organic produce. More unexpected is the strong no-smoking policy (pool and darts room excepted). At the back, a large walled garden with dreamy vale views. The village, with its wide main street and solid stone buildings, has a timeless feel; glorious walks start from the door.

directions	From A170 Helmsley to Kirkbymoorside, left towards Fadmoor.
meals	12pm-1.45pm; 6.30pm-8.45pm (7pm-8.45pm Sundays). Main courses £8.50-£15.95.
closed	2.30pm-6.30pm (3pm-7pm Sunday).

Neil & Rachael Nicholson
The Plough Inn,
Main Street, Fadmoor,
Kirkbymoorside,
Yorkshire YO62 7HY
tel 01751 431515

map: 13 entry: 571

directions	Off A170, 5 miles west of Pickering.
meals	12pm-3pm (Sundays); 7pm-11pm. Main courses £7.95-£13.90.
closed	Mondays.

Janet Frank
Moors Inn,
Appleton le Moors,
Kirkbymoorside,
Yorkshire YO62 6TF
tel 01751 417435

map: 13 entry: 572

The Blacksmith's Arms
Lastingham

Rows of tankards suspended from low black beams, glowing fires, timeworn saddles, a ghost called Ella and a pint of Daleside Blond. It's a rural dream. You almost slide down to the lovely little village, so deep is it sunk into the valley. The low, rambling, dimly-lit pub has provided shelter and comfort to monks, shepherds and travellers since 1693; now it is visited by gamekeepers, walkers and church enthusiasts; St Mary's (1030) sits next door and, rumour has it, a secret tunnel runs between the two. Once an impoverished priest with 13 children ran both pub and church, to the dismay of his bishop; the current landlord is approved of by all. The little dining rooms are not quite as atmospheric as the bar with its lit range, but this is a great place for a gossip, a pint and an old-fashioned steak and ale pie.

directions	Left off A170 Kirkbymoorside-Pickering road.
meals	12pm-2pm (2.30pm in winter); 7pm-9pm. All day weekends in winter. No food 2 weeks in November. Main courses £7.95-£10.95.
closed	2.30pm-6pm; Tuesday lunchtimes in winter. Open all day Friday-Sunday & in summer.

Peter & Hilary Trafford
The Blacksmith's Arms,
Front Street,
Lastingham, Pickering,
Yorkshire YO62 6TL
tel   01751 417247

map: 13 entry: 573

The Birch Hall
Beck Hole

Two small bars with a shop in between, unaltered for 70 years. Steep wooded hillsides and a stone bridge straddling the rushing river and, inside, a fascinating glimpse of life before World War II. The Big Bar has been beautifully repapered and has a little open fire, dominoes, darts and service from a hatch; the benches and tables come from the station waiting room at Beck Hole. The shop (stacked with postcards, traditional sweets, ice creams) has its original fittings, as does the Little Bar with its handpumps for three cask ales. The original 19th-century enamel sign hangs above the door. Food is simple and authentic: local pies, specially baked stotties or baps, homemade scones and delicious beer cake. Steep steps take you to the terraced garden that looks over the inn and across the valley. Parking is scarce so show patience and courtesy in this old-fashioned place.

directions	9 miles from Whitby towards Pickering.
meals	11am-3pm; 7.30pm-11pm (10.30pm Sun). All day in summer. Sandwiches & pies £1.50-£2.50.
closed	3pm-7.30pm & Monday evenings in winter. Open all day in summer.

Glenys & Neil Crampton
The Birch Hall,
Beck Hole, Goathland,
Yorkshire YO22 5LE
tel   01947 896245
web   www.beckhole.com

map: 13 entry: 574

Yorkshire

Wheatsheaf Inn
Egton

Unlike many pubs in this area, the Wheatsheaf has shirked expansion and held onto its character. It sits so modestly back from the wide main street you could pass it by – and miss a good deal. The first entrance brings you into the main room with bar, a restful room with dark green walls, low beams and comfy old settles, but the main treat here is the locals' bar, dominated by its Yorkshire range. This drinkers' den takes 12 at a push and is hugely popular with walkers and fishermen and dogs. A range of cask ales ensures plenty of chatter, while the restaurant dishes up game in season and meat and veg from local farms. The river Esk at the foot of the steep hill is famous for fly-fishing and so there is, unsurprisingly, fishing memorabilia on the walls, and a few angling pictures. Egton is lovely – and worth a linger.

directions	Off A171; 6 miles west of Whitby.
meals	12pm-2pm; 6pm-9pm. No food Sunday evenings & Mondays. Main courses £8-£14.
closed	Monday lunchtimes. Open all day weekends.

Nigel Pulling
Wheatsheaf Inn,
Egton,
Whitby,
Yorkshire YO21 1TZ
tel   01947 895271

map: 13 entry: 575

Yorkshire

Fox & Hounds
Goldsborough

Don't be fooled by the swirly carpets and artex walls of this small stone inn in the middle of nowhere. The food served is as delicious as you will find anywhere. Jason Davies brings London expertise, Sue Wren adds local charm and together they are producing some of the best pub meals in Yorkshire. Eat cosily by the winter fire or out in the summer garden. Wisely, the daily-changing menu restrains itself to half a dozen starters and mains, one pudding and a cheeseboard. Loving care is applied to spanking fresh fish from the Whitby inshore fleet, game from the North York Moors, local meat and organic vegetables. Star turns include pea and mint risotto; slow-roast belly pork and mash; halibut with fennel, new potatoes and lemon oil. Pudding might be a chocolate terrine; cheese is served with Ampleforth apples and oatcakes. Small being so beautiful, it's wise to book. *No smoking throughout.*

directions	Village signed off A174 north of Whitby.
meals	12pm-2pm; 6pm-9.30pm. No food Sunday evenings. Main courses £8.50-£16.
closed	Winter: Monday; Tuesday; Wednesday lunchtime. Summer: Monday; Tuesday lunchtime.

Jason Davies & Sue Wren
Fox & Hounds,
Goldsborough,
Whitby,
Yorkshire YO21 3RX
tel   01947 893372

map: 13 entry: 576

Pub awards

Local, Seasonal & Organic Produce Award

The Pot Kiln, entry 9

The George & Dragon, entry 250

The Appletree Country Inn, entry 568

Authentic Pub Award

The Tinners Arms, entry 61

The Queen's Head, entry 36

Ye Olde Gate, entry 109

Pub with Rooms Award

The Queen's Arms, entry 430

For information about our Pub Awards see pages 28–29

The Halfway Bridge, entry 461

Community Pub Award

The Old Crown, entry 96

The Halfway House, entry 429

The Plough & Harrow, entry 591

wales

Ship Inn
Red Wharf Bay

The boatmen still walk across from the estuary with their catch. Inside The Ship, fires roar in several fireplaces and bars share nautical bits and bobs. There are pews and benches and bare stone walls, and huge blackboards where the daily specials change almost by the hour. At night, the menu proffers Welsh seafood based on the best the boats have brought in: grilled turbot served with lemon and seasonal vegetables; dressed crab. But the old Ship is so much more – a family-friendly public house where, for 30 years, regulars and visitors have been enjoying great ales and freshly prepared food, from 'brechdanau' – sandwiches – to 'pwdin'. Fine Welsh cheeses, too. These lovely people are as proud of their hospitality as they are of their language – and the vast sea and sand views from the front terraces are inspiring. Bag a table if you can.

Ye Olde Bulls Head Inn
Beaumaris

This was a favourite haunt of Samuel Johnson and Charles Dickens and now attracts drinkers and foodies like bees to clover. In the rambling, snug-alcoved bar there's draught Bass on offer, while in the contemporary brasserie in the stables you have a choice of ten wines by the glass to match your sarnies or Indian-spiced spatchcock poussin. Spot the ancient weaponry and old ducking stool, which contrasts with the sophisticated remodelling of the restaurant upstairs under hammer-beamed eaves. Here, Welsh dishes are designed around seafood from the Menai Strait, and as much beef, lamb and game as the chefs can find on the island. The results: sticky short rib of Welsh black beef, breast of duck with purple figs, and fillets of local brill, seasoned as required with Anglesey sea salt. Service comes with warmth and charm.

directions	Off B5025, north of Pentraeth.
meals	12pm-2.30pm; 6pm-9.30pm (12pm-9pm Sundays). Main courses £7.95-£15.95; bar meals £2.95-£5.85.
closed	Open all day.

Neil Kenneally
Ship Inn,
Red Wharf Bay,
Anglesey LL75 8RJ

tel	01248 852568
web	www.shipinnredwharfbay.co.uk

map: 6 entry: 577

directions	Castle Street is main street in Beaumaris.
meals	12pm-2pm; 6pm-9pm. Restaurant 7pm-9.30pm only (not Sundays). Main courses £6-£12; set menu £35.
closed	Open all day.

David Robertson
Ye Olde Bulls Head Inn,
Castle Street, Beaumaris,
Anglesey LL58 8AP

tel	01248 810329
web	www.bullsheadinn.co.uk

map: 6 entry: 578

Carmarthenshire

The Brunant Arms
Caio

Miles from anywhere, the Vale of Cothi is a place of mystery and legend – the final resting place of John Harries, one of Wales's last wizards. In this lovely, secluded, time-warp village, the pub feels warm, cared-for, cosy and at the community's heart. Samantha and David say, modestly, they do "good pub food", but what you get is succulent Welsh black rump steak marinated in red wine and Brecon ostrich on potato rosti – enhanced by delightful service and candlelight. They also do proper meals for children, while walkers drop by for ploughman's and baked potato with chilli. Ale is from the tap. In the lounge bar are traditional tables and chairs, a couple of high-backed settles, logs in the grate, books and bagatelle – it's a snug, carpeted corner away from the TV, darts, piano and pool of the public bar. No garden, but a lovely, flower-bedecked wooden patio.

directions	Signed from A482 midway between Lampeter & Llanwrda.
meals	12pm-2pm; 6.30pm-9pm. Main courses £7.95-£12.25.
closed	2.30pm-6pm. Open all day weekends.

Samantha & David Phillips
The Brunant Arms,
Caio,
Llanwrda,
Carmarthenshire SA19 8RD
tel   01558 650483

map: 7 entry: 579

Carmarthenshire

Angel Inn
Salem

A warm, candlelit, unselfconsciously styled grotto of a place – run by special people doing their own thing. Former Welsh chef of the year Rod Peterson rules the kitchen, but this isn't one of those restaurants masquerading as a pub – you'd feel equally happy just sinking into the comfy sofa with a malty pint of Rev James. The bar, one of the cosiest in Wales, has a quirky, homely charm – squishy sofas covered in throws, fairylights on corkscrew branches, the odd pot plant or Art Deco mirror – while the dining room is a revelation, its dark glossy floors broken up by lovely antique dressers and carved gothic arches. Staff are smart and attentive and the food divine; in the bar, find quiche of duck and lovage with apricot chutney; in the restaurant, braised shoulder of Welsh lamb with pulse ragout and Paloise sauce. No designer vegetables here: portions are hearty and satisfying. Enchanting in every way.

directions	Off the A40 towards Talley, 3 miles north of Llandeilo.
meals	12.15pm-2pm; 7pm-9pm. Restaurant evenings only. Main courses £9.95-£18.50; bar meals £3.95-£12.95.
closed	Sundays; Mondays; Tuesday lunchtime; 2 weeks early January.

Liz Smith
Angel Inn,
Salem,
Llandeilo,
Carmarthenshire SA19 7LY
tel   01558 823394

map: 7 entry: 580

Carmarthenshire

Y Polyn
Nantgaredig

Mark and Susan Manson have stepped happily into this pub that sits by a fork in the roads, one leading to Aberglasney, the other to the National Botanic Garden of Wales. They know their onions – Susan was head chef at the Worshipful Company of Innholders, Maryann chef-patron at the Four Seasons in Nantgaredig – and have smartened up the interior with bold colours, herringbone matting, local art, fresh flowers and candles. A leather sofa and armchairs by the fire encourage the easy feel, while the restaurant has a happy mish-mash of tables and chairs. The short menu is pleasingly simple: fresh ingredients well put together and presented. Start with chicken liver parfait with rhubarb chutney, move onto roast rump of Gower saltmarsh lamb with onion, garlic and thyme purée, finish with nectarine and frangipane tart. The emphasis is on food, but you are equally welcome to pop in for a drink.

directions	Off junction of B4300 & B4310 between A48 & A40 east of Carmarthen.
meals	12pm-2pm; 7pm-9.30pm. Main courses £8.50-£17.50; set menus £13.50-£25.50.
closed	Saturday lunchtimes; Sunday evenings; Mondays. Call for opening times.

Mark & Susan Manson,
Simon & Maryann Wright
Y Polyn,
Nantgaredig, Carmarthen,
Carmarthenshire SA32
tel   01267 290000

map: 6 entry: 581

Carmarthenshire

New Three Mariners
Laugharne

In one of Wales's most romantic, beautiful, weatherworn towns (Dylan Thomas haunt and inspiration behind Llareggub in *Under Milk Wood*) is one of Wales's finest community pubs. In the largest part of the old boozer, dark panelling has been painted white while further spaces are blinkingly bright as coastal light pours through big old windows onto stylishly low tables, slate floors and wicker loungers. Pot plants add to the greenhouse feel and there are boaty pictures on the walls. If all this sounds too New England to be true, then turn right into the cosy pubby part for dartboard, jukebox, (stylish) leather sofas, woodburning stove and weathered locals. Food is pub traditional – local faggots, local fish and chips, paninis for trendies. Neil Morrissey (owner) frequently drops by to play Mr Hosty, joined, more often that not, by actor chums. It all adds to the fun.

directions	Laugharne is on A4066, south of A40 at St Clears.
meals	12pm-3pm; 5pm-9pm; 12pm-9pm summer. No food Sunday & Monday in winter.
closed	Open all day.

Richard Pearce
New Three Mariners,
Victoria Street,
Laugharne,
Carmarthenshire SA33 4SE
tel   01994 427426

map: 6 entry: 582

Ceredigion

The Harbourmaster Hotel
Aberaeron

The old spit-and-sawdust pub has become decidedly chic with an inspirational restaurant and bar; among the Georgian frontages on the bay, its is an unmissable blue. Inside is a space that's cosy but cool: soft shades, a curving bar, blocked-oak tables, an open fire. In the restaurant (booking recommended) daily menus are studded with the best local produce: Aberaeron prawns, Loughor mussels, Cardigan Bay lobster. The chef's food zings: skate wing poached with lime and coriander, chargrilled Welsh Black beef with square-cut chips, coconut crème brûlée with mango sorbet. Lobster boats at lunch, twinkling harbour lights at dinner, real ale, well-chosen wines, dazzling service. The Ceredigion Coastal Path runs past the hotel, while the beaches of New Quay lie just five miles south – what a place to come back to! The Heulyns' dedication to all that is best about Wales shines forth.

directions	Between Aberystwyth & Cardigan off A487.
meals	12pm-2pm; 6.30pm-9pm. Main courses £11.50-£18.50.
closed	Sunday evenings; Monday lunchtimes. Open all day.

Glyn & Menna Heulyn
The Harbourmaster Hotel,
Pen Cei, Aberaeron,
Ceredigion SA46 0BA
tel   01545 570755
web   www.harbour-master.com

map: 6 entry: 583

Conwy

Kinmel Arms
St George

In St George – just a handful of cottages – a sparkling pub-restaurant with rooms. Enter a light, open-plan space of cool, neutral colours, hard wood floors and a central bar, then a conservatory restaurant with marble-topped tables and Tim's photographs of glorious North Wales. Tim and Lynn take pride in what goes on the plate – Conwy Bay seafood and top quality local meats. Weekly changing guest ales and wines by the glass are an added bonus when dining on wild mushroom tart with Welsh blue cheese and guinea fowl supreme. You're a hop from Snowdonia and that stunning coast – walks start from the door – so treat yourself to one of the four dreamy suites, each with French windows to a decked seating area and a fabulous bathroom with vast towels. *No smoking throughout. No children or dogs overnight.*

directions	A55 for Conwy. After Bodelwyddan exit, take next exit, for St George. Left at junc.; up for 200yds.
meals	12pm-2pm (4pm Sunday); 6.30pm-9.30pm. Main courses £8.95-£18.95.
rooms	4 suites £135-£175.
closed	3.30pm-6.30pm; Mondays (except bank holidays); Sunday evenings.

See page 43 for bedroom details.

Tim & Lynn Cunnah-Watson
Kinmel Arms,
The Village, St George,
Abergele, Conwy LL22 9BP
tel   01745 832207
web   www.thekinmelarms.co.uk

map: 7 entry: 584

Denbighshire

White Horse Inn
Hendrerwydd

An old drover's inn with bags of character. There's a tremendous little Poacher's Bar, all quarry-tiled floors, huntin' shootin' and fishin' ephemera, open fire, careworn benches and chairs and a hatch servery dispensing three real ales and grand bar meals to ramblers and locals. In contrast: a classy dining room, created by the absorption of next door's cottages into the 400-year-old building, and a new bistro/family room. There's a chic feel to the web of polished-floorboarded rooms, ready-set for dining, the tables and old reclaimed chairs contrasting with striking sculptures, textile prints, frescoes and fresh cream-washed and brick walls. Diners lounge in comfy sofas at the bar-side fireplace, considering a choice of game and venison pâté, roast shoulder of local lamb, and wonderful Welsh cheeses. The setting is sublime, the pub huddled beneath the beautiful Clwydian Mountains, and you can savour stunning views from the newly landscaped garden. Heaven!

directions	3 miles north of Ruthin just off B5429 between Llandyrnog and Llanbedr-Dyffryn-Clwyd.
meals	12pm-2.30pm; 6pm-9.15pm. Main courses £4.25-£13.
closed	Mondays; Sunday evenings.

Ruth & Vit Vintr
White Horse Inn,
Hendrerwydd, Denbigh,
Denbighshire LL16 4LL
tel   01824 790218
web   www.white-horse-inn.co.uk

map: 7 entry: 585

Denbighshire

The Corn Mill
Llangollen

The 18th century has been left far behind in this renovated corn mill beside the swiftly flowing Dee. Not only is the interior light, airy and well-designed, but the busy menu is laced with contemporary ingredients and ideas. There are also gorgeous views onto the river whether you're enjoying your pint of Boddingtons in the fabulous bar, or settling down to eat in one of the comfortable upper-floor dining areas. The decked veranda-cum-walkway is a stunner, built out over the cascading rapids, a gangway overhanging one end, beyond the revolving water wheel. Watch dippers and grey wagtails as you tuck into bacon, brie and tomato toasted ciabatta, fried chicken with baked potato and coleslaw, and scrumptious puddings like waffle with honeycomb ice cream. The Brunning & Price formula is a tried and tested one, known for its 'something-for-everyone' appeal – and the setting is supreme.

directions	Off Castle Street, (A539) just south of the river bridge.
meals	12pm-9.30pm (9pm Sundays). Main courses £7.95-£14.50; bar meals £3.95-£8.45.
closed	Open all day.

Andrew Barker
The Corn Mill,
Dee Lane, Llangollen,
Denbighshire LL20 8PN
tel   01978 869555
web   www.cornmill-llangollen.co.uk

map: 7 entry: 586

The Boat
Erbistock

An old riverside favourite that draws crowds in summer. Spruced up but not without charm, this 17th-century pub has open fires, stone floors, bare brick walls, heavy oak beams and squishy sofas. You eat in a bright conservatory extension of marble-topped tables and metal-and-wicker chairs, before a view of the fast-flowing Dee and a bank lined with picnic benches. The setting is unquestionably special. Open and closed sandwiches by day yield to white onion and tarragon soup in the evening, trout with pine nuts and lemon butter, and pan-fried chicken breast with caramelised onions; the kitchen employs "the best of everything that is Welsh". Wine choices, though limited, are global and there are eight by the glass; there is a regularly changing choice of real ales and Addlestone's Cloudy cider on handpump. Cheery, youthful staff whizz around at quite a pace.

Pant-yr-Ochain
Gresford

A long drive snakes through landscaped parkland to this magnificent old country house sheltered by trees. It's multi-gabled with colourwashed walls pierced both by tiny, stone-mullioned and tall, orangery-style windows. To one side a huge conservatory opens up views across terraces to the estate lake; within, a jigsaw of richly panelled rooms and drinking areas lures both those who come to dine and those in search of the hop. Intimate corners, they're there, as are huge refectory tables, comfy alcoves and private snugs, with open fires, quarry tiles and bare boards below an eccentric ceiling-line. Everywhere there is a cornucopia of bric-a-brac: penny slots and cases of clay pipes, bills and flyers, caricatures and prints. It sounds OTT but fits comfortably here, and the usual good quality Brunning & Price menu of home-cooked and locally sourced food is available. Beer aficionados revel in nine real ales.

directions	From Wrexham A483 for Chirk; A359 to Erbistock.
meals	12pm-2.30pm; 6.30pm-9pm (9.30pm Fridays & Saturdays); 12pm-9pm Sunday. No food Sunday evenings in winter. Main courses from £6.95 (lunch), £9.95-£18.95 (dinner).
closed	Open all day Sunday.

Paul Rothery
The Boat,
Erbistock, Wrexham,
Denbighshire LL13 0DL
tel   01978 780666
web   www.theboatinn.co.uk

map: 7 entry: 587

directions	Gresford signed off A483 Wrexham bypass.
meals	12pm-9.30pm (9pm Sundays). Main courses £8.25-£14.95.
closed	Open all day.

Lindsey Douglas
Pant-yr-Ochain,
Old Wrexham Road, Gresford,
Wrexham, Denbighshire LL12 8TY
tel   01978 853525
web   www.pantyrochain-gresford.co.uk

map: 7 entry: 588

Flintshire

The Stables at Soughton Hall
Northop

In a vast landscaped parkland – a grand space for weddings – is the former Bishop's Palace, Soughton Hall. The old stable, itself listed, is somewhat smaller. Inside – a dazzling transformation: the cobbled floors have been varnished and the blacksmith's bellows recycled (now a table among old pews, chairs and benches). Metal bar stools – once seed-drill seats – front a bar dispensing beers from local craft breweries, huge wrought iron light-holders hang from rough-hewn beams over tables named after racehorses, and a rear room is still replete with saddles and tack. Upstairs, through the impressive on-site wine shop, is a relaxing restaurant in a huge-raftered roof, all colourwash and candlelight. Treat yourself to posh pub grub, or push out the boat and order roast brace of quail from a long menu. Outside, estate cattle chew contentedly as customers relax with a drink in the peaceful beer garden.

directions	West of Chester, follow Northop sign from A55; A5119 through village & follow brown signs for Soughton Hall.
meals	12pm-9.30pm. Main courses £7.50-£18.95.
closed	Open all day.

	John & Rosemary Rodenhurst
	The Stables at Soughton Hall, Soughton Hall, Northop, Mold, Flintshire CH7 6AB
tel	01352 840577
web	www.soughtonhall.co.uk

map: 7 entry: 589

Glamorgan

The Blue Anchor
East Aberthaw

Inglenooks and open log fires, stories of smugglers and derring-do – it's rich in atmosphere. Inside is a warm warren of little rooms and doorways less than five feet high. The Colemans have cheerfully nurtured this 700-year-old place for almost half a century and restored the pub to its former glory following a fire in 2004. Dine in winter on pheasant from their local shoot, in summer on sewin from Swansea Bay and salads from the vegetable garden. You can pop in for a roast ham baguette and a pint of well-kept Wye Valley – or dip into the chef's selection of regional cheeses. Under the eaves of a classic thatched roof, the restaurant delivers spinach and cream cheese mousse, roast monkfish with sauce vièrge and crispy seaweed, shank of lamb with roasted shallot sauce, Sunday roasts (do book). It's pubby, good looking and wonderful at doing what it knows best.

directions	2 miles west of Cardiff Airport just off B4265.
meals	12pm-2pm (2.30pm Sundays); 6pm-8pm. Restaurant 7pm-9.30pm only. Main courses £7-£14.75.
closed	Open all day.

	Jeremy Coleman
	The Blue Anchor, East Aberthaw, Glamorgan CF62 3DD
tel	01446 750329
web	www.blueanchoraberthaw.com

map: 2 entry: 590

Plough & Harrow
Monknash

The kind of pub you wish was your local — and it is as welcoming to single drinkers as it is to groups. Originally part of a monastic grange, today's Plough & Harrow is so convivial that sometime-Aussie landlady Paula can vouch for the presence of the piratical ghosts that many say have been hanging around for centuries. Ancient, low white walls draw you to the front door. There are low ceilings and low lights in the rooms to either side, each with a big fireplace filled with churchy candles or crackling winter logs, and the bar groans with an impressive array of handpumps — up to 11 ales are served. Happy yellow walls, original floors, a well-loved assortment of furniture — and a trombone used to play 'Happy Birthday' the other day. Traditionalists will enjoy gammon and chips on the lunch menu, but for the more adventurous there are dishes such as summer crab salad and more restauranty but fantastic value food in the evenings (moules marinière, a roasted duck breast on potato fritters). A brilliant atmosphere, a great find.

directions	Village signed off B4265, between St Brides Major & Llantwit Major, 6 miles SW of Cowbridge.
meals	12pm-2pm (2.30pm weekends); 6pm-9pm. No food Sunday evenings. Main courses £4.95-£13.95.
closed	Open all day.

SPECIAL AWARD
see pages 28-29

David & Debbie Woodman & Paula Jones
Plough & Harrow,
Monknash, Cowbridge,
Glamorgan CF71 7QQ
tel   01656 890209
web   www.theploughandharrow.com/foodgastro.asp

map: 2 entry: 591

Gwynedd

Penhelig Arms Hotel
Aberdyfi

The Dyfi estuary can inspire awe in the fiercest storm or lie like a millpond under the full moon. It's a place to share with someone special, such is the hospitality shown by the Hughes family and their staff. In front is the tiniest harbour, while along the quay come the fishermen, butchers, bakers and various smallholders who deliver their daily produce to the kitchen. The seemingly inexhaustible menus are up-dated at every session to reflect what's wettest and freshest that day. At white-clothed tables sample Mediterranean fish soup, plaice with a buttery prawn velouté sauce, chargrilled leg of Welsh lamb steak with roast vegetables, panna cotta with fresh fruit. Soup and sandwiches are the staples of the pub bar, smartly cosy with a central log fire; on sunnier days they'll serve you at your chosen spot astride the harbour wall. Robert is in charge "of the ales and wines only" — but all are well chosen and in the right spirit.

directions	From Dolgellau, A470 for Porthmadog; A493 to Aberdyfi.
meals	12pm-2pm; 7pm-9pm (bar meals from 6pm). Main courses £8.95-£13.95; set menu £28; Sunday lunch £17 (restaurant only).
closed	3pm-5.30pm (5pm weekends).

Robert & Sally Hughes
Penhelig Arms Hotel,
Aberdyfi,
Gwynedd LL35 0LT
tel   01654 767215
web   www.penheligarms.com

map: 6 entry: 592

Gwynedd

Bryn Tyrch
Capel Curig

Bang in the heart of Snowdonia National Park, a simple roadside inn perfect for walkers and climbers. Its interior is well-worn, its style laid-back and in winter there's a great big fire. The lunch menu sensibly strays no further than sandwiches (ham and local Welsh cheese), jacket potatoes with sausage and onion, and Welsh rarebit made with Caerphilly and local ale. Evening blackboards suggest a breezy and generous approach to vegetarian and vegan dishes (coconut and vegetable curry, say), alongside meaty choices such as Hungarian goulash and local lamb shank. Massive desserts include lemon meringue pie. Picture windows run the length of the main bar with strategically placed tables making the most of the view, there are comfy sofas to sink into by the fire, and a pool table in the bare-bones hikers' bar. Friendly staff will advise you on the best climbs and walks.

directions	On A5, 5 miles west of Betws-y-Coed.
meals	12pm-3pm; 6pm-9pm. Bar meals served to 6pm. Main courses £8.95-£12.95; bar meals £3.80-£6.95.
closed	Mondays & Tuesdays November-February.

Rita Davis
Bryn Tyrch,
Capel Curig, Betws-y-Coed,
Gwynedd LL24 0EL
tel   01690 720223
web   www.bryntyrch-hotel.co.uk

map: 7 entry: 593

Monmouthshire

Llanthony Priory Hotel
Llanthony

Reached by a winding country road is this a secret cluster of buildings; once upon a time only walkers and pony-trekkers knew Llanthony was here. What was the abbot's cellar is now an ivy-tumbled house with tower cradled by lush and vertiginous hills. No mobile reception, no cars, just beauty and birdsong. The pub is the cellar, a white vaulted room with an atmospheric hotchpotch of wooden tables and high-backed pews; in summer people wander through the ruins, then rest, pint of Hubby's in hand, on the grass. The restaurant has an old range, grandfather clock and carved antique sideboard; its leaded windows overlook the gracious ruins. Ian the barman is friendly and knowledgeable, so are the locals. Food is simple: homemade beefburgers, spicy lamb casserole, proper espresso, no corners cut. It is romantic, otherworldly, special.

directions	Village signed off A465 north of Abergavenny & south of B4350 at Hay-on-Wye.
meals	12pm-3pm; 7pm-9pm. Main courses £5.45-£8.95.
closed	Mondays (except bank holidays); Tues-Fri lunchtimes & Sun eves Dec-Mar. Open all day in summer & Saturdays in winter.

Geoff Neil
Llanthony Priory Hotel,
Llanthony, Hay-on-Wye,
Monmouthshire NP7 7NN
tel   01873 890487
web   www.llanthonypriory.supanet.com

map: 7 entry: 594

Monmouthshire

Bell at Skenfrith
Skenfrith

Indulge the senses at this classy 17th-century coaching inn in a lovely village on the banks of the Monnow. Inside is immaculate but informal, and the place is run with warmth – Janet treats young staff like members of the family. Expect the best of everything: proper coffee, mostly organic food and superb wine and cognacs – there's even an organic menu for children (Mash Bang Wallop etc). Bedrooms are country smart with Farrow & Ball colours and beds dressed in cotton piqué and Welsh wool; plus homemade biscuits, Cath Collins toiletries and a hi-tech console by the bed so you can listen to music in your bath. Descend for Usk Valley lamb and iced mango parfait in the restaurant overlooking the terrace, toast the occasion with local cider or champagne, then flop into a sofa by the fire.

directions	From Monmouth B4233 to Rockfield; B4347 for 5 miles; right on B4521 for Ross. Pub 1 mile.
meals	12pm-2.30pm; 7pm-9.30pm (9pm Sunday). Main courses £11.90-£19.
rooms	8: 5 doubles, 3 suites £95-£170. Singles £70-£110 (not weekends).
closed	Mondays Nov-Mar; 2 weeks end Jan/early Feb. Open all day.

See page 43 for bedroom details.

William & Janet Hutchings
Bell at Skenfrith,
Skenfrith,
Monmouthshire NP7 8UH
tel   01600 750235
web   www.skenfrith.co.uk

map: 7 entry: 595

Hunter's Moon Inn
Llangattock Lingoed

Enthusiastic owners have taken on this deep-country inn just off Offa's Dyke. The original building, with its low ceilings and 1217-flagged floors, was constructed by stonemasons establishing a place to stay before building the neighbouring church. Book ahead – the 'table for the evening' policy ensures proper care is taken with the locally-sourced food that is Sara's domain. Specials include chicken schnitzel and pheasant wrapped in smoked bacon; puddings are homemade. Haydn looks after the wet side of things; the local and guest ales are well-kept and the wine list well chosen. Two chocolate labs are a star turn and have their own outdoor seating arrangements. You, too, can sit out – under parasols overlooking the churchyard or in the beer garden. A drying room for walkers, too.

directions	A465 Abergavenny-Hereford; for Skenfrith on B4521 thro' Llanvetherine. Signed left to Llangattock Lingoed.
meals	12pm-2.30pm Sunday; 7pm-9pm Tuesday-Saturday. No food on Monday or Tuesday evenings in winter. Main courses £10-£15.
closed	Lunchtimes October-end February.

Haydn Jones & Sara Collin
Hunter's Moon Inn,
Llangattock Lingoed, Abergavenny,
Monmouthshire NP7 8RR
tel 01873 821499
web www.hunters-moon-inn.co.uk

map: 7 entry: 596

The Clytha Arms
Clytha

The inn stands on the old coaching route into border country, in gorgeous surroundings. You may sit outside in fine weather and enjoy cockles, crab sandwiches or a ploughman's that promises three local cheeses. Inside, two bars: one high-ceilinged, non-smoking, with a button-back sofa, the other more rustic, with stripped floors and bar games; both have cheery fires. The restaurant is smart with marbled walls and white linen tablecloths. In the kitchen is Andrew Canning, the local genius who rustles up monkfish with crab and laverbread sauce, and rack of lamb with garlic mash and rosemary sauce. The monthly set menu will tempt you with steak and oyster pudding, and iced tequila and citrus soufflé. Wines, local beers and Herefordshire ciders are excellent, and there's homemade perry for the bibulously curious.

directions	6 miles east of Abergavenny off old Abergavenny to Raglan road.
meals	12.30pm-2.15pm; 7pm-9.30pm. No food Sunday eves & Mondays. Main courses £11.50-£23; bar meals £5.25-£11; set menu £19.95.
closed	Monday lunchtimes. Open all day weekends.

Andrew & Sarah Canning
The Clytha Arms,
Clytha, Abergavenny,
Monmouthshire NP7 9BW
tel 01873 840206
web www.clytha-arms.com

map: 7 entry: 597

Monmouthshire

The Boat Inn
Penallt

Years ago the barrels arrived by train at Penallt Halt – at this, the Welsh end of an iron viaduct across the river Wye. Dr Beeching scuppered the trains; now the gravity-dispensed beers are delivered along a web of one-track lanes tumbling to this strand of riverside cottages in the gorge. The Boat is a friendly, unfussy, reliable little local. Its steep, terraced garden is bounded by waterfalls dropping to the river, while the Wye Valley Walk passes the door. Beyond the modest veranda are two small rooms; the main L-shaped bare-stone bar is warmed by an inglenook stove and dotted by careworn tables, chairs, sofa and benches; the side room is colourwashed and dappled with prints and old photos. Straightforward meals accompany the beers (many from local breweries) which are still aged in a 'cellar' hewn from the sandstone hillside behind.

directions	Park at Millennium Green car park in Redbrook, on A466 Monmouth-Chepstow road; cross footbridge; look for pub signs.
meals	12pm-2.30pm (3pm Sundays in winter); 6pm-9pm (12pm-9pm weekends in summer). Bar meals £3-£6.
closed	Open all day.

Don Ellis
The Boat Inn,
Lone Lane,
Penallt, Monmouth,
Monmouthshire NP25 4AJ
tel   01600 712615

map: 7 entry: 598

Monmouthshire

Beaufort Arms
Raglan

There's no missing the gracious old coaching inn on the High Street, dressed in shades of wheat and cream. Inside, a big welcoming entrance hall, immaculate leather and wicker chairs, open fires, slate floors and an abundance of cosy corners. The place is big enough to get lost in, has a brilliant buzz, just about everybody comes here and Eliot and Jana head a friendly, dedicated team. The good-looking and contemporary restaurant has a menu to match, and the menu frequently changes. There are Beaufort beef burgers with chargrilled veg, minted pea and asparagus risotto, creamy fish pie. Wines range from classic to modern, real ales include a changing guest, continental beers are on tap. Bedrooms – the best in the main house – are as pleasing as all the rest: fresh, spotless and new. Try to get one with a church view and you'll be like the cat who got the cream.

directions	Village centre, 0.5 miles from A449/A40 junction between Monmouth and Abergavenny.
meals	12pm-3pm; 6pm-9pm (8.30pm Sundays). Main courses £8.50-£16.95.
rooms	15: 7 double, 7 twin, 1 single £85-£95. Singles £60.
closed	Open all day.

See page 44 for bedroom details.

Eliot & Jana Lewis
Beaufort Arms,
High Street, Raglan, Usk,
Monmouthshire NP15 2DY
tel   01291 690412
web   www.beaufortraglan.co.uk

map: 7 entry: 599

Monmouthshire

Raglan Arms
Llandenny

Two reasons to stop here – the castle and the pub. The Raglan Arms effortlessly combines its function of village local and excellent place to eat and new owner Andrew Davis plans to keep it that way. A sense of anticipation mounts as you read the daily-changing blackboards from plush leather sofas arranged around the log fire. You won't be disappointed… confit of duck for starters, heaps of fresh fish and shellfish – sea bream with lemon and tarragon sauce – wild boar with apple and stilton sauce, and hearty casseroles like creamy lamb with cumin and ginger and Italian-style beef stew. Cheeses come from the best local suppliers, as does the meat. There's a conservatory restaurant, too, but only 12 tables in all – do book. Real ales come from small local breweries – Wye Valley and Breconshire – and very fairly priced wines from a short but global list are the icing on the cake. Worth the small detour to get here.

Black Bear
Bettws Newydd

The first thing you see is the bar with a band of regulars quaffing their Timothy Taylor's. Beyond the glowing fire (chef-proprietor Molyneux drove off in mid-interview to get more coal!) is a dining room that hints at a passion for the Sport of Kings. At the lower end are more dining tables in what looks like a 1930s tea room… but the Black Bear dates from the 16th-century and the lovely old character remains. Stephen Molyneux uses produce in season, Usk salmon, pheasant, venison and duck. And you may taste warm salad of fresh scallops, turbot with avocado, wine and cream, beef fillet with stilton, Welsh rack of lamb, and – heaven on a plate – Baileys Irish Cream cheesecake. "Whatever comes out of the kitchen" will be unusual, unpredictable and rather good. The Black Bear is worth negociating the many country lanes it takes to get here.

directions	In the centre of Llandenny.
meals	12pm-2pm; 7pm-9.30pm. Main courses £9.75-£15.
closed	Sunday evenings; Mondays (except bank holidays).

	Andrew Davis
	Raglan Arms,
	Llandenny,
	Usk,
	Monmouthshire NP15 1DL
tel	01291 690800

map: 7 entry: 600

directions	On B4595 2 miles north of Usk.
meals	12pm-2pm; 6pm-9pm (later if booked). Main courses £10-£16.
closed	Monday lunchtimes (January-November).

	Stephen Molyneux
	Black Bear,
	Bettws Newydd,
	Usk,
	Monmouthshire NP15 1JN
tel	01873 880701

map: 7 entry: 601

Monmouthshire

Cherry Tree Inn
Tintern

Across a stream and slotted into a jumble of houses, this looks like a wild west general store. It pretty much is – Steve and Jill Pocock run the porch-fronted local shop and post office as well the pub (follow the several signs up a steep flight of steps). Stepping through the door delivers a wallop of 160-year-old pub atmosphere: slate floors, bare bricks and wood; even the modern bits feel old. Tempting aromas waft into the red-walled dining room. Offerings on the billboard-sized blackboard include homemade soup, wild boar pâté and Welsh steak (local organic ingredients whenever possible). In the oldest part of the pub (more steps), musical instruments on the wall are handy for impromptu roistering, or there's a tottering pile of magazines to accompany some CAMRA browsing. Hancock's HB is the host beer; guests might include Great Dane or Butty Batch. The wine cellar is well-stocked and cider drinkers aren't neglected.

directions	Take narrow lane off A466 beside the Royal George; pub signed.
meals	12pm-3pm; 6pm-9pm (8.30pm Sunday). Main courses £5.95-£9.95.

Steve & Jill Pocock
Cherry Tree Inn,
Raglan Road, Tintern,
Monmouthshire NP16 6TH
tel 01291 689292
web www.thecherry.co.uk

map: 7 entry: 602

Monmouthshire

The Greyhound Inn
Usk

Nick is enthusiastically committed to running this excellent country inn; it takes a little finding on the back roads out of Usk but anyone local will point you in the right direction. Outside, the 17th-century Welsh longhouse brims with summer flower baskets. Inside are inter-connecting bars with open fires and hanging hops; there are darts and dominoes in one room, cosy armchairs in another, and a long menu. Welsh smoked venison with juniper and orange, lamb cutlets with redcurrant and red wine sauce, sirloin steak with port and stilton, filo ricotta parcels with tomato and pepper sauce, meringue gâteau. Usk-caught salmon or trout is a favourite. Choose from several real ales, classic bottled ciders and wines of the month at giveaway prices. Staff couldn't be friendlier, and families and dogs are welcomed.

directions	From Usk centre, signs to Llantrissant for 2.5 miles.
meals	12pm-2.15pm; 6pm-10.30pm. No food Sunday evenings. Main courses from £8.
closed	4pm-7pm Sunday. Open all day Monday-Saturday.

Nick Davies
The Greyhound Inn,
Llantrissant, Usk,
Monmouthshire NP15 1LE
tel 01291 672505
web www.greyhound-inn.com

map: 7 entry: 603

Monmouthshire

Newbridge Inn
Usk

As darkness falls, the old stone bridge is floodlit, its arches reflected in the glassy waters of the Usk. The setting is seductive, the garden runs prettily down to the river and the trellises are decked with flowers. The Newbridge is everything a gastropub should be: warm, inviting and beautifully turned out. In several rooms on several levels, willow twigs emerge from aluminium buckets, church candles squat in cast-iron candelabras, the paintwork – caramels, terracottas, creams – glows and the interior, stripped of fuss and muddle, reveals the naked beauty of floorboards and beams. The staff are professional, the air is filled with happy chat and the food is worth saving up for – organic Tidenham Chase chicken on wild mushroom tagliatelle, rack of Monmouthshire lamb with dauphinoise potatoes. But don't feel you have to dine here; drinkers are welcome and there's room for all.

directions	From Usk A449 towards Caerleon; 2 miles after Llangibby, left for Tredunnock; inn beside river.
meals	12pm-2.30pm (3pm Sunday); 6.30pm-9.30pm (7pm-8.30pm Sunday). Main courses £13.15-£18.
closed	Open all day.

Vanessa Redmond
Newbridge Inn,
Tredunnock, Usk,
Monmouthshire NP15 1LY

tel	01633 451000
web	www.thenewbridge.co.uk

map: 2 entry: 604

Neath

Dulais Rock
Aberdulais

If the Rock were any closer to the Aberdulais Falls it would be in the splash pool – you can hear the roar from the deck at the back. Inside is modern but not minimalist – warm wood, slate floors, retro lighting and a vast wood-burning stove. Bar food ranges from local smoked salmon to steak pie. John is passionate about his food, and in the three-tier restaurant the menu is modern Welsh: Welsh-bred meats, fish landed at Swansea, organic vegetables from John's parents' Glyn Fach Farm (one of Rick Stein's food heroes). Try a roasted duck breast on puy lentils with caramelised pears. There's proper coffee, and two real ales in summer, one in winter. Up in the eaves, bedrooms are smartly cream, white and cocoa brown; two share a balcony overlooking trees, rockface and glimpses of the stunning falls.

directions	From M4 junc. 43, A465 to Neath; then signs for Aberdulais Falls.
meals	12pm-9.30pm Tues-Sat. No bar food Sat eve. Set menus £19.50 & £24.50; bar meals £5.50-£9.95.
rooms	3 doubles £62.50.
closed	Sun & Mon eves in winter. Open all day Fri, Sat & in summer.

See page 44 for bedroom details.

John Peace
Dulais Rock,
Main Road, Aberdulais,
Neath SA10 8EY

tel	01639 644611
web	www.dulaisrock.co.uk

map: 7 entry: 605

Pembrokeshire

The Old Point House Inn
Angle

Lonely, windswept, so close to the sea they're cut off at spring tide. Weary fishermen have beaten a path to the old inn's door for centuries; part-built with shipwreck timbers, it started life as a bakehouse for ships' biscuits. The tiny bar, its bare walls papered with old navigation charts, is utterly authentic, the restaurant is cosy by night, and in fine weather you may sit out and devour vast prawn sandwiches. Doug, ex-fisherman, welcomes everyone, from weathered regulars meeting over pints of Felinfoel to families in for Sunday lunch. Son Lee is a good cook and the specials board is full of fish: haddock with Welsh cheeses, halibut with lemon butter, red snapper with chilli pepper sauce, Milford cod fishcakes with piles of chips. No need to rush home. Three simple, fresh, white and blue bedrooms await upstairs; ask for the quiet twin with the stunning bay view.

directions	From Pembroke follow signs for Angle. There, from Lifeboat Trust, cross beach to pub.
meals	12pm-2.30pm; 6.30pm-9pm. Main courses £7.75-£22.
rooms	3 twins/doubles £50. Singles £25.
closed	Tuesdays November-March.

See page 44 for bedroom details.

Doug, Carol & Lee Smith
The Old Point House Inn,
Angle,
Pembroke,
Pembrokeshire SA71 5AS
tel   01646 641205

map: 6 entry: 606

Pembrokeshire

Cresselly Arms
Cresswell Quay

The day we called, trainer Peter Bowen's Cresswell Quay had just won his fourth race of the season and there was an air of euphoria. We were treated to beer that was far better than we had any right to ask – and the horse was paying! The walls of this old pub are hung with wisteria; pick an outside table and gaze onto the estuary and the tranquil woods. Inside, ale is poured from a jug; there's no truck with modern innovation here. Well-kept pints are downed by all and sundry and you are surrounded by memorabilia of a past age: shiny brown paintwork, red-and-black tiling, a coal-fired Aga in the parlour. And, of course, pictures ancient and new of famous nags. The local talk (and occasionally TV) will be of horses and history. When the tide is up, you can get here by boat... and you won't be late for lunch, there isn't any. Take home instead a jar of the famous lemon curd. Utterly authentic.

directions	Off A4075 between A40 & A477.
meals	No food served.
closed	2.30pm-6pm.

Maurice & Janet Cole
Cresselly Arms,
Cresswell Quay,
Tenby,
Pembrokeshire SA68 0TE
tel   01646 651210

map: 6 entry: 607

Pembrokeshire

The George
Haverfordwest

Nothing in Pembrokeshire can hold a candle to John and Lesley's café-pub and restaurant. Up on the hillside, overlooking castle and town, its walled, driftwood-furnished garden has stupendous views. The old brewhouse is much as it always was, only funkier, and now you can buy all sorts of eco-friendly items – hemp bags, leather sandals, candles. There is an inexhaustible supply of coffee, too, along with real ales and splendid wines. Home-cooked meals span the globe for inspiration while ingredients are closer to home, and include organic vegetables from the Lewis's own farm. You get Cardigan Bay crab cakes with toasted pine nuts; fillets of sewin in a lime and fennel butter; creamy hummus; 'raw food energy salad'. John and Lesley can claim a real food menu that stands out from the crowd – and it's very well priced.

directions	Follow signs for town centre & then St Thomas Green. Left into Hill St; left opp. cinema into Market Street.
meals	10.30am-5pm; 6.30pm-9.15pm Friday & Saturday only. Main courses £5.50-£9.50.
closed	Sundays. Open 10.30am-5.30pm Monday-Thursday (10.30pm Friday & Saturday).

John Glasby & Lesley Lewis
The George,
24 Market Street,
Haverfordwest,
Pembrokeshire SA61 1NH
tel   01437 766683

map: 6 entry: 608

Pembrokeshire

The Sloop
Porthgain

Perfectly in keeping with its seawashed setting, the Sloop has been welcoming fisherfolk since 1743. The village remains a fishing harbour – the landlord catches his own lobster, mullet and crab – but, until the Thirties, Porthgain was more famous for bricks and granite. The tide used to come up to the Sloop's walls before the harbour was built; now there's a little seating area out front. Weatherbeaten on the outside, the pub is surprisingly cosy within. Expect bare beams, some bare boards, a happy melée of furniture, a table made from an old mill wheel, a canoe suspended from the ceiling, a board announcing 'the catch of the day'. Tuck into homemade mackerel pâté or lobster thermidor on tomato rice; breakfast too (open to all) sounds a treat. Holiday-makers descend in summer but the rest of the year this is a community pub, with a proper games room and real fires. Staff are perfect all year round.

directions	Village signed off A487 between Fishguard & St Davids.
meals	9.30am-11am; 12pm-2.30pm; 6pm-9.30pm. Main courses £7-£17.50.
closed	Open all day.

Matthew Blakiston
The Sloop,
Porthgain, St Davids,
Pembrokeshire SA62 5BN
tel   01348 831449
web   www.sloop.co.uk

map: 6 entry: 609

Pembrokeshire

Dryffryn Arms
Pontfaen

Miss the small sign peeping out of Bessie's well-tended garden and you'll miss the pub – which would be a shame, because it's a treasure. Bessie has been here half a century and nothing has changed in that time, including the outside loos. A trooper possessed of a dry wit she shows no sign of tiring, keeps the place spotless and serves from a hatch in the wall seven days a week. The bar has the proportions of a domestic front room so you'll fall into easy conversation with the locals (farmers, hunters and the like). Old quarry tiles on the floor, an embroidered picture of the Queen on the wall, fresh flowers on the window sill, peanuts, crisps and Bass from the barrel – it is timeless inside and out. To the left of the pub is a garden with a bench under Bessie's washing line from which you may drink in the peace and the view: of the verdant little valley below, threaded by a silver river.

directions	Pontfaen is on the Gwaun Valley road off the B4313 east of Fishguard,
meals	No food served.
closed	Open all day.

Bessie Davies
Dryffryn Arms,
Cwm Gwaun,
Pontfaen,
Pembrokeshire SA65 9SG
tel 01348 881305

map: 6 entry: 610

Pembrokeshire

Tafarn Sinc
Preseli

The highest pub in Pembrokeshire is the quirkiest pub in the world – or a close contender. It was speedily erected in 1876 as a hotel on the GWR railway; now the giant, red-painted, corrugated zinc building oversees a tiny railway platform complete with mannequin-travellers and a Victorian pram. It is beautifully tended outside and in, with a prettily trellised garden and an arresting Alpine-panelled public bar. Hams and lamps hang from the ceiling, there's sawdust on the floors and two big woodburners belch out heat. It's warm and welcoming and full of merry walkers. Hafwen, the perfect landlady, and husband Brian oversee the cosy, constant buzz and serve a solidly traditional menu (Preseli lamb burgers, faggots with onion gravy), and their own excellent beer. Tons of character, a touch of the surreal and a fabulous setting, high in the Preseli hills. No further introduction is needed – just a visit.

directions	Rosebush is on the B4329 Haverfordwest to Cardigan road.
meals	12pm-2pm; 6pm-9pm. No food Sunday evening. Main courses £7.90-£13.90.
closed	Mondays in winter. Open all day.

Brian & Hafwen Davies
Tafarn Sinc,
Preseli, Rosebush,
Clunderwen,
Pembrokeshire SA66 7QT
tel 01437 532214

map: 6 entry: 611

Pembrokeshire

Nag's Head Inn
Abercych

Behind the vibrant orange exterior is a feast of bare wood and stone. The lighting is soft and warm, there's a rustic chicken-wire sideboard crammed with old beer bottles, a glass cabinet displaying the famous 'rat' of Abercych (actually a stuffed coypu) and a photo of old Emrys, the treasured regular after whom the home-brewed beer is named. And there's Gizmo, resident fluffball cat. The Nag's Head has a simple, tasteful charm, is full of old tales and curios and quirkery and serves the best kind of hearty pub food, from cheese and onion toasties with salad to steak and Old Emrys ale pie, and local sewin in summer. Come with the family and explore the pushchair-friendly ClynFyw sculpture trail – it starts from here. There's a play area too, in the long, lovely riverside garden. By a bridge on the river bank, at the bottom of a steep hill, the setting alone is worth the trip.

directions	Off A4332 between Cenarth & Boncath.
meals	12pm-2pm; 6pm-9pm. Main courses £7-£15.
closed	Mondays. Open all day Sunday.

Steven & Sam Jamieson
Nag's Head Inn,
Abercych,
Boncath,
Pembrokeshire SA37 0HJ
tel   01239 841200

map: 6 entry: 612

Powys

The Bear Hotel
Crickhowell

Viewed from the square of this small market town, the 16th-century frontage of the old coaching inn looks modest. Behind the cobbles and the summer flowers, it is a warren of surprises and mild eccentricity – bars and brasserie at the front, nooks and crannies carved at the back – behind which is the family- and dog-friendly garden. The beamy lounge has parquet, plush seating and a mighty fire; settle in and savour their good beers, wines, whiskies and ports. There are two dining areas where at night you can feast on Welsh Black beef, Usk salmon, Brecon venison and locally grown seasonal vegetables and regional farmhouse cheeses. Homemade ice creams, mousses and puddings are equally sumptuous. We've never seen the place empty and Mrs Hindmarsh is still firmly in charge of an operation that rarely comes off the rails.

directions	On A40 between Abergavenny & Brecon.
meals	12pm-2pm; 6pm-10pm (7pm-9.30pm Sun). Main courses £12.50-£18.20; bar meals £5.75-£15.95.

Judy Hindmarsh
The Bear Hotel,
High Street, Crickhowell,
Powys NP8 1BW
tel   01873 810408
web   www.bearhotel.co.uk

map: 7 entry: 613

Nantyffin Cider Mill Inn
Crickhowell

On the other side of the road, the river Usk pours down the valley. Diners pour in here for a sight of menus that feature livestock from the owners' estate at the foot of the Brecons. A whole network of small suppliers provides fresh produce, from courgette flowers to line-caught sea bass, while autumn brings mushrooms from their "secret patch" and game from the Glanusk estate. A cider press from the pub's previous life – it stretches back 350 years – occupies the middle of the main dining room, but you may also sit in one of two intimate bars, choosing from blackboard specials or a fixed-price menu. Expect good, honest, country cooking concocted with minumum fuss and maximum flavour – plus real ales and ciders on tap, delicious wines by the glass, hot punch in winter, homemade lemonade in summer and organic apple juices. Note: winter opening hours may be erratic.

directions	1 mile outside Crickhowell on A40 to Brecon.
meals	12pm-2.30pm; 6.30pm-10pm (9pm in winter). Main courses £10.95-£15.95.
closed	3pm-6.30pm & Mondays.

Glyn Bridgeman
Nantyffin Cider Mill Inn,
Brecon Road, Crickhowell,
Powys NP8 1SG
tel   01873 810775
web   www.cidermill.co.uk

map: 7 entry: 614

The Farmer's Arms
Crickhowell

This cracking place takes some beating, with Barney the dobermann in residence by the log stove, and the regulars propping up the bar. Filled with farm folk on Saturdays, there's no escaping the infectious laughter that fills the place. Commendable meals emanating from an open kitchen are a tribute to the produce from the farms and fisheries that dot this corner of The Beacons. Real ales and ciders are local too, and the careful choice of a handful of good quality wines is sensibly priced. Eat royally from the single menu – rack of lamb, baked halibut, rib-eye steak with all the trimmings – either in the flagstoned bar hung with dried hops or in the fancier dining room beyond, where vintage photographs and informal table settings add to a warm atmosphere. A favoured lunch spot for pony-trekkers and walkers in love with the Black Mountains.

directions	On A40, right onto A479; after 3 miles on right in centre of village.
meals	12pm-2pm; 7pm-10.30pm. Main courses £6-£15.
closed	Monday & Tuesday lunchtimes.

Andrew & Sue Lawrence
The Farmer's Arms,
Cwmdu, Crickhowell,
Powys NP8 1RU
tel   01874 730464
web   www.thefarmersarms.com

map: 7 entry: 615

The White Swan
Llanfrynach

The front resembles the row of cottages the pub once was. Its cavernous interior has been recently remodelled and its central bar is a split-level zone, making bar staff appear unnaturally tall as they serve Brains Bitter and other fine ales or wines. Make the most of the open fire, while you consider the Specials Board; it majors in fish so there could be seared scallops with spicy salsa, and baked sea bass with chilli and basil – as well as haunch of Brecon venison with beetroot risotto, red wine and juniper sauce. The restaurant menu includes Hereford beef, Brecon lamb, local pheasant; the cheeses are Welsh, the digestive biscuits homemade. There are farmhouse tables, leather sofas, big woodburners, and a trellised patio at the back – gorgeous in summer. You're spoilt for walks here, so stride off into the Brecon Beacons – or potter along the towpath of the Mommouthshire & Brecon canal.

directions	Signed from A40 3 miles east of Brecon on Crickhowell road.
meals	12pm-2pm (2.30pm Sundays); 7pm-9.30pm (9pm Sundays). Main courses £10.45-17.50.
closed	Mondays & Tuesdays.

Byron Lloyd
The White Swan,
Llanfrynach, Brecon,
Powys LD3 7BZ
tel 01874 665276
web www.the-white-swan.com

map: 7 entry: 616

The Felin Fach Griffin
Brecon

Stylish but cosy, fresh but not fussy. This bold venture mixes the buzz of a smart city bistro with the easy-going pace of Welsh country living, and it's popular. Full of bright elegance, downstairs fans out into several eating and sitting areas, with stripped pine and old oak furniture. Make for three giant leather sofas around a raised hearth, or opt for the rustic backroom bar. A Dutch chef stars in the kitchen, turning out simple but sensational dishes for smartly laid tables: Black Mountain smoked salmon, braised ox cheeks with mash, vanilla crème brûlée. Breakfast is served around one table in the morning room; wallow with the papers and make your toast on the Aga. Bedrooms are in a modern style, clean and simple, with a few designer touches: tulips in a vase, check curtains, snowy white towels and linen. Charles hosts with aplomb.

directions	On A470, 3.5 miles NE of Brecon.
meals	12.30pm-2.30pm; 7pm-9.30pm. Main courses £7.95-£9.95 (lunch); £13.50-£17 (dinner).
rooms	7: 4 twins/doubles, 3 four-posters £92.50-£115. Singles from £67.50.
closed	2.30pm-6pm; Monday lunchtimes (except bank holidays).

See page 44 for bedroom details.

Charles & Edmund Inkin
The Felin Fach Griffin,
Felin Fach, Brecon,
Powys LD3 0UB
tel 01874 620111
web www.eatdrinksleep.ltd.uk

map: 7 entry: 617

The Harp
Old Radnor

Landlord Erfyl meets and greets you like a mate, and sure as eggs you soon become one. Being so small – with arguably the tiniest bar counter in the county – it needs to be booked ahead, at least for Thursday's steak and fish nights. Enjoy a pint of John Roberts XXX or Timothy Taylor's with a Herefordshire rump steak, trout fillet with parmesan and basil cream, or maybe homemade lamb and leek pie. (There are ploughman's and baguettes, too.) The interior is spick-and-span: 14th-century slate flooring in the bar; tongue-and-groove in a tiny room that seats a dozen diners; crannies crammed with memorabilia, an ancient curved settle, an antique reader's chair, two fires. Life in this tiny village remains unchanged; from your seat under the sycamore you can overlook the spectacular valley at will, but don't expect much action after sunset.

The Talkhouse
Pontdolgoch

From the outside it looks like a nice, ordinary pub. Which is what it once was. Today it serves over 70 'niche boutique' wines. Stephen and Jacqueline have a winning formula in their 17th-century drovers' rest: intimate, attentive service, marvellous food. The first room you come into is a sitting room with comfy armchairs and sofa – just the place for pre-lunch drinks or after-dinner coffee. The bar has beams, log fire and sumptuous sofas; the claret-and-cream dining room has French windows that open to the garden in summer so you can dine outside. Classical, seasonal cooking – the lightest sweet potato and butternut soup, juicy, plump scallops with confit tomatoes and lemon dressing, delicately cooked Welsh lamb, a lavender panna cotta with raspberries – is a treat, the daily-changing menu using the finest local produce. A small, perfect find in the rolling wilderness of mid-Wales.

directions	From Kington A44; after 3 miles left for Old Radnor.
meals	12pm-2pm (weekends only); 7pm-9pm. Main courses £8.75-£10.50.
closed	Mondays (except bank holidays); Tuesday-Friday lunchtimes.

Heather & Erfyl Price
The Harp,
Old Radnor,
Powys LD8 2RH
tel   01544 350655

map: 7 entry: 618

directions	On A470 1 mile west of Caersws & 5 miles from Newtown.
meals	12pm-1.30pm; 6.30pm-8.45pm. Main courses £12-£16.50.
closed	Sunday evenings, Mondays, Tuesday lunchtime. Bookings only Wednesday & Thursday lunchtimes in winter.

Stephen & Jacqueline Garratt
The Talkhouse,
Pontdolgoch, Caersws,
Powys SY17 5JE
tel   01686 688919
web   www.talkhouse.co.uk

map: 7 entry: 619

Powys

Wynnstay Hotel
Machynlleth

Trucking through the gastronomic desert that is mid Wales, you'll be happy to discover this rambling old coaching inn in this quaint market town. It's rather more hotel than pub – but there's a cracking bar with original oak floors, low beams, scrubbed tables, and, at night, a cosy, candlelit feel. Bag a seat by the log fire in winter and peruse chef Gareth Johns's appealing menus over a pint of Reverend James. He applies his skills to fine local produce: Conwy mussels, Barmouth lobster, bass from Cardigan Bay, salmon and sewin from the river Dyfi, Welsh Black beef and lamb from the valley, game shot by the landlord. Bay scallops with wilted Ynyslas chard and black pepper oil may precede roast leg of saltmarsh lamb with orange and laver gravy, and excellent Welsh cheeses to finish. Thanks to family connections with Italy, there are some wonderful wines from small Italian growers and a traditional pizzeria at the back.

directions	In the centre of Machynlleth.
meals	12pm-2pm; 6.30pm-9pm. Main courses £5.95-£14 (lunch), £8.95-£16 (dinner); set dinner £25; Sunday lunch £10.95 & £12.95.

Charles & Sheila Dark
Wynnstay Hotel,
Machynlleth,
Powys SY20 8AE

tel	01654 702941
web	www.wynnstay-hotel.com

map: 7 entry: 620

Swansea

No Sign Bar
Swansea

The name is not a marketing contrivance, but goes back to 1690s licensing laws. In contrast to the characterless drinking halls of Wind Street, the No Sign is quirky and cosy, its Dickensian interior a match for the frontage: worn flagstones, ragged walls, shelves of books and cabinets of old curios. Slump into a leather armchair with a newspaper from the rack. (Dylan Thomas drank here when he worked at the *Evening Post* – as present-day scribblers do.) There's a terrace to the rear, and the longest-ever back room, new and furnished in a similarly haphazard style. Three ales are well-kept but it's the wine list that deserves heritage listing (and 'Wined' Street it once was): 40 bottles, 12 by the glass. Homemade food is served by friendly staff; the tapas and hand-cut chips are a hit, and when your insides need warming try the homely lamb cawl. Avoid the weekend crowds and slip upstairs.

directions	M4 junc. 41 to Swansea. Follow signs for city centre. Right at Sainsbury's onto Wind Street.
meals	12pm-10pm (Sundays to 9pm). Main courses £6.50-£10.
closed	Open all day.

Philippa Shipley
No Sign Bar,
56 Wind Street,
Swansea SA1 1EG

tel	01792 465300

map: 2 entry: 621

England

This section includes pubs that have recently changed hands and foodie pubs that we belive are on the up. All are well worth seeking out.

Bath & NE Somerset

The Raven, 7 Queen St, Bath, BA1 1HE   01225 425045
Ordinary looking city centre pub in a wonderful cobbled street that seduces with its cosy atmosphere and hidden depths, cracking beer (try the Raven Ale!) and an interesting, modern take on pub food.

Bedfordshire

The Cock, Broom, SG18 9NA   01767 314411
Remarkably unspoilt village boozer. Beers tapped from the cask in the orignal tap room – there's a rarity! Plain pine-panelled rooms and a proper skittles room too.

Hare & Hounds, Bedford, SG18 9HQ   01767 627225
Old village pub that's been given a gastropub overhaul within – loads of leather and funky colours. Excellent food on short, seasonal, produce-led menu.

The Five Bells, Stanbridge, LU7 9JF   01525 210224
Likeable country pub noted for engaging bar with head-cracking beams, winter fires, and candlelit restaurant. Now part of the select Bel & Dragon restaurant group. Reports please.

Berkshire

The Red House, Marsh Benham, RG20 8LY   01635 582017
Thatched gastropub in the Kennet Valley with French owner and chef. Set bistro lunch menu and an inventive carte served in the smart, book-lined restaurant. Super summer alfresco dining.

Crown & Garter, Inkpen, RG17 9QR   01488 668325
Lost among a web of lanes below Inkpen Beacon, Gillian Hern's old pub sits surrounded by fields and woodland. There's an inglenook in the bar to warm your cockles, Berkshire beers to quaff, delicious food and a glorious garden for summer sipping.

Black Boys Inn, Hurley, SL6 5NQ   01628 824212
The 16th-century building may look like a country pub but inside has a restaurant feel. Still, there's Brakspeare on tap and some seasonally inspired cooking from a pedigree chef.

The Highwayman, Checkendon, RG8 0UA   01491 682020
A secluded hamlet on the edge of the Chilterns and an atmospheric old inn. Revitalised under new owners, its character restored, it draws walkers and foodies for pints of Pride and simple, fresh food.

England

Birmingham

The Beacon, Bilston St, Sedgley, DY3 1JE   01902 883380
Fine pub with its own microbrewery. Little's changed since WWII, with a fascinating period piano bar and smoking lounge. The Victorian till is as ornate as they come. Sandwiches only.

Bristol

Robin Hood's Retreat, Gloucester Rd, Bristol, BS7   0117 924 7880
Victorian red-brick boozer with a smart makeover, a new honeypot for Bristol foodies. Chef Nathan Muir (ex-Bibendum) offers a modern European menu and eight real ales on tap. Arrive early if you want a table.

The King's Head, 60 Victoria St, Bristol, BS1 6DE   0117 927 7860
Classically Victorian inside, 1660 out. A charming period narrow bar and exceptionally cosy, panelled rear snug, splendid mirrored back bar, photos of old Bristol and gallons of Smiles.

The Merchants Arms, 5 Merchants Rd, Bristol, BS8   0117 904 0037
Honest and real, done-up without a whiff of modern pretension. Simple, friendly, Bath Ales-owned, with excellent beers and good snacks.

Old Duke, 45 King St, Bristol, BS1 4ER   0117 927 7137
There's a New Orleans speakeasy, British-pub feel to this shrine to jazz and blues not far from Bristol Old Vic. Music is served up nightly along with the occasional curry or stew.

Hope & Anchor, 38 Jacobs Wells Rd, Bristol BS8   0117 929 2987
Unpretentious and with a dedicated following – from arty youth to well-shod Cliftonites – who come for pub grub without the gastro-pomp and ales that change according to the landlord's whim.

Wellington Inn, Gloucester Rd, Bristol, BS7 8UR   0117 951 3022
Imposing red-brick pub on Horfield Common, a drop-kick's distance from the Memorial Stadium. Something of a flagship for Bath Ales, plus solid pub food, a buzzing atmosphere and occasional live blues and folk.

Buckinghamshire

Lions of Bledlow, Bledlow, HP27 9PE   01844 343345
Ideal base for tackling one of the local walks into the Chiltern Hills, this time-worn 16th-century pub delivers a good range of real ales, a pleasant garden, but average food.

Photos 1. & 6. www.paulgroom.com 2. Crown & Garter, Inkpen 3. Jo Boissevain
4. The Red House, Marsh Benham 5. Hope & Anchor, Bristol

The Rising Sun, Little Hampden, HP16 9PS 01494 488394
Walkers love this inn – the menu of delicious fresh goodies is enough to satisfy any hearty appetite. A civilised dining pub in pretty countryside (but smokers not welcome).

Stag & Huntsmen, Hambleden, RG9 6RP 01491 571227
The setting's the thing and the picture-book village is perfect. Bars are small and traditional, carpeted and lively; the dining room modern. Hearty food, excellent ale.

The White Hart, Preston Bissett MK18 4LX 01280 847969
Thatched, timbered and latched – a deeply cosy village pub where locals in thick socks prop up the bar. Logs fires, daily papers, local ale on tap and a recent revamp under newish owners – reports please.

The White Horse, Hedgerley, SL2 3UY 01753 643225
Super local in easy reach of the M40 (junc. 2). Swap the services for flagstones, inglenook, beamed bar and perfect ploughman's lunch. Seven real ales are tapped from the barrel.

The Crown, Little Missenden, HP7 0RD 01494 862571
An unspoilt brick cottage pub in a pretty village, run by the same family for over 90 years. Excellent beers, good wines and sandwiches, a big garden and walking all around.

Full Moon, Chesham, HP5 2UH 01494 758959
The landlord claims this ancient inn used to be a brothel. Nothing so unsalubrious now, just food (organic meat), good beers and bags of atmosphere.

The Swan, Salford, MK17 8BD 01908 281008
Stylish new opening from pub group Peach Pubs. Trendy revamp of an ordinary village boozer; leave the M1 (junc. 13) for great antipasti nibbles and enjoyable modern pub food, all day.

Old Queen's Head, Penn, HP10 8EY 01494 813371
David and Becky Salisbury's fourth pub venture opened in 2006. Sure to be a success, big on dining, informal and relaxed. The extended 16th-building oozes old oak, flagstones, rich fabrics, cosy corners.

Cambridgeshire
Cambridge Blue, 85 Gwydir St, Cambridge, CB1 01223 361382
Away from the centre, this simple local has a warm atmosphere and stacks of rowing paraphenalia. A wide choice of ales, among them Adnams and Nethergate – but no room for smokers.

England

White Pheasant, Fordham, CB7 5LQ   01638 720414
Very welcoming dining pub with bare boards, wooden tables, crackling logs, fresh fish and farmhouse cheeses. Handpumped Woodforde's Wherry and a dozen wines by the glass. Reports please.

Dyke's End, Reach, CB5 0JD   01638 743816
Real community hamlet whose "splendid pub" (to quote the Prince of Wales) is owned by the village. A lovely old place, well worth a visit, but food can be over ambitious.

The Boathouse, Ely   01353 664388
From the folk who brought you The Crown & Punchbowl and The Cock, a more restaurant-led venture that incorporates a wow of a waterside location and brasserie menu. Works best as a lunchtime venue.

Cheshire

Old Harkers Arms, Russell St, Chester, CH1 5AL   01244 344525
A buzzy atmosphere and a great range of microbrewery ales at this beautifully converted warehouse down by the canal. Run by Brunning & Price pubs – good modern pub food.

The Dog, Over Peover, WA16 8UP   01625 861421
Respected dining pub deep in the Manchester broker belt. Carpeted rooms, paintings and prints, and a traditional locals' bar complete with pub games, tiled floor and local Weetwood ales.

Sutton Hall, Sutton, SK11 0HE   01260 253211
Authentically 16th century: big fires, stained glass and flagstones. Decent handpumped ales, lovely grounds with duck pond, gothic windows in the bedrooms.

Dusty Miller, Wrenbury, CW5 8HG   01270 780537
Hugely popular pub in a beautifully converted watermill beside the Shropshire Union Canal. Local food is ever-present on the imaginative menus. Super alfresco areas.

Nags Head, Haughton Moss, CW6 9RN   01829 260265
Spic-and-span 17th-century pub with real fire and all the trimmings. Conservatory extension deals in views and fresh local food, and there's a big garden and bowling green.

The Old Harp, Little Neston, CH64 0TB   0151 336 6980
Small and unassuming in a stunning location at the edge of the Dee Marshes. Watch marsh harriers or little egrets as you sup real ales and enjoy views across the estuary to North Wales.

Photos 1. & 2. www.paulgroom.com 3. Ben Peace 4. John Coe
5. Lions of Bledlow, Princes Risborough 6. Chris Banks

Swettenham Arms, Swettenham, CW12 2LF   01477 571284
Remotely sited hamlet and pub in the Dane Valley next to the
Quinta Arboretum. Top-notch food, locally brewed beers.
Handy for the Jodrell Bank radio telescope and science centre.

Cornwall

The Rashleigh, Polkerris, PL24 2TL   01726 813991
A pub *on* the beach in a tiny cove! The old coastguard station is
cosy in winter, unbeatable in summer; down a pint of real ale and
watch the sun set across St Austell bay.

The Earl of St Vincent, Egloshayle, PL27 6HT   01208 814807
Flower-decked 15th-century inn filled to the rafters with rich
furnishings and an amazing collection of clocks, all in perfect order.
'Time' is called by a cacophony of chimes, bongs and cuckoos.

The Rising Sun, St Mawes, TR2 5DT   01326 270233
Delightful harbour views from the sunny terrace at St Austell
Brewery's flagship inn-hotel. Smartly decorated, lively bar,
conservatory restaurant and good food.

The New Inn, Manaccan, TR12 6HA   01326 231323
Unfussy thatched village local with that 'lost in the old country'
feel. Walk over from Helford for heart-warming pub grub,
pints of Doom Bar and a natter with the locals.

The Ship, Porthleven, TR13 9JS   01326 564204
A hit with holidaymakers and locals, this harbourside pub revels
in its fun, smuggler-meets-fishing-boat interior, and offers
surprisingly good food alongside Cornish ales.

The White Hart, Ludgvan, TR20 8EY   01736 740574
Granite stone 14th-century pub with ochre-coloured walls, low
beams and real ale from the cask. Come for intimate boxed
seating areas and log-burning fires.

Bay View Inn, Widemouth Bay, EX23 0AW   01288 361273
Sip a pint of Sharp's and watch hot-shot surfers carving up choice
Atlantic rollers – this is one of the best beach/surf watching pubs
on the north coast. The deck area, BBQ and interesting menu are
all rightly popular.

Cumbria

The Pheasant Inn, Casterton, LA6 2RX   01524 271230
18th-century inn overlooking Casterton's green and nearby fells of
the Lune Valley. Great base for walking and a popular eating venue.

England

The Sun Inn, Dent, LA10 5QL   015396 25208

Dent is an unspoilt Dales village of cobbles and cottages. After an invigorating walk pile into the Sun for log fires and pints of Dent beers, brewed up the valley.

The Pheasant, Bassenthwaite, CA13 9YE   017687 76234

The snug at the Pheasant is wonderful, a reminder of past times: it was a busy coaching inn, now it's a hotel with pristine rooms. Jennings on tap, good bar food, glorious gardens.

Bridge Hotel, Buttermere, CA13 9UZ   01768 770252

On the one hand it fits the bill with its stunning position and pubby bar for walkers – complete with real ales and hearty bar food. On the other hand, it's a smart hotel with formal restaurant.

Fat Lamb Country Inn, Ravenstonedale, CA17 4LL   015396 23242

Remote, rambling 17th-century farmhouse with a lived-in feel, expansive fell views, and a wetland nature reserve at the bottom of the garden. Coal fires, hearty food, tip-top Tetleys and wonderful walks.

Derbyshire

Old Crown, Shardlow, DE72 2HL   01332 792392

A fine pub for beer and cider drinkers on the banks of the Trent. Three house ales, up to seven guest beers and plenty of real ciders in the summer. Reasonable pub food.

The Barley Mow, Kirk Ireton, DE6 3JP   01335 370306

A pub your great-grandfather would have liked. Rambling roses climb the Jacobean façade, inside is austere, dimly lit, addictive. Classic tap room, snug bar with a Dickensian feel – for locals, ramblers and pub historians, a gem.

Eyre Arms, Hassop, DE45 1NS   01629 640390

Traditional pub covered by Virginia creeper, close to Hassop Hall and good walks. Beams, log fires, lamplight, ancient knick-knacks and country cooking that's great value.

Barley Mow, Bonsall, DE4 2AY   01629 825685

An unchanging, quirky little pub on the edge of the Peak District. Good filling grub, wonderful fire, UFOs and tall tales abound. Limited opening, but good beers and great craich.

Devon

The London Inn, Molland, EX36 3NG   01769 550269

Honest and unpretentious village local in the Exmoor foothills full of locals, dogs, hunters and shooters. Few frills in rambling flagstoned rooms – hearty food and great beer.

Photos 1. & 4. John Coe 2. The Earl of St Vincent, Egloshayle
3. Chris Banks 5. The Barley Mow, Kirk Ireton 6. The Maltsters Arms, Tuckenhay

Tuckers Arms, Dalwood, EX13 7EG   01404 881342

Postcard-pretty thatched pub in the tranquil Axe valley. Originally a manor house, parts date back 700 years; old stone floors, beams aplenty, big log fires, enjoyable food.

The King's Arms, Stockland, EX14 9BS   01404 881361

A barn of a place and a working locals' pub – plenty of noise from the Ladies Skittles Teams! Good ales, a varied menu and Sunday roasts; tuck in after a hike on the Blackdown hills.

The Anchor Inn, Cockwood, EX6 8RA   01626 890203

Fine views of Cockwood's landlocked harbour are to be had from this 460-year-old former fisherman's cottage. Fitting then to find an awesome 30 mussel dishes on a long, fishy menu. Good real ales, too, but tricky parking.

The Cherub, Dartmouth, TQ6 9RB   01803 832571

Dartmouth's oldest building (1380) creaks with age: a magnificent timbered house with an overhanging beamed façade. Good ales in tiny bar with inglenook; pub food in restaurant.

The Start Bay Inn, Torcross, TQ7 2TQ   01548 580553

Packed the minute it opens (arrive late at your peril), for this modest 14th-century beachside inn arguably serves the best fresh fish and chips in Devon.

The Church House Inn, Harberton, TQ9 7SF   01803 863707

Darkly atmospheric Devon longhouse with fantastic beamed ceiling, oak panelling, medieval glass and respectable list of real ales. Food shows ambition.

The Maltsters Arms, Tuckenhay, TQ9 7EQ   01803 732350

More lively London brasserie than rural Devon inn, it's the good food, local ales, and spectacular setting on Bow Creek that make this 16th-century pub a popular spot.

The Sloop Inn, Bantham, TQ7 3AJ   01548 560489

A 16th-century smuggler's pub smack on the coastal path in the glorious South Hams and a stroll from the beach – the perfect stop-off for fresh fish and a pint of Palmers IPA.

The Mill Brook Inn, South Pool, TQ7 2RW   01548 531581

Arrive by boat (high tide) at this 400-year-old village pub on the Salcombe estuary. Cosy bars, great crab sandwiches, Bass from the barrel, farm cider and a tiny streamside terrace.

England

Manor Inn, Lower Ashton, EX6 7QL   01647 252304
Small, traditional Teign Valley local overlooking field and valley.
Crackling log fires in cosy bars, honest grub, local cider and
excellent west country ales.

Northmore Arms, Wonson, EX20 2JA   01647 231428
A treasure buried down tiny lanes on the edge of Dartmoor.
Wonderfully unspoilt, simple beamed rooms, homemade food,
great beer, exceptional walking. Open all day.

Cricket Inn, Beesands, TQ7 2EN   01548 580215
Unassuming outside, open plan within, but a real local feel. The
great seaside location is matched by a good fish menu. Expect jazz
with your Sunday lunch.

Fountain Head, Branscombe, EX12 3BG   01297 680359
Old-fashioned and unspoilt 500-year-old stone pub, formerly a
blacksmith's forge and cider house. Panelled walls, flagstone floors,
home-brewed beers and simple food in great walking country.

Fox & Goose, Parracombe, EX31 4PE   01598 763239
By a stream in a valley between Exmoor and the dramatic
coastline, an unassuming pub worth seeking out for its big
blackboard menus: fish from local boats, meats from surrounding
farms and great local ales.

The Pilchard Inn, Burgh Island, TQ7 4BG   01548 810514
Walk across the sand or take the sea tractor to this atmospheric
smugglers' pub on the tidal island made famous by Agatha Christie.
Beams, flagstones, roaring log fires, BBQs, cliff walks. Unique!

Turf Hotel, Exminster, EX6 8EE   01392 833128
Reached only on foot (20-min walk), by bike or by boat, a unique,
rambling old pub overlooking Exe estuary mudflats. Bareboard bar
with big bay windows for winter wader-watching and top-notch
Otter Ales. Closed Dec-Feb.

Dorset
The Anchor Inn, Chidcock, DT6 6JU   01297 489215
A cracking coastal path watering hole below Golden Cap. The big
sun terrace and gardens overlook a pebbly beach. Open fires, pints
of Palmers and crab sandwiches.

Photos 1. The King's Arms, Stockland 2. & 6. John Coe 3. The Start Bay Inn, Torcross
4. Russell Wilkinson 5. The Anchor Inn, Cockwood

The Royal Oak, Cerne Abbas, DT2 7JG 01300 341797
Crackling log fires throughout the three flagstoned rooms
add to the charm of this creeper-clad, thatched and historic pub.
Great for drink, but approach the long and unseasonal menu
with caution.

The Three Horseshoes, Powerstock, DT6 3TF 01308 485328
Victorian stone inn in a drowsy village down twisting lanes below
Eggardon Hill. Fresh food and tip-top Palmers ale, best savoured on a
balmy evening on the terrace watching the sun slide over the valley.

The Brace of Pheasants, Plush, DT2 7RQ 01300 348357
In rolling downland, one of Dorset's prettiest pubs — two thatched
cottages in a rural hamlet. A fine summer garden and great
walkers' pitstop; great atmosphere and good food at a price!

Langton Arms, Tarrant Monkton, DT11 8RX 01258 830225
Five microbrewery ales and a bistro-style menu using meat from
the owners' farm draw locals and walkers to this rose-and-creeper-
clad, thatched 17th-century village pub. Beautifully restored
following a serious fire.

The Marquis of Lorne, Nettlecombe, , DT6 3SY 01308 485236
Isolated inn with gardens (good for kids) at the base of Eggardon
Hill. Worth the trip down tortuous lanes for log fires, Palmers
ales, lovely food and valley views across Powerstock.

Rose & Crown, Trent, DT9 4SL 01935 850776
A rural Dorset gem — thatched, unpretentious and rustic with rug-
strewn stone floors, log fires, four ales on tap and views across open
fields to rolling hills. Peaceful end-of-lane location by the church.

Vine Inn, Pamphill, BH21 4EE 01292 882259
Former bakehouse run by the Sweatland family for generations,
now owned by the National Trust. Two timeless bars, London
Pride on tap and sandwiches for sustenance. Close to Kingston
Lacy House and Badbury Rings.

Stapleton Arms, Buckhorn Weston, SP8 5HS 01963 370396
Rupert and Victoria Reeves who transformed the fortunes of the
Queens Arms in Corton Denham revamped this village pub in
March 2006 — have they worked the same magic? Reports please.

England

Greyhound, Sydling St Nicholas, DT2 9PD 01300 341303

Having made a huge success of the West Bay down by the sea, John Ford and Karen Trimby (plus chef) moved inland in 2006 to this rambling village local in a sleepy valley north of Dorchester. The fish should be good.

Ship in Distress, Mudeford, BH23 3NA 01202 483997

Quirky and crammed with nautical clutter as befits its name, this entertaining local is a fish fancier's dream. Arrive early for fresh Mudeford crab or grilled scallops, first-class fish and chips or a tureen of Breton-style fish soup.

Durham

Lord Crewe Arms, Blanchland, DH8 9SP 01434 675251

Here lie the remains of Blanchland's 12th-century abbey lodge set in cloistered gardens. One of England's finest inns, replete with grand fireplaces and a vaulted crypt bar.

Essex

The Mole Trap, Tawney Common, CM16 7PU 01992 522394

The single-track drive through miles of gloriously unspoilt countryside is the 'wow' of this very rural pub. Excellent beers (Ridley, Couch Vale, Fullers London Pride).

Peldon Rose, Peldon, CO5 7QJ 01206 735248

A 14th-century smugglers' inn rescued from decay. Wonky walls, head-cracking beams and huge fires – wonderful. Fine wines, scrummy food and stylish, simple bedrooms.

The White Hart, Great Yeldham, CO9 4HJ 01787 237250

Classic half-timbered pub that impresses inside too, with beams, panelling, open fires and bare boards galore. New owners appear to be concentrating on the restaurant and offer good set lunches.

Blue Boar, Maldon, CM9 4QE 01621 855888

Old coaching inn, now a hotel, with a smart but pubby bar. Its own microbrewery churns out Farmers Ale, Blue Boar Bitter and Hotel Porter stout, all tapped from the cask.

Gloucestershire

Wild Duck, Ewen, GL7 6BY 01285 770310

Impressive, creeper-clad 15th-century inn close to Cotswold Water Park. Rambling rustic interior with roaring log fires and red walls.

The Bull Inn, Hinton, SN14 8HG 0117 937 2332
Fine 16th-century stone pub set back from a deep-cut Cotswold lane. Enticing with tiny windows, low beams, open fires and an inventive menu. Sunny south-facing terrace.

The Baker's Arms, Broad Campden, GL55 6UR 01386 840515
Traditional Cotswold pub that serves home-cooked food and a good selection of well-kept beers. Good walking all around and a welcome for children.

Twelve Bells Inn, Circencester, GL7 1EA 01285 644549
Quirky backstreet pub with glowing fires, scrubbed pine tables and rugs on old tiled floors in three lively, low-ceiling rooms. Characterful landlord, decent fresh fodder and five cracking real ales. A must for beer drinkers.

The Old Fleece, Rooksmoor, GL5 3NB 01453 872582
A fine, mullion-windowed Cotswold stone roadhouse. Mammoth sandwiches all day; real ales and ciders; a dozen wines by glass and over 50 eclectic menu items.

Red Lion, Ampney St Peter, GL7 5SL 01285 851596
Well-preserved time-warp pub beside A417 east of Cirencester. Hatch bar, handpumped Hook Norton, two simple flagstoned rooms with crackling log fires, and long-serving landlord. Closed weekday lunchtimes.

Mill Inn, Withington, GL54 4BE 01242 890204
Ancient, mossy-roofed inn beside the babbling river Coln in a secret Cotswold valley. Low beams, flagstones and blazing log fires in rambling rooms that remain delightfully untouched. Sam Smiths on tap and great local walks.

Priory Inn, Tetbury, GL8 8JJ 01666 503534
Modern makeover in 2005 for historic town centre inn. Now a gastropub with rooms, a big welcome for families and a passion for buying fresh produce from local farms and suppliers.

The Beehive, Cheltenham, GL50 2XE 01242 579243
Attractive corner pub hidden among the antiques shops and cafés of Cheltenham's bohemian quarter. Traditional, reassuringly laid-back, serving decent real ales and good simple gastropub fare accompanied by a warm buzz.

England

Hampshire

The Mayfly, Testcombe, SO20 6AX   01264 860283
Unrivalled tranquil river scenes draw summer crowds to this beamed
old farmhouse on the banks of the Test. Comfortable bar, pubby food
and splendid terrace. Arrive on foot or by bike via the Test Way.

The Fleur de Lys, Pilley, SO41 5QB   01590 672158
History is as much of a pull as a good pint at this thatched pub.
Deeply traditional, serving hearty food in beamed bars. Roaring
fires, lovely garden, forest walks from door.

The Tichborne Arms, Tichborne, SO24 0NA   01962 733760
Real ales from the cask, homely pub food and a glorious summer
garden draw folk to this red-brick, thatched pub in a serene rural
hamlet in the Itchen valley. The Wayfarer's Walk and the Itchen Way
almost pass the door.

The Hawkley Inn, Hawkley, GU33 6NE   01730 827205
A chatty mix of locals and walkers from the Hangers Way Path fill
this honest, no-frills inn. Had a fine reputation for its ales and robust,
unpretentious food – has new owner Nick Troth changed anything?

The Trooper Inn, Petersfield, GU32 1BD   01730 827293
Rustic and remote downland inn with laid-back atmosphere of
candlelit, wood-floored bars, cracking real ale and solidly good,
monthly-changing menus.

The Oak Inn, Bank, SO43 7FE   023 8028 2350
New Forest walks radiate in every direction from this friendly, low-
beamed 18th-century pub. Walkers, cyclists and locals pour in. Ale
tapped from the cask, hearty home-made food – more reports please.

The Jolly Sailor, Old Bursledon, SO31 8DN   023 8040 5557
Reached via 45 steps or by boat, this former shipbuilder's house
overlooks the river Hamble. Watch all things nautical from the
terrace and from big windows in the newly refurbished bars.

The Bell, Alresford, SO24 9AT   01962 732429
Respected licensees Brian and Lynn O'Callaghan continue to work
their magic on this faded Georgian inn. Stylishly reworked bar and
dining area, upgrading of bedrooms and modern pub menus.

The Bugle, Hamble, SO31 4HA   023 8045 3000
Celebrated the world over by the sailing fraternity, an ancient
hostelry beautifully remodelled in 2005. Beams, timbers, flagstones,
fires, decent pub food and boatish views from the front terrace.

Carnarvon Arms, Whitway, RG20 9LE 01635 278222
Former coaching inn for Highclere Castle, reopened in 2005 as
'fine dining, traditional country inn'. Expect stylish surroundings
and skilled cooking from Robert Clayton, ex Priory Hotel Bath.

Herefordshire

The Saracens Head, Symonds Yat, HR9 6JL 01600 890435
Large, jolly 16th-century inn on the east bank of the Wye. Go for
the beer, imaginative menu featuring local produce, and
entertainment provided by watching the ancient hand-ferry plying
across the river.

The Boot, Orleton SY8 4HN 01568 780228
Half-timbered village inn beloved of locals with orchard garden,
horsebrasses, big fire. Real ales and cider matched by traditional
pub roasts, grills, curries and casseroles.

Kilverts, Hay-on-Wye, HR3 5AG 01497 821042
Trendy town-centre inn with a sense of fun, olde-worlde-style
bar, Wye Valley and Hancocks beers on tap, and a global menu
to choose from. Easy atmosphere, but varying service – open
all day.

Hertfordshire

The Holly Bush, Potters Crouch, AL2 3NN 01727 851792
An immaculate, 18th-century country pub elegantly furnished with
antiques and big oak tables candlelit at night. Fabulous Fuller's
ales, straightforward food, nice garden.

The Brocket Arms, Ayot St Lawrence, AL6 9BT 01438 820250
Gem of a local that dates from the 14th-century. It's a
beer drinkers' haven, with darts and dominoes instead of
piped music, and a courtyard and walled garden when the
weather's warm.

The Jolly Waggoner, Ardeley, SG2 7AH 01438 861350
Pretty rural pub with pink walls, bare floorboards, blazing fires
and lots of knick-knacks. Blackboards list popular bar specials and
there's a cottagey restaurant next door.

Isle of Wight

The Spyglass Inn, Ventnor, PO38 1JX 01983 855338
Famous and fascinating 19th-century inn on Ventnor Esplanade
overlooking the sea. Seafaring memorabilia fills rambling
rooms; good seafood specials, local ale and seating by the
sea wall.

England

Red Lion, Freshwater, PO40 9BP 01983 297171

A short stroll from the tidal river Yar and a handy stop-off for local Goddards ale and special food. Sofas, flagstones and fires in the open-plan bar; very civilised.

Kent

The Gate Inn, Marshside, CT3 4EB 01227 860498

A charming rural local, run for years by a landlord who resists change. Two small, well-worn bars, log fires, Shepherd Neame tapped from the cask, and simple, hearty food.

The Tiger, Stowting, TN25 6BA 01303 862130

Hard to find yet civilised country boozer with friendly locals, rugs on bare boards, candles om scrubbed tables, roaring winter fire, cracking real ales (festival in summer), and splendid live jazz evenings.

The Ringlestone Inn, Ringlestone, ME17 1NX 01622 859900

Drink in the 400-year-old atmosphere of this country inn, located by the Pilgrim's Way on the North Downs. Expect low beams, brick floors, cosy corners, fires in winter and a glorious summer garden.

Spotted Dog, Smarts Hill, TN11 8EE 01892 870253

Ancient, low-beamed, panelled, nooked, crannied and rambling – everyone loves this textbook country pub. But will the food continue to impress under new management? Reports please.

Rock Inn, Chiddingstone Hoath, TN8 7BS 01892 870296

A timeless, tile-hung brick cottage in a glorious location. Scuffed and delightfully laid-back, the perfect walker's stop for a pint of Larkins and a satisfyingly thick sandwich.

The Greyhound, Leigh, TN11 8LZ 01892 870275

Hard to find down winding country lanes but worth it. Beautifully cared-for traditional interior and homely local fare. Adnams, Kings and Barnes Sussex on handpump.

The Great House, Gills Green, TN18 5EJ 01580 753119

Former Elizabethan cottages with an alluring mix of beams, open fires and pretty garden. Continental feel to the menu with tapas in the bar, French brasserie dishes in the restaurant.

George Hotel, Cranbrook, TN17 3HE 01580 713348

Fine old town centre inn from the 13th century. Past the ancient front door and there's contemporary styling and modern cooking – plus a few pub classics.

Photos 1. Getty 2. & 4. Spotted Dog, Smarts Hill 3. Chris Banks
5. Russell Wilkinson 6. Hare & Hounds, Fullbeck

The Yew & Ewe, Brookland, TN29 9QR   01797 344215

Next to an ancient country church, this 16th-century pub has been thoroughly gastropubbed – the sophisticated interior comes as quite a surprise. Food is from the Med, beer from Adnams and smoking is banned.

Lancashire

Spread Eagle, Sawley, BB7 4NH   01200 441202

A 17th-century inn on the banks of the Ribble. A serious pub-restaurant; soup and sandwiches in the bar. Great for a riverside drink in summer.

John O'Gaunt, Lancaster, LA1 1JG   01524 65356

Small city-centre pub with terrific atmosphere. Décor is 1930s, enhanced by low-key trad jazz that often floats through. Good range of beers and great choice of simple food – the cullen skink is outstanding.

Leicestershire

Fox & Goose, Illston on the Hill, LE7 9EG   0116 259 6340

A good old-fashioned local. No food; the only animals in this shrine to country pursuits are stuffed or on the walls. Excellent beers in a charming rural setting.

The Crown, Old Dalby, LE14 3LF   01664 823134

Creeper-covered old inn loved for its ales and sweeping summer lawns. A warren of tiny, unspoilt rooms filled with oak settles, antique tables, coal fires and a quaint hatchway bar from which guest beers are tapped from the cask.

Bewicke Arms, Hallaton, LE16 8HB   01858 555217

Fishermen love this pretty 400-year-old inn for its proximity to Eyebrook Reservoir and for its traditional, scrubbed bar. Tourists descend for the setting, and annual bottle-kicking contest on Easter Monday.

Lincolnshire

Chequers, Gedney Dyke, PE12 0AJ   01406 362666

Popular dining pub at the mouth of The Wash, specialising in fish dishes and imaginative daily blackboard specials cooked by landlady-chef. Nicely refurbished – reports please.

Hare & Hounds, Fulbeck, NG32 3JJ   01400 272090

The old stone coaching inn was established in the early 1600s, grew in the 18th and 19th centuries, and was used as a maltings until 1910. Previous owners created a successful small business – reports please of the new regime.

England

London

The Alma, 499 Old York Rd, Wandsworth, SW18 020 8870 2537
At the time of going to press, Charles Gotto was in the process of
handing this quirky pub opposite Wandsworth station back to
Young's. Always a stylish place in which to savour a pint or a glass
of wine – reports please.

The Coopers Arms, 87 Flood St, Chelsea, SW3   020 7376 3120
Under Charles Gotto's amiable stewardship, the Coopers was a
refreshing, if unusual, pit stop with its retro décor and contemporary
feel. Now run by Young's Brewery – has it lost its sparkle?

Fox & Hounds, 29 Passmore St, Chelsea, SW1W   020 7730 6367
Lovely unpretentious boozer, all the cosier for being decked out in
hunting red. Be entertained by the 'Wicked Wit' blackboards from
a corner pew as you tuck into doorstep sandwiches.

The Bridge, Barnes, SW13 9DW   020 8563 9811
Near Hammersmith Bridge, the perfect spot to stop after a
riverside walk. Tuck into a delicious fresh menu with a pint of
Ruddles Best in the sleek interior, or on decking in summer.

The Latchmere, Battersea Park Rd, Battersea, SW11 020 7223 3549
A pub and a theatre rolled into one. Spruced up high-ceilinged bar,
leather sofas, warm fire, bags of smoky atmosphere and a mini-
theatre to watch new comic talent.

The Cow, Westbourne Park Rd, Ladbroke Grove, W2 020 7221 5400
A restaurant in disguise, but Tom Conran has done it very well.
Superb fish and crustacae: you can eat up or down. Laid-back staff
serve a laid-back crowd – and it's friendly.

The Archery Tavern, 4 Bathurst St, Bayswater, W2   020 7402 4916
Everyone loves this place, once the haunt of the London
Toxophilite Society. The Hyde Park stables are in the mews behind,
so ponies clop by. Excellent beers on tap, simple food.

Warrington Hotel, Warrington Cres, Maida Vale, W9   020 7286 2929
Cavernous, splendid, Victorian. Good beers, 22 wines by the glass
and Thai food, too. The bar has a huge arched ceiling and a
magnificent staircase. Good for celeb spotting.

Cumberland Arms, Dartmouth Rd, Hammersmith, W14 020 7371 6806
As sister pub to the nearby Atlas and Fox & Hounds (Battersea),
the food here is of the same high calibre. A magnet for office
workers at lunchtimes but draws the locals for pints at sundown.

Photos 1. Quentin Craven 2. www.paulgroom.com 3. The Alma, Wandsworth 4. The
Coopers Arms, Chelsea 5. The Westbourne, Notting Hill 6. Ye Olde White Bear,
Hampstead

The Salusbury, Salusbury Rd. Queen's Park, NW6 020 7328 3286
Lively gastropub with a deli on the side. Red walls are covered
with seminal jazz album sleeves. Delicious, mainly Italian food and
a lengthy wine list.

Lord Palmerston, Dartmouth Park Hill, Archway, NW5 020 7485 1578
Bustling gastro pub stripped down to bare boards and wooden
tables, with food that's quite something (Moroccan touches,
great steaks) and good wine and beer. Garden for summer.

William IV, 786 Harrow Rd, Kensal Green, NW10 020 8969 5944
There's excellent food and wine in the elegant and sedate
restaurant – and a laid-back bar with sofas, fires and music. Also a
garden for summer at the back.

Spaniards Inn, Spaniards Rd, Hampstead, NW3 020 8731 6571
A legendary hangout with a history. Oak-panelled snugs, open fires
and delightful garden with aviary (packed in summer). Ciabattas,
risottos, Sunday roasts, smiley staff.

Ye Olde White Bear, Well Rd, Hampstead, NW3 1LJ 020 7435 3758
Backstreet pub with country looks and higgledy-piggledy interior
warmed by an open fire. Good beers, selection of wines, smashing
pub grub.

The Northgate, 113 Southgate Rd, Islington, N1 020 7359 7392
Gastro bar with a terrific reputation for fish (menu changes daily).
Loll on couches and admire the art; take a wine onto the terrace,
heated for late summer drinking. A joy.

King's Head Theatre Pub, Upper St, Islington, N1 020 7226 0364
Don't imagine this pub plays second fiddle to the drama upstairs –
it is a vibrant, wooden-floored local with a late licence, live music
every night and food for those who watch the show.

Viaduct Tavern, 126 Newgate St, St Paul's, EC1A 020 7600 1863
The only unaltered gin palace in London, wonderfully lavish and
famous for its triptych oil painting of four Viaduct statues. Join city
lunchtime throng for good beer and bar food.

Prince of Wales, 48 Cleaver Sq, Kennington, SE11 020 7735 9916
Once a gangland boozer, now an intimate little place
serving good Spitfire to students and yuppies. Packed in
summer when locals gather in the lovely square to play
boules.

England

Manchester

Marble Arch, 73 Rochdale Road, Manchester   0161 832 5914
Marvellous tiled interior, with mosaic friezes high up in the
vaulted roof and a deceptive sloping floor. A microbrewery at the
rear produces an enticing array of organic vegan beers. Much loved
pub in Rochdale Road area.

Arden Arms, 23 Millgate, Stockport, SK1 2LX   0161 480 2185
A superb tiled lobby bar, hidden snug, real fires and sublime
Edwardian wood and glass bar, in the shadow of the monstrous
ASDA. The limited lunchtime food is of restaurant quality.

Rain Bar, 80 Bridgwater Street, Manchester   0161 235 6500
Wrestled from the shell of an umbrella factory in 1999, an
inspired mix of bistro and traditional pub beside the Rochdale
Canal in the city centre. Decent fodder and J W Lee's beers.

Circus Tavern, 86 Portland Street, Manchester   0161 236 5818
One of Britain's smallest pubs, thrice as deep as wide, with a tiny
under-stairs bar and two magnificent, panelled roomettes. Twenty
punters (supping Tetleys Bitter) is a crowd here.

Cross Keys, Uppermill, OL3 6LW   01457 874626
Superlative moorland-edge setting four miles east of Oldham high
above the Tame Valley, with stone-flagged floors, terrific fire-blacked
range, excellent food (try the savoury puddings). Lee's beers.

Norfolk

Fat Cat, Norwich, NR2 4NA   01603 624364
Victorian corner pub and beer drinkers' heaven. Over 20 real ales
with some on handpump, others tapped from cask. The owners
proudly keep this a traditional and simple drinking pub.

Buckinghamshire Arms, Blickling, NR11 6NF   01263 732133
Handsome, National Trust-owned Jacobean inn standing close to
the gates of the grand hall. Glowing woodburners in old pine
furnished bars, serving locals in winter and full of tourists in
summer. Big lawn and courtyard.

The George, Cley-next-the-Sea, NR25 7RN   01263 740652
Norfolk Naturalists Trust was formed at this rambling Edwardian inn
overlooking saltmarshes. New landlord Dan Goff owns the White
Horse in Blakeney so expect standards to rise. Reports please.

Photos 1. The Angel, Corbridge 2. John Coe 3. Buckinghamshire Arms, Blickling
4. The Star Inn, Sulgrave 5. The Lifeboat Inn, Thornham 6. Three Horseshoes, Warham

Red Lion, Stiffkey, NR23 1AJ   01328 830552
The new landlord has wisely left the rustic interior unchanged.
Reports please, especially on the short blackboard menu focusing on
local fish. Regarded by locals and walkers as something of a gem.

Three Horseshoes, Warham, NR23 1NL 01328 710547
Plain rooms that have barely changed since the 1930s – gas lights,
rough deal tables, Victorian fireplaces – and East Anglian ales
tapped straight from the cask. Good home cooking too.

The Lifeboat Inn, Thornham, PE36 6LT   01485 512236
The glowing lamps and open fires of this bags-of-character inn
beckon. It's been an ale house since the 16th century – and they
still serve a decent pint. The sea is a brisk, bracing walk
across fields.

Northamptonshire
The Star Inn, Sulgrave, OX17 2SA   01295 760389
A short stroll from Sulgrave Manor, the ivy-clad stone pub dates
from 1700 and draws the crowds for its unchanging atmosphere –
flagged floors, settles, inglenook fireplace. Reports on new
regime welcome.

The Windmill, Badby, NN11 3AN   01327 702363
Thatched 17th-century inn with hotel extension close to Althorp
Park and Sulgrave Manor. Warmly decorated flagstoned bar has log
fires, cask ales and traditional/modern menu.

Northumberland
The Star Inn, Netherton, NE65 7HD   01669 630238
Timeless gem lost in remote countryside north of Rothbury. Little
has changed in 70 years – simple 'living room', excellent Castle
Eden ale; no food. Ring for opening times.

The Angel, Corbridge, NE45 5LA   01434 632119
New owners and big changes at this splendid 17th-century inn in
pretty Corbridge. Cosy panelled lounge with big open fire;
brasserie style dining area – reports please.

The Ship, Holy Island, TD15 2SJ   01289 389311
Rustic bare boards and beamed bars – a spotless little pub that sits
in a terrace of cottages on a fascinating tidal island. Hadrian and
Border ales and good seafood.

England

Allenheads Inn, Allenheads, NE47 9HJ   01434 685200
In one of England's highest villages, a fascinating 18th-century pub with a thousand artefacts: sup and browse. Simple pub food, great walks.

Nottinghamshire

Black Horse, Caythorpe, NG14 7ED 0115 966 3520
A tiny, carpeted bar where Sharron Andrews sells beer brewed on the premises and the fish menu is so popular that booking is essential. Dick Turpin once hid in the gents, apparently.

Robin Hood, Elkesley, DN22 8AJ   01777 83859
A far better pitstop than the roadside 'restaurants' on offer: take the Elkesley turning off the A1 for a decent ploughman's or a lamb confit with mint pesto, garlic and thyme sauce.

Bottle & Glass, Harby, NG23 7EB   01522 703438
They put the emphasis on fish at this deceptively spacious village gastropub – even down to fish and chip takeaway suppers on a Friday evening. Good selection of real ales too, and plenty of wines by the glass.

Oxfordshire

The Greyhound, Rotherfield Peppard, RG9 5HT   0118 972 2227
Hugely attractive and ancient tiled and timbered pub north of Reading. Impressive country venue for new owner Anthony Worrall Thompson and his grill-restaurant formula – 35-day aged beef steaks and his own suckling pigs.

The Five Horseshoes, Maidensgrove, RG9 6EX   01491 641282
A super pub with magnificent views. The garden's a wonderful place to drink in the Oxfordshire beauty and spot the wheeling resident Red Kites. Inside, sup pints of Brakspears and tuck into decent homemade pies.

The Lamb Inn, Burford, OX18 4LR   01993 823155
Classic coaching inn that is now owned by a small hotel chain who have shifted emphasis onto rooms and restaurant. Bar food is pricey, but for location, character and super garden it's hard to beat.

The Swan, Swinbrook, OX18 4DY   01993 822165
Old water mill in a lovely Cotswold village on the Devonshire Estate – an ale-lover's paradise. Flagstones, settles and open fires, cheerful chatter and hearty food – but limited opening hours!

Photos 1. Stag's Head, Swalcliffe 2. John Coe 3. The Swan, Swinbrook
4. Russell Wilkinson 5. Fleece on the Green, Witney 6. The Lamb Inn, Burford

King William IV, Hailey, OX10 6AD   01491 681845
Take an OS map to locate this rural treat tucked down single-track lanes in the Chilterns. Spick-and-span traditional interior, the full range of Brakspear ales, grassy front garden with peaceful views – super after a hike in the hills.

Turf Tavern, Tavern Bath Place, Oxford, OX1 3SU   01865 243235
Rambling, lively, classic 18th-century tavern where ale reigns supreme – 200 guest ales are served during the year. Three flagstoned courtyards, roasted chestnuts and steak and ale pie.

Rose & Crown, 14 North Parade Av., Oxford   01865 510551
No music or mobile phones at this characterful, three-room Victorian city pub – just conversation, great ales, traditional lunchtime food, and a heated back yard.

The Bear, 6 Alfred Street, Oxford, OX1 4EH   01865 728164
Oxford's oldest boozer, popular with town and gown, has a low-beamed, shambolic interior, many years' worth of framed, frayed ties (it's a long story) and good ale.

Fleece on the Green, Witney, OX28 4AZ   01993 892270
Georgian pub overlooking the green that's getting the thumbs up from locals for the all-day sandwiches (bacon sarnies at 8.30am), pizzas and brasserie dishes. Great formula from Peach Pubs.

Stag's Head, Swalcliffe, OX15 5EJ 01295 780232
Shakespeare is said to have supped at this pretty village pub. There's oodles of character in the cosy series of rooms and a real local feel. It's a first venture for new owners – reports please.

Hand & Shears, Church Hanborough, OX29 8AB 01993 883337
Sister pub of the White Hart in Wytham, a civilised boozer with a wide range of food. Sink into wing chairs by a cosy, flower-crowned fireplace to read the papers.

Three Horseshoes, Witney, OX28 6BS   01993 703086
A romantic's treasure – low candlelight, open brickwork and a tantalising menu. A cosy place for winter warmers on a chilly night.

King's Head, Wooton, OX20 1DX 01993 811340
Come for homemade bread with lunchtime soups and a modern British menu at dinner – all freshly prepared. Hook Norton ales and cosy beamed bars, too. Reports please.

England

Anchor Inn, Oxford, OX2 6TT   01865 510282

Bold new venture for Jamie and Charlotte King who made a success of the Star In at Sulgrave. The 1930s Art Deco style pub in the Jericho area has been restored: expect good food, Wadworth beers and a big welcome. Reports please.

Rutland

Old White Hart, Lyddington, LE15 9LR   01572 821703

Spick-and-span country pub with old black beams, tiled floors, roaring log fires, seasonal menus, good ales, and a walled garden with 12 floodlit petanque pitches.

The Grainstore Brewery, Oakham, LE15 6RE   01572 770065

Working brewery with a bare bones bar delivering nine cracking ales and simple pub food. Tours can be arranged in advance.

Shropshire

The Crown, Hopton Wafers, DY14 0NB   01299 270372

Faded but comfortingly traditional and hidden away in a tranquil valley. The food is good and a fire burns in winter in the carpeted bar. New owners are extending the place – expect big changes.

The Royal Oak, Cardington, SY6 7JZ   01694 771266

At the foot of Caer Caradoc, a 500-year-old pub loved by muddy-booted ramblers – with a dependable range of real ales, cider and inexpensive daily specials from local suppliers.

The Plough, Wistanstow, SY7 8DG   01588 673251

Pretty village tucked off A49/A489. A friendly Shropshire Lad with well-above-average pub food: steak and ale pie, venison casserole, Sunday roasts. Woods Brewery lives next door.

The Miners Arms, Priest Weston, SY7 8EW   01938 561352

On the wild Welsh borders an unspoilt pub that's the hub of hamlet life – they sell dog food, groceries and gas, put on folk nights and harvest thanksgiving. Wonderful red tiled locals' bar with big inglenook; food on request.

Clive Restaurant with Rooms, Bromfield, SY8 2JR   01584 856565

Handsome building that's not particularly 'pubby' but noted for a decent pint of Hobson's, good choice of wines in the bar and some ambitious cooking in the restaurant.

Photos 1. & 2. The Crown, Hopton Wafers 3. & 6. The Grainstore Brewery, Oakham
4. Clive Restaurant with Rooms, Bromfield 5. The Royal Oak Inn, Withypool

Countess's Arms, Weston Heath, TF11 8RJ   01952 691123
Unassuming roadside pub transformed by the Earl of Bradford into
a chic dining venue. Expect rough brick walls lined with modern
art, blazing log fires, chandeliers in galleried eating areas,
impressive wines, global food.

Sun Inn, Rosemary Lane, Leintwardine, SY7 0LP
No airs or graces at this terraced house beside the river Teme. Just
two basic rooms with scrubbed tables, stone floors, barrels of beer
and cider stillaged in the kitchen. Unchanged since the Ark, and
landlady Floss in her 80s. No phone.

Somerset

The Notley Arms Inn, Monksilver, TA4 4JB   01984 656217
Isolated, pretty village pub with a welcoming intimate feel – perfect
for cold nights. Dependable range of local ales and good food.

Pilgrim's Rest, Lovington, BA7 7PT   01963 240597
More of a restaurant with a 'pubby' style delivering Champflower Ale
on handpump and a menu of interesting modern dishes.

The Royal Oak Inn, Withypool, TA24 7QP   01643 831506
It's a magical drive across the moor to this small forgotten place.
Oak trestles, beams, crackling log fires and home-cooked food –
perfect after a hike to Tarr Steps.

Carpenter's Arms, Pensford, BS39 4BX   01761 490202
Rambling, rose-clad stone inn overlooking the Chew Valley.
Civilised beamed bar with cosy fires, rustic furnishings and
modern pub food.

Kingsdon Inn, Kingsdon, TA11 7LG   01935 840543
Weary A303 travellers should take note of this postcard-pretty
thatched cottage as it is the ideal spot to relax over a good
home-cooked lunch or supper. Minutes from the Podimore
roundabout.

The Helyar Arms, East Coker, BA22 9JR   01935 862332
Fine gastropub that's worth a detour – for the food that goes from
strength to strength, and for the handsome feudal village it lives in.
Real ales, Somerset cider and global wines are well priced.
Landlord plans to sell in 2006.

England

Cat Head Inn, Chiselborough, TA14 6TT   01935 881231
Striking hamstone village pub in rolling countryside close to
Montacute. Spotless flagstoned rooms, fresh imaginative food,
Otter bitter on tap and attractive garden with peaceful views over
the village.

The George, Ilminster, CA19 0DG   01460 55515
Spick and span town-centre pub opposite the buttercross, nicely
furnished, yellow walls hung with hunting prints, classical music,
interesting chalkboard menu, and a genuine welcome. Just off A303.

Blue Flame, Nailsea, BS48 4DE   01275 856910
Spartan, well-worn 19th-century rural local frequented by farmers
and real ale and cider enthusiasts. Two basic rooms, one with coal
fire, barrels on stillage, filled rolls, pub games and big garden;
open all day in summer. A rarity!

Staffordshire
Anchor Inn, Old Lea, ST20 0NG   01785 284569
Largely unaltered old boatman's pub beside the Shropshire Union
Canal. Beer and cider from jugs filled in the cool cellar beside
the canal trough. Approached by boat or down grass-centred
lanes. No food.

Suffolk
The Swan, Hoxne, IP21 5AS   01379 668273
Still a feel of times past at this restored village local. A great buzz –
and hearty helpings of home-cooked food.

Victoria, Earl Soham, IP13 7RL   01728 685758
Inauspicious whitewashed village local by the green, famous
for its home brewed beers – Earl Soham Brewery. Easy-going
atmosphere and few frills in the rustic main bar but you will find
hearty pub food and a cracking pint of Victoria Ale.

The Bell Inn, Walberswick, IP18 6TN   01502 723109
A 600-year-old inn set in a tiny summer-soft, winter-bleak fishing
village. Enjoy good local ales and homely bar food surrounded by
ancient beams, flagstones, wooden settles and open fires.

Photos 1. Anchor Inn, Nayland 2. The Helyar Arms, East Coker 3. Henry Morriss
4. The Randolph Hotel, Reydon 5. John Coe 6. The Bell Inn, Walberswick

Eels Foot Inn, Eastbridge, IP16 4SN   01728 830154

This plain, backwater village pub is not just for locals; they may stop talking when you walk in but are quick to welcome 'grockles' in the midst of the tourist season. Good honest food, and a real craic on music nights.

Ramsholt Arms, Ramsholt, IP12 3AB   01394 411229

Idyllic – on the shore of the river Deben. Sup a pint of Nethergate on the terrace, listen to the calls of the curlew. Cosy fires, game in season and great fish and chips.

The Angel, Lavenham, CO10 9QZ   01787 247388

A delightful ancient inn overlooking Lavenham's market place and famous timbered guildhall. Dining area has huge inglenook fireplace. East Anglian ales and daily-changing menus.

Anchor Inn, Nayland, CO6 4JL   01206 262313

The old country inn with its great riverside location has been thoroughly renovated – with some detriment to the atmosphere. However, regulars from Colchester, as well as tourists, are drawn by the posh gastropub food.

Butt & Oyster, Chelmondiston, IP9 1JW   01787 280245

Impossibly charming riverside pub with old settles, tiled floors and fine views across the Orwell. Arrive early if you want one of the window seats.

The Randolph Hotel, Reydon, IP18 6PZ   01502 723603

As good for a quick bite and a pint of Adnams as for a three-course meal that takes in local fish and game, this late Victorian pub-hotel. It sports sleek, modern good looks within, sunny gardens without.

The Queens Head, Brandeston, IP13 7AD   01728 685307

Revamped Adnams pub in sleepy backwater a short drive from Framlingham Castle. Airy and spacious rooms with limed panelled walls and polished pine tables, fresh flowers, logs in the inglenook, and 'pub food with a difference'. Reports please.

England

The Bell, Cretingham, IP13 7BJ   01728 685419
Beams, beams and more beams – a lovely old style pub,
all that an inn should be, with rugs on worn boards, moody
red or yellow walls, big fireplaces and contemporary style
menus favouring fresh fish. Reports welcome.

The Henny Swan, Great Henny, CO10 7LS   01787 269238
Refurbishment has not lost the soul and style of this middle-of-
nowhere riverside pub well worth the longish drive. Lovely light
lunch menu and Suffolk ales.

Plough & Sail, Snape Maltings, IP17 1SR   01728 688413
Set at the front of the Maltings, next to the road, this busy
bustling Adnams pub-restaurant delivers a sound, globally
inspired menu to a vast array of tables. A tourist magnet on
weekends and holidays.

Surrey
Punch Bowl Inn, Dorking, RH5 5PU   01306 627249
15th-century charm: a roaring inglenook, scrubbed tables and
uneven flagged floors. The tile-hung pub is in superb walking
country. Summer BBQs and Badger beers.

The White Cross, Richmond, TW9 1TJ   020 8940 6844
Real fires in cosy bars and huge windows overlooking the Thames
– what views! Enjoy a pint or three on the terrace, hugely popular
in summer. Bar food is swiftly served.

Old School House, Ockley, RH5 5TH   01306 627430
Some of the best fish and seafood here at Bill Bryson's former
boys' boarding school. Expect fresh Selsey crab and Loch Fyne
oysters alongside Gales beers.

The Albert Arms, Esher, KT10 9QS   01372 465290
Lavish refurbishment of a high street corner pub has created
an impressive pub-with-rooms. Sleek bar area offering cask
ales, many wines by the glass and eclectic menus.
Live weekend jazz.

The Parrot, Forest Green, RH5 5RZ   01306 621339
The Gotto family have left their mini-empire of London pubs and
taken over this substantial pub near their organic farm. Expect
high standards and modern menus featuring rare-breed meats.
Reports please.

Photos 1. Sheila Clifton 2. The Rainbow Inn, Cooksbridge 3 & 5. John Coe
4. www.paulgroom.com 6. Getty

Sussex

Well Diggers Arms, Petworth, GU28 0HG 01798 342287
Rustic, rendered old roadside pub that may not immediately
appeal. Step inside for Young's ales and winter game, huge
casseroles, properly hung steaks, real pies and seafood – perfect.
Character landlord too.

Black Jug, Horsham, RH12 1RJ 01403 253526
Victorian town centre pub owned and revamped by Brunning and
Price. Expect classic wooden panelling, wooden floors, trademark
bookcases and modern pub served all day.

Six Bells, Chiddingly, BN8 6HE 01825 872227
Gary Glitter, Led Zeppelin and Leo Sayer have all played in this
quirky little boozer renowned for its music. Logs fires, atmosphere
and great value food.

Blue Ship, Billingshurst, RH14 9BS 01403 822709
Lost down a web of Sussex lanes, an unassuming Victorian exterior
and charming 15th-century core. Classic main bar with worn brick
floor, low heavy beams, crackling fire in the inglenook and beer
from the barrel.

The Rainbow Inn, Cooksbridge, BN8 4SS 01273 400334
Pleasing roadside pub north of Lewes that draws foodies for excellent
seasonal food. Cosy clubby bar for pints of Harveys, charming private
dining rooms, decked terrace with views to the South Downs.

Three Moles, Selham, GU28 0PN 01798 861303
Built to serve Selham Station in 1872, now a truly unspoilt and
old-fashioned rural local with simple furnishings. Great beer, farm
cider, monthy sing-songs, long-serving landlady, no food.

The Chimney House, Brighton, BN1 5DF 01273 556708
Brighton boozer transformed into a non-smoking food pub by
former Tate Gallery restaurant manager. Stripped boards, eclectic
furnishings, big mirrors and an open kitchen producing fresh food
from local produce.

Warwickshire

The Bell, Alderminster, CV37 8NY 01789 450414
Cheerful bar and bistro in converted coaching inn. Fresh food
on daily chalkboards, in bar rooms or restaurant, and popular
musical suppers. Conservatory and garden with valley views.

England

Wiltshire

The Lamb at Hindon, Hindon, SP3 6DP   01747 820573

New tenants for this old coaching inn in sleepy Hindon. Rambling rooms ooze character, deep red walls groan with old prints, big bay windows look across the street, settles front blazing log fires. Food is on the up.

The Red Lion, Lacock, SN15 2LQ   01249 730456

Little has changed since Jane Austen's day with big open fires, rugs on flagstones, bare boards, timbers. Modern touches include fine home-cooking and compact Georgian-style bedrooms.

The Neeld Arms, Grittleton, SN14 6AP   01249 782470

True country boozer with friendly locals, two glowing inglenooks, fresh tasty food, good beers and drinkable wines. Four-poster beds upstairs, breakfast feasts.

The Three Crowns, Brinkworth, SN15 5AF   01666 510366

Intimate, old-style bars and a huge no-smoking conservatory. Real ale, good wine, a garden with views and a large, surprising menu result in a winning formula.

The Bell, Ramsbury, SN8 2PE   01672 520230

On the square of this quaint market town, a handsome, bay-windowed, whitewashed 17th-century inn with a sympathetic makeover... a woodburner in the small bar and a stylish dining room. Reports welcome.

The Linnet, Great Hinton, BA14 6BU   01380 870354

With enthusiasm, dedication and bags of talent, chef-patron Jonathan Furby has turned the Linnet into a popular pub-restaurant. Good value lunches, unusual combinations and everything homemade.

The Barge Inn, Seend Cleeve, SN12 6QB   01380 828230

Former wharf house beside the Kennet & Avon Canal converted to an attractive and bustling pub with a quirky barge-themed décor. Moorings outside, towpath walks, waterside garden and Wadworth ales.

Rising Sun, Bewley Common, SN15 2PP   01249 730363

Unpretentious stone pub high on a hill above Lacock. Escape the crowd for the terrace and unrivalled Avon Valley views, sup a pint of Moles as hot-air balloons drift across the sky on summer evenings.

Worcestershire

The King's Arms, Ombersley, WR9 0EW 01905 620142

A wonderful, unpretentious little place, all woodsmoke, heavy oak-beamed ceilings, glowing fires and dimly lit nooks and crannies: the centuries stand still at this fine, timber-framed building. Taken over by next door (Crown & Sandy's) in 2005.

Bell & Cross Inn, Clent, DY9 9QL 01562 730319

A cosy atmosphere with open fires to enjoy good pub food (the owner was chef to the English football squad) and a selection of real ales. A surprisingly unspoilt little pub so close to Birmingham.

Colliers Arms, Clows Top, DY14 9HA 01299 832242

Food with a view! A top quality menu and wine list and a 'gourmet evening' to tickle foodie tastebuds.

Yorkshire

The Three Hares, Bilbrough, YO23 3PH 01937 832128

16th-century pub in an unspoilt rural setting (sheep eyeball you as you sip your wine). Revamped interior and an interesting, balanced menu strong on seasonal produce.

The Crab & Lobster, Asenby, YO7 3QL 01845 577286

Rambling, characterful pub-restaurant. A bohemian, whacky interior and ceilings that are a riot of memorabilia provide the backdrop for extravagant seafood.

The Fox & Hounds, Pickering, YO62 6SQ 01751 431577

Old coaching inn in a sleepy backwater below the North York Moors. Expect homely panelled bars with open fires and well-presented modern pub food.

The Fat Cat, Sheffield, S3 8SA 01142 494861

In Sheffield and desperate for a pint, follow signs to the Kelham Island Museum to locate this bustling backstreet boozer. Cracking home-brewed beers and six guest ales await, and good value pub grub.

The Buck Inn, Thornton Watlass, HG4 4AH 01677 422461

Archetypal village pub set next to the village green and perilously close to the cricket pitch. Good, ever-changing range of local ales and a wide ranging menu. Homely, traditional interior, summer barbecues and children's play area.

England

Black Sheep Brewery, Masham, HG4 4EN   01765 689227
Follow a fascinating tour of Theakston's high-flying brewery with a
perfect pint of Riggwelter or a hearty meal in the informal bar-
bistro: try shank of lamb with Square Ale sauce.

Fox & Hounds, Carthorpe, DL8 2LG   01845 567433
Slip off the hectic A1 for peace and nourishment at this pristine
village pub. Come for traditional interiors, delicious wines and
fresh food with a fishy slant.

The Laurel, Whitby, YO22 4SE   01947 880400
A super little pub in an unspoilt fishing village with views out to
sea. Few frills other than a roaring fire, tip-top Theakston ales and
good sandwiches.

The George, Hubberholme, BD23 5EJ   01756 760223
Sympathetically updated but fairly basic Dales pub with
good beer and traditional pub food. Stands next to a bridge across
the River Wharf in stunning walking country. JB Priestley's
favourite watering hole; he's buried in the church opposite.

Charles Bathurst Inn, Arkengarthdale, DL11 6EN   01748 884567
Retreat after a bracing walk to the Codys' wonderful inn tucked
high above Swaledale. Rustic pine-furnished interiors; hearty
dishes of local produce.

The Greyhound, Saxton, LS24 9PY   01937 557202
Unchanging 13th-century stone inn next to Saxton's church.
Packed with ornaments, plates and brasses in three cosy rooms
with blazing winter fires. Sam Smiths from the cask.

Hack & Spade, Whashton, DL11 7JL   01748 823721
Good seasonal food, Black Sheep beers and bin-end wines at this
soft stone pub in an off-the-beaten-track hamlet. Log fires and
long views across fertile farming country complete the picture.

Queens Arms, Litton, BD23 5QJ   01756 770208
Good walks onto the moors and alongside the river Skirfare f
rom this homely 16th-century inn beside a winding lane in the
remote Dales. Return for warming fires, home-brewed ales,
hearty food, stunning views.

Wales

Cardiff
Waterguard, Cardiff Bay, CF10 4PA   029 2049 9034
Fascinating old buildings fill the Cardiff Bay area and this half-historic customs house is full of cosy charm – plus a bold extension with floor-to-ceiling glass framing the view across the bay.

Carmarthenshire
White Hart Inn, Llanddarog, SA32 8NT   01267 275330
An oddity for west Wales, a thatched pub whose low-beamed rooms ooze fairytale charm. Real log fires, real homemade pies and real beers (home-brewed) – worth leaving the A40 for.

Conwy
The Queen's Head, Llandudno Junction, LL31 9JP   01492 546570
Old wheelwright's cottage with low beams, polished tables and a roaring fire in the bar. Come for pints of Burton ale, home-cooked food – Conwy crab, local fish or Welsh lamb.

Groes Inn, Ty'n y Groes, LL32 8TN   01492 650545
A 500-year-old drovers' inn notable for its fabulous views over the Conwy Valley. Cosy bars, rambling dining areas, real ale, a conservatory and gardens.

Denbighshire
Plough Inn, St Asaph, LL17 0LU   01745 585080
North Wales's best example of gastropubbery. Real ale bar; wine shop; fresh fish and steaks waiting on crushed ice to be cooked to order; Art Deco bistro. Gets busy.

Flintshire
Glasfryn, Sychdyn, CH7 6LR   01352 750500
Former farmhouse smartly made-over by the upmarket Brunning & Price group. Big buzzy bar, impressive beers, distinctive dining areas, modern pub food all day, and great views.

Glamorgan
The Bush, St Hilary, CF71 7DP   01446 772745
Wonderfully traditional thatched pub in gentle countryside. Cul-de-sac location makes outside benches popular in summer. In winter head for the roaring fire.

Wales

Gwynedd

Pen-y-Gwryd Inn, Nant Gwynant, LL55 4NT 01286 870211
Snowdonia's ex-mountain rescue HQ and training base for the
1953 Everest expedition. See their boots in the bar; dine by
candlelight; stay the night. A treasure.

The George, Penmaenpool, LL40 1YD 01341 422525
One of Wales's finest views across the Mawddach estuary towards
Snowdonia. Family-friendly basement, beamed and flagstone bar
and tables on the water's edge. New owners are making an effort
with the food – reports welcome.

Monmouthshire

The Wheatsheaf, Llanhennock, NP18 1LT 01633 420468
Solidly traditional, utterly unpretentious country pub a few miles
from Caerleon. A smiling welcome, good home cooking and real
ales all guaranteed.

The Hardwick, Hardwick, NP7 9AA 01873 854220
Chef Stephen Terry is back in Abergavenny, down the road from
his old restaurant (The Walnut Tree). Opening as we go to
press. Simple, locally sourced foods and weekend brunches.
Reports please.

Pembrokeshire

Pendre Inn, Cilgerran, SA43 2SL 01239 614223
Tiny, old and special, this village inn delivers gargantuan portions of
good pub grub and decent ales in flagstoned rooms – at low prices!

Stackpole Inn, Stackpole, SA71 5DF 01646 672324
Former village store and post office of this hamlet on the fringe of
spectacular NT coastline. Great choice of fresh local dishes in
whopping portions.

Powys

The Traveller's Rest, Talybont-on-Usk, LD3 7YP 01874 676233
Wonderfully warm and inviting pub-restaurant on a quiet back
road with views across fields and a canal passing by. Tasteful
interior retains rustic charm; food is modern and good. Open
evenings and weekends only.

Royal Oak, Gladestry, HR5 3NR 01544 370669
Stone-built local, smack on the Offa's Dyke Path beneath Hergest
Ridge. Filled with farmers and booted walkers supping pints of
Woods in front of roaring fires and tucking into good value food.

Photos 1. Jackie King 2. Henry Morriss 3. & 6. Jules Richardson
4. John Coe 5. Russell Wilkinson

Bhurtpore Inn Aston, Cheshire, entry 48
The Watermill Ings, Cumbria, entry 84
The Bridge Inn Topsham, Devon, entry 138
Culm Valley Inn Culmstock, Devon, entry 144
The Swan Little Totham, Essex, entry 161
The Ostrich Inn Newland, Gloucestershire, entry 174
The Royal Oak Fritham, Hampshire, entry 201
The Sun Inn Bentworth, Hampshire, entry 209
The Cow & Plough Oadby, Leicestershire, entry 265
The White Horse Parsons Green, London SW6, entry 289
The Victoria Beeston, Nottinghamshire, entry 359
The Falkland Arms Great Tew, Oxfordshire, entry 384
The Crown Churchill, Somerset, entry 427
Halfway House Pitney, Somerset, entry 429
Plough & Harrow Monknash, Glamorgan, entry 591
Cherry Tree Inn Tintern, Monmouthshire, entry 602

Photo The White Horse, entry 289

Best for... own breweries

Pot Kiln Frilsham, Berkshire (West Berkshire Brewery) entry 9
The Watermill Ings, Cumbria (Ings Mill Brewery) entry 84
Drunken Duck Inn Barngates, Cumbria (Barngates Brewery), entry 87
Kirkstile In Loweswater, Cumbria (Loweswater Brewery), entry 92
Old Crown Hesket Newmarket, Cumbria (Hesket Newmarket Brewery), entry 96
The Queen's Head Inn Tirril, Cumbria (Tirril Brewery), entry 97
Dartmoor Union Holbeton, Devon (Union Brewery), entry 115
The Flower Pots Inn Cheriton, Hampshire (Cheriton Brewhouse), entry 210
The Swan on the Green West Peckham, Kent (Swan Brewery), entry 246
The Church Inn Uppermill, Lancashire (Saddleworth Brewery), entry 263
The Bell East Langton, Leicestershire (Langton Brewery), entry 266
Greenwich Union Greenwich, London SE7 (Meantime Brewery), entry 299
Baltic Fleet Liverpool, Merseyside (Wapping Brewery), entry 322
Dipton Mill Inn Hexham, Northumberland (Hexhamshire), entry 354
All Nations Madeley, Shropshire (Worfield Brewery), entry 401
St Peter's Hall St Peter South Elmham, Suffolk (St Peter's Brewery), entry 437
Old Cannon Brewery Bury St Edmunds, Suffolk (Old Cannon Brewery), entry 449
The Plough Coldharbour, Surrey (Leith Hill Brewery), entry 454
The Talbot Knightwick, Worcestershire (Teme Valley Brewery), entry 526
The Sair Inn Linthwaite, Yorkshire (Linfit Brewery), entry 530
Foresters Inn Carlton in Coverdale, Yorkshire (Wensleydale Brewery), entry 547
Nag's Head Inn Abercych, Pembrokeshire, (Nags Head Brewery), entry 612

Photo St Peter's Hall, entry 437

King William Bath, Bath & N.E. Somerset, entry 3
The Pot Kiln Frilsham, Berkshire, entry 9
The Harris Arms Lewdown, Devon, entry 132
Digger's Rest Woodbury Salterton, Devon, entry 139
The Bell at Sapperton Sapperton, Gloucestershire, entry 169
The Stagg Inn Titley, Herefordshire, entry 215
Three Crowns Ullingswick, Herefordshire, entry 225
George & Dragon Speldhurst, Kent, entry 250
The Three Fishes Mitton, Lancashire, entry 257
Bay Horse Forton, Lancashire, entry 252
Red Lion Inn Stathern, Leicestershire, entry 269
The Duke of Cambridge Islington, London, entry 311
The Goose Britwell Salome, Oxfordshire, entry 369
The Olive Branch Clipsham, Rutland, entry 388
The Waterdine Llanfair Waterdine, Shropshire, entry 392
Canal Inn Wrantage, Somerset, entry 413
Anchor Inn Walberswick, Suffolk, entry 439
The Queens Head Bramfield, Suffolk, entry 440
The Tollgate Inn Holt, Wiltshire, entry 511
The Coachman Inn Snainton, Yorkshire, entry 567
The Appletree Country Inn Marton, Yorkshire, entry 568
The Star Inn Harome, Yorkshire, entry 570

Photo The Pot Kiln, entry 9

Best for... cheese

The Pheasant Keyston, Cambridgeshire, entry 42
The Nobody Inn Doddiscombsleigh, Devon, entry 136
The Stagg Inn Titley, Herefordshire, entry 215
The Freemasons Arms Wiswell, Lancashire, entry 258
Farmers Arms Lincoln, Lincolnshire, entry 270
The White Hart Lydgate, Greater Manchester, entry 321
Dipton Mill Hexham, Northumberland, entry 354
Martin's Arms Colston Bassett, Nottinghamshire, entry 360
Crown Country Inn Munslow, Shropshire, entry 396
The Camelot South Cadbury, Somerset, entry 431
Jolly Sportsman East Chiltington, Sussex, entry 475
The Blacksmiths Arms Westow, Yorkshire, entry 565
The Star Inn Harome, Yorkshire, entry 570
White Horse Inn Hendrerywdd, Denbighshire, entry 585

Photo Christopher Hubbard

The Bell Inn Aldworth, Berkshire, entry 10
The Queen's Head Newton, Cambridgeshire, entry 36
The Star Inn St Just, Cornwall, entry 60
Tinners Arms Zennor, Cornwall, entry 61
Old Crown Hesket Newmarket, Cumbria, entry 96
Ye Olde Gate Inne Brassington, Derbyshire, entry 109
Rugglestone Inn Widecombe-in-the-Moor, Devon, entry 128
The Bridge Inn Topsham, Devon, entry 138
The Square & Compass Worth Matravers, Dorset, entry 148
The Boat Inn Ashleworth, Gloucestershire, entry 177
Harrow Inn Steep, Hampshire, entry 212
All Nations Madeley, Shropshire, entry 401
Yew Tree Cauldon, Staffordshire, entry 435
Royal Oak Wineham, Sussex, entry 473
The Case is Altered Five Ways, Warwickshire, entry 502
The Fleece Bretforton, Worcestershire, entry 525
The Falcon Inn Arncliffe, Yorkshire, entry 544
White Horse (Nellie's) Beverley, Yorkshire, entry 563
The Birch Hall Beck Hole, Yorkshire, entry 574
Cresselly Arms Cresswell Quay, Pembrokeshire, entry 607
Dryffryn Arms Pontfaen, Pembrokeshire, entry 610

Photo Dryffryn Arms, entry 610

The Mole & Chicken Easington, Buckinghamshire, entry 27
The Pheasant Inn Higher Burwardsley, Cheshire, entry 50
Hanging Gate Sutton, Cheshire, entry 56
The Halzephron Gunwalloe, Cornwall, entry 62
The Drunken Duck Inn Barngates, Cumbria, entry 87
Brackenrigg Inn Watermillock, Cumbria, entry 93
The Ancient Camp Inn Ruckhall, Herefordshire, entry 222
Carpenter's Arms Walterstone, Herefordshire, entry 224
The Gun Docklands, London, entry 300
The White Horse Brancaster Staithe, Norfolk, entry 337
The King William IV Mickleham, Surrey, entry 452
Duke of Cumberland Arms Henley, Sussex, entry 462
Three Horseshoes Elstead, Sussex, entry 465
The Griffin Inn Fletching, Sussex, entry 477
The Castle Inn Edgehill, Warwickshire, entry 493
The Millbank Mill Bank, Yorkshire, entry 533
The Harp Old Radnor, Powys, entry 618

Photo The White Horse, entry 337

Dundas Arms Kintbury, Berkshire, entry 8
The Shipwright's Arms Helford, Cornwall, entry 64
The Pandora Inn Mylor Bridge, Cornwall, entry 65
The Ship Inn Noss Mayo, Devon, entry 114
The Ferry Boat Inn Dittisham, Devon, entry 122
The Royal Oak Langstone, Hampshire, entry 213
The Inn at Whitewell Whitewell, Lancashire, entry 256
The Ship Wandsworth, London, entry 293
The Gun Docklands, London, entry 300
The White Horse Brancaster Staite, Norfolk, entry 337
The Trout at Tadpole Bridge Oxfordshire, entry 377
The Riverside Inn Cressage, Shropshire, entry 398
Ship Inn Red Wharf Bay, Anglesey, entry 577
The Harbourmaster Hotel Aberaeron, Ceredigion, entry 583
The Corn Mill Llangollen, Denbighshire, entry 586
The Boat Erbistock, Denbighshire, entry 587
Penhelig Arms Hotel Aberdyfi, Gwynedd, entry 592
The Old Point House Inn Angle, Pembrokeshire, entry 606

Photo The Boat, entry 587

The White Lion Barthomley, Cheshire, entry 54
The Mason's Arms Cartmel Fell, Cumbria, entry 80
Ye Olde Gate Inne Brassington, Derbyshire, entry 109
Duke of York Iddesleigh, Devon, entry 133
The Wykeham Arms Winchester, Hampshire, entry 204
The White Horse Inn Priors Dean, Hampshire, entry 211
Harrow Inn Steep, Hampshire, entry 212
The Three Chimneys Biddenden, Kent, entry 248
Martin's Arms Colston Bassett, Nottinghamshire, entry 360
The Falkland Arms Great Tew, Oxfordshire, entry 384
The Royal Oak Inn Luxborough, Somerset, entry 405
Halfway House Langport, Somerset, entry 429
King's Head Laxfield, Suffolk, entry 441
The Blue Lion East Witton, Yorkshire, entry 548
White Swan Pickering, Yorkshire, entry 569
The Blacksmith's Arms Lastingham, Yorkshire, entry 573
Plough & Harrow Monknash, Glamorgan, entry 591

Royal Oak Bovingdon Green, Buckinghamshire, entry 31
The Mason's Arms Knowstone, Devon, entry 145
The Shave Cross Inn Shave Cross, Dorset, entry 146
The Riverside Inn Aymestrey, Herefordshire, entry 214
The Dove Dargate Kent, entry 240
Hundred House Hotel Norton, Shropshire, entry 402
Lord Poulett Arms Hinton St George, Somerset, entry 414
The Devonshire Arms Long Sutton, Somerset, entry 416
The Stag Eashing, Surrey, entry 455
The Lickfold Inn Lickfold, Sussex, entry 460
The Fox Goes Free Charlton, Sussex, entry 468
The Star Inn Old Heathfield, Sussex, entry 486
The Howard Arms Ilmington, Warwickshire, entry 495

Photo Lord Poulett Arms, entry 414

Pub & wc access for wheelchair users

England

Bedfordshire 6
Berkshire 10 • 12 • 13
Birmingham 17
Bristol 19
Buckinghamshire 25 • 26 • 28 • 29 • 30 • 31 • 33
Cambridgeshire 35 • 38 • 39 • 41
Cheshire 45 • 47 • 48 • 49 • 50 • 51 • 56 • 59
Cornwall 60 • 65 • 69 • 74
Cumbria 80 • 83 • 84 • 86 • 87 • 89 • 91 • 92 • 93 • 99
Derbyshire 102 • 106 • 108 • 109 • 110 • 111 • 112 • 113
Devon 114 • 115 • 116 • 118 • 121 • 123 • 124 • 125 • 129 • 132 • 135 • 136 • 137 • 140 • 141 • 143 • 144
Dorset 146 • 147 • 148 • 149
Durham 151 • 153 • 155

Essex 160 • 161 • 164
Gloucestershire 166 • 167 • 168 • 169 • 172 • 175 • 176 • 183 • 184 • 185 • 190 • 191
Greater Manchester 195
Hampshire 198 • 199 • 201 • 202 • 203 • 205 • 207 • 208 • 211 • 212
Herefordshire 216 • 218 • 220 • 225 • 226 • 227 • 229 • 230
Hertfordshire 231 • 232
Isle of Wight 236 • 237
Kent 243 • 246 • 249
Lancashire 253 • 254 • 255 • 257 • 258 • 262
Leicestershire 264 • 265 • 267 • 268
Lincolnshire 270 • 272
London 279 • 280 • 286 • 287 • 288 • 289 • 290 • 291 • 292 • 294 • 297 • 298 • 300 • 308 • 310 • 312 • 313 • 314
Manchester 321
Merseyside 323
Norfolk 328 • 331 • 332 • 334 • 335 • 336 • 337 • 338 • 340
Northamptonshire 341 • 343 • 345
Northumberland 349 • 350 • 352 • 353 • 354
Nottinghamshire 359 • 360 • 362
Oxfordshire 364 • 365 • 367 • 368 • 370 • 372 • 373 • 374 • 376 • 377 • 379 • 381 • 383 • 385
Rutland 388 • 389 • 390 • 391
Shropshire 393 • 395 • 398 • 399 • 400 • 402
Somerset 404 • 408 • 409 • 410 • 414 • 415 • 416 • 417 • 419 • 425 • 431
Staffordshire 434 • 435
Suffolk 437 • 438 • 439 • 446 • 447
Surrey 453 • 454 • 456

Photo Hundred House Hotel, entry 402

Wales

Pubs with special bedrooms

See individual entries and pages 30-44 for more details.

England

Wales

Photo Beaufort Arms, entry 599

50% or more local produce
used, and a significant
percentage of organic

England

Wales

No piped music

Photo The Drunken Duck, entry 87

Live music

England

Wales

Photo Cat's Back, entry 291

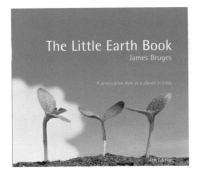

The Little Earth Book
Edition 4, £6.99
By James Bruges

A little book that has proved both hugely popular – and provocative. This new edition has chapters on Islam, Climate Change and The Tyranny of Corporations.

The Little Food Book
Edition 1, £6.99
By Craig Sams, Chairman of the Soil Association

An explosive account of the food we eat today. Never have we been at such risk – from our food. This book will help clarify what's at stake.

The Little Money Book
Edition 1, £6.99
By David Boyle, an associate of the New Economics Foundation

This pithy, wry little guide will tell you where money comes from, what it means, what it's doing to the planet and what we might be able to do about it.

www.fragile-earth.com

Celebrating the triumph of creativity over adversity.

An inspiring and heart-rending story of the making of the stained glass 'Creation' window at Chester Cathedral by a woman battling with debilitating Parkinson's disease.

"Within a few seconds, the tears were running down my cheeks. The window was one of the most beautiful things I had ever seen. It is a tour-de force, playing with light like no other window ..."
Anthropologist Hugh Brody

In 1983, Ros Grimshaw, a distinguished designer, artist and creator of stained glass windows, was diagnosed with Parkinson's disease. Refusing to allow her illness to prevent her from working, Ros became even more adept at her craft, and in 2000 won the commission to design and make the 'Creation' Stained Glass Window for Chester Cathedral.

Six Days traces the evolution of the window from the first sketches to its final, glorious completion as a rare and wonderful tribute to Life itself: for each of the six 'days' of Creation recounted in Genesis, there is a scene below that is relevant to the world of today and tomorrow.

Heart-rending extracts from Ros's diary capture the personal struggle involved. Superb photography captures the luminescence of the stunning stained glass, while the story weaves together essays, poems, and moving contributions from Ros's partner, Patrick Costeloe.

Available from Alastair Sawday Publishing £12.99

ALASTAIR SAWDAY'S
SPECIAL ESCAPES

Home ▪ Search ▪ Hotlist ▪ Owners ▪ Links

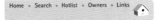

The Flat, Sloane Square

London, England

You're in the heart of town, yet tucked up in a smart residential street. Sloane Square tube is on your doorstep, you can be on the King's Road within three minutes and the No. 19 bus whisks you off to Knightsbridge and beyond. The apartment is dreamy; you will linger in the morning, then find an excuse to bolt home in the afternoon. Climb up to the third floor to discover an enormous glass roof flooding the hall with light. Glittering elegance comes in the form of Farrow & Ball paints, a 1793 Chatelet great-grandfather clock, a walnut dining table, a gilded Venetian bedhead and halogen lights. The sofa, covered in raw silk, was too big to come through the door so the delivery man pulled it up single-handedly, tottering on the tiny balcony. Best of all is the exquisite art that hangs on the walls (Frederique represents several artists and holds shows in New York). A super-comfy double bed wears crisp Egyptian cotton, a leaf from a Burmese bible graces the sitting room wall and a mellow marble bathroom pampers. The kitchen is similarly resplendent with dishwasher, hanging pots and stainless steel oven. Exceptional.

Sloane Gardens.

Details for The Flat

Contact Frederique Browne	**sleeps:**
tel: 020 7823 4704	**rooms:** 2: 1 double, 1 single, sharing bathroom.
@ Send E-mail Enquiry	**price:** £0 – £850.
≫ Visit Web Site	**closed:** Never.
	changeover: Flexible.

Hall.

? Details Explanation

€ Currency Converter

↗⊼ 🗑   ? Symbol Explanations

Living area in Flat 4.

Why Come Here?

Checklist	Points Of Interest
✓ Dishwasher	● Two minutes away from Royal Court Theatre.
✓ Electricity included	● Near to Peter Jones department store.
✓ Washing machine	
✓ Television	● Battersea Park a 10-minute walk away.
✓ Land line telephone**	● 5 minutes from the river and the Chelsea Flower Show.
✓ Restaurant nearby	This information is provided by owners and is not endorsed by ASP. If you have questions about it, please contact the owners.
✓ Iron & ironing board	
✓ Public transport	
✓ Music system***	

** May only be for incoming calls
*** Not necessarily including CD player

More details here »

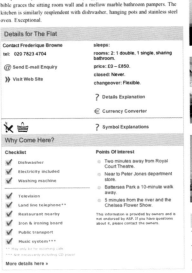

Master bedroom in Flat 4.

Now what?

● Add The Flat to your Hotlist »

● Find other Special Escapes in London »

● Booking Advice for Special Escapes »

A whole week self-catering in Britain with your friends or family is precious, and you dare not get it wrong. To whom do you turn for advice and who on earth do you trust when the web is awash with advice from strangers? We launched Special Escapes to satisfy an obvious need for impartial and trustworthy help – and that is what it provides. The criteria for inclusion are the same as for our books: we have to like the place and the owners. It has, quite simply, to be 'special'. The site, our first online-only publication, is featured on www.thegoodwebguide.com and is growing fast.

www.special-escapes.co.uk

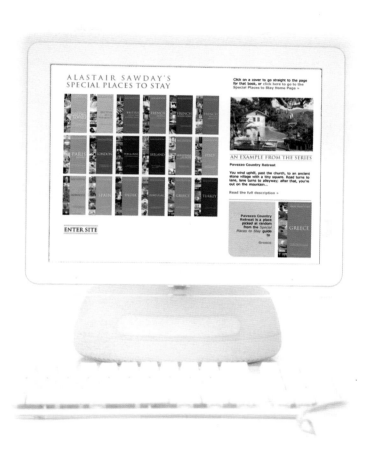

The World Wide Web is big – very big. So big, in fact, that it can be a fruitless search if you don't know where to find reliable, trustworthy, up-to-date information about fantastic places to stay in Europe, India, Morocco and beyond....

Fortunately, there's www.specialplacestostay.com, where you can dip into all of our guides, find special offers from owners, catch up on news about the series and tell us about the special places you've been to.

www.specialplacestostay.com

Order form

All these books are available in major bookshops or you may order them direct.
Post and packaging are FREE within the UK.

Bed & Breakfast for Garden Lovers	£14.99
British Hotels, Inns & Other Places	£13.99
British Bed & Breakfast	£14.99
French Bed & Breakfast	£15.99
French Hotels, Châteaux & Other Places	£14.99
French Holiday Homes	£12.99
Greece	£11.99
India	£10.99
Ireland	£12.99
Italy	£14.99
London	£9.99
Morocco	£11.99
Mountains of Europe	£9.99
Paris Hotels	£9.99
Portugal	£10.99
Pubs & Inns of England & Wales	£13.99
Spain	£14.99
Turkey	£11.99
The Little Earth Book	£6.99
The Little Food Book	£6.99
The Little Money Book	£6.99
Six Days	£12.99

Please make cheques payable to Alastair Sawday Publishing   Total £ _____

Please send cheques to: Alastair Sawday Publishing, The Old Farmyard, Yanley
Lane, Long Ashton, Bristol BS41 9LR. For credit card orders call 01275 395431
or order directly from our web site www.specialplacestostay.com

Title   First name   Surname

Address

Postcode   Tel

PUB3

If you do not wish to receive mail from other like-minded companies, please tick here ☐
If you would prefer not to receive information about special offers on our books, please tick here ☐

Report form

If you have any comments on entries in this guide, or if you have a favourite pub or inn you would like to recommend, we would love to hear about it. You can return this form, email info@sawdays.co.uk, or visit www.specialplacestostay.com and click on 'contact'.

Existing entry

Name of pub: _____

Entry number: _____   Date of visit: ___ / ___ / ___

New recommendation

Name of pub: _____

Landlord/ lady: _____

Address: _____

Postcode: _____   Tel: _____

Your comments

What did you like (or dislike) about this pub? Were the people friendly? What sort of food, beer and/or wine did they serve? What was the location like?

_____

_____

_____

_____

_____

_____

_____

_____

_____

_____

Your details

Name: _____

Address: _____

Postcode: _____   Tel: _____

PUB3

How to use this book

Somerset

Canal Inn
Wrantage

Blink and you could miss the rustic whitewashed pub by the A378 – closed for years until Pedro and Clare picked up on its potential in 2003. It's much more than the no-frills ale house it appears to be. Enjoy the best local ales for miles – foaming pints of Blackdown Ditch Water – in the bare-boarded bar, or sample Somerset scrumpy-style ciders and a host of Belgian beers. Yet the key to its success in winning favour with the community is its passion for local produce. Menus proudly list the small suppliers, all within a five-mile radius – eggs and veg from Mr & Mrs Titman, vintage local cheeses, allotment veg. A farmers' market in the bar on the last Saturday of the month brings customers and suppliers together. So food miles are kept to a minimum and trade receives a boost – ingenious. Regular fish nights, Monday fish and chips (eat-in or take-away), music nights and an annual beer festival complete the picture.

directions	Beside A378 towards Langport, 2 miles east of A378 Taunton-Ilminster road
meals	12pm-2pm; 6.30pm-9pm. Main courses £6-£10 (lunch), £10-£15 (dinner).
closed	2.30pm-5pm (7pm weekends); Monday lunchtimes.

Pedro Aparacion & Clare Paul
Canal Inn,
Wrantage, Taunton,
Somerset TA3 6DF
tel 01823 480210
web www.thecanalinn.com

map: 2 entry: 413

① Somerset

Lord Poulett Arms
Hinton St George

② There's an upbeat yet elegant feel to this wonderful 400-year-old inn. And it sits in a ravishing village. Traditional trappings – hops, pewter tankards, country antiques – rub shoulders with quirky bits: *Carry On* posters on the wall, a hammock in the divine summer garden, a chess set laid out to play. Floors are bare flags or age-worn boards, the bar is simple and uncluttered, there's space and intimacy at the same time, a huge old fireplace crackling with logs, cider from the jug. The chef trained in Japan so the Dorsetshire fish and the Exmoor game might come with an oriental touch. Try spinach and pea soup, wild sea bass with exotic mushrooms in a sake and teriyaki sauce, Lovington's ice creams and west country cheeses. Contemporary wallpapers set the tone for super bedrooms upstairs – along with open-stone walls, brass bedsteads and seagrass floors; Roberts radios add a fun touch. Brilliant value, friendly to dogs.

directions	Village signed off A30, west of Crewkerne. ③
meals	12pm-2pm; 7pm-9pm. Main courses £9-£15. ④
rooms	4 twins/doubles £72. Singles £48. ⑤
closed	3pm-6.30pm & Monday lunchtimes. ⑥

See page 38 for bedroom details.

⑦ Steve Hill
Lord Poulett Arms,
High Street, Hinton St George,
Crewkerne, Somerset TA17 8SE
tel 01460 73149
web www.lordpoulettarms.com

⑨

⑧ map: 3 entry: 414